THE
HANDBOOK
OF
MORTGAGE
BANKING

**A Guide to the
Secondary Mortgage Market**

THE
HANDBOOK
OF
MORTGAGE
BANKING

A Guide to the
Secondary Mortgage Market

Edited by

James M. Kinney
President
Guild Mortgage Company
San Diego, California

Richard T. Garrigan
Professor of Finance
DePaul University
Chicago, Illinois

DOW JONES-IRWIN
Homewood, Illinois 60430

ISBN 0-87094-434-7

Library of Congress Catalog Card No. 84–71128

Printed in the United States of America

3 4 5 6 7 8 9 0 K 2 1 0 9 8 7 6

Foreword

The secondary mortgage market is a classic example of an industry laboring in relative obscurity before suddenly being thrust onto center stage. This new-found attention is well deserved: The industry has developed new distribution channels and new products, attracted new investors, and provided affordable financing for homebuyers during some of the worst years in housing's history.

As this is written, in 1985, the secondary mortgage market is vastly more sophisticated than it was just five years ago, and this trend is accelerating. There are many examples: The growth of the mortgage-backed security and, more recently, the collateralized mortgage obligation; the adjustable rate mortgage; and the increased use of computer technology.

Moreover, the secondary market has become of critical importance to the housing finance system. A decade ago, the size of the secondary mortgage market was only about one quarter of newly originated mortgages; in 1983, it accounted for three quarters of new originations.

This is the first time that a handbook describing these changes has been compiled. The editors and contributors to this work are to be commended for providing a comprehensive guide for those seeking to understand—and participate in—the secondary mortgage market.

David O. Maxwell
Chairman and CEO
Federal National Mortgage Association

Preface

The Handbook of Mortgage Banking is a unique business management book written by businessmen and women and their advisors in the mortgage banking field and related businesses. Its setting is the rapidly changing and increasingly sophisticated primary/secondary mortgage, financial futures, and capital markets. It is specifically designed to inform the mortgage executive or student of business management about the management principles of mortgage banking and to help them analyze the significance of industry changes on secondary mortgage market participants. The *Handbook* focuses on practical knowledge, informed perspectives, and results-oriented management guidelines used by experienced managers and specialists in the mortgage banking and related real estate finance industries.

The *Handbook* emphasizes

1. External factors which may or should influence decision making in the mortgage banking industry.
2. Internal corporate general management policies and principles directly affecting profit-making decisions.

The Handbook of Mortgage Banking consists of 29 chapters organized within several major divisions. Part One, The Institutional Setting, consists of two sections. Section A, The Structural Environment, focuses upon how the supply of mortgage credit has been affected by the major changes occurring in the institutions and instruments which form the structure of the secondary mortgage market. Section B, The Legal and Regulatory Environment, provides an overview of how the activities of secondary market participants are shaped by both law and regulation.

The next four parts of the *Handbook* comprise its managerial core. Unlike most existing literature about the secondary mortgage market, the *Handbook* is not a "how-to" book. Rather than stressing how to make a good loan, the *Handbook* focuses on managing a profitable mortgage banking business. This emphasis is immediately apparent in the two sections that form Part Two, Secondary Mortgage Market Operations. The chapters in Section A are concerned with Strategic Considerations, while those contained in Section B cover Originating and Marketing Policies. Part Three, in turn, pertains to the Administration of a Servicing Portfolio, while the chapters contained in Parts Four and Five deal with Finanacial Management and Investor Considerations.

Part Six, Specialty Lending, contains the final chapters of the *Handbook*.

Material in these chapters depicts many of the latest mortgage financing arrangements.

In recent years, the continuing evolution of the secondary mortgage and capital markets has become a virtual revolution. Fundamental structural and product changes have occurred at an accelerating rate against a backdrop of increased interest rate volatility and market sophistication. To discern the significance between the effect of changing external factors on the mortgage banking business and the need to pursue successful management principles in light of changed external variables is the challenge presented to the reader. The *Handbook* attempts to aid the reader in this task by focusing on enduring mortgage banking general management principles, not on increasingly less relevant specific prescriptions.

Because the *Handbook,* as of its date of publication, represents a contemporary viewpoint of successful practitioners and industry experts, it summarizes the significant external variables and management principles affecting informed decision making. Thus, the student of mortgage banking management need be primarily concerned only with management literature published after the *Handbook* or literature that discusses or analyzes particular topics not sufficiently addressed in the *Handbook.*

The editors wish to express their deep gratitude to the nine members of the Editorial Advisory Board, the 39 Contributing Authors, and the 45 Consulting Editors who are acknowledged within these introductory pages. Without their dedication and willingness to make time available for *The Handbook of Mortgage Banking,* this project would still be but an idea.

In particular, we would like to extend our sincere personal appreciation to Susie Rapp, Helen Gaither, Billie Smith, and David A. Child, whose diligent struggles with legibility, changes, rewrites, and deadlines provided us with the support to edit the many and varied manuscripts into a meaningful focus on the management of mortgage banking.

James M. Kinney
Richard T. Garrigan

Contributing Authors

Robert E. Adams
Vice President, Investment Banking
World Wide Group, Inc.

William W. Bartlett
Vice President
Shearson Lehman Mortgage Securities
Shearson Lehman/American Express, Inc.

Caryl S. Bernstein
Executive Vice President, General Counsel
and Secretary
Federal National Mortgage Association

Leland C. Brendsel
Executive Vice President Finance
and Chief Financial Officer
Federal Home Loan Mortgage Corporation

JoAnn Carpenter
Assistant General Counsel
Federal National Mortgage Association

Robert F. Dall
Managing Director
Salomon Brothers Inc

Richard A. Dorfman
Managing Director
Lehman Commercial Paper, Inc.
Shearson Lehman/American Express, Inc.

James S. Dunne
Vice President
Salomon Brothers Inc

Delbert R. Ellis
Senior Vice President
First Federal Savings and Loan of Arizona

Robert B. Ferguson, Jr.
President and Chairman of the Board
Security Pacific Mortgage Corporation

David R. Ganis
President
Northern Futures Corporation

F. Allen Graham
Executive Vice President
Bloomfield Savings and Loan Association, F.A.

James H. Hammond, Jr.
Partner
Peat, Marwick, Mitchell & Co.

Joycelyn Harris
President
Builders Mortgage Company

Christopher W. Hart
Assistant Professor of Economics, Marketing,
and Tourism
School of Hotel Administration
Cornell University

Peter E. Kaplan
Partner
Witkowski, Weiner, McCaffrey & Brodsky, P.C.

Kurt Kettenmann
Vice President
Bankers Trust Company

Phillip E. Kidd
Director of Strategic Planning—Real Estate
Finance Business
Chase Manhattan Bank

James M. Kinney
President
Guild Mortgage Company

William H. Lacy
President
Mortgage Guaranty Insurance Corporation

Thomas S. LaMalfa
Vice President
Mortgage Guaranty Insurance Corporation

William E. Long
President
Talman Home Mortgage Corporation

Richard G. Marcis
Senior Vice President
Trident Financial Corporation

Roswald K. McMullen
Senior Vice President
Mortgage and Trust, Inc.

Allen P. Miller
Regional Vice President
Federal National Mortgage Association

Richard L. Mower
President and Chief Executive Officer
Transamerica Mortgage Company

Robert J. Mylod
President
Federal National Mortgage Association

James J. O'Meara
Vice President-Mortgage Finance
The First Boston Corporation

Norman H. Peterson
Manager, Loan Acquisition
Federal National Mortgage Association

Elizabeth B. Qutb
Staff Vice President, Mortgage Finance Division
National Association of Home Builders

Richard M. Schapiro
Vice President
Salomon Brothers Inc

David F. Seiders
Senior Staff Vice President
for Housing Policy and Mortgage Finance
National Association of Home Builders

Dexter E. Senft
Managing Director
The First Boston Corporation

John W. Starke
Managing Director
Westchester Mortgage Company

Kenneth J. Thygerson
President
Federal Home Loan Mortgage Corporation

David D. Tibbals
Vice President
Salomon Brothers Inc

Dennis M. Wiggins
President
Sybran Corporation/Mortgage Data Service

George I. Wilson
Executive Vice President
The Lomas & Nettleton Company

Hunter W. Wolcott
President
Reserve Financial Management Corporation

Donald B. Vaden
President and CEO
Chase Home Mortgage Corporation

Lester A. Werling
Senior Vice President
Guild Mortgage Company

William A. Wildhack
Chairman
Wildhack & Associates, Inc.

Walter B. Williams
President
Continental, Inc.

Contents

PART ONE
The Institutional Setting **1**

   PART ONE—SECTION A: The Structural Environment **3**

  1. **Supply and Demand for Mortgage Credit in the 1980s**
      Phillip E. Kidd **3**
      Demographics and Housing Demand. Housing Finance: Its Problems
      and Its Potential. Thrift Industry. Other Sources of Housing Funds. The
      Role of Government Mortgage Agencies. How Many Dollars Are
      Needed?

  2. **Residential Mortgage and Capital Markets**
      David F. Seiders **21**
      The Mortgage Lending/Investment Process: *Primary-Market Instruments
      and Participants. Secondary-Market Institutions and Instruments.
      Mortgage Investors.* Development of Pass-Through Markets and
      Implications for Mortgage Lending and Investment Patterns:
      *Development of Pass-Through Markets. Sales of Loans into Secondary
      Markets. Implications for the Investor Base. Mortgage/Securities Swaps.*
      Federal Policy toward Mortgage Pass-Through Securities: *Creation of
      New Trust Device. Tax Treatment of Recovered Discount. Establishment
      of Federal Quality Standards. Treatment under Pension-Fund Law and
      Regulation. SEC Registration Requirements. Marginability of Securities.
      State Blue-Sky and Legal-Investment Statutes. Deposit Liabilities and
      Recourse Arrangements.* Outlook for Mortgage Securities Markets.
      Epilogue: Policy Update

  3. **Federal Government-Related Mortgage Purchasers**
      Kenneth J. Thygerson **57**
      Overview. Federal National Mortgage Association (Fannie Mae).
      Federal Home Loan Mortgage Corporation (Freddie Mac). Government
      National Mortgage Association (Ginnie Mae). Other Government
      Involvement: *Federal Housing Administration (FHA). Veterans
      Administration (VA). Farmers Home Administration (FmHA).*

4. **The Role of Mortgage Securities**
    Robert F. Dall and Richard M. Schapiro   **73**
    Historical Development: *Introduction of the GNMA Pass-Through
    Program. Trading and Distribution. GNMA Pass-Through Securities
    Problems. Wall Street Involvement. New Programs.* Private-Sector
    Mortgage Securities: *Conventional Mortgages. Wall Street and the
    Mortgage Markets.*

5. **Conventional Mortgage-Backed Securities**
    Leland C. Brendsel   **87**
    Introduction. Rationale and Early Development. Evolution of the
    Concept. Other Programs: *Other New Entrants.* Relative Role of
    Conventional Securities and Market Potential. Issues Ahead for
    Conventional Securities: *Standardization. Active Management of Pools.
    The Quality of the Guarantee.* Conclusion.

6. **The Role of the Rating Agencies: A Standard & Poor's Perspective**
    James J. O'Meara and David D. Tibbals   **97**
    *Rating Approach to Mortgage-Related Securities. Overview of Mortgage
    Securities.* Mortgage Pass-Through Certificate: *Credit Quality and Loss
    Protection. Financial Strength of Entity Providing Loss Protection.
    Servicer's Cash Advance Capability. New Mortgage Instruments.*
    Mortgage-Backed Bonds: *Quality of the Collateral. Quantity of
    Collateral. Creditworthiness of the Issuer. Review Process.* Mortgage
    Pay-Through Bonds: *Credit Risk. Reinvestment Risk. Cash Flow
    Coverage. Issuer Considerations. Advantages of Pay-Through Bonds.*
    Summary. Appendix: Debt Rating Definitions.

7. **Interest-Rate Futures**
    David R. Ganis and James S. Dunne   **125**
    History of Futures Trading: *Major Regulated Exchanges. Futures
    Markets on Fixed-Income Securities.* Interest Rate Futures Contracts:
    *Advantages of Use. Dealer Markets and Futures Markets. Trading
    Volume and Open Interest. Speculation and Hedging. Hedge Planning.
    Margin.* Conclusion: *Effective Controls and Accounting.*

8. **The Role of the Private Mortgage-Insurance Industry**
    William H. Lacy and Thomas S. LaMalfa   **137**
    Historical Review of the Private Mortgage Insurance Industry: *Pre-
    Depression Era. Government Mortgage Insurance. Private Mortgage
    Insurance Reborn. Growth of the Industry.* Operation of the Private

Mortgage Insurance Industry: *Standardization of Practices.*
Underwriting Functions. Claims Functions. Financial Strength. Role in
the Primary and Secondary Markets: *Primary Market Involvement.*
Secondary Market Involvement. Involvement in Mortgage Securities and
Conduits. Current Coverage Issues. Conclusion.

PART ONE—SECTION B: The Legal and
Regulatory Environment   **155**

9.   **The Legal Environment: An Overview**
     Caryl S. Bernstein and JoAnn Carpenter   **155**
Introduction. Federal Laws: *Real Estate Settlement Procedures Act of*
1974. Equal Credit Opportunity Act of 1974. Truth in Lending Act.
Home Mortgage Disclosure Act of 1975. Fair Housing Act. Community
Reinvestment Act of 1977. Employee Retirement Income Security Act of
1974. Securities Laws. Chartering of Savings and Loan Associations.
Garn-St Germain Depository Institutions Act of 1982. State Laws:
Usury. State Foreclosure Laws and the Uniform Land Transactions Act.
Doing Business. Securities. Lending Powers of State Savings and Loan
Associations. Chartering. Uniform Simplification of Land Transfers Act.
Uniform Condominium Act.

10. **The Regulatory Environment: An Overview**
     Peter E. Kaplan and Elizabeth B. Qutb   **183**
Introduction. Primary Regulators. Depository Institutions: *Savings*
Institutions. FS&L Service Corporations and Holding Company
Subsidiaries. Banks. Bank-Owned Mortgage Companies. Mortgage
Bankers: *Mortgage Companies. Bank Holding Company (BHC)*
Subsidiaries. FHA/VA: *Approval. Operational Requirements.* Federally
Related Conduits and Purchasers. Approval: *Government National*
Mortgage Association (GNMA). Federal National Mortgage Association
(FNMA). Federal Home Loan Mortgage Corporation (FHLMC).
Operational Requirements: *GNMA. FNMA. FHLMC.* Product Eligibility:
GNMA. FNMA. FHLMC. Mortgage-Insurance Companies. Regulations
Affecting the Structure and Marketing of the Security. Security
Structure: *IRS and SEC Requirements. Securities Rating.* Dealer
Regulation: *SEC, NYSE and Self-Regulation. "Good Delivery"*
Requirements. Federal Reserve Board-Regulation T. Blue-Sky Laws.
Futures and Options Exchanges: *GNMA Futures Markets. Exchange-*
Traded Options. Life Insurance Companies. Pension Funds: *ERISA.*
Public Funds. Conclusion.

PART TWO
Secondary Mortgage Market Operations 215
PART TWO—SECTION A: Strategic Considerations 217

11. **Determining Lending Strategy**
    Robert J. Mylod and James M. Kinney 217
    Types of Lending: *Income-Property Lending. Residential Lending.
    Builder Loans. Spot Loans. Spot versus Builder. Wholesale
    Distribution. Direct to Consumer. The Consumer: Market Segments.
    Types of Loans.*

12. **The Value of Mortgage Banking**
    John W. Starke 235
    Introduction. Approaches to Value: *Income Approach. Business Plan.
    Cost Approach. Application of Methods.* Income Approach: *Analysis
    Method. Assumptions. Projected Cash Flow.* The Value of Servicing:
    *Servicing Income. Servicing Cost. Escrow Income. After-Tax Value.
    Expected Value. Cancellation Risk. Present Value. Computing Present
    Value.* The Cost Approach: *Net-Asset Value. Value of the Organization.
    Value of the Firm.* Comparison of Values.

13. **Market Analysis**
    Richard L. Mower and Dennis M. Wiggins 255
    Market Demand: Analysis of a Location's Economy: *Economic Factors.
    External Factors. Demographic Study. Summary of Market Demand.*
    Market Supply: Analysis of Competitors: *Motivation. Performance.
    Summary of Market Supply.*

14. **Purchase and Sale of Servicing Portfolios**
    Hunter W. Wolcott 269
    The Market. Servicing as a Corporate Investment: *Required Current
    Portfolio Information. Historical Portfolio Information. Field
    Examination.* Executing the Purchase or Sale: *The Buyer's Perspective.
    The Seller's Perspective. Closing the Purchase or Sale.* Summary.
    Appendix: GNMA Servicing Transfer Checklist.

PART TWO—SECTION B: Originating and Marketing Policies 283

15. **Production-Department Management**
    Robert B. Ferguson, Jr. 283
    Determining Goals and Objectives. Incentives: *Management. Loan
    Officers.* Organization: *Regional Manager. Branch Manager.
    Underwriting. Quality Control. Compliance and Training. Purchased
    Loans.* Branch Administration: *Processing the Loan. Closing the Loan.*

Customers. Pricing. Pricing Communication. Duration. Timing. Delivery. Interest-Rate Changes. Variations. Management Considerations. Reporting and Control. Coordination with Agencies. Conclusion.

16. **Inventory Philosophy, Reporting, and Control**
    F. Allen Graham **301**
    Inventory Defined. Identifying Risks: *Origination Risks. Selling Risks.* Inventory Exposure: *Mechanical. Strategic. Analysis. Market Exposure. Administrative Exposure.* Summary.

17. **Hedging Alternatives**
    William E. Long **315**
    The Need to Hedge. Interest Rate Volatility. Interest-Rate Uncertainty. The Ways to Hedge. Forward-Delivery Commitments—Whole Loan. Forward-Delivery Commitments—Participations. Forward-Delivery Commitments—MBSs: *GNMA. FNMA. FHLMC.* Other Price Protection Alternatives: *GNMA Futures. Other Futures Contracts. Options Market. Servicing-Released.* Specific Hedging Alternatives: *FNMA. FHLMC. GNMA MBSs. FNMA/FHLMC MBSs. Conduit Companies. Private Investors. Second Mortgages.* Summary.

18. **Collateral Management**
    Jocelyn Harris **331**
    Investor Commitments: *FNMA and FHLMC.* Types of Loan Sales: *Whole Loan and Participation Sales. Mortgage-Backed Securities (MBSs).* Documentation: *New Loan Files. Warehousing-Funding Package.* Quality Control. Follow-Up. Reports. Summary.

PART THREE
Administration of a Servicing Portfolio **341**

19. **Loan Administration**
    George I. Wilson **343**
    The Servicing Agreement: *Standard Provisions. Desirable Provisions.* Organization and Primary Responsibility. Loan Accounting and Cashiering: *Control of Cash Received. Types of Remittances. Disbursements for Taxes and Insurance. Billing the Subsidy.* Collection and Foreclosure: *Collection Procedures. Property Inspections. Foreclosure.* Escrow Administration: *Tax Disbursements. Insurance Coverage. Lienable Items. Analysis of Escrow Accounts.* Relating to Those Outside the Company: *The Investor. The Mortgagor. Government Agencies. State Laws and Regulations. Insurance Agents and Tax*

*Collectors. Reports, Standards, and Data Processing. Reports Showing
the Total Work Flow of Activity. Reports Showing the Exception Cases.
Standards. The Role of Data Processing.*

PART FOUR
Financial Management   361

20. **Financial Planning**
      Delbert R. Ellis   **363**
      Strategic Planning: *Planning Process. Key Assumptions. Contingency
      Plans.* Determining Capital Requirements: *Ownership and Size. Cash
      Flow Projections.* Budgeting: *Relation to Strategic Plan. Goals and
      Objectives. Forecasting Loan Volume. Implementation and Monitoring.*
      Controls: *Cost Accounting. Responsibility Centers. Controllable Items.
      Reports. Communications. Internal Controls.* Analysis: *Origination.
      Marketing. Servicing. Warehousing. Overhead.*

21. **Short-Term Financing Requirements and Capabilities**
      Roswald K. McMullen   **377**
      Management Considerations: *Interest Rate. Flexibility and
      Administrative Ease. Risk of Corporate Assets.* Short-Term Financing
      Alternatives: *Bank Lines of Credit. Documented Discount Notes.
      Commercial Paper. Repurchase Arrangements. Variations. Alternatives.*

22. **Accounting Policies**
      James H. Hammond, Jr.   **395**
      Mortgage Loans Held: *Loans Held for Sale or Market Recovery. Loans
      Held for a Long-Term Investment. Loans Sold under Repurchase
      Agreements.* Definition of Lower of Cost or Market: *Current Industry
      Practice. Computation of Market.* Committed Loans and GNMA
      Securities. Uncommitted Loans. Uncommitted Mortgage-Backed
      Securities. Costs Associated with Bulk Purchases. Valuation Dates and
      Subsequent Changes in Market Conditions: *Valuation Dates.* Subsequent
      Recoveries of Previous Write-Downs. Bulk Purchases and Sales of
      Loans and Servicing Rights. GNMA Mortgage-Backed Securities
      (MBSs): *Operating Procedures. Initial Deposit of Interest in Custodial
      Account.* Accounting for Futures Contracts. Allowances for Loan
      Losses: *Individual Evaluation Method. Timing of Evaluations.* Mortgage
      Origination Costs. Excess of Purchase Price over Sales Price of
      Mortgages Purchased and Sold. Revenues: *Loan-Administration Fees.
      Loan-Origination Fees.* Interest Income: *Fees Relating to Loans Held
      for Sale. Fees Relating to Loans not Held for Sale.* Recognition of
      Interest Income. Discontinuance of Recognition of Interest Income.

Financial Statement Presentation and Disclosure: *Disclosures. Sample Financial Statements.*

PART FIVE
Investor Considerations   415

23. **Analyzing Warehousing Credits**
    Kurt Kettenmann   **417**
    Choosing the Customer: *Warehouse Lending Risks. Price Risk: Nonhedged Inventory. Price Risk: Overhedged Inventory. Price Risk: Nonviable Investor Commitments. Secondary Risks.* Monitoring Inventory Risks. Analyzing the Risks: *Character, Credit, and Capacity. Financial Analysis. Capital. Financial Statements. Assets. Liabilities. Income and Expenses. Reporting Procedures and Practices. Operational Analysis.* Documentation: *Warehousing Agreement. Collateral.* Types of Secured Lending: *Direct Warehousing. Participations. Pooling.* Standby Letters of Credit and Backup Commitments: *Documented Discount Notes. Repurchase Agreements (Repos). Commerical Paper. Other Customer Needs.* Required Reports. Audits. Summary.

24. **Analyzing and Monitoring Originators and Servicers**
    Allen P. Miller and Norman H. Peterson   **437**
    Production Capability and Portfolio Needs: *Past Record. Internal Audit. Financial Condition. Quality of Servicing.* Monitoring Servicing Performance: *Cash Flow Analysis. Routine Servicing.* Types of Reports. Primary Problem Areas. Future Considerations. Conclusion.

25. **Liquifying Portfolio Loans**
    Richard A. Dorfman   **447**
    The Importance of Accounting Policies. Planning a Liquification: *Analytical Phase. Strategic Phase. Reinvestment Phase. Execution Phase: Sale of Loans, MBSs, or Bonds.* Portfolio Segmentation. Sample Segmentation. Portfolio Financings (Hypothecations). Segmentation, Schematics, and Summary.

26. **Mortgage Investment Determinants**
    William W. Bartlett   **459**
    Foreword. Product Diversity: *Mortgages versus Mortgage-Backed Securities. MBSs versus Bonds. Liquidity Lends Intrinsic Value. Loan Participations. Risk Considerations—Market versus Credit. Market Risk. Call Protection. CMO Protection. Credit Risk. Other Yield Considerations. Forecasting Funds Available for Investment. Forward-Delivery Transactions. Disadvantages. Accounting Considerations.*

Discount with High Speed. Discount with Slow Speed. Tax Questions:
Accrued Interest. Accrual-Basis Taxpayer. Cash-Basis Taxpayer.
Summary.

27. **Determining the Yield**
    Dexter E. Senft   **473**
    What Is a Mortgage? Qualifying for a Mortgage. Servicing. Where
    Does Mortgage Money Come From? What Types of Properties Are
    Mortgaged? Nontraditional Mortgages: *Graduated Payment Mortgages
    (GPMs). Pledged-Account Mortgages (PAMs). Buy-Down Loans.
    Growing Equity Mortgages (GEMs). Midgets. Variable-Rate Mortgages
    (VRMs). Price-Level-Adjusted Mortgages (PLAMs). Shared-Appreciation
    Mortgages (SAMs).* Pass-Through Securities: *The Underlying
    Mortgages. Payments to Investors. Guarantees.* Prepayments.
    Measuring Prepayments. *SMM Experience. FHA-Experience. Pros and
    Cons of FHA Experience.* Factors Affecting Prepayments. Average Life,
    Half-Life, and Duration. Yield Measurement: *Mortgage Yield.*
    Drawbacks of Mortgage Yield. HTG Yield. Corporate Bond Equivalent
    Yield. Parity Price. Taxation. Prepayment Consistency: *The Law of
    Averages. Arguments against Consistency. An Alternative.* Risk versus
    Reward. The Future: New Security Structures. Appendix: Formulas
    Relating to Mortgages and Pass-Throughs.

PART SIX
Specialty Lending   563

28. **The Future for Alternative Mortgage Instruments**
    Richard G. Marcis   **565**
    Introduction. Current AMI Activity. AMIs and the Selection Process.
    Evolving Mortgage Forms. Is There a Future for the Fixed-Rate
    Mortgage? Impact of AMIs on the Housing Market. Summary and
    Concluding Observations.

29. **Resort Timeshare Financing**
    Robert E. Adams and Christopher W. Hart   **577**
    Growth. Consumer Satisfaction. Forms of Ownership. Timesharing
    Exchange. Consumer Profile. Financing. Type of Financing: *Consumer
    End-Load Financing. Acquisition and Construction Financing. Joint
    Venture Financing.* Why Lend on Timeshares? Risk Analysis: *The
    Developer(s). The Project. Location. Project Design. Feasibility
    Studies. Appraisals. Marketing and Sales. Management and
    Maintenance. Legal and Regulatory Requirements. Administrative
    Processing.* Summary.

Index   593

PART ONE

The Institutional Setting

— PART ONE —— SECTION A ——

The Structural Environment

— Chapter 1 ——

Supply and Demand for Mortgage Credit in the 1980s

Phillip E. Kidd
Director of Strategic Planning—Real Estate Finance Business
Chase Manhattan Bank

      The purpose of this chapter is to develop estimates of the amount of residential credit that may be required in the 1980s. The chapter begins with a review of demographic issues, specifically the effect of the post-World War II baby boom on aggregate housing demand and on the mix of units (ownership versus rental, single-family versus multifamily). Next, the discussion turns to financial topics, specifically the impact on mortgage availability of changes in both the sources of mortgage funds and in the mortgage instrument. Then high and low projections of the net change in outstanding residential mortgage debt are made. A range is presented to illustrate the difference in mortgage financing requirements between some reasonable estimate of actual housing activity and the amount needed to satisfy all the potential housing demand of the 1980s.

3

Demand for housing finance is derived from the population's need for shelter. In satisfying that need, people make choices. They can live in single- or multifamily dwellings, use existing structures or new construction, and buy or rent their living space. Both their age and family situation and their ability to finance their housing selections, which depends on their real incomes and the cost and availability of mortgage credit, affect their plans. Significantly, their demographic characteristics and financial conditions are continuously changing, creating a dynamic environment for housing finance.

For example, in the second half of the 1970s, consumers' real incomes were improving, mortgage funds were expanding, and the real cost of mortgages after allowing for taxes and inflation was minimal. Housing starts and resales climbed rapidly. Homeowners aggressively upgraded their housing. First-time home buyers poured into the market. Housing was unquestionably considered the best investment/inflation hedge for most people.

In contrast, in the early 1980s, the deterioration in consumer's real incomes combined with the growing scarcity of mortgage money and record high interest rates served to slash housing demand. Consumers either could not find mortgages, or they could not afford them. Both housing starts and home resales fell dramatically, and consumers and speculators alike questioned housing's value as an investment/inflation hedge.

Significantly, the demographic demand for housing and housing finance was exceptionally strong in both periods. In the late 1970s, the supply of mortgage credit satisfied a large real demand for housing. In the early 1980s, because the supply of credit was insufficient, effective housing demand collapsed, leading to a sizable accumulation of unsatisfied demand for housing. Thus, the key questions for the remainder of the 1980s become: How strong will the demographic demand for housing and housing finance be? How will the supply of mortgage credit adjust to that demand? This chapter focuses upon the answers to these questions.

Demographics and Housing Demand

The total U.S. population is no longer growing rapidly. In the 1980s, it is projected to increase at a rate of less than 1 percent compounded annually. Consequently, shifts in the population's age structure, not its overall growth, will most affect housing. The major demographic movement will be the passage of the post-World War II babies through the ages of 25 to 44—the predominant age group of first-time home purchasers.

People born between 1946 and 1964 are now the *largest* group in the country, accounting for one third of the population. However, they are not a homogeneous group. Within the postwar baby boom, there were two distinct waves (see Figure 1). In the first wave (1946 to 1954), births, which had been 2.9 million in 1945, abruptly jumped to 3.4 million in 1946 and then crept

Figure 1 • Annual Births in the United States: 1935–1982

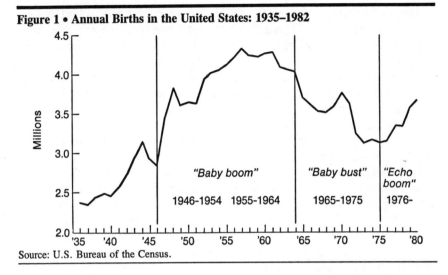

Source: U.S. Bureau of the Census.

erratically upwards, passing 4 million in 1954. During those nine years, births averaged 3.8 million per year, or 45 percent higher than the annual birth rate in the previous 15 years. In the second wave (1955 to 1964), births averaged nearly 4.2 million per year.

Thus, births escalated rapidly during the first wave and then leveled off at an exceptionally high plateau during the second. Equally important, people in the first wave are presently in a very different stage of their life than those in the second. Currently, people from the large first wave are prime first-time home buyers; most have left school, found jobs, and are forming households (see Table 1). In contrast, people from the even larger second wave are currently between 18 and 27; some are in school, while others are in the process of finding jobs and starting households.

Household formations are the most significant factor affecting new residential construction.[1] They generate two thirds to three quarters of the demand for new building. Replacements, second homes, and vacancies make up the rest.

Table 1 • Ages of the Postwar Babies

Born	1970	1975	1980	1985	1990
1946–1954	16–24	21–29	26–34	31–39	36–44
1955–1964	6–15	11–20	16–25	21–30	26–35

---

[1] In an equilibrium situation, the formation of a household immediately creates the demand for another housing unit. However, there is nothing in this concept to imply that either the demand is promptly satisfied or that the recently formed household actually occupies the new unit. Consequently, household formations (or their breakup) can create supply/demand imbalances in the residential market and affect the mix and level of new and existing housing transactions.

During the early 1970s, as some of the first wave left home and set up their own residences, household formations jumped 37 percent (see Table 2). Later in the decade, when most of the first wave and a few of the second wave were on their own, new households rose still higher. Currently, with the first wave nearly through creating households but more and more of the second wave establishing their independence, household formations are expected to level off. Later in this decade, when most of the second wave will be in their own households and the first people from the relatively small baby bust years (1965–75) will be moving out on their own, household formations should start inching downwards (see Figure 1).

In the 1970s, household formations also received a boost from the surge in single-person units due to the rapid expansion in the number of people in their 20s living alone, the rising divorce rate, and the fact that more older people are living by themselves. In the 1980s, these trends will persist because the second wave will pass through its 20s; the divorce rate, even if it levels off, will be much higher than in the early 1970s; and the number of elderly women outliving their husbands will continue to rise.

Another factor influencing housing demand is the nation's high rate of migration, especially to the South and West. Significantly, people in their 20s are the most prone to move (see Table 3). Given that age group's proclivity for movement and living alone, the passage of the large first wave through their 20s gave housing demand a twin boost in the 1970s. However, as people grow older, their families and jobs will increasingly hold them in the same location. In the 1980s, the first wave will become less mobile. In contrast, the much larger and younger second wave will become more mobile. Consequently, migration, although likely to level off, will remain at a very high rate through most of this decade.

While a useful indicator of future demand, data on household formations do not reveal the type of housing wanted (single-family or multifamily, existing or new, buy or rent). The age distribution of household formations and the

Table 2 • Average Annual Net Change in Households by Age Group

Between the Years	Age Group						
	Under 25	25–34	35–44	45–54	55–64	Over 65	All Ages
1961–1965	171	41	79	129	200	308	927
1966–1970	186	365	−45	163	246	278	1,194
1971–1975*	305	655	35	140	110	395	1,640
1976–1980*	115	630	440	−50	200	415	1,750
1981–1985	100	455	590	90	100	365	1,700
1986–1990	−30	340	645	300	20	350	1,625

*Adjusted to allow for the additional 1.4 million households found in the *1980 Census* compared to previous estimates of 1980 households.
Sources: U.S. Bureau of the Census, *Current Population Surveys, 1980 Census, and Population Projection p-25, No. 805.*

Table 3 • Population Mobility

During any five-year period approximately:
3 out of every 4 people in their 20s will move.
1 out of 2 people in their 30s and early 40s will move.
1 out of 4 people over 45 will move.

Source: U.S. Census Bureau, *Geographical Mobility Survey*.

ownership-rental relationships in various age groups provide useful insights into people's housing preferences.

People usually begin thinking seriously about buying their first home in their middle 20s (see Table 4). The switch from rental to ownership occurs most rapidly between the late 20s and early 30s and then continues at a diminishing rate through the late 30s and early 40s.

Throughout the 1980s, many households in the first wave will be seeking to purchase their first home. By the middle of the 1980s, more and more of the second wave will join them in looking for their first home to buy. Meanwhile, the primary rental group—those under 25—will shrink. Even the significant gains in households over 65 (an age group when some people sell their homes) will not offset the passage of the postwar babies out of the rental market. Consequently, housing demand in the 1980s is expected to place significant emphasis on homeownership.

In the mid 1970s, the mix of shelter production (housing starts plus mobile homes) began changing. Gradually, the 65/35 division between single-family and multifamily units moved towards a 75/25 ratio. Recent economic conditions have reversed that trend, raising the share of multifamily starts.

In the early 1980s, rising housing prices along with increasingly scarce mortgage credit and record high mortgage rates forced potential home buyers of all ages to rethink their housing options. Nondetached single family housing ownership became increasingly popular because of its affordability. Many multifamily units were sold as condominiums, propping up multifamily building. Condominiums accounted for a third of all multifamily starts. The rehabilitation and conversion into condominiums of existing apartments and even some nonresidential structures grew. In addition, mobile-home (also known as manufactured housing) units gained greater consumer acceptance.

Significantly, people have been using the existing housing stock more intensively to satisfy their shelter needs. While figures on rehabilitations and conversions are elusive, comparing total shelter production against net increases in the housing stock does indicate how the existing stock has been used during periods with quite different levels of demographic demand for housing. During the post-World War II housing boom, only 1.8 million units of the existing housing stock were replaced through new production (see Figure 2). In the 1960s, when demand pressures were easing and the emphasis was on upgrading the quality of the housing, 6.4 million existing units were replaced by new production. In the 1970s, replacement through new production dropped to 1.7

Table 4 • Occupancy Status by Age of Household Head

Occupancy Status:	All Ages	Under 25	25–29	30–34	35–39	40–44	45–54	55–64	65+
Homeowner	100%	100%	100%	100%	100%	100%	100%	100%	100%
	68	26	47	63	73	76	80	82	74
Renter	32	74	53	37	27	24	20	18	26

Source: U.S. Census Bureau, *Current Population Reports*, series P–20, No. 366.

Figure 2 • Net Changes in Housing Stock During the 1950s, 1960s, and 1970s

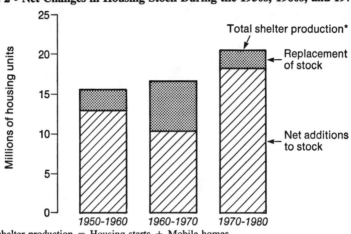

*Total shelter production = Housing starts + Mobile homes
Source: U.S. Bureau of the Census.

million units as rehabilitation and conversions were used to preserve and add to usable living space.

With prospective demand at an extraordinarily high level, extensive fixing up of the existing building stock will continue in the 1980s. In addition, exceptional pressures will be brought to bear on housing production (see Table 5). An enormous pent-up demand for housing, especially ownership units, was created because of the low level of housing starts in the early 1980s compared to the high level of household formations.

Unfortunately, it is effective demand (desire backed up by purchasing power), not potential demand, that matters. To transform this large potential into effective housing demand is clearly dependent on the nation's ability to restructure the economy and to resolve its financial and fiscal problems. Interwoven in this overall effort is the continued reshaping of the residential mortgage finance system to assure ready access to funds at competitive terms.

Housing Finance: Its Problems and Its Potential

Until the early 1980s, residential housing activity roughly followed a five-year cycle. Each cycle consisted of a year of very low activity, two years of expansion, a peak year, and then a year of slippage. The increasing scarcity and rising cost of mortgage credit generally would pull housing off its peak and into a steep decline. As the rest of the economy weakened and other long-term credit demands eased, funds would return to the mortgage market, lowering credit costs and increasing the availability of mortgage money, sparking a housing recovery.

Table 5 • Housing Demand and Supply: 1971–1990 (annual averages, in thousands of dwelling units)

	1971–75	1976–80	1981–85	1986–90
Demand:				
Net households formed	1,650	1,750	1,700	1,625
Removals*	700	550	500	500
2nd Homes, vacancies, etc.	200	200	200	200
Unmet demand carry over	—	—	200	575
Total	2,550	2,500	2,600	2,900
Supply:				
New housing starts	1,800	1,700	1,400	1,800
Mobile homes	450	250	275	350
Conversions*	300	350	350	350
Total	2,550	2,300	2,025	2,500
Unmet potential demand	—	200	575	400

*Removals include demolitions, merged units, and residential units transferred to other uses. Conversions include subdivision of existing units into more units and transformation of nonresidential structures into residential uses. Figure for removals and conversions are judgmental but were derived from a study of the trends in the *Annual Housing Surveys*.
Sources: U.S. Census Bureau and U.S. Department of Housing. Source for the format idea is George A. Christie, Chief Economist, McGraw-Hill Information Systems Company.

Availability of mortgage money is often characterized in terms of feast or famine. However, when net changes in mortgage debt are viewed in five-year intervals and compared to the rest of the capital markets (all mortgages, stocks, and bonds), the feast or famine view is questionable (see Table 6). Over the past three decades, which include periods of war, moderate inflation, and rampant inflation, residential finance consistently accounted for one fifth to one quarter of the total long-term funds raised (except between 1971 and 1975 when the severe plunge in stock values in 1973 and 1974 threw off the relationship).

In the middle of those years, the 1966 credit crunch created substantial doubts about the future of mortgage-market institutions and instruments. Subsequently, innovations in mortgage and savings instruments occurred: the FNMA commitment auction (1968), GNMA mortgage-backed security (1970) and FHLMC participation certificates (1972); and an assortment of new savings accounts with higher maximum interest rates and different maturities and minimum-balance requirements. Such developments enabled the housing market in the 1970s to continue to attract considerable mortgage funds in an increasingly inflationary environment.

Today, the residential mortgage market is adjusting to the aftermath of many years of insidious inflation that ruined investors' appetites for long-term, fixed-rate loans and strongly influenced the rapid deregulation of thrift institutions. Significantly, deregulation has brought to the market new mortgage and savings instruments that will be vital in competing successfully for funds in the 1980s.

Table 6 • Net Change in Outstanding Long-Term Debt and Equity for Selected Time Periods

	1951–1955	1956–1960	1961–1965	1966–1970	1971–1975	1976–1980
Long-term debt and equity ($ billions)	235	262	479	443	596	1,937
Percent distribution	100%	100%	100%	100%	100%	100%
Long-term debt	27	49	38	64	102	61
Bonds:	3	19	11	33	47	28
U.S. Treasury	−16	−3	−1	1	8	9
Federal credit agencies*	1	2	1	6	7	4
State and local government	9	9	6	8	12	6
Corporate	8	10	4	17	18	8
Foreign	1	1	1	1	2	1
Mortgages:	24	30	27	31	55	33
Single-family	18	20	17	17	32	24
Multifamily	2	3	4	5	7	2
Other	4	7	6	9	16	7
Equities (at market value)	73	51	62	36	−2	39
GNP deflator (average for the period)	2.6%	2.6%	1.7%	4.6%	7.5%	8.2%

*Excludes mortgage pools, which are included with mortgages, but includes some short-term debt.
Source: Federal Reserve Board, *Flow of Funds*.

Thrift Industry

The efforts of the thrift industry (mutual savings banks and savings and loan associations) to rebuild net worth after their serious financial troubles of the early 1980s epitomizes the problems and potential of the residential mortgage market. Thrifts traditionally invested significant sums in mortgages, accounting for nearly three fifths of the single-family mortgages outstanding and for almost one half of the multifamily mortgages outstanding in the early and mid 1970s (see Tables 7 and 8).

Their share of direct mortgage holding began shrinking in the latter part of the 1970s because of several factors. Most important were the laws and regulations that bound the thrift industry to the residential market and forced them to borrow "short" and to lend "long." In periods where short-term rates were lower than long-term rates (the 1950s and early 1960s), these were acceptable investment strategies. However, they became progressively more dangerous tactics during the 1970s, when short-term rates periodically exceeded long-term rates, triggering large deposit outflows from these institutions.

To minimize the damage from "disintermediation," thrift institutions sought to improve the liquidity of their mortgage investments within the confines of their regulatory constraints. The development of GNMA MBSs and FHLMC PCs provided liquidity because these marketable securities could be used as collateral for repurchase agreements and other borrowing programs, or sold outright if market conditions warranted. (Editor's note: The efforts by FHLMC and FNMA to help thrifts liquify their portfolio have been ongoing, varied, and comprehensive and are discussed in Chapter 3 of this handbook.)

Thrift institutions also sought more flexibility in adjusting their portfolio yields to changes in interest rates and in matching up the term structure of their assets and liabilities. During the 1970s, federal and state legislatures clung to the concept of thrifts as specialized institutions servicing the housing market.

Table 7 • Year-End Holdings of Single-Family Mortgage Loans by Type of Investor: 1972, 1976, and 1983

	1972	1976	1983
Outstandings ($ billions)	328	493	1,016
Lenders (percent distribution)	100%	100%	100%
Thrift institutions	63	62	44
Commercial banks	15	16	16
Government credit agencies (including state and local)	8	8	12
Mortgage pools	3	8	24
Others*	11	6	4

*Life insurance companies, pension funds, mortgage companies, and REITs.
Source: Department of Housing and Urban Development.

Table 8 • Year-End Holdings of Multifamily Mortgage Loans by Type of Investor: 1972, 1976, and 1983

	1972	1976	1983
Outstanding ($ billions)	61	87	124
Lenders (percent distribution)	100%	100%	100%
Thrift institutions	45	46	44
Life insurance companies	27	21	15
Government credit agencies (including state and local)	16	21	23
Others*	12	12	18

*Commercial banks, pension funds, mortgage companies, REITs, and mortgage pools.
Source: Department of Housing and Urban Development.

Repeated bouts with disintermediation gradually modified these attitudes, and regulators slowly improved the interest rates and terms on some high-balance time and savings accounts. However, Congress continued to fix the rates on these and other deposit accounts. Thus, whenever open-market rates surpassed those ceilings, thrift institutions were vulnerable to disintermediation. Not until the introduction in 1978 of six-month money market certificates (MCCs) did deposit institutions finally obtain authority to issue a market rate savings instrument.

While piecemeal deregulation of the liability side of their balance sheet proceeded, very little was done for the asset side until legislators were confronted with the very real possibility of a thrift industry collapse in the early 1980s. Within two years, Congress passed two pieces of landmark deregulation legislation: the Depository Institutions Deregulation and Monetary Control Act of 1980 (DIDA) and the Garn-St Germain Act of 1982. DIDA expanded the thrift industry's investment authority in such short-term instruments as commercial paper and consumer loans, and in such long-term lending as corporate bonds and commercial real estate. It established the Depository Institutions Deregulations Committee (DIDC) to eliminate both the interest rate differential (Regulation Q) and interest rate ceilings on time and savings certificates. In response to DIDA's liberalization spirit, the Federal Home Loan Bank Board (FHLBB) permitted savings and loan associations to originate and invest in alternative mortgage instruments and granted service corporations the powers to issue letters of credit and engage in securities activity, including advising, underwriting, distributing, and selling securities.

The Garn-St Germain Depository Institutions Act of 1982 (Garn-St Germain Act) enabled federal thrifts to invest in commercial, corporate, business, and agricultural loans on the same basis as national banks and to engage in equipment leasing. In addition, their educational lending powers were expanded and asset-percentage restrictions were substantially eased for amounts invested in nonresidential real estate and consumer loans. The Garn-St Germain Act also directed DIDC to create a money market deposit account (MMDA) for thrift institutions and commercial banks to compete with Wall Street's money market funds (MMFs). MMDAs were an immediate success. Three months after their introduction, they exceeded $300 billion, of which approximately $125 billion flowed to thrifts, effectively ending two and a half years of disintermediation.

Although deregulation has greatly expanded their ability to compete in these new areas, there are still significant reasons that thrift institutions will remain large suppliers of housing funds in this decade. Neither deregulation bill altered the strong tax incentives that thrifts have for investing in residential mortgages. In addition, the growing use of adjustable rate mortgages, hedging techniques, and MBSs has made it easier for thrift institutions to manage the term and interest rate risks in funding housing-related assets.

In contrast, to redeploy their assets will be difficult and time-consuming. These other markets are much smaller than the housing market. The largest— consumer lending—is less than half the size of the residential market (see Table 9). Furthermore, each of these markets is already fiercely competitive, and most thrifts are not staffed with the necessary in-house specialized lending skills to make an immediate, dramatic impact.

Interestingly, thrift holdings of residential mortgages, including MBSs, were about 53 percent of the total residential debt outstanding at the end of 1983, down from their 60 percent share in 1972. While this percentage may slip further as these institutions search for a balance between asset diversification and the attraction of residential lending, thrifts still should be supplying nearly half of all housing funds at the end of the decade.

Table 9 • Outstanding Consumer, Corporate, Construction, and Mortgage Loans on December 31

	$ Billions			Compound Growth Rate 1972–1983 (p.a. percent)
	1970	1975	1983	
Mortgages:	470	801	1,822	11%
Single-family	295	490	1,214	12
Multifamily	60	101	149	5
Other	115	210	459	10
Construction loans:	n.a.	41	108	13
Single-family	n.a.	13	32	12
Multifamily	n.a.	11	22	9
Nonresidential	n.a.	17	54	16
Consumer credit:	172	268	608	11
Installment	106	172	396	11
Other	66	96	212	10
Corporate business loans:	104	172	402	11

n.a. = not available.
Sources: Federal Reserve Board and Department of Housing and Urban Development.

Other Sources of Housing Funds

Although the thrift industry has been the dominant lender, the residential market has always attracted funds from others. With thrifts actively diversifying, the housing market will need even more funds from others to satisfy the enormous potential demand for housing.

Among the remaining private financial institutions, commercial banks hold approximately 15 percent of the residential debt outstanding (see Tables 7 and 8). In the future, they are not likely to increase their percentage for the same reasons that thrift institutions want to diversify their lending.

Life insurance companies are significant contributors to the multifamily market, primarily in the income-producing rental segment. Although their direct investment in home mortgages is relatively small, they do indirectly finance single-family loans through their purchases of FNMA, GNMA, and FHLMC securities. However, the major thrust of their real estate activity remains in the income-producing nonresidential market, where they are the dominant lender.

With the likelihood of little gain in commercial bank and life insurance company involvement, the residential market will increasingly look to the pension funds for more money. The attraction is twofold: First, assets of private and public (state and local) pension funds are expected to nearly quadruple in the 1980s, rising from over $600 billion in 1980 to nearly $2,250 billion in 1990; second, relatively few of their assets are invested in the residential mortgage market, either through direct holdings of mortgages or indirectly through purchases of housing agency securities or MBSs. Unfortunately, the business and government sectors also view pension funds as prospective funding sources. Consequently, the residential market will encounter considerable competition for pension fund dollars.

Pension funds have broad discretionary investment powers. This permits them to choose among investments, selecting those that can best protect their principal against inflation, provide high relative real returns (including the possibility of equity ownership), and have good liquidity. MBSs meet many of their criteria, because they usually provide very favorable spreads over other long-term financial instruments. Moreover, MBSs often offer safety in the form of government guarantees and provide liquidity through an effective secondary market. However, because MBSs are now primarily backed by long-term, fixed-rate loans, their market value could be sharply affected in a volatile financial environment.

To capture a $250 billion to $400 billion of the growth in pension fund assets (about 15 to 25 percent of their expected increase), the residential mortgage market must develop an effective method of packaging adjustable rate home loans into MBS. Significantly, federal mortgage agencies, such as GNMA, FNMA, and FHLMC are taking an active part in creating such securities.

The Role of Government Mortgage Agencies

Federal and state governments created mortgage agencies to maintain order in the residential mortgage market, which generally meant buying loans whenever private institutions could not. In addition, these agencies are often directed to support various federal or state housing subsidy efforts. Such programs are likely to continue with increasing focus on subsidizing elderly and low-income multifamily housing. Consequently, agency holdings of apartment mortgages are likely to rise in the 1980s, while single-family mortgage holdings may decline.

With the development of a GNMA mortgage-backed security in 1970, federal mortgage agencies shifted their emphasis from merely holding loans toward the development and support of mortgage instruments that could be sold and resold to others, adding much needed liquidity to residential mortgage investment.

Initially, FHA/VA mortgages were selected for the GNMA MBS because of their wide acceptance among mortgage investors, their uniform mortgage documentation, their well-established criteria for evaluating housing construction and mortgagor credit, and their government mortgage insurance or guaranty against borrower default. Subsequently, FHLMC and, and later, FNMA devised standardized loan documentation and credit criteria, including the use of private mortgage insurance, for conventional loans. Their standards quickly spread throughout the mortgage-lending community. Today, there is a large and growing volume of conventional MBSs.

In the 1970s, some mortgage lenders began using alternative mortgage instruments that distributed the interest and inflation risks between borrowers and lenders. FHLMC and FNMA supported those efforts through special programs to purchase a wide variety of adjustable-rate mortgages. More recently, they, as well as private institutions, have been developing techniques for securitizing alternative mortgage instruments. In the 1980s, such innovations will continue as the residential market seeks ways to expand mortgage availability and affordability.

How Many Dollars Are Needed?

The dwelling-unit forecast for the 1980s in Table 5 is based on the view that housing activity will not match potential demand through most of the decade because of the relative scarcity of mortgage credit. To fund even this forecast level of transactions will require an estimated $1,550 billion in net new-mortgage debt (see Table 10), approximately two times the net increase in the 1970s.

In this projection, the residential recovery, begun in late 1982, is expected to struggle upwards for another two years against the combined weight of rising

Table 10 • Net Change in Residential Mortgage Debt Outstanding and Total Number of Dwelling Units Started, Sold, or Shipped in the 1960s, 1970s, and 1980s

	1961–1970	1971–1980	1981–1990 Projections	
			Low*	High
Net change in mortgage debt ($ billions):				
Single family	153	684	1,400	2,350
Multifamily	39	77	130	165
Mobile homes	n.a.	10†	20	35
All loans	192	771	1,550	2,550
Dwelling units (millions):				
Housing starts	14.2	17.5	16.0	17.4
Existing home sales	n.a.	28.3	30.0	33.5
Mobile-home shipments	2.4	3.5	3.1	3.3

n.a. = not available.
*The housing starts and mobile-home shipments were derived from the annual averages in Table 5.
†Estimate.
Sources: For the years 1961–70 and 1971–80, the dollar figures are from the Federal Reserve Board, while the dwelling unit numbers are from the Census Bureau and the National Association of REALTORS®.

interest rates and diminishing availability of mortgage money. At its peak in 1985–86, shelter production (housing starts and mobile-home shipments) barely exceeds 2.1 million units, at a time when prospective demand could be nearly 2.5 million units. Housing then slumps for two years, before regaining its strength late in the decade. In the decade's final year, shelter construction (including mobile homes) moves above 2.4 million units, spurred on by better mortgage conditions.[2]

Normally, when potential demand consistently outruns supply, increases in housing prices accelerate rapidly. Although new and existing home prices in the forecast rise and fall with the different phases of the residential cycle, their average yearly gain for the 1980s is barely 6 percent, compared to 10 percent per year in the 1970s.[3] This is partly the result of down-sizing in detached new homes and partly the greater attraction of condominiums in new and converted buildings. However, the primary reasons are the anticipated poor availability of mortgage credit and its expected high cost. The persistent difficulties in finding home buyers that can qualify for mortgages will slow increases in home prices.

Nevertheless, price increases, not gains in activity, cause the enormous change in mortgage debt in this projection. For example, at a 6 percent annual

---

[2]Existing home sales, following the same course as new-home activity, tops out at 3.3 million units in 1985–86, declines for two years, and then recovers to exceed 3.8 million units in 1990.

[3]Advances in mobile-home prices are around 8 percent per year because of the expected greater use of double-wides and improved quality in both construction and permanent site locations.

growth rate, the average new-home price will advance from nearly $79,000 in 1980 to $140,000 in 1990 (based on the Census Bureau's price index of houses sold). In turn, the average home price for the decade will be nearly $110,000, compared to the $50,000 average for the 1970s, a 220 percent appreciation. Meanwhile, single-family starts will average 1,060,000 units per year, 7.5 percent lower than the average annual rate for the 1970s.

By itself, the $1,550 billion net increase is a staggering figure. However, it does not satisfy all the potential demand for housing in the 1980s (see Table 5). The question arises: How much would be needed to eliminate the shortfall between demand and supply? To answer that, another dwelling-unit forecast is made that assumes complete satisfaction of prospective demand in the 1980s. In addition to the $1,550 billion, this projection indicates that mortgage debt will have to rise another $1,000 billion to fund the necessary building (see Table 10). The total of $2,550 billion is nearly three and a half times the net change registered in the 1970s.

Because of the very low level of activity in 1981 and 1982, shelter production will have to achieve an unprecedented rate of building (over 2 million units in seven consecutive years, 1984–90) in the remainder of the decade to fulfill all the potential demand. Using a cyclical pattern similar to the one in the low projection, shelter construction at the next peak (in 1985–86) will have to exceed 2.4 million units. That level has only been surpassed in the three-year period 1971–1973, when both rental apartment building and mobile-home shipments were at record levels. Although falling in the next two years, starts plus shipments will still have to total more than 2 million units, something that has never happened in previous housing slumps. Finally, shelter production will have to recover and eventually advance beyond 2.5 million units in 1990. For the entire decade, this projection means an annual average of 2,060,000 units, which is 150,000 units per year higher than the low projection but 40,000 units per year less than was actually built in the 1970s.[4]

For the high protection to be met, the assumed high cost and poor availability of mortgage credit would have to be alleviated, so that the substantial number of potential buyers could qualify for mortgages. If all potential buyers were able to qualify, they would create a surge in effective demand, and housing prices would respond with double-digit increases. Consequently, new-, existing-, and mobile-home prices would grow at a 10¼ percent annual rate, compared to 6 percent in the low projection and 10 percent in the 1970s.

In the high projection, most of the addition to mortgage debt comes from escalating prices with some expansion in new and existing home sales. The average new-home price approaches $210,000 in 1990 versus $140,000 in the low projection. As a result, the average new price for the decade would be

---

[4]In the high projection, existing home sales would average 3,350,000 units, or 350,000 units per year higher than the low projection and 520,000 units per year higher than the yearly average in the 1970s.

$132,000, or 260 percent more than the average price for the 1970s. However, single-family starts would average 1,190,000 units per year, only 4 percent higher than the 1970s average annual rate.

There are several elements common to both projections: Only about one third of the growth in mortgages in each prediction is expected to occur in the first half of the decade; and both forecasts anticipate a much stronger economy in the second half of the decade than in the first half.

The mix of total shelter production in both estimates emphasizes housing for sale because of the exceptionally large number of households in the first-time home buying age. Single-family detached housing accounts for nearly 55 percent of the total. Mobile homes make up another 16 percent. Condominiums for sale in multifamily structures are almost 15 percent. Thus, nearly 85 percent of shelter construction is expected to be aimed at the ownership market, leaving only 15 percent for rental apartments. However, the combination of rental apartments and condominiums reveals that close to 30 percent of new units started are in multifamily buildings.

Both projections are based on net changes in outstanding first mortgages. Because of inadequate statistics, no attempt is made to project second-mortgage formations, although second-mortgage loans could provide several hundreds of billions of dollars for mortgage finance.

At the end of 1980, there were more than $1,130 billion in residential mortgages outstanding.[5] By the end of this decade, that amount could range between $2,675 billion and $3,675 billion. Over 90 percent of those loans are expected to be single-family mortgages ($2,400 billion to $3,350 billion). Most of those loans will also be written on standardized forms, regardless of whether they are fixed-rate or some type of adjustable mortgage instrument. Consequently, even if the mortgages are initially held in portfolio, institutions can later raise money by pooling them and issuing MBSs. In turn, much of the estimated expansion in single-family debt may ultimately flow through the secondary market, which will provide needed liquidity to the residential mortgage market.

Near record increases in household formations assure a very strong demographic demand for housing in the 1980s. Since three fifths of the new households will be in the age of first-time home purchase, most of their aspirations will be directed towards the ownership market, rather than the rental market. However, scarcity of mortgage funds and historically high mortgage rates in the first few years of the decade have held shelter production well under its potential. That has forced more and more consumers to modify their desires for a detached single-family home and instead to concentrate on finding affordable housing, even if it means accepting condominiums, mobile homes, or units in rehabilitated or converted residential and nonresidential structures. Simulta-

---

[5]At the end of 1980, single-family mortgages outstanding were nearly $980 billion, multifamily mortgages outstanding were nearly $137 billion, and mobile-home loans outstanding were more than $17 billion.

neously, the deregulation of thrifts and the widespread investor aversion to long-term, fixed rate mortgages has spurred the residential market's search for new techniques for attracting funds, such as adjustable rate mortgages and new types of mortgage-backed securities.

In response to the large demographic demand for housing, both the push for financial innovation and the increasing shift in home buyer attitudes will continue throughout the second half of the decade. An enormous volume of funds will flow into the residential market, financing a very high level (by recent standards) of new and existing housing transactions. Nevertheless, because of the sheer size of this potential demand, not all of it can be satisfied in the 1980s, promising a continuation of strong housing activity in the early years of the next decade.

Chapter 2

Residential Mortgage and Capital Markets

David F. Seiders
Senior Staff Vice President for Housing Policy
and Mortgage Finance
National Association of Home Builders

Residential mortgage credit can flow to borrowers through a number of channels, or *circuits,* in the financial system. Ultimately, mortgage capital comes primarily from the saving of private nonfinancial sectors of the economy—the household and business sectors—which invest their funds either in financial intermediaries or directly in financial market instruments issued by private or governmental entities.[1] In some cases, the ultimate savers lend directly to mortgage borrowers—i.e., by buying mortgage instruments "issued" by borrowers. But most mortgage lending is done by private or governmental intermediaries that receive funds either through deposits placed with them by savers, through issues of their own debt instruments in the markets, or through resales of mortgages to institutions that, themselves, raise funds from savers in one way or another.

Depository institutions traditionally have been the major force in housing finance in the United States, both making *(originating)* large amounts of mortgage loans and holding large amounts of mortgage assets in their portfolios. Through the process of financial intermediation, the depositories have provided a number of valuable services to both savers and mortgage borrowers, including *denomination intermediation* (taking small amounts of funds from individual savers and making large mortgage loans to borrowers) and *maturity intermediation* (taking short-term funds from liquidity-conscious savers and making long-term loans to purchasers of real estate assets having long service lives). Some types of depositories—savings and loan associations and savings banks—actually have been required by federal or state laws or regulations, and have been encouraged by federal tax law, to concentrate their investments in residential mortgage assets. Furthermore, systems of federal and state deposit insurance have facilitated the process of intermediation by relieving savers of concern either about the quality of assets acquired by depository institutions

---

[1]Government and foreign sectors may also be ultimate sources of mortgage capital.

with their funds or about the interest-rate risk incurred by depositories that channel their short-term funds into long-term mortgage assets.

The importance of depository institutions in the housing finance system could decline markedly in the future. Legislation such as the Garn–St Germain Depository Institutions Act of 1982 has substantially broadened the investment choices available to savings and loan associations and savings banks, and the serious financial problems encountered in recent years by depositories that had concentrated their investments in long-term residential mortgages have encouraged usage of the new powers. It is possible that the depositories increasingly will act like mortgage bankers, retaining their profitable mortgage origination and servicing functions but selling the bulk of their mortgage production on secondary markets.[2] Unless government-related secondary market credit agencies acquired these mortgages—an unlikely prospect in view of the apparent desire of Congress and the current administration to contain the governmental presence in the nation's financial system—additional mortgage investment would be needed from private institutions that are not required or encouraged by public policy to acquire mortgage assets. If heavier mortgage investment were not forthcoming from such private sources, mortgage interest rates would rise relative to yields on other capital market instruments and the total volume of mortgage lending would decline.

In order to attract a broad range of private investors, mortgage instruments will have to compete effectively in the nation's capital markets with corporate and government securities. To date, only mortgage-related securities carrying the guarantees of federal agencies or federally sponsored enterprises have been effective forces in the capital markets. If the process of integration between mortgage and capital markets is to proceed successfully without further proliferation of federally guaranteed mortgage-related securities, further development of markets for private alternatives is essential.

This chapter lays out background material on the evolving need for secondary mortgage market transactions and the developing role of mortgage-backed securities in the process of integration of mortgage and capital markets. The first section provides an overview of primary and secondary mortgage markets, examining the roles of private and federal instruments and institutions. The second section focuses upon the markets for mortgage pass-through securities, discussing the development of these markets to date and the effects the securities have had on mortgage lending and investment patterns. The third section deals with federal policy toward the pass-through securities markets. Emphasis is placed upon a major initiative, stemming from the 1982 report of the President's Commission on Housing, that is designed to further the development of fully private mortgage pass-through securities. The final section considers the

---

[2]The likelihood of this scenario varies directly with the degree of difficulty to be encountered by depository institutions in marketing adjustable-rate mortgages to household borrowers, in lengthening their liability structure, or in hedging their portfolio interest-rate risk through financial futures markets or other means.

outlook for private securities under alternative government policies toward the programs of federally sponsored enterprises.

The Mortgage Lending/Investment Process

The housing finance system in the United States includes many private and public institutions and several levels of market activity. In simple terms, the mortgage lending/investment process involves the provision of housing credit to borrowers by institutions and individuals who hold housing loans in their portfolios. However, a number of institutions may come between borrowers and ultimate investors, and the characteristics of the mortgage asset may be transformed along the way as insurance and guarantees are attached and as securities replace the original mortgage loans.

Primary-Market Instruments and Participants

Residential mortgage loans are made (originated) in *primary markets* where lenders and borrowers transact business. Borrowers obtain mortgage credit in these markets mainly from depository institutions or mortgage banking companies that maintain lending offices in communities throughout the country. Since the 1930s, mortgage loans made in primary markets typically have been long-term, fixed-rate instruments with level payments that fully pay off *(amortize)* the principal balance over the loan term. However, new types of mortgage instruments have emerged recently to serve the various needs of borrowers and investors in an environment of inflation and heightened interest rate uncertainty, a development facilitated by adjustments to a number of federal and state laws and regulations. Most of the new mortgage instruments provide for adjustable interest rates, graduated payment schedules, or some combination of these two features.

Repayment of mortgage loans made in primary markets may be insured or guaranteed by third parties. The need for such coverage depends primarily on the size of the loan relative to the market value of the property and the financial status of the borrower. The federal government underwrites fixed-rate residential mortgages (both level-payment and graduated-payment mortgages), primarily under the insurance programs of the Federal Housing Administration (FHA) and the guarantee programs of the Veterans Administration (VA).[3] In recent years, FHA/VA loans have accounted for roughly one fifth of the total dollar volume of home mortgages originated.

Private mortgage insurance has become an important factor in primary markets since the early 1970s. In recent periods, the private mortgage insurance industry—now made up of 14 companies—has insured roughly the same num-

---

[3]On July 30, 1984, an FHA insurance program for adjustable-rate home mortgages was inaugurated.

ber of home mortgage loans as the FHA and VA combined. Unlike the FHA and VA, these companies have insured adjustable-rate as well as fixed-rate loans. Still, noninsured conventional mortgages (ordinarily contracts with loan-to-value ratios below 80 percent) still account for about 60 percent of all mortgage credit originated in this country.

Table 1 shows institutional distributions of residential mortgage originations in primary markets, broken down by type of mortgage: FHA/VA and conventional. Thrift institutions (savings and loan associations and savings banks) traditionally have been the most important originators of residential mortgages, and they have specialized in conventional rather than FHA/VA loans. This specialization developed primarily because of somewhat higher net yields on conventional loans and limited needs by these institutions for liquid mortgage assets. In the FHA/VA market, mortgage companies have been dominant, originating about four fifths of the total in recent years. These companies also have accounted for a rising share of originations in the conventional loan market. Commercial banks originated a bit more than one fifth of total residential mortgage credit during the past decade. Banks have been a relatively minor factor in the FHA/VA loan market, but have accounted for roughly a fourth of origination activity in the much larger conventional loan market.

Secondary-Market Institutions and Instruments

Institutions operating in primary mortgage markets may hold the mortgages they originate, adding them to their asset portfolios. In many cases, however, originators sell their loan production on secondary markets, thereby replenishing their supplies of loanable funds. Transfers of outstanding *(seasoned)* mortgages among mortgage investors also take place on secondary markets.

Sales of mortgage loans from originators to investors inevitably involve some cost, but such transfers can be necessary for effective functioning of the housing finance system. Secondary market transactions may be needed to correct interregional imbalances in the supply of and demand for mortgage credit, as evidenced by interregional mortgage interest rate differentials. Secondary market transactions may also be needed to move mortgage assets from one type of institution to another within the same market area. The latter need arises within a system characterized by specialization and division of labor. One type of institution may perform a mortgage banking function, specializing in mortgage origination and servicing and selling mortgage assets to investors who choose not to perform these functions. Such a division of functions can be encouraged by federal or state regulations governing the activities of various types of institutions.

Mortgage originators may sell their loans on secondary markets through a number of channels. The particular channel to be employed depends, first of all, on whether the loans are government-underwritten or conventional, and on whether or not they are standard fixed-rate, level-payment contracts. Given the

Table 1 • Origination of Residential Mortgages by Type of Mortgage and Institution (institutional shares of property-type totals, in percent)

	1970	1971	1972	1973	1974	1975	1976	1977	1978	1979	1980	1981	1982	1983
Total residential mortgages														
Thrift institutions	45%	50%	53%	54%	49%	56%	60%	58%	53%	48%	48%	44%	39%	46%
Commercial banks	18	19	21	21	21	17	21	22	23	21	21	21	25	22
Mortgage companies	26	23	19	17	21	19	14	16	19	24	23	26	27	27
All other	11	8	7	8	9	8	5	4	6	7	9	9	9	5
FHA/VA mortgages														
Thrift institutions	15	18	17	17	15	16	17	12	11	9	11	9	5	8
Commercial banks	13	11	10	11	6	8	11	8	8	6	6	6	9	12
Mortgage companies	70	69	71	69	77	73	70	78	78	82	81	81	83	78
All other	3	2	2	3	2	2	2	2	3	3	3	4	3	2
Conventional mortgages														
Thrift institutions	60	64	64	62	58	66	67	67	62	59	57	53	49	58
Commercial banks	21	22	24	24	25	19	23	24	26	25	25	25	29	25
Mortgage companies	4	5	5	6	7	5	3	5	7	8	7	12	14	13
All other	16	11	8	9	11	9	6	5	6	8	11	10	8	4

Note: Data include originations of long-term residential mortgages (excluding construction loans) by 10 types of institutional lenders.
Source: U.S. Department of Housing and Urban Development.

loan type, the choice of channel depends on relative sales prices and marketing costs, as well as on relative servicing fees (and servicing responsibilities) that will prevail during the lives of the loans.

In general terms, mortgage originators have three major sales alternatives. First, they may sell whole loans or *mortgage participations* (portions of mortgage loans) to private investors, with or without another institution serving as intermediary or broker. The standardization of fixed-rate mortgage instruments provided by government insurance and guarantees has made FHA/VA loans acceptable to a variety of secondary market investors. Private mortgage insurance, as well as uniform mortgage documents developed during the past decade, have helped to make conventional loans more marketable.

Second, mortgage originators may sell their loans through the markets for pass-through securities. Using this technique, lenders pool homogeneous groups of loans (generally fixed-rate loans) and sell shares in these pools by issuing pass-through securities that entitle holders to portions of the flow of principal and interest payments on the underlying mortgages in the pools. The payments to securities holders ordinarily are guaranteed by government or private institutions, even when the mortgages in the pools backing the securities carry insurance or guarantees against default loss.

Third, mortgage originators may sell fixed- or adjustable-rate loans to federal or municipal government agencies that either issue debt (taxable or tax-exempt) and hold mortgages in their portfolios or resell the mortgages to private investors. In the event that agencies resell by issuing pass-through securities that they guarantee, they perform a so-called conduit function.

The extent to which seasoned mortgage assets (as opposed to newly originated loans) are bought and sold on secondary markets depends critically on their *liquidity*. Liquidity is an investment characteristic related to the speed at which transactions can be effected, the extent to which a sale influences the going market price, and the transactions costs (commissions and bid-asked price spreads) involved in selling and buying. Generally, the liquidity of a mortgage asset varies directly with both the amount outstanding and the degree of standardization of the asset (particularly standardization with respect to delinquency and default risk). As a general rule, federally underwritten (FHA/VA) mortgages are more liquid than fixed-rate conventional mortgage loans, even though the amount of conventional loans outstanding far exceeds the amount of FHA/VA loans. Adjustable-rate conventional loans are quite illiquid because of both limited amounts outstanding and lack of homogeneity.

The major development in secondary mortgage markets during the past decade has been the introduction and growth of federally related pass-through securities issued against pools of government-underwritten and conventional residential mortgage loans (primarily fixed-rate contracts). The predominant pass-through securities are those guaranteed by the Government National Mortgage Association (GNMA), a full-fledged federal agency. These securities, which represent shares in pools of federally underwritten mortgages (primarily

FHA-insured and VA-guaranteed), are issued by private mortgage originators (generally mortgage banking companies) and are held by a variety of private investors. Major securities dealers make primary and secondary "cash" markets in these securities, providing for both immediate and forward delivery. Moreover, futures markets in GNMAs have been organized on major exchanges, and exchange-based GNMA options have been authorized by the SEC.

The Farmers Home Administration (FmHA) is the only full-fledged federal agency that both issues and guarantees mortgage pass-through securities. The FmHA securities program has opened a channel between mortgage markets and the broader capital markets even though most of these instruments are not held by private investors. The securities are issued against pools of residential mortgages originated at FmHA offices through various home loan programs of this agency. Since the mid-1970s, the securities have been sold exclusively to the Federal Financing Bank, and proceeds from these sales have replenished a revolving fund used by FmHA to acquire additional mortgages. Via this mode of operation, therefore, the FmHA program has been channeling substantial amounts of funds raised by the Treasury into rural housing markets.

The Federal Home Loan Mortgage Corporation (FHLMC), a federally sponsored enterprise owned by the Federal Home Loan Bank System, issues and guarantees pass-through securities backed by pools of conventional residential mortgages. These mortgage pools traditionally have consisted of newly originated loans acquired from private institutions (primarily thrift institutions) by FHLMC through various purchase programs. Since the mid-1970s, pass-through securities have been marketed by FHLMC to private investors through a syndicate of securities dealers. Recent program changes also provide for pooling of seasoned residential mortgages and permit institutions that sell loans to FHLMC to market the pass-through securities on their own in connection with the so-called mortgage/securities swap programs.

The Federal National Mortgage Association (FNMA), a federally sponsored enterprise owned by private stockholders, began to issue and guarantee pass-through securities in 1981. In some cases, the mortgage pools consist of newly originated conventional home loans purchased by FNMA from lenders, and FNMA sometimes markets the securities through dealers. But like FHLMC, FNMA also has instituted securities programs involving seasoned mortgages and has permitted private institutions to swap pools of mortgages for FNMA-guaranteed pass-through securities.

Some mortgage pass-through securities have been issued by private institutions without the benefit of federal guarantees on either the pooled mortgages or the securities. However, the volume of such issues has been quite limited to date, despite the immense size of the conventional mortgage market and strenuous efforts by major financial intermediaries and the securities industry to develop this pass-through market (partly through the use of large private conduit firms). Price/cost relationships in the market generally have favored issuance of federally guaranteed securities by private institutions (GNMAs) and by federally sponsored enterprises (FNMA and FHLMC). Private securities have made significant footholds only in markets where they have not had to compete head-to-head with the federal varieties. In this regard, some success has been recorded with private placements tailored to the demands of investors like private and public pension funds. Public offerings by private conduit firms have been particularly successful when pools have been composed of large mortgage loans beyond the size limits set by Congress for FHLMC and FNMA ("non-conforming" loans).

Tables 2 and 3 provide information on the structure of secondary market activity.[4] Table 2 shows the composition of mortgage sales, by type of institution and mortgage. Mortgage companies traditionally have been the major sellers of residential mortgages, although their share of the total has declined somewhat since the early 1970s. The decline has occurred in the conventional component of the market, as these companies have continued to account for the lion's share of sales of FHA/VA loans. Thrift institutions, the major originators of conventional loans, have also been the principal sellers of these mortgages, accounting for about half the total in 1983.

Table 3 shows the composition of mortgage purchases, by type of mortgage and institution. Thrift institutions traditionally have been the largest single purchasers of conventional mortgages, just as they have been the principal sellers. Large transfers of conventional loans within the S&L industry have occurred to correct interregional imbalances in the supply of and demand for mortgage credit existing under a system of nationwide deposit-rate ceilings, limitations on outside borrowing powers of S&Ls, and restrictions on branching. In recent years, an excess of sales over purchases of conventional loans at thrifts has reflected, to a large degree, acquisitions by these institutions of FHLMC-guaranteed pass-through securities (not counted as mortgage purchases). The FHLMC program, in fact, has helped move large amounts of conventional loans from S&Ls in the capital-short western part of the country to S&Ls in the capital-surplus northeast region.

In the FHA/VA market, GNMA pools have become the major "purchasers" of loans sold on secondary markets (reaching 76 percent in 1983). In essence, mortgage companies—the principal originators and sellers of FHA/VA loans—have increasingly marketed their loan production by issuing GNMA-guaranteed securities and by selling these instruments to securities dealers or to private investors. At the same time, federally related agencies, particularly FNMA, have deemphasized government-underwritten loans in their purchase programs.

---

[4]Note that Tables 2 and 3 exclude transactions associated with mortgage/securities swap programs of FHLMC and FNMA as well as transfers of loans between FmHA and the Federal Financing Bank.

Table 2 • Sales of Residential Mortgages by Type of Mortgage and Institution (institutional shares of property-type totals, in percent)

	1970	1971	1972	1973	1974	1975	1976	1977	1978	1979	1980	1981	1982	1983
Total residential mortgages														
Thrift institutions	7%	10%	13%	13%	15%	18%	21%	25%	23%	24%	27%	26%	42%	29%
Commercial banks	10	10	9	8	7	11	10	11	10	8	12	9	7	9
Mortgage companies	71	68	61	62	65	53	44	52	54	58	54	56	41	54
All other	12	12	18	18	13	18	25	12	13	10	6	9	10	8
FHA/VA mortgages														
Thrift institutions	5	6	7	4	5	6	7	5	5	4	8	9	2	2
Commercial banks	13	10	7	7	5	6	7	6	7	5	6	5	6	9
Mortgage companies	81	79	75	73	84	69	68	87	84	87	82	76	76	82
All other	1	4	11	16	5	19	18	2	4	4	4	10	16	8
Conventional mortgages														
Thrift institutions	14	22	26	26	29	35	35	43	39	45	47	41	64	52
Commercial banks	5	9	11	9	9	17	14	15	13	12	18	13	7	10
Mortgage companies	35	32	31	44	40	33	19	22	27	29	27	38	22	30
All other	46	37	32	21	22	14	32	20	21	15	8	8	7	8

Note: Sales of conventional mortgages have been adjusted to exclude FHLMC and FNMA mortgage/securities swap programs, transfers of loans from the Farmers Home Administration to the Federal Financing Bank (through FmHA pools), and transfers of loans from the Federal Financing Bank to the Farmers Home Administration (sales out of FmHA pools back to FmHA).

Sources: U.S. Department of Housing and Urban Development, Federal Home Loan Mortgage Corporation, and Federal National Mortgage Association.

Table 3 • Purchases of Residential Mortgages by Type of Mortgage and Institution (institutional shares of property-type totals, in percent)

	1970	1971	1972	1973	1974	1975	1976	1977	1978	1979	1980	1981	1982	1983
Total residential mortgages														
Thrift institutions	37%	48%	49%	36%	27%	29%	33%	30%	21%	19%	21%	20%	31%	27%
Commercial banks	4	6	4	4	2	1	2	3	3	3	7	6	3	2
Federal and related agencies	37	19	19	32	36	37	23	17	30	21	18	16	22	15
Mortgage pools	13	21	19	18	27	27	35	40	36	41	36	36	31	42
Federally related	13	21	19	18	27	27	35	40	34	39	34	34	28	40
Private	0	0	0	0	0	0	0	0	2	2	2	2	3	2
All others	9	6	9	10	8	6	7	10	11	16	18	21	13	14
FHA/VA mortgages														
Thrift institutions	36	47	48	28	15	20	22	13	10	5	3	0	5	2
Commercial banks	4	7	4	3	1	1	1	2	1	1	1	2	2	2
Federal and related agencies	49	22	23	35	38	33	11	8	22	14	17	10	4	0
GNMA pools	3	18	14	19	33	40	57	61	49	63	64	60	65	76
All others	8	6	11	15	13	6	9	16	17	17	15	28	24	20
Conventional mortgages														
Thrift institutions	41	52	51	47	40	42	48	48	31	33	38	35	43	48
Commercial banks	3	3	4	5	4	1	3	5	4	5	12	10	4	3
Federal and related agencies	3	10	10	26	33	42	37	25	37	29	20	21	30	27
Mortgage pools	43	27	29	17	19	9	8	19	23	19	9	18	15	13
Federally related	43	27	29	17	19	9	8	18	20	15	6	14	11	10
Private	0	0	0	0	0	0	0	1	3	4	3	4	4	3
All others	10	8	4	5	0	6	4	6	6	14	21	16	8	9

Note: Purchases of conventional mortgages have been adjusted to exclude FHLMC and FNMA mortgage/securities swap programs, transfers of loans from the Farmers Home Administration to the Federal Financing Bank (through FmHA pools), and transfers of loans from the Federal Financing Bank to the Farmers Home Administration (purchases out of FmHA pools by FmHA). Purchases by mortgage pools are synonymous with issues of pass-through securities.
Sources: U.S. Department of Housing and Urban Development, Federal Home Loan Mortgage Corporation, Federal National Mortgage Association.

Mortgage Investors

Mortgage investors are the ultimate suppliers of mortgage credit. Table 4 shows trends in holdings of mortgage loans, by major types of institutions, since 1950. Depository institutions have clearly been the dominant mortgage holders, generally accounting for three fifths or more of the total. Savings and loan associations, alone, have held about 40 percent, on average, since the mid-1960s. The market share of depository institutions declined substantially after the late 1970s, however, as many thrift institutions encountered severe financial difficulties, allocated larger proportions of their investments to short-term nonmortgage assets, and swapped large amounts of mortgage assets for pass-through securities guaranteed by FNMA or FHLMC.

The share of residential mortgages held by federal agencies and federally sponsored enterprises has more than doubled during the past three decades, although the federal share of the total has remained relatively constant since 1970. Within the federal and related agency total, FNMA has been dominant, accounting for nearly four fifths of the total at the end of 1983.

Growth of mortgage pools that back issues of federally related pass-through securities has been striking. This component rose from a negligible amount in 1970 to one fifth of total residential mortgage debt outstanding at the end of 1983. The mortgage pools, of course, are not actually investors in mortgage assets. The ultimate suppliers of mortgage funds are the holders of the pass-through securities. In Table 5, pass-through securities have been allocated to major institutional groups to show trends in the investor distribution of total residential mortgage assets (mortgage loans plus pass-through securities). This table will be discussed further in the following section.

Development of Pass-Through Markets and Implications for Mortgage Lending and Investment Patterns

This section has several purposes: first, to describe the current state of development of the various markets for pass-through securities, in absolute terms and relative to the size of appropriate components of the mortgage market; second, to consider the relationship between the development of pass-through markets and the proportion of mortgage loans moved from primary markets into secondary markets; third, to examine the effect of mortgage securities on the structure of the investor base for residential mortgage assets; and, fourth, to provide some perspective on federally related mortgage/securities swap programs that have burgeoned since late 1981.

Development of Pass-Through Markets

More than $90 billion in residential mortgage pass-through securities were issued in 1983 (Table 6). More than $278 billion of such securities were out-

Table 4 • Residential-Mortgage Debt Outstanding by Type of Institution (percentage shares of total amount outstanding)

| End of Period | Depository Institutions | | | | Life Insurance Companies | Federal and Related Agencies | Federally Related Mortgage Pools† | All Others‡ |
	Total	Savings and Loan Associations	Mutual Savings Banks*	Commercial Banks				
1950	56%	24%	13%	19%	20%	3%	0%	21%
1955	60	30	15	15	21	3	0	15
1960	63	35	15	13	18	5	0	14
1965	69	40	16	13	15	3	0	14
1970	66	39	14	13	12	7	1	15
1975	67	42	11	14	6	8	5	14
1980	63	41	7	15	3	7	12	15
1981	61	39	7	15	3	7	12	16
1982	57	35	7	15	3	7	16	17
1983	55	32	8	15	2	7	20	16

*MSB data for 1983 include holdings of FSLIC-insured stock federal savings banks.

Sources: Board of Governors of the Federal Reserve System, Flow of Funds Accounts.

†Mortgages in pools backing pass-through securities issued and/or guaranteed by the Government National Mortgage Association, Federal Home Loan Mortgage Corporation, Federal National Mortgage Association, and Farmers Home Administration.

‡Includes mortgage-banking companies, real estate investment trusts, private pension and retirement funds, state and local government credit agencies and retirement funds, credit unions, individuals, and private mortgage pools.

Table 5 • Holdings of Residential Mortgage Loans and Pass-Through Securities by Type of Investor (percentage shares of total residential mortgage debt outstanding)

End of Period	Thrift Institutions			Diversified Private Investors†	Federal and Related Agencies‡	State and Local Government Agencies	Memo	
	Total	S&Ls	MSBs*				Individuals§	Diversified Private Institutions‖
1970	53%	39%	14%	39%	7%	1%	5%	34%
1971	54	41	14	38	7	1	6	32
1972	55	42	13	37	7	1	5	32
1973	54	42	12	37	7	2	5	32
1974	54	42	12	36	8	2	6	30
1975	54	43	11	35	9	2	6	29
1976	56	45	11	34	8	2	6	28
1977	57	46	11	34	7	2	6	28
1978	56	46	10	34	8	2	6	28
1979	53	44	9	37	8	2	7	30
1980	52	43	9	37	8	3	8	29
1981	50	42	8	39	8	3	9	30
1982	48	40	8	40	9	3	10	30
1983	48	38	10	40	9	3	8	32

*MSB data for 1983 include holdings of FSLIC-insured stock federal savings banks.
Sources: Board of Governors of the Federal Reserve System, Federal Home Loan Bank Board, National Association of Mutual Savings Banks, and U.S. Department of Urban Development.
†Includes individuals and private institutional investors other than thrift institutions.
‡Includes Federal Financing Bank holdings of Certificates of Beneficial Ownership issued by the Farmers Home Administration since 1975.
§Includes first and second mortgages as well as land contracts but excludes pass-through securities held by individuals (Federal Reserve staff estimates).
‖Includes all pass-through securities not held by thrift institutions or the federal government (Federal Financing Bank).

Table 6 • New Issues of Residential-Mortgage Pass-Through Securities by Type of Guarantee on Security ($ millions)

Period	Total	GNMA-Guaranteed	FHLMC-Guaranteed	FNMA-Guaranteed	FmHA-Guaranteed	Private*	Memo: Non-Swap Issues Sold to Private Investors†
1970	$ 1,968	$ 452	$ 0	$ 0	$1,516	$ 0	1,968
1971	3,963	2,702	67	0	1,194	0	3,963
1972	5,584	2,662	494	0	2,428	0	5,584
1973	4,907	2,953	317	0	1,637	0	4,907
1974	6,728	4,553	52	0	2,123	0	6,728
1975	11,235	7,447	554	0	3,234	0	8,001
1976	16,973	13,764	1,362	0	1,820	27	15,153
1977	24,881	17,440	4,500	0	2,686	255	22,195
1978	26,150	15,358	6,212	0	3,609	971	22,541
1979	33,480	24,940	4,546	0	2,286	1,708	31,194
1980	29,752	20,648	2,527	0	5,462	1,115	24,290
1981	24,693	14,256	4,377	717	4,158	1,185	17,512
1982	60,603	16,012	24,171	13,972	4,367	2,081	23,476
1983	90,322	50,496	19,692	13,341	4,039	2,754	61,823

*All securities without guarantees of federal agencies or federally related enterprises. Most issues carry private pool insurance, although some are backed by bank standby letters of credit or by subordination arrangements under which issuers hold subordinated securities.
†Excludes FHLMC and FNMA swap issues and FmHA issues of Certificates of Beneficial Ownership sold to the Federal Financing Bank. Prior to 1975, all FmHA-guaranteed pass-through securities were sold to the public; since early 1975, all FmHA securities have been sold to the Federal Financing Bank in the form of CBOs.
Sources: Government National Mortgage Association, Federal Home Loan Mortgage Corporation, Federal National Mortgage Association, Farmers Home Administration, and U.S. Department of Housing and Urban Development.

standing at the end of the year—accounting for a fifth of all residential mortgage debt outstanding (Table 7). For markets that generally did not exist prior to 1970, these certainly are impressive figures.

Some breakdowns of the pass-through totals are essential for analysis of the implications of mortgage securities for the structure of housing finance. For one thing, mortgage/securities swap programs of FHLMC and FNMA (discussed in some detail below) have swollen the new-issue figures without necessarily involving the transfer of mortgage assets among institutions. Secondly, the pass-through securities program of the FmHA, as discussed previously, simply transfers mortgage assets from one federal entity to another. Adjustment for these two factors provides a measure of non-swap issues sold to private investors (shown in the last column of Table 6). This measure totalled $62 billion in 1983. Such issues have been heavily dominated by the GNMA-guaranteed securities program. In fact, during 1983, issues of GNMAs accounted for 82 percent of all non-swap securities issues sold to private investors.

GNMAs have become the major secondary marketing vehicle for FHA/VA loans. As shown in Table 8, issues of single-family GNMAs actually exceeded the volume of FHA/VA home loans originated during 1983 (through 1983, virtually all securities issued against pools of FHA/VA loans were GNMAs);[5] furthermore, issues of GNMAs accounted for 93 percent of all sales of FHA/ VA home loans, both newly originated and seasoned mortgages. By contrast, non-swap issues of single-family conventional pass-through securities (both federally underwritten and private securities) accounted for only 7 percent of the originations of single-family conventional mortgages and made up only about 18 percent of the total sales of conventional home loans in 1983.

New-issue volume (adjusted), therefore, reveals a clear pattern. Most government-underwritten home mortgages originated in primary markets have been sold to private investors through the GNMA-guaranteed securities market. On the other hand, only small proportions of conventional mortgages originated in primary markets have been sold through the pass-through securities markets, and most of these issues have been guaranteed by federally sponsored enterprises (FNMA and FHLMC). Data on outstanding securities reveal much the same picture. Table 9 shows the evolving importance of mortgage pass-through securities in the portfolios of residential mortgage assets (mortgage loans plus pass-through securities) held by all types of private investors, broken down by the types of mortgages in the pools.[6] Since 1970, pass-through securities held by private investors have grown from less than 1 percent to one fifth of all

---

[5]Although GNMAs are issued only against pools of newly originated FHA/VA loans (those less than one year old), GNMA issues can exceed FHA/VA originations in a given period if the originations were higher in the previous period. FHA/VA originations rose sharply during the second half of 1982 in the wake of large declines in market interest rates, and peaked around year-end.

[6]This table includes securities obtained by investors via swap transactions with FNMA and FHLMC.

Table 7 • Residential Mortgage Pass-Through Securities Outstanding by Type of Guarantee on Security ($ millions)

End of Period	Total	GNMA-Guaranteed	FHLMC-Guaranteed	FNMA-Guaranteed	FmHA-Guaranteed	Private*	Memo: Total as Percent of Residential Mortgage Debt Outstanding
1970	$ 2,592	$ 347	$ 0	$ 0	$ 2,245	$ 0	1%
1971	6,832	3,074	65	0	3,693	0	2
1972	11,093	5,504	441	0	5,148	0	2
1973	14,252	7,890	766	0	5,596	0	3
1974	19,424	11,769	757	0	6,898	0	4
1975	29,344	18,257	1,598	0	9,489	0	5
1976	44,021	30,572	2,671	0	10,751	27	7
1977	63,944	44,896	6,610	0	12,156	282	8
1978	82,008	54,347	11,892	0	14,516	1,253	9
1979	110,975	75,787	15,180	0	17,047	2,961	11
1980	134,099	93,874	16,854	0	19,295	4,076	12
1981	153,425	105,790	19,853	717	21,804	5,261	13
1982	208,045	118,940	42,964	14,450	24,349	7,342	17
1983	278,625	159,850	57,895	25,121	25,494	10,265	20

*Cumulative issues of private pass-through securities, not adjusted for amortization and prepayments.
Sources: Government National Mortgage Association, Federal Home Loan Mortgage Corporation, Farmers Home Administration, U.S. Department of Housing and Urban Development, and Federal Reserve Board.

Table 8 • Non-Swap Issues of Pass-Through Securities Sold to Private Investors by Type of Mortgage in Pool

| | Dollar Volume of Issues ($ Millions) | | | | | Percent of Mortgage Originations (by Type) | | | | |
| | Single-Family | | Multifamily | | | | Single-Family | | Multifamily | |
Period	FHA/VA	Conventional	FHA	Conventional	Total	Total	FHA/VA	Conventional	FHA	Conventional
1970	$ 452	$ 1,491	$ 0	$ 25	$ 1,968	4%	4%	6%	0	0%
1971	2,702	1,209	0	52	3,963	6	15	3	0	1
1972	2,511	2,882	151	40	5,584	6	15	5	5	3
1973	2,775	1,876	178	78	4,907	5	22	3	6	2
1974	4,362	1,925	191	250	6,728	8	35	3	6	3
1975	7,248	554	199	0	8,001	9	48	1	9	0
1976	13,494	1,389	270	0	15,153	12	77	1	14	0
1977	17,088	4,755	352	0	22,195	12	67	3	16	0
1978	15,084	7,183	274	0	22,541	11	49	5	10	0
1979	24,632	6,254	308	0	31,194	15	62	4	8	0
1980	20,311	3,642	337	0	24,290	17	75	3	9	0
1981	13,745	3,256	511	0	17,512	16	76	4	13	0
1982	15,686	7,464	326	0	23,476	22	82	10	8	0
1983	49,556	11,327	940	0	61,823	28	104	7	36	0

Note: FHLMC and FNMA swap issues and certificates of beneficial ownership issued by the Farmers Home Administration have been excluded. Negligible amounts of FHLMC pass-throughs issued against pools of conventional multifamily mortgages have been included under single-family conventional issues. Securities issued against pools of FHA and VA mortgages reflect only the GNMA program; small amounts of FNMA pass-through securities backed by seasoned FHA/VA mortgages are included in the conventional issues for 1982 and 1983.

Sources: Government National Mortgage Association, Federal Home Loan Mortgage Corporation, Federal National Mortgage Association, Farmers Home Administration, and U.S. Department of Housing and Urban Development.

Table 9 • Outstanding Pass-Through Securities Held by Private Investors by Type of Mortgage in Pool

End of Period	Volume Outstandings ($ millions)					Percent of Mortgage Assets (by Type) Held by Private Investors				
		Single-family		Multifamily			Single-family		Multifamily	
	Total	FHA/VA	Conventional	FHA	Conventional	Total	FHA/VA	Conventional	FHA	Conventional
1970	$ 2,592	$ 347	$ 2,185	$ 0	$ 60	1%	0%	1%	0%	0%
1971	6,831	3,074	3,659	0	98	2	4	2	0	0
1972	11,093	5,353	5,458	151	131	3	6	2	1	0
1973	14,252	7,561	6,224	329	138	3	8	2	3	0
1974	19,424	11,249	7,539	520	116	4	12	2	5	0
1975	26,066	17,538	7,318	719	491	5	18	2	7	1
1976	38,747	29,583	7,742	989	433	6	27	2	8	1
1977	56,513	43,555	11,244	1,341	373	8	37	2	11	0
1978	71,620	52,732	16,947	1,615	326	9	42	3	11	0
1979	97,637	73,853	21,577	1,934	293	11	52	3	11	0
1980	118,233	91,602	24,088	2,272	271	12	57	3	11	0
1981	134,857	103,007	28,818	2,783	249	12	60	4	13	0
1982	186,712	115,831	67,537	3,109	235	16	63	8	14	0
1983	255,622	155,801	95,562	4,049	210	20	72	11	17	0

Note: Excludes certificates of Beneficial Ownership held by the Federal Financing Bank but includes securities issued under FNMA and FHLMC swap programs. Negligible amounts of FHLMC pass-throughs issued against pools of conventional multifamily loans have been included under single-family conventional issues. Securities issued against pools of FHA and VA mortgages reflect only the GNMA program; small amounts of FNMA pass-through securities backed by seasoned FHA/VA mortgages are included in the conventional issues for 1982 and 1983.

Sources: Government National Mortgage Association, Federal Home Loan Mortgage Corporation, Federal National Mortgage Association, Farmers Home Administration, U.S. Department of Housing and Urban Development, and Board of Governors of the Federal Reserve System.

residential mortgage assets held by these entities. In the case of FHA/VA single-family mortgages, this share has grown to nearly three fourths. Large amounts of FNMA and FHLMC swap activity raised the proportion for single-family conventional mortgages substantially in 1982 and 1983, but the securities share still was only 11 percent at year-end 1983.

Sales of Loans into Secondary Markets

It generally has been assumed that growth of the pass-through securities markets (non-swap securities) has been associated with a rise in the importance of mortgage banking activity—that is, with the sale of newly originated loans in secondary markets by new issues of these securities. Rising ratios of mortgage sales to mortgage originations frequently have been cited as evidence of this phenomenon. However, analysis of available data suggests that sales of loans by issues of pass-through securities have largely substituted for sales through other channels, and that rising ratios of sales to originations reflected, to some degree, sales of seasoned mortgages by financially troubled thrift institutions.

As noted above, new issues of single-family GNMAs actually exceeded the volume of originations of FHA/VA home mortgages in 1983. This fact might suggest that development of the GNMA market has resulted in a greater flow of FHA/VA loans from primary to secondary markets. However, as shown in Table 10, the ratio of sales to originations for FHA/VA home mortgages has not shown a persistent trend since 1970 (when the GNMA program began), averaging 103 percent during this period.[7] This pattern largely reflects the fact that, at the primary market level, the FHA/VA market has traditionally been dominated by mortgage companies that sell their production of long-term loans as a matter of course.

The ratio of sales (swap-adjusted) to originations of conventional home loans has been relatively high in recent years, particularly in 1982 (Table 10). This development, however, does not primarily reflect the issuance of pass-through securities (government underwritten or private). As noted above, the ratio of new non-swap issues of conventional pass-throughs to originations of single-family conventional loans has risen only moderately in recent years.

The rise in the sales/originations ratio for conventional home loans reflected primarily a rise in this ratio (swap-adjusted) at thrift institutions—from 14 percent in 1978 to 26 percent by 1981, followed by a leap to 70 percent in 1982.[8] Some of the increase undoubtedly was associated with a rise in mortgage bank-

---

[7]The ratio can exceed 100 percent for two reasons: (1) sales of newly originated loans lag originations to some degree, and (2) sales of seasoned FHA/VA loans take place among secondary market investors. Sales of outstanding GNMAs do not affect the FHA/VA sales figures.

[8]The thrift share of primary market activity held up rather well during this period; these institutions accounted for half of total originations of conventional home mortgages in 1982, down from 62 percent in 1978.

Table 10 • Ratio of Mortgage Sales to Mortgage Originations by Type of Property and Mortgage (percent)

	1970	1971	1972	1973	1974	1975	1976	1977	1978	1979	1980	1981	1982	1983
Total residential mortgages	36%	29%	30%	29%	30%	32%	33%	31%	34%	39%	41%	46%	61%	55%
FHA/VA	83	76	94	108	85	96	107	93	94	91	98	109	100	113
Conventional	12	10	13	13	16	16	19	20	22	25	26	30	50	39
Home mortgages	40	32	32	31	33	33	34	32	34	39	43	47	63	59
FHA/VA	90	84	106	124	103	104	112	97	97	95	104	117	102	112
Conventional	12	9	12	13	17	16	20	20	21	25	27	31	53	42
Multifamily mortgages	20	18	22	20	12	20	20	24	33	32	27	37	48	25
FHA	37	27	36	39	16	43	63	52	69	56	54	70	90	116
Conventional	15	15	18	15	10	15	12	19	24	24	14	22	26	11

Note: Sales of conventional home mortgages have been adjusted to exclude FHLMC and FNMA mortgage/securities swap programs, transfers of loans from the Farmers Home Administration to the Federal Financing Bank, and transfers of loans from the Federal Financing Bank back to the Farmers Home Administration.
Sources: U.S. Department of Housing and Urban Development, Federal Home Loan Mortgage Corporation, and Federal National Mortgage Association.

ing activity by thrifts that sought to generate origination and servicing income while limiting portfolio interest-rate risk. Both FNMA and FHLMC have been ready markets for conventional home loans originated by the thrifts. But the rise in the ratio has also reflected large sales of seasoned mortgages out of thrift portfolios, particularly during 1981 and 1982. In September 1981, the Federal Home Loan Bank Board made an important adjustment to its regulatory accounting procedures, permitting deferral and amortization of losses from sales of low-rate assets. By protecting net worth positions for regulatory purposes, this adjustment facilitated mortgage sales as part of *funds redeployment strategies,* at least for mutual associations that need not adhere to generally accepted accounting principles in their financial statements. Sales of seasoned mortgage assets can lead to higher current net income through reinvestment in higher yielding instruments, generation of origination and servicing fees on assets acquired, retention of servicing on loans sold, and recapture of previously paid income taxes (if current losses are shown)[9]

Sales of mortgages out of portfolio also have occurred subsequent to thrift mergers treated under so-called purchase accounting rules. This phenomenon became particularly important after mid-1982 as falling market interest rates created opportunities for capital gains upon sale of low-rate assets that previously had been marked down to market values. In this regard, it also should be noted that managers of private pension funds (both uninsured plans and those managed by life insurance companies under guaranteed income contracts) have exhibited preferences for deeply discounted (low coupon) mortgage assets. This is because of the superior *call protection* (protection against early prepayment) afforded by such instruments.

Implications for the Investor Base

It commonly has been assumed that the growth of the markets for mortgage pass-through securities has resulted in a broader institutional base of mortgage supply, because the securities are closer substitutes for bonds than are whole mortgages or mortgage participations. However, the structure of supply has changed remarkably little as the pass-through securities markets have developed. While it is impossible to say how the investor distribution of mortgage assets would have evolved in the absence of the pass-through markets, empirical observation suggests that there has been a good deal of substitution between pass-through securities and other mortgage assets in the portfolios of investors.

Table 5 showed changes in the investor distribution of total residential mortgage assets (mortgages plus pass-through securities) broken down by thrift institutions (that receive special federal tax incentives to invest in mortgage as-

---

[9]For tax purposes, the entire capital loss is deductible in the period of the asset sale, and a 10-year loss carryback rule may be utilized.

sets);[10] federal, state, and local government agencies; and diversified private investors. These data indicate that the thrift share of total mortgage assets changed little during the 1970–78 period. This share dropped by several percentage points during 1979–82 as the industry encountered severe financial difficulties and funneled unusually large amounts of funds into liquid assets to take advantage of short-run arbitrage opportunities.[11] The other major components all gained in relative terms during the period, with diversified private investors showing the largest increase. The increase in this category, however, was traceable to a rise in mortgage credit held by home sellers. This rise was generated through the spate of "creative" financing arrangements that blossomed as market interest rates climbed to unprecedented levels in 1979–1982. The share of total residential mortgage assets held by diversified private institutions (diversified private investors less individuals) crept up to 32 percent by the end of 1983 (the same as in the early 1970s). Diversified private institutions would be expected to gain in relative terms, of course, if development of the pass-through markets attracted bond investors into mortgage assets.

The FHA/VA market may be singled out for special consideration. This is the component of the mortgage market where development of pass-through securities has been most striking. As with total residential mortgage assets, the broad investor distribution of total FHA/VA mortgage assets (FHA/VA mortgage loans plus GNMAs) has changed remarkably little since the inception of the GNMA program. This suggests that the degree of substitution between GNMAs and FHA/VA mortgages has been substantial, while substitution of GNMAs for nonmortgage investments such as corporate and government bonds has been limited.[12] As shown in Table 11, the S&L share has changed little as the GNMA market has developed. The thrift share has eroded substantially since the early 1970s because of a marked decline at mutual savings banks. However, part of this decline may represent an increase in registration of MSB-owned GNMAs under street names, partly to facilitate RP transactions.[13] The share accounted for by diversified private investors changed little through 1978, and then increased to slightly more than two fifths. This percentage is overstated to the extent that GNMAs owned by MSBs are registered in street names.

---

[10]Mortgage pass-through securities are treated the same way as mortgage loans under federal tax law in calculation of the special bad-debt reserve provision available to thrift institutions.

[11]The market share of mutual savings banks actually has been trending downward since the mid-1960s, partly reflecting relatively weak housing activity and stringent usury ceilings in the primary markets served by these institutions.

[12]It also is unlikely that there has been much substitution of GNMAs for conventional mortgages. If investment quality and liquidity ranked high in an investor's scale of preferences, it is likely that mortgage assets held prior to the availability of GNMAs would have been concentrated in FHA/VA rather than conventional loans.

[13]At S&Ls, where data on both ownership and registration of GNMAs are available, it is evident that registration under street/nominee names has increased in importance during recent years.

Table 11 • Holdings of FHA/VA Mortgage Loans and GNMA-Guaranteed Pass-Through Securities by Type of Investor (percentage shares of total FHA/VA mortgage debt outstanding)

End of Period	Thrift Institutions			Diversified Private Investors	State and Local Government Agencies	Federal and Related Agencies	Memo: FHA/VA Share of Total Residential Mortgage Debt
	Total	S&Ls	MSBs				
1971	44%	20%	24%	35%	0%	20%	30%
1972	48	24	24	31	0	21	29
1973	49	25	24	26	1	23	26
1974	47	25	22	26	1	26	25
1975	47	26	21	26	1	26	25
1976	46	26	20	31	1	22	23
1977	43	24	20	36	1	20	21
1978	41	23	18	37	2	21	20
1979	37	21	16	41	2	20	20
1980	37	22	15	40	3	20	20
1981	35	21	14	42	3	20	20
1982	36	23	13	42	4	18	20
1983	38	25	13	44	4	14	20

Note: Figures for MSBs are understated, and those for diversified private investors are overstated, by the extent to which MSBs hold GNMAs in street names or nominee accounts. MSB data for 1983 include holdings of FSLIC-insured stock federal savings banks.

Sources: Board of Governors of the Federal Reserve System, Federal Home Loan Bank Board, Government National Mortgage Association, and U.S. Department of Housing and Urban Development.

Mortgage/Securities Swaps

Mortgage/securities swap programs of FHLMC and FNMA, introduced during the last half of 1981, have become prominent features in the markets for mortgage pass-through securities. Twenty-five billion dollars of securities were issued under these programs during 1983—$16 billion at FHLMC and $9 billion at FNMA—accounting for 28 percent of all pass-throughs issued.

Through swap transactions, private institutions exchange mortgages held in their portfolios for mortgage pass-through securities guaranteed by FNMA or FHLMC. In the process of a swap, FNMA and FHLMC technically buy mortgages from swapping institutions at par, resell the mortgages by issuing securitites with the same par value, and place the mortgages in legal trusts for which the agencies are trustees. This process is virtually instantaneous. In fact, the mortgages never appear as assets on the balance sheets of FNMA or FHLMC.

Institutions that engage in swap transactions with FHLMC or FNMA pay commitment fees and give up some interest return on their asset portfolios because FNMA and FHLMC deduct guarantee fees calculated in terms of basis points. For the swapping institution, these costs may exceed any increase in expected return associated with holding higher quality assets in portfolio. This result is inevitable when the swapping institution retains the primary risk of borrower default.[14] In any case, the quality of swapped loans typically is high to begin with. On seasoned loans, borrowers ordinarily have accumulated substantial equity which inhibits defaults, and both FNMA and FHLMC require private mortgage insurance on newly originated conventional contracts with loan/value ratios of 80 percent or more.

Thus, incentives other than a simple upgrading of asset quality at swapping institutions have been necessary to drive the swap programs. Such motives include the following:

—To obtain collateral that is eligible, under applicable regulations, for use in retail (customer) RPs, or collateral that is acceptable to banks and securities dealers for wholesale RPs (reverse repurchase agreements). Conventional mortgage loans ordinarily are neither eligible nor acceptable for these purposes.
—To improve liquidity positions for regulatory purposes. FHLMC/FNMA-guaranteed securities generally are not eligible for regulatory liquidity under FHLBB rules because of their long contract maturities, but swaps can be used to free eligible liquid assets that have been tied up in RPs.
—To prepare for sales of low-rate assets following mergers treated under "purchase" accounting, or to prepare for sales of such assets as part of a funds redeployment strategy to increase current net income. Because of their superior liquidity or marketability, pass-through securities issued against pools of mortgages may command higher market prices than the mortgages

---

[14]Both FNMA and FHLMC operate programs exposing them to loss only in the event of default by the swapping institution.

themselves, even if guarantee fees paid to the agencies equal or exceed the increase in credit quality perceived by investors.

—To market newly originated loans in the secondary mortgage market. Mortgage swaps, and subsequent sales of the securities to investors or dealers, can be used by mortgage originators as an alternative to sales of conventional mortgages to FHLMC or FNMA under the standard purchase programs of these agencies, sales to private investors or to managers of conduit operations, or sales through issuance of fully private mortgage pass-through securities.

Through the end of 1982, swap transactions involved primarily seasoned fixed-rate conventional home mortgages held by savings and loan associations, and the primary S&L motive for swaps was to acquire assets eligible or acceptable for use in retail or wholesale RPs. Indeed, S&L net sales (sales less purchases) of mortgages and net sales of mortgage pass-through securities moved sharply in opposite directions after late 1981, while S&L net sales of total mortgage assets (mortgages plus securities) changed little. While this inverse relationship suggests that swapping for resale was relatively unimportant, there were instances of swaps and subsequent sales, particularly following markdowns of seasoned low-rate mortgage assets in connection with purchase accounting.

Usage of swaps by thrift institutions to obtain collateral for retail RPs, or to maintain RP volume while boosting regulatory liquidity, has fallen since December 1982 in the presence of the money market deposit account. Retail RPs were structured primarily to compete with money market mutual funds at a time when thrift institutions did not have a deposit instrument to compete effectively with the money funds.[15] Use of swaps in conjunction with purchase accounting should also decline in the wake of a ruling by the Financial Accounting Standards Board (FASB) that reduces the appeal of this type of accounting. FASB ruled that the period of time over which "goodwill" accounts can be depreciated cannot exceed the period of time over which discounts on assets (that had been marked down to market values) can be taken into income. And the large declines in market interest rates after mid-1982 damped incentives for thrifts to sell low-rate assets as part of funds redeployment strategies.

Thus, the incentives that led to heavy issuance of FHLMC/FNMA-guaranteed securities for purposes largely unrelated to flows of mortgage credit have weakened. On the other hand, since early 1983, swaps have become more important as a way for mortgage originators to transform their new loans into pass-through securities, either for addition to portfolio or for sale through the dealer community. Although the swap programs initially were designed and marketed by FNMA and FHLMC with seasoned mortgages in mind, both agen-

---

[15]Institutions that engaged in swaps primarily to obtain collateral for RPs thus may discover that the activity turned out to be exorbitantly expensive, since guarantee fees must be paid to FNMA and FHLMC over the entire life of a security.

cies now permit new loans to be swapped, and the programs have been adjusted to better accommodate these loans. Both enterprises see new-loan swaps as an effective way to earn both commitment and guarantee fees while minimizing their expenses and completely eliminating any financing risk. In this regard, it may be noted that although both sponsored enterprises have incorporated optional delivery features into their swap programs, issuance of such options does not expose the enterprises to interest-rate risk (since they do not actually take the mortgages into their portfolios).

If the swap programs become widely used for newly originated mortgages, these transactions could largely substitute for the so-called benchmark FNMA and FHLMC programs that have involved the outright purchase of mortgages from loan originators. Such purchases historically have been financed by agency issues/sales of pass-through securities (FHLMC's primary mode of operation) or by agency issues of debt (FNMA's primary procedure). Moreover, by swapping securities for new loans, both FHLMC and FNMA would operate more like GNMA, attaching guarantees to securities that are sold (marketed) by private institutions that both originate mortgages and package them in pools. FHLMC's Charter Act apparently would enable this federally sponsored enterprise to operate like GNMA, but FNMA's congressional charter does not permit the guarantee of securities issued by other entities. Early in 1983, FNMA proposed a change to its charter that would permit this sponsored enterprise to guarantee securities issued by institutions eligible to sell loans to FNMA.

Federal Policy toward Mortgage Pass-Through Securities

Throughout the 1970s, Federal policy actively encouraged development of markets for federally related mortgage pass-through securities. More recently, federal policy has been swinging away from support of federally related pass-through securities. Indeed, the Reagan administration has indicated that it wants to substantially alter the balance of federally related and private securities in the secondary mortgage markets, favoring a shift toward securities issued and backed by wholly private entities.

The president established a housing commission in June 1981. The President's Commission on Housing was charged, among other things, to develop options and recommendations with respect to federally related secondary mortgage market programs and private sector alternatives. The housing commission submitted its report to the president and to the secretary of the Department of Housing and Urban Development in April 1982, providing a comprehensive set of recommendations on the mortgage pass-through securities markets. The recommendations covered the programs of federal agencies (the Government National Mortgage Association and the Farmers Home Administration), federally sponsored enterprises (the Federal National Mortgage Association and the Federal Home Loan Mortgage Corporation), and wholly private securities. In each of these areas, the commission generally tried to identify appropriate long-term positions as well as means of transition from current arrangements.

Basically, the housing commission called for eventual elimination of the GNMA and FmHA pass-through programs, virtually complete privatization of both FHLMC and FNMA, and development of viable private sector alternatives to the programs of the federal agencies and federally sponsored enterprises.[16] The commission concluded that wholly private mortgage securities had been at a substantial disadvantage in the capital markets for three reasons: (1) federally related mortgage securities had crowded out private issues, (2) provisions of federal and state laws or regulations had created unnecessary and largely unintended problems for private securities, and (3) lack of standardization of private securities had limited their marketability (liquidity) and inhibited development of an efficient dealer market with small bid-asked price spreads.

In the commission's plan, the competitive advantages of federally guaranteed securities were to be reduced as federal programs were scaled back and the federal connections of the relevant sponsored enterprises were peeled away. This process was not to take place, however, until policy measures were implemented to strengthen the private pass-through markets.

Since the release of the housing commission report, federal policy toward mortgage pass-through securities has been broadly consistent with the commission's perspective. Although the Administration's budget documents have proposed reductions in GNMA's commitment authority and stressed the goal of complete privatization of the federally sponsored enterprises, emphasis has been placed on development of private sector alternatives and no concerted effort has yet been made to phase down the federally related programs. Credit budget ceilings have not been used to effectively hold down the volume of GNMA guarantees or the volume of FHA-insured loans that can go into GNMA pools. Furthermore, the federal connections of FNMA and FHLMC have not been materially altered, and these federally sponsored enterprises have not been made subject to the discipline of the federal credit budget.[17]

Following upon the work of the housing commission, the Administration has been working on a package of legal and regulatory measures designed to improve the markets for private mortgage pass-through securities, and the 1984 and 1985 budget documents stressed the importance of this initiative. The various components of the package have been designed to increase the prices at

---

[16]For a more detailed discussion of the commission's recommendations in these areas, and of the process by which they were reached, see David F. Seiders, "Mortgage Pass-Through Securities: Progress and Prospects," *AREUEA Journal*, Summer 1983.

[17]In 1982, the administration failed to support legislation that would have restructured FHLMC along the lines proposed by the commission for the short run, primarily because the bill contained no schedule for moving FHLMC to a truly private status over the longer term. In the administration's view, the bill—which would have given FHLMC authority to raise capital through public stock issues—would have fostered rapid growth of an entity that would continue to qualify as a federally sponsored enterprise.

which mortgage originators can sell their loans by issuing wholly private securities, to lower the cost of issuance, or to broaden the investor base for private pass-throughs.[18]

A number of federal and federally related agencies have been involved with various aspects of the Administration's private market initiative, and substantial progress has been made in some regulatory areas. Furthermore, in August 1983, legislation was introduced in the Senate addressing a number of adjustments requiring statutory change (S. 1821 and S. 1822). The following discussion outlines the major components of the initiative, reviews progress made through the end of 1983[19], and considers some potential regulatory issues that have received little attention—issues associated with the regulation of deposit liabilities and recourse arrangements at depository institutions.

Creation of New Trust Device

The housing commission felt that the trust device currently available under federal tax law to issuers of both federally guaranteed and private mortgage pass-through securities had been a major obstacle to market development. This device, called the *grantor trust,* is quite inflexible and has prevented innovation with respect to both the types of pass-through securities issued against a pool of mortgages and the management of pool assets or cash flows by issuers/servicers. Under the grantor trust, income generated by a mortgage pool can become taxable at both the trust and the investor levels if the issuer (1) sells classes of securities that do not represent proportional interests in all funds flowing into the mortgage pool or (2) engages in any active management of either the asset structure of the trust or the cash flow produced by trust assets. These constraints have prevented issuers from marketing different classes of securities tailored to the cash-flow preferences of different types of investors, and have subjected investors to uncertainties about cash flows and effective maturities of their securities, as well as to associated uncertainties about effective yields on securities purchased at prices different from par.

The administration's initiative on private mortgage securities involves the creation under federal tax law of a new type of trust device, dubbed the TIM (Trust for Investment in Mortgages). This trust would be similar in certain respects to real estate investment trusts (REITs) and regulated investment companies (mutual funds). In particular, issuers of TIM securities would be permitted to market different classes of securities against a mortgage pool, and to engage in certain types of pool management, without incurring the danger of double federal taxation on income generated by assets in the trust.

TIM proponents, in consultation with various trade groups, have identified a number of possibilities concerning multiple classes of securities with different

---

[18]For an assessment of the prospects for success of the so-called "TIMs" initiative, see Seiders, "Mortgage Pass-Through Securities: Progress and Prospects."

[19]An update through the fall of 1984 is provided at the end of the chapter.

types of claims on cash flows from a fixed mortgage pool. Two prominent candidates have emerged: (1) senior/subordinated classes, where the subordinated securities bear all risk of delinquency and foreclosure on the entire mortgage pool (similar to arrangements constructed by Crocker National Bank and Home Federal S&L) and (2) fast-pay/slow-pay classes, where holders of the fast-pay securities receive all retirements of principal (including prepayments) flowing to the pool until the portion of principal represented by this class is fully distributed. The latter scheme would provide some investors with short-lived assets and others with securities having cash flows more like bonds than like standard mortgage pass-throughs.

Concerning management of pool assets and cash flows, several possibilities have been identified: (1) distribution of interest and/or principal payments to investors on a semiannual or annual basis, rather than monthly as mortgage payments flow into the pool. This is intended to meet the preferences of institutions that traditionally have invested in corporate or government bonds. (2) Reinvestment of mortgage principal retired through scheduled payments or prepayments, in order to fashion securities with durations suitable to the preferences of different types of investors. Both types of arrangements could involve outside reinvestment contracts, under which a third party (such as a bank) would guarantee reinvestment of interest and/or principal at the original pass-through rate.

Tax Treatment of Recovered Discount

Price discounts on pass-through securities are "recovered" by investors as mortgages in the pools are repaid, or prepaid, at par. The housing commission had recommended an adjustment to the Internal Revenue Code to permit investors to classify the recovery of secondary market discounts on private mortgage pass-through securities as capital gains rather than as ordinary income.[20] This adjustment was recommended to provide parity with the tax treatment accorded corporate and government interest-bearing securities.

The Treasury Department proved reluctant to support an amendment to the IRC to provide the tax treatment recommended by the commission for mortgage pass-through securities, primarily because of revenue considerations. However, if TIMs were set up as corporate entities—a possibility under recent legislative proposals (S.1822)—the recovery of secondary market discounts on TIM securities could become eligible for corporate tax treatment.

Establishment of Federal Quality Standards

The housing commission had recommended further study of the need for government efforts to promote standardization of the private mortgage securi-

---

[20]The Commission did not recommend a change in the tax treatment of primary market (original-issue) discounts, the recovery of which is classified as ordinary income for all types of securities under the tax code.

ties market—a topic on which the commission was divided. The original TIM proposal, drafted shortly after the commission submitted its report, envisioned that the Treasury Department or some other federal agency would establish stringent criteria that a mortgage trust would have to meet in order to win the TIM designation. The criteria covered factors such as the composition of mortgage pools, private pool insurance, letters of credit, and reserves funded by pool managers.

In more recent forms, however, there has been a swing away from stringent quality criteria toward minimum criteria that a broad range of securities could meet. The proposed "Trust for Investment in Mortgages Act" (S. 1822) would require only that the securities be able to obtain an investment grade rating from a nationally recognized rating agency.[21] To date, public offerings of private mortgage pass-through securities have generally exceeded the minimum investment grade standard. Such a minimum standard would provide for a good deal of flexibility in the market, but it would do little to enhance the marketability or liquidity of TIM securities because of the lack of homogeneity that could result.

Treatment under Pension-Fund Law and Regulation

Staff at the Labor Department have indicated that TIM securities could, by administrative action, be defined as *plan assets* under the Employee Retirement Income Security Act of 1974 (ERISA) if quality standards were established by federal law or regulation. Such treatment would parallel that accorded shares in regulated investment companies and federally guaranteed mortgage pass-through securities. This would relieve fiduciaries of private pension funds of the responsibility to assure that each and every loan in a TIM mortgage pool meets the many ERISA requirements, a burdensome requirement that has deterred most fiduciaries from even considering private pass-through securities as pension fund investments. TIM securities also could be provided an administrative class exemption from various technical restrictions related to parties in interest problems and associated prohibited transactions under ERISA.[22]

It might be argued that the rather weak investment grade standard that has been proposed should not qualify TIM securities for the same type of treatment as federally guaranteed securities, since the interests of pension plan beneficiaries could conceivably be compromised. However, the Department of Labor may view favorable treatment of TIMs as a reasonable response to political pressure for mandated investment in mortgage instruments by pension funds.

---

[21]The top four categories (AAA, AA, A and BBB under Standard & Poor's designations) commonly are referred to as "investment grade."

[22]These technical problems are discussed on pages 142–43 of the housing commission report.

SEC Registration Requirements

The SEC traditionally required that the prospectus for a public offering of private mortgage pass-through securities contain complete and final information on all mortgages in the pool. This requirement prevented public offerings of securities on a forward basis (while mortgage pools were being assembled). It clearly would not fit the proposed TIM securities, since the composition of mortgage pools backing these securities may be subject to change (because of pool management). The SEC also turned down requests to make shelf registration procedures available to private mortgage pass-through securities. Recognizing these problems, the housing commission had recommended streamlined registration requirements tailored to mortgage securities, to facilitate forward sales and issuance of small amounts in series.

In 1983, the SEC agreed to substantially alter the registration requirements for private mortgage pass-through securities. First, issuers of securities carrying an investment grade rating may now conduct public offerings on a *blind pool* basis, including in the prospectus only a general, or generic, description of mortgages to be pooled. Actual pool data may be provided later on separate forms filed with the commission and sent to investors.[23] This change in procedures reduces the holding-period risk of issuers (the risk of change in market value of mortgages assembled into pools prior to sale of the securities), and facilitates management of mortgage pools after issuance.

Second, the commission's Rule 415 shelf registration procedures were made available for public offerings of private mortgage securities carrying an investment grade rating. Issuers now can offer several series of mortgage pool certificates, over a period of up to two years, pursuant to a single registration statement. This change in procedures not only reduces the total registration costs of issuers but also provides issuers flexibility in timing their sales to accord with changes in market conditions.

Third, periodic disclosure requirements imposed upon issuers after an offering has been sold have been tailored to the unique activities of issuers *(sponsors)* of mortgage pass-through securities. The requirements are less elaborate than those applying to issuers of corporate securities, and thus are less costly. Issuers of mortgage pass-through securities, of course, are not floating their own debt instruments, and the information relevant to prospective buyers of outstanding securities is quite different from the information relevant to buyers of outstanding corporate obligations.

Despite the fact that these changes in SEC registration requirements and certain features of the TIM proposal (particularly the authority for sponsors/ issuers to engage in management of mortgage pools after issuance) establish close similarities between TIM securities and shares in mutual funds, the SEC

---

[23]The rating agencies do not actually rate blind-pool securities before the mortgage pools are created. At the time such securities are offered to investors, issuers make a commitment to obtain a specified investment-grade rating at the time the offering is closed.

has confirmed the availability of an existing exemption for mortgage-backed securities from the Investment Company Act of 1940. Registration as investment companies, of course, would subject TIM issuers/sponsors to additional regulatory requirements.

Marginability of Securities

In response to housing commission recommendations and the TIMs initiative, the Federal Reserve Board amended its Regulation T in January 1983, specifying that private mortgage-backed securities may be used as collateral for margin credit at securities brokers and dealers. The criteria established by the board basically parallel those currently used for so-called OTC margin bonds (nonconvertible debt securities not traded on national exchanges), and deal with availability of information on issues and issuers/servicers, the performance of issuers/servicers in carrying out their responsibilities, and the marketability of securities. The board tailored the marketability criterion, which is expressed in terms of issue size, to special features of mortgage securities. Because of the "wasting" nature of such securities and the need of issuers to market small amounts in series, the requirement established for minimum issue size ($25 million) applies at time of issuance rather than at the time margin credit is extended. Moreover, issue size may include the aggregate of securities issued in series under a single registration statement.[24] The board also held open the possibility of fundamental change in this requirement, noting that individual issue size would become less relevant to marketability if a large market for homogeneous private mortgage-backed securities eventually developed.

State Blue-Sky and Legal-Investment Statutes

The housing commission had noted problems created for private mortgage pass-through securities by state blue-sky and legal-investment statutes and had made general recommendations for change, leaving it up to the National Conference of Commissioners on Uniform State Laws (NCCUSL) to devise specific adjustments. Establishment of federal quality standards (even the weak investment grade standard) might help secure favorable treatment of TIM securities under such statutes. Another possibility, embodied in the Secondary Mortgage Market Enhancement Act introduced in the Senate (S. 1821), would involve federal preemption of state legal-investment and blue-sky laws for investment grade mortgage-related securities.

---

[24]The $25 million requirement was adopted from the "OTC margin bond" section of Regulation T.

Deposit Liabilities and Recourse Arrangements

Issuers of private mortgage pass-through securities have been able to secure high ratings for their issues in a number of ways: (1) by purchasing pool insurance from private mortgage insurance companies, (2) by issuing standby letters of credit, or (3) by holding securities representing subordinated interests in the mortgage pools or trusts.[25] Whenever a depository institution retains some responsibility to maintain payments to securities holders in the event of defaults on mortgages in the pools, issuance may be viewed by supervisory authorities as borrowing rather than as sales of mortgage assets. Indeed, there is a danger that regulatory authorities will construe issuance to involve creation of deposit liabilities that automatically become subject to regulations dealing with reserve requirements (Regulation D).[26] This problem could arise with the proposed TIM securities as well as with private pass-through securities that do not bear the TIM designation.

The Federal Reserve Board generally has ruled that issues of mortgage pass-through securities by commercial banks constitute sales of assets rather than borrowing. However, the board has also decided that issuance of wholly private securities by a depository institution could give rise to a deposit liability if the mortgages in the pool were of questionable quality or if the institution's exposure to loss exceeded a certain proportion of the size of the issue. This decision, in fact, has been incorporated into Regulation D. Pass-through securities issued and sold to third-party investors do not give rise to deposit liabilities as long as the pools are made up of conventional one- to four-family mortgages and the bank's obligation is not more than 10 percent. Such requirements could constrain various issues envisioned by supporters of the TIMs vehicle.

Although a sale of assets with recourse need not give rise to a deposit liability, generation of substantial contingent obligations under recourse arrangements (which fall below the bottom line on balance sheets) could undermine the strength of the issuing institution in the event of widespread mortgage defaults. The Federal Reserve Board recognized this potential problem in considering bank proposals to issue private mortgage pass-through securities when standby letters of credit or subordinated pool securities were part of the proposals. In the past, the board has been of the opinion that adequate procedures are available to supervise the risks to banks associated with these types of arrangements. The board may, of course, reconsider this question at any time. Recent substantial growth in bank use of standby letters of credit to support a variety of contractual arrangements (such as corporate commercial paper) has raised questions about the risk exposure of banks. Moreover, the recent soft-

---

[25]Some large banks found that use of letters of credit or subordinated pool securities, instead of private pool insurance, enabled them to obtain higher investment ratings at lower cost.

[26]The Federal Reserve Board has determined that issuance of mortgage pass-through securities can create deposit liabilities for issuing banks if the securities are the "functional equivalent of repurchase agreements."

ness of home prices and relatively high mortgage delinquency and foreclosure rates, if extended for some time into the future, would increase the probability of bank losses on recourse arrangements established for private mortgage pass-through securities.

Outlook for Mortgage Securities Markets

The future size and structure of mortgage securities markets will depend not only on evolving underlying needs for secondary market channels but also on the evolution of federal policy toward these markets. Public policy has promoted development of federally related mortgage pass-through securities since 1970, and these securities are now an important part of the housing finance system. Recent efforts to further the development of fully private mortgage-related securities—evidenced by the TIMs initiative, related legislation introduced in the Senate, and pronounced intentions by the Reagan administration to promote private mortgage securities—could presage significant expansion of the channels through which funds flow from capital market investors to borrowers in primary mortgage markets.

The administration may not support substantial development of private mortgage securities markets, however, unless provisions are made to contain, or actually scale back, the federally related securities programs. Containment or reduction could be accomplished by excluding FNMA and FHLMC from the TIMs market and preventing them from issuing TIM-like securities (such as FHLMC's Collateralized Mortgage Obligations), by restricting the size of mortgage loans that FNMA and FHLMC can buy, and eventually by "privatizing" these sponsored enterprises by cutting their federal connections. These and other steps have been under consideration by the Cabinet Council on Economic Affairs.

Control of federally related mortgage securities is favored by the current administration as part of a general effort to reduce the presence of the federal government in the nation's financial system. It should also be recognized that housing does not enjoy the priority status it once had in this country. Thus, the Administration is reluctant to support a package of proposals that might promote a shift of capital toward housing and away from business plant and equipment. A shift of mortgage securities from federal to private forms is viewed as highly desirable. An increase in the proportion of capital flowing into housing is not viewed so favorably.

EPILOGUE: POLICY UPDATE

During 1984, a number of important developments occurred with respect to federal policy toward the mortgage-related securities markets. These developments, relating primarily to the policy issues discussed above, fall into three categories:

1. The TIMs initiative: the administration had planned to submit its own version of the "Trust for Investment in Mortgages Act" to the Senate early in 1984. This version would have completely excluded FNMA and FHLMC from the TIMs pass-through market, would have prevented FNMA and FHLMC from issuing TIM-like bonds (such as FHLMC's CMOs), and would have made FNMA and FHLMC securities ineligible as collateral for TIM-like bonds issued by private entities (such as home builders). Opposition to this approach by housing interests and FNMA was intense. In April, the administration decided not to promote TIMs legislation during 1984. TIMs may or may not resurface after the elections.

2. The "Secondary Mortgage Market Enhancement Act of 1984" was enacted on October 3, 1984. Title I, designed to enhance development of the private mortgage securities markets, amended federal securities laws and preempted certain state laws. The major provisions, applying primarily to securities backed directly or indirectly by first liens on residential property, may be summarized as follows:

   —Statutory limitations on investment in private mortgage-backed securities by federally chartered depository institutions are removed, leaving it up to the regulators to specify investment limits.

   —Sales contracts made by brokers and dealers for forward or delayed delivery (within 180 days) of private mortgage-backed securities do not involve extensions of credit to or by the brokers/dealers. This provision is intended to facilitate development of forward-delivery markets for fully private securities.

   —State blue-sky and legal-investment statutes are preempted for high-grade private mortgage-backed securities (those rated in one of the two highest categories by at least one nationally recognized statistical rating organization) subject to reversal by the states within seven years. Thus, such securities need not be registered with state supervisory agencies, and they may be purchased by state-regulated financial institutions (such as pension funds and insurance companies) as if they were federally issued or guaranteed securities. Title II dealt with the secondary market programs of FNMA and FHLMC.

   Provisions important to the competitive relationship between issuers of private mortgage securities and the federally sponsored enterprises may be summarized as follows:

   —Limits on sizes of single-family mortgages that may be purchased by FNMA and FHLMC apply to the total loan size even if only a portion of a loan (i.e., a loan participation) is purchased.

   —FHLMC is specifically prohibited from guaranteeing mortgage-backed securities issued by others.

3. Tax treatment of recovery of market discounts: although capital gains treat-

ment of the recovery of market discounts on mortgage-related securities has not been provided, the treatment afforded corporate and government securities was changed by The Deficit Reduction Act of 1984; as a result, the recovery of market discounts by holders of corporate and government securities now is treated as ordinary income (as with original issue discounts). Thus, the competitive disadvantage that mortgage-related securities had experienced, vis-à-vis other types of securities in the capital markets, has been addressed.

—— Chapter 3 ——————————————————

Federal Government-Related Mortgage Purchasers

Kenneth J. Thygerson
President–Chief Executive Officer
Federal Home Loan Mortgage Corporation

Overview

This chapter covers the development of the secondary market for home mortgages, from its beginnings in the 1930s to its current multibillion-dollar-per-year level. The chapter focuses on the role of government-related organizations in this development. The role of the secondary market is to integrate mortgage markets and capital markets. In this way it supplies a ready source of funds for housing at market interest rates.

The secondary market is the collection of institutions involved in the trading of mortgages and mortgage-related securities. In the primary market, lenders deal directly with homebuyers; they underwrite loans, appraise property, and then service the loans by receiving monthly payments from borrowers and passing them on to a conduit or to the investor in the loans.

The main originators of mortgages are also the main sellers in the secondary mortgage market: (1) thrift institutions (savings and loan associations and mutual savings banks), (2) mortgage banking companies, and (3) commercial banks. Thrift institutions, by tradition, charter, and tax treatment, have held a major share of their assets in mortgages, financing them with deposits. In recent years, however, thrifts have sold a steadily rising percentage of their mortgage originations in the secondary market. Commercial banks, on the other hand, have consistently sold 15 to 20 percent of the mortgages they originate. Mortgage banking companies, which are not depository institutions, sell virtually all of the loans they originate.

From the late 1930s through the 1960s, the development of the secondary market was a slow, evolutionary process. It was instituted and sustained by federal government actions intended to make a market for mortgages originated by private lenders and insured by the Federal Housing Administration (FHA) or guaranteed by the Veterans Administration (VA). Trading in conventional mortgages was not common during this period for two reasons. First, these loans were considered risky by investors because they lacked federal guarantees or insurance. Second, neither the loan documents nor credit underwriting procedures were standardized.

Federal government actions to develop a national secondary mortgage market began essentially in 1938 with the chartering of the Federal National Mortgage Association (Fannie Mae) by Congress. Fannie Mae provided a secondary market for FHA/VA loans by buying these mortgages from originators and holding them in portfolio. Fannie Mae financed this portfolio by issuing short-term debt. In 1968, several roles performed by Fannie Mae were transferred to the Government National Mortgage Association (Ginnie Mae), a newly formed entity within the U.S. Department of Housing and Urban Development (HUD). The secondary market for federally insured mortgages expanded further in 1970 when Ginnie Mae began guaranteeing mortgage-backed pass-through securities representing shares in pools of FHA/VA loans.

The securities, called *pass-throughs* because funds are passed through to investors, were successful in attracting nontraditional mortgage investors to housing for a number of reasons. The owner of a pass-through receives a *pro rata* share of the monthly payments on the underlying mortgages. These include scheduled principal and interest payments, prepayments of principal, and, in the event of default, recovery of principal. This mechanism avoids the problems investors face in buying individual whole loans. Nontraditional investors typically do not have the expertise or the inclination to originate and service mortgage loans, and they are not generally in a position to underwrite and accept the full risk of default. By pooling the mortgages, this risk is diversified. By choosing a guaranteed security, investors can reduce (and, in the case of Ginnie Mae securities, eliminate) their losses in the event of default. For the same reasons, the pass-through is a more marketable instrument than a whole loan in the event the investor decides to sell it.

By the 1970s, the secondary market in federally insured home mortgages was well established. In contrast, there remained a glaring absence of an organized market for the sale of conventional mortgages. A new era of interest-rate volatility and periodic liquidity crises among mortgage lenders prompted Congress in 1970 to authorize the purchase of conventional loans by Fannie Mae and to charter the Federal Home Loan Mortgage Corporation (Freddie Mac). Although Freddie Mac was authorized to purchase FHA/VA as well as conventional loans, its main purpose was to spur the development of a conventional secondary market.

In 1971, Freddie Mac introduced the first conventional mortgage pass-through, the Mortgage Participation Certificate (PC). Rather than holding loans in portfolio, the corporation's financing strategy involved paralleling its purchases with PC sales to investors. In 1973, Freddie Mac and Fannie Mae cooperated in the development of a standard loan application and property appraisal report. The widespread adoption of the standard loan applications and underwriting guidelines by lenders led to substantial increases in the trading of conventional mortgages in the secondary market.

The success of the Ginnie Mae and Freddie Mac pass-through programs resulted in the first issuance of a nongovernment-related conventional pass-through security by a single lender, the Bank of America, in 1977. Following that, issues of conventional pass-throughs by other conduits began to emerge. The conduits pool mortgages from multiple lenders and market them as pass-through securities.

The volume of publicly issued private pass-throughs has been small, however, only about $6 billion through 1983 compared to almost $300 billion for government-related issues. The importance of the federally related guarantee and economies of scale seem to be factors in their limited market share. In addition, Ginnie Mae, Freddie Mac, and Fannie Mae mortgage-backed securities have benefitted from special legal, regulatory and tax treatment. For example, these securities are exempt from Securities and Exchange Commission (SEC) registration requirements, which are time-consuming and costly. The SEC has considerably eased the registration procedures for private issuers recently, reducing their disadvantage.

In the last few years, another development—thrift portfolio restructuring—has expanded the volume of loans sold in the secondary market. In addition to purchasing new originations, Fannie Mae and Freddie Mac purchase seasoned mortgages from lenders' portfolios. Simultaneously, the lenders purchase the securities backed by the loans they have sold. Such transactions, referred to as *swaps,* increase the liquidity of the mortgages, as well as the lenders' ability to use them as collateral for their own borrowing. Lenders can use Fannie Mae and Freddie Mac to swap current production as well as seasoned loans.

The most important function of the secondary market is to provide an elastic supply of funds to the mortgage market. That is, it ensures that the supply of funds expands and contracts in response to demand, keeping mortgage rates in line with capital market rates. During the 1970s, it did this in two ways. First, secondary market activity moved funds from areas of the country with a surplus of mortgage funds to areas with a deficit. For example, institutions in the Northeast and North Central regions, with somewhat lower mortgage rates (reflecting relatively weak loan demands and state-imposed usury ceilings) and large savings inflows, purchased mortgages for their portfolios, while those in the fast-growing Sunbelt sold newly originated loans in order to continue to meet their heavy loan demands.

Second, secondary market activity was able to offset the cyclical disintermediation in the thrift industry. Because thrift institutions were subject to deposit rate ceilings, they experienced significant outflows of deposit funds when interest rates rose rapidly. As a result, their ability to finance mortgage loans was significantly impaired. Sales of mortgages in the secondary market resulted in inflows of funds from nontraditional mortgage investors. Many now see the role of the secondary market expanding to meet the increasing mortgage credit demands of the 1980s.

Federally related organizations have played important roles in the development of secondary mortgage markets. In what follows, we examine in more detail the background and current operations of Fannie Mae, Freddie Mac, and Ginnie Mae. These operations, however, are subject to continual change in response to the needs of the marketplace. The roles of FHA, VA, and the Farmers Home Administration (FmHA) are also briefly discussed.

FEDERAL NATIONAL MORTGAGE ASSOCIATION (FANNIE MAE)

The concept of the Federal National Mortgage Association first emerged in the National Housing Act of 1934, which authorized the creation of entities to be known as national mortgage associations. These associations were expected to mobilize private capital to alleviate the liquidity problems of private mortgage lenders brought on by the Depression and the widespread use of short-term balloon mortgages. In addition, the associations were expected to counteract high interest rates, particularly in developing areas of the nation, by shifting mortgage funds from capital-rich to capital-poor areas.

Private capital proved difficult to attract, however, and no national mortgage associations were created. In 1938, the National Mortgage Association of Washington was chartered by Congress as a subsidiary of the Reconstruction Finance Corporation (RFC). Soon after it was chartered, the organization's name was changed to the Federal National Mortgage Association. Fannie Mae, as it came to be called, differed in one key respect from the earlier associations. Congress appropriated funds for its initial operations and further authorized it to issue debentures to finance purchases of FHA-insured residential mortgages.

In 1950, Congress transferred Fannie Mae from the RFC to the Housing and Home Finance Agency (HHFA), the forerunner of the Department of Housing and Urban Development (HUD). In response to criticism of government ownership of Fannie Mae, in 1954 Congress arranged for Fannie Mae's secondary market function to be converted eventually to private ownership through the retirement of Treasury stock. Fannie Mae's functions were divided into three areas (1) the secondary market operations, (2) special assistance functions, and (3) management and liquidation operations. By 1968, however, Fannie Mae's Treasury stock had not been retired (in fact, it was increased), and Fannie Mae remained a mixed-ownership corporation.

In 1968, Congress took steps to make Fannie Mae a privately owned corporation. The Housing and Urban Development Act of 1968 partitioned Fannie Mae into two separate entities, Fannie Mae and the Government National Mortgage Association (Ginnie Mae). Fannie Mae was to continue the secondary market functions as a government-sponsored private corporation; the new Ginnie Mae was given the special assistance and management and liquidation functions.

The Departments of Treasury and Housing and Urban Development have some regulatory authority over the corporation. Further, the Treasury may extend a line of credit to Fannie Mae. As a result of these government ties, Fannie Mae is viewed as having *agency status,* which enables it to issue debt at a lower rate than if it were viewed as a totally private entity.

Fannie Mae stock is traded on the New York Stock Exchange. Each year, the corporation's 30,000 stockholders elect 10 of the corporation's 15 directors; the additional 5 are appointed by the president of the United States. In 1982 Fannie Mae employed approximately 1,200 people in its Washington, D.C., headquarters and regional offices in Philadelphia, Atlanta, Chicago, Dallas, Los Angeles, and in its fiscal office in New York.

Initially, Fannie Mae purchased only FHA/VA loans. In 1970, it was authorized to purchase conventional mortgages as well. Most of its purchases were federally insured loans, and its most active sellers were mortgage bankers, who primarily originate this type of loan. Gradually, as sales by thrift institutions and commercial banks increased, Fannie Mae's conventional loan purchases expanded. In recent years, Fannie Mae's conventional volume has exceeded its FHA/VA volume. Fannie Mae's portfolio in 1983 was about 60 percent conventional loans. Out of a total of $18 billion in purchases for its portfolio that year, $200 million were FHA/VA loans.

Each year, Congress sets the maximum size for a single-family loan that Fannie Mae may purchase, based on an index of average new and existing house prices. As of January 1985, this limit was $115,300. The same limit applies to Freddie Mac. Limits are higher for two- to four-family dwellings.

Fannie Mae's mortgage purchases are based on its issuance of commitments. Under such commitments, Fannie Mae agrees in advance to purchase a specified dollar amount of loans at a specified yield. The commitment system helps protect lenders from the risk of an increase in mortgage rates during the life of the commitment. Such an increase would otherwise increase the yield required by Fannie Mae (and decrease the price it is willing to pay). Lenders usually pay fees for these commitments, although there is no commitment fee currently for standard adjustable-rate mortgages under Fannie Mae's 30-day mandatory delivery program.

Fannie Mae offers on a daily basis one- or two-month mandatory delivery commitments for fixed-rate first and second mortgages; one-, two-, three- or four-month mandatory commitments and four-month optional commitments for adjustable rate mortgages; nine or 12-month standby commitments; and three-month resale and refinance optional commitments. Fannie Mae sellers can request commitments under any of the corporation's standard programs by calling the corporation during each business day between 11 A.M. and 5 P.M. EST. Mandatory delivery commitments are issued at posted yields; standby commitments carry no yield.

As part of its strategy to match assets and liabilities more closely Fannie Mae introduced eight standard adjustable-rate mortgage plans in 1981, and began to purchase a wide variety of ARMS on a negotiated basis. In 1983 the corporation reduced its standard ARM products to three: one-, three- and five-year instruments tied to respective U.S. Treasury rates. Interest and payment adjustments occur simultaneously, and borrowers may elect a payment cap if desired. The plans can be combined with graduated payment features to reduce the initial monthly payment.

The minimum commitment amount is $25,000 for first and second single-family mortgages. In addition to the standard program offerings, commitments can be issued by Fannie Mae's regional offices on a negotiated basis for a variety of standard and nonstandard products.

Fannie Mae's fee structure varies, reflecting the different services provided under its various programs. Sellers who wish to retain servicing must own Fannie Mae stock. (This requirement was reduced to one share, for loans purchased after January 31, 1983.) Servicers receive a minimum fee of 0.375 percent of the original unpaid principal balance for fixed-rate first mortgages, 0.500 percent for adjustable-rate mortgages, and at least 0.25 percent for second mortgages. A sizeable portion of Fannie Mae's earnings are generated from fees charged to lenders in its mortgage purchase operations.

Fannie Mae purchases 50 to 90 percent participation interests (in 5 percent increments) in pools of conventional fixed-rate, one-to-four-family mortgages, in addition to buying whole loans. It also has programs that purchase rehabilitation, manufactured-housing, and conventional second-mortgage loans. In its resale and refinance program, Fannie Mae purchases loans required to sell or refinance the existing mortgages it currently owns. From approved lenders, the corporation buys Ginnie Mae-guaranteed certificates backed by FHA-insured or VA-guaranteed mobile-home loans as well. Fannie Mae also issues commitments for various types of FHA-insured project mortgages.

To participate in any purchase program, a seller must obtain Fannie Mae's approval. To qualify, sellers must originate real estate loans as a primary activity and have a minimum net worth of $250,000 plus 0.2 percent of the amount of their Fannie Mae servicing portfolio.

After loans are accepted for purchase, Fannie Mae performs a computer edit of the loan data from a mortgage-submission voucher. If the submission matches the contract on file, a check is cut and mailed to the seller.

Under its purchase programs for single-family mortgages, conventional participations, conventional second mortgages, and its mortgage-backed securities program, the seller warrants that the loan meets Fannie Mae's requirements. Because of this policy, loan submission can be funded rapidly. Fannie Mae sets aside contingency reserves for losses, and performs post-purchase spot checks to ensure that the loans meet its standards.

Fannie Mae also offers financing for investment properties. Additionally, under two of its programs the agency will give prior approval to entire condominium projects, planned unit development (PUD) projects, or subdivisions to facilitate later purchases of conventional mortgages in such communities. Fannie Mae's regional offices may also purchase spot loans in PUDs or condominiums.

Traditionally, Fannie Mae held in portfolio all of the mortgages acquired through its purchase activities, in this sense acting much the same as a thrift institution in the primary mortgage market. Of course, unlike S&Ls, Fannie Mae does not take retail deposits. It issues debt directly in capital markets. Although the funding of the portfolio has been assisted by interest income, fees charged to loan sellers, and sales of stock, the major source of funding has been the issuance of long-term debentures and short-term discount notes to investors.

Because of its use of short-term debt to finance long-term investments, Fannie Mae has been exposed to substantial interest-rate risk. During the past decade, Fannie Mae's earnings have varied widely over interest-rate cycles, declining when borrowing rates rose above the yield on the portfolio, and increasing when borrowing rates declined. Nevertheless, Fannie Mae has never drawn on its $2.25 billion line of credit with the U.S. Treasury.

In the future, Fannie Mae is likely to rely somewhat less on issuance of debt and somewhat more on less risky means of funding mortgage purchases—mortgages pass-through securities, for example. In December 1981, after it received approval from HUD and the U.S. Treasury, Fannie Mae made its first public offering of guaranteed mortgage pass-through certificates, in the amount of $250 million. The pass-throughs were backed by seasoned conventional loans and Fannie Mae guaranteed the timely payment of principal and interest. As of the end of 1983, the total volume of mortgage-backed securities (MBSs) issued by Fannie Mae exceeded $25 billion. Fannie Mae expanded both the types of loans eligible for pooling and its selling and distribution system in reaching this level of activity. However, the diversity of instruments currently being purchased by Fannie Mae limits the extent to which the pass-through vehicle can be used to finance the corporation's purchases.

MBSs are issued to sellers who submit loans under pool purchase or swap agreements, after Fannie Mae receives a certified schedule of mortgages (from an approved document custodian) indicating a seller has delivered the necessary documents. The minimum pool size for swaps is $1 million. Lenders may create single or joint (multiple-lender) pools. Within a pool, loan coupons may vary within a range of two percentage points. Fannie Mae has also separately pooled growing equity mortgages that it purchased and seasoned FHA and VA loans from its portfolio.

The amount of spread between the mortgage rate in a pool and the security's rate is based on whether the security is sold with or without *recourse;* that is, whether the lender or Fannie Mae assumes the risk of borrower default. The spread is 30 basis points if Fannie Mae assumes the risk of loss from defaults, and 25 basis points if the risk is assumed by the lender.

To the extent that Fannie Mae continues to hold mortgages in portfolio, it can be expected to attempt to match the terms of these assets to the terms of its liabilities in order to reduce its interest-rate risk. Fannie Mae's emphasis on purchasing adjustable-rate mortgages represents a move in this direction. The adjustable-rate mortgage is a more interest-rate-sensitive mortgage asset, in effect shortening the maturity of the loan.

FEDERAL HOME LOAN MORTGAGE CORPORATION (FREDDIE MAC)

The Federal Home Loan Mortgage Corporation was chartered by Congress in 1970 to develop a conventional secondary market. The corporation's initial capital came from the sale of $100 million in nonvoting common stock to the twelve district Federal Home Loan Banks. These banks, in turn, are owned by those savings and loan associations in their districts that belong to the Federal Home Loan Bank System (FHLBS).

The corporation's board of directors is composed of the three members of the Federal Home Loan Bank Board who are appointed by the president of the United States. The board of directors has the authority to require the Federal Home Loan Banks to guarantee the corporation's obligations. However, this power has never been used. In addition, Freddie Mac can use the FHLBS to raise funds. Further, until January 1, 1985 the corporation is tax exempt. For these reasons, Freddie Mac, like Fannie Mae, is classified as a quasi-governmental organization, and its debt offerings are also accorded agency status.

Freddie Mac's sources of new capital have included undivided profits, additions to reserves, and the sale of subordinated debentures to investors. In October 1982, Freddie Mac was granted authority to issue preferred stock.

In 1982 Freddie Mac employed approximately 600 employees in its Washington, DC headquarters, its regional offices in Arlington, Atlanta, Chicago, Dallas, and Los Angeles, and its underwriting offices in Denver, San Francisco, and Seattle.

Unlike Fannie Mae, Freddie Mac retains very few of the mortgages it purchases in portfolio. Instead, it matches its purchases with sales of PCs to investors. The practice of buying and selling mortgages at a positive spread avoids interest-rate risk and has enabled Freddie Mac to operate profitably in an environment that has severely tested unhedged portfolio lenders.

The PC was introduced in 1971 and became the principal method of funding purchase activities in 1976. In 1975 Freddie Mac introduced another mechanism for financing its purchases, guaranteed mortgage certificates or GMCs, which it may continue to issue on a limited basis. These are modified passthroughs which pay principal to investors annually, and interest semi-annually. GMCs are intended to attract traditional corporate bondholders.

With PCs, principal and interest are passed through to investors monthly. The corporation guarantees the timely payment of interest and full payment of principal on the mortgages underlying PCs. Freddie Mac sets aside contingency reserves against losses on the loans backing the PCs, and generally requires that mortgages with loan-to-value (LTV) ratios above 80 percent have private mortgage insurance.

In 1983 Freddie Mac issued another type of mortgage security, the collateralized mortgage obligation (CMO). Issued as general obligations of the corporation, CMOs are uniquely structured to attract different types of investors. A bond backed by long-term, fixed-rate mortgages purchased by the corporation, the CMO creates fast-, intermediate-, and slow-pay classes. All classes receive semi-annual interest payments; owners of the fast-pay class receive all payments of principal, both scheduled and unscheduled, until they are fully paid. Then intermediate-class owners receive principal payments. Finally, slow-pay class investors receive payments. Long-term investors, and particularly pension funds, have invested in the intermediate and slow-pay classes. S&Ls invested most heavily in the fast-pay class.

On the purchase side of its operation, Freddie Mac offers a selection of mortgage programs on a daily basis. Its purchase programs are designed to attract investment-quality mortgages. Freddie Mac buys conventional one- to-four family whole loans and participations for both adjustable-rate mortgages and long- and intermediate-term fixed-rate mortgages; whole loans and participations in long- and intermediate-term fixed-rate multifamily mortgages, and home improvement loans (HILS). Sellers have a choice of terms in which to deliver mortgages under the various programs. Mandatory delivery contracts are available in 30-, 60-, 90-, or 120-day terms under the one- to-four family fixed-rate and adjustable-rate mortgage programs. Sixty-day mandatory delivery contracts are available for HILs.

Under its optional delivery programs, Freddie Mac agrees in advance to purchase a specified dollar amount of loans at a specified yield. These optional commitments protect lenders from changes in mortgage rates during the life of the commitment. If interest rates rise during the commitment period, the lender may deliver loans at a lower yield than that required in the spot (immediate delivery) market; if rates drop, the lender may exercise the option not to deliver under the commitment.

Freddie Mac offers four-month optional commitments for adjustable- and fixed-rate home mortgages. An eight-month optional is available for fixed-rate home mortgages only.

For multifamily mortages, Freddie Mac offers a prior approval commitment as well as a 30-day immediate delivery contract. The prior approval process provides lenders with a firm 60-day commitment to purchase a specific multi-family mortgage at a specified maximum rate. If the lender chooses to deliver the loan to Freddie Mac when it is closed, he or she may elect the lower of the commitment rate or the immediate delivery rate. The prior approval process offers lenders the opportunity to obtain a firm commitment for the loan before it is closed, while providing the rate protection afforded by an optional commitment. Sellers have the option of making both assumable or nonassumable loans in the multifamily programs. The maximum amount for assumables is $20 million; for non-assumables it is $7.5 million. There is no limit on the amount a lender may commit to sell over time, except that the number of prior approval requests a lender has in process at any one time may be limited by Freddie Mac, at its discretion.

Commitment fees are not charged under Freddie Mac's mandatory delivery programs. Optional delivery commitments are issued with commitment fees that are determined by market conditions. A fee of 2 percent is charged for multifamily prior approval requests, with half the fee refunded when a loan is delivered and purchased.

Freddie Mac offers financing for single-family homes owned as second homes, and for one- to-four unit properties owned for investment purposes, at the same rates available for loans on owner-occupied homes.

A delivery fee is charged for each investor property loan purchased by Freddie Mac. The fee is based on the unpaid principle balance of the delivered loan.

Freddie Mac also offers approval of entire condominium and planned unit development projects that are under construction or renovation, or which are still controlled by the developer. This approval facilitates purchases of loans from these communities.

Until October 1982, the corporation charged a commitment fee based on the purchase amount to all sellers who were not members of the Federal Home Loan Bank System. The fee was dropped to encourage broader participation in the corporation's purchase programs by mortgage bankers, commercial banks, mutual savings banks, and credit unions.

The great bulk of Freddie Mac's purchase activity results from the fixed-rate home mortgage programs. However, the corporation has placed increasing emphasis on adjustable-rate mortgage programs in recent months in response to portfolio lenders' preference for mortgage instruments with more interest-rate sensitivity. Freddie Mac's current adjustable-rate mortgage programs include one-, three- and five-year ARMS indexed to one-, three-, and five-year Treasury rates respectively. The one-year ARM replaced the corporation's original one-year ARM program, which was indexed to the Bank Board's contract rate. Payment cap options were introduced in 1984. The corporation expects to begin purchasing ARMs with interest rate caps.

To make an offer to sell mortgages, a lender telephones Freddie Mac on any business day and gets immediate confirmation of the commitment. The four- and eight-month optional delivery programs are offered every Tuesday. Freddie Mac announces required net yields at which it will consider offers for fixed-rate mortgages and the margin over the index for adjustable-rate mortgages on its commitment line. Minimum required net yields on optional delivery programs are announced on Tuesdays; the line also carries required spreads under guarantor. Offer amounts over $25 million are considered on a negotiated basis through the corporation's regional offices.

Minimum commitment amounts have recently been dropped for most programs. For multifamily loans, the minimum is currently $100,000 per contract. For HILs it is $25,000.

A package of loans delivered to Freddie Mac must include the documentation prescribed by the corporation for each purchase program. By means of a streamlined underwriting process, computer selection of single-family loans that meet certain criteria eliminates the need for manual review of credit documentation by the underwriting staff. Properties may be inspected, selectively or randomly, and the homeowners' credit is analyzed. Freddie Mac typically rejects a small percentage of the loans submitted. The turnaround time from the delivery of a loan to funding is usually less than 21 days. Under the corporation's quick funding program for fixed-rate mortgages, introduced in 1981, Freddie Mac reduced its turnaround time to about 11 days for certain lenders by reducing documentation requirements.

Freddie Mac purchases mortgages each day until 2 P.M. EST. At that time it begins the process of selling these mortgages. On the sales side, Freddie Mac has two programs for issuing PCs backed by conventional fixed-rate mortgages on one-to-four family homes. Freddie Mac sells PCs to investors and issues PCs to lenders in exchange for mortgages. (Adjustable-rate mortgages and home improvement loans are currently held in portfolio.) PCs are now available in denominations as small as $25,000. Savings and loans have offered PCs obtained in swaps to customers at the retail level, as well as using them to back retail repurchase agreements, which offer savers a high-yield, short-term investment option.

Freddie Mac holds daily auctions of PCs to investors based on commitments to purchase issued that day. Freddie Mac works through a 13-member selling group and the corporation's own retail sales staff. The number of PCs offered and the certificate rate for various settlement dates are announced through the dealers. Additionally, a sale of PCs for optional delivery is held every Tuesday to coincide with the four- and eight-month optional delivery purchase programs.

Dealers submit offers by 2:20 P.M. Bids may be made on a competitive or noncompetitive basis. Noncompetitive bidders specify the amount of their offer only, agreeing to accept the average weighted yield at which competitive offers are accepted.

Offers are accepted or rejected based on whether they fall within an acceptable range as determined by the corporation. Based on the result of the auction and yields of PCs already trading, required net yields are set for the next day's purchase commitments. The corporation's pricing objective is to obtain a positive spread between the yield received in its mortgage purchase commitments and the yield it agrees to pay on the PCs. This spread is necessary to cover Freddie Mac's operating costs and to provide additions to reserves. For this reason, the corporation's purchase activities and PC sales are closely coordinated on a continuing basis.

Investors purchasing PCs receive confirmation and settlement notices the afternoon following the transaction. Chemical Bank is transfer agent for the PCs. Regardless of the number of PCs held, the investor receives one check each month.

The corporation's second method of issuing PCs is its guarantor, or swap, program, introduced in 1981. Lenders sell mortgages either at below-market coupon rates or current rates, and simultaneously buy Freddie Mac-guaranteed PCs backed by those same mortgages. The PCs are substantially more liquid than the underlying unpooled mortgages. Lenders may use them as collateral for repurchase agreements and other borrowing, or they may sell them to investors. The program was originally designed to aid lenders in converting low-yielding seasoned mortgages to securities as they struggled to cope with the earnings problems created by a high-interest-rate environment. It was later enhanced to attract current production mortgages once lenders adopted the swap concept.

In the guarantor program, which, like the PC sales program, is available daily, Freddie Mac purchases conventional mortgages and seasoned FHA and VA mortgages in exchange for securities. Freddie Mac requires a minimum spread of 25 basis points without recourse (in which the corporation assumes the risk of borrower default), and 20 basis points with recourse (in which the risk is assumed by the lender). In using the guarantor program, the seller must specify the offer amount and delivery period for which the commitment is desired. Two delivery periods, 90 and 180 days, are available; a commitment fee of 0.01 percent is charged for 180-day optional delivery. Bids are in terms of a spread between the yields on the mortgages offered and on the resultant PCs. The minimum eligible coupon rate on whole loans is equal to the PC certificate rate, plus the administered bid, plus a 37.5 basis-point minimum servicing fee. The PC rate plus the administered spread determines the minimum coupon rate for participation pools. The minimum pool size is $1 million for swaps.

Lenders may deliver loans originated in more than one state to fulfill purchase commitments as well as guarantor contracts. Nationwide lenders may handle commitments, delivery, and monthly accounting functions under all of Freddie Mac's programs through the Freddie Mac offices serving the area in which their principal office is located, if they so desire.

As lenders' inventories of seasoned low-rate mortgages decline, the use of the Guarantor program to provide liquidity may change. In fact, lenders are increasingly viewing the program as an alternative to the traditional method for delivering mortgages. For example, it may be less costly for large lenders who do not need Freddie Mac's selling services to convert newly originated mortgages into guaranteed pass-through securities using swaps. Given the similarity of this to the Ginnie Mae mechanism, a substantial volume of new production swaps may be expected to result.

Freddie Mac's activity can be expected to change in other ways as well. For example, programs for graduated payment mortgages and adjustable rate mortgages are being developed that are designed to encourage standardization. Further, the corporation expects to use its expertise in financial markets to assist lenders in other ways, such as in developing hedging strategies for their portfolios.

GOVERNMENT NATIONAL MORTGAGE ASSOCIATION (GINNIE MAE)

The Government National Mortgage Association was created as a wholly owned government corporation in 1968 by the National Housing Act. Ginnie Mae was given responsibility for certain functions previously performed by Fannie Mae. The Housing and Urban Development Act of 1968 established jurisdiction over Ginnie Mae in the newly created HUD. Ginnie Mae's president is a presidential appointee who receives general policy direction from the secretary of HUD. Ginnie Mae's offices are located in the HUD headquarters in Washington, DC. Ginnie Mae has about 55 employees.

In addition to its mortgage-backed security program, Ginnie Mae has two other major activities. One is its special assistance function. Under it, Ginnie Mae purchases mortgages to fulfill two statutory objectives: (1) to provide assistance for financing certain types of housing for which financing is not readily available (as for low-income families); and (2) to counter declines in mortgage lending and housing construction over business cycles. In the so-called tandem program, Ginnie Mae purchases below-market-interest-rate FHA-insured multifamily mortgages. These loans are then sold, primarily at bimonthly auctions, at a discount that results in a market yield to the investor. Ginnie Mae's other major activity is to manage and liquidate a portfolio of federally owned mortgages, including loans transferred to it by other federal agencies.

Ginnie Mae launched its mortgage security program in 1970, when it gave its first guarantee on a pool of FHA/VA loans originated by a private lender. The program experienced rapid growth over the 1970s, and by the end of 1982 the cumulative volume of mortgage pass-through securities guaranteed by Ginnie Mae reached $141 billion. This is more than double the amount backed by all other government and private organizations combined. In 1982 approximately 75 percent of FHA/VA loans were packaged in Ginnie Mae pools. The minimum size of a pool is $1 million, and the minimum certificate that can be bought has a $1,000 initial face value.

Each new Ginnie Mae pass-through is created on the initiative of a private lender who wishes to sell the kinds of loans eligible for inclusion in the pools. Typically, approved issuers are mortgage bankers; they may also be S&Ls, mutual savings banks, commercial banks, and credit unions. Lenders assemble mortgages insured by FHA or guaranteed by VA or FmHA less than one year prior to the date Ginnie Mae guarantees the pool. The loans must be similar with respect to interest rate, maturity, and type (level payment or graduated payment; single family or multifamily; 15- or 30-year). In its traditional programs, the lender obtains a commitment to guarantee securities backed by the pooled mortgages, and upon completion of a pool proceeds to actually issue securities based on the commitment. The Ginnie Mae guarantee of timely payment of principal and interest carries the full faith and credit of the U.S. government.

Ginnie Mae plays a relatively minor role in the physical production of the securities. It supplies standardized securities instruments and underlying contractual agreements and assures that the mortgages in the pool exist and are held securely on behalf of Ginnie Mae. Ginnie Mae is able to play this limited role because, unlike the current Freddie Mac and Fannie Mae programs, Ginnie Mae does not actually purchase the mortgages. It only adds its guarantee to mortgage securities that are issued by private lenders.

The FHA/VA mortgages underlying Ginnie Mae pools have interest rates 50 basis points above the coupon rate of the security. Of this 50 basis points, the issuer receives 44 basis points as a servicing fee and as compensation for the risk of advancing principal and interest when borrowers' payments are late. Ginnie Mae keeps the remaining 6 basis points as its fee. This fee has more than covered Ginnie Mae's operating costs and losses on default, and has resulted in a large accumulation of reserves.

Ginnie Mae takes very little default risk. All of the mortgages underlying the pools are already government-insured or guaranteed. In addition, Ginnie Mae imposes minimum net worth requirements on its issuers. Moreover, under its contract with the issuer, Ginnie Mae can take an issuer's entire Ginnie Mae servicing portfolio to recover any losses if the issuer defaults. Since it started selling servicing contracts in 1976, Ginnie Mae has had only 23 cases of default by issuers, and only one has required more than a marginal payment from reserves. Ginnie Mae securities, known as Ginnie Maes, trade in a well-organized market. They can be bought and sold with relatively low transaction costs because of the large volume of activity, particularly for recent issues.

Ginnie Mae introduced major innovations in August 1983 in the way its securities are issued and administered. Ginnie Mae II may be used by lenders in addition to or as an alternative to the traditional Ginnie Mae mortgage-backed security program, now known as Ginnie Mae I.

The focal point of Ginnie Mae II is the feature of a central paying agent. As central paying and transfer agent, Chemical Bank makes all principal and interest payments to investors, enabling holders of more than one Ginnie Mae II certificate to receive a single check. This feature provides a more efficient and convenient means of paying investors, transferring securities, reporting principal factors, and issuing new pools.

Loans with different interest rates within a one percentage point range may be mixed within the same pool. Pools may also include loans originated by lenders in various parts of the country. The jumbo or multiple-issuer pool option aggregates packages submitted by various issuers for a particular issue date and securities interest rate, and combines them into a single pool that backs a single issue of securities. Investors have indicated an interest in the more consistent cash flow provided in such jumbo pools.

Several months prior to each issue date Ginne Mae announces the securities coupon rates for multiple-issuer pools. When setting the rates, Ginnie Mae provides the type of loan, issue date, and face interest rate of the securities. Each issuer under a multiple-issuer pool is responsible for marketing the portion of the securities that corresponds in amount of the outstanding principal balance of the loan package contributed by it. The issuer makes all necessary arrangements for the sale of the securities to investors, either directly or through securities brokers or dealers. The issuer also makes all necessary arrangements for its receipt of payment for the securities it issues.

Investors holding Ginnie Mae I securities can in many instances convert them to Ginnie Mae IIs and thus receive a single monthly check for most or all of their Ginnie Mae holdings.

As with other securities, holders of Ginnie Maes are vulnerable to price changes as market rates of interest fluctuate. Hedging against this risk has been made easier by the development of an organized futures market in Ginnie Mae securities, and may be further facilitated by the Ginnie Mae options market that has been proposed. The Ginnie Mae futures market is one of only two futures markets for long-term securities, the other being for U.S. Treasury debt. Ginnie Mae's role in fostering the development of the futures and options markets may be one of its most important contributions.

OTHER GOVERNMENT INVOLVEMENT

A number of other government agencies are involved in housing finance as direct lenders, mortgage insurers, and participants in the secondary market. The three agencies whose loans are guaranteed in Ginnie Mae pools are discussed briefly.

Federal Housing Administration (FHA)

The Federal Housing Administration was created by Congress in 1934 to provide federal insurance for home mortgages. As a result, it was able to standardize the (then innovative) long-term, low-downpayment mortgage.

To be eligible for FHA insurance, mortgages have to meet certain standards with respect to loan, borrower, and property characteristics. Mortgage-loan applications and property appraisal reports, as well as the mortgage document itself, became standardized. Further, there is a limit on the maximum loan amount. This is currently $67,500 (more in high-cost areas).

Until recently HUD set interest-rate ceilings for loans with FHA insurance. Even with the ceilings, the mortgages and insurance were not subsidized. That is, except for certain high-risk loans, the insurance program is actuarially sound. Further, private lenders originated the loans. When the ceiling rate was less than market interest rates, lenders charged points up front (each point is 1 percent of the amount borrowed) to establish a market yield. Technically, the home buyer could only pay one point, with the seller paying the rest. The seller was often compensated by increasing the price of the house, which offset the cost of the mortgage points. With the Housing Act passed in November 1983, both the interest rate and the payment of points were deregulated.

FHA continues to play a role in establishing innovative mortgage instruments. In 1977, FHA began insuring graduated-payment mortgages (GPMs). Ginnie Mae guarantees pools of GPMs in addition to the pools of 30-year fixed-rate loans. FHA began insuring adjustable-rate mortgages in 1984, and Ginnie Mae announced a related program. The future role of Ginnie Mae, in terms of volume and the types of mortgages pooled, depends on the future role of FHA.

Veterans Administration (VA)

The Veterans Administration was created by Congress in 1944 as an independent arm of the federal executive branch to assist veterans of military service in a variety of ways. Because of shortages of housing and mortgage credit at that time, the agency was authorized to guarantee privately originated mortgage loans to veterans that had low or no downpayments. In addition, the VA conducted a direct-loan program for veterans until Congress ended it in 1980. VA-guaranteed loans are purchased by Fannie Mae and are included in Ginnie Mae pools.

Farmers Home Administration (FmHA)

The Farmers Home Administration was created by Congress in 1946. Its purpose is to provide rural housing and development financing for individuals and businessess unable to obtain market-rate conventional loans. The agency makes available direct loans, loan guarantees, and grant programs.

The most important FmHA direct-loan programs are the rural housing program, the rural cooperative housing program, and the rural housing loan program. Interest rates under these programs are set by FmHA and interest rate subsidies may bring effective rates down to one percent.

Direct loans made by the FmHA are generally held by the agency and serviced by its district offices. Some FmHA-guaranteed mortgages are packaged into Ginnie Mae pass-through securities. FmHA pass-throughs are not offered publicly, but are sold to the Federal Financing Bank.

—— Chapter 4 ——————————————————————

The Role of Mortgage Securities

Robert F. Dall
Managing Director
Salomon Brothers Inc.

Richard M. Schapiro
Vice President
Salomon Brothers Inc.

Historical Development

The secondary market for residential mortgages evolved after the Great Depression in response to a series of actions taken by the federal government to meet the critical shortage of mortgage funds being made available by the thrift, banking, and life insurance industries. During this period, the federal government realized that declining real estate values would further depress the economy, thereby delaying its revitalization. In order to stabilize the real estate market and alter the highly illiquid position which threatened the viability of most financial institutions, several programs were initiated by the government.

Of primary importance was the establishment in 1934 of the Federal Housing Administration (FHA). The FHA offered the government's first mortgage-default insurance. With this insurance of principal, lenders were able to accept lower downpayments on FHA-insured mortgage loans. More importantly, the FHA was the first to standardize objective mortgage-quality criteria and evaluation practices for program eligibility. Many of these standards, such as the 80 percent loan-to-value ratio and the 30-year term, were subsequently adopted as industry conventions.

The establishment of such industry standards laid the groundwork for the secondary market. Uniformity of underwriting criteria and the financial security of the FHA insurance gave mortgage originators the confidence to buy and sell mortgages through the Federal National Mortgage Association (FNMA), which was established in 1938 to provide a market for FHA-insured loans. In 1948 FNMA expanded its program to Veterans Administration (VA) guaranteed loans, which were considered equivalent to FHA loans from a quality standpoint. The marketing of mortgage loans through FNMA and the standardization

AUTHORS' NOTE: The authors wish to thank Keith M. Maillard for his invaluable assistance in completing this article.

of industry guidelines facilitated the first attempts to tap mortgage funds on a national scale and to close disparities in regional economies.

Despite these positive first steps, the secondary market remained small and fragmented. Throughout the 1960s, housing theorists, politicians, academicians, and economists struggled with the problem of improving the delivery system of single-family loans to the mortgagor. Although a number of highly respected economists had begun to question the efficacy of alloting so many GNP dollars to housing, more specifically FHA and VA housing, the American Dream of home ownership was a compelling political fact of life.

Introduction of the GNMA Pass-Through Program

A program to aid the development of the secondary market was finally agreed upon in late 1970 and the Government National Mortgage Association pass-through program was put into effect. The Government National Mortgage Association (GNMA) was spun off from FNMA in 1968 and, prior to the introduction of its pass-through program, had not been very well known except as the guarantor of a small number of bond issues. GNMA was established as a government corporation within the Department of Housing and Urban Development to administer mortgage support programs which could not be transferred to the private sector.

In late 1970, GNMA announced its guaranteed securities programs, which would provide full-faith-and-credit support of the U.S. government. The mortgage-backed securities programs were viewed as a means of channeling funds from the nation's securities markets into the housing market. Since the mortgage market had traditionally been localized, with local lenders supplying regional financing needs, the pass-through program was conceived as a means of bringing the resources and economies of the national securities market to the mortgage market. Funds raised through the issuance of these securities could then be recycled by mortgage originators into new mortgage loans. Through this process, the program could increase the overall supply of credit available for housing and help ensure that such credit would be available at reasonable interest rates. More importantly, the GNMA security format provided a means for investors to invest in mortgages without the cumbersome process of reviewing individual loan files. Each investment represented a pro rata share in pools of mortgages which were either insured by the FHA or guaranteed by the VA. The pooling concept allowed investors to spread their risk over a large universe of mortgage loans, thereby diversifying their credit exposure.

The securities were the following:

1. Straight pass-throughs—a 30-year fixed-maturity security with monthly payment of principal and interest to investors *if* collected by the issuer. In essence, only those funds collected would be remitted.
2. Fully modified pass-throughs—a 30-year fixed-maturity security with

monthly payment of principal and interest to investors *whether or not collected* by the issuer.

The pass-through rate is stated on the face of the GNMA certificate. This rate is the interest rate on the FHA and VA mortgages which comprise the mortgage pool, less a guaranty fee of 6 basis points (a basis point is equal to one hundreth of 1 percent, i.e., .01 percent) and the prescribed servicing fee (44 basis points) set by GNMA. For example, if the FHA/VA mortgage rate were 12.50 percent, the GNMA rate would be 50 basis points less, or 12.00 percent. It should also be noted that the minimum size for each pool of GNMA pass-throughs was $1,000,000, with the proviso that the pools could be broken down into individual units as small as $25,000.

The earliest participants in the program involving the purchase and ultimate distribution of the GNMA pass-throughs were commercial banks and nonbank government bond dealers who had experience and expertise in dealing with U.S. government and federal-agency securities. Investment banking houses which did not specialize in U.S. government or federal-agency securities also established departments in these areas in anticipation of the program's success. The full-faith-and-credit guarantee of the U.S. government attracted investors who were otherwise prohibited from purchasing participations in mortgage loans. Finally, new partnerships and corporations were established to deal in these securities (in the GNMA program). Investment in and creation of such securities was a relatively simple process since U.S. government guaranteed securities are not subject to SEC registration requirements, thereby eliminating the need to build a large staff to perform the time-consuming due-diligence, analysis, and financial-structuring functions typically required in other securities underwritings.

The natural issuers of the pools of securities to be guaranteed by GNMA were the originators of FHA-insured and VA-guaranteed mortgages. These included savings and loan associations, mutual savings banks, commercial banks, and mortgage bankers. Mortgage bankers initially dominated this market, since their operations were geared towards originating mortgage loans for immediate resale while other financial institutions at that time typically retained such loans for their own portfolios.

The orgination and distribution of GNMA securities are diagramed in Figure 1.

Trading and Distribution

There are two standard over-the-counter markets in which GNMA securities are traded—the immediate and future delivery market.

Cash Immediate Market.   This market is traded in the current month, and is analogous to the market in corporate bonds. It is characterized by firm obli-

Figure 1 • How the GNMA Mortgage-backed Securities Program Works

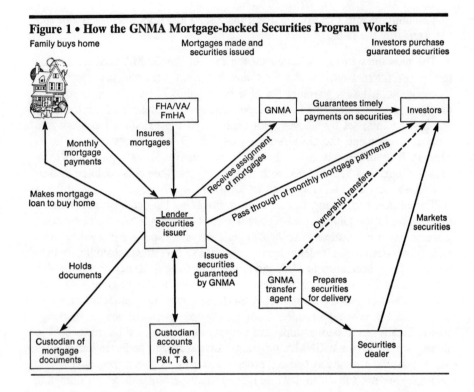

gations to buy and sell, differentiating it from some of the vehicles in the future
delivery markets, such as standbys and futures contracts on the Chicago Board
of Trade or the American Commodity Exchange. The cash immediate market
is the most widely used method of GNMA delivery.

Cash Forward Market (TBA Market). The over-the-counter market for
trading in future months is the *cash forward market*. It is also called the TBA
(to-be-announced) market. It is a mandatory-buy or mandatory-sell market, and
settlements can range forward from one to six months, and occasionally as far
forward as one year. Forward contracts may be satisfied with GNMA pools
already in existence, or with pools that may be formed by a mortgage banker
between the date of contract and the forward settlement date.

The GNMA market is composed of various coupons, but only one of those
coupons is called the *current coupon*. The GNMA current-coupon is a function
of the latest mortgage rate and is 50 basis points less than this rate.

Transactions involving the forward delivery of GNMA securities are consummated at a specific price today, irrespective of the movement in the market in

the future. Such a practice locks in the future price that an institution will deliver loans into a forward commitment, thereby defining the exposure due to interest-rate moves.

GNMA Pass-Through Securities Problems

The new GNMA pass-through security presented a number of new elements to the securities market which inhibited immediate growth and caused some abuses as a result of varying knowledge of the nature of the security. Some of these are the following:

1. The real housing-production cycle for the FHA and VA tract building projects is somewhere between 90 and 120 days. Consequently, mortgage bankers and other traditional originators (who must pre-fix their costs), had to sell the GNMA security on a forward basis. The security was sold at a fixed price, regardless of the uncertainty as to whether all the loans could be closed at the same price. Dealers accepted that fact and bought the securities for forward delivery. They simultaneously sold the securities for forward delivery without recognizing that every sale by an originator to a dealer was a short sale. A short sale for a fixed forward delivery date had credit implications which were ignored until increased volatility in the marketplace resulted in a number of embarrassing and costly failures to receive securities that had been pre-sold.

2. Some participants began to trade for forward delivery dates beyond the real production cycle. Such practice was purely speculative.

3. The GNMA pass-through security with a 30-year fixed maturity was presumed to have a 12-year average life (based upon FHA statistics) and were traded accordingly. The pass-throughs may have had a propensity to trade to a 12-year average life. However, the real average life was unknown, since acceleration or deceleration of mortgage prepayments could dramatically affect the average life and, therefore, the ultimate yield of any specific security. Many transactions were initiated in the early years without a full understanding of this phenomenon.

4. The GNMA current coupon was set 50 basis points below the FHA origination rate. The 50 basis points included 44 basis points for servicing (to be retained by the originator) and 6 basis points to GNMA as guarantor. Since the FHA rate was not determined solely on the basis of market conditions, aberrations occurred in the market whenever political or other considerations prevented the FHA rate from moving in concert with real interest rates.

5. Since all prepayments or defaults were at par (100 percent), there was a natural resistance by dealers to own a GNMA pass-through at a premium. This limited the upside potential of the security for any investor who held a GNMA which he thought would appreciate in price in the event of a decline in interest rates.

6. The monthly pay feature of the pass-through, coupled with the irregularity of the payment size (a result of prepayments and defaults), were foreign to the investment community. Investors resisted the purchase of a security which was difficult not only to understand but also to track from a cash flow and accounting standpoint.

7. Since individual mortgagors could prepay at any time without penalty, the security had no inherent call protection.

Wall Street Involvement

As the GNMA programs developed, the bank and nonbank government-bond dealers typically assigned traders with various degrees of experience to the GNMA securities. In most cases, GNMA pass-throughs were traded by the government-bond departments despite the unique cash flow characteristics of the security.

Eventually, dealers involved in the GNMA business began to hire people with mortgage industry related experience to work directly with mortgage bankers in order to gain access to the origination of the securities. While most dealers already had contacts with financial-institution originators, efforts were stepped up to cover other major originators (such as savings and loan associations).

Dealers entered into standby arrangements under which mortgage bankers paid a fee for the right to sell GNMAs to the dealer at a specified forward date and an agreed-upon price. This practice provided protection for the mortgage banker against adverse moves in interest rates. The dealers, in turn, paid a fee to institutional investors either to pair off the fees received (with a modest spread) or to protect (hedge) their own positions.

In the early 1970s purchasers of GNMA securities tended to be institutions related to the mortgage industry. To attract nontraditional investors, yields on GNMAs rose rapidly, and at one time were more than 250 basis points above long Treasury bonds. The historical yields and spreads of GNMA securities relative to the yields of 10- and 30-year Treasuries are set forth in Figures 2 and 3. About half of the GNMAs outstanding today are held by investors who are not directly connected to the mortgage industry. (See Table 1.) With this increased market interest has come an increased growth in outstanding GNMAs—from $56.7 billion at year-end 1978 to $170.9 billion at June 30, 1984. (See Table 2.) Included in Table 3 is a summary of all GNMA mortgage-backed securities traded in the secondary market, from April 1972 to July, 1984.

New Programs

Since the advent of its original program, GNMA has introduced a number of additional securities which bear mentioning.

Figure 2 • Time Chart of Yield Levels and Spreads

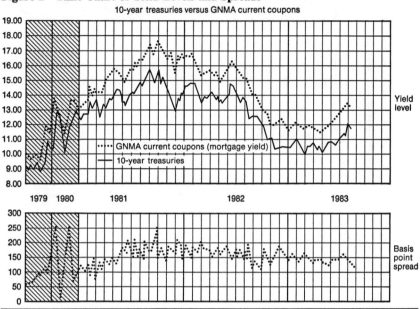

Figure 3 • Time Chart of Yield Levels and Spreads

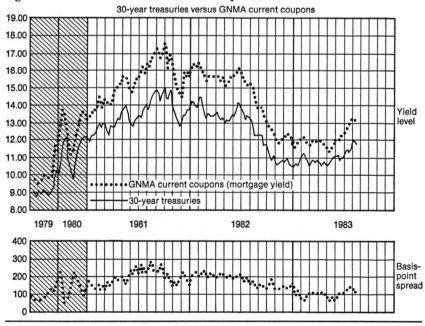

Table 1 • Government National Mortgage Association Mortgage-Backed Securities Program (holdings of GNMA securities, by type of holder—$ billions)

Investors groups	1984 Month Ended						
	January	February	March	April	May	June	July
Mutual Savings Banks	$ 12.3	$ 12.4	$ 13.0	$ 13.3	$ 13.3	$ 12.8	$ 12.8
Commercial Banks	7.6	7.7	7.6	7.7	7.6	7.4	7.4
Savings and Loan Associations	38.5	39.9	40.4	41.6	42.8	42.2	42.3
Public Retirement/Pension Funds	13.4	13.6	13.8	13.8	13.7	13.8	13.9
Private Retirement/Pension Funds	.6	.6	.6	.6	.6	.6	.7
Mortgage Bankers	3.7	3.8	3.8	3.8	3.7	4.1	4.2
Securities Brokers/Dealers	18.1	18.2	20.0	20.2	20.9	21.5	22.3
Nominees	67.7	68.3	67.7	67.1	67.8	68.5	68.8
Corporations/Partnerships	7.2	7.2	7.2	7.2	7.0	7.2	7.0
Private Individuals	4.1	4.1	4.2	4.4	4.5	4.5	4.7
Credit Unions	2.9	3.0	2.8	2.8	2.9	2.9	2.9
Life Insurance Companies	5.8	5.9	5.8	5.9	6.3	6.8	7.0
Other Insurance Companies	.8	.8	.8	.8	.8	.8	.8
State and Local Government General Funds	5.3	5.3	5.2	5.3	5.3	5.2	5.0
Fiduciaries—Individual	1.4	1.4	1.4	1.4	1.4	1.4	1.5
Fiduciaries—Institutional	4.1	4.3	4.4	4.8	4.9	6.0	6.5
Others	1.0	1.0	1.2	1.2	1.2	1.2	1.3
Total	194.5	197.5	199.9	201.9	204.7	206.9	209.1
Terminated Issues	1.9	1.9	2.0	2.0	2.0	2.0	2.1
Total Issues	$196.4	$199.4	$201.9	$203.9	$206.7	$208.9	$211.2

*Amounts shown are original amount of issuances and do not reflect current balances.
Source: Prepared by the office of the secretary, GNMA—August 20, 1984.

Table 2 • Government National Mortgage Association Mortgage-Backed Securities Program (outstanding securities balances, end of month—$ thousands)

	1979	1980	1981	1982	1983	1984
January	$56,716,466	$78,849,086	$ 95,061,526	$106,588,555	$120,849,504	$162,107,991
February	57,878,488	79,900,352	96,291,628	107,433,714	123,739,452	164,562,150
March	59,138,602	80,843,221	97,183,599	108,592,408	127,939,408	166,260,936
April	60,201,766	82,419,479	98,405,070	109,240,400	131,391,311	167,554,604
May	61,398,494	83,384,636	99,143,592	110,142,385	134,960,774	169,493,107
June	62,840,859	84,281,705	100,558,241	111,458,726	139,275,939	170,892,674
July	64,780,700	85,633,871	101,581,443	112,317,758	143,897,647	
August	66,735,518	88,030,929	102,742,503	113,175,290	146,516,454	
September	69,008,019	89,452,126	103,749,969	114,776,204	151,596,573	
October	71,456,466	91,425,074	104,293,199	115,935,336	154,776,823	
November	73,463,744	92,573,781	104,822,872	117,068,081	156,687,026	
December	75,787,135	93,873,647	105,789,613	118,940,232	159,849,816	

Source: Prepared by the office of the secretary, GNMA—August 8, 1984.

Table 3 • Government National Mortgage Association Mortgage-Backed Securities Program (mortgage-backed securities transferred in secondary market—$ millions)

	1972	1973	1974	1975	1976	1977	1978	1979	1980	1981	1982	1983	1984
January		$ 250	$ 432	$ 660	$ 1,193	$ 3,388	$ 4,021	$ 3,580	$ 4,802	$ 4,136	$ 5,354	$ 12,196	$ 13,512
February		283	495	805	1,475	3,177	3,491	2,820	3,876	3,475	4,648	11,237	15,283
March		218	735	1,002	1,959	4,711	3,105	3,177	4,304	4,943	7,042	16,857	16,733
April	$ 240	273	668	1,313	2,440	3,164	2,747	2,830	3,886	4,008	5,852	13,682	14,692
May	307	170	532	972	2,513	3,732	2,724	2,987	4,210	3,548	5,636	17,642	15,227
June	243	309	529	935	1,901	3,588	2,775	3,230	4,728	4,774	7,127	17,641	13,692
July	186	396	495	1,151	2,190	3,596	2,534	4,392	5,369	4,529	6,100	13,026	14,099
August	192	303	454	773	2,169	3,525	3,030	5,093	5,312	3,898	7,036	14,150	
September	140	165	447	817	2,783	3,985	3,043	4,365	5,457	3,990	8,393	14,840	
October	187	218	511	851	2,886	3,319	3,408	5,990	5,119	4,375	9,896	15,875	
November	247	259	429	786	3,392	3,331	3,086	4,744	3,920	5,060	11,377	14,566	
December	224	296	555	1,099	4,120	3,432	2,966	5,016	4,344	6,717	12,192	17,300	
Total	$1,966	$3,140	$6,282	$11,164	$29,021	$42,948	$36,930	$48,224	$55,327	$53,453	$90,653	$179,012	$103,238

Source: Prepared by the office of the secretary, GNMA—August 20, 1984.

A brief outline of several of the products appear below:

1. GNMAs backed by single-family mortgages with 15-year maturities (15-year GNMAs) were introduced to the mortgage securities market in 1982. They were initially originated by a single mortgage banker in the summer of 1982. By December of 1982, 10 other major mortgage originators had begun issuing this type of mortgage.

The 15-year GNMA security is similar to the widely traded 30-year GNMA, in that both represent a pro rata share in a pool of mortgages either insured by the FHA or guaranteed by the VA. Also, both have a 50 basis point service fee and a 45-day delay until first payment. The primary difference between the two lies in the maturity of the underlying mortgages (15 years versus 30 years) and in the absence of a current coupon for the 15-year certificate. This implies that the 15-year mortgages may be originated with a choice of coupons, some of which could represent a substantial discount from the 30-year current coupon. The 15-year GNMA is an intermediate term security, and its yield is quoted to a 7-year average life.

2. The GNMA graduated payment mortgage pass-through (GNMA-GPM) was first issued in April, 1979. The GPM consists of fractional undivided interests in mortgage loans whose monthly payments graduate (increase) for a predetermined number of years. They are issued in minimum denominations of $25,000 with a round lot for trading consisting of $1,000,000 principal amount. Graduated payment loans are usually 30-year loans on mortgages on owner-occupied one-to-four family dwellings. As is the case in level-payment GNMAs, mortgage bankers are the primary issuers. FHA designed the GPM for younger home buyers who may not have, at time of purchase, the income necessary to support a more expensive purchase, but whose potential for substantial increased income in the near future makes them worthwhile credit risks for a larger mortgage amount. The yield calculation on the GPM is based on the standard 12-year prepayment structure.

3. The GNMA mobile home program began in 1973, but experienced very little success before 1976. Financing for mobile homes was constrained during 1973–74 as the recession deepened and loan delinquencies and repossessions of financed units rose. Private mortgage issuers experienced heavy losses from 1974–76. Mobile home loans were cited as one of the factors contributing to losses from the high rate of default. Repossession rates, however, have declined significantly since 1975 and as construction standards have improved for manufactured homes, the market for these securities has grown dramatically.

GNMA mobile-home securities represent fractional undivided interests in pools of FHA-insured or VA-guaranteed mortgage loans on mobile homes. The securities contain the same full-faith-and-credit guarantee for timely payment of principal and interest as GNMA single-family securities. However, the maturity on mobile-home mortgages is considerably shorter and the yield is quoted on a 5- to 9-year average life depending upon its maturity.

As of July 31, 1984, approximately $4.4 billion GNMA mobile-home securities had been issued. Changes in HUD regulations and the price attractiveness of manufactured housing (compared to single-family housing) should ensure a rapid growth of GNMA mobile-home securities.

4. In July 1983, GNMA introduced a new program called Phase II. The Phase II program was designed to eliminate the administrative inefficiencies of the old GNMA security. Most significantly, a central paying agent is utilized under Phase II, thereby eliminating the receipt of multiple remittances for investors owning pass-through securities representing different mortgage pools. In addition, Phase II allows the formation of multiple-issuer pools of mortgages allowing mortgage originators the ability to create pools that may be smaller in size than the standard delivery amount of $1 million. The primary GNMA program permits only a single issuer for each mortgage pool.

5. FHA announced in July 1984 that it would begin to insure certain forms of adjustable rate mortgage loans (ARMs). GNMA correspondingly stated that it would begin a securities program utilizing these FHA-insured ARMs. The ARMs have been standardized as to their percentage increase, their index, and other applicable characteristics.

Private-Sector Mortgage Securities

Conventional Mortgages

In the late 1970s, securities were created for mortgages other than those of the U.S. government insured and those that were federal-agency guaranteed. These private sector mortgages make up 75 to 80 percent of all outstanding mortgages. A number of securities were created to package these mortgages.

Mortgage Pass-Throughs. The first conventional mortgage pass-through was issued by the Bank of America in September 1977. This device involved the conveyance of conventional mortgage loans (one-to-four family loans) into a legal entity called a *grantor trust* and the sale of undivided interests in that trust to investors. The investors received principal and interest payments from the trustee of the pool. Timely advances were to be made by the Bank of America in amounts equal to a pool policy provided by mortgage guaranty insurance. The pool policy amounted to 5 percent of the original face amount of the mortgages in the pool and declined only in the event of actual losses. While this issue was unrated, subsequent issues which had the benefit of additional insurance protection achieved investment grade ratings which were AA (Standard & Poor's). Later, when the private mortgage insurance was replaced by the bank's own letter of credit, the issues were rated at the same level as Bank of America's debt—AAA. Currently, through combinations of pool and private-mortgage insurance these securities can achieve "AAA" ratings from Standard & Poor's.

Mortgage-Backed Bonds. Thrift institutions were able to tap the intermediate-debt markets by pledging, with a high degree of over-collateralization, deep-discount mortgages with shorter average maturities. Because of the quantity and high credit quality of the collateral, high-investment-grade ratings (including AAA ratings) could be obtained. In 1984, a similar security incorporating overcollateralization of GNMA's and other mortgage-backed securities was introduced to the European capital markets. These securities were issued predominantly by subsidiaries of thrifts and, because of the significant overcollateralization, were rate AAA.

Variable Rate Pass-Throughs. These securities have been issued on two occasions by the Home Savings and Loan Association in Los Angeles which set a coupon and a price at issuance, with periodic coupon adjustments tied to an index. This was the first mortgage security that allowed for the inclusion of mortgage loans with variable interest rates. With the growing interest by the potential homeowner in the adjustable rate loan, it is expected that the variable or adjustable rate pass-through may prove to be a widely used vehicle for secondary market funding of these loans.

Conduit Conventional Pass-Throughs. Pass-throughs were soon introduced in which a variety of corporate entities collected mortgages from various originators and offered pass-through securities modeled on those issued by the Bank of America and Federal Home Loan Mortgage Corporation PCs.

Pay-Through and Cash Flow Bonds. These bonds were the next logical step. These instruments combine attributes of both mortgage-backed bonds and conventional pass-throughs and have particular appeal to debtors who need to take advantage of installment sales-tax treatment. The security is structured so that it is a borrowing on the books of the issuer.

The most recently developed type of mortgage-backed security is the collateralized mortgage obligation (CMO). While CMOs are clearly a type of cash flow bond, they represent a notable development, in that the cash flow of the underlying mortgage pool is apportioned to different classes of bonds to create short-term and long-term securities from the steady but declining cash flows of the mortgage pool. Most significantly, the CMO enables the issuer to target maturities which have specific appeal to certain investors. The first CMO was issued by the Federal Home Loan Mortgage Corporation in June 1983. The $1 billion issue was comprised of three classes of bonds with differing maturities. All principal payments are applied to the short maturity bonds until retired, then to the intermediate-maturity bonds, and finally to the long maturity bonds.

The CMO structure provided further entry into the capital market for mortgage securities. Since June of 1983, approximately $11 billion in CMOs have been issued. CMOs have primarily been issued by builders, looking to finance their home production, and other institutions looking to take advantage of market arbitrage between the mortgage and capital markets.

Dealers have been beset by an array of new conventional securities. Adjustable-rate securities, the sought-after panacea of thrift institutions, have been held out for distribution by dealers. The issuance of an adjustable rate CMO supported by the cash flow if ARMs is not long in coming. In 1984 approximately 60 percent of all conventional mortgage production was in ARMs. The secondary market funding of these ARMs will probably take the form of the current state of the art—CMO's.

Wall Street and the Mortgage Markets

In the Salomon Brothers Inc bond market research report ("1984 Prospects for Financial Markets"), it is estimated that the total demand for credit in calendar 1984 will amount to $543.4 billion. Of that total, $173.0 billion represents total net increases in all mortgage debt outstanding by the end of 1984. More importantly, the total of privately held mortgages of all classes is estimated at $1,319.5 billion by December 31, 1983. It is obvious from these figures that the mortgage market constitutes an enormous segment of the capital markets. With the expected increased growth in housing starts, the mortgage segment of the capital markets should continue to grow as a percentage of the total capital markets. In addition, the security markets will be called upon to supply an increasing share of the needs of the mortgage markets with the result being that traditional market relationships may very well change.

The mortgage markets of the future will continue to look more and more like the traditional securities markets where secondary-market liquidity helps to provide optimal primary-market pricing with a resultant minimum cost of housing to the mortgagor. As more mortgage originators and securities dealers become active participants in the secondary mortgage market, new innovations and efficiencies will undoubtedly result.

Conventional Mortgage-Backed Securities

Leland C. Brendsel
Executive Vice President Finance
and Chief Financial Officer
Federal Home Loan Mortgage Corporation

Introduction

Long before a formal secondary market existed, mortgage lenders sought and found investors in residential mortgages. The introduction of the conventional mortgage-backed security in 1971 provided the market with a more efficient mechanism for bringing together the mortgage lender and the mortgage investor. The conventional mortgage-backed security is backed by a pool of individual mortgages. The instrument thus created represents a more marketable investment that attracts investors who traditionally would not invest in mortgages.

Introduced only 12 years ago, the conventional mortgage-backed security is a relatively new addition to the investments that are available to the large capital-market investor. With a total of about $100 billion in public and private pass-through securities issued through the end of 1983, the conventional mortgage-backed security has more than adequately succeeded in establishing its viability as an investment instrument capable of attracting large sums of capital-market funds. By demonstrating its effectiveness in channeling capital-market funds into housing during that industry's severe depression of 1981–82, the conventional mortgage-backed security has emerged from that tumultuous period as the linchpin of the secondary-mortgage market that now supplies a substantial portion of mortgage funds to homebuyers.

Mortgage originators have three broad options when they decide to trade mortgages for other assets: (1) they may sell mortgages directly to other lenders; (2) they may sell mortgages for cash through the standard programs of intermediaries such as Freddie Mac and Fannie Mae; or, (3) they can swap mortgages for securities that are guaranteed by the intermediaries. With the swap option, lenders take responsibility for marketing the security if they should decide to sell it.

This chapter defines the conventional mortgage-backed security, explores its development and the progress it has made over the past decade, discusses its market potential, and addresses the issues affecting its future development.

Rationale and Early Development

While mortgages may offer investors attractive yields—and the opportunity to support a social objective is also considered by many to be desirable—they are complex instruments with cash flow, maturity, marketability, risk characteristics, and servicing requirements that translate into disadvantages in the competition for capital-market funds. For example, consider the harried mortgage lender trying to execute a deal to sell a group of whole mortgages to a life insurance company through a broker/dealer. As the lender listens, the voice on the other end of the phone drones on: "And we'll also need the loan-tovalue ratios . . . a listing of the locations of the properties . . . a breakout of the terms, maturities, amortization schedules. . . ." The questions are posed by the broker in trying to arrange the purchase for the insurance company. They are necessary to gather information the company needs to underwrite the package. The mortgage lender may well have to repeat this process three or four times with different brokers or investors to determine the best price (mortgage packages can be evaluated in a variety of ways). The process itself may require a total of several weeks before the sale will be completed.

In contrast, consider the lender who has swapped mortgages for securities, and who then decides to sell the securities. This time the transaction requires less than a few minutes, and the only terms to be discussed are the price, based on the coupon, and the settlement date. The quality, terms, and marketability of the mortgage-backed security are understood by brokers and investors, providing smaller price differences among participants than might occur on the sale of a group of individual mortgages.

One obvious advantage of securitizing loans prior to selling them is greater certainty about the quality of the asset being priced by the buyer and about the structure of the market in which it is being sold. When a seller determines that the market is right for a sale, a mortgage security can be sold with a phone commitment in an active secondary market. A whole-loan package, in contrast, might be offered to various buyers in the whole-loan market, where wide discrepancies in valuation occur, and it must be described in detail to each prospective buyer. The certainty of the agreement is also much greater in the security market than in the whole-loan market. A phone commitment for a specified coupon, price, and settlement in the security market is not subject to review on delivery. By contrast, whole-loan sales are contingent on the execution of the commitment agreement, the quality of the loan package, and the mutual understanding of the terms of the commitment. Market movements that reduce the value of the loans before purchase may increase the incentive for finding fault with the agreement.

Evolution of the Concept

The conventional mortgage security provides an efficient mechanism for bringing the mortgage originator and the mortgage investor together. It does this by offering investors a liquid security backed by a pool of mortgages. With a mortgage security, an investor obtains an undivided interest in the pool of mortgages. The security entitles the holder to a portion of the flow of principal and interest payments on the underlying mortgages. These payments are passed through to the investors, usually on a monthly basis, hence the name *pass-through.*

The pass-through concept has a precedent in the mortgage-backed securities known as Ginnie Maes, which have been authorized since 1968 and which are backed by FHA and VA mortgages. Timely and full payment of Ginnie Maes are guaranteed by the full faith and credit of the United States, and the FHA and VA mortgages underlying them also carry the guarantee of government agencies. Conventional mortgages, in contrast, could offer only the protection provided by private-mortgage insurance. And the conventional mortgage-backed security would not be guaranteed by the United States government, but rather, to the extent permitted by tax regulations, by the issuer. In 1970, Congress chartered the Federal Home Loan Mortgage Corporation (Freddie Mac) for the purpose of creating a national secondary market for the growing volume of conventional residential mortgage originations. S&Ls had traded in participations between themselves since the early sixties, but no organized national market existed.

As a federally sponsored corporate entity (without, however, the benefit of federal appropriations), Freddie Mac had the advantage of offering securities that could trade in the government securities markets. This was critical to the successful start-up of the conventional mortgage-backed security.

Freddie Mac began issuing securities called mortgage participation certificates (PCs) in 1971, to achieve its objective of providing an available supply of credit for conventional mortgages. The PC was the first conventional pass-through security. With $66 billion issued through 1983, the PC had achieved substantial liquidity and an active secondary trading market. The security offers monthly distributions with timely interest and full return of principal guaranteed by Freddie Mac.

The introduction of the conventional mortgage-backed security in 1971 was intended to develop the possibilities of a secondary market in conventional, or non-guaranteed mortgages, in contrast to government-insured FHA and guaranteed VA mortgages. Proponents of the conventional mortgage security envi-

sioned that the integration of the mortgage and capital markets would result in
the continuous availability of conventional mortgage credit at market rates of
interest, without regard to cyclical and regional influences. Such a system
would mean that homebuyers' efforts to obtain mortgages would no longer be
thwarted by thrift disintermediation or the mismatch between deposit flow and
the demand for mortgage credit in a particular area.

Early efforts undertaken by Freddie Mac to ensure the viability of the new
instrument included establishing uniform mortgage documents and using appraisal and underwriting standards uniformly throughout the country. Standardization of the underlying mortgages was essential to ensure the quality of the
mortgages and the reputation of the PC as a desirable vehicle for investing in
them.

Table 1 shows that, in 1982, more than half of the investors in Freddie
Mac's standard programs were investors other than thrift institutions. Eighteen
percent of these PCs were held by pension funds.

Freddie Mac also offered a second type of mortgage security, the guaranteed
mortgage certificate (GMC), in 1975. Like the PC, the GMC represents an
undivided interest in a pool of mortgages that have been purchased by the
corporation. However, the GMC pays interest at the certificate rate semi-
annually; principal is paid annually. The GMC's schedule of payments for principal and interest was arranged to avoid the problems associated with receiving
and reinvesting monthly payments. Approximately $3 billion in GMCs were
issued from 1975 to 1979.

In 1981 Freddie Mac introduced a program called Guarantor, which enabled
lenders to swap mortgages for PCs. In contrast to the standard purchase and
sales programs, lenders are responsible for marketing the PCs they receive
through swaps. Initially the program attracted lenders needing to sell seasoned
low-yielding loans. It was later enhanced to appeal to lenders selling current
production as well. Over $24 billion in PCs have been issued in the guarantor

Table 1 • PC Investor Profile (Standard Program) August 1982 (in percent)

Investor Type	Percent of Total
S&Ls	45.1%
Public and private pensions	18.1
Insurance companies	9.7
Mutual savings banks	6.5
Dealers	2.4
State and local governments	2.1
Bank trusts	1.3
Others	14.8
Total	100.0%

Note: A substantial volume of Freddie Mac PCs are actually held in nominee accounts. Nominees
are firms that perform securities transactions on behalf of other investors. In the distribution
above, the holdings of nominees have been allocated to the various investor groups in accordance
with a survey of nominee managers conducted by Freddie Mac in 1982.

program through 1982. In 1983 the program was expanded to include purchase of seasoned FHA and VA mortgages in exchange for FHA/VA PCs.

Continuing the effort, pioneered by the GMC, to increase the certainty of principal distributions and attract a more diverse group of investors, Freddie Mac issued collateralized mortgage obligations (CMOs) in June of 1983. The first issue was offered as a general obligation of the corporation and sold in multiples of $25,000. The CMO differs from most mortgage securities in the manner in which principal and interest are passed on to investors. The concept was based on maturity preference techniques widely used in municipal revenue bond issues. The CMO has three distinct classes with short, intermediate, and long-term payment characteristics. All classes receive semiannual payments of interest.

Investors holding the first fast-pay class receive all payments of principal, both scheduled amortization and prepayments, until they are fully paid. Then the second class begins to receive principal payments. Similarly, when the first two classes are fully paid, the third class begins to receive principal payments. Freddie Mac guarantees a minimum schedule of payments to holders of CMOs.

The offering attracted investors with different preferences for the maturities of their assets. Investors in the first class were primarily savings and loans seeking a relatively short-term asset to match their short-term liabilities. Institutional investors, seeking intermediate or long-term assets to match their long-term obligations, purchased most of both the second and third classes. Life insurance companies and pension funds made large purchases in class two, and pension funds purchased most of class three.

Since the first CMO, Freddie Mac has completed two additional issues backed by current coupon mortages, and one backed by seasoned low coupon loans. The later CMOs include a fourth class for which interest accrues but is not paid until the shorter classes are retired. In addition, other issuers have entered the market. In just over one year, there have been 34 issues totaling $12 billion. Freddie Mac's CMOs account for about one quarter of this total.

Other Programs

Private issues of mortgage securities from private institutions first appeared in 1977 when Bank of America became the first to make a large public offering of pass-through securities. First Federal Savings and Loan of Chicago and Glendale Federal made similar offerings a short time later.

Through 1982, approximately 50 nonagency issuers had issued private pass-through securities. The total volume of such offerings reached approximately $3 billion by the end of 1982. Private issues have accounted for a small portion of the total mortgage-security market for several reasons, including obsolete investment eligibility laws and investor preferences influenced by ERISA. In addition, the interest-rate climate throughout the late 1970s and the early 1980s held down volume, making it hard to construct large pools. Costly federal and state securities registration and private security-rating requirements have also hampered the growth of private mortgage-security issues. The Secondary Mortgage Market Enhancement Act, enacted in October 1984, removes or reduces many of these restrictions.

In 1981, the Federal National Mortgage Association (Fannie Mae) began to issue and guarantee conventional mortgage-backed securities. Before 1981, Fannie Mae held its mortgage purchases in portfolio, financing them with short- and intermediate-term debt. The mortgage pools backing Fannie Mae's conventional programs consist of conventional home loans Fannie Mae has purchased from lenders, including both new originations and loans from portfolio. The program was later expanded to include FHA and VA mortgages. Like Freddie Mac, by swapping securities for mortgages during the 1981–82 period, Fannie Mae was able to take advantage of lenders' need to turn low-yielding, seasoned mortgages into a source of improved liquidity, and thereby built its security program rapidly. At the end of 1982, Fannie Mae had issued approximately $15 billion securities in mortgage securities.

Other New Entrants

The conventional mortgage-security market has attracted new players to the secondary mortgage market arena, including (1) financial institutions seeking to expand their lines of business, and (2) financial "supermarkets" with networks of housing-related businesses. The significant recent developments include the following examples:

Residential Funding Corporation (RFC), a private conduit owned by Norwest Mortgage Inc. (formerly Banco Mortgage Company), purchases primarily nonconforming mortgages, those whose balance is above the $115,300 maximum for single-family loans currently placed on Freddie Mac and Fannie Mae. Maximum loan amounts on some of RFC's programs range from $150,000 to $500,000. RFC's securities have a double-A rating from Standard and Poor's.

General Electric Credit Corporation (GECC), traditionally a source of financing for consumer appliances, has created a network of housing-related subsidiaries, including two mortgage insurance companies and a mortgage-banking subsidiary. GECC has privately placed a AAA-rated $65 million issue with a pension fund. Like RFC, GECC has focused on jumbo loans, those exceeding the current federal individual-mortgage limit for Freddie Mac and Fannie Mae.

Through its Coldwell Banker Real Estate Group subsidiary, Sears now offers mortgage pass-through certificates backed by fixed-rate conventional mortgages. Sears' subsidiary, Seraco, has also announced plans to offer Sears customers an opportunity to invest in "retail" mortgage securities through its financial services centers. Sears' mortgage-finance network includes Coldwell Banker, Allstate Insurance, and Dean Witter Reynolds Inc.

Relative Role of Conventional Securities and Market Potential

The Ginnie Mae market, consisting of securities guaranteed by the Government National Mortgage Association, is approximately twice as big as the conventional mortgage-security market, but conventionals are steadily closing the gap. In the mid-seventies, the volume of Ginnie Maes issued was five times greater than conventionals. Much of the anticipated growth in conventional mortgage securities is expected to occur within the remainder of this decade.

Of the $1 trillion in mortgages outstanding, more than 75 percent are conventional mortgages. Even after subtracting the $100 billion already backing securities, and the $100 billion in adjustable rate mortagages, over $500 billion in conventional mortgages remain for potential securitization. With the growing trend towards securitization of mortgages—as financial institutions restructure their balance sheets and methods of doing business—the conventional mortgage security may be on the verge of major growth. The interest expressed by the variety of new players suggests that others have reached similar conclusions about the potential market for the instrument.

Portfolio lenders seem increasingly disposed to securitize mortgage purchases. Securities provide them greater flexibility in managing their portfolios and therefore in matching assets and liabilities. Securities facilitate portfolio restructuring when necessary and act as collateral for borrowings. At the same time, securities provide a mechanism for employing excess funds and make possible an expanded line of services.

Swapping or selling loans in the secondary market may also contribute to an increase in fee income, if it increases the volume of originations. And swapping or selling loans helps build a servicing portfolio, which produces income over time. The selection of secondary-market products available today also makes it possible for lenders to offer a broad product line to an expanding customer base.

Interest among investors in mortgage securities supports their prospects for growth as well. For example, the large quantity of pension-fund assets, estimated at $800 to $900 billion, represents a great potential source of funds for housing. Through mortgage-backed securities, pensions have an opportunity to invest in safe, relatively high-yielding assets, while at the same time avoiding the problems traditionally associated with whole loans.

ISSUES AHEAD FOR CONVENTIONAL SECURITIES

Standardization

The availability of a variety of alternative mortgage instruments over the past two years, such as adjustable-rate and early ownership mortgages, gives borrowers, lenders, and investors additional flexibility in meeting their financial objectives. Yet there are also some costs associated with this flexibility in the context of the secondary-mortgage market, and specifically in securities. A wide range of alternative mortgage instruments works against the market's need for large, homogeneous volumes of mortgages. A challenge ahead is to find the mortgage instruments that reflect a convergence of what is attractive to borrowers, lenders, and investors. Such standardization is what makes it possible to trade securities in a large enough volume to reap the benefits of an efficient secondary market. Such standardization may ultimately result in a steadier flow of funds and lower borrowing costs for home buyers.

Developments such as the CMO, previously discussed, suggest that the industry has made strides in rising above the lock-step between mortgage payments and investor receipts. The flexibility of the CMO permits the tapping of a variety of investor interests.

Active Management of Pools

Legislation was introduced in Congress in 1983 that would provide for a new type of investment vehicle, the Trust for Investment in Mortgages (TIM), intended to attract private-sector capital to the secondary market for home mortgages. The 1982 report of the president's housing commission recognized a number of statutory and regulatory obstacles to complete market acceptance of mortgage-backed securities, including constraints on flexible pool management and the resulting taxability of actively managed trusts at the issuer level.

The TIMs legislation would allow active management of mortgage trusts. Such a trust would be allowed to issue multiple class securities similar to the CMO, and to reinvest income and principal received from the mortgages in the pool. The TIM itself would not be subject to the federal income tax, and items of income, gain, and loss would be passed through to the TIM shareholder. The major advantage relative to the CMO is treatment as an asset sale for tax purposes, rather than as a debt financing. This could benefit certain potential issuers such as mortgage bankers and certain investors such as thrifts. The TIMs legislation has not passed, but most likely will be reintroduced in 1985.

The Quality of the Guarantee

The question of how to evaluate the quality of the guarantee backing the conventional mortgage security presents another important issue. Conventional mortgage-backed securities are being issued in a variety of shapes and sizes by new players. Some of these securities are backed by homogeneous mortgages, others are backed by mortgages that are diverse. As a result, the conventional security—until recently a fairly simple instrument—has entered a new experimental phase of development.

Any guidelines developed for gauging the quality of the guarantee attached to the security should include the following factors:

- the financial strength of the issuer: what is the capital base and the profitability picture of the organization?
- the underwriting and servicing standards applied to the mortgages underlying the security: how thorough are they and how strongly enforced?
- asset quality: what is the prospect for loss from individual mortgage defaults?
- the issuer's ability to handle administration and processing responsibilities efficiently.

Conclusion

Conventional mortgage securities transform investment in residential mortgages in ways that overcome many of the traditional obstacles perceived by pension funds and other institutional investors.

For the investor, conventional securities provide an advantage over mortgages because (1) they reduce the problems associated with default risk and the need for staff underwriting expertise; (2) they offer standardization of mortgages in large volume; (3) they are more liquid than mortgages; and (4) they reduce administrative transaction costs. For the originator, mortgage securities also make a great deal of sense, because they give portfolio managers greater flexibility in managing their assets. As these advantages become even better understood by both capital-market investors and by lenders who elect to sell mortgages in the secondary market or swap mortgages for securities, the conventional mortgage security should enjoy rapid growth and an even more central role in the nation's emerging housing finance system.

Chapter 6

The Role of the Rating Agencies: A Standard & Poor's Perspective*

James J. O'Meara
Vice President–Mortgage Finance
The First Boston Corporation

David D. Tibbals
Vice President—Mortgage Finance
Salomon Brothers Inc.
(Formerly Vice Presidents of Standard & Poor's Mortgage Group)

In a typical year, approximately $125 billion of bonds are issued in the U.S. public-debt market. Another $15–20 billion are privately placed. The annual number of issuers exceeds 1,000 and includes such diverse entities as steel companies, bank holding companies, municipalities, utilities, and other entities that need to raise long-term capital. Moreover, bonds may be unsecured general obligations of the issuer, or they may be secured by a particular revenue stream or by specific collateral. In short, the myriad of bond issuers and the increasing complexity of their issues necessitate an analytical staff that few investors can afford to maintain, giving rise to the need for professional assessors of bond quality.

Credit ratings help investors by providing an easily recognizable, simple tool that couples a possibly unknown issuer with an informative and meaningful symbol of credit quality. Credit ratings have become an important facilitative factor in the sale and trading of bonds in U.S. capital markets. Letter rating symbols and the opinions they represent, however, cannot describe the extensive effort that is put into each rating judgement and the detailed rationale that stands behind each rating.

Ratings are of value only as long as they are credible. Rating credibility arises primarily from the objectivity which results from the rater being independent of the issuer's business. When enough investors are willing to accept the judgement of a particular rating, that rater gains recognition as a rating agency. Credibility is fragile. A rating agency operates with no governmental mandate, subpoena powers, or any other official authority.

Today, two rating agencies assign ratings to most public debt issues: Standard & Poor's Corp., a subsidiary of McGraw-Hill, Inc., and Moody's Inves-

---

*Reviewed by S&P Mortgage Group

tors Services, a Dun & Bradstreet unit. Additional rating firms include Fitch Investor Services, Duff & Phelps, and McCarthy, Crisanti and Maffei. Standard & Poor's, Moody's, and Fitch are, to date, the primary firms involved in the rating of mortgage securities. The focus of this chapter will be on the rating approach used by Standard & Poor's.

S&P rated its first corporate bond in 1923 and its first municipal bond in 1940. Today, ratings are assigned to a wide variety of instruments such as debentures, first mortgage bonds, commercial paper, preferred stock, and tax anticipation notes. S&P currently has ratings on issues of some 2,000 domestic and foreign corporations and 8,000 municipalities, states, and foreign nations. In addition, there are commercial paper ratings on over 1,100 issuing entities. S&P's staff of rating professionals exceeds 160. Ratings are published in several of its printed and electronic services and are distributed by the general and financial news media.

A S&P rating is a current assessment of the creditworthiness of an obligor with respect to a specific obligation. This assessment takes into account the likelihood of principal and interest being repaid on a timely basis in accordance with the terms of the obligation. Moreover, the rating evaluation considers security provisions and relative creditor standing in bankruptcy. Definitions of S&P's bond ratings can be found in the Appendix.

As a matter of policy, S&P rates most public bond issues of $10 million and over with or without a request from the issuer. There are, however, some exceptions to this policy. Private placements, mortgage-related financings, and certain other types of issues are rated only upon request (with the issuer having publication rights to the rating). For private placements, there is no ongoing rating surveillance beyond the initial rating assessment.

A rating is not a recommendation to purchase, sell, or hold a security because it does not comment on market price or suitability for a particular investor. Although many questions are asked in a number of areas as S&P proceeds through the rating process, a rating does not mean that S&P has performed an audit, nor does it attest to the authenticity of the information provided by the issuer upon which the rating is based. Ratings can be changed, suspended, or withdrawn as a result of changes in information or its unavailability.

It is interesting to note the exclusive nature of the AAA category. Only twenty industrial corporations in the United States, for example, presently carry AAA ratings on their public debt. In the structured financing area where collateral and third party support agreements can be utilized, however, the number of AAA ratings increases dramatically.

Rating Approach to Mortgage-Related Securities

In assigning a rating to a mortgage-related security, S&P follows a multiple-step process. First, the issuer or its investment banker contacts S&P to request a rating and submits pertinent information regarding the issuer and the security to the S&P rating group specializing in this area. Next, representatives of

S&P's rating staff usually meet with members of the issuer's senior management, their investment bankers, and/or lawyers to discuss the issuer's operations and the specific terms of the security. The primary and secondary analysts assigned to the issue then conduct the final analytical review of the legal documents and the issuer's operations and prepare a written rating presentation. The presentation of the analysis is made to a rating committee consisting of five to seven S&P analysts. The primary and secondary analysts are included, along with other analysts specializing in the structured financing area. Once the rating is determined, the issuer is notified of the rating and the major considerations in the evaluation. The issuer has the option of appealing the rating decision by furnishing additional information, in which case the rating committee reconsiders its position before rendering a final rating decision.

The area within S&P responsible for rating mortgage securities is the financial institutions/mortgage department. Both tax-exempt housing issues and taxable mortgage financings are rated by this department. A professional staff of 25 analysts is assigned on a full-time basis to the rating of these securities.

Overview of Mortgage Securities

The mortgage securities market, since its inception in the early 1970s, has been dominated by government agencies. Government National Mortgage Association (GNMA), Federal Home Loan Mortgage Corporation (FHLMC), Federal National Mortgage Association (FNMA), and state and local housing agencies have issued (or guaranteed in the case of GNMA) approximately $312 billion of securities involving single-family mortgage loans. In recent years a growing number of mortgage securities have been sold out of the private sector. These securities have been issued by thrifts, banks, mortgage bankers, homebuilders and insurance companies. In total about $25 billion of these securities have been issued and rated by Standard & Poor's.

The focus of this chapter will be on the criteria used by S&P in rating mortgage securities issued out of the private sector. Since 1975, when S&P became the first agency to rate mortgage securities, a considerable amount of time and effort has been spent developing criteria to evaluate the new forms of mortgage securities that have been rated. These rated securities can be placed into three major groups:

1. *Mortgage pass-through certificates.* This security represents an ownership interest in a pool of mortgage loans. Payments made on the mortgage loans are passed through to certificateholders in an amount sufficient to repay principal and interest at the pass-through rate. The certificates are created from a sale of assets and are thus not a general obligation of the issuer. Traditional single-family mortgage loans as well as other types of mortgage loans have been sold using the pass-through structure. Rated pass-through certificates have been issued by thrifts, mortgage bankers, commercial banks, and conduit companies. Since 1977, S&P has issued ratings on about $7 billion of pass-through certificates, the majority of which received AA private ratings.

2. *Mortgage-backed bonds*. These bonds are a general obligation of the issuer, typically secured by conventional single-family mortgage loans. The mortgage collateral is regularly valued and maintained by the issuer at a specified percentage of the outstanding bond balance. In the event of the issuer's default or a collateral insufficiency, the bond trustee liquidates the collateral to repay bondholders in full. To date, approximately $6 billion of public and private bond issues have been rated. Almost all of these bonds have been issued by thrift institutions.

3. *Mortgage pay-through bonds*. This relatively new security is a bond, but incorporates many of the characteristics of a pass-through certificate. It is structured so the collateral pool, generally consisting of conventional single-family mortgages or GNMAs, will generate a sufficient cash flow to provide for the full and timely repayment of the bonds. The reliance on the mortgages' cash flow rather than market value is the key factor which distinguishes this instrument from the standard mortgage-backed bond. S&P has rated pay-throughs issued by homebuilders, mortgage bankers, and thrifts. The total amount of pay-throughs rated to date equals about $12 billion.

Mortgage Pass-Through Certificate

A mortgage pass-through certificate differs from the typical bond issue that S&P is accustomed to rating in that it is not a debt obligation. Since the certificateholders have an ownership interest in the pooled loans, they are entitled to only those payments made under a pure pass-through structure. If only half of the mortgagors' scheduled payments are collected, for example, the certificateholders receive only this amount. A rating on this basis, of course, would be meaningless. It would address the probability of investors receiving what they had actually collected; hence, all issues would have to be rated AAA regardless of their credit strength.

In order to provide a meaningful rating, S&P views the pass-through certificate as a debt instrument. Consequently, it is assumed that investors expect to receive at a minimum all contractually scheduled payments owed on the mortgage loans, whether or not made by the mortgagors. A support system therefore must exist to cover payment shortfalls caused by mortgage delinquencies and foreclosures. This support system may include mortgage insurance policies, servicer advances, performance bonds and other sources of payment protection. The rating process, in an effort to determine the likelihood of certificateholders receiving scheduled mortgage payments in a full and timely manner, focuses on three major factors:

1. The credit quality of the loan pool and the amount of loss protection.
2. The financial strength of the mortgage insurer or the source providing the loss protection.
3. The cash advance capability of the servicer.

Credit Quality and Loss Protection

The first factor considered in the rating evaluation is the credit quality of the loans in the pool. In assessing the credit quality, an estimate is made of the largest amount of potential losses that could occur because of foreclosures. This estimate of potential losses is then compared to the amount of loss protection provided. So long as the loss coverage is sufficient to handle the perceived degree of credit risk, pass-throughs can qualify for S&P's highest ratings. All types of loans are thus eligible for inclusion in pass-through pools provided that their credit risk can be quantified and adequate loss protection can be supplied.

To quantify credit risk, two critical assumptions must be made: (1) the number of loans in the pool that will be foreclosed (the *foreclosure frequency*) and (2) the average loss that will be realized upon these foreclosures (the *loss severity*). The amount of potential credit losses is then equal to the product of the assumed foreclosure frequency and loss severity. In deriving these two assumptions, the various characteristics of the loans in the pool are assessed, including their lien status, interest-rate and payment terms, secured property types, loan-

---

Table 1 • Characteristics of a Prime Mortgage Pool

Prime Characteristics	Rationale
Mortgage security: first lien on single-family (one-unit) detached property.	This property is perceived as having lowest credit risk because of its widest acceptance among homeowners.
Mortgage payments: fixed-rate, level payment, fully-amortizing loans.	This payment structure avoids refinancing risk and uncertainty over whether mortgagor can make increased payments.
Mortgagor status: secured properties are mortgagor's primary residences.	Mortgagor is more likely to keep his primary residence rather than his vacation home if encountering financial difficulties.
Location of properties: well-dispersed throughout an area having a strong and diversified economic base.	Wide dispersion minimizes effect of localized economic downturns and a strong economic area reduces foreclosure risk and strengthens property values.
Loan-to-value ratio: 80% or less.	Smaller downpayments (i.e., higher LTV ratios) reduce incentive to repay loans thus increasing the likelihood of foreclosure.
Number of loans: 300 or more.	Since an actuarial approach is used in quantifying credit risk, a large pool is needed to reduce the probability of statistical aberrations occurring.
Size of loans: average loan size not exceeding FHLMC limit (currently $115,300) with maximum loan size not greater than $200,000.	High-priced properties have a more limited market and thus are more vulnerable to larger price declines.
Loan underwriting: should meet FHLMC/FNMA standards.	Use of FHLMC/FNMA standards should minimize presence of high risk mortgagors.

to-value ratios, average and maximum loan size, and geographic location. When pass-throughs were first developed, the loan pools created were of prime quality. (Table 1 lists those characteristics that S&P views as constituting a prime pool). These prime loans have performed exceptionally well over the last 40 years. The loan-default rate has remained consistently low and foreclosure losses have been minimal.

To qualify for a high rating, pass-through certificates must be able to withstand losses that could be realized under a worst-case scenario. For fixed-rate mortgages, the worst-case scenario is assumed to be a depressionary period of high unemployment and sharply declining real estate values. In order to determine the amount of loss protection needed under such a scenario, S&P looked to the experience of the 1930s.

There are limitations, of course, in looking to the experience of the Great Depression as an indicator of what a worst-case loss scenario may be for pass-through pools. First, the social and economic infrastructure of the 1930s was much different from that of today. Second, the typical single-family mortgage in the 1930s was different from the prime mortgage loan of today in two respects: it had a large balloon payment due at maturity and a low loan-to-value ratio at origination. Third, liberal forebearance policies and the fact that many states passed foreclosure-moratorium laws may have disguised the number of problem loans to a substantial degree. Hence, it is difficult to determine precisely from the available data what the actual loss experience was during this period on loans with characteristics similar to those found in today's prime pass-through pools. Nevertheless, S&P believes this period provides the best data for establishing loss-protection levels because the favorable loss experience of recent years has been aided by the appreciation in the loans' underlying property values.

According to studies and industry experts, about 15 percent of all fully amortizing loans originated during the late 1920s and early 1930s are estimated to have entered foreclosure. The loss severity on the loans foreclosed is more difficult to determine. Single-family property values, however, are thought to have declined between 25 and 30 percent during this period, which would mean even larger price declines for foreclosed properties. Based on these estimates, S&P developed the loss-protection levels needed for prime loan pools. Table 2

Table 2 • Minimum Loss Protection Levels for Prime Pools

Rating Category	Loss Coverage*	Foreclosure Frequency	Loss Severity
AAA	7%	15%	47%
AA	4	10	40
A	2.8	8	35

Note: All percentages are based on the initial aggregate pool balance. *Loss coverage is the product of the foreclosure frequency and loss severity. Lower loss coverage levels are used for AA and A ratings because less severe economic conditions are assumed.

shows the levels that are used for the three highest rating categories and their respective foreclosure-frequency and loss-severity assumptions.

At the AAA rating category, for example, the minimum level of loss protection needed is 7 percent of the initial aggregate mortgage balance. This level is derived from assuming the 1930s foreclosure frequency of 15 percent and a loss severity of 47 percent. The loss severity of 47 percent reflects a 37% average decline in the market value of the foreclosed properties and foreclosure expenses equal to 25 percent of their initial mortgage balances (see Table 3 for an example of this loss-severity calculation). It should be noted that S&P's AAA loss assumptions for a prime pool implicitly assume a depressionary period less severe than the 1930s experience. The foreclosure frequencies and property-value declines estimated to have occurred during the 1930s were based on the national experience. Substantial regional variations, however, did occur. Thus, the AAA loss levels for prime pools, which typically have a relatively small number of loans and a regional concentration, do not assume a recurrence of a 1930s style depression. Nonetheless, these loss levels are extremely conservative and should be sufficient to cover losses during periods of severe economic stress, more severe than any period experienced during the post-World War II era.

Many pass-throughs have loans with characteristics that would prevent the pool from meeting the prime definition. In such cases, higher loss levels are assumed. Table 4, for example shows how variations in two of these prime characteristics (the loan-to-value ratio and the type of secured property) affect the foreclosure-frequency and loss-severity assumptions and thus the needed level of loss coverage for a AA rating, the rating most frequently assigned to pass-through certificates.

Once the amount of credit protection is determined, an analysis of the type of protection provided is necessary. Since mortgage insurance policies pay

---

Table 3 • Example of Loss-Severity Calculation for Prime Loans (AAA rating assumptions)

Purchase price of home	$100,000	
Loan balance (80% of purchase price)		$80,000
Market-value decline (37% of purchase price)*	(37,000)	
Market value at foreclosure sale	(63,000)	$63,000
Market loss		$17,000
Foreclosure costs (25% of loan balance)†		+20,000
Total		$37,000

Total loss divided by loan balance = severity of loss
$37,000/$80,000 = 47%

*Derived from estimated decline in properly values during the 1930s (25%–30%) adjusted to reflect fire sale price at foreclosure
†Foreclosure costs include accrued interest (12%), brokerage fees (5%), legal fees (3%), taxes (3%), and other miscellaneous items including property maintenance expenses (2%). Mortgage loan is assumed to have an interest rate of 12%, and foreclosure period is expected to last 12 months.

Table 4 • Effect of Loan-to-Value Ratio on Loss Coverage

LTV	Foreclosure Frequency	Loss Severity	AA Coverage
80	10%	40%	4.0%
90*	15	29	4.5
95*	30	27	8.1
Property Type	**Foreclosure Frequency**	**Loss Severity**	**AA Coverage**
Single-family, detached	10%	40%	4%
Low-rise condominium (4 stories or less) attached, two-family	12	42	5
High-rise condominium (more than 4 stories) three-four-family	20	45	9

*Insured with primary mortgage insurance down to 75% LTV.

claims only if the property is conveyed to the insurer in its original condition (less normal wear and tear), protection against bankruptcy and hazard losses is necessary. Bankruptcy filings can prevent foreclosures on nonprimary residences and thus the insurer may not have title and not pay a claim. Therefore, S&P requires bankruptcy coverage of 1 percent of the pool.

Since the insurer may not pay a claim if the property is not in its original condition, protection against hazard losses is needed. All loans, therefore, are required to have standard homeowner policies (or a servicer blanket policy).

Moreover, all loans with secured properties located in designated flood areas should have federal flood insurance. In addition, a special hazard policy should be provided to insure against losses, such as those caused by earthquakes or mudslides, that are not covered by the standard homeowner policies. Generally speaking, the amount of special hazard coverage equals the greater of 1 percent of the initial aggregate principal balance of the loans or the sum of the two largest loans in the pool.

Financial Strength of Entity Providing Loss Protection

The next consideration in the rating evaluation is the financial strength of the entity providing the credit-loss protection. The reason for this is obvious. Unless absolutely no losses are expected to be incurred, this entity must be called upon to cover losses. In most rated pass-throughs the loss coverage is provided by mortgage-insurance policies. Two different types of policies are used: (1) the primary policy which insures each loan with a high loan-to-value ratio (in excess of 80 percent) for the top 20 or 25 percent of its balance and (2) the pool policy which insures losses realized on all loans up to a specified percentage of the initial pool balance.

To determine the claims-paying ability of the mortgage insurance company (MIC), S&P performs a thorough evaluation of its operations. In this evaluation, S&P looks for the following factors:

1. A suitable period of time in business to produce a meaningful track record.
2. A good geographic spread of business.
3. A prudent investment policy.
4. A strong capital position.
5. A favorable underwriting experience.
6. A capable management team.

S&P has rated the claims-paying ability of thirteen MICs: all of the ratings were either AA or AAA. In some cases, the presence of a third-party surety bond or reinsurance policy enabled S&P to look to another, stronger entity.

The analysis of MICs takes into account their ability to pay claims under economic conditions that are consistent with those assumed in the derivation of pool loss levels. Under the worst-case scenario, the MICs' loss experience, however, is expected to be much less than that for pools because of the larger number of loans and better geographic dispersion in their insured book of business. With the advent of uncapped, adjustable-rate loans with negative amortization potential, however, a new worst-case loss scenario could evolve, one with sharply rising interest rates combined with declining housing values (caused by the small number of homebuyers that could qualify for financing). This scenario could conceivably generate greater losses for MICs than those assumed under depression conditions. Needless to say, if these loans become the predominant instrument insured by MICs, without stronger capital positions or increased premiums to offset the higher risks, the evaluations of MICs' claims paying abilities may have to be lowered.

A source other than an insurance policy can be used to provide credit-loss protection. One such source is a bank letter of credit (LOC). The LOC approach has been used by banks issuing pass-throughs who want to avoid the cost of insurance and to substitute their own credit rating for the typical AA mortgage insurer's evaluation. S&P evaluates the LOC in the same manner as it does mortgage insurance policies. The LOC should have no exclusions, be irrevocable for a period of time coincident with the certificate life, and be written by a bank whose unsecured credit rating is not less than the pass-through rating.

Servicer's Cash Advance Capability

In assessing the servicer, S&P's primary focus is on its ability to make cash advances. Loan-collection procedures and foreclosure policies are also evaluated. In addition, the treatment of the certificate account and the back-up servicing responsibilities are other important servicer-related considerations.

The cash advance capability is important because the timeliness of payment to the certificateholder can be affected. A delinquent mortgage can cause a payment shortfall until either the delinquency is cured by the mortgagor or foreclosure is completed and a claim is paid under the insurance policy. While the insurance claim settlement will include the payment of interest accrued during the default period, this payment is not timely (accept in the case where the policy has an advance-claims payment provision where the insurer will make advances to cover delinquent payments until the mortgagor cures the delinquency or the servicer obtains title to the property). S&P therefore looks to the servicer to advance delinquent mortgage payments, when such advances will be recoverable from future payments made by the delinquent mortgagors or from insurance claim settlements.

To determine whether a servicer can be counted on to make cash advances, S&P must rate its creditworthiness. This rating evaluation calls for a comprehensive analysis of the servicer's operations and financial condition. In performing this analysis, S&P follows the same approach that would be used if the servicer's debt obligations were being rated. Generally speaking, only major institutions would have sufficient credit strength to be relied upon to make cash advances.

A mechanism such as a servicer performance bond or an advance-claims payment provision under the insurance policy, however, can be substituted for the servicer's cash advance function. This cash advance mechanism must be of sufficient size to cover advances on delinquent loans that will eventually foreclose as well as loans only temporarily delinquent. With this mechanism, the creditworthiness of the servicer can be ignored. All entities with demonstrated servicing expertise, including both regulated and nonregulated entities, could thus qualify.

Another servicer-related consideration is the certificate account in which homeowners' payments are deposited pending monthly distribution to certificateholders. These funds are expected to be protected against loss in the event of bankruptcy of the depository institution. To protect against loss, the certificate account can be maintained at a highly rated bank or can be held in a trust department with all monies invested in assets meeting specified standards.

When a pass-through security is rated the same as or lower than the issuer/servicer, S&P takes comfort in the fact that the servicer cannot resign from that position, thus eliminating concern about the quality of a replacement. If S&P is to rate a pass-through issue higher than the servicer, however, the acknowledgement of the possibility that the servicer may cease operations while certificates are outstanding is implied. Therefore, to make sure the loans are always being serviced, the trustee for the issue is expected to be required not only to replace a poor servicer but also to take over servicing if no one else can be found, and to do so at the originally stipulated servicing fee.

New Mortgage Instruments

To date, mortgage pools have consisted primarily of fixed-rate, fully amortizing, first-lien mortgage loans. Given conditions in the mortgage market and the desire of investors for shorter maturities and more interest-sensitive loans, future pass-through pools will undoubtedly reflect nontraditional mortgage instruments to a greater extent. S&P has reviewed several of these mortgage instruments and has come to general conclusions regarding their relative risk.

Second Mortgages.   The recent loss experience on second mortgages, particularly those in California, has been very poor. The mortgage-insurance companies that have insured these loans have realized substantial losses. Two reasons appear to explain this bad experience: (1) sloppy underwriting standards, particularly those used by loan brokers; and (2) overvalued appraisals. The absence of a sales price makes it more difficult to determine the market value of the property.

An analysis of the mortgage-insurance companies' loss data on second mortgages shows that purchase-money mortgages have much less default risk foreclosure frequency) than do home-improvement and equity loans. This seems to be explained partly by the fact that with purchase-money mortgages the purpose of the loan is known. It is less likely that such a loan will cause the borrower financial difficulties (compared to an equity loan which is used to start a new business or fund an expensive vacation). In addition, a sale price is available to assess the accuracy or the property appraisal. The foreclosure frequency for purchase-money mortgages, in fact, is very similar to that experienced in first mortgages. On the other hand, a very high loss severity is incurred upon foreclosure for both purchase-money and home-improvement and equity loans because of the second-lien position.

Table 6 • Minimum Loss-Protection Levels for Prime Second-Mortgage Loan Pools (in percent)

	Loss Coverage	Foreclosure Frequency	Loss Severity
AAA rating category			
Purchase Money loans	15%	15%	100%
Home Improvement/Equity Loans	22.5	22.5	100
AA rating category			
Purchase Money	10%	10%	100%
Home Improvement/Equity Loans	15	15	100
A rating category			
Purchase Money	8%	8%	100%
Home Improvement/Equity Loans	12	12	100

Notes:
(1) All loans have those prime characteristics defined for first mortgages except for the difference in lien status (note: combined loan-to-value ratio doesn't exceed 80%).
(2) Income tests and property appraisals must be in accordance with FNMA/FHLMC standards for *first* mortgage loans.
(3) Each loan must have a minimum balance of $10,000 (small second mortgage loans have been shown to have significantly higher default risk)
(4) No primary insurance policies are assumed to be present (if available, this coverage results in lower severity assumptions)

In quantifying the needed level of loss protection for second mortgages, S&P assumes higher foreclosure frequencies for home-improvement and equity loans than for first mortgages. It also assumes a 100 percent loss severity for all second mortgages, in contrast to the 35–50 percent loss severity typically used for first-mortgage loans. Table 6 describes the loss-protection levels needed for pool of prime second-mortgage loans.

Term Loans. These loans have experienced a revival in popularity recently owing to the attractiveness of their shorter maturities to lenders and investors. Term loans have the same credit characteristics as fully amortizing loans, other than the obvious risk of the homeowner being unable to refinance. If all the loans in the pool come due over a short interval, a firm take-out commitment is expected to be in place covering the full aggregate loan balance of the pool. Furthermore, the take-out commitment must be unconditional, or potential losses due to any preconditions for funding must be covered by another source. If the loan maturity dates are spaced over several years, commitment coverage of less than 100 percent may be acceptable, with the precise amount dependent on the maturity distribution of the loans. The financial strength of the entity providing the take-out commitment will be assessed in accordance with S&P's weak-link rating approach, with the pass-through rating being no higher than this assessment.

Shared Appreciation Mortgages (SAMs). Because S&P rates the probability of receiving only scheduled principal payments and interest at the pass-through rate, there is no major analytical problem in rating SAMs where it is clear that the appreciation is shared only to the extent realized. It should be emphasized, however, that the rating evaluation will assess the legal ability of the mortgagee to collect his share of the appreciated value. Consequently, the SAM documents must provide a clear and equitable method for quantifying and allocating the realized appreciation.

Pledged Account Mortgages (PAMs)/Buy-Down Mortgages. These mortgages call for the creation of a pledged account which is used to subsidize the mortgagor's payments during the early years of the loan's life. The subsidized amount gradually declines over time resulting in the need for higher mortgagor payments. In quantifying the differential risk associated with the PAM structure, primary emphasis is placed on the number of years in which the mortgage payments are subsidized and on what the maximum annual payment increase will be. Obviously, the longer the subsidized period and the larger the payment increase, the more likely the mortgagor will be to experience difficulties when the subsidy expires.

Graduated Equity Mortgages (GEMs). These loans are similar to PAMs in that future payment increases are determined at the time the loans are originated. The major differences, however, are that the annual payment increases occur over the life of the loan and that all payment increases are applied toward reduction of principal. Thus, the GEM is repaid faster and its loan-to-value ratio improves correspondingly. The faster build-up in the equity position gives the mortgagor greater incentive to meet payments. Nonetheless, the rising payment schedule makes the GEM somewhat riskier than the traditional level-payment mortgage.

Graduated-Payment Mortgages (GPMs).   Negative amortization is introduced along with payment increases in GPMs. The negative amortization that occurs during the graduated-payment period causes the loan-to-value ratio to increase, typically reaching a maximum of about 120 percent at the end of the fifth year. In quantifying loss-protection levels for GPMs, S&P makes the conservative assumption that if the loan defaults, the foreclosure will occur at the time the loan-to-value ratio is at its peak, resulting in a high severity of loss. Moreover, a sharp increase in the foreclosure frequency assumption (about five times that used for a prime pool) is necessary to reflect the additional risk associated with the 12 percent loan-to-value ratio. Special primary-mortgage insurance policies, however, have been developed which cover the full amount of negative amortization; the presence of these primary policies can substantially reduce the increase in needed pool insurance coverage.

Adjustable-Rate Mortgage (ARMs).   S&P has developed preliminary criteria for rating pools with adjustable rate mortgages. These criteria will be refined when ARM programs become more standardized and empirical data can be collected on their performance. In developing the criteria the factors considered most important were annual and lifetime interest rate or payment caps and the presence of negative amortization. Other factors include the income tests used in underwriting a loan, and the presence of initial discounts or "teaser rates." Standard & Poor's also looks for full disclosure to the mortgagor regarding the terms of the ARM.

Uncapped ARMs are viewed as having substantially more credit risk because all interest-rate risk is shifted from the lender to the mortgagor. Historically, there has been a fairly strong correlation among changes in inflation, interest rates, personal income, and housing values. Nevertheless, these economic variables do not always move together over short periods of time. Housing values and borrowers' incomes, for example, could remain constant while mortgage interest rates rise sharply. In assessing the needed protection levels for these loans, the frequency of potential rate changes, the volatility of the index on which the mortgage rate is based, and the potential for negative amortization are considered.

S&P does not believe that these loans are suitable for inclusion in pass-through pools unless an overwhelming amount of loss coverage is provided.

The problem with these loans is that once they are sold through a pass-through security, the servicer does not have the flexibility to renegotiate payments if interest rates rise sharply. The failure of the mortgagor to meet the higher payments requires the servicer to foreclose. If these loans are not securitized, temporary problems caused by rising interest rates may be averted by forebearance policies.

In addition, quantifying the incremental credit risk inherent in these loans is extremely difficult because there is virtually no empirical data currently available to indicate how the loans will perform during an adverse interest-rate scenario. Consequently, S&P is taking a very conservative approach in quantifying the level of loss protection needed for these loans until a sufficient record exists.

This list is by no means exhaustive. Yet-to-be-devised variations of single-family mortgage loans, as well as commercial and multifamily loans, may be included in pass-through pools in the future. S&P, in fact, is already exploring the possibility of rating commercial and multifamily loan pools.

Mortgage-Backed Bonds

The issuer of an MBB owns the collateral and is entitled to retain all cash flow generated by the collateral (barring exceptionally large prepayments) so long as no default on the bonds occurs. If a bond default does occur due to a missed interest or principal payment or the failure to maintain the collateral at a certain level, the trustee for the bondholders sells the collateral and uses the proceeds to redeem all outstanding bonds. In order for a bondholder to suffer a loss, the market value of the collateral has to decline below the outstanding bond balance at the same time the issuer defaults.

Both the creditworthiness of the issuer and the amount of the collateral affect the likelihood of the bondholder being repaid in full. Ratings, therefore, address the probability of two events—an issuer default and a collateral shortfall—occurring at the same time. It should be emphasized, however, that the ratings reflect only the probability of repayment of full principal and interest. They do not take into account the likelihood of bonds being repaid prior to their maturity from the liquidation of the collateral.

A major concern, of course, is that no legal or regulatory impediment prevents the timely liquidation of the collateral if the issuer defaults. If a mortgage-backed bond issuer were subject to the bankruptcy laws, for example, its insolvency would result in judicial action that could affect the trustee's ability to liquidate the collateral. Most issuers of rated MBBs, however, have been thrifts and banks, which are not subject to the bankruptcy laws. In the event of their insolvency, either the FSLIC or the FDIC would be the appointed receiver. Based on a review of banking regulations, and discussions with the regulators, S&P is convinced that the FSLIC and the FDIC could not, nor would be willing to, take any action to jeopardize bondholders' interests. This assumes that the bondholders have a perfected security interest in the collateral and that the terms of the transaction are in accordance with state law.

In rating MBBs, three factors play an important role in the analysis:

1. The quality of the collateral.
2. The quantity of the collateral.
3. The creditworthiness of the issuer.

Quality of the Collateral

In the event of a MBB default, the collateral must be quickly sold to repay the bondholders. Hence, the marketability of the collateral is of critical importance. Only those assets that have a well-developed secondary market are eligible for inclusion in collateral pools. The collateral for rated MBBs typically consists of prime conventional mortgage loans. A few issues, however, have pools composed exclusively of GNMAs or FHA/VA mortgages.

To ensure that the collateral be highly marketable, the conventional mortgages pledged must be of prime quality. The characteristics associated with a prime collateral pool are the same as those discussed for pass-through pools (see Table 1). Not all of the mortgages in the pool, however, must necessarily possess every one of these characteristics in order to be considered highly marketable. Most rated issuers have allowed a limited basket of mortgages with more liberal characteristics. This basket has permitted the following three types of loans:

1. Loans with balances ranging from the current FHMLC limit to a specified dollar amount over this limit (the maximum dollar size permitted varies among issuers depending upon the average value of single-family homes in the issuers' market area).
2. Loans with original loan-to-value above 80 percent to 90 percent (these loans must have primary-mortgage insurance).
3. Loans secured by low-rise condominiums (*low-rise* is defined as four stories or less).

The basket has not exceeded 35 percent of the collateral pool and has not contained any loans having more than one of these three special characteristics. In addition, no more than 25 percent of the collateral pool can be high balance or high LTV loans and condominiums are limited to 10 percent of the pool.

Quantity of Collateral

The bond indenture requires the collateral to be valued on a regular basis, usually quarterly. The valuation method typically calls for the market value of the conventional mortgages to equal the present value of the expected cash flow (assuming an average life of 12 years) discounted at a rate equal to the most recent rate for mandatory commitments posted by FHLMC or FNMA. The issuer must then maintain the collateral's market value at a specified percentage (the maintenance level) of the outstanding bond balance. Failure to meet this maintenance level for any reason, except for regulatory restrictions, is an event of default.

In assessing the adequacy of the maintenance level for a conventional-mortgage collateral pool, three types of risk are assessed: (1) credit risk, (2) prepayment risk, and (3) interest-rate risk. The first two risks are considered to be rather modest, since the collateral pool is assumed to be most vulnerable during a period of sharply rising interest rates. In this environment, S&P believes losses due to credit risk would be minor. Since no value is given to delinquent mortgages in the collateral pool on valuation dates, the maximum time exposure to credit risk is only about five months: three months from the last valuation date plus the amount of time needed by the trustee to liquidate the collateral. Moreover, even if a large percentage of mortgages were to become seriously delinquent between valuation dates, the foreclosure recovery value would probably exceed the assumed market value of the mortgages. For example, a 9 percent mortgage discounted at a 20 percent rate would have a market value equal to only one-half of its par amount.

A prepayment risk exists if mortgage prepayments can be released between valuation dates to the issuer. This obviously would reduce the amount of collateral securing the bonds. This risk again is minor when S&P's worst-case scenario of rising interest rates is assumed, since prepayment rates are likely to be very low in this environment. Recent bond issues, in fact, eliminate this risk entirely by prohibiting prepayment proceeds to be released if the collateral maintenance level is not being met.

The decline in the market value of the collateral pool caused by rising interest rates is by far the greatest risk. The degree of interest-rate risk is influenced by a number of factors:

1. Frequency of valuing the collateral: this obviously affects the time exposure to interest-rate risk.

2. Length of the cure period: this is the time which the issuer has to value the collateral and replenish any shortfall, which again affects the time exposure to rate risk.

3. Type of collateral: the degree of price risk varies with the general characteristics of the collateral. For example, GNMA securities have less price risk than conventional mortgages because they are more liquid investments.

4. Creditworthiness of the issuer: the weaker the issuer, the greater the need to rely on the collateral. In assessing the issuer's creditworthiness, S&P generally makes only two distinctions, is the issuer investment grade or subinvestment grade.

Table 7 presents the collateral maintenance levels for conventional mortgages, FHLMC/FNMA certificates, and GNMA securities that S&P thinks are

Table 7 • Minimum Collateral Maintenance Levels Needed

	Frequency of Collateral Valuations		
	Quarterly	Bimonthly	Monthly
AAA rating category			
Investment Grade Obligor			
Prime Conventional Mortgages	170%	165%	160%
GNMA Securities	150	145	140
FHLMC/FNMA Certificates	160	155	150
Noninvestment Grade Obligor			
Prime Conventional Mortgages	180	175	170
GNMA Securities	160	155	150
FHMLC/FNMA Certificates	170	165	160
AA rating category			
Investment Grade Obligor			
Prime Conventional Mortgages	160	155	150
GNMA Securities	140	138	135
FHLMC/FNMA Certificates	150	148	145
Noninvestment Grade Obligor			
Conventional Mortgages	170	165	160
GNMA Securities	150	145	140
FHLMC/FNMA Certificates	160	155	150
A rating category			
Investment Grade Obligor			
Prime Conventional Mortgages	150	150	145
GNMA Securities	138	133	130
FHLMC/FNMA Certificates	145	143	140
Noninvestment Grade Obligor			
Prime Conventional Mortgages	160	155	150
GNMA Securities	140	138	135
FHLMC/FNMA Certificates	150	148	145

Notes:
(1) Collateral maintenance levels are expressed as a percentage of the outstanding bond balance.
(2) Cure period in all cases is 30 days.
(3) No collateral prepayments can be released between valuation dates unless the maintenance
     level continues to be met.

appropriate for its three highest rating categories based on an evaluation of historical market value declines. The effect on the collateral levels due to the frequency of collateral valuations and the financial conditions of the issuer is also illustrated.

Creditworthiness of the Issuer

The vast majority of MBBs have been issued by savings and loan associations. In evaluating these associations, S&P assesses their historical performance and prospects as well as the overall industry's financial condition and outlook. In addition to the industry risk analysis, the rating evaluation focuses on seven key areas: market position and area, profitability, asset and liability management, liquidity, asset quality, capital adequacy, and management.

A detailed discussion of S&P's approach to evaluating S&Ls is beyond the scope of this chapter. It should be noted, however, that S&P scores the S&L industry well below average relative to the overall rating universe. This low score reflects the industry's major asset/liability mismatch. This mismatch was caused by the past practice of borrowing short to lend long. This in turn caused massive operating losses and rapidly deteriorating capital positions. Very few S&Ls would qualify for an investment grade rating on an unsecured basis. In fact, most S&L's unsecured rating evaluations would fall in the B category.

Review Process

Both the increasing volatility of interest rates and the changing financial condition of the issuer can have a negative effect on the credit quality of MBBs and hence, the rating. Market preferences also change. To maintain maximum protection to bondholders and the highest quality ratings, S&P monitors interest rate volatility and secondary market preferences. In addition, each issue is reviewed on a quarterly basis, and the financial condition of investment grade issues is monitored continually. This review process has not affected those issues sold in the last few years, however, it has affected those issues sold prior to 1981.

As a result of the rapid rise in interest rates in early 1980, two indenture changes were made to issues outstanding at that time. First, the frequency of collateral pricing was increased. Originally, the collateral was valued on a semi-annual basis; however, in the summer of 1980, the indentures of publicly rated bonds were amended to reflect more frequent pricing (typically quarterly). Second, the maximum time permitted to price and replenish the collateral pool was changed from 60 to 30 days, in order to reduce the pool's time exposure to rising interest rates.

In regard to the financial condition of the issuers, it's clear that the creditworthiness of almost all the issuers has weakened since their bonds were first sold. In fact, the financial condition of most issuers declined to the point where they found it necessary to increase their bonds' collateral maintenance level in order to retain S&P's AAA rating.

Therefore, in spite of increasingly volatile interest rates and the weakening financial condition of the issuers, MBB issuers have had the ability to maintain ratings by taking action to improve the credit strength of the collateral. S&P will continue to review closely the volatility of interest rates to ensure that collateral maintenance levels are sufficient to cover interest-rate risk. In addition, S&P will be monitoring the secondary market's perception of what constitutes a prime mortgage pool to be sure that MBB collateral can be quickly liquidated to repay bondholders in the event of an issuer default.

Mortgage Pay-Through Bonds

Pay-throughs are designed so that the mortgage collateral will generate a cash flow sufficient to provide for the full and timely repayment of the bonds. The mortgage collateral pool can be structured to accommodate any desired bond repayment schedule, provided the collateral cash flow is adequate to meet scheduled bond payments. The bond's cash flow, for example, can be dedicated to one class of bondholders at a time, thereby increasing call protection to bondholders. This type of bond is known as a Collateralized Mortgage Obligation (CMO), the most popular form of pay-through bonds. Other bonds can take on the characteristics of the underlying mortgages and be fully amortizing with level payments of principal and interest. The central focus of the analysis, in all cases, is to determine the likelihood of the expected collateral cash flow being adequate to meet debt service on the bonds.

In rating mortgage pay-through bonds, four key factors are considered in the evaluation:

1. The credit risk inherent in the mortgage collateral.
2. The reinvestment risk on mortgage prepayments and foreclosure recoveries.
3. Collateral cash flow coverage of scheduled bond payments.
4. The issuer and the effect of its insolvency on the bonds.

Credit Risk

In assessing the credit risk inherent in the mortgage collateral, the same approach used in rating mortgage pass-through pools is applied. That is, the degree of credit risk assumed is basically a function of the characteristics of the collateral and the rating desired. The mortgage characteristics are reviewed to determine the worst-case foreclosure frequency and loss severity for the specified rating category. The needed level of credit protection is then equal to the product of the assumed foreclosure frequency and loss severity.

The requisite level of credit protection can be provided by mortgage-insurance policies of the same type used for mortgage pass-through certificates. As an alternative to insurance policies, however, the mortgage collateral itself can be used to cover credit losses. In fact, substantial credit coverage in the form of overcollateralization may already exist because of the bond's structure. The coupons on the mortgage collateral, for example, could be much lower than the bond rate, thereby requiring an aggregate mortgage balance much larger than the amount of bonds sold. This in order to generate a cash flow sufficient to meet the debt service on the bonds. To illustrate this concept, a hypothetical pay-through issue is provided in Table 8.

In this simplified example, the $100 million collateral pool provides a

Table 8 • Hypothetical Pay-Through Example

Mortgage Collateral Pool	$100 million of 7%, 30–year fully amortizing mortgages with monthly level payments.
Pay-through Bonds	$50 million of 15 ¾%, 30–year fully amortizing bonds with monthly level payments.
Monthly Scheduled Mortgage Cash Flow	$665,000
Monthly Scheduled Bond Payments	$662,000
Required Mortgage Over-collateralization	$ 50 million*
Required Over-collateralization Percentage	50%†

*Equals the difference between the initial aggregate collateral balance and the initial bond balance.
†Equals the required mortgage over-collateralization divided by the initial aggregate mortgage collateral balance.

monthly scheduled cash flow of $665,000, which is just sufficient to fund the scheduled monthly bond payments. To generate adequate cash flow to service the bonds, $50 million of required over-collateralization is needed. Expressed differently, the amount of the bonds that can be supported by this collateral pool is equal to the present value of the collateral's cash flow discounted at the bond rate.

The over-collateralization required to service the bonds is available to mitigate the effect of credit losses. The required over-collateralization percentage of 50 percent ($50 million over-collateralization divided by $100 million of mortgages) indicates that the mortgages' discounted value is worth 50 percent less than its face amount. All the mortgages therefore could lose half of their value upon foreclosure and the recovery proceeds would be sufficient to repay the principal amount of the bonds. The assumed loss-severity rate (the total expected loss upon foreclosure divided by the mortgage balance) can thus be reduced by the required over-collateralization percentage when quantifying the needed level of loss protection.

The amount of required over-collateralization available, of course, can vary depending upon the mortgage coupons, the bond rate, and the maturities of the mortgages and the bond. Also, since the mortgages in the collateral pool may have different coupons and maturities, the required over-collateralization percentage may vary for each mortgage. For example, if a 15¾ percent mortgage were present in the collateral pool described in Table 8, it would need no over-collateralization.

When relying upon required over-collateralization as a source of credit protection, S&P assumes that those mortgages having the lowest amount of required over-collateralization (those with the highest coupons and shortest remaining maturities) are the ones that will go into foreclosure. This assumption is necessary in order to be certain that the required over-collateralization will be available to absorb credit losses. It should be recognized that the required over-collateralization only becomes available if the mortgage prepays or is foreclosed. The larger amount of required over-collateralization that is available on lower coupon mortgages, for instance, cannot be counted on to cover credit losses realized on the higher coupon mortgages. Hence, when determining the expected loss-severity rate for the collateral pool, credit is only given to the lowest required over-collateralization that exists.

The required over-collateralization for most issues is either not present or insufficient in itself to cover the assumed credit losses. In which case, excess collateral can be provided; that is, a level of collateral that would generate scheduled cash flow in excess of the amount needed to meet bond payments. Table 9 presents three simple examples to clarify this concept. In Example A, the mortgages have the same interest rate and payment terms as the bonds. Since over-collateralization is not required to equate the mortgage and bond payment streams, no source exists to cover credit losses.

The only change in Example B is that there are now $95 million of bonds outstanding, thereby resulting in $5 million of *excess* over-collateralization. Since this excess over-collateralization is not needed to fund scheduled bond payments, the full dollar amount will always be available to cover the pool's aggregate credit losses. The excess over-collateralization will thus be adequate so long as total credit losses don't exceed $5 million.

Example C shows a situation where both required and excess over-collateralization are present. The mortgage coupons are now assumed to be 11½ percent, below the bond rate of 15¾ percent. Mortgage over-collateralization is therefore first required to equate the cash flows. The $71 million of bonds require a monthly cash flow of $940,000. Since the $100 million of mortgages generate a monthly cash flow of $990,000, only $95 million of mortgages are

---

Table 9 • Three Pay-Through Bond Examples

Example A
Collateral = $100 million of 15¾%, 30–year fully amortizing loans.
Bonds   = $100 million of 15¾%, 30–year fully amortizing bonds.

Required Mortgage Over-collateralization = 0

Example B
Collateral = $100 million of 15¾%, 30–year fully amortizing loans.
Bonds   = $95 million of 15¾%, 30–year fully amortizing bonds.

Required Mortgage Over-collateralization = 0.
Excess Mortgage Over-collateralization   = $5 million.

Example C
Collateral = $100 million of 11½%, 30–year fully amortizing loans.
Bonds   = $71 million of 15¾%, 30–year fully amortizing bonds.

Required Mortgage Over-collateralization* = $24 million ($95 million
                                                          less $71 million)
Excess Mortgage Over-collateralization   = $ 5 million

*Monthly cash flow off $95 million of mortgage collateral equals approximately $940,000, which could support $71 million of bonds (with monthly payments of $940,000). Required over-collateralization percentage is 25% ($24 million divided by $95 million).

needed to cover the bond payments. Hence, $5 million of excess mortgage collateral is available.

To illustrate how these two different forms of over-collateralization are treated in the rating evaluation, assume the collateral pool in Example C experiences a foreclosure frequency of 10 percent and a loss severity of 50 percent, thereby requiring a 5 percent level of loss protection. In assessing whether these assumed losses would be covered by the over-collateralization, the loss severity of 50 percent would first be reduced by 25 percent ($24 million divided by $95 million) to reflect the amount of required over-collateralization available. In other words, half of the assumed losses would be covered by the required over-collateralization, which has the same effect as a *primary* mortgage insurance policy in reducing the loss severity. The remaining $2.5 million of assumed losses (the foreclosure frequency of 10 percent times the adjusted loss severity of 25 percent times the $100 million of mortgage collateral) would then be compared to the full amount of excess over-collateralization. In this example, the $5 million of excess collateral, acting like a mortgage *pool* insurance policy, is thus sufficient to cover the remaining losses.

To summarize, the credit risk inherent in the mortgage collateral can be covered by either mortgage insurance (or other external sources such as a bank letter of credit) or by the collateral pool itself. If mortgage insurance is provided, the amount needed is similar to those levels discussed for mortgage pass-throughs. The analysis of the ability of collateral pool to cover losses can become complex because the evaluation takes into account both the required level of over-collateralization resulting from the discounting of the mortgages and the excess collateral that may be available. Generally speaking, the requisite ·amount of excess collateral would be comparable to the amount of pool insurance policies provided for pass-throughs, after adjusting for the presence of required over-collateralization.

Reinvestment Risk

The second key rating consideration is the reinvestment risk. This risk is present when mortgages prepay, because these mortgage prepayment proceeds have to be reinvested at a rate at least equal to the bond rate until they are passed through to the bondholders, which usually takes place on the next bond payment date. To illustrate this point, assume a 12 percent mortgage is being used to support a 12 percent bond with semi-annual payments. If this mortgage prepays on the day the bond is issued, the prepayment proceeds will have to be reinvested at a rate of at least 12 percent for the next six months in order to repay the bond in full with accrued interest.

In quantifying the loss potential due to the reinvestment risk on mortgage prepayments, several factors need to be considered:

1. The interest rate on the bonds.
2. The frequency of bond payments.

3. The percentage of the mortgages that will prepay.
4. The timing of the prepayments.
5. The minimum assumed-reinvestment rate.

The terms of the issue, of course, will determine the first two factors. In regard to the others, when S&P issues its highest ratings conservative assumptions are made. Specifically, S&P assumes: (1) that all of the mortgages could prepay over the life of the bonds; (2) that they could do so soon after a bond payment date, thereby having to be invested for up to the maximum period of time between bond payment dates; and (3) that the reinvestment rate could be as low as 3 percent.

The potential loss due to the reinvestment risk on prepayments is generally covered by the required level of overcollateralization. For example, in the event the mortgage has a coupon less than the bond rate, the proceeds realized upon its prepayment, plus the assumed reinvestment income, would usually exceed its discounted value. In situations where the required level of over-collateralization would be insufficient, a cash reserve is typically provided.

Cash Flow Coverage

A major concern, of course, is that the collateral pool be able to fund the bond payments on time. If the bond repayment terms are not similar to those of the pledged mortgages, the scheduled cash flow off the mortgages should be sufficient to fund the bond payments. The issue should not have to rely on mortgage prepayments to meet bond payments. Since mortgage prepayment rates are highly sensitive to interest-rate levels, S&P feels uncomfortable in having to count on prepayments being available to meet bond debt service.

The effect of mortgage defaults on the cash flow coverage is also assessed. Obviously, the risk characteristics of the mortgage collateral pool are an important factor in quantifying the needed level of cash flow coverage. Moreover, the level of mortgage coupons is considered: the higher the coupons, the larger the cash flow reduction caused by mortgage delinquencies. In addition, the frequency of bond payments is a factor. Since most mortgage delinquencies are eventually cured by the mortgagors, the issue's vulnerability to fluctuations in the mortgage delinquency rate can be reduced by lengthening the time between bond payment dates.

The cash flow coverage can be provided in two different ways. One way is through some source external to the collateral pool, such as a cash reserve, performance bond, or bank letter of credit. These sources of protection have to be as strong as the rating on the issue implies. A pay-through bond collateralized by a low-risk mortgage pool generally needs cash flow coverage in this form equal to about 1 percent of the initial mortgage pool. This reserve is maintained at the requisite amount for the life of the bonds. Therefore, if the reserve is drawn down, it has to be replenished from future excess cash flow before any funds can be released to the issuer.

The other way of providing this cash flow coverage is through excess over-collateralization. Under this structure, the collateral pool generates a scheduled cash flow above that needed to fund the bond payments. The amount of excess overcollateralization needed to ensure adequate cash flow coverage is dependent on the three previously mentioned factors, particularly the frequency of bond payments. If the bonds have monthly payments, for example, the monthly cash flow would have to cover the highest monthly mortgage delinquency rate deemed possible. On the other hand, with semi-annual bond payments, there would be six months of excess cash flow available to cover delinquencies, and much less exposure. It's therefore difficult to generalize as to what amount of excess overcollateralization is needed to provide adequate cash flow. For our highest ratings, the needed level of excess overcollateralization for a prime collateral pool could range from a low of 5 percent to a high of 25 percent depending upon the bond's payment characteristics.

Issuer Considerations

Pay-throughs are structured to obviate the need to assess the creditworthiness of the issuer. All issuers regardless of their financial strength have the ability to obtain S&P's highest rating on their pay-through issues. While S&P doesn't concern itself with the creditworthiness of the issuer, it does evaluate the issuer's mortgage underwriting and servicing capabilities. An evaluation of the issuer's underwriting procedures is given additional emphasis when the mortgage collateral is not covered by a pool insurance policy. If there has been no second underwriting of the collateral pool by a mortgage insurer, S&P has to be convinced that the collateral is of high quality and that no adverse selection has occurred in the collateral pool's formation. Otherwise, a second underwriting of the collateral by a mortgage-insurance company may be necessary.

A major concern is whether pay-through bonds will continue to work as structured in the event of the issuer's insolvency. For example, if an issuer were to become bankrupt, the courts could disrupt the collateral package and prevent the bondholders from being repaid in a timely manner. Therefore, the issuing entity should be structured to prevent adverse effects that could occur because of a bankruptcy filing. To accomplish this, the issuer can create a wholly owned, single-purpose subsidiary that holds the collateral and issues the bonds. If structured properly, the likelihood of the subsidiary becoming bankrupt should be the same as the likelihood of the collateral cash flow not being sufficient to meet bond debt service. This can be accomplished by strictly restricting the company's business to only issuing mortgage backed securities. The company must be restricted from incurring any liabilities other than highly rated debt or debt that is subordinate and where creditors have agreed not to file bankruptcy petitions.

In S&P's opinion, a single-purpose corporation isn't needed in certain cases where the issuer's insolvency would not come under the bankruptcy laws. Therefore, a thrift or bank could issue the pay-through bonds directly. The FSLIC or the FDIC would be the appointed receivers if an insolvency occurred. S&P is convinced these agencies would permit bond payments to be made in a timely manner.

One issue, however, that remains uncertain is how the regulators would treat the collateral in the event the issuer becomes insolvent and the market value of the collateral at such time exceeds the outstanding bond balance. S&P believes that the regulators may liquidate the collateral and repay the bondholders in full (and thus recapture the excess collateral value), even though the indenture gives the bondholder the right to foreclose on the collateral and keep the bonds outstanding by continuing to utilize the collateral cash flow to meet the scheduled debt service. Because of this uncertainty, S&P will not rate pay-through bonds issued by banks or thrifts unless the possibility of an earlier repayment due to the issuer's insolvency is fully disclosed to investors.

Advantages of Pay-Through Bonds

Like the mortgage-backed bond, the pay-through enables the issuer to use low-yielding mortgages to raise cash, without having to sell them and realize a loss. Moreover, even when the mortgage collateral bears market rates, home builders by issuing a pay-through can produce the same effect as an asset sale while reaping special tax benefits. This because the installment method of income recognition can be used in accounting for their housing sales. In addition, the pay-through has several distinct advantages over the standard mortgage-backed bond:

Expanded Collateral Eligibility. A substantial expansion of collateral eligibility is possible because it is the collateral's cash flow rather than its market value which is looked upon to repay the bonds. Hence the marketability of the collateral is not a consideration. Many types of mortgages, such as those secured properties that are not single-family detached can be included in pay-through pools without limitations. Inclusion of these loans does increase credit risk, but this incremental risk can be offset by higher mortgage insurance or additional collateral.

No Need for Collateral Valuation and Replenishment. The pay-through issuer does not have to go to the trouble of regularly marking the mortgage collateral to market, as required under the mortgage-backed bond. If interest rates rise and reduce the collateral's market value, the collateral pool does not have to be replenished. In fact, collateral substitutions are not necessary if mortgages go into default because the initial composition of the pool can be fixed.

Lower Collateral Coverage. Since the focus is on the cash flow generated by the collateral, the potential for future erosion in the collateral's market value due to rising interest rates can be ignored. Moreover, the fact that the collateral pool can be fixed from the date of the bond's issuance with no future maintenance requirements obviates the need to assess the creditworthiness of the issuer. Collateral coverage may thus be significantly lower, especially if the bond payment terms are similar to those of the mortgages.

Summary

S&P's approach to rating mortgage securities has been an evolving one. Since the first mortgage security was rated in 1975, rating criteria have been developed to assess many different types of mortgage-related financings. A substantial increase in the volume of mortgage securities is expected in the future. Securities involving single-family mortgages are likely to be used to a much greater extent as lending institutions, particularly the thrifts, may have difficulty in funding the strong demand for mortgage credit. Moreover, current legislative initiatives such as TIMs, if successful, should dramatically expand the presence of the private sector in the mortgage-securities market.

Given the strong growth potential for mortgage securities issued out of the private sector, the rating agencies in the future should play a more important role in the mortgage-securities market. As new issuers and investors enter this market, there will be a greater need for an independent and reliable system to evaluate credit quality. By ensuring that investors are made aware of the various degrees of risk involved in the different mortgage securities, the rating agencies provide a valuable service and help increase market efficiency.

In an effort to be more responsive in meeting the needs of investors and homebuyers, continued innovations in the forms of mortgage financing will likely occur, necessitating further expansion of S&P's rating criteria. It is also anticipated that securities involving mortgages on commercial and multifamily properties will represent an important new area of mortgage financing. The S&P rating approach to mortgage securities should therefore continue to evolve as S&P attempts to rate the creditworthiness of all new forms of mortgage-related financings.

APPENDIX: DEBT RATING DEFINITIONS

A Standard & Poor's debt rating is a current assessment of the creditworthiness of an obligor with respect to a specific obligation. This assessment may take into consideration obligors such as guarantors, insurers, or lessees.

The debt rating is not a recommendation to purchase, sell, or hold a security, inasmuch as it does not comment as to market price or suitability for a particular investor.

The ratings are based on current information furnished by the issuer or obtained by S&P from other sources it considers reliable. S&P does not perform an audit in connection with any rating and may, on occasion, rely on unaudited financial information. The ratings may be changed, suspended, or withdrawn as a result of changes in such information or its unavailability, or in other circumstances.

The ratings are based, in varying degrees, on the following considerations:

1. Likelihood of default: capacity and willingness of the obligor for the timely payment of interest and repayment of principal in accordance with the terms of the obligation.
2. Nature of and provisions of the obligation.
3. Protection afforded by, and relative position of, the obligation in the event of bankruptcy, reorganization, or other arrangement under the laws of bankruptcy and other laws affecting creditor's rights.

The ratings are as follows:

AAA Debt rated AAA has the highest rating assigned by Standard & Poor's. Capacity to pay interest and repay principal is extremely strong.

AA Debt rated AA has a very strong capacity to pay interest and repay principal and differs from the highest rated issues only to a small degree.

A Debt rated A has a strong capacity to pay interest and repay principal although it is somewhat more susceptible to the adverse effects of changes in circumstances and economic conditions than debt in higher rated categories.

BBB Debt rated BBB is regarded as having an adequate capacity to pay interest and repay principal. Whereas it normally exhibits adequate protection parameters, adverse economic conditions or changing circumstances are more likely to lead to a weakened capacity to pay interest and repay principal for debt in this category than in higher rated categories.

BB Debt rated BB, B, CCC, or CC is regarded, on balance, as predominantly B speculative with respect to capacity to pay interest and repay principal in accordance with the terms of the obligation. BB

CCC indicates the lowest degree of speculation, and CC the highest degree of speculation. While such debt is likely to have some quality and protective characteristics, these are outweighed by large uncer-

CC tainties or major risk exposures to adverse conditions.

C This rating is reserved for income bonds on which no interest is being paid.

D Debt rated D is in default, and payment of interest and/or repayment of principal is in arrears.

Plus (+) or Minus (−): The ratings from AA to B may be modified by the addition of a plus or minus sign to show relative standing within the major rating categories.

NR   Indicates that no rating has been requested, that there is insufficient information on which to base a rating, or that S&P does not rate that particular type of obligation as a matter of policy.

Debt obligations of issuers outside the United States and its territories are rated on the same basis as domestic corporate and municipal issues. The ratings measure the creditworthiness of the obligor but do not take into account currency exchange and related uncertainties.

Bond Investment Quality Standards: Under present commercial bank regulations issued by the Comptroller of the Currency, bonds rated in the top four categories (AAA, AA, A, and BBB, commonly known as *investment-grade ratings*) are generally regarded as eligible for bank investment. In addition, the laws of various states governing legal investments impose certain rating or other standards for obligations eligible for investment by savings banks, trust companies, insurance companies, and fiduciaries generally.

—— Chapter 7 ——————————————

Interest-Rate Futures

David R. Ganis
President
Northern Futures Corporation

James S. Dunne
Vice President
Salomon Brothers Inc.

History of Futures Trading

The principles that helped create the interest-rate futures markets in 1975 find their roots in ancient Greece and Rome. There already existed there a fixed time and place for trading commodities, a marketplace, and a practice of contracting for future delivery. The Roman Empire, at its height, had as many as 19 sales markets which served as distribution centers for the commodities collected from around the world.

The principle of the central marketplace survived the dark ages and developed in the late 1100s into a series of trade fairs. Merchants traveled from fair to fair selling their commodities. Most trading at the fairs was done in the spot (cash) market. By the 13th century, however, the practice of contracting for future delivery was reestablished, with standards of quality established by samples.

As the modern city grew, these trade fairs declined in importance. What took their place were market centers in the city, which in Europe became known as bourse, boerse, and beurs, and in Spain, as bolsa.

The growth of these specialized trading markets was not limited to the West. In the East, spot- or cash-market trading in rice began in 1700, and forward trading on the Osaka Rice Exchange began in 1730.

In the early 1800s it was common for farmers to bring their produce to market at a regional exchange at a given time each year. Often the supply of meats and grains exceeded existing demand, and the prices bid for the commodities would be very low. Sometimes the produce was dumped in the streets for lack of buyers.

Major Regulated Exchanges

Within four to six months, however, demand would be far in excess of supply and prices for produce would experience a large increase. The price fluctuations were not acceptable either to farmers or to merchants. Both parties therefore began making contracts for forward delivery. The practice was used in Chicago. In 1848, a group founded the Chicago Board of Trade. In the late 1800s, the rules of futures trading were formalized; contracts were standardized; and rules of conduct, clearing, and settlement procedures were established. Futures contracts then became legally enforceable agreements for either the purchase or sale or a commodity, for delivery at a future date and at a presently agreed-upon price.

The Chicago Mercantile Exchange was started in 1874 as the Chicago Produce Exchange. The Kansas City Board of Trade was organized in 1856. The Mid-America Commodities Exchange was founded in 1868. In New York the Commodities Exchange, Inc. (Comex) was started in 1933.

As the interest-rate futures markets expanded, new exchanges were created. The International Monetary Market, a division of the Chicago Mercantile Exchange, was founded in 1972. Another exchange created to trade interest-rate futures contracts was the New York Futures Exchange (NYFE). It was founded in 1980. A recent addition to exchanges created to trade interest-rate futures was the London International Financial Futures Exchange (LIFFE).

Futures Markets on Fixed-Income Securities

After much research, discussion, and debate within the financial community, a futures market was started in October 1975 in Government National Mortgage Association (GNMA) Certificates. The market opened on the Chicago Board of Trade. A few months later, in January 1976, a market in 90-day U.S. Treasury Bills was opened on the International Monetary Market Division of Chicago Mercantile Exchange. The number of contracts traded in that first short year was 20,125. In 1981, the total number of interest-rate futures contracts traded exceeded 21 million.

The need for the organization of interest-rate futures trading was created by the sharp rise and fall of interest rates in 1969–1970 and 1973–1974. Interest-rate fluctuations since 1979 have made the advantages of using the interest-rate futures market even more obvious and have encouraged the tremendous growth in trading volume. Even as interest rates climbed to their highest levels in the century, and as they suffered short periods of extreme fluctuation, interest-rate futures were not used as much as they could have been for commercial hedging purposes by a very large percentage of potential market participants. There were several reasons for this. There were and still are, to some extent, regulatory restrictions. Even where permitted, the use was limited because of misinformation about futures markets in general. Another primary reason was lack of knowledge about interest-rate futures—their applications, advantages, and risks.

Interest Rate Futures Contracts

A *futures contract* is a legally enforceable agreement between two parties. It is similar to many other written agreements in that it decribes the terms of the transaction and the conditions to which both buyer and seller must adhere. The terms and conditions of the futures contract are not subject to negotiation by the parties buying and selling. Instead, a standard contract, which may not be revised in any manner, is established by the exchange. That agreement, along with the trading rules of the exchange, is binding on all members.

Advantages of Use

This creates two very important benefits for users of a futures market: first, only price is determined by buyers and sellers on the exchange floor. This permits transactions to be concluded quickly without negotiating terms. Second, since all contracts for delivery in the same month are identical, commitments are easily made on the floor of the exchange. This increases liquidity and allows contracts to be offset, or closed out, prior to delivery.

An order previously executed on a futures exchange to buy (or sell) can be offset by executing the opposite order to sell (or buy) in the same contract for the same delivery month on the same exchange. The second transaction does not require the participation or even the knowledge of the party on the other side of the initial transaction. The initial buyer and seller are not linked permanently in that relationship since the clearing unit of the exchange assumes the opposite side of each trade at the end of each trading day. The clearing unit of the exchange will match a new seller to the initial buyer or a new buyer to the initial seller.

Dealer Markets and Futures Markets

A market could be defined as a fixed location where transactions are concluded under uniform rules by buyers and sellers meeting face-to-face, as in the interest-rate futures markets. Another way to define a market would be as a place where buyers and sellers are trading under any terms they agree upon by telephone or wire from locations anywhere in the world, as is the practice in dealer markets.

Historically, what we know today as interest-rate futures markets started as dealer markets and grew in scale and diversity until the conditions were such as to justify an organized futures market. The most important of these conditions is the risk resulting from price fluctuations. Futures markets come into existence because those engaged in the trade prefer not to assume the price and performance risks associated with buying and selling exclusively in a dealer market.

Dealer markets and futures markets serve two different purposes. The economic purpose of most dealer markets in fixed-income securities is to distribute new issues to investors. This entails delivery of the security against immediate payment and transfer of ownership. By contrast, the economic purpose of a futures market is to provide commercial interests with a secure method of hedging price risks that arise in the normal course of business. These risk-transfer transactions usually do not entail actual delivery, since price risk alone is at issue for a hedger. The futures position will be closed out through an offsetting purchase or sale at a later time.

Another important difference between a dealer market and a futures market is that dealer transactions are on a principal-to-principal basis, while futures are executed on an agency basis, with the exchange acting as principal to both buyer and seller. This permits open futures positions to be liquidated simply by taking an offsetting position.

Role of the Exchange.   An organized exchange regulated by the Commodity Futures Trading Commission (CFTC) is the central feature of all futures trading. Everything important or unique about futures trading can be traced back to the structure or functions of the exchange. The exchanges, including their clearing organizations, set margin-deposit levels and enforce required daily settlements among members. The exchange also establishes the standardized contracts to be traded, as well as the rules and procedures for fair and orderly trading.

Role of the Clearing Organization.   A futures exchange serves two purposes: (1) it provides trading facilities: a trading floor and a complex communications system; and (2) it provides order-execution and market-making by its members and trade-reporting, trade-clearing, market surveillance, and other support activities by its staff. Members and officers of the exchange also function as a self-regulating body, to assure fair and orderly trading.

An essential function found in every futures exchange is performed by the clearing organization: collecting margin deposits from members for newly opened positions and collecting and paying cash after marking-to-market all open positions at the end of each trading day. Marking-to-market involves relating all positions still open to closing daily prices and computing gains or losses, crediting gains to the customers' account, or calling upon other customers to make up all losses. This transforms a futures exchange from a passive, order-matching marketplace into an active role as the financial guarantor behind all open positions. To accomplish this, the clearing organization of the exchange becomes, for daily cash settlement purposes, the opposite side of every open position—the buyer to every seller, the seller to every buyer. A gain from the day's price change will be credited immediately to appropriate member accounts, whether or not cash has been collected from the adversely affected member accounts. The total resources of the clearing organization, plus the combined resources of all clearing members, are committed to protect the opposite party in the event one party to the transaction defaults.

The benefit of the clearing organization as the "credit" on either side of every trade is that all cleared trades bear the credit of the exchange. This serves to facilitate order executions and improves market liquidity because there is no need to discriminate among buyers and sellers of differing financial quality.

Trading Volume and Open Interest

The two most general measurements of liquidity and depth for any futures market are trading volume and open interest. *Trading volume* is the number of contract-unit transactions during a period of time. *Open interest* is the number of open contract units at a given point in time.

Futures trading volume is reported as one side only. A daily volume might be 12,000 contracts bought and 12,000 contracts sold. Buys and sells are not added together. (The number of contracts bought always equals the number sold since there must be a buyer for every seller.) A large volume of trading is a good indication of a liquid market. Liquidity can be gauged by the ability of market participants to execute commercial-size orders quickly at a price close to the price of the last transaction. Judgements will vary as to what is *quick* and *close*.

There are three major groups of market participants: (1) a commercial group comprised of fixed income investors, dealers, and borrowers; (2) nonmember individual speculators; and (3) member floor traders. Estimates of the speculative share of total fixed-income futures trading are frequently based on the combined activities of nonmember individuals and floor traders. Putting the two together blurs the important distinction between the two groups and tends to inflate the speculative share of the total. Unlike the nonmember individual, whose major source of income is from another activity and who speculates in futures part-time, the floor trader has a substantial investment in a membership and usually devotes full-time to the market-making function which is essential for prompt executions of all orders. Under the auction-market rules of a futures exchange, the function of the floor trader is much closer to a stock market specialist than to a nonmember speculator.

Open interest is the number of contracts recorded with the exchange at the close of business each day as transactions that have not been offset by an opposite trade or settled by delivery. Open interest, like trading volume, counts one side only; an open interest of 17,000 is 17,000 bought positions and 17,000 sold positions.

Speculation and Hedging

Participants in all futures markets fall into one of three groups, based on their motivations and the degree of risk associated with their actions. Speculators are motivated by the profit potential of anticipated price changes, and they assume significant financial risks in that pursuit. Hedgers are motivated by their desire to avoid potential losses resulting from price-level fluctuations that affect their commercial activities, and by hedging they reduce their overall risk exposure. Arbitragers are motivated by the profit potential of detecting temporary price relationship distortions while assuming very little financial risk.

Speculators commit risk capital as margin deposits with the expectation that their profits from skillful futures trading will provide an unusually high return on investment. Futures markets give speculators an opportunity to realize these rates of return through the workings of leverage. On an initial margin of $2,000 for example, a price change of 2 points (2 percent of par) in a bond or GNMA futures contract would result in a 100 percent return on investment:

Buy	Sell	
1 Sept. T-Bond on 6/1	1 Sept. T-Bond on 7/1	
@ $70,000	@ $72,000 = $2,000 profit	
2 pts. = $^{64}\!/_{32}$ × $31.25 =	Margin deposit 6/1	$2,000
$2,000	Profit on trade	$2,000
	= 100% return	

Price changes of that order are not uncommon. It should be emphasized that leverage also works the other way. A relatively small adverse price change could lead to the complete loss of the initial margin deposit:

Buy	Sell	
1 Dec. T-bond on 9/15	1 Dec. T-bond on 11/12	
@ $65,000	@ $63,000 = 2 pts. loss	
2 pts. = $^{64}\!/_{32}$ × $31.25 =	Margin deposit 9/15	$2,000
$2,000	Loss on trade	$2,000
	= 100% net loss	

It is for this reason that only high-risk capital should be committed to speculation in futures. *Risk capital* may be defined as the amount that may be lost without significantly changing the speculator's overall financial condition.

By acting in their own self-interest, speculators produce an important but unintended social benefit: they add liquidity to futures markets enabling commercial enterprises to transfer unwanted business risks. A lower level of risk in the activities of a business should reduce the risk-premium component of its costs. In this respect, the pool of risk capital supplied by futures-market speculators is analogous to the capital of insurance underwriters, who assume the risks of hurricanes, fires, and other potential losses that businesses generally attempt to avoid.

Most business organizations operating in markets subject to large or erratic price changes hedge the resulting financial risks in one form or another. They accomplish this by forward delivery contracts, by options, or by futures. In each case, the objective is to establish a known price in advance of an actual transaction. A futures position, bought or sold at a fixed price, is a hedge if it serves as a temporary substitute for an intended transaction and actual delivery at a later date:

Futures	Cash
Sell 10 Dec. GNMA on 8/15 at 75	A S&L commits to originate 10-$100,000 loans at 97 on 8/15
Buy 10 Dec. GNMA on 12/1 at 77 = 2 pt. loss per contract	The S/L closes the loans and sells them to an insurance company on 12/1 at 99 for a 2-pt. gain = $2,000.00 per loan

Futures Transaction (loss) $20,000
Cash Transaction (gain) $20,000
Net effect of the Hedge   =   0

The objective is to reduce the risk of an unfavorable price-level change during the period between the time the transaction takes place on the exchange and the actual delivery transaction. While a properly constructed hedge is effective, no hedging transaction precisely offsets gains and losses.

Institutional participation in the fixed-income futures markets has expanded consistently for a number of years. The rate of growth, however, in commercial activity has suffered some important constraints. One constraint has been the time required to gain a sufficient understanding of futures markets and establish internal procedures. Another much more important constraint has been the apparent confusion at the regulatory and senior-management levels about the difference between hedging and speculation: the risk exposure before and after taking a futures position and the expected results of price movements in the future market. A commercial organization uses futures to establish in advance a price level or price relationship for an intended transaction when potential price fluctuations create a risk of unfavorable prices at the time of the actual transaction. The magnitude of risk is less after taking a futures position. Speculators use a futures market as a means of profiting from anticipated price changes. The speculator starts with no risk; in the act of taking a futures position a risk is taken. Thus, the hedger's exchange of risk for less-risk is the exact opposite of the no-risk to risk transfer for the speculator. The hedger looks at price changes in a futures position as one side of a two-sided unit, the actual or intended cash position being the other side. The amount of gain or loss in futures does not stand by itself. It must be viewed in relation to better or worse in the actual or anticipated cash position. A speculator has no other side, and, indeed, does not want one. An expected gain from the futures position is the only reason for taking it. Any loss in futures is a real loss. The second distinction, then, is between the hedger's expectation that either a futures gain or loss will neutralize a loss or gain elsewhere, or the speculator's expectation of an absolute gain from a futures position.

After the need for a hedge is established, the hedger must determine the appropriate contract to use, the amount of the hedge, and the contract months to use. A successful hedging strategy depends to a great extent upon the hedger fully understanding the interest-rate futures markets and their relationship to the risk the user of the futures market is hedging.

Hedge Planning

There are various risks a hedger can incur in cash-market instruments where there is a similar instrument traded on a futures or options exchange; Ginnie Maes, for example. There may, however, be a difference in the price of the two instruments (cash and futures), because the futures contract is a standard contract, where the cash instrument may carry a different rate or maturity. There may also be risks in the cash market which have no direct similar instrument in the futures or options market; for example, a loan tied to a floating prime rate and CD futures. The price relationship between the risk being hedged and the contract being used as the hedge vehicle is called the *basis:*

GNMA Futures Market	GNMA Cash Market
Price for March	Price for 12%
Delivery = 85	GNMA = 99
	99
	85
	14 pt. = Basis (unadjusted
	for yield equivalency)

The *basis relationship* is an important part of the overall hedging strategy. The change of the futures price and the price (rate) of the cash-market risk should be compared over a period of at least two years. Through mathematical correlation and regression analysis the relationship can be properly depicted. Determining the futures market that has the highest degree of correlation with the movement of price in the cash market is an important first step in hedge planning. The use of correlation and regression analysis is important in determining the proper ratio of futures contracts to use in relation to the risk being hedged. The assumption is that while two sets of price movements may be closely related, they do not move exactly with each ohter. A *hedge ratio* is arrived at to smooth out the price movement inequities.

The basis change over time, and any process used to determine the basis, should be continually reviewed. A hedger can be over or under-hedged if there has been a fundamental change in the basis, and only a continual analysis of price relationships would reveal such a change.

Time Adjustment. The next step in determining the hedge is time. If a hedger were going to have $1 million with a one-year maturity at risk and the risk could best be hedged in the T-Bill futures market, he would use four contracts, not one, multiplied by the proper ratio arrived at through the correlation analysis. A one basis-point change in a T-bill futures contract results in a dollar change of $25 because the contract calls for delivery of a 90-, 91-, or 92-day Treasury bill. To get the effect of a full year of risk, four contracts would be used, not one, since a basis-point change over a full year on $1 million is $100. The contracts would be spread out over a year's time.

Contract Option Months.   Another key question in hedge planning is what *contract months* to use. A two- or three-year risk would be difficult to hedge by using the distant months in a futures contract. These months are not nearly as liquid as the nearby months and could cause price distortion if a hedger were trying to place a position. The nearby months are more liquid, and through the process of placing a hedge in the nearby months, closing out the position as time passes, and rolling the positions forward, a risk of a long-term nature can be properly hedged.

Timing.   The last factor in hedge planning is *timing*. The basis, as mentioned before, will change. From time to time, due to temporary aberrations in either the cash market or the futures market, the basis relationship will be distorted so that the futures market will be rich or cheap. *Richness* implies a narrower-than-normal basis, so that when the relationship adjusts, prices in the futures market will fall more rapidly relative to a decline in prices in the cash market. *Cheapness* refers to a wider than normal relationship. In the event of a drop in prices in a cheap market, the cash-market prices will fall faster relative to the decline in futures prices. A good rule of thumb to follow: a futures market should be sold when it is rich and bought when it is cheap.

Margin

The term *margin* in the futures industry does not have the same meaning as margin in stock transactions. Buying shares of common stock on margin means making a down payment and borrowing the balance required to pay the full purchase price from a broker.

By contrast, a futures transaction is an agreement to buy or sell at a later date. It is not a purchase and sale that results in immediate delivery, payment, and transfer of ownership. The purpose of a margin in connection with futures trading is to serve solely as a performance bond or good-faith deposit held by the clearing organization of the exchange. This guarantees that both parties to the agreement will perform when required to make or take delivery in the future.

Each exchange establishes the minimum margin deposits requried for specific contracts traded on that exchange. Margins may differ for hedgers and speculators. The difference reflects the fact that a hedger's net exposure to price fluctuations is reduced by opposite positions in the cash market. Brokerage firms may set higher but not lower margin levels for their customers. These minimum margin amounts reflect exchange officials' and members' judgement of market conditions. When safe to do so, margin deposits will be set low to encourage public participation in the market and minimize the cost of commercial hedging. If price volatility increases, however, protecting the financial integrity of the exchange assumes priority. Minimum margin deposits will be increased to maintain adequate reserves against the greater risks created by larger and more frequent price changes. Under conditions deemed to be an emergency, the exchange may give its members one hour's notice for additional margin requirements during trading hours. Futures margin deposits are set as specific dollar amounts per contract. Any resulting percentage relationship between the margin amount and the value of the asset underlying the futures contract is incidental.

The exchanges also make it a practice to set two levels of margins—initial and maintenance—although in some cases they may be equal. An *initial margin* is the deposit made when a new position is opened. A *maintenance margin* is the level to which the initial deposit may be depleted by adverse price changes before additional cash is required to restore the initial deposit amount. As an example, assume that initial is $2,000 and maintenance is $1,500. On the first day, $2,000 is segregated as the initial margin for one newly opened futures contract. If the account is marked to the market on the second day down $400, there would be no call for cash because the balance of $1,600 is still above the maintenance level. If the account is marked to the market down another $200 on the third day, the account balance would be less than $1,500 and there would be a call for $600 in cash. This is the amount necessary to bring the account balance back to $2,000. Maintenance calls are for cash because a loss in an account that bought (or sold) must generate a corresponding gain in a different account that sold (or bought). The gain may be withdrawn from the clearing organization the next day in cash. The source of that cash is the account experiencing the loss.

Initial and maintenance margins are deposited in segregated accounts. Segregated accounts are required by federal regulation to provide customer protection. Brokerage firms must account separately for the funds of each futures customer. Special bank accounts, not subject to lien or offset, are maintained to prevent commingling of brokerage-house and customer funds. The broker must keep at all times sufficient funds or government securities in segregated accounts to ensure that no customers' losses offset other customers' profits.

Conclusion

A later chapter in this book will examine the interest-rate futures markets as one of many alternatives which can be used in reducing inventory price risk, as well as inventory carry cost. The futures markets can be used successfully to reduce risk. Their use, however, depends on the amount of time spent learning about the markets. The most productive and efficient use of the interest-rate futures markets will be possible only when each potential user commits the time to learn about the various markets.

Effective Controls and Accounting

Key ingredients in the learning process are the proper choice of a broker through whom to execute hedging transactions and proper control of the hedging process itself. At least at the start, a user of the futures markets would be well advised to use a broker who has an established interest-rate futures department from which help and advice on a professional level can be expected.

Most major accounting firms have positions pertaining to the use of the futures markets and how hedge profits and losses, as well as margin deposits, are to be treated for accounting purposes. In addition, most regulatory agencies have rules and policies governing the use of the futures markets. Familiarity with the accounting and regulatory policies and the laws governing the use of the futures markets is an important requirement before the actual use of the markets.

Adequate administrative control of a hedging program is also important. Proper audit controls must be established, which include trading authority limits, reporting limits, and board resolutions.

—— Chapter 8 ——————————————————

The Role of the Private Mortgage Insurance Industry

William H. Lacy
President
Mortgage Guaranty Insurance Corporation

Thomas S. LaMalfa
Vice President
Mortgage Guaranty Insurance Corporation

Mortgage guaranty insurance, or private mortgage insurance, is generally defined as the indemnification of mortgage lenders for losses incurred by reason of nonpayment of a mortgage loan.

For one-to-four family residences, private mortgage insurance acts as a substitute for the reduced equity down payment in a high-ratio mortgage loan, spreading the mortgage lending risk and assisting more than 5 million families nationwide to purchase homes they otherwise would not be able to afford. This financial guaranty makes mortgage investments more attractive by reducing the risk while increasing the liquidity and fluidity of credit. Private mortgage insurance protects the mortgage lending industry against losses, and by sharing the risk inherent in mortgage lending, mortgage insurance allows lenders to continue making loans during difficult economic times.

Historical Review of the Private Mortgage Insurance Industry

Pre-Depression Era

The modern private mortgage industry dates back only to the late 50s, yet the business of guaranteeing mortgages actually evolved from the title insurance business in the late 1800s. Most of the early mortgage guaranty activity centered in the state of New York, where it was an outgrowth of the liberal interpretation of an 1885 state statute regarding title insurance. The first legislation enacted specifically to permit the insuring of actual mortgage debt was passed in New York in 1904. The law was expanded in 1911 to allow insurance companies to buy and sell mortgages, and the business grew rapidly during the prosperous 1920s.

Those early mortgage insurers guaranteed principal and interest payments only, not the payment of taxes and other related expenses. No actuarial calculations existed yet to relate the assumed risk to the insurance rate charged. Losses were of little concern in an era when it was easy to sell foreclosed properties at a profit.

In addition to guaranteeing whole mortgages, insurance companies dealt in participations beginning in 1906. Later known as mortgage bonds, these participations allowed multiple investors to hold a mortgage or group of mortgages.

In the early mortgage insurance industry, a lack of regulations and restraints was coupled with abuses and malpractices. These weaknesses went largely unnoticed in the heyday of the 20s, but became increasingly apparent during the Depression years when the bank holiday of 1933 prompted the liquidation of all the New York mortgage guaranty companies.

Several factors contributed to the industry's collapse. First, insurers failed to observe even the most rudimentary rules of sound credit granting and underwriting. Second, reserve requirements had been established at levels that proved to be inadequate. The guaranty fund was in no way related to the amount of coverage outstanding. Third, the law provided that part of a company's reserves could be invested in its own or other insured mortgages, discouraging diversification and giving rise to numerous conflicts. Since many mortgages were not backed by sound appraisal practices, the value of such holdings could vary and prove inadequate to cover the guaranty. Because a portion of a company's holdings could be in nonamortizing mortgages, much of the value of a portfolio was only paper value. The real estate boom of the 20s masked defects in accounting, appraisal, underwriting, and pricing. The lack of a common understanding as to what constituted value proved a major failing in the industry.

In 1934 George W. Alger led a committee investigation of the collapse of the New York title and mortgage guaranty companies. The committee endorsed the concept of private mortgage insurance and went on to recommend a strict regulatory framework for the industry. The Alger report called for investment and accounting reforms, standardized appraisal techniques, prohibition of subsidiary corporations to the insurance company, and full separation of guaranty insurance companies from other real estate institutions. It also urged strict underwriting criteria, sizable reserve funds set aside in investments that were not subject to severe price cycles, and a specific limit on the ratio of contingent insurance risks to a company's capital and surplus. More than 20 years passed before the recommendations of the Alger Committee influenced the shape of a new private mortgage insurance industry.

Government Mortgage Insurance

Coincident with the Alger report, Congress enacted the National Housing Act of 1934 in an effort to revitalize the depressed housing industry. In addition to provisions designed to stimulate construction, the act created the Federal Housing Administration (FHA) to provide government-backed mortgage insurance to lenders making real estate mortgages for one-to-four family residences. The Mutual Mortgage Insurance Fund (MMIF) was established within the FHA as a self-supporting insurance system. MMIF is funded by premiums paid by mortgagors, and lender claims are satisfied from this fund. Other reserve funds exist for specific loan categories.

Although FHA insurance made housing possible for millions of families, the program was less than satisfactory from some lenders' perspectives. Savings and loan associations especially complained of complex procedures, excessive paperwork, and time-consuming credit investigations and property inspections. Such lack of acceptance of FHA insurance, together with the Alger recommendations, made the rebirth of private mortgage insurance possible.

Private Mortgage Insurance Reborn

As the FHA program reestablished the soundness of insuring mortgages, the private sector became increasingly interested in the potential of a restructured private mortgage insurance industry. In 1957 Max H. Karl founded Mortgage Guaranty Insurance Company (MGIC) in Milwaukee, Wisconsin, under new legislation based on the Alger report.

Growth of the Industry

Since 1957, the mortgage-guaranty insurance industry has grown at an impressive rate, with growth since 1970 illustrated in Table 1. Initially, some lenders, perhaps familiar with the early mortgage guaranty business, questioned the viability of modern mortgage insurance. In 1958, federally chartered savings and loan associations were given the authority to make loans up to a 90 percent loan-to-value ratio. Because such loans were regarded as greater risks, there was incentive to use MGIC insurance. Two additional private mortgage insurance companies joined the scene in 1961, with the field continuing to expand in following years. Federally chartered savings and loans were granted the power to make 95 percent loan-to-value ratio mortgages in 1971, and industry growth was spurred again. Growth trends in the private mortgage insurance industry are in contrast to the experience of FHA and VA programs, as illustrated in Table 2.

Table 1 • Mortgage Originations for One-to-Four Family Homes ($ millions)

Year	Total Originations	Conventional	FHA	VA	Percent of Total Originations That Are Insured	MICs	MIC Percent of Insured Originations
1970	$35,587	$22,972	$8,769	$3,846	38.7%	$1,162	8.4%
1971	57,789	39,964	10,994	5,830	36.7	3,430	16.1
1972	71,820	59,660	8,456	7,748	35.3	9,158	36.1
1973	79,125	66,364	5,185	7,578	32.1	12,627	49.0
1974	67,508	55,088	4,533	7,889	32.1	9,219	42.6
1975	77,913	62,811	6,265	8,837	32.2	10,024	40.0
1976	112,786	95,361	6,998	10,424	28.4	14,600	45.6
1977	161,974	136,523	10,470	14,881	29.0	21,595	46.0
1978	185,036	154,429	14,581	16,027	31.3	27,327	47.2
1979	187,088	147,479	20,772	18,838	34.7	25,324	39.0
1980	133,762	106,704	14,955	12,102	34.5	19,035	41.3
1981	98,212	80,141	10,538	7,534	37.5	18,719	50.9
1982	94,918	75,867	11,472	7,580	39.8	18,749	49.6
1983	199,445	151,967	28,602	18,876	45.0	42,360	47.1

Source: Mortgage Insurance Companies of America.

Table 2 • Comparison of Private versus Government Mortgage Insurance (number of mortgages insured)

Year	Private Insurers	FHA	VA	Private Insurers Percent of Total
1976	450,810	230,371	328,612	44.6%
1977	617,398	284,294	399,098	47.5
1978	695,620	300,551	354,776	51.5
1979	578,038	415,866	356,105	43.0
1980	392,808	332,738	266,256	40.0
1981	353,466	175,052	142,180	53.0
1982	315,973	123,553	92,957	59.3
1983	661,802	422,028	285,696	48.3

Source: Mortgage Insurance Companies of America.

Operation of the Private Mortgage Insurance Industry

Standardization of Practices

A major lesson learned from the collapse of early mortgage insurance companies was the importance of standardized appraisal, underwriting, and general insurance practices throughout the industry. Today, industry standards are founded on legislative models, trade association guidelines, and eligibility requirements of the Federal Home Loan Mortgage Corporation (FHLMC) and the Federal National Mortgage Association (FNMA).

The basic legal framework of the reborn mortgage insurance industry lies in the law passed by the Wisconsin legislature in 1956 to allow the establishment of MGIC. As mortgage insurance expanded into other states, this law became the model for other state legislatures. Even more stringent laws were passed in California and Illinois in the 1960s. Mortgage insurance companies must comply with the regulations of their states of domicile as well as those of each state in which they insure mortgages. Certainly, there are some differences between state laws. In general, the laws establish basic standards for paid-in capital and surplus, exposure limits, and surplus and contingency reserves.

The Mortgage Insurance Companies of America (MICA) was founded in 1973. This trade association serves as a listening post, catalyst, and advocate of industry positions on legislative and regulatory matters emanating from Washington. MICA acts as a liaison for the industry with FNMA and FHLMC relative to secondary market activities and generally seeks to enhance the understanding of the mortgage insurance industry by the private and public sectors.

The third force affecting the standardization of industry practices is the requirements of FNMA and FHLMC that must be met by private mortgage insurance companies before the loans they insure are eligible for purchase by these agencies. The FHLMC eligibility requirements, also generally followed by FNMA, encompass mortgage insurer operations, including underwriting policies and procedures, claims procedures, capital structure, solvency, corporate organization, conflicts of interest, and accounting procedures.

Taken together, these three controlling forces guide the operation of the private mortgage insurance industry.

Underwriting Functions

Underwriting is the selection process through which undesirable risks are eliminated and exposures are spread among risk classifications. Mortgage insurance underwriting has four basic elements: (1) the selective qualification of eligible lenders, (2) continuous spot checks of lender appraisals and credit reports, (3) the selective review of individual applications for mortgage insurance, and (4) analysis of the mortgage instrument features.

The process generally begins with the issuance of a master policy to qualified lenders. A master policy is a statement of terms and conditions the lender and insurer will follow when conducting business. Prior to issuing a master policy, the mortgage insurance company evaluates the lender's net worth and quality of assets, servicing ability, method for handling delinquent loans, and the professional capability of the appraisal and underwriting staffs. Once approved, the lender may submit individual loans to the insurance company to be insured or rejected on a case-by-case basis.

Through the underwriting process, the insurer attempts to qualify borrower, mortgage instrument, and property, and relies on both internal and external sources of information. Lenders are required to provide extensive documentation with the application for insurance, including verification of employment, credit report, loan application, property appraisal, photograph of the property and mortgage program description. Insurance company underwriters rely on current statistical studies on every aspect of the mortgage market, as well as studies of borrower characteristics. When the underwriting process has been completed with satisfactory results, a commitment is issued to the lender guaranteeing insurance for the mortgage. This commitment becomes a certificate of insurance upon receipt of the premium by the mortgage insurance company.

Mortgage insurance companies continually monitor their master policyholders to ensure satisfactory performance. Three main indicators are used by insurers to evaluate a lender's performance: (1) rejection ratios for applications submitted, (2) loss experience on policies issued, and (3) results of spot checks of lender-supplied credit report and property appraisals.

The introduction in the late 1970s of creative new financing instruments increased the need for high-quality loan underwriting. New mortgage features, such as adjustable rates, buydowns, and graduated payments, introduced a new class of mortgage risk. The risks associated with the long-term, fixed-rate mortgage were known and understood. Risk of default was limited to radical changes in borrower income or debt obligations. Today mortgage insurers are concerned about erosion due to negative amortization and about the safety and attractiveness of mortgages to the investor.

The job of mortgage insurance underwriter now includes responsibility for mortgage instrument analysis to ensure that the risks of the mortgage are reasonable for borrower, lender, investor and insurer.

Claims Functions

Clearly, the function of mortgage insurance is to protect the mortgage noteholder against loss resulting from default of the buyer. According to the terms of the master policy, the lender must report delinquencies to the insurer and begin foreclosure or other appropriate proceedings upon recurring default. The lender submits a claim, including evidence of merchantable title to the property, to the mortgage insurance company, and the insurer selects one of the following methods to satisfy the claim:

Option 1: Pay the entire claim amount to the lender and take title to property.

Option 2: Pay 20 percent, 25 percent, or other percentage of the claim amount, depending on the policy, with the lender retaining title to property.

Table 3 shows an example of a claim. The total amount of the claim is $46,562. The insurer would pay the entire amount to the lender under Option 1, taking title to the property for resale. Under Option 2, if the mortgage insurance policy provided 25 percent coverage, the insurer would pay $11,640.50 to the lender to settle the claim. Title to the property would remain with the lender.

Financial Strength

As major purchasers of low down payment mortgage loans backed by private mortgage insurance, FNMA and FHLMC continually evaluate the financial strength of the insurance companies. The Arthur D. Little Inc. study of the private mortgage insurance industry, done under contract to FNMA and FHLMC, found that the typical mortgage insurance company could withstand economic hardship as severe as that experienced during the Depression.

The strength of modern mortgage insurance companies lies in their reserve

Table 3 • Example of Claim Settlement

Principal balance due	$40,946
Accumulated interest (excludes penalty interest and late charges)	3,200
Subtotal	44,146
Attorney's fees (maximum 3 percent of subtotal)	1,324
Property taxes paid	584
Hazard insurance premiums advanced	242
Preservation of property (includes such items as securing the property and winterizing)	160
Disbursement and foreclosure proceedings	386
Subtotal	46,842
Less: Escrow balance and rent received	(280)
Total claim	$46,562

structure. Unlike most other types of insurance companies, mortgage insurers must maintain reserves sufficient to cover potential losses for a given year as well as catastrophic losses associated with a severe economic downturn. Three separate reserves are maintained by all private mortgage insurance companies:

1. **Contingency reserves** are required by law to protect policyholders against the type of catastrophic losses which can occur in a depressed economic period. Half of each premium dollar earned goes into this reserve and may not be accessed by the insurer for a 10-year period unless losses in a calendar year exceed 20 to 35 percent of earned premiums, depending on the state of domicile, and even then only with the approval of the insurance commissioner of the state where the insurance company is domiciled.

2. **Unearned premium reserves** consist of premiums received for the term of the policy. The method by which the premiums are earned for this reserve is established by state law to match premiums with losses and loss exposure.

3. **Loss reserves** are established to cover losses on a case-by-case basis as the insurer learns of defaults and foreclosures.

The underwriting experience and aggregate assets and reserves for the private mortgage insurance industry are presented in Tables 4 and 5.

Role in the Primary and Secondary Markets

Primary Market Involvement

The presence of the mortgage insurance companies in the primary market provides direct benefits for loan originators and borrowers. The traditional role of this guaranty against loss has encouraged the expanded use of high-ratio

Table 4 • Industry Underwriting Experience ($ millions)

	1983	1982	1981	1980	1979	1978	1977
Net premiums written	$522.9	$364.5	$329.7	$313.0	$315.9	$301.3	$215.8
Premiums earned	449.3	348.8	329.8	311.1	305.2	260.3	191.3
Losses	356.8	209.9	93.8	58.7	39.3	39.2	35.7
Expenses	191.0	175.0	161.4	141.0	134.0	116.7	77.7

Note: Table changed to uniformly reflect data from pages 4 and 7 in the statutory statements. Source: Mortgage Insurance Companies of America.

Table 5 • Industry Reserves and Assets ($ millions)

	1983	1982	1981	1980	1979	1978	1977
Admitted assets	$2,371	$2,036	$1,827	$1,656	$1,458	$1,261	$1,035
Unearned premium reserve	347	273	258	259	258	246	211
Loss reserve	244	181	100	75	55	43	36
Statutory contingency reserve	1,076	1,052	985	834	684	543	422
Policyholders surplus	623	476	427	455	425	409	332

Source: Mortgage Insurance Companies of America.

lending. This has increased the number of eligible homebuyers in the market-place which, in turn, increases the mortgage originations of lenders. The benefits of private mortgage insurance can include: lower premium costs, faster loan processing, a variety of insurance coverage options, flexible underwriting policies and higher maximum loan amount limits.

Unlike the FHA, which usually insures 100 percent of the principal amount due on a mortgage, the private mortgage insurance companies typically insure only the top 20 to 25 percent of the mortgage, depending on the loan-to-value (LTV) ratio and the insurance coverage option desired by the lender. First-year premium amounts vary with the LTV, amount of coverage desired, and premium payment plan. Renewal rates for private insurers typically are ¼ to ⁵⁄₁₀ of 1 percent of the outstanding loan balance. Private insurance may be canceled at the option of the lender.

Lenders may select from a variety of coverage options and payment plans, depending on their needs or the needs of an investor. Available coverages range from the top 12 percent to 30 percent of the loan. Premium payment plans are available both on an annual basis (premium paid once each year) or on a single prepaid basis (premium paid in advance for a specified number of years). For example, on a 90 percent LTV loan with top 20 percent coverage, the first year premium would be .80 percent of the original loan balance and .35 percent of the declining balance each year thereafter.

In Table 6, the default risk for an assumed uninsured 80 percent LTV con-

Table 6 • Comparison of Uninsured and Insured Conventional Loan Default Risk

	80 Percent Conventional Uninsured Loan (@ 12½%)		90 Percent Conventional Insured Loan (@ 12¾%)	
Sales price	$100,000		$100,000	
Down payment	20,000		10,000	
Original loan amount	80,000		90,000	
Interest during:				
Default period (4 months)	3,332		3,824	
Foreclosure (2 months)	1,665		1,910	
Redemption period (6 months)	4,988		5,725	
Taxes due during foreclosure	2,000		2,000	
Hazard insurance during foreclosure	250		250	
Foreclosure costs	500		500	
Attorney's fees (up to 3%)	2,400		2,700	
Property maintenance	300		300	
Investment at acquisition	95,435		107,209	
Less: MIC claim payment	—	(0%)	21,442	(20%)
Sales price needed to break even	95,435		85,767	
Disposal price under distress sale	95,000		95,000	
Less: Broker's commissions (@ 6%)	5,700		5,700	
	89,300		89,300	
Sales price needed by lender for break-even	(95,435)		(85,767)	
Lender's margin of safety (loss)	$(6,135)		$ 3,533	

ventional loan is compared to that for an insured 90 percent LTV conventional loan. The MIC claim payment results in the margin of safety shown for the insured loan in comparison to the loss shown for the uninsured loan. This margin of safety can reduce the financial risks associated with the other holding period costs incurred by a lender prior to the sale of the property.

Private mortgage insurance is based on the concept of shared risk. Thus the private insurance companies rely on information supplied by the lender when underwriting a loan for insurance rather than duplicating this information. They establish acceptable standards of risk selection and leave the task of gathering information such as credit and employment data to the lender. They normally apprise a lender of acceptance or rejection of an individual loan within 24 hours after receipt of an application and supporting documentation.

Changing lifestyles affect borrower needs and increase the risks of long-term lending. Through use of flexible underwriting standards, the private insurers maintain the ability to respond to changes in the lending environment. Recognizing that home prices have risen steadily since the mid-1970s, the mortgage insurance companies raised the traditional 25/33 percent underwriting ratios. These ratios, which dated from the 1930s, have been reevaluated and established at either 28/36 percent or 33/38 percent, depending on the type of mortgage. These new ratios were based on an analysis of delinquencies, defaults, and foreclosures for different types of instruments.

The private insurance companies insure higher loan amounts than those for mortgages that may be purchased by FHLMC or FNMA. Often referred to as nonconforming loan amounts, these higher balance mortgages have become more prevalent during the past decade as a result of rapidly increasing home prices.

Secondary Market Involvement

The mortgage insurance companies were among the pioneers in the private secondary market. MGIC, for instance, can trace its secondary market customer assistance program back to 1967. Their experience demonstrated to the other insurers that mortgage lenders would use mortgage insurance in greater quantity if the insurers provided their customers with assistance in selling their loans. By the mid-1970s secondary market services became a significant way for the mortgage insurance companies to earn new business. Since then, their importance has grown as greater numbers of lenders turn to the secondary market for capital to support their lending operations.

In order to provide the primary market with an adequate supply of funds, mortgage originators need the ability to access capital from all sectors of the debt market. In addition, lenders need to do so at rates that are competitive with other investments, such as corporate bonds.

The genesis of the secondary market was the outgrowth of the mortgage market's need to seek and attract capital from sources other than depositories. These institutions, especially savings and loan associations, had become the major suppliers of capital for mortgage finance by the 1960s. By the late 1960s savings associations and, to a lesser extent, savings banks and commercial banks provided the bulk of funds for residential mortgage lending.

Housing's sensitivity to interest rates made this economic sector subject to periods of "feast or famine," however. Cyclicality, in combination with periodic bouts of disintermediation, also adversely affected both the demand for and the supply of mortgage capital. As a result of these conditions, the housing market was regularly characterized by imbalances; either too much or too little capital was available relative to demand. Moreover, funds for mortgage lending were seldom uniformly distributed. Depositories in some regions of the country were capital rich, while other areas, chiefly those with strong local demand, were capital short. Too much capital in a given area with light demand forced portfolio lenders to cut their mortgage-lending rates in order to maintain their market share objectives. Elsewhere, rates were considerably higher and borrower demand was stronger, but funds were scarce. Lenders and would-be lenders suffered at both ends: Those with excess capital relative to demand hurt their portfolio yields by bidding down interest rates; others reduced their lending despite strong demand in order to allocate their limited funds.

Regulatory relief beginning in the late 1960s allowed savings associations to invest a portion of their funds outside their normal lending areas. Further liberalization by the regulatory authorities, especially the Federal Home Loan Bank Board, empowered associations to invest growing percentages of their funds outside their local markets. These moves helped ameliorate supply and demand factors, thereby smoothing out the flow of funds and providing better returns to the exporters of capital. Both parties to such transactions benefited as the supply of funds was more evenly spread out across the country.

Mortgage insurance companies were aware of the market's imbalances and began to assume the role of secondary market middlemen or "matchmakers." The mortgage insurance companies' niche within the secondary market grew as their insurance operations expanded, making them increasingly more cognizant of regional mortgage market conditions. By the early to mid-1970s mortgage insurers could readily identify areas and institutions with excess capital, as well as those lenders who had loans to sell. As the baby boom generation blossomed into adulthood and as new demand surfaced when the population began shifting to the south and western portions of the country, even greater numbers of lenders turned to the secondary market for funds. The important role of the mortgage insurance companies as matchmakers grew in tandem.

While introducing buyers to sellers—and vice versa—was the mortgage insurance industry's initial role, their financial success allowed them to expand the size of their secondary market operations. Their early involvement, moreover cast them into a position of prominence. The industry's secondary market personnel were regarded by many as experts at a time when a majority of primary market lenders were just beginning to explore the idea and mechanics of selling and buying loans. By the mid-1970s the mortgage insurance companies were sponsoring workshops and seminars to train new entrants in the ways and means of the secondary market. More insurance business led to bigger secondary market staffs at the mortgage insurance companies.

From observers of the market to matchmakers to teachers to "experts": that is largely the way mortgage insurance companies' role evolved and mushroomed. Larger staffs allowed the mortgage insurance companies to reach greater numbers of would-be participants. More and more lenders became aware of the secondary market's value to their operations and their earnings. The mortgage insurance companies' secondary market networks flourished.

Today, mortgage insurance companies continue to take bids and offers from buyers and sellers just as they did a decade or more ago. Their position in the market is now as much or more that of an advisor as it is a deal facilitator: Mortgage insurance company staffs help lenders structure different types of transactions, keep them abreast of FNMA and FHLMC yield requirements and a myriad of programs, share information on market conditions, assist lenders in designing primary market marketing programs, and train new personnel for their customers. In addition, hundreds of buyer and seller contacts, many of which began through mortgage insurance company introductions, continue to thrive and support the secondary market infrastructure that the mortgage insurance companies helped develop.

As needs changed and opportunities arose, the mortgage insurance companies attempted to respond to the challenges and changing directions, in part, through their secondary market operations.

Table 7 shows conventional residential mortgage originations and purchases and sales data from 1970 through 1983. This data indicates the growth of both the primary (or origination) market and purchases and sales volumes in the secondary market. Table 8 provides some limited information on the volume of secondary market activity that the mortgage insurance companies have helped place. Collectively, the mortgage insurers represent the second largest factor in volume after the federally sponsored agencies. MICA, the mortgage

Table 7 • Ratio of Total Mortgage Sales to Originations for One- to Four-Family (Nonfarm) Mortgage Loans: 1970–1983

Year	Total Sales ($ billions)	Total Originations ($ billions)	Ratio of Sales to Originations (percent)
1970	$ 14.2	$ 35.6	39.9%
1971	18.5	57.8	32.1
1972	24.1	75.9	31.8
1973	24.9	79.1	31.4
1974	23.1	67.5	34.2
1975	29.7	77.9	38.1
1976	40.9	112.8	36.3
1977	55.4	162.0	34.2
1978	67.8	185.0	36.6
1979	76.6	186.6	41.0
1980	65.8	133.8	49.2
1981	53.2	98.2	54.2/51.8*
1982	100.6	97.0	103.7/69.9*
1983	148.1	199.5	74.3/61.9*

*Ratio adjusted for FHLMC and FNMA swaps to approximate the ratio of current year originations sold in the secondary market in those years.
Sources: The Supply of Mortgage Credit 1970–1979; and selected reports of the "Survey of Mortgage Lending Activity," for the Fourth Quarter 1981, Fourth Quarter 1982, and for the year 1983. (Washington, D.C.: Office of Financial Management, U.S. Department of Housing and Urban Development).

Table 7 • Ratio of Total Mortgage Sales to Originations for One-to-Four Family (Nonfarm) Mortgage Loans: 1970–1983

Year	$ Billions	Percent of Aggregate Conventional Loan Sales
1978	$ 3.3	9.1%
1979	6.3	16.1
1980	4.6	12.2
1981	6.7	20.9
1982	13.0	25.8

Source: Mortgage Insurance Companies of America.

insurance companies trade association, discontinued monitoring secondary marketing involvement by individual mortgage insurance companies at the end of 1982. Nonetheless, MGIC's tracking of secondary market activity suggests that their volume (and it is probably fair to suggest that the volume of the other mortgage insurance companies as well) grew substantially since 1982. In 1983, MGIC credited itself with assisting in the placement of $9.3 billion for their mortgage insurance customers.

In addition to their trading networks, most mortgage insurance companies provide their customers with a wide array of marketing and technical support services. Fundamental changes within the mortgage finance industry, resulting from deregulation, heightened competition for funds, high interest rates, technological developments, new mortgage instruments and new securities—to name some factors currently affecting mortgage lending—have increased the level of sophistication needed by lenders to operate efficiently. The mortgage insurance companies have sought to stay abreast of these developments and to provide their customers with services and products to match their changing needs.

In the secondary market, several mortgage insurers have established or sponsored conduit operations to purchase large quantities of mortgage loans for placement with nontraditional investors such as insurance companies and pension funds. Conduits, which are discussed in the next section, have brought billions of dollars of new capital to the mortgage lending industry. Deregulation, meanwhile, has opened the mortgage industry to dozens of new mortgage instruments. To keep the industry informed of what lenders are doing in other markets, especially when these efforts are successful, the mortgage insurance companies began using survey research techniques to inform lenders of various developments and aspects of these new instruments. For example, if lenders in one area of the country experimented with a specific instrument which subsequently was abandoned, the dissemination of this fact along with supporting reasons for its failure could be conveyed to other lenders, in the hope that such information would save them time and money. Mortgage insurance companies were also among those who embraced and promoted technological advancements. Computer applications ranging from complex instrument and/or program analysis to rapid delivery of commitment certificates, for instance, were advanced and promulgated by the mortgage insurers. Finally, such services as newsletters and training manuals were disseminated in order to keep lenders apprised of market conditions and trends. Research papers providing accurate and authoritative information on specific subject matters, such as regulatory disclosure requirements, have been sponsored by the mortgage insurance companies.

Involvement in Mortgage Securities and Conduits

As stated earlier, one of the principal purposes for the establishment of secondary market operations in the private mortgage insurance industry was to attract new sources of capital to mortgage lending, thereby alleviating the periodic disruptions in the availability of mortgage credit.

In recent years, considerable progress has been made in integrating the mortgage market into the capital or bond markets. This trend has been supported by mortgage market participants who have sought to make it less dependent on traditional sources of mortgage funds.

The mortgage and bond markets were initially linked through the development and growth of mortgage-backed securities. In 1970, the Government National Mortgage Association (GNMA) pass-through security program first introduced nonmortgage investors to mortgage-backed securities. This mortgage and bond market amalgamation has also been facilitated by the Federal Home Loan Mortgage Corporation through its issuance of mortgage-backed securities (MBS) collateralized by conventional residential mortgage pools. In 1981, the Federal National Mortgage Association inaugurated a mortgage securities program and joined the growing ranks of MBS issuers.

Today, private-sector companies are entering the securities business along with FNMA, FHLMC, and GNMA. One such experiment, Residential Funding Corporation, began in late 1982. Residential Funding, like its public sector counterparts, purchases loans individually or in bulk, packages them into securities, and sells the securities to investors through an investment banking firm. MGIC is a cosponsor of the Residential Funding operation, a conduit.

The purpose of the conduit is to access a national pool of investment money for local mortgage markets. Additionally, the conduit should reduce the cost of the funds by tapping the less expensive funds of the bond market. This objective is achieved by introducing standardization and marketability to the mortgage market.

The mortgage insurance companies were forerunners in mortgage-backed security design and conduit operations. Their involvement began with the Bank of America issue in 1977 in which MGIC developed pool and hazard insurance policies to enhance the issues' marketability.

Mortgage-backed securities can be divided into two basic groups: mortgage-backed bonds (MBB) and pass-through certificates. A mortgage-backed bond, defined as a financial instrument that is a general obligation of the issuing institution, is collateralized by a mortgage on a pool of mortgages, and has a stated maturity. They differ from corporate bonds in that they are secured by mortgage assets but otherwise have many characteristics of bonds. For example, mortgage-backed bonds generally have a fixed-note rate, are payable semiannually, and are overcollateralized. Since they have many of the fixed and certain cash flow features of corporate bonds, they appeal to traditional bond buyers.

Mortgage-backed bonds are usually rated by an investment rating agency. Ratings indicate the payment capability of the issuer and are important determinants of the interest cost of a bond issue. The ratings are predicated on such considerations as the quality and type of collateral and its value relative to the amount of borrowing in the issue. Overcollateralization ensures that sufficient collateral exists in the pool so that the aggregate market value of the underlying mortgages will always exceed the principal due on the outstanding bonds. This, in turn, reduces the risk exposure of the bondholders and simultaneously shifts the emphasis from the creditworthiness of the issuer to the collateral.

Mortgage-backed, pass-through certificates are collateralized by mortgages grouped into pools. Fractional interests in the pools are then sold to investors. As payments from the pool are received by the issuer, they are passed through to the certificateholders. As a result, the investor is assured of a minimum yield in monthly principal and interest payments. Each certificateholder in the pool shares in the interest income and principal prepayments and repayments generated by the underlying mortgages.

Since prepayments and delinquencies are possible, the cash flow on a pass-through can vary from payment to payment. This distinguishes it from the fixed and certain cash flow features of mortgage-backed bonds. In addition, pass-throughs, unlike mortgage-backed bonds, are not issuer obligations but rather constitute a sale of assets. The mortgage pool, not the issuer, represents the security and repayment source to the investor.

Because pass-throughs are not general obligations of the issuer, the investor must rely on the quality of the collateral, the private mortgage insurance, and the hazard insurance for protection against loss of principal and interest. While most pass-through issues have been rated AA by Standard & Poor's, several recent issues have obtained AAA ratings. Mortgage insurance helps the issuer obtain a higher rating and thus helps broaden the investor market while simultaneously holding down the issuers' expense. The following criteria are used by Standard & Poor's in rating pass-throughs: (1) the capabilities of the servicer and trustee, (2) the capabilities of the mortgage insurer, (3) the level and nature of any equity reserve, and (4) the characteristics of the mortgage pool.

The term *conduit* refers to the process of aggregating loans into a large pool. Principal and interest payments on the pool are passed through to investors in the form of payments on a bond or pass-through certificate. The entity that passes the payment to the investor is the conduit. GNMA and FHLMC were the first conduit and first conventional conduit, respectively. Private conduits began with the Bank of America's historic issuance of mortgage-backed securities mentioned earlier. Since then, conduits have increased in number and design. Some are oriented toward a single product, while others offer a myriad of commitment types for an array of different types of mortgage products.

Conduit companies, several of which are sponsored by the mortgage insurance companies, were designed to be of special help to small- and medium-sized financial institutions. They have helped mortgage sellers participate more fully in markets that were previously only available to large issuers. Conduits strive to access nontraditional sources of mortgage capital and save individual originators a substantial amount of time and money by relying on economies of scale to minimize the underwriting, legal, accounting, and rating expenses that normally would be incurred directly and totally by the originator when packaging and placing securities.

For the issuer, conduits eliminate pool-size constraints and loan eligibility restrictions, while offering the investor the opportunity to obtain rated securities from a single source with the safety and spread of risk of a geographical and lender diversified portfolio. Investors are spared the cost and inconvenience of evaluating each loan, checking legal details, and monitoring loan servicing. Conduits usually act as the master servicer. In this role, conduits monitor the performance of the individual subservicers and fulfill the functions established under the pooling and servicing agreements.

Current Coverage Issues

As long as the real estate market remains dynamic, private mortgage insurance companies must remain alert to changing financial trends, consumer attitudes, and the needs of mortgage lenders. The current lending environment demands foresight and responsiveness on the part of mortgage insurers.

Early in 1981, mortgage lenders received the authority to make adjustable rate mortgages (ARMs). This type of loan helps lenders continue to make mortgage loans during volatile interest rate periods, because the interest rate on these loans can be adjusted periodically. The flexibility of ARMs has created uncertainty about ARM behavior under different economic conditions. It has also created a different kind of lending risk for lenders, mortgage insurers, and secondary market investors.

In-depth risk analysis of the new adjustable rate mortgages led private mortgage insurance companies to introduce insurance coverage flexible enough to keep pace with the changeable ARM. Unlike traditional mortgage insurance policies, the new constant dollar exposure coverage limits lender exposure to a given percentage, typically to 75 percent of the original property value, regardless of the loan balance at the time of an insurance claim. This coverage adjusts with the loan balance and provides dollar-for-dollar coverage.

Conclusion

The private mortgage insurance industry has historically taken an active role in both the housing and financial arenas. Today, the industry continues to significantly augment the flow of funds through the secondary market.

— PART ONE —— SECTION B —

The Legal and Regulatory Environment

— Chapter 9 —

The Legal Environment: An Overview

Caryl S. Bernstein
Executive Vice President, General Counsel, and Secretary
Federal National Mortgage Association

JoAnn Carpenter
Assistant General Counsel
Federal National Mortgage Association

Introduction

The federal government has been instrumental in the development of housing law, particularly since the 1930s. This involvement has been evidenced by the creation of the FHA and VA programs to assist homebuyers in obtaining financing, the network of federally chartered thrift institutions that are chartered and supervised by the Federal Home Loan Bank Board (FHLBB), and the establishment of major participants in the secondary mortgage market: the Federal National Mortgage Association (FNMA), the Government National Mortgage Association (GNMA), and the Federal Home Loan Mortgage Corporation (FHLMC).[1] Since the 1970s, the federal government has expanded its involvement beyond the financing of housing to the regulating of individual mortgage

---

[1]See Chapter 3 for a discussion of FNMA, GNMA, and FHLMC, each of which is federally chartered.

transactions through such legislation as the Real Estate Settlement Procedures Act of 1974.

The following sections summarize federal and state laws that are pertinent to housing finance and, therefore, directly or indirectly to the secondary mortgage market. Since these sections provide only a general overview, the reader may wish to refer to the various legislative enactments in order to gain a fuller understanding of the law applicable to real estate finance.

Federal Laws[2]

Real Estate Settlement Procedures Act of 1974

The enactment of the Real Estate Settlement Procedures Act of 1974, as amended, (RESPA)[3] effected a number of changes in the settlement process for residential real estate. The provisions of RESPA are applicable to any *federally related mortgage loan,* which is defined to include a first mortgage loan on a one- to four-family residence that is (1) made by a federally regulated or federally insured lender or (2) intended to be sold by the originating lender to FNMA, GNMA, or FHLMC.[4] RESPA is implemented by Regulation X,[5] which was promulgated by the Department of Housing and Urban Development (HUD).

Pursuant to RESPA, lenders of such loans must provide their borrowers with a booklet, as prescribed by the secretary of HUD, that contains specific information regarding the nature and costs of real estate settlement services. The lender must also include with the booklet a good faith estimate, stated in either a specific dollar amount or in a dollar range, of the charges the borrower is likely to incur for specific settlement services. Regulation X provides that the "good faith estimate must bear a reasonable relationship to the charge a borrower is likely to be required to pay at settlement, and must be based upon experience in the locality or area in which the Mortgaged Property is located." The booklet and the good faith estimate must either be delivered or mailed to the borrower not later than three business days after the borrower's loan application is received by the lender.

Regulation X also requires that the person conducting settlement in every

---

[2]See also State Laws, Usury, *infra,* for a discussion of the federal law that preempts state usury laws as they apply to first mortgages.

[3]The Real Estate Settlement Procedures Act of 1974 was amended by the Real Estate Settlement Procedures Act Amendments of 1975, Pub. L. No. 94–205, 89 Stat. 1157 (1976), and Section 461 of the Housing and Urban-Rural Recovery Act of 1983, Pub. L. No. 98–181, 97 Stat. 1155, 1230 (1983). The discussion is based on the Act, as amended, 12 U.S.C. §2601 *et seq.*

[4]See Section 3 of RESPA for other examples of a federally related mortgage loan. (24 C.F.R. §3500.5(b) limits the definition to loans involving a transfer of legal title of the mortgaged property.) Mortgage loans exempt from the coverage of RESPA are identified in 24 C.F.R. §3500.5(d).

[5]24 C.F.R. §3500.1 *et seq.*

federally related mortgage loan settlement transaction use a uniform settlement statement form, HUD-1, regardless of whether or not such person is the lender. (The form need not be used if the borrower is not required to pay any settlement charges or if the borrower is required to pay a fixed amount for settlement charges and has been informed of this amount when applying for the loan.) The form is to be completed to itemize all charges to be paid by the borrower and all charges to be paid by the seller in connection with the settlement. Charges not imposed by the lender and which the borrower or seller contracts to pay apart from the settlement need not be disclosed on HUD-1. Information regarding settlement charges to be paid by the borrower may be deleted from the copy of the form that is to be furnished to the seller and vice versa. Upon the borrower's request, the person conducting settlement must permit the borrower to inspect HUD-1, completed insofar as possible, one business day prior to settlement. (The borrower has no right to such advance inspection if the borrower or the borrower's agent does not attend settlement.) HUD-1 must be delivered or mailed to the borrower and the seller at or before settlement, subject to limited exceptions.

RESPA also prohibits certain practices in connection with the settlement of federally related mortgage loans. For example, the payment or receipt of any fee, kickback, or thing of value that is compensation for the referral of business incident to a real estate settlement service is expressly prohibited. Also prohibited is the payment or receipt of any portion of a charge made or received for a settlement service other than for services actually performed.[6]

Among the exemptions from these prohibitions are "payments pursuant to cooperative brokerage and referral arrangements or agreements between real estate agents and brokers." In addition, the seller of property may not require the buyer to purchase title insurance from any particular title company.[7] RESPA also prohibits the lender from charging a fee for the preparation and distribution of HUD-1. Finally, RESPA places limitations on the amount of escrow funds a lender may require of a borrower for the payment of taxes, insurance premiums, or other charges with respect to the property.

Equal Credit Opportunity Act of 1974

The Equal Credit Opportunity Act of 1974 (ECOA) prohibits discrimination on the basis of sex or marital status by financial institutions and other firms engaged in the extension of credit. In 1976, ECOA was amended to prohibit discrimination in the extension of credit on the following additional bases: race,

---

[6]The penalties for violating the prohibition against kickbacks and unearned fees include the following: civil liability equal to three times the amount of any charge paid for the settlement service; the possibility that court costs and reasonable attorney's fees can be recovered; and a fine of not more than $10,000 or imprisonment for not more than one year, or both.

[7]The penalty for violation of this prohibition is civil liability equal to three times the charges for such title insurance.

color, religion, national origin, age (provided the applicant has the capacity to contract), receipt of income from any public assistance program, or the good faith exercise of any right under the Consumer Credit Protection Act. ECOA, as amended,[8] is implemented by Regulation B,[9] which was promulgated by the Board of Governors of the Federal Reserve System (the Federal Reserve Board). Twelve federal agencies enforce ECOA and Regulation B; the specific jurisdiction depends on the particular class of creditors.

Regulation B prohibits a creditor from discriminating against any applicant on any of the nine prohibited bases concerning any aspect of the credit transaction. A *creditor* is defined, in part, as "a person who, in the ordinary course of business, regularly participates in the decision of whether or not to extend credit." Discrimination means "to treat an applicant less favorably than other applicants."

In addition to the general proscription against discrimination, Regulation B also sets forth rules concerning applications, evaluations of applications, and extensions of credit. Under these rules, a creditor may not make statements that would, on a prohibited basis, discourage a reasonable person from applying for, or pursuing an application for, credit. They also prohibit a creditor from requesting certain information in conjunction with a credit application. This information includes, subject to certain exceptions, the sex or marital status of the applicant, the applicant's intention to bear children, and the race, color, religion, or national origin of the applicant. A creditor may request information about a spouse or former spouse only under specified circumstances: if the spouse will be liable for repayment of the debt, for example.

Regulation B prohibits a creditor from discriminating against an applicant on a prohibited basis in evaluating the applicant's creditworthiness. In a judgmental evaluation system, a creditor is permitted to consider an applicant's age or receipt of income from public assistance only for the purpose of determining a pertinent element of creditworthiness. For example, a creditor may consider the applicant's occupation and length of time to retirement to determine whether the applicant's income justifies the duration of the extension of credit. In evaluating a credit application, a creditor may not use assumptions or statistics concerning the likelihood that a group of persons will receive less income in the future because of the bearing or rearing of children. A creditor must consider alimony, child support, or separate maintenance payments as income, to the extent such payments are likely to be consistently made, if the applicant relies on such payments in applying for credit.

In extending credit, a creditor may not refuse to grant an individual account to a creditworthy applicant on any prohibited basis. If an applicant for individual credit qualifies under the creditor's standards for the amount and terms of the credit requested, a creditor may not require a cosigner on the note, subject

---

[8] 15 U.S.C. §1691 *et seq.*
[9] 12 C.F.R. §202.1 *et seq.*

to certain exceptions. For example, if an applicant requests secured credit, a creditor is permitted to require the signature of the applicant's spouse on any instrument if the creditor believes that signature to be necessary to make the secured property available to satisfy the debt in the event of default, that is, to create a valid lien, pass clear title, waive inchoate rights to property, or assign earnings.[10]

Certain classes of transactions are afforded special treatment under Regulation B. Public utilities credit, securities credit, incidental consumer credit, business credit, and governmental credit are exempted from specified provisions. In addition, in the case of special-purpose credit programs designed to benefit economically disadvantaged groups, a creditor may require all program participants to share certain characteristics and may request and consider information concerning the common characteristics required for eligibility. Such common characteristics may be those of race, color, religion, national origin, sex, marital status, age, or receipt of income from a public assistance program.

Regulation B also specifies that lenders must request, but may not require, that applicants for consumer credit relating to the purchase of residential real property, to be secured by a lien on such property, provide information regarding race, national origin, sex, marital status, and age. Such information is to be used for monitoring purposes and may not be used to discriminate against applicants on those bases.

Regulation B sets forth specified time periods within which a creditor must notify an applicant concerning the creditor's action regarding a loan application. Subject to limited exceptions, within thirty days after receiving a completed application, a creditor must notify the applicant of the creditor's approval of, or adverse action regarding, the application. A notification of adverse action must contain: (1) a statement of the action taken, (2) an ECOA notice, (3) the name and address of the federal agency administering ECOA vis-a-vis the creditor, and (4) specific reasons for the action taken or a disclosure of the applicant's right to a statement of reasons.

Truth in Lending Act

The Truth in Lending Act (TILA),[11] which became effective on July 1, 1969, was enacted "to assure a meaningful disclosure of credit terms so that the consumer will be able to compare more readily the various credit terms available to him and avoid the uninformed use of credit . . . ." TILA has been amended several times, for example, by the Truth in Lending Simplification and Reform Act (Title VI of the Depository Institutions Deregulation and

---

[10]For example, "Unofficial Staff Interpretations of Regulation B," *Federal Reserve Regulatory Service* 6–181, states that FNMA's requirement that a cosigner or guarantor on a residential mortgage loan execute the mortgage as a co-mortgagor is permissible under Regulation B.

[11]15 U.S.C. §1601 *et seq.*

Monetary Control Act of 1980).[12] TILA is implemented by Regulation Z,[13] which was promulgated by the Federal Reserve Board. Nine federal agencies share enforcement of TILA and Regulation Z.[14]

Regulation Z generally applies to individuals or businesses that regularly offer or extend to consumers[15] credit[16] that: (1) is subject to a finance charge or by written agreement[17] is payable in more than four installments and (2) is primarily for personal, family, or household purposes. In the case of credit transactions secured by dwellings, a creditor (as defined by Regulation Z) that has extended credit more than five times a year is deemed to regularly extend consumer credit. The following types of transactions are specifically exempt from Regulation Z: (1) business, commercial, agricultural, or organizational credit; (2) credit over $25,000 not secured by real property or a dwelling;[18] (3) public utility credit; (4) securities or commodities credit; (5) home fuel budget plans; and (6) student loan programs. A transaction involving the acquisition of property that is not, or is not intended to be, owner-occupied is considered to be for business purposes.[19]

Regulation Z sets forth separate rules for open-end and closed-end credit transactions. Open-end credit is extended by a creditor under a plan that involves repeated credit transactions, the imposition of a finance charge on the outstanding unpaid balance, and the reinstatement of the credit available to the consumer to the extent any outstanding balance is repaid. For example, the extension of credit under a revolving credit card account is an open-end credit transaction. All consumer credit that does not qualify as open-end credit is

---

[12]Pub. L. No. 96–221, 94 Stat. 132, 168 (1980).

[13]12 C.F.R. §226.1 et seq. See Scoptur, "Truth in Lending: New Light on Reg. Z," *Mortgage Banking*, Feb. 1983, at 32, for a discussion of compliance with Regulation Z by a mortgage lending institution.

[14]The civil penalties for certain violations of TILA and Regulation Z include actual damages, statutory damages, attorney's fees, and court costs. The criminal penalty for willful and knowing violations of TILA and Regulation Z is a fine of not more than $5,000, imprisonment for not more than one year, or both.

[15]The definition of "consumer" excludes guarantors, sureties, and endorsers. "Federal Reserve Board Official Staff Commentary," *Federal Reserve Regulatory Service* 6–1163.5 [hereinafter cited as "Official Staff Commentary"].

[16]A mortgage assistance plan administered by a government agency in which a portion of the consumer's monthly payment amount is paid by the agency is not considered credit for purposes of Regulation Z. "Official Staff Commentary," *supra* n. 15, at 6–1162.1.

[17]A letter merely confirming an oral agreement does not constitute a written agreement. "Official Staff Commentary," *supra* n. 15, at 6–1162.4.

[18]Credit secured by a mobile home that is used or expected to be used as the principal dwelling of the consumer does not fall within this exemption. "Official Staff Commentary," *supra* n. 15, at 6–1163.9.

[19]See "Background and Summary of Regulation Z," *Federal Reserve Regulatory Service* 6–1142.

classified as closed-end credit. Real estate transactions generally are closed-end credit transactions.[20]

In closed-end credit transactions, the creditor must disclose certain information in a clear and conspicuous written form that the consumer may keep. Information, as applicable, must be disclosed about the following: (1) identity of the creditor, (2) amount financed, (3) itemization of amount financed,[21] (4) finance charge,[22] (5) annual percentage rate, (6) variable rate provisions,[23] (7) payment schedule, (8) total of payments, (9) demand feature, (10) total sales price, (11) existence of prepayment penalties, (12) late payment charges, (13) creation of a security interest in property, (14) insurance, (15) certain security interest charges, (16) reference to the appropriate contract document, (17) assumption policy, and (18) required deposit.

Creditors that are involved in closed-end residential mortgage transactions subject to RESPA must make good faith estimates of the disclosures required by Regulation Z before consummation of the transaction or within three business days after receiving a consumer's written application, whichever is earlier. (The three-day time period for disclosing credit terms coincides with the time period within which creditors subject to RESPA must provide good faith estimates of settlement costs.) Regulation Z provides for a tolerance in deviation from the actual annual percentage rate. The tolerance rate for regular transactions is one-eighth of one percent; for irregular transactions, one-fourth of one percent. (An irregular transaction is a transaction with multiple advances, irregular payment periods other than an odd first period, or irregular payment amounts other than an odd first or final payment.) If the creditor's estimate subsequently turns out to be beyond these tolerances, the creditor must disclose the changed terms before or at the time of the consummation of the transaction.[24]

If a creditor expressly agrees in writing to permit a consumer to assume an existing residential mortgage, the creditor must make new disclosures to the consumer, based on the remaining obligation. Regulation Z also provides that a consumer has the right to rescind a closed-end credit transaction that involves the retention or acquisition of a security interest in a consumer's principal

[20]An exception is a plan pursuant to which negotiated advances are made under an open-end real estate mortgage that meets all three criteria of the open-end credit definition. "Official Staff Commentary," *supra* n. 15, at 6–1162.9.

[21]Regulation Z provides that good faith estimates of settlement costs involved in transactions subject to RESPA may be disclosed instead of the itemization of the amount financed.

[22]See 12 C.F.R. §226.4 for examples of finance charges and charges excluded from the finance charge.

[23]Information provided in accordance with variable rate regulations of other federal agencies may be provided instead of the variable rate information required under Regulation Z.

[24]The term "consummation" refers to the time the consumer becomes contractually obligated under the credit transaction, rather than the time the consumer pays a nonrefundable fee. "Official Staff Commentary," *supra* n. 15, at 6–1163.6.

dwelling, subject to certain exceptions. The consumer may exercise this rescission right within three business days from the later of (1) consummation of the transaction, (2) delivery of a notice of the consumer's right to rescind, or (3) delivery of all material disclosures. The right to rescind is specifically not applicable to mortgage transactions to finance the acquisition or initial construction of the consumer's principal dwelling. Rather, a right of rescission may exist only if the secured property is currently used as the borrower's principal dwelling, for example, home improvement loans, second mortgages, and certain refinancings.[25]

Regulation Z also specifies disclosure rules for advertising closed-end credit.[26] Messages that invite, offer, or otherwise announce generally the availability of credit transactions to prospective customers are covered by Regulation Z. For example, newspaper messages and telephone solicitations are advertisements for the purposes of Regulation Z, whereas informational material, such as interest rate memos that are distributed only to business entities and oral or written communications relating to the negotiation of a specific transaction, are not covered by Regulation Z.[27] Advertisements covered by Regulation Z that state a rate of finance charge must also use the term *annual percentage rate* in describing the rate. In addition, if certain credit terms are stated in an advertisement, other terms must also be stated. The terms that trigger additional disclosure are: (1) the amount or percentage of any down payment, (2) the number of payments or the period of repayment, (3) the amount of any payment, or (4) the amount of any finance charge. The disclosure of any of these terms requires that the advertisement also state: (1) the amount of percentage of the down payment, (2) the terms of repayment, and (3) the annual percentage rate.

Home Mortgage Disclosure Act of 1975

The Home Mortgage Disclosure Act of 1975, as amended, (HMDA)[28] was enacted to enable the public "to determine whether depository institutions are filling their obligations to serve the housing needs of the communities and neighborhoods in which they are located and to assist public officials in their determination of the distribution of public sector investments in a manner de-

---

[25]"Background and Summary of Regulation Z," *supra* n. 19, at 6–1158. See 12 C.F.R. §226.15 for the consumer's right to rescind under an open-end credit plan secured by the consumer's principal dwelling.

[26]Section 144 of TILA, which specifies certain requirements for advertising closed-end credit, states that it is not applicable to residential real estate advertisements except to the extent the Federal Reserve Board requires by regulation. Such requirements are applicable to residential real estate advertisements because of the general applicability of Regulation Z to residential real estate credit transactions. For example, see 12 C.F.R. §226.3, which does not include residential real estate transactions in the list of transactions exempt from Regulation Z.

[27]"Official Staff Commentary," *supra* n. 15, at 6–1161.4.

[28]12 U.S.C. § 2801 *et seq.*

signed to improve the private investment environment." HMDA is implemented by Regulation C,[29] promulgated by the Federal Reserve Board. The authority granted by HMDA expires on October 1, 1985.

HMDA requires certain depository institutions to compile and make available to the public, for inspection and copying, information regarding the number and total dollar amount of mortgage loans that were originated or purchased by the institution during each year. HMDA applies to any commercial bank, savings bank, savings and loan association, building and loan association, homestead association (including cooperative banks), or credit union that meets the following criteria set forth in Regulation C: (1) total assets of more than $10 million on the preceding December 31; (2) a home office or any branch office located in a standard metropolitan statistical area as defined by the U.S. Office of Management and Budget; (3) not a state-chartered institution in a state exempted from HMDA by the Federal Reserve Board; and (4) the making of federally related mortgage loans. Regulation C defines a *federally related mortgage loan* as a first lien on residential real property designed for one to four families that is: (1) made by a depository institution that is insured or regulated by the federal government; (2) made, insured, or guaranteed by HUD or another federal agency; or (3) intended to be sold by the originating depository institution to FNMA, GNMA, or FHLMC, or to a financial institution from which it is to be purchased by FHLMC.

Fair Housing Act

The Fair Housing Act (FHA),[30] which is Title VIII of the Civil Rights Act of 1968, as amended, prohibits discrimination in housing on the basis of race, color, religion, sex, or national origin. Specifically, FHA outlaws discrimination in: (1) the sale or rental of housing, (2) the financing of housing, and (3) the provision of brokerage services, for example, the participation in a multiple-listing service. The prohibition against discrimination in the financing of housing applies to any bank, building and loan association, insurance company, or other entity in the business of making commercial real estate loans. Discrimination includes the denial of a loan on a prohibited basis or the discrimination on a prohibited basis in the fixing of the amount, interest rate, duration, or other terms or conditions of a loan. FHA also makes it unlawful to coerce, intimidate, threaten, or interfere with any person in the exercise of, or because they have exercised, rights granted by certain provisions of the FHA. FHA provides an exception to its prohibition on housing discrimination in the case of certain activities conducted by religious organizations or private clubs.

---

[29]12 C.F.R. § 203.1 *et seq.*
[30]42 U.S.C. § 3601 *et seq.*

Community Reinvestment Act of 1977

The Community Reinvestment Act of 1977 (CRA)[31] was enacted in response to the practice of redlining—the refusal by a lender to grant loans in certain neighborhoods. CRA applies to national banks, state-chartered banks that are members of the Federal Reserve System, bank holding companies, state-chartered nonmember banks and savings banks insured by the Federal Deposit Insurance Corporation (FDIC), savings and loan associations insured by the Federal Savings and Loan Insurance Corporation (FSLIC), and savings and loan holding companies. Under CRA, each institution is assigned an appropriate federal financial supervisory agency from among the Comptroller of the Currency, the Federal Reserve Board, the FDIC, or the FHLBB.

As part of its examination of each institution, the federal financial supervisory agency must "assess the institution's record of meeting the credit needs of its entire community, including low- and moderate-income neighborhoods, consistent with the safe and sound operation of such institution . . . ." The supervisory agency is also directed to consider such record in evaluating an institution's application for a *deposit facility*. *Deposit facilities* include national bank or federal savings and loan association charters, deposit insurance for certain newly chartered institutions, establishment of a domestic branch or other facility that accepts deposits, relocation of a home or branch office, and certain mergers, consolidations, acquisitions of assets, and assumptions of liabilities.

Each of the four supervisory agencies has adopted virtually identical regulations implementing CRA,[32] under which each regulated financial institution is required to prepare a map that delineates the local community or communities that comprise its entire community. These regulations define a *local community* as the "contiguous areas surrounding each office or group of offices, including any low- and moderate-income neighborhoods in those areas." Each institution is also required to adopt a CRA Statement for each delineated local community listing the specific types of credit within certain categories that the institution is prepared to extend within that community. The institution must also post a CRA notice, which advises the public that it may review and comment on the CRA Statement and may request announcement of applications covered by CRA. In addition, the institution must maintain, available for public inspection, a file that consists of recent CRA Statements, written comments by members of the public on the CRA Statements, and responses to such comments.

The regulations also specify those factors that the supervisory authority will consider in assessing the institution's record of performance in meeting the credit needs of its entire community. Some of these factors are: (1) the insti-

---

[31]12 U.S.C. § 2901 *et seq.*

[32]12 C.F.R. § 25.1 *et seq.* (Comptroller of the Currency), 12 C.F.R. § 228.1 *et seq.* (Federal Reserve Board), 12 C.F.R. § 345.1 *et seq.* (FDIC), and 12 C.F.R. § 563e.1 *et seq.* (FHLBB).

tution's activities to ascertain the credit needs of its community, (2) the extent of the programs to make the community aware of the credit services offered, (3) the geographic distribution of credit extensions and denials, (4) the opening and closing of offices, and (5) the origination of various types of loans within the community. The regulations specify that the institution's record of performance may be the basis for the denial of an application for specified depository facilities.[33]

Employee Retirement Income Security Act of 1974

Private pension plans, whose investments may include real estate mortgages, are governed by the Employee Retirement Income Security Act of 1974, as amended (ERISA).[34] ERISA protects the interests of pension participants and their beneficiaries by (1) providing: minimum standards for participation, vesting and funding; (2) requiring that information be disclosed to participants and beneficiaries; and (3) establishing standards of conduct, responsibility, and obligation for fiduciaries of employee benefit plans. ERISA is administered by the Department of Labor and the Internal Revenue Service.

Section 404 of ERISA sets forth the duties of fiduciaries of employee benefit plans. Fiduciaries must discharge their duties solely in the interest of the participants and beneficiaries for the exclusive purpose of: (1) providing benefits to participants and their beneficiaries and (2) defraying the reasonable administrative expenses of the plan. Fiduciaries are also subject to a "prudence" rule. They must discharge their duties "with the care, skill, prudence and diligence under the circumstances then prevailing that a prudent man acting in a like capacity and familiar with such matters would use in the conduct of an enterprise of a like character and with like aims."[35] In addition, fiduciaries are required to diversify the plan's investments in order to minimize the risk of large losses, unless to do so would be clearly imprudent. Finally, fiduciaries must discharge their duties in accordance with the plan's governing documentation as long as such documentation is consistent with certain provisions of ERISA.

---

[33]For example, regulations adopted by the Comptroller of the Currency require that the Comptroller assess (1) the applicant's record of performance in considering an application for conversion from a state bank charter to a national bank charter and (2) the applicant's proposed CRA Statement in considering an application for a national bank charter submitted by an applicant other than a state bank. 12 C.F.R. § 25.8 (b) and (c).

For a discussion of the impact of protests filed under CRA on the grant or denial of applications, see Eisman, "The Community Reinvestment Act in Perspective," 8 *Seller-Servicer* 18 (1981).

[34]29 U.S.C. § 1001 *et seq.* See Martell and Antsen, "A Mortgage Banker's Guide to ERISA," *Mortgage Banking,* Sept. 1984, at 8, for a discussion of the applicability of ERISA to transactions by a mortgage lending institution.

[35]The Department of Labor has adopted a regulation that provides a "safe harbor" for satisfying the requirements of the "prudence" rule. See 29 C.F.R. § 2550.404a-1.

Section 406 of ERISA specifies that certain transactions between a plan and a party in interest are prohibited, unless subject to an exemption.[36] (A *party in interest* is defined in Section 2(14) of ERISA to include, among others, any fiduciary of the employee benefit plan, a person providing services to the plan, an employer with any employees covered by the plan, and an employee of such employer.) The following transactions between a plan and a party in interest are prohibited: (1) the sale, exchange, or leasing of any property; (2) the lending of money or other extension of credit; and (3) the furnishing of goods, services, or facilities. In addition, fiduciaries are prohibited from engaging in any transaction involving: (1) the transfer to, or use by or for the benefit of, a party in interest, of any asset of the plan or (2) the acquisition, on behalf of the plan, of any employer security or employer real property in violation of other provisions of ERISA. Finally, fiduciaries are prohibited from engaging in transactions for their own benefit or transactions that are adverse to the interests of the plan or the interests of its participants or beneficiaries.

A plan's acquisition of mortgages might violate the prohibited transaction provisions because of certain relationships between the parties. For example, a plan's purchase of mortgage loans made to employees of the plan's contributing employer might violate the prohibitions against: (1) the lending of money or other extension of credit between a plan and a party in interest; and (2) a transfer to, or use by or for the benefit of, a party in interest, of any asset of the plan.[37] This type of transaction is covered by a class exemption issued by the Department of Labor.[38]

The Department of Labor has also issued a regulation that describes the

---

[36]See also § 4975 of the Internal Revenue Code of 1954 (Title II, Subtitle B of ERISA), which provides for a tax on certain transactions involving a plan and a disqualified person. The Department of Labor has granted both individual and class exemptions for certain transactions that would otherwise be prohibited by ERISA and the Internal Revenue Code of 1954. For example, Prohibited Transaction Exemption 84-14 provides a class exemption for various parties related to employee benefit plans to engage in transactions involving plan assets if certain conditions are satisfied. 49 Fed. Reg. 9494 (1984).

[37]See 46 Fed. Reg. 59335, 59337 (1981), which proposed a class exemption for transactions involving certain residential mortgage financing arrangements. The proposed exemption was modified and adopted in 1982 as Prohibited Transaction Exemption 82-87. See n. 38.

[38]See Prohibited Transaction Exemption 82-87, 47 Fed. Reg. 21331 (1982), which provides an exemption for the following transactions of employee benefit plans if certain conditions are met: (1) the issuance of commitments for the provision of mortgage financing to purchasers of residential dwelling units, (2) the receipt of a fee in exchange for the issuance of such commitment; (3) the making or purchase of loans or participation interests therein pursuant to such commitments; and (4) the direct making, purchase, sale, exchange, or transfer of mortgage loans or participation interests therein. One of the conditions requires that the mortgage loan be a "recognized mortgage loan," which is defined as a loan on a residential dwelling unit which, when originated, was eligible for purchase through an established program of FNMA, GNMA, or FHLMC. See also Prohibited Transaction Exemption 81-7, 46 Fed. Reg. 7520 (1981), which exempts, under certain conditions, transactions involving the acquisition and holding by employee benefit plans of certain mortgage-backed securities and the servicing and operation of mortgage pool investment trusts. This exemption was expanded and superseded by Prohibited Transaction Exemption 83-1, 48 Fed. Reg. 895 (1983).

assets that a plan is considered to own, for purposes of ERISA's fiduciary responsibility provisions, when it invests in certain guaranteed governmental mortgage pool certificates.[39] (The term *guaranteed governmental mortgage pool certificate* is defined to include a mortgage pool certificate with respect to which interest and principal payable pursuant to the certificate is guaranteed by FNMA, GNMA, or FHLMC.) The regulation states that the plan's assets include "the certificate and all of its rights with respect to such certificate under applicable law, but do not, solely by reason of the plan's holding of such certificate, include any of the mortgages underlying such certificate." If plan assets were deemed to include the underlying mortgages in the pool, the manager of such a pool might be a fiduciary with respect to the plan. (The term *fiduciary* is defined in ERISA to include persons who exercise authority or control respecting the management or disposition of plan assets.) Because of the regulation, however, the manager of a governmental mortgage pool would not be a fiduciary of the plan solely by reason of the plan's investment in the pool.

Securities Laws

Certain transactions involving mortgage-related securities are exempt from the registration provisions of the Securities Act of 1933 (Securities Act).[40] Section 4(5) of the Securities Act provides a registration exemption for the offer or sale of promissory notes, or participations in such notes, that are secured by first mortgages on commercial or residential real property and that are originated by a savings and loan association, savings bank, commercial bank, or similar banking institution supervised and examined by a federal or state authority. The availability of the exemption is subject to the fulfillment of three conditions: (1) the minimum aggregate sales price per purchaser may not be less than $250,000; (2) the purchaser must pay cash either at the time of sale or within 60 days thereafter; and (3) the purchaser must buy for his own account only. If the securities are originated by a HUD-approved mortgagee,[41] the registration exemption is available if the preceding three conditions are satisfied and if the offeree or purchaser is one of the institutions previously described, a supervised insurance company, FNMA, GNMA, or FHLMC.

In addition, the registration exemption applies to transactions involving nonassignable contracts to buy or sell the above-described mortgage-related securities, provided that: (1) the contracts are to be completed within two years, (2) the seller and purchaser are entities that qualify for the exemption, and (3) the three exemption-availability conditions described are fulfilled. Section 4(5) also

---

[39]29 C.F.R. § 2550.401b-1.

[40]15 U.S.C. § 77a *et seq.*

[41]Presumably, a HUD-approved mortgagee that is also one of the financial institutions previously described would need only comply with the registration exemption requirement applicable to such institutions, as described *supra*.

states that the exemption will apply to resales of the mortgage-related securities
only if certain specified conditions are satisfied.

Transactions in mortgage-related securities may also be exempt from registration if such securities are sold by an issuer in a private offering. Section 4(2)
of the Securities Act provides that transactions by an issuer not involving any
public offering are exempted transactions to which the registration provisions
of Section 5 of the Securities Act do not apply. Section 3(b) of the Securities
Act gives the Securities and Exchange Commission (SEC) authority to exempt
classes of securities by reason of the small amount involved or the limited
character of the public offering, but only if the offering of such securities does
not exceed $5 million. Regulation D, adopted by the SEC pursuant to Sections
3(b) and 4(2) of the Securities Act, establishes three exemptions from the registration requirements of the Securities Act. The regulation, which consists of
Rules 501–506, sets forth limitations (depending on the exemption) regarding
the aggregate offering price,[42] the manner of offering, the maximum number
and qualifications of the offerees, the furnishing of information, and the resale
of the securities.

Several rules adopted pursuant to the Securities Exchange Act of 1934 (Exchange Act)[43] also provide exemptions for mortgages and interests in mortgages. For example, Rule 3a12–1 states that mortgages sold by FHLMC are
exempt from the provisions of the Exchange Act, insofar as the Exchange Act
is inapplicable to exempted securities. In addition, Rule 3a12–4 provides that
certain mortgage securities are deemed exempted securities for the purpose of
certain Exchange Act provisions regarding the registration and regulation of
brokers and dealers.

Securities issued by certain participants in the secondary mortgage market
are also deemed to be exempted securities. Section 311 of the FNMA Charter
Act provides that securities issued by FNMA and GNMA are deemed to be
exempted securities within the meaning of laws administered by the SEC to the
same extent as securities that are direct obligations of, or obligations guaranteed as to principal or interest by, the United States.[44] Section 306(g) of the
FHLMC Act provides the same exemption for securities issued or guaranteed

---

[42]Transactions under Rule 506 are not subject to an aggregate offering price limitation as is the
case with transactions under Rule 504 ($500 thousand) and Rule 505 ($5 million).

[43]15 U.S.C. § 78a *et seq.* The Secondary Mortgage Market Enhancement Act of 1984, which
was enacted on October 3, 1984, amended the Exchange Act by adding the term "mortgage related
security" and providing that, subject to regulations adopted by the Federal Reserve Board, the
"forward trading of such securities for up to 180 days does not constitute an extension
of credit or borrowing for purposes of [Sections 7 and 8 of the Exchange Act.]"
H.R. Rep. No. 98-994, 98th Cong., 2d Sess. 12, *reprinted in* 1984 U.S. Code Cong. & Ad.
News 2827, 2833.

[44]12 U.S.C. § 1723c. Subsections 304(d) and (e) of the FNMA Charter Act also provide that
FNMA's mortgage-backed securities and subordinated obligations, respectively, are deemed to be
exempted securities. 12 U.S.C. § 1719(d) and (e). GNMA guarantees GNMA mortgage-backed
securities issued by others pursuant to Subsection 306(g)(1) of the FNMA Charter Act, which
provides that "[t]he full faith and credit of the United States is pledged to the payment of all

by FHLMC (other than securities guaranteed by FHLMC that are backed by mortgages not purchased by FHLMC).[45] Section 3(a)(2) of the Securities Act provides that, except as otherwise expressly provided, it is inapplicable to "[a]ny security issued or guaranteed by the United States . . . ." Section 3(a)(12) of the Exchange Act defines *exempted security* to include "securities which are direct obligations of, or obligations guaranteed as to principal or interest by, the United States . . . ." The exemption granted under these statutory sections, however, does not exempt issuers of the securities from the antifraud provisions of the federal securities laws (for example, Section 17 (a) of the Securities Act and Section 10(b) of the Exchange Act and Rule 10b–5 thereunder).

Chartering of Savings and Loan Associations

Section 5(a) of the Home Owners' Loan Act of 1933 (HOLA)[46] authorizes the FHLBB to issue charters to associations to be known as federal savings and loan associations and federal savings banks, which are to provide credit for housing.[47] In issuing such charters, the FHLBB is required to give "primary consideration to the best practices of thrift institutions in the United States." Section 5(e) of HOLA provides that a charter can be granted only if the following factors can be found to exist: (1) charter recipients are of good character and responsibility; (2) a necessity exists for such an institution in the community to be served; (3) there is a reasonable probability of the institution's usefulness and success; and (4) there will be a lack of undue injury to properly conducted existing local thrift and home-financing institutions resulting from the establishment of the proposed institution. Regulations adopted pursuant to HOLA set forth the forms of the charters that are issued to federal savings and loan associations and federal savings banks.[48]

Garn–St Germain Depository Institutions Act of 1982

Section 341 of the Garn–St Germain Depository Institutions Act of 1982 (Garn–St Germain Act)[49] governs the ability of mortgage lenders and their assignees and transferees to enforce due-on-sale clauses. A due-on-sale clause permits a lender to declare a mortgage note due and payable if the mortgaged

---

amounts which may be required to be paid under any guaranty under this subsection." 12 U.S.C. § 1721(g)(1)

[45]12 U.S.C. § 1455(g). Section 210 of the Secondary Mortgage Market Enhancement Act of 1984, Pub. L. No. 98–440, 98 Stat. 1689, 1697 (1984), subsequently added new Subsection 306(h), which specifically prohibits FHLMC from guaranteeing securities that are backed by mortgages not purchased by FHLMC. 12 U.S.C. § 1455(h).

[46]12 U.S.C. § 1464(a).

[47]FHLBB regulation of these institutions is discussed in Chapter 12.

[48]See 12 C.F.R. §§ 544.1 and 552.3.

[49]12 U.S.C. § 1701j-3.

property is sold or transferred without the lender's prior written consent.

The Garn–St Germain Act, subject to certain exceptions, preempts state statutory and case law that prohibits the enforcement of due-on-sale clauses. An exception to this preemption was provided for mortgage loans (originated by entities other than federal savings and loan associations and federal savings banks) made or assumed in certain states during the period beginning on the date the state, by statute or statewide court decision, prohibited the enforcement of due-on-sale clauses and ending on October 15, 1982, the effective date of the Garn–St Germain Act. These loans, known as *window period loans,* are subject to the state-law restrictions in force during the window period until October 15, 1985, unless the state acts to otherwise regulate these loans by that date. Mortgage lenders, however, may require any successor or transferee of the borrower to meet customary credit standards. In addition, the Garn–St Germain Act provides that, prior to October 15, 1985, the Comptroller of the Currency[50] and the National Credit Union Administration Board (NCUA Board)[51] may regulate, as otherwise authorized, such mortgage loans originated by national banks and federal credit unions, respectively.

The Garn–St Germain Act also enumerates the following nine circumstances under which lenders may not enforce due-on-sale clauses: (1) the creation of a subordinate lien without a transfer of rights of occupancy in the property; (2) the creation of a purchase-money security interest for household appliances; (3) the transfer by devise, descent, or operation of law on the death of a joint tenant or tenant by the entirety; (4) the granting of a leasehold interest of three years or less not containing an option to purchase; (5) the transfer to a relative resulting from the borrower's death; (6) the transfer to the borrower's spouse or children; (7) the transfer to the borrower's spouse pursuant to a decree of dissolution of marriage, legal separation agreement, or property settlement agreement; (8) the transfer into an inter vivos trust of which the borrower is, and remains, a beneficiary and which does not relate to a transfer of rights of occupancy in the property; and (9) transfers described in regulations prescribed by the FHLBB.[52]

Under Section 341(e)(1) of the Garn–St Germain Act, the FHLBB has adopted regulations governing the due-on-sale practices of federal associations and other lenders.[53] These regulations clarify various terms used in the Act. For example, they define *sale or transfer* of property broadly to include various

---

[50]The Comptroller of the Currency has adopted regulations governing the enforcement of due-on-sale clauses by national banks. 12 C.F.R. § 30.1.

[51]The NCUA Board has adopted regulations governing the enforcement of due-on-sale clauses by federal credit unions. 12 C.F.R. § 701.21-6(d).

[52]Subsequent legislation limits these exceptions to enforcing due-on-sale clauses to real property loans secured by liens on residential real property containing less than five dwelling units, including liens on the stock allocated to dwelling units in cooperative housing corporations, or on residential manufactured homes. Pub. L. No. 98–181, § 473, 97 Stat. 1155, 1237-38 (1983).

[53]12 C.F.R. § 591.1 - § 591.6. Certain provisions of the regulations do not apply to national banks and federal credit unions to the extent the Comptroller of the Currency and the NCUA Board adopt regulations governing due-on-sale enforcement.

categories of real estate financing techniques that have been used to circumvent the enforcement of due-on-sale clauses. Instead of listing the window period states, the regulations define two categories of state laws that create a window period. These are state laws that prohibit the unrestricted exercise of due-on-sale clauses by providing that a due-on-sale clause may be enforced only if: (1) the lender's security interest or likelihood of repayment is impaired or (2) the lender must accept an assumption without an interest-rate change or with an interest-rate change below the lender's current market interest rate for similar loans. The regulations also provide that the list of statutory restrictions on the exercise of due-on-sale clauses applies only to loans made on homes occupied or to be occupied by the borrower.

State Laws

Usury

Usury is the imposition or exaction of an interest rate in excess of that permitted by law. Most states have usury statutes that specify a maximum legal interest rate.[54] Some of the usury statutes provide exemptions for certain classes of lenders (savings and loan associations), certain types of loans (FHA-insured loans), or loans over a specified amount. In interpreting usury statutes, courts generally require that the following elements be present before they find a loan to be usurious: "(1) a loan or a forbearance, either express or implied, of money or its equivalent; (2) an understanding between the parties that the principal shall be repayable absolutely; (3) the exaction of a greater profit than is allowed by law; and (4) an intention to violate the law."[55] Penalties range from forfeiture of excess interest to forfeiture of all interest and principal.

Section 501 of Title V of the Depository Institutions Deregulation and Monetary Control Act of 1980 (DIDC)[56] establishes a federal preemption of state usury laws as they apply to first mortgage loans.[57] DIDC preempts state con-

---

[54]For a discussion of what charges exacted in connection with a mortgage loan are deemed to be interest, see *Usury Laws and Modern Business Transactions*, 73-149 (Practising Law Institute 1981), and Nosari and Lewis, "How Usury Laws Affect Real Estate Development," 9 *Real Est. L.J.* 30 (1980).

[55]Rollinger v. J.C. Penney Co., 86 S.D. 154, 158, 192 N.W.2d 699, 701 (1971). Some courts have found the required intent for a usury violation if the lender intended to exact interest and the rate of interest exceeds that permitted by law.

[56]Pub. L. No. 96-221, 94 Stat. 132, 161-63 (1980), 12 U.S.C. § 1735f-7 note.

[57]The National Bank Act provides that the maximum interest rate on loans made by national banks is the greater of (1) the interest rate allowed by the laws of the state in which the bank is located or (2) one percent above the Discount rate on 90-day commercial paper in effect at the Federal Reserve Bank in the Federal Reserve district where the bank is located. 12 U.S.C. § 85. Sections 521, 522, and 523 of Title V of DIDC provide a similar "most favored lender" status to FDIC-insured state banks, FSLIC-insured institutions, and federally insured credit unions, respectively. 12 U.S.C. §§ 183ld, 1730g (amended by Pub. L. No. 97-457, § 33, 96 Stat. 2507, 2511 (1983) to include FDIC-insured federal associations) and 1785 (g). States, however, may adopt laws overriding these preemptions.

stitutional and statutory provisions that limit the rate or amount of interest, discount points, finance charges, or other charges in connection with a loan secured by a first lien on: (1) residential real property, (2) all stock allocated to a dwelling unit in a residential cooperative housing corporation,[58] or (3) a residential manufactured home.[59] The preemption applies only to federally related mortgage loans, defined in Section 527(b) of the National Housing Act[60] as modified by Section 501(a)(1)(C) of DIDC, that are made after March 31, 1980.[61]

DIDC permitted states to override the preemption by specific action before April 1, 1983,[62] but such state action could not affect: (1) mortgages made pursuant to commitments entered into during the period from April 1, 1980 to the date of the state action and (2) mortgages that are rollovers of existing mortgages (as described in regulations of the FHLBB) that were made or committed to during the period from April 1, 1980 to the date of the state action. DIDC is implemented by regulations contained in 12 C.F.R., Part 590, promulgated by the FHLBB.

State Foreclosure Laws and the Uniform Land Transactions Act

A typical mortgage instrument contains a number of covenants, the default of which by the borrower gives the lender the right to declare the remaining amount of the mortgage loan due and payable. If the borrower does not pay this amount, the lender may elect to exercise its right to foreclose on the mortgaged property. The lender's right to foreclose, however, may be barred by the borrower's subsequent compliance with a state statute that specifies how the default may be cured and the mortgage reinstated.

State statutes specify the manner in which the mortgagee may foreclose on the mortgaged property. The most common method of foreclosure is by sale of

---

[58]Before the enactment of Section 324 of the Housing and Community Development Act of 1980, Pub. L. No. 96-399, 94 Stat. 1614, 1647-48 (1980), this category read as follows: "stock in a residential cooperative housing corporation where the loan . . . is used to finance the acquisition of such stock."

[59]The preemption applies to first liens on residential manufactured homes only if the terms and conditions of the loans comply with the consumer protection provisions in regulations adopted by the FHLBB. See 12 C.F.R. § 590.4.

[60]12 U.S.C. § 1735f-5(b).

[61]The Housing and Community Development Act of 1980, *supra* n. 58, expanded the federal preemption to apply also to certain loans made by individuals financing the sale or exchange of their owner-occupied residential real property. The Omnibus Budget Reconciliation Act of 1981, Pub. L. No. 97-35, § 384, 95 Stat. 357, 432 (1981), further expanded the preemption to such loans involving residential manufactured homes.

[62]The following jurisdictions have enacted laws specifically overriding the preemption: Colorado, Georgia, Hawaii, Iowa, Kansas, Massachusetts, Minnesota, Nebraska, Nevada, North Carolina, Puerto Rico, South Carolina, South Dakota, and Wisconsin. 5 *Fed. Banking L. Rep.* (CCH) ¶ 58,910.02. The DIDC also specifically permits states to adopt laws placing limitations on the discount points or such other charges on loans otherwise covered by the preemption.

the property, either pursuant to court order or a power-of-sale provision in the mortgage instrument. In states where the law requires a judicial foreclosure, the mortgagee must institute an action to foreclose the mortgage by filing a complaint or petition against the mortgagor and all other parties that have a right of redemption in the property. A court of equitable jurisdiction must then determine whether the mortgagee has the right to foreclose. If the court finds that a default has occurred, the court enters a decree or judgment that specifies the amount due the mortgagee, the period of redemption, and the period during which notice is to be given to the public that the property is to be publicly auctioned. Thereafter, the property is sold by an officer designated to conduct the sale. In states where the law permits foreclosure under a power-of-sale provision in the mortgage instrument, the property is publicly sold after the mortgagee gives notice of its intention to foreclose the mortgage. The mortgagor's only recourse in such a state is to petition the court for an injunction to prevent the proposed sale of his property.[63]

The Uniform Land Transactions Act (ULTA),[64] which was drafted by the National Conference of Commissioners on Uniform State Laws in 1975 and amended in 1977,[65] deals with foreclosure and other aspects of contractual transfers of real estate. One of the purposes of ULTA is "to provide uniformity in state law which will facilitate the creation of a legal atmosphere which encourages development of a widespread secondary mortgage market."[66]

ULTA consists of three articles: Article 1 contains definitions and general provisions, Article 2 deals with contracts for the sale and lease of real property, and Article 3 deals with security interests in real property.

Article 2 provides that contracts to convey real estate, to be judicially enforceable, must be evidenced by a writing signed by the party against whom enforcement is sought. However, there are certain exceptions. For example, if the buyer has taken possession of the real estate and has paid all or part of the contract price, the contract to convey need not be in writing. A contract to convey does not fail for indefiniteness, even though one of its terms is left for future agreement of the parties, as long as there is a reasonably certain basis for giving an appropriate remedy.

Article 2 also specifies the rights and obligations of the parties to a real estate contract. A seller in a contract to convey real estate (other than a leasehold) must: (1) provide marketable title at the time of the conveyance, (2) give

---

[63]The preceding discussion was drawn from Madway, "A Mortgage Foreclosure Primer," 8 *Clearinghouse Rev.* 146 (1974).

[64]At the time of this writing, no state has adopted either ULTA or the Uniform Simplification of Land Transfers Act, discussed *infra*. These laws, however, are indicative of the reforms needed in the laws governing contractual transfers of real estate as well as the laws governing the recording of instruments and rules of priority among conflicting interests in real property.

[65]The American Bar Association approved ULTA in 1978. Copies of ULTA may be obtained from the National Conference of Commissioners on Uniform State Laws, 645 N. Michigan Ave., Chicago, Illinois 60611.

[66]ULTA, Commissioners' Prefatory Note 2.

a deed that contains certain implied warranties, and (3) transfer possession of the property if a possessory interest is being conveyed. A buyer has the right to revoke acceptance of the real estate in case the seller substantially breaches the contract. Revocation must occur within specified time frames and before there is any substantial adverse change to the real estate other than that caused by the breach. If the buyer materially breaches the contract, the seller's remedies include: (1) reselling the real estate and recovering the amount by which the unpaid contract price exceeds the resale price, plus the excess of any incidental and consequential damages over any expenses avoided because of the buyer's breach; (2) recovering damages; or (3) recovering the contract price in certain cases. In case of the seller's failure to convey, the buyer: (1) may recover any part of the contract price already paid and (2) is generally entitled to damages equal to the difference between the fair market value at the time for conveyance specified in the contract and the contract price, plus the excess of any incidental and consequential damages over any expenses avoided because of the seller's breach. In the alternative, the buyer is entitled to specific performance. The buyer is also entitled to a recordable lien against the real estate if the nonconveying seller wrongfully refuses to return any part of the contract price paid by the buyer. The statute of limitations provides a six-year period for suits for the breach of any obligation arising out of either a contract to convey or a conveyance; however, the parties to the transaction may by contract reduce the period to not less than one year.

Article 3 governs security interests in real property. Its three requirements for creating a security interest are: (1) a security agreement containing a description of the collateral and signed by the debtor, (2) value given, and (3) an interest in the collateral by the debtor. The article provides that as between unrecorded security interests, the first to attach has priority. In addition, it sets forth rules regarding the priority of future advances made pursuant to a recorded security interest.

In order to achieve uniformity in the area of interest-rate calculation, Article 3 specifies items that are to be considered part of the finance charge. It also requires that an actuarial method of computation be used in allocating payments between interest and the amount financed. Article 3 specifically fails to set a maximum finance charge, except as to real estate transactions involving specified protected parties.

In the event of the debtor's default, Article 3 provides rules governing the rights of the secured party, who may sue on the debtor's personal obligation, if any, and foreclose the security interest. Before a secured party forecloses, the debtor is entitled to receive detailed notice of the secured party's intention to foreclose. Where the parties' agreement provides for foreclosure by exercise of a power of sale, the foreclosure must be conducted in a reasonable manner, including prior notification of the intended sale to the debtor and other persons having an interest in the real estate. In foreclosure by judicial proceeding, the court enters a judgment for the amount due and prescribes how the court official is to conduct the sale. Regardless of the mode of foreclosure, the debtor is liable for a deficiency judgment unless: (1) the debtor is a *protected party*[67] under ULTA and (2) the obligation secured is a purchase-money security interest. ULTA provides for no right of redemption after sale of the property. However, the debtor in default is given the right to cure his default prior to: (1) the execution of a contract for sale or sale of the secured property under a power of sale or (2) before the time specified in a decree of judicial foreclosure.

Doing Business

Corporations that engage in mortgage activities out of state may be subject to the various state *doing business* statutes. Whether a particular activity such as the purchase or sale of mortgages out of state constitutes doing business depends on the applicable state statutes and judicial decisions.

> 'Doing business' may involve buying and selling (anything), suing or defending a suit, maintaining offices or agents, lending and borrowing, transferring securities, opening bank or savings association accounts, making other investments, owning or leasing land, participating in joint ventures, or making a contract of any nature. On the other hand, any one of these activities may *not* be deemed the 'doing of business.'[68]

If a particular activity constitutes doing business in a state, then an out-of-state corporation must obtain permission to carry out such activity in the foreign state. Usually, such permission takes the form of a certificate of authority to do business within the state. Doing business in a state without the necessary qualification to do so can subject a corporation to a number of penalties, which may include denial of access to the foreign state's courts, inability to enforce the corporation's contracts (foreclosure of mortgages, for example), and liability of the corporation's officers and directors. In addition, a corporation doing business in a foreign state, whether qualified or not, may be liable for taxes on the corporation's business activities in the foreign state.[69]

As a result of its study of the various doing business laws, the U.S. League of Savings Associations has compiled a summary chart of activities in which

---

[67]Section 1-203(a) of ULTA defines "protected party" as follows:

> (1) an individual who contracts to give a real estate security interest in, or to buy or to have improved, residential real estate all or a part of which he occupies or intends to occupy as a residence; (2) a person obligated primarily or secondarily on a contract to buy or to have improved residential real estate or on an obligation secured by residential real estate if, at the time he becomes obligated, that person is related to an individual who occupies or intends to occupy all or a part of the real estate as a residence; or (3) with respect to a security agreement, an individual who acquires residential real estate and assumes or takes subject to the obligation of a prior protected party under the real estate security agreement.

[68]Prather, "What Constitutes 'Doing Business,'" XXV *Legal Bulletin* 65, 67 (1959).

[69]The preceding discussion was based on "Savings Associations, Service Corporations, and the 'Doing Business' Laws," XLIX *Legal Bulletin* 173 (1983).

an out-of-state savings association may engage with reasonable safety in the 50 states and the District of Columbia.[70] The chart categorizes the jurisdictions according to whether the following activities of an out-of-state savings and loan association carried on in the state constitute the doing of business in that state: (1) making loans, including participations therein; (2) purchasing locally originated loans or participations therein; or (3) utilizing the collection procedure, especially foreclosure. The chart indicates that 21 states and the District of Columbia consider the making of loans in the jurisdiction to be doing business there, but that out-of-state entities can purchase loans and collect payments on them without being considered to be doing business in the state.

Securities

All of the states have enacted blue sky laws, which regulate the offer and sale of securities on the state level, and certain states have enacted laws that specifically govern the offer and sale of securities backed by real estate or mortgages.[71] In a majority of the states, the blue sky law is the Uniform Securities Act (the Act) or a modification thereof.[72] The Act, which was adopted by the National Conference of Commissioners on Uniform State Laws in 1956 and thereafter amended, consists of four parts: (1) fraudulent and other prohibited practices; (2) registration of broker-dealers, agents, and investment advisers; (3) registration of securities; and (4) general provisions.

Part III of the Act provides that "[i]t is unlawful for any person to offer or sell any security in this state unless (1) it is registered under this act or (2) the security or transaction is exempted under [this act]." There are three types of registration: by notification, coordination, or qualification. Registration by notification is available for any security whose issuer has been in continuous operation for at least five years and satisfies certain requirements regarding: (1) the absence of default in the payment of principal, interest, or dividends on securities with a fixed maturity or a fixed interest or dividend provision and (2) specified average net earnings. This type of registration becomes effective two business days after the filing of the registration statement, subject to certain exceptions.

Registration by coordination is available for any security for which a regis-

---

[70]*Id.* at 177.

[71]See N.Y. Gen. Bus. Law § 352–e and N.J. Stat. Ann. § 49:3–27 *et seq.*, which govern real estate syndication offerings. The recently enacted Secondary Mortgage Market Enhancement Act of 1984 exempts (1) securities offered and sold pursuant to Section 4(5) of the Securities Act and (2) "mortgage related securities" (as defined in newly added Section 3(a)(41) of the Exchange Act) from state laws requiring registration or qualification of securities or real estate to the same extent as any obligation issued by, or guaranteed as to principal and interest by, the United States or any agency or instrumentality thereof. States may override this preemption by statute no later than October 2, 1991.

[72]The Act, as amended is reprinted in VII *Martindale-Hubbell Law Directory* Part VI 199 *et seq.* (1984).

tration statement under the Securities Act has been filed with the SEC in connection with the same offering. This type of registration becomes effective when the federal registration statement becomes effective, if certain conditions are satisfied. Finally, registration by qualification is available for any security. This type of registration becomes effective when the state securities administrator so orders.

The Act provides certain exemptions from the registration requirement for specified securities and for specified transactions. Included among the exempted securities are: (1) any security issued or guaranteed by the United States, by any state, or by any agency or instrumentality thereof and (2) any security listed on one of the specified stock exchanges. The transactions that are exempt include: (1) any transaction in an evidence of indebtedness that is secured by a real estate mortgage if the entire mortgage, together with the evidence of indebtedness, is offered and sold as a unit; (2) any offer or sale to a bank, savings institution, trust company, insurance company, investment company, pension or profit-sharing trust, or other financial institution; and (3) any transaction pursuant to an offer directed to not more than ten persons, subject to certain conditions.[73]

Lending Powers of State Savings and Loan Associations

Savings and loan associations in all the states are authorized to make loans on the security of residential real estate. This authority, however, is limited in most states by requirements regarding loan-to-value ratio, maximum loan maturity, maximum amount of the loan, and prescribed lending area. Some state statutes provide that a savings association may make loans that do not conform to the basic requirements up to a specified percentage of the association's assets. Other states have followed the approach of the Model Savings Association Act, which requires savings associations to maintain at least 60 percent of their nonliquid assets in first-lien direct-reduction real estate loans on home and primarily residential properties, subject to certain restrictions. The remaining portion of the association's nonliquid assets (liquid assets must comprise 5 percent of the association's savings liabilities) may be invested in other real estate loans, subject only to the statutory limitation on loans to one borrower and specified sound lending standards.

In a majority of states, savings associations are specifically authorized by statute to make construction loans. Nearly all the states also specifically authorize savings associations to invest in U.S. government guaranteed and insured loans (such as loans guaranteed by the Administrator of Veterans' Affairs or insured by the Federal Housing Administrator). In addition, most state savings

---

[73]See Maloney, "Blue Sky Regulation of Federally Exempt Offerings: An Update," 16 *Rev. Sec. Reg.* 977 (1983), for the status of state exemptions available for offerings exempt from federal securities law registration under Regulation D.

associations are authorized to purchase and sell loans, subject to the condition that an association may purchase only loans that it could make.[74]

A number of state legislatures have adopted statutes designed to give state associations parity with federal associations. The impetus for such parity legislation is the desire to make state savings associations competitive with federal savings and loan associations operating in the same state. The statutes vary in the degree to which parity is accorded to the state savings association. For example, the Arizona parity statute confers upon federally insured state associations the same rights, powers, and privileges as those of federal associations doing business in Arizona. (Ariz. Rev. Stat. Ann. § 6–402B.) The Wyoming parity statute grants the state association all the powers of federal associations, but provides that the state examiner of savings associations may restrict or limit such powers. (Wyo. Stat. § 13–7–102(b).) The Hawaii parity statute authorizes state associations that are members of the Federal Home Loan Bank to exercise all the rights and privileges of local federal associations, subject to the prior consent of the state regulatory authority. (Hawaii Rev. Stat. § 407–55.) The Ohio parity statute is an example of the most common type of parity statute. It permits the state regulatory authority to grant to state associations, by rule, any of the rights or powers possessed by local federal associations. (Ohio Rev. Code Ann. § 1155.18.)[75]

A number of states that permit savings associations to make adjustable-rate mortgages (mortgages whose interest rates change, based on a predetermined index such as the six-month Treasury bill rate, the rate for three-year Treasury securities, or the lender's cost of funds) subject such mortgage loans to a number of conditions. For example, several states place legal restrictions on adjustable mortgage loans that allow negative amortization. (*Negative amortization* is the increase of the unpaid principal balance of a loan by the amount by which the interest due on the loan exceeds the loan payments.) Many state statutes also limit other aspects of adjustable-rate mortgages, such as providing ceilings on interest-rate increases and limiting the indices that may be used as the basis for interest-rate adjustments.

Title VIII of the Garn–St Germain Act indirectly preempts state laws governing adjustable-rate mortgages by providing that nonfederally chartered housing creditors may make, purchase, and enforce alternative mortgage instruments if such instruments conform with regulations issued by certain federal

---

[74]The preceding discussion was drawn from Harth and Weeks, "Statutory Lending Powers of State Savings Associations," XXXVI *Legal Bulletin* 179 (1970), and "Model Savings Association Act," XLV *Legal Bulletin* 181 (1979). See "Savings Association Legislation and Litigation—1982," XLVIII *Legal Bulletin* 251 (1982), for a discussion of recent changes in the lending powers of certain state savings associations.

[75]See " 'Tie-in' Statutes: State-by-State Study," XLIX *Legal Bulletin* 45 (1983), and " 'Tie-in' Statutes: State-by-State Study Supplemented," XLIX *Legal Bulletin* 182 (1983), for a study of the various state parity statutes.

agencies.[76] States may override Title VIII by specific action before October 15, 1985, but such state action may not affect: (1) mortgages made pursuant to an agreement entered into during the period from October 15, 1982 to the date of the state action and (2) renewals, extensions, refinancings, or other modifications of the mortgages that were entered into during the period from October 15, 1982 to the date of the state action.

Chartering

Various state laws authorize the creation of such financial institutions as state banks and state savings and loan associations. In order to operate, such institutions must be granted charter approval by the appropriate regulatory authority (the state banking board, the superintendent or commissioner for state banks, or the superintendent or commissioner for savings and loan associations.)[77]

For example, the Ohio superintendent of building and loan associations must examine all the facts regarding the formation of a proposed building and loan association prior to the recordation of the association's articles of incorporation by the secretary of state. The superintendent is empowered to refuse to certify the articles of incorporation if, among other things, "the character and general fitness of the persons proposed as incorporators in such corporation are not such as to command the confidence of the community in which such corporation is proposed to be located, [and] the public convenience and advantage will not be promoted by its establishment . . . ." (Ohio Rev. Code Ann. §1151.03.) If the association does not commence business within one year of the issuance of its articles of incorporation, the association will cease to exist and the articles will become void. In addition, the state statute specifies capital and other requirements that must be met in order for a building and loan association to commence business in Ohio.[78]

Uniform Simplification of Land Transfers Act

The Uniform Simplification of Land Transfers Act (USOLTA) was drafted and approved by the National Conference of Commissioners on Uniform State

---

[76]12 U.S.C. §3801 *et seq.* An example of an "alternative mortgage transaction" is "a loan . . . secured by an interest in residential real property . . . in which the interest rate or finance charge may be adjusted or renegotiated." Alternative mortgage instruments of (1) state-chartered banks, (2) state-chartered credit unions, and (3) all other nonfederally chartered housing creditors, including savings and loan associations, mutual savings banks, and savings banks, must comply with the applicable regulations of the Comptroller of the Currency, NCUA Board, and FHLBB, respectively, in order for the preemption to apply.

[77]See *Issues in Financial Regulation* 6 (F. Edwards ed. 1979).

[78]See "Regulating State Chartered Savings Associations: An Introduction to the Ohio Scheme," 11 Akron L. Rev. 399 (1978), for a comprehensive discussion of the chartering of building and loan associations under Ohio law.

Laws in 1976 and amended in 1977.[79] The purposes of USOLTA include
"the furtherance of the security and certainty of land titles, the reduction of
the costs of land transfers, the balancing of the interests of all parties in the
construction lien area, and the creation of a more efficient system of public land
records."[80]

USOLTA consists of seven articles. Article 1 contains definitions and general provisions. Article 2, which deals with the conveyancing and recording of
land transfers, provides that a conveyance is effective if it: (1) reasonably identifies the grantor, grantee, and property; (2) contains a manifestation of an
intent to make a present transfer; and (3) is in writing and signed by the grantor. A deed delivered by an escrow agent to a good faith purchaser for value
is effective against third parties, even though such delivery is in violation of
the grantor's instruction. Article 2 also provides that a grantor may convey
directly to himself and another, thereby eliminating the requirement under
common law for an intermediate conveyance to a "strawman."

Pursuant to Article 2, a document may be recorded if it is capable of being
processed by the recording office's equipment, is accompanied by the proper
recording fee, and includes specified indexing information. The document need
not be witnessed or acknowledged. Certain presumptions, such as the genuine-
ness of the document and the voluntariness thereof, are created by the recordation of a signed document pertaining to title to real estate. The article also
provides for the recording of affidavits containing facts relating to real estate,
its use, or its ownership.

Article 3 establishes priorities and provides for marketable record title and
extinguishment of claims. Documents must be referred to in other documents
by their record location in order to be in the record chain of title. A person has
a marketable record title to property, subject only to specified claims, if the
person has an unbroken chain of title for 30 years or more. Technical defects
in a signed real estate document are cured by the lapse of one year from the
date of recording.

Article 4 deals with the recording of statutory liens and pending judicial
proceedings. Article 5 replaces existing state mechanics' lien laws. Pursuant to
this article, any person who furnishes material or services under a contract for
the improvement of real estate has the right to a construction lien against the
real estate to the extent provided in the article. An owner may record a *notice
of commencement,* which acts as a notice to third parties that construction liens
may be claimed against the real estate. A lien claimant's priority then begins
on the date such notice is recorded if the lien claimant records his lien during
the effective period of the notice of commencement. The article permits the

---

[79]As mentioned in n. 64, no state has adopted USOLTA at the time of writing. Copies of
USOLTA may be obtained from the National Conference of Commissioners on Uniform State
Laws, 645 N. Michigan Ave., Chicago, Illinois 60611.

[80]USOLTA, Prefatory Note 3.

state to adopt one of two alternatives concerning the liability of the owner for the payment of the lien.

Article 6 contains instructions to recording officers for the maintenance of geographic indices of public land records. Article 7 specifies the effective date of USOLTA and identifies those statutes that are repealed by the adoption of USOLTA.

Uniform Condominium Act

The creation of condominiums is governed by state statutes in each of the 50 states. The various state statutes differ in terminology and detail, thereby "[making] it difficult for a national lender to assess the appropriateness of condominium documents and of condominium financing arrangements . . . ."[81] In response to the differing condominium statutes, the National Conference of Commissioners on Uniform State Laws drafted and approved the Uniform Condominium Act (UCA),[82] which is designed to unify and modernize the law of condominiums. The original version of UCA, which was promulgated in 1977,[83] has been enacted into law in Minnesota, Pennsylvania, and West Virginia. UCA was amended in 1980 and in its amended form was enacted into law in Maine, Missouri, Nebraska, New Mexico, and Rhode Island.[84]

UCA consists of five articles. Article 1 contains definitions and general provisions governing such matters as taxation, applicability of local ordinances, and eminent domain. The term *condominium* is defined to mean "real estate, portions of which are designated for separate ownership and the remainder of which is designated for common ownership solely by the owners of those portions. Real estate is not a condominium unless the undivided interests in the common elements are vested in the unit owners." Each unit, together with its interest in common elements, constitutes a separate parcel of real estate, with certain exceptions, for tax purposes. Local ordinances are expressly prohibited from discriminating against the condominium form of ownership.

Article 2 provides for the creation, alteration, and termination of the condominium. A developer may create a condominium only by executing and recording a declaration that must contain certain information. Specifically, the declaration must state, among other things, the maximum number of units that may be created, any development rights reserved by the developer, and any restrictions on the use, occupancy, and alienation of the units.

---

[81]Uniform Condominium Act, Prefatory Note 1.

[82]Copies of UCA may be obtained from the National Conference of Commissioners on Uniform State Laws, 645 N. Michigan Ave., Chicago, Illinois 60611.

[83]The American Bar Association approved UCA in 1978.

[84]Because the Virginia condominium law resembles UCA in most major respects, the Uniform Law Commissioners recognize Virginia as having enacted a "substantially similar" version of the 1980 UCA.

Article 3 requires that a unit owners' association be established to manage the condominium. The article details the powers of the association and also delineates the association's tort and contract liability and its obligation to obtain insurance. In addition, the article establishes the association's right to have a lien on a condominium unit for unpaid assessments or fines.

Article 4 specifies the consumer protection measures that must be afforded to condominium unit purchasers. Pursuant to this article, the developer must prepare a detailed public offering statement before offering any interest in a condominium unit to the public. If this statement is not delivered to the purchaser more than 15 days before the execution of the purchase contract, the purchaser may cancel the contract within 15 days after receipt of the statement, but before the conveyance of the unit. The article also specifies the information that the unit owner must give to a purchaser in the event of resale of a unit.

Article 4 also deals with condominium conversions. Residential tenants must be given at least 120 days' notice to vacate if their building is being converted to condominiums. The tenants must also be afforded the right to purchase their units during the 60-day period following the notice to vacate. If a tenant declines to purchase his unit on the terms offered, the developer may not offer the unit at a lower price or upon more favorable terms to a third party for at least 180 days.

Article 5 is an optional article that establishes an administrative agency to regulate the activities of condominium developers.

—— Chapter 10 ——————————————

The Regulatory Environment: An Overview

Peter E. Kaplan
Partner
Witkowski, Weiner, McCaffrey & Brodsky, P.C.

Elizabeth B. Qutb
Staff Vice President, Mortgage Finance Division
National Association of Home Builders

Introduction

From its inception, the secondary mortgage market has had a close federal nexus. Even today that market is still primarily federalized. As such, it is a regulated market, but not necessarily in the classic sense of that term. The major product, FHA and VA mortgages, is regulated, yet the major originators of that product, mortgage banking companies, enjoy only minimal direct regulation, particularly when compared to the real estate activities of commercial banks and thrift institutions. HUD, in fact, classifies most mortgage bankers as unsupervised lenders. The major secondary market entities—those institutions that purchase the mortgage product—are either federal or quasi-federal agencies. Thus, their requirements and procedures are inherently regulatory in nature. Yet, they would be the last to characterize themselves as regulators.

Many of the laws and regulations that apply to secondary market transactions are not limited solely to such transactions, but have equal impact upon primary market transactions as well. An FHA loan, originated by a lender to be held in portfolio, is, for the most part, treated no differently from a regulatory standpoint than a loan sold in the secondary market. Furthermore, most loans are originated in conformance with secondary market standards even though they may never leave the lender's portfolio. Obviously, there are some regulations that only apply to secondary market transactions. With more than half of all loans now being sold in the secondary market these regulations will take on increasing importance.

What follows below is not intended to even highlight all the major regulations with which secondary market participants need be concerned, but rather to give a flavor of the all-pervasive regulatory framework that envelopes that market. New participants should not be deterred, however, merely forewarned.

PRIMARY REGULATORS

Depository Institutions

Depository institutions are the most closely and strictly regulated of all financial firms, and generally fall under the jurisdiction of two or more regulatory authorities. The financial condition of banks and thrifts is the foremost object of regulatory scrutiny, the goal of which is to protect depositors. Regulatory examination and supervision are intended to ensure to the greatest extent possible the safety and soundness of the institution, with consequent emphasis on liquidity, net worth, capital resources, reserves, and general financial strength. Consequently, virtually all ongoing depository institutions find that they also meet the capital requirements necessary to participate in the secondary markets as HUD-approved mortgagees or as FNMA- or FHLMC-approved seller/servicers. Banks and thrifts may encounter limitations, however, on their investments in real estate loans, since regulators view control over investments as the key to controlling risk to the institution. Thus, depository institutions experience greater constraints in choosing and developing product lines than most other mortgagees.

Savings Institutions

The Federal Home Loan Bank board regulates all federally chartered savings and loan associations, and through its subsidiary, the Federal Savings and Loan Insurance Corporation, all FSLIC-insured state-chartered S&Ls. All 50 states also have state savings (and loan) association commissioners or their equivalents (District of Columbia S&Ls are all federally chartered. Minnesota anticipated dissolution of its state commission in 1982 after its remaining state S&Ls converted to federal charters.) Four states maintain their own deposit insurance funds for state-chartered thrift institutions: Massachusetts, Ohio, North Carolina, and Maryland.

Mutual savings banks, which operate in only 12 states, are traditionally state-chartered and regulated. They may be insured by a state fund or by the FDIC. They are eligible for membership in the Federal Home Loan Bank System, and in 1980, the FHLBB was authorized to grant federal charters for savings banks.

Federal S&Ls and FSLIC-insured state S&Ls must maintain a net worth within a statutory range of 3 to 5 percent of qualified assets, this range having been set by the FSLIC. (In 1982, FSLIC lowered the minimum from 4 percent to 3 percent.) Quarterly reports must be submitted to the FHLBB and FSLIC, and all institutions are subject to semiannual audits. In addition, the FSLIC prescribes accounting procedures which S&Ls must follow.

In August 1982, the FHLBB home-lending rules for federal S&Ls were largely deregulated, enabling S&Ls to originate virtually all types of loans already introduced, as well as virtually any type of loan that might be introduced in the future. Savings and loan associations were permitted to purchase or sell any whole loan or participation interest which they could legally originate. These regulations were amended in May 1983 to implement the broad new powers granted to federally chartered thrifts in Title III of the Garn–St Germain Depository Institutions Act of 1982 (DIA); part of an effort to strengthen home mortgage lenders and ensure the availability of mortgage credit.

DIA provided that federal associations may make "loans on the security of liens upon residential or nonresidential real property," subject to a forty percent-of-assets limitation for investments in nonresidential real property. *Residential real estate* (or *residential real property*) includes homes, multifamily dwellings, combinations of either of these, business property, farm residences, combinations of farm residences and commercial farm real estate, and property that will be improved by the construction of such structures. *Nonresidential real estate* (or *nonresidential real property*) includes all other real estate.

A federal association may now originate, invest in, sell, purchase, service, or participate in real estate loans subject to the limitations of the HOLA (Home Owners' Loan Act of 1933) and Part 545. The final regulations expressly include the brokerage and warehousing of loans within the authority to otherwise deal in real estate loans in order to clarify that such activities are permissible.

In addition, the regulations allow an association to adjust the interest rate, payment, balance, or term to maturity on a real estate loan (other than a home loan secured by borrower-occupied property) to the extent permitted by the loan contract. The FHLBB's amendments to the real estate lending regulations imposed limitations on the adjustments that an association could make on any home loan. The final amendments provide that only those home loans that are secured by borrower-occupied property are subject to the regulatory limitations on adjustments. For all other real estate loans, adjustments are a matter to be negotiated and incorporated into the loan contract.

A loan will be considered to be secured by real estate if: (1) the security property is real estate under state law, (2) the association's security interest may be enforced as a real estate mortgage or its equivalent under state law, (3) the security property is capable of being separately appraised, and (4) the association relies substantially on real estate as primary security for the loan. If the security property is a leasehold or another interest for a term of years, it must extend or be subject to extension at the option of the association for at least five years beyond maturity of the loan. Under the revised regulation, an association may make a real estate loan on the security of a time-share unit if the security property is real estate under state law.

Several provisions of Part 545 prescribe various terms and conditions for *home loans*, a subset of the real estate lending category. A home loan is defined as one made on the security of homes, including a unit of a condominium or cooperative, a combination of homes and business property, farm residences, and commercial farm real estate, and the regulation states the applicable limitations. The existing maximium term of 40 years for a home loan still applies, as does the requirement for semiannual payments of interest, except as expressly authorized. Home loans must be repaid in semiannual installments, except for those loans that are nonamortizing (interest-only loans), or that are line-of-credit loans. Nonamortizing loans, by their nature, require no repayments of principal until maturity.

A home loan may be fully amortizing (principal payments made over the term of the loan), partially amortizing (balloon loan), nonamortizing (interest-only loan), or a line-of-credit loan (either an open-end or closed-end loan). In addition, the loan contract may provide for negative amortization of a portion of the interest on a loan, or of all interest (a reverse-annuity mortgage).

An association may also receive part of the consideration for making a home loan in the form of a share of the property's appreciation since origination. The loan-to-value provisions that are applicable to home loans provide that, at origination, the ratio may not exceed 100 percent of the appraised value of the property. Loans originated in excess of 90 percent of the value must contain private mortgage insurance for the value of the loan that exceeds 80 percent, and board-of-director approval is required. During the loan term the ratio may increase above the limits if the increase is due to an adjustment (these are discussed below), but the ratio generally may not increase above 125 percent of the original value of the security property as a result of such adjustments.

The FHLBB promulgated regulations allowing adjustments to the terms of home loans, subject to certain conditions, with limitations that were deemed necessary when the loan is secured by the borrower's residence. For such home loans, the adjustments to the interest rate, payment balance, or term must be made in compliance with the regulations.

In connection with multifamily dwellings and nonresidential real estate, DIA deleted the statutory requirement that loans on the security of nonresidential real estate must be secured by a first lien, and allowed investment in such property to 40 percent of an association's assets.

The loan-to-value ratio requirements for each of these types of loans may not exceed the limits established by the association's directors. If the loan exceeds 90 percent, however, it must also be approved by the directors. The loan term may not exceed 30 years, except that nonamortized loans (interest-only loans) must be repaid within 5 years.

Construction loans on nonresidential real estate must be repayable within six years, making the period the same as for multifamily dwelling construction loans. The regulation requires semiannual payment of interest, except to the extent that the loan contract provides for negative amortization. The ratio of the loan balance to the initial appraised value of the property, however, may not exceed 100 percent as a result of any negative amortization.

FS&L Service Corporations and Holding Company Subsidiaries

A federal S&L may invest up to 3 percent of its assets in service corporations to be owned, either wholly or jointly, with other S&Ls. The activities of service corporations are regulated by the FHLBB. These corporations may engage in any activity which is permissible for the parent, as well as in additional activities that are reasonably related to the business of the parent. Thus, service corporations enjoy greater flexibility in lending and product expansion, in both residential and income-property activities. Until recently, a service corporation could operate only in the state of the parent (or multiple parents within the same state). Currently, however, all geographic restrictions for service corporations have been removed.

Permissible activities of multi-S&L holding company subsidiaries are regulated by the FHLBB, which has the authority to examine them. Although single-S&L holding companies and their affiliates were exempt from FHLBB regulatory overview, § 335 of the Garn–St Germain Act provided a three-year period during which such entities will become subject to the requirements applicable to multi-S&L holding companies.

Banks

General Supervision.   Almost all banks are regulated by at least one of the federal agencies: the Office of the Comptroller of the Currency (the OCC) for national banks; the Board of Governors of the Federal Reserve System (insured state member banks); and the Federal Deposit Insurance Corporation (insured state nonmember banks and savings banks). These three agencies operate independently of one another. State banks are additionally subject to the regulations of 50 state banking commissioners or their counterparts (all District of Columbia institutions are federally chartered).

Minimum net capitalization for a national bank is generally $1,000,000, although the OCC may require more, or, occasionally, less (the statutory minimum is $100,000). State banks can be chartered with as little as $25,000 capitalization, but generally their capital requirements range between $100,000 and $500,000. National banks must accumulate unimpaired surplus up to 20 percent of paid-in-capital prior to commencing business. All banks are required to increase their unimpaired surplus accounts by a certain percentage each year, generally by one-tenth of 1 percent of their net profits.

The FDIC insures almost all banks in the country and monitors net worth requirements according to a system for grading a bank's financial strength. Generally, banks are expected to maintain a net worth of 5 percent of assets. Additionally, the Federal Reserve requires member banks to maintain reserves, the level of which is set by regulation.

Virtually all banks are required to submit quarterly (semiannual for some states) *call reports* of condition and operations to the OCC, the Federal Reserve, the FDIC, or the state banking commissioners, or any combination of these. The OCC is required to examine its banks twice each year, of which one examination in each two-year period may be waived. Most states require a minimum of one examination per year, usually two. The Federal Reserve must examine state member banks, but may waive this requirement where it deems state examination to be sufficient. Even at that, the Fed usually performs its own examination every 1–3 years. FDIC usually performs an annual examination of insured banks, and may do so more frequently if a bank's financial condition warrants.

Real Estate Authority. Prior to the October 15, 1982 enactment of the Garn–St Germain Depository Institutions Act, national banks were subject to a variety of restrictions, including loan-to-value ratios, amortization requirements, maturity requirements, and limitations on the aggregate amount of loans secured by real estate that a national bank could make. The Garn–St Germain Act deleted the language of old Section 24 of the Federal Reserve Act (12 U.S.C. 371), thereby removing all statutory restrictions on real estate loans, and instead, authorized national banks to make loans in accordance with regulations prescribed by the OCC.

Old Section 24 set maximum loan to value ratios at 66-2/3 percent for unimproved property; 75 percent for property with off-side improvements or property in the process of being improved; and 90 percent for improved property. Under the revised statute, the OCC eliminated limitations on the amount that a national bank may loan relative to the appraised value of the property securing the loan, making this decision the responsibility of each bank's directorate and management.

Under the prior law, loans exceeding 75 percent of the appraised value of the property and loans on one-to-four-family dwellings were required to be repaid in installment payments sufficient to amortize the entire principal of the loan within 30 years. The amortization schedule had to reflect regular payments, at least annual payments, in an amount sufficient to repay the principal during the life of the loan.

The OCC elected to eliminate requirements regarding amortization, including limits on negative amortization, and maturity limitations in connection with real estate lending. The OCC stated that it is the responsibility of bank officers and directors to prudently manage real estate lending activities to avoid exposing the bank to undue or unwarranted risk.

Finally, old Section 24 imposed two primary limitations on the aggregate amount of real estate lending by a national bank: (1) a national bank was prohibited from making or purchasing real estate loans in excess of the amount of either its unimpaired capital and surplus, or its time and savings deposits, whichever is greater; and (2) the aggregate of amounts unpaid on real estate loans secured by other than a first lien, when added to unpaid prior mortgages, liens, and encumbrances, could not exceed 20 percent of the bank's paid-in-capital and unimpaired capital stock, plus 20 percent of its unimpaired surplus fund. The OCC elected to remove all of these limitations from its regulation, thereby allowing national banks to increase their participation in the real estate lending market.

The OCC was motivated by the fact that market forces and management philosophies are the real determinants of a bank's real estate lending practices. The OCC also concluded that significant developments had occurred in the mortgage market during recent years, and that if the restrictions were retained, national banks would be constrained in their response to changes in the real estate market. Therefore, in order to make it easier for national banks to conform their lending program to secondary market requirements, the OCC elected to remove these restrictions, subject to general safety and soundness considerations.

The maximum per-borrower lending limit for all types of loans (which was formerly 10 percent of paid-in-capital and unimpaired capital, plus 10 percent of unimpaired surplus) was increased by the Garn–St Germain Act to 15 percent of capital and surplus, plus an additional 10 percent if this latter amount is secured by readily marketable collateral.

Bank-Owned Mortgage Companies

Mortgage companies directly owned by national banks (rather than by bank holding companies) are considered, for all practical purposes, as departments of the bank, regardless of their separate corporate identity. These subsidiaries are initially organized under state corporation laws, but are subsequently governed by the Federal Reserve Act and the regulations of the Comptroller of the Currency. They are examined by the OCC. All national bank subsidiary mortgage companies are consequently deemed *supervised* for HUD approval, as are subsidiaries of federal S&Ls.

The statutes of many states do not specifically authorize state banks to own corporate subsidiaries, but effectively permit them by not prohibiting them. Consequently, they are not regulated by state banking laws, but by other applicable state laws. A few states prohibit subsidiaries, although mortgage departments of state banks may operate through loan production offices. A few states do regulate and examine state bank subsidiaries, thereby making these banks eligible for a *supervised* designation for HUD's purposes.

Most state bank-owned companies, however, must operate under HUD's requirements for unsupervised lenders. Nevertheless, the Federal Reserve usually examines state member bank subsidiaries annually.

Mortgage Bankers

Once small, independent entrepreneurs, mortgage bankers are today most often part of a larger organization such as a bank holding company (BHC). The special considerations arising from bank holding company affiliation are described below. (Bank-owned mortgage companies and S&L service corporations were covered in the previous section.) There are of course many other possibilities. While organizational form is one major regulatory determinant, the firm's product line is of at least equal importance. Thus, a mortgage banker's regulatory environment typically includes the approval and operational requirements of FHA and VA (Section I-C), as well as those of GNMA, FNMA and FHLMC (Section II).

Mortgage Companies

Mortgage companies are organized under the laws and regulations of the individual state or states in which they do business. These companies may be independent, "captive," owned by nondepository firms or holding companies, owned by bank holding companies or S&L holding companies, or be unregulated companies owned by state banks. Regardless of their form of organization, they must meet the requirements of state partnership and corporation laws, including stock requirements and registration, licensing laws, and doing business laws.

A mortgage company may also fall under the doing business laws of states in which it does not have an office, but in which it originates loans (as many other lenders). The company may also come under those laws if it purchases or services whole or participation loans from that state, or carries out collection procedures within that state. All these companies are subject to federal credit laws, under the jurisdiction of the Federal Trade Commission. Additionally, they are subject to any state credit laws governing such areas as usury, adjustable-rate loans, and other alternative mortgage instruments, enforcement of due-on-sale clauses in mortgage contracts, interest charged on interest, interest paid on escrowed funds, and consumer disclosures.

Few, if any, mortgage companies must submit detailed financial reports to the state corporation commission, although certain stock reports and annual independent audits may be required for public companies or subsidiaries of public companies. Nevertheless, most mortgage companies are subject to audits by outside government agencies and investors. These may include audits by an independent public accountant (IPA), financial institutions examiners, FNMA, FHLMC, and additional IPAs retained by private investors.

Because independent mortgage companies rely upon their ability to sell their real estate loans, their operations and products are essentially regulated by the requirements of HUD, FHA/VA, and FmHA, and of the institutional secondary markets: FNMA, FHLMC, and GNMA. Unless otherwise restricted by state laws, independent companies enjoy the most flexibility in developing products for private investors, with or without approval of the state corporation commission or its equivalent.

Bank Holding Company (BHC) Subsidiaries

Certain types of activities are prohibited for BHCs and their subsidiaries by the Federal Reserve Board, which regulates BHCs. Few of these restrictions, however, affect one-to-four-family residential lending operations of mortgage company subsidiaries.

Under Regulation Y (which implements Section 4(c)(8) of the Bank Holding Company Act), BHC-affiliated mortgage companies may originate, purchase, and sell loans; lease real property; service loans; act as custodian or escrow agent for funds deposited for special use; advise mortgage and real estate investment trusts; invest in community rehabilitation; and sell or broker credit-related insurance.

Within the scope of these permissible activities, BHC subsidiaries are governed by state laws for doing business, licensing, etc., to the same extent as if they were independent or otherwise unaffiliated with regulated depository institutions. (This is true for subsidiaries of savings and loan holding companies as well.) HUD determines the supervised or nonsupervised lender status of BHC subsidiaries on a case-by-case basis. In general, most are considered unsupervised, although a few which are able to meet a complex set of criteria of affiliation with a national bank may be deemed supervised.

The Fed has the authority, but is not required, to examine the mortgage company subsidiaries of BHCs and of state member banks, and usually audits such companies annually. The opening of new offices, or the adding of activities (such as second mortgages or mobile-home loans), requires *de novo* notification to the Federal Reserve Board by the mortgage company's parent, and subsequent permission.

OCC has the authority to examine bank holding companies, and their non-bank subsidiaries, where national banks are members of the holding company, but it rarely does so. The FDIC also has statutory authority to examine the affiliates of insured banks.

FHA/VA

Approval

Federal Housing Administration. Mortgage bankers must comply with the requirements outlined for nonsupervised mortgagees in order to become a HUD-approved mortgage. A *nonsupervised mortgagee* is an institution which has as its principal activity the lending or investment of funds in real estate mortgages, and is not subject to the inspection or supervision of a government agency other than the Federal Reserve. HUD approval for both supervised and nonsupervised lenders is obtained through submission of Form HUD-92001. HUD-approved status permits the lender to submit applications for the insurance of mortgages and to purchase, hold, service, and sell HUD-insured mortgages. Mortgagees must maintain a minimum net worth of $100,000 in assets acceptable to HUD. To obtain approval, an applicant must provide evidence, in the form of an audit report prepared by an independent public accountant, that it meets this financial requirement. It must also maintain a reliable warehouse line of credit or other mortgage funding program that is acceptable to HUD, which provides at least $250,000 of available funds for use in the origination of mortgages. Approved mortgagees must also have the capacity to segregate all escrow funds received from mortgagors. These escrow funds must be deposited in a special custodial account in a financial institution in which deposits are insured by the FDIC, FSLIC, or NCUSIF.

HUD also requires approved mortgagees to submit an application to maintain a branch office as a prerequisite to the submission of applications for mortgage insurance by a bank. For each branch office, Form HUD-92001B, Branch Office Notification, must be submitted to the field office in whose jurisdiction the branch office is located. The mortgagee remains fully responsible to HUD for the actions of its branch offices. HUD requires a nonrefundable fee to accompany each application. The application fees for the main office and each branch office is $250 and $50, respectively. In addition, HUD assesses annual fees for the main office and each branch office of $150 and $50, respectively. These fees are submitted together with the Yearly Verification Report, Form HUD 9200 IV.

Veterans Administration. Participation in the VA Prior Approval Loan Guaranty Program is open to nonsupervised lenders. The VA does not set forth specific requirements such as net worth, experience, or office approval. Generally, a nonsupervised lender approved by the FHA is also eligible to submit loans on a prior-approval basis to VA.

The Veterans Administration does have specific requirements for nonsupervised lenders eligible to participate in automatic processing. These were significantly changed in November 1982. In order to be an approved VA automatic lender, a minimum of $50,000 of working capital must be maintained. (This is defined as the excess of current assets over current liabilities.) The lender must submit a current financial statement with the application for automatic processing. Only those nonsupervised lenders who have actively engaged in origination and servicing of VA mortgages for the five years preceding the date of application will be considered eligible. Lenders having three years' experience may be considered if each principal officer actively engaged in origination and servicing activities has had at least five years' confirmed experience in managerial functions in the field of VA mortgages. Résumés must be submitted with the application. Approved automatic lenders must have one or more lines of credit aggregating at least $1 million. If the automatic lender sells the loans which it originates, it must have a minimum of two permanent investors. The lender's servicing portfolio must contain a minimum of 500 loans, 250 of which must be VA loans. An alternative procedure has been established whereby a lender who has originated at least 100 loans, 50 of which are VA loans, and who can show a delinquency rate over a period of one year which is no higher than the national average for all mortgage loans, can qualify for VA automatic approval. Builder-related lenders must meet additional criteria regarding independence in underwriting.

Operational Requirements

Federal Housing Administration. HUD-approved mortgagees must originate and service HUD-insured mortgages in accordance with generally accepted prudent lending practices for financial institutions and HUD's requirements. Each mortgagee is required to establish and maintain an adequate written quality control plan for loan origination and servicing on a systemwide basis. This includes its branch offices. Although HUD does not prescribe standards for a mortgagee's internal-management controls, it does indicate that the quality control system must be consistent with the need to assist corporate management in determining whether HUD requirements and the mortgagee's policies and procedures are being followed by its personnel.

All HUD-approved mortgagees are required to submit a yearly verification report (HUD Form 92001-V) to update the mortgagee's status and the operations of the main and branch offices. In addition, an annual fee of $150 for the main office and $50 for each branch office must accompany the report. Nonsupervised mortgagees must also file an audit report within 75 days of the close of the mortgagee's fiscal year. HUD Handbook LG4000.3 REV., Audit Guides for Audits of HUD-Approved Nonsupervised Mortgagees for Use by Independent Public Accountants prescribes the standards to be followed in conducting such audits.

HUD sets forth a mortgagee's responsibilities to establish and maintain escrow accounts. These procedures are defined in the Mortgagee Approval Handbook, 4060.1. Basically, each month the mortgagee must collect from the mortgagor an amount sufficient to pay all escrow obligations prior to delinquency. The regulations clearly state that escrow funds are to be used only for the purpose for which they are collected. Under no circumstances can a lender use escrow funds for delinquent payments, late charges, assumption fees, or any other charges. HUD regulations neither forbid nor require that escrow account bear interest. However, some state laws require that interest be paid on the mortgagors' escrow accounts. These requirements must be met by HUD-approved mortgagees. HUD does not permit mortgagees to invest escrowed funds unless the net income is paid or credited to the mortgagor's account. Detailed guidelines on escrow administration can be found in HUD Handbook 4330.1, Administration of Insured Mortgages.

HUD provides approved mortgagees with detailed handbooks covering every phase of loan processing, servicing, and reporting. The following handbooks should be consulted for a complete understanding of HUD's operational requirements.

4000.4 Mortgagee's Guide to Direct Endorsement

4060.1 Mortgagee Approval Handbook

4115.1 Administrative Instructions and Procedures for Home Mortgage Insurance

4125.1 Underwriting - Technical Direction for Home Mortgage Insurance

4135.1 Subdivision Analysis and Procedures Handbook

4145.1 Architectural Processing and Instructions

4150.1 Valuation Analysis for Home Mortgage Insurance

4155.1 Mortgage Credit Analysis

4330.1 Administration of Insured Mortgages.

The application process for HUD single-family insurance, outlined in 4150.1 and 4155.1, consists of three steps. The first of these is the application for conditional commitment. This involves the submission by the mortgage lender of an appraisal on a specific property. If the property is eligible, HUD agrees, through the issuance of a conditional commitment, to insure the mortgage on that property, provided it is sold to a purchaser who is found to be qualified by HUD standards. The second step is the application for firm commitment, which involves the submission by the lender of a mortgage credit application and supporting documentation for analysis of the borrower's credit worthiness. If the lender is eligible, HUD, through the issuance of a firm commitment, agrees to insure a mortgage on the specific property, for a named borrower, in an amount and on terms set forth in the commitment. The third step is the request for insurance endorsement. This involves submission by the mortgage lender of evidence that the mortgage has been closed in accordance with the terms of the firm commitment.

Over the years HUD has experimented with a number of alternatives to its standard procedures for processing loans. These alternative plans have generally had an underlying common objective—more responsibility upon the lender. The most notable of these programs have been: (1) the Certified Agency Program (CAP), (2) the Coinsurance Program, and (3) the Demonstration Program of Outreach and Delegated Processing. The CAP program was discontinued in 1966, the coinsurance program has never generated any significant volume, and the delegated-processing program was succeeded by a program known as *Direct Endorsement Processing* (DEP) in May of 1883. DEP is not a demonstration program, but is rather a standard operating procedure.

Under DEP, HUD does not issue conditional and firm commitments, except for proposed construction. The lender has full responsibility for underwriting the loan, including all property-appraisal and mortgage-credit aspects. The lender closes a loan and forwards it to HUD for endorsement (insurance), which is the first time HUD actually reviews the loan. Technically a lender closes at risk as HUD can refuse to endorse it. The regulations, however, make it clear that HUD will endorse if all statutory (as opposed to regulatory) requirements have been met. There is no intention on the part of HUD to reunderwrite a loan before endorsing it. HUD will conduct a more intensive postendorsement review and can suspend mortgages for unsatisfactory performance.

Since HUD relies solely on the analysis and judgment of the lender in the underwriting of these mortgages, participation in the DEP will be permitted only for those mortgagees who have demonstrated qualifications, experience, and expertise. To participate in DEP, a mortgagee must be HUD-approved in good standing. This includes supervised mortgagees, nonsupervised mortgagees, and governmental institutions. They must have five years' experience in the origination of single-family mortgages or have a principal officer with a minimum of five years' managerial experience in the origination of single-family mortgages. If nonsupervised, a mortgagee must be approved as a FNMA seller, or approved as a GNMA issuer of single-family mortgage-backed securities, or have a net worth (in assets acceptable to HUD) of at least $250,000. It must have on staff underwriters who meet HUD's qualifications and who have implemented a quality control plan.

The mortgagee must have on staff a full-time employee to serve as underwriter, who is either a corporate officer with signatory authority or is otherwise authorized to bind the mortgagee in matters involving the origination of mortgage loans. The underwriter must have a minimum of three years' full-time experience reviewing credit and property applications. Each application for mortgagee approval is to include a nomination for the individual to serve as the mortgagee's underwriter. The nomination includes a verification by the president or vice president that the nominee has the authority to bind the corporation. A résumé or the applicable portion of HUD Form 92563 must be submitted.

Mortgagees may use their own staff to perform appraisals, inspections, and mortgage-credit analysis. If the lender chooses to use members of HUD fee panels, HUD will make assignments to fee personnel. An appraiser must have a total of five years' experience. This experience must include at least two years' specialized experience in the valuation of property that demonstrates a knowledge of the ability to apply the principles, practices, methods, and techniques of appraising. The remaining experience may be general experience.

A mortgage-credit examiner must have three years' experience in examination and analysis of financial and credit risk factors involved in the granting of loans. As with the underwriter, a résumé or the applicable portion of Form HUD–92563 is to be submitted for each nominee. Before the underwriter and staff technicians can perform functions under the direct-endorsement program, they must attend field-office training sessions.

Veterans Administration.   The Veterans Administration (VA) operational requirements are outlined in its Lenders Handbook, VA 26–7. It is the lender's responsibility to determine whether the veteran is eligible for VA loan guaranty and the amount of the entitlement due to the veteran. Under the prior-approval submission program, the lender packages the loan and sends it to the VA field office for approval. The loan cannot be closed until receiving the VA guaranty. The lender is responsible for providing the VA with documentation relating to the creditworthiness of the borrower and the appraisal of the property.

There is no limit on the amount of the loan which may be guaranteed, except that the loan amount cannot exceed the reasonable value established by VA. Also, the interest rate on the loan cannot exceed the rate in effect on the date the loan is closed. Generally speaking, the veteran borrower cannot be charged fees, except those expressly permitted under schedules established by VA. The veteran may pay reasonable fees for inspections and appraisals, recording fees and taxes, credit reports, initial tax and insurance escrow payments, hazard insurance, and title examination and insurance. Loan discounts may be paid by the borrower only for the refinancing of existing indebtedness.

In addition to the prior-approval processing, VA also has an automated processing program. Lenders who are authorized to do so may make loans that are automatically guaranteed. The lender may close the loan without issuance of evidence of guaranty. A certificate of commitment is issued when the loan report shows that a portion of the loan proceeds has been escrowed.

As is the case in FHA-insured loans, the lender is responsible for servicing the loan after it is closed (again, unless it is sold to another approved VA lender). Section F of the VA lenders handbook details the servicing guidelines for guaranteed loans. VA regulations permit a late charge provision, not to exceed 4 percent, to be included in the loan instrument. It also permits the borrower to prepay, without assessment of a fee, the entire or partial indebtedness.

VA servicing regulations also include forebearance procedures, collection and disbursement of taxes and insurance, sale of the property, release of veterans from personal liability, release of security, notice of default, and reinstatement.

FEDERALLY RELATED CONDUITS AND PURCHASERS

Approval

Government National Mortgage Association (GNMA)

To be approved to issue GNMA-guaranteed mortgage-backed securities, an applicant must first be an FHA-approved mortgagee and either a FNMA- or a GNMA-approved servicer. The prospective issuer must have as a principal element of its business operation the origination or servicing of mortgage loans, and meet standards of managerial and financial strength. State or local government instrumentalities are eligible, but the bulk of active issuers are private financial institutions.

The issuer must have at least three full-time officers and one additional employee, each with sufficient experience in mortgage origination or servicing to assure an ability to manage the pool on a long-term basis. Résumés are to be submitted with the initial application. The issuer's offices must be self-contained and separate from those of any other entity.

An applicant must submit audited financial statements for the three most recent fiscal years, and, once approved, supply new statements at least annually. These are reviewed by GNMA (using criteria similar to the FHA standards regarding acceptable and unacceptable assets) with a view to assuring the issuer's ability to advance funds to cover shortfalls in the pool accounts. Issuers must have adjusted net worth equal to specified percentages of the total of existing security balances plus outstanding commitments. For single-family mortgages the formula is $100,000, plus 1 percent of the amount between $5 and $20 million, plus 0.2 percent of the amount over $20 million.

Federal National Mortgage Association (FNMA)

In order to be approved as a FNMA seller/servicer, a lender must have a minimum net worth of $250,000, plus 0.2 percent of the outstanding principal balance of the lender's FNMA servicing portfolio, including loans pooled under FNMA's mortgage-backed securities program. Lenders are approved on a national, rather than a regional or state-by-state, basis. Newly approved lenders may be required to submit mortgage documents to FNMA for prior approval during an initial time period.

Approved FNMA lenders may sell FNMA loans originated by nonapproved lenders; the approved lender, however, must make all warranties and is held solely accountable for the loan quality. A lender may also designate another FNMA-approved lender as the servicer.

In order to participate in FNMA's guaranteed mortgage pass-through securities program, an institution must first be approved as a conventional loan seller/servicer under the regular program, and own at least one share of FNMA stock. In addition, FNMA reserves the right to issue pool purchase contracts at its discretion. At a minimum, an eligible seller/servicer must at all times maintain net worth (in assets acceptable to FNMA) of $250,000, plus 0.2 percent of all outstanding principal amounts of mortgages pooled pursuant to all existing pool purchase contracts. The seller/servicer is responsible for compliance with the mortgage terms and all applicable law and must maintain adequate fidelity and errors-and-omissions coverage. The seller/servicer must also notify FNMA of any contemplated or actual changes in its financial, corporate, or organizational status that might affect its ability to comply with the foregoing.

Separate approval is also needed to service second mortgages. Applicants must have qualified personnel trained in second mortgage lending and maintain a minimum net worth of $250,000, plus 0.2 percent of all loans serviced for FNMA. Approval is not necessary to sell first mortgages to FNMA.

Federal Home Loan Mortgage Corporation (FHLMC)

FHLMC, like FSLIC, operates as a subsidiary within the Federal Home Loan Bank Board. Sellers must be actively engaged in mortgage origination and servicing and may be members or nonmembers. A member is a Federal Home Loan Bank, the FSLIC, or a financial institution that is a member of the Federal Home Loan Bank System. Eligible nonmembers are: (1) financial institutions, the deposits or accounts of which are insured by an agency of the United States or by a state agency (if the total time and savings deposits insured by that agency exceeds 20 percent of all deposits in that state), and (2) HUD-approved mortgagees.

All Federal Home Loan Bank members have been approved as eligible sellers. In the case of savings banks, commercial banks and other federal- or state-insured depository institutions, FHLMC determines approval on a case-by-case basis according to mortgage origination and servicing experience.

In the case of HUD-approved mortgagees, there are detailed specifications, including financial requirements. A seller first must be approved for its normal lending territory (defined as the state in which it is headquartered, plus any other areas within 100 miles of the home office). Subsequently, a lender may apply for approval as a nationwide lender.

Financial requirements for HUD-approved mortgagees include adjusted net worth equal to a specified percentage of assets. Percentages vary: 5 percent for closed inventory with take-outs, 10 percent for most construction loans, 50 percent of single-family Real Estate Owned (REO) held over a year. The ratio of total assets to adjusted net worth should not exceed 25 to 1. There are also liquidity requirements. The seller/servicer must have been originating conventional loans for at least a year, have originated at least $1,000,000 in the last

12 months, and be servicing at least $5,000,000 of conventional loans, exclusive of purchased servicing. FHLMC applies these requirements flexibly.

Operational Requirements

GNMA

GNMA's operational requirements center in two main areas: proper pool administration and prudent securities marketing practices. The HUD office of inspector general has developed an audit guide for audits of GNMA-approved issuers of mortgage-backed securities for use by independent accountants. The guide also provides for a review of the custodial operation of the commercial bank holding the underlying mortgage documents. In addition, FNMA, under a contract with GNMA, conducts an operational-compliance audit of the issuer.

Chapter 11 of the GNMA mortgage-backed securities guide outlines the proper procedures for segregating and applying the cash flow from the underlying mortgages and paying the security holders. A key aspect of the GNMA mortgage-backed securities program is the issuer's obligation to remit all payments due to holders, whether or not received from the mortgagor, so that holders can reasonably expect to receive their installments by the 15th calendar day of each month. This means that the issuer must regularly advance his own funds. There are also a number of periodic reporting requirements designed to inform investors of the current status of a particular pool.

Because imprudent securities-marketing practices undermine both the soundness of individual issuers and the integrity of the program as a whole, GNMA attempts to assure that issuers carry out their securities marketing and trading activities in a manner consistent with prudent business practices and their own and others' financial capacity. Requirements include a suitability rule, prudent business practice rules, minimum forward-delivery mark-to-market deposit requirements, and record-keeping and reporting requirements. Both the audit guide and direct GNMA inquiries are used to check compliance.

Although the GNMA mortgage-backed securities bookkeeping burdens were heavy. Lenders had to maintain registers of securities holders and issue monthly checks to each investor for each security held. Large-scale investors, for their part, received multiple checks.

Changes in technology have made it possible to streamline this process and have led to the introduction of a new generation of GNMA mortgage-backed securities in August 1983. A chief feature of the new program, called GNMA II, is the use of a central paying agent to consolidate most bookkeeping operations. Each month issuers mail a single check to the central paying agent and the central paying agent issues a single payment to each security holder, generally by the 20th of the month.

FNMA

In December 1981, FNMA undertook to move away from the detailed regulation of its lender underwriting and servicing procedures that had formerly characterized its operations. For example, underwriters and appraisers no longer need be approved by FNMA, and lenders are authorized to use their best judgment in carrying out the intensive servicing of delinquent loans, without having to obtain prior approval to begin foreclosure.

Lenders now submit underwriting and purchase documents at the time of delivery for purchase. If, within 180 days, FNMA determines that the loan does not meet its criteria, the lender will be required either to correct the deficiency or repurchase the loan.

FNMA does prescribe in detail the proper procedures for handling, applying, and remitting funds to FNMA. There is a strong emphasis on the lender's internal control mechanisms. FNMA conducts an annual compliance audit, and can require remedial action, suspend a lender, or collect damages if the lender has violated the warranties contained in the selling contract and its supplements.

FHLMC

In addition to the requirements for initial approval described above, FHLMC sets out detailed servicing, reporting, and remittance requirements in its servicers' guide. These generally follow standard secondary market practices. FHLMC relies heavily on warranties given by the seller servicer as part of the purchase agreement.

FHLMC seller/servicers are required to remit scheduled payments, whether or not received from mortgagors, but are not required to carry loans in foreclosure or to absorb losses. A delinquency rate higher than the average for that state can cause a seller to be dropped from the program.

All FHLMC seller/servicers must submit an independent audit of mortgage accounts annually. The audit program is described in FHLMC Form 16, which covers servicing procedures, proper application of funds, handling of escrow and trust funds, and sufficiency of insurance, both on the mortgages and for the institution. In addition, most seller/servicers are required to submit audited financials except where the FSLIC permits internal auditors to perform this function, or when, as a matter of practice, the servicer does not have an independent audit.

Product Eligibility

GNMA

All mortgages pooled must be FHA-insured, or VA- or FmHA-guaranteed home mortgages, but not all types of FHA, VA, or FmHA mortgages are eligible for GNMA pools. The GNMA mortgage-backed securities guide defines the eligible types of mortgages and establishes certain restrictions on eligible products. These are designed to enhance the soundness and marketability of the resulting pools.

Similar mortgages are grouped into the following pool types: single-family (level- and graduated-payment mortgages), multifamily (interim and permanent loans), and mobile-home loans. Multifamily pools contain only one mortgage, but single-family pools must have at least 11 loans, with no single loan representing more than 10 percent of the original principal balance. Loans must be less than one year old.

In recent years most FHA/VA production has been packaged as GNMA securities, so that eligibility for pools is a key determinant in the success of any new FHA or VA home mortgage program. GNMA has expanded its eligible product list to include FHA 203(k) home improvement loans, certain FHA and VA graduated-payment mortgages, and is considering growing equity mortgages. Currently, no adjustable-rate, not fully amortizing, or shared-appreciation mortgages are permitted.

GNMA II also permits the use of large multiple-issuer pools. GNMA periodically announces coupon rates available for each pool each month. Issuers may submit loan packages as low as $250,000 and market securities based on a prorated portion of the whole pool. It is hoped that the use of multiple-issuer pools with greater geographic diversity will allow greater prepayment certainty.

Custom pools, in the minimum amount of $1 million for standard loans and $500,000 for GPMs, will continue to be available.

GNMA II also permits the mixing of interest rates within a range of 1 percent. This should make it easier to assemble pools during times of fluctuating interest rates or in the event that FHA moves to negotiated interest rates.

There will be separate pools for each of the following FHA/VA mortgages:

Single-family level-payment mortgages.

Graduated-payment mortgages.

Growing equity mortgages.

Manufactured-housing loans.

FHA adjustable-rate mortgages.

Buy-downs may be mixed indiscriminately in GNMA II pools, although they are still not permitted in GNMA I pools.

The GNMA II program does not replace the traditional GNMA program. Lenders may choose one or the other when pools are submitted for processing.

Multifamily mortgages must be insured by FHA under any section of the National Housing Act, except Title X and Section 244.

FNMA

FNMA buys mortgages for its own portfolio through both its regular programs and through special negotiated transactions. It also swaps mortgages for

FNMA-guaranteed mortgage-backed securities. The regular programs have been expanded to include a wide variety of mortgage instruments, such as adjustable-rate and graduated-payment mortgages, second trusts, and growing equity mortgages, as well as the traditional FHA/VA and conventional fixed-rate mortgages. Almost all FHA-insured projects are eligible for sale, as are conventional multifamily mortgages meeting FNMA criteria. In recent years, an increasing share of FNMA's activity has been in single-family conventional mortgages.

Almost any mortgage design will be considered for a negotiated transaction or mortgage-backed security, provided it meets basic statutory requirements, one of the most important of which is the maximum loan size (currently $115,300 for the contiguous states).

Historically, FNMA's underwriting standards have played a key role in the standardization and evolution of the conventional market. The uniform documents developed with FHLMC are now used almost universally by conventional lenders. Acceptance of privately insured, low down payment mortgages, and equal treatment for condominiums and manufactured housing—first by FNMA and FHLMC and then by other lenders—represent important milestones in the evolution of U.S. housing. As a portfolio investor, FNMA has also been concerned with protecting the enforceability of due-on-sale clauses.

Beginning in 1981, FNMA began to de-emphasize detailed underwriting criteria and prior approval of loans by the FNMA staff. Delegated underwriting, formerly reserved for certain select seller/servicers, became the norm. FNMA also sought to increase its activity with savings and loans by offering to buy participations and loans more than one year old, the latter primarily through the mortgage-backed securities program.

FHLMC

FHLMC has always been primarily concerned with conventional loans, and because of its association with the savings and loan industry, these have typically been participations rather than whole loans. Accordingly, FHLMC has traditionally placed more reliance on seller/servicer warranties than on extensive review of loan submissions. FHLMC document submission requirements are less extensive than FNMA's, but FHLMC underwriting criteria generally parallel, and are adjusted in tandem with, FNMA's. One exception is FHLMC's insistence on owner occupancy.

FHLMC prefers to package and resells its purchases as mortgage-backed securities. Because of this bent, its list of eligible products has not been extensive until recently. Although the bulk of its activity is in traditional fixed-rate, level-payment first mortgages, FHLMC has recently begun to promote the use of adjustable-rate mortgages and the short-term, 15-year loan. At this writing FHLMC purchases a 1-year ARM indexed to the Federal Home Loan Bank Board average-contract interest rate for existing homes and a 3-year and a 5-

year ARM indexed to the corresponding Treasury securities. To date, FHLMC has not permitted negative amortization. However, beginning December 19, 1983, FHLMC added a 1-year ARM indexed to the 1-year Treasury bill. In addition, the one-, three- and 5-year ARMS will feature an optional payment cap. At each adjustment period the buyer may elect a 7-½ percent cap on the increase in payments. If the cap is chosen, negative amortization will accrue. However, at no time will the principal be permitted to exceed 125 percent of the original loan amount. The current 1-year ARM program is expected to be dropped. FHLMC is also considered an ARM tied to a cost-of-funds index and a conventional graduated-payment mortgage. To date, ARM volume has been limited to permit the development of a securities program.

FHLMC also swaps mortgages for participation certificates through its guarantor program. Begun in August 1981, the guarantor program was originally intended to help lenders improve liquidity by getting old, low-yield loans off the books without having to realize a loss. Now, however, the program is widely used with new loan production by lenders who want to keep their assets more liquid.

There are two separate programs, one for conventional loans and another for FHA/VA loans that are at least a year old. The program applies only to fixed-rate loans on one-to-four-family homes. No adjustable-rate mortgages, growing equity mortgages, multifamily loans, or home-improvement loans are permitted. Coupon rates on the mortgages must be within a range of 200 basis points.

Loans may be delivered to FLHMC on a recourse or non-recourse basis. (*Recourse loans* are those a lender agrees to repurchase should the borrower default.) Recourse loans may be delivered to FHLMC at a slightly lower required spread.

Mortgage-Insurance Companies

Mortgage-insurance companies (MICs) are subject to state regulation and, because of the large number of insured loans delivered to FNMA and FHLMC, must for all practical purposes be approved by those agencies. FHLMC has published formal eligibility requirements that include minimum capital and surplus of $5 million, and no more than 60 percent of risk concentrated in any one state.

Currently about half the states have regulations governing mortgage insurers, and a model law has been drafted. Because of both the high level of activity there and its application of the principle of externality, the California commissioner has been a key factor in the evolution of state regulation. As mortgage insurers move from the business of insuring individual loans to writing insurance on pools of mortgages, the views of Standard & Poors and other rating agencies take on increased importance as well.

Mortgage insurers are monoline corporations and must form subsidiaries to write other types of business. Three types of reserves are required: (1) an unearned premium reserve, (2) a cash reserve, and (3) a contingency reserve equal to one-half of earned premiums. These are held for 10 years. An insurer's contingent liability is limited, usually by statute, to 25 times the sum of its statutory surplus and contingency reserve. S&P accepts this ratio for individual mortgage business, but requires a 7 to 1 ratio of pool policy liability to capital. California has also adopted extensive regulations governing pool insurance.

State regulations limit the mortgage insurer's concentration of business in a particular locality or subdivision. FNMA, FHLMC, and S&P also have diversification standards.

Mortgage insurers normally do business with lenders under a master policy. Once the lender is reviewed and a policy issued, the insurer does not set operational requirements, except as they relate to claims and foreclosures. They do, however, underwrite the individual mortgages submitted for coverage. MIC willingness to insure a new mortgage design is a key element in the success of any innovation. Generally, MICs have themselves been among the more inventive in this area and are insuring a variety of new products developed by themselves and others.

REGULATIONS AFFECTING THE STRUCTURE AND MARKETING OF THE SECURITY

Security Structure

IRS and SEC Requirements

Because pools and mortgages do not qualify statutorily for investment-company treatment under Section 851 of the Internal Revenue Code, they do not have the flexibility of mutual funds. Instead, the grantor-trust format has been used in practically all offerings of mortgage packages. To qualify as a grantor trust, the pool must be fixed at the outset and be self-liquidating with no reinvestment of cash flow and with no power to alter it after its formation. A passive trust of this nature is not subject to taxation as a corporation. The IRS has also ruled that certificates evidencing interests in mortgage trusts are mortgages for the purpose of thrift tax treatment and state legal investment laws, and that they qualify for the mortgage-transaction exemption under Section 4(5) of the Securities Act of 1933. It is this same logic that leads the Department of Labor to look through the MBS certificate and discover prohibited transactions involving the underlying mortgage assets.

Mortgages can also be sold using limited-partnership, real estate investment trust, and limited-purpose corporation formats. These are all used for commercial and multifamily rental properties. Limited-purpose corporations are being increasingly used by single-family builders to issue mortgage-backed bonds, but the GNMA, FHLMC-PC, and FNMA CMBS all use the grantor trust pass-through and it remains the classic format.

GNMA, FHLMC, and FNMA mortgage-backed securities are exempt from SEC registration requirements by virtue of their federal status, but issuers voluntarily comply with SEC disclosure requirements. Public offerings of private issues must be registered with the SEC. An issuer may use the shelf registration technique by preparing a general prospectus, to be supplemented by information covering the specifics of each sub-offering as it occurs. The need to disclose the geographic location and other characteristics of the underlying mortgages limits the ability to sell forward prior to origination.

Securities Rating

Although rating agencies have no official mandate or authority, their views have a major impact on the structure of and collateral eligible for a nonfederally related mortgage security. A rating is a simple statement of probability of timely payment of interest and repayment of principal. The rating process, however, is a complex weighing of a myriad of variables and tends to be a negotiation process. As a practical matter, all public offerings must be rated, and many private placements are rated as well.

Although all the major rating agencies have looked at mortgage-related instruments, Standard & Poors (S&P) has been the most active. S&P has published basic guidelines and actively sought to educate market participants regarding mortgage-related investments.

The major emphasis in S&P's rating process has centered around four key areas:

The nature of the pool.

The capabilities of the servicer.

The level and nature of the insurance or other back-up coverage.

The capabilities of the mortgage insurance company or other provider of back-up coverage.

S&P has a strong preference for single-unit, detached, owner-occupied housing. Townhouses and condominiums, however, have gradually become acceptable, provided the issuer can show that they are of equal quality. Geographic and economic (broad employment base) diversity are also considered key factors. There should be at least 100 mortgages in the pool; loan sizes should be mid-range for their local markets; and only a limited number of loans should have loan-to-value ratios in excess of 80 percent.

Under the *modified weak-link theory* the servicer is evaluated primarily in terms of its originating and servicing competence, and its ability to fund cash shortfalls on an interim basis. Accordingly, properly structured pools may be rated one grade higher than the servicer would be classified.

For an investment grade rating, S&P requires special-hazard insurance (usually 1 percent of the pool balance) covering events not covered by normal homeowner insurance. In addition, there must be some form of reserve or insurance to fill the gap that credit losses may cause in the underlying mortgage pool. This has most frequently been a 5 percent mortgage insurance pool policy, but it can be a cash reserve, a letter of credit, or other arrangement. If the back-up coverage is provided by a third party, then its financial strength becomes a key consideration. A pool will not be rated higher than the mortgage insurer. S&P also considers the separate underwriting typically performed by an insurer a valuable addition.

In order to arrive at a rating, S&P requires at a minimum the following information:

1. Five years of audited financial statements, plus interim reports for the current year;
2. The prospectus and other legal documents pertaining to the issue;
3. Copies of all insurance reports; a trustee's certification that mortgage documents are in order;
4. Description of the selection process for the pool and the geographic distribution of the mortgages; and
5. Geographic distribution of all the issuer's residential mortgages and the performance record of similar mortgages originated by the issuer.

Mortgage-backed bonds and pay-through bonds differ from pass-through securities in several important aspects. The instrument is a debt of the issuer rather than a sale of assets, so that the financial strength of the issuer is of ultimate importance. On the other hand, sufficient over-collateralization can reduce the probability of a cash shortfall to negligible proportions. Greater over-collateralization can offset a weak issuer and substitute for pool insurance. Unlike a pass-through, bond structures require interim investment of proceeds and therefore reinvestment risk becomes a factor. S&P assumes a 3 percent reinvestment rate.

Standard & Poors also evaluates secured commercial paper (collateral trust notes or mortgage-backed notes). Such paper provides an alternative to bank warehousing and can be issued directly by a very large mortgage lender, or, more commonly, on the lender's behalf by a major financial institution. In this case the creditworthiness—in terms of both liquidity and financial stability—of the mortgage banker or other issuer is crucial. The quality and level of the collateral, however, and the additional protection of the indenture and financing agreement can be used to support a higher rating than that of the issuer itself.

Dealer Regulation

SEC, NYSE and Self-Regulation

The regulation of the securities markets and dealers is organized around the principle of self-regulation with governmental oversight. In practice, this means that dealers are regulated by membership organizations, such as the New York Stock Exchange (NYSE), the National Association of Security Dealers (NASD) and the Chicago Board of Trade (CBOT). These are, in turn, overseen by the Securities Exchange Commission (SEC) or, in the case of futures, the Commodity Futures Trading Commission (CFTC).

Most dealers active in mortgage-backed securities are members of the NYSE, and it is through the NYSE that SEC requirements are enforced. NYSE members, however, must meet net capital criteria more stringent than those imposed by the SEC. As a consequence, many NYSE member firms have created separate nonmember subsidiaries to handle certain facets of their business, such as government securities. Known as *GSIs,* these subsidiaries trade GNMAs, FHLMC-PCs, FNMA CMBSs, and other exempt securities, but not private CMBSs. (A private issue backed by FHA mortgages has, in at least one instance, been exempted from registration by the SEC.)

The minimal degree of regulation to which a GSI is subject has combined with heightened market volatility to produce some serious problems. In 1980, SEC and the Federal Reserve Board released a study (in which the Treasury participated, but which it did not endorse) recommending a systematic regulatory framework for the regulation of trading in exempt mortgage-backed securities.

This prospect, plus heightened realization of the market risks involved, spurred a concerted effort by the major dealers to enhance their own internal control of procedures and to create a meaningful system of self-regulation. Under the aegis of the Public Securities Association (PSA), uniform practices for the clearance and settlement of mortgage-backed securities were developed and a MBS clearing corporation established. Both the NYSE and SEC continue to adjust their net capital rules to reflect current market conditions, but there is no effort to impose systematic market regulation.

The current system emphasizes suitability (with absolute position limits for each customer), hedging techniques (such as computerized systems for aggregating and continuous marking-to-market), and requiring market-maintenance deposits where necessary. The clearing corporation imposes the same discipline on interdealer trades. Many dealers systematically hedge their open positions in the futures market. The use of optional delivery commitments has been sharply reduced, but may rebound as exchange-traded options develop.

The regulation and practice of dealers interacts with, and reinforces, regulations imposed on buyers and sellers by GNMA, the Federal Home Loan Bank

Board (FHLBB), and the various bank regulators. GNMA's requirements are sketched in Section I-B. In May 1979, the FHLBB amended its regulations to discourage imprudent use of forward commitments as a fee-generating device. FHLBB policy continues to evolve, and was recently amended to give more recognition to *bona fide* hedging strategies.

"Good Delivery" Requirements

Both the PSA uniform practices and the MBS clearing corporation specify exactly what and how GNMA or FHLMC securities are to be delivered in fulfillment of a commitment. These rules, which are often more exacting than those of GNMA, are imposed by dealer members on their customers. For example, the number and exact amount of securities for various sizes of commitments are specified, as well as the timing and method of payment. Problems sometimes arise when a new FHA or VA procedure is instituted and accepted by GNMA, but is not yet accepted by either the MBS clearing corporation or by the Chicago Board of Trade as constituting good delivery.

Clearing corporations operate on the presumption that market participants will deliver the cheapest product that meets their criteria, and therefore attempt to exclude pools that may tend to decrease the value of the product as a class.

Federal Reserve Board-Regulation T

Reg T governs the extension of credit by dealers to customers. Previously, mortgage-backed securities could not be sold on margin in the manner of corporate bonds. Nevertheless, the federally related securities can be used for repurchase agreements subsequent to the initial purchase. It was primarily the private issues that suffered from what was apparently unintentional discrimination.

In December 1982, however, the Federal Reserve Board amended Reg T to include private mortgage pass-through securities in the definition of OTC margin bonds. Although buying private MBSs on margin is a readily acceptable proposal, the board's amendment authorized only pass-through securities having a minimum original issue of $25 million.

Blue-Sky Laws

The Uniform Securities Act, a model state code which has been substantially adopted by 39 states, does not exempt mortgage-backed securities from registration, even though the issuers' bonds may be exempt. As a result, private issuers must either register or confirm exemption in each of the states in which the security will be marketed, which is a time-consuming and expensive process. FNMA and FHLMC maintain blue-sky compliance for their programs.

Futures and Options Exchanges

GNMA Futures Markets

In 1975, the Chicago Board of Trade (CBOT) launched the GNMA–CDR (collateralized depository-receipt) contract. Since that time, the board and other exchanges have introduced other GNMA futures contracts, but none has been able to sustain substantial liquidity. The Chicago Board of Trade is a self-regulatory membership organization subject to Commodity Futures Trading Commisssion (CFTC) oversight. In addition, the CFTC has recently approved the National Futures Association (NFA) as a self-regulatory body for futures commission merchants, somewhat analagous to the National Association of Securities Dealers (NASD).

The CFTC must give prior approval to proposed new contracts and to major changes in existing contracts or exchange rules. The exchanges, however, have broad emergency powers to act on their own.

Long the province of large commercial hedgers and sophisticated speculators, futures markets have not emphasized elaborate customer protection and broker surveillance regulation. Instead, there is a small initial margin requirement, equal to one day's maximum price fluctuation, plus a marking-to-the-market. Because daily price movements are subject to a limit (for example, 2 percent of par for GNMAs), the initial margin is normally sufficient to permit brokers to protect themselves by closing out a customer's position, if additional funds are not provided overnight.

The major exchanges are strongly capitalized and stand behind each trade. Nevertheless, it is the broker, not the customer, who is a party to the trade and to whom the customer must look in the event of a dispute. Thus, while a customer need not be concerned with the party on the other side of the transaction, he does need to be concerned with the financial strength and integrity of his broker. All brokers must register with the CFTC, and those who are clearing members of a particular exchange must meet additional financial and operational standards imposed by the exchange.

Exchange-Traded Options

The trading of options on GNMA futures, GNMA securities, and other financial instruments should soon commence, with congressional clarification of the jurisdictional division between the SEC and the CFTC now behind us. In the interim, Treasury-bond options can be used as a cross-hedge. Much of the regulatory framework has already been established. The Federal Reserve Board has completed Reg T changes regarding margin, and the FHLBB has specified the conditions under which federal savings and loans may participate in the market.

Life Insurance Companies

Life insurance companies are regulated at the state level, typically by a state insurance commissioner. Regulations are designed to protect policyholders, and they affect the mortgage market primarily in the manner in which they prescribe investment criteria and statutory accounting requirements.

Life insurance companies have long been major investors in agricultural, residential, and commercial real estate. Accordingly, investment in mortgages is normally permitted, but there may be restrictions, such as a maximum 75 percent loan-to-value ratio or a maximum loan size, among others. Loans often may be accommodated by a basket provision permitting a limited amount of investment in securities not otherwise eligible. In some cases, prior regulatory approval is required for this category. Some states also limit the out-of-state investments of companies chartered in their state, or require out-of-state companies to invest in the state in proportion to the volume of business done there.

In addition, state regulations often specify the maximum percentage of assets that can be invested in specific categories such as stocks, bonds, and mortgages. Within these regulations, however, life insurance companies have broad discretionary powers and can switch significant sums of money, especially between bonds and mortgages. Although life insurance companies are permitted to originate mortgages directly, they typically do not, preferring instead to rely on a local third party, such as a mortgage banker, for origination and service.

Statutory accounting practices are relevant because they permit investments in bonds and mortgages to be carried at their amortized cost (they need not be marked-to-market). Common stock and perpetual preferred stocks, on the other hand, must be carried at market and a securities-valuation reserve established as a cushion. Reserves are calculated on the basis of a very conservative return assumption, and because liquidity is not a priority of the regulators, mortgages are considered a highly appropriate investment.

Pension Funds

ERISA

Private, corporate and union (but not state and local) employee benefit plans are subject to the Employee Retirement Income Security Act of 1974 (ERISA). The ERISA requirements affecting mortgage investment primarily involve fiduciary responsibilities. Some of these reflect traditional practices. For example, fiduciaries are required to act for the exclusive benefit of participants, to diversify investments, and to act ". . . with the care, skill, prudence and diligence . . . that a prudent man acting in a like capacity and familiar with such matters . . ." would use.

ERISA, however, also contains a list of prohibited transactions, some of which may be beneficial to the plan participants and to other parties involved. The statute does provide a procedure by which exemptions may be granted by the Department of Labor (originally IRS approval was also required). The prohibited transaction rules are enforced by severe IRS sanctions, and the Department of Labor may and does bring suit.

Prohibited transactions under ERISA are sales, exchanges, leasing, loans or other extensions of credit, or transfers of assets between a plan and a *party in interest* (anyone connected with the plan, such as a trustee, investment manager, employer, union, employee, or service provider). There are also prohibitions against self-dealing by fiduciaries, which extend from receiving consideration from an interested party for unrelated transactions to a limitation on securities issued by the plan and real estate transactions involving the plan. Despite the passive nature of the grantor trust format, administrators of pools are considered fiduciaries by the Department of Labor.

With the important exception of GNMA, FHLMC, and FNMA securities, the Department of Labor looks through the security and regards the underlying mortgages to be the assets acquired by the plan. As a consequence, almost any real estate or mortgage investment is potentially a prohibited transaction, requiring a special exemption from the Department of Labor. Special exemptions require extensive review, including publication in the *Federal Register*. They are therefore not usually practical in today's marketplace. Consequently, the industry has sought class exemptions covering the most common types of instruments. Class exemptions eliminate the need for prior approval by the Department of Labor for transactions meeting the specified criteria. For residential mortgage investments, the two most important class exemptions are 81–7 covering conventional mortgage-backed securities (CMBS) and 82–87 covering sales of whole loans and participations. In addition, the Department of Labor has made clear that mortgages backing GNMA, FNMA, and FHLMC securities are not plan assets, and therefore do not give rise to interested-party relationships. Additionally, normal pool administration functions are exempt from the fiduciary provisions.

The CMBS exemption is limited to pools backed by single-family mortgages. The pool itself must provide additional credit support, such as pool insurance, equal to the greater of 1 percent of the pool, or the full balance of the largest mortgage in the pool. There must be a binding pooling and servicing agreement. The initial sale of certificates between the pool sponsor and the plan is exempt from the fiduciary self-dealing requirements, provided that: (1) the pool is sold at a market rate; (2) the pool is reviewed by a third-party fiduciary; (3) the sponsor receives no additional compensation for the sale; (4) the plan does not purchase more than 25 percent of the total offering; and (5) at least 50 percent of the total offering is acquired by a person independent of the sponsor, trustee, or insurer. These last restrictions limit the exemption's usefulness for private placements. Class Exemption 83–7 expands 81–7 to cover second liens and optional delivery commitments.

Class Exemption 82–87, dated May 8, 1982, covers sales of whole loans and participations. Its applicability is limited to single-family mortgages which are eligible for purchase, through an established program, by FNMA, GNMA, or FHLMC. The loan must be originated by an established mortgage lender (defined as a HUD-approved mortgagee), a FNMA- or FHLMC-approved seller/servicer, or a state housing finance agency. The decision to purchase, sell, or issue a commitment must be made by an independent qualified real estate manager.

Public Funds

The funds of state and local employee retirement plans currently are not subject to regulation at the federal level, although pending federal legislation (the Public Employee Retirement Investment Security Act) would impose such a requirement. In most cases, these funds are subject to a state legal investment statute similar to those enacted for state-chartered financial institutions. Because of their federal status, GNMA, FHLMC, and FNMA mortgage-backed securities are permissible investments under most such statutes. Private MBSs have not been eligible, except in those cases where they could be encompassed within an authorization to invest in mortgage loans or a general prudent-investor clause. A 1980 legal-investment survey found the Aaa-rated Bank of America issue to be not legal for public funds in 26 states. With the growing interest in special in-state mortgage investment programs, a number of states are revising their laws to include private MBSs.

Interpretation and implementation of the pension fund's legal-investment statute normally falls to the state treasurer's office, which may also become involved in the detailed review of any proposed private placement. Either by statute or as a matter of policy, many states limit mortgage and MBS investments to in-state properties. There may also be loan limits and special priorities for the employees of that fund. In contrast, a few funds are concerned about overconcentration of investments in one geographic location, and seek securities backed by out-of-state mortgages for diversification purposes.

Other state regulations regarding mortgage insurance companies and policies may affect the structure of a private mortgage-backed security. Also, doing business laws and issuer retainage requirements may shape efforts to organize a specially tailored private placement with a state fund.

Conclusion

Although increasingly a single national market, the secondary market encompasses highly diverse institutions and activities. It therefore has become the province of an equally diverse set of regulators, each with its own set of responsibilities. While there is considerable overlap and an occasional gap or contradiction, the resulting patchwork quilt of regulation has proved remarkably resilient. It survived a period of severe testing over the past few years as both the mortgage and securities markets underwent revolutionary change. It may even be that the decentralized, multiple regulatory framework improved the ability of the system to accommodate rapid change and growth. Much of the credit for this success, however, belongs to a few key regulators. They recognized their interdependence and worked cooperatively to solve problems in a way that assured that the individual pieces would continue to fit together as a strong, workable whole.

The market continues to grow geometrically in terms of both dollar volume and the variety of products and participants. The primary regulators have responded by streamlining and standardizing requirements in the origination and servicing areas. There is increased delegation of responsibility to lenders with emphasis on specified performance criteria and post-audit review to control quality and assure compliance. Securitization of the secondary market has provided the standardization necessary for large volume to be handled easily, but has brought new regulation in the marketing area from both primary regulators of mortgage institutions and from the traditional regulators of the securities market.

The products offered and operational methods of individual firms are increasingly determined by the federally related conduits whose regulations and policies are geared to limiting their own risk as security guarantors and assuring the marketability of their product. The emphasis on the standardization and marketability of securities has also brought informal regulation from Wall Street. Its views will undoubtedly become even more important as the nonfederally related sector continues to grow.

PART TWO

Secondary Mortgage Market Operations

— PART TWO —— SECTION A —

Strategic Considerations

—— Chapter 11 ——

Determining Lending Strategy

Robert J. Mylod
President
Federal National Mortgage Association

James M. Kinney
President
Guild Mortgage Company

As a middleman, the mortgage banker is more than just a loan broker, for he maintains a responsible presence from the time the mortgage loan is created until it is paid in full. The mortgage banker functions in a continuum extending from the seller/builder of the property to the seller's agent, to the mortgage borrower, to the mortgagee, to the mortgage investor. A mortgage banker's unique competence, to use Peter Drucker's phrase, is found in this continuum as the mortgagee. For only mortgage bankers specialize in the origination or production of mortgage loans for sale to the secondary mortgage market. Other mortgage lenders make or buy loans. Others sell loans. Still others service loans. Only mortgage bankers, however, link all three functions.

A mortgage banker knows that if he can sell a loan, he can usually originate it. Secondary mortgage market investors impose standard requirements for acceptable loans. Given the requisite qualifications for access to these secondary mortgage market investors, what types of lending should a mortgage banker pursue? Who are the mortgage banker's customers? What type of service organization is appropriate? What mortgage product line should be offered? This chapter discusses various answers to these questions, which, when weighed against corporate objectives, available resources, and management values, determine origination or lending strategy.

Types of Lending

The two primary types of lending in mortgage banking are income-property lending and residential lending. Income-property loans (shopping centers, office buildings, industrial buildings, apartment houses) have been typically originated by mortgage bankers who were appointed *correspondents* of mortgage investors (typically, major life insurance companies and pension funds). In the past, correspondent appointments were normally made on an exclusive basis; only designated correspondents could represent certain income-property investors in specified areas. As a result, any available correspondencies were limited to any new originator of income property loans.

However, the subtle changes evolving in recent years have changed the correspondent system. Many correspondent relationships are no longer exclusive. The local correspondent in a given area may not originate a loan that he later services. The rationale appears to be a desire on the part of the insurance company or pension fund to obtain more exposure to the market by accepting loan offerings from many sources. Thus, the income-property lending mortgage banker has, of necessity, added a mortgage-brokerage capability to his available services.

The originator of income property loans also has access to a secondary mortgage market if he originates more standardized loans, such as FHA-insured construction or FHA project loans, which can be sold as collateral for GNMA securities. Some of the management considerations involved in deciding to make construction loans are developed below, following the discussion on builder loans. FHA-project loans, however, are such a small part of the secondary mortgage market today that to discuss their unique requirements and risks may distort their overall significance. Suffice it to say that FHA project loans are originated and sold to the secondary market but are comparatively insignificant when contrasted to the predominance of residential loans on the secondary mortgage market.

Income-property lending is a specialized field that defies operating generalizations. While there are well-defined analytical and underwriting guidelines, geographic, demographic, and economic variables have a definite impact on the success of a mortgage banker. The lack of standardization in income-property financing procedures and documentation (as contrasted to the almost rigid residential procedures in the secondary market) limits income-property financing activities in the secondary mortgage market.

Residential loans constitute the bulwark of both mortgage banking lending activity and secondary mortgage market sales and trading activity. Sometimes described as single-family lending, residential lending actually involves originating loans on one-to-four-family residences. Mortgage bankers have historically dominated the origination of residential government-backed (FHA and VA) loans, while savings and loan associations have traditionally dominated conventional loan originations. Residential lending is open to virtually every company which meets the minimum net worth and staff experience requirements of the most important secondary-market investors.

Each type of lending has certain economic and management characteristics that should be evaluated for their compliance with corporate objectives, the resources required for success and management's comfort level:

Income-Property Lending

1. Project oriented.
2. High unit profitability (or loss); few units.
3. Large dollar units; long time-period to originate.
4. Sporadic cash flow from fees and commissions.
5. Relatively large fixed costs per unit.
6. Negotiated price; however, negotiation is limited, as prices are often tied to relatively short-term cost of funds; originate to a specific investor take-out.
7. Specialized product; unique, technical expertise required; premium put on analysis and underwriting.
8. More vulnerable to personnel turnover because of limited qualified labor pool.
9. Intimate knowledge of local markets required.
10. Competitiveness keyed to investors (correspondents) represented.
11. Relatively few investors represented; limited money available (although there has been an evolution into brokerage services in order to expand the investor pool).
12. Relatively low administrative servicing cost.
13. Requires relatively few managers.
14. Few regulations.
15. Larger owner/development client usually a sophisticated borrower; many have staff capability to package and place deals. Mortgage banker must seek out and service smaller client and offer wider exposure.

Residential Lending

1. Process oriented; a continual flow of loans, unlike discrete projects.
2. Low unit profitability (or loss); many units.
3. Small dollar units; short time frame to originate.
4. Relatively predictable cash flow from fees and commissions.
5. Relatively small fixed costs per unit.
6. Market-determined price; high-risk exposure to interest-rate changes.

7. Standardized product(s); relatively low degree of technical expertise required; premium on sales ability and hedging interest rates.
8. Less vulnerable to personnel turnover; large labor pool available.
9. Local-market knowledge not a key factor.
10. Competitiveness a function of individual service, price, and product line.
11. Virtually unlimited money available from secondary market.
12. Large servicing staff required; more diversified servicing portfolio.
13. Requires many managers.
14. Many regulations and agencies to deal with.
15. Requires warehouse line of credit.

To succeed in either type of lending, management must develop a strategy that reflects these operating realities.

Whether governmental or conventional loans, residential lending for a mortgage banker can be further differentiated between *builder* (subdivision or tract) *loans* and *spot loans*. The derivation of the term *spot* is disputed, but two theories prevail. One theory holds that, unlike builder loans in a given subdivision, spot loans are spotted around various neighborhoods, because they are usually resales of currently existing houses. The other theory contends that spot loans are so named because they are processed one at a time instead of in batches, as are loans from a builder for a weekend's sales in his subdivision. Whichever theory is correct, spot loans usually are on currently existing houses; builder loans are on new construction.

Builder Loans

Providing financing services to residential builders can be demanding, risky, and rewarding. Traditionally, new-construction residences have been sold to upscale buyers. Because these buyers have historically generated low delinquencies and higher (than resale or *spot*) loan balances, a higher value has been assigned by the market to their servicing value. In recognition of this, builders have typically driven harder bargains than real estate brokers. Builders argue that high volume and upscale buyers justify better volume than spot business. The risks of dealing with builders on a forward-commitment basis are discussed in the chapters on inventory management and production-department management.

Some lenders have separate sales organizations for builder loans and spot loans. Some have builder-loan specialists working out of the same office as does the spot-loan sales staff. Some firms have national account representatives who cultivate the multimarket builders. In larger offices, the same loan officer rarely deals with both types of customers. A builder-loan representative usually keeps builder prospects informed of available mortgage products and provides local services for the convenient taking of loan applications and for loan processing.

As well as the appraisal of the project, the builder's credit, balance sheet status and record should be analyzed to determine whether he is a good candidate for issuance of a mortgage commitment. Generally, builder loans must have HUD, FNMA, or FHLMC approval of subdivision plans in order to be saleable on the secondary market. When sales take place, the lender assists the builder's homebuyers by obtaining their mortgage-loan approval.

The builder's market is shown in Table 1. Builders of 10 or fewer homes a year formed nearly 60 percent of the total in 1981, but produced only 15 percent of the houses. These builders are the most likely to have limited bank lines and the most likely to require that mortgage lenders also provide construction loans. At the other extreme, builders of more than 100 houses a year made up about 3 percent of the total, yet produced nearly 30 percent of the houses. Large and medium builders (those who build 50–100 houses a year) often have several subdivisions under way at the same time.

A still smaller number of builders, probably fewer than 100, build in several markets at once. These multimarket builders produce more than 5 percent of all the houses. Many of them are publicly owned. Some have their own mortgage banking subsidiaries.

Credit ratings among builders do not usually correspond to size. Building is a high-risk, highly leveraged business and even quite large builders may be overextended. Credit standings should never be taken for granted.

Construction Lending. Many mortgage bankers make construction loans to builders because that is a profitable activity, regardless of who gets the permanent end loans. Other mortgage bankers extend only construction credit because they believe this is a sound way to obtain the permanent loans. Others tie construction and permanent loans together; indeed, it is not uncommon for them to *roll over* the construction loan into various permanent loans. Construction loans, however, introduce construction risk to residential lending. To properly assess and manage this risk requires experienced and knowledgeable construction loan officers. It also requires strict policies, procedures, and underwriting guidelines to ensure against losses and prevent an undesired inventory of *real estate owned*.

Large mortgage banking firms may have a regional office system for per-

Table 1 • Profile of Builders of Single-Family Homes in 1981

Number of Houses Built	Number of Builders	Percent of Builders	Number of Houses	Percent of Houses
1–10	22,620	58%	98,980	14%
11–25	10,140	26	162,610	23
26–50	3,510	9	127,260	18
51–100	1,560	4	113,120	16
101 +	1,170	3	205,030	29
Total	39,000	100%	707,000	100%

Source: Builder studies conducted by NAHB Research Foundation Inc., Rockville, MD, for Housing Industry Dynamics, Inc.

manent and construction loan underwriting, but most require home or central office approval. Needless to say, the loan submission from the branch or satellite office must include all the necessary documents so that the loan can flow through the approval and funding process. The construction loan is usually approved by the residential loan director or regional vice president, depending on the structure of the mortgage banking firm. Normally, loans over a specific amount take loan committee approval. Once the loan is closed, the banking department must prepare the loan for disbursements according to the draw schedule specified in the construction loan agreement.

The mortgage banker should inspect the property prior to advancing any draw request. This inspection should be made by the loan officer, branch manager, or a designee who has experience with building construction. The mortgage banker should enforce the construction loan agreement, so that the builder will not be allowed to fall behind the disbursement schedule, thus putting the mortgage security in jeopardy.

Along with loan underwriting, the collection of construction interest is one of the most important aspects of interim or construction lending. A leading indicator that a builder has financial problems is the nonpayment or slow payment of construction interest. A systematic follow-up of past-due borrowers by the loan officer or branch manager will help curb the default rate in the construction loan portfolio. In addition, any further loan approvals or advances on existing loans should be curtailed unless interest is in a current status and any liens (or notices of intent to lien) filed by suppliers and subcontractors are satisfied. Construction lenders should be familiar with state laws before advancing funds where known liens exist.

Whereas residential foreclosures are handled by the servicing department for permanent loans in service, construction loan foreclosures are handled by the production department. Should a foreclosure occur, immediate steps must be taken to complete construction or to secure the property and arrange for disposal as soon as possible. The branch manager or loan officer should obtain an appraisal of the current market value and list the property with an active real estate broker familiar with the area. A periodic inspection of the property is necessary to ensure against vandalism or weather damage. Proper yard and exterior maintenance is necessary to ensure that the property is in good marketable condition. Extra incentives should be offered to local branch managers normally primarily concerned with residential production to ensure quick disposal of the property. In addition, a penalty system should be devised so that the branch is charged with a portion of the cost of carrying the property during the period it is not an interest-earning asset.

Spot Loans

For builder loans, the customer of the mortgage originator is obviously the builder. For spot loans, the customer is the real estate broker or his agent, the real estate sales person. Accordingly, spot-loan volume is generated by loan officers who call on real estate offices to provide such services as taking loan applications at the buyer's convenience, prequalifying applicants, obtaining necessary approvals, and monitoring the required appraisals. Customers are usually captured by the quality of the loan officer's service—unique product knowledge and speed, accuracy, and skill in solving processing problems. While price is a major determinant and often what makes the deal, the most skilled loan officers and managers form strong, durable relationships with substantial sources of business.

Spot-loan origination offices are usually staffed by a manager (who may originate loans), loan officers, who usually work on a commission basis; and a processing/closing staff. In some cases, there are satellite offices with only sales staff. The processing is done at a larger nearby office. This is a potentially costly distribution system. Commissions and incentives must be high enough to retain skilled performers. Even so, there is always high turnover. Maintaining a consistent quality of service, underwriting, and documentation requires substantial investments in manpower, management resources, training, and hardware. In downturns, staffs are usually not reduced as fast as volume (even with commissioned loan officers), and when there are surges of volume they usually cannot be expanded fast enough. This system of personal service to a continuing user (a realtor or a broker) enhances the originator's identity in the local mortgage market. It builds a reputation for quality and develops customer loyalty. It also provides a more consistent and more predictable volume than do alternative wholesale loan-origination systems.

The real estate brokerage office typically is a fairly small business. Currently, almost 90 percent of real estate firms have only one office. Almost 20 percent of all firms are affiliated with national franchises, and the larger the firm, the more likely it is to be affiliated. The trend towards larger firms appears to have been affected by the downturn in real estate market conditions, at least temporarily. (See Table 2, Figures 1, 2, and 3, and Table 3.)

The head of a real estate brokerage office does not always control the office's mortgage business. In a number of large firms, individual sales agents

Table 2 • Trends in the Size of Firms in Terms of Real Estate Offices: 1979–1982 (percentage distribution)

Number of Offices	1979	1980	1981	1982
1	85.7%	85.4%	83.7%	89.0%
2	8.8	9.5	10.1	7.1
3	2.7	1.7	2.7	1.5
4	1.0	0.9	1.2	0.6
5	0.4	0.4	0.3	0.7
6–10	0.9	1.1	0.9	0.9
Over 10	0.5	1.0	1.1	0.2
Total	100.0%	100.0%	100.0%	100.0%

Figure 1 • Comparison of the Size of Firm and the Percent of Salespersons Affiliated with Different Size Firms (percentage distribution)

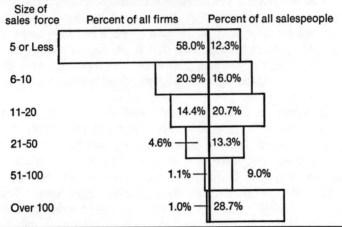

Size of sales force	Percent of all firms	Percent of all salespeople
5 or Less	58.0%	12.3%
6-10	20.9%	16.0%
11-20	14.4%	20.7%
21-50	4.6%	13.3%
51-100	1.1%	9.0%
Over 100	1.0%	28.7%

may be separate sources of referrals. Even though franchisers may at times enter into special arrangements with a particular lender, it is usually up to the local affiliates as to how much volume they will generate under this arrangement.

Spot versus Builder

While spot and builder businesses differ widely, some generalizations can be useful for planning lending strategy. The following paragraphs outline some points of concern.

Spot loans form a much larger market, approximately three to four times the builder market in most locations. It is an easier market to enter because one does not have to offer construction financing to get the first crack at the business. It is a more consistent market, less subject to the significant fluctuations that recessions or tight money cause in the builder business. Some lenders find the spot loan business less sensitive to pricing considerations than builder loans. (Part of almost every builder advertisement refers to monthly payment or financing costs.)

Builder loan business has the advantage of lower origination costs, occasional higher front-end income, and (without major interest-rate changes) a more predictable volume. The close relationship developed with a builder by a mortgage banker, particularly if he or she is also the construction lender, helps to create loyalty. Issuing forward commitments for a front-end fee helps to keep the builder from straying to a competitor. Realtors do not have this incentive.

Figure 2 • Trends in the Percent of Firms in Various Size Categories: 1979–1982 (percentage distribution)

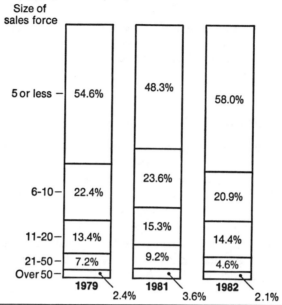

There are larger risks and different staff requirements in doing builder loans. For a construction lender, there are concerns about the builder's ability to complete a project, the time necessary to complete it, and the ultimate saleability of the product. When securing builder commitments in the secondary market, the need for long forward commitments presents problems for mortgage bankers, particularly if a wide variety of financing alternatives is required.

Figure 3 • Franchise Affiliation of Firms: 1977–1982 (percent of firms)

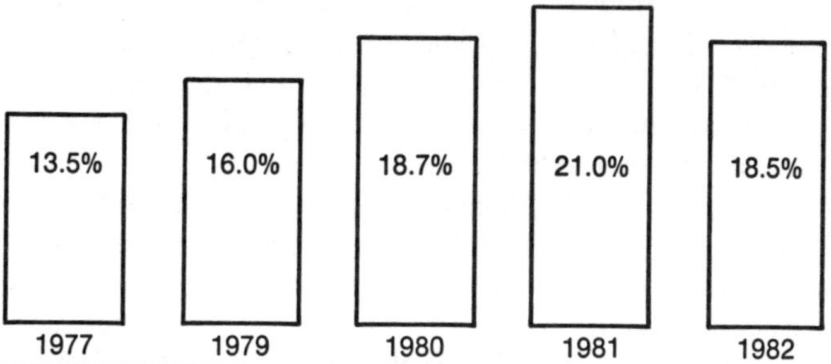

13.5%	16.0%	18.7%	21.0%	18.5%
1977	1979	1980	1981	1982

Table 3 • Firms Affiliated with Franchises: 1979–1982 (percent of firms)

Year	All Firms	10 or Less	11–20	21–50	Over 50
			Size of Sales Force		
1982	18.5%	12.1%	43.9%	40.5%	35.0%
1981	21.0	13.6	41.8	47.1	51.4
1980	18.7	15.9	39.0	48.1	30.4
1979	16.0	15.1	32.3	46.0	31.1

Wholesale Distribution

The relatively high cost of maintaining spot loan origination branches has led to an increasing use of wholesale methods of obtaining loans. In one pattern, noncontractual relations are established by mortgage bankers with mortgage brokers or with other lenders who act as brokers. The brokers secure and process the loan and submit it to the wholesaler for underwriting, closing, and funding. Wholesale offices are usually staffed only by a manager and a clerical force and may not be local. (A regional office is adequate for providing the effective management of documentation.) Since the wholesaler does the underwriting and closing, control is maintained over the quality of the loan. These loans are usually closed into the mortgage banker's own warehouse. This option to avoid warehousing risks is often the primary incentive for other lenders to broker loans to wholesaler mortgage bankers.

Another wholesale alternative is the purchase of loans already closed by another lender, that is, loans with servicing. The servicing purchased by this method is typically made up of FHA and VA loans, because only government loans do not require re-underwriting by the wholesaler. Often, the sellers of such servicing are mortgage bankers who enter into firm contracts to deliver a given percentage of their government closings to the wholesaler. Originating for sale to wholesalers may attract mortgage bankers who are too small to package their own GNMA securities, or who have a greater need for immediate income than for long-term servicing income, or who have either no or insufficient warehousing lines of credit.

Although many wholesaler mortgage bankers have regional offices, this system can be managed from a centralized home office. Overhead and start-up costs are usually minimal, and personnel costs per loan are usually the lowest of any other method of origination. If the wholesaled loans are priced at closing, there is usually little secondary-market risk. While volume in this system is difficult to predict, surges are more easily managed.

As compared to the branch-origination spot loan system, wholesale methods of originating have much less market recognition and customer loyalty. There is little to differentiate one wholesaler from another, except price or being first in a given local market. Wholesalers of the first category, those buying loans before closing, can partly offset this by offering types of loans that are difficult

Table 4 • Advantages and Disadvantages of Using Different Mortgage-Originator Distribution Systems

	Advantages	Disadvantages
Branches using a sales force	Dependable sources Quality control Name identity Involvement with consumer	Large capital investment Difficulty and high cost of managing volume surges High interest-rate risk Need for administrative management
Centralized without using a sales force	Low overhead Ease in managing volume surges	Less dependable sources Reduced name identity Potentially high interest-rate risk Limited geographic spread Relative noninvolvement with consumer
Wholesale: loan purchase	Low start-up and operating expenses Ease in managing volume surges Lessened interest rate risk	Reduced quality control Reduced name identity Price competitive
Wholesale: purchase of servicing	Low start-up and operating expenses Handles volume surges well No interest rate risk	Capital intensive Reduced quality control Lack of name identity Very price competitive

to obtain elsewhere in addition to standard mortgages. The relative advantages and disadvantages of using different mortgage originator distribution systems are graphically presented in Table 4.

Direct to Consumer

An alternative wholesale method for originating loans is to bypass the intermediary and go directly to the consumer. This is quite common in refinancing existing first mortgages and in generating both new and existing second-mortgage loans. Historically, thrifts have appealed to their customers this way, not only for loans but for savings as well. Many companies have access to lists of loans with high interest rates—both in their own servicing portfolio and in the portfolios of others—which they use to solicit owners with offers of lower interest-rate loans. Usually, interested owners are directed to contact local origination offices.

Sometimes there is no outside sales force. Offices are staffed by a manager and a processing/closing team. Traffic is generated by persistent advertising, typically direct mail and newspaper advertising which stresses low-rate financing. Using this method, the lender retains full control of product quality, maintains identity in the market (particularly if affiliated with another type of local lender), and may retain servicing on a loan which would otherwise have been lost to competition. Surges and slowdowns in volume are usually easily managed, partly by turning advertising on or off. If no sales force is involved, the savings in sales commissions can be substantial. However, these savings may be insufficient to offset the costs of advertising plus the pricing subsidies that may be necessary to attract the customer.

The Consumer: Market Segments

When mortgage originators speak of customers, they rarely mean the mortgage applicant. The customer is usually another intermediary—the builder or real estate broker—who brings them the applicants. Still, it is the mortgage applicants who make up the ultimate market for the mortgage originator's services. The consumer segment is the market in which the mortgage banker's primary customers must deal, and it is important to understand which income level and social class of applicant the primary customers address. There are three broad categories:

Middle Income Applicants.   These applicants comprise the mass market. Applicants range from blue-collar workers (generally the higher paid and higher seniority individuals) through white-collar workers to those in middle management, small businesses and professionals. (Many of these households also have two incomes.)

This market segment generates the most loan volume. It is the most sensitive to price competition. It can sustain significant fluctuations in volume, and sales will be affected by high interest rates. It is the market in which most mortgage applicants qualify for loans and in which more seller financing is used. As in other segments, sales are affected by recessions, since there are fewer employee transfers and fewer decisions to trade up.

These applicants usually prefer conventional loans, although there will be swings to FHA/VA when FHA/VA maximum loan amounts are sufficiently high or when low discount points prevail. In markets in which housing costs are not so high (the South and the Southeast), there is a substantial acceptance of FHA/VA loans at all times.

Recent consumer and lender surveys have shown differences within the markets in the acceptance of adjustable-rate mortgages and other alternative mortgage instruments, particularly some of the more exotic instruments. Upwardly mobile executives and professionals seem to understand more about the need for these types of loans and are more willing to accept them. Most borrowers are concerned about budgeting their income and do not know how to deal with the uncertainty of possible future payment increases. Acceptance, as might be expected, is also greater where the local economy is strong and borrowers are therefore more confident of future increases in income. Also, in a strong economy, there may be fewer choices. However, most people still prefer fixed-rate loans with no possibility of negative amortization.

Lenders serving this market need the capability of originating conventional and FHA/VA loans. Also, after periods during which there has been extensive seller financing, there is significant potential for refinancing volume when rates decline.

Low to Moderate Income Applicants. This borrower is one with a lower disposable income, who has to commit a higher percentage of that income to housing. In many instances there is limited credit history, or one in which credit payment records have to be carefully reviewed. Most of these customers have primarily blue-collar or service occupations. Hence, they are highly vulnerable to recessions and unemployment and to increases in monthly mortgage-payment requirements caused by higher interest rates. In some markets, a significant portion are minority families. Some are households headed by single parents, most often female. Because of a traditionally higher percentage of delinquencies, these loans have a higher-than-average servicing cost.

This market is made up almost solidly of government loans; it is predominantly a spot loan market. Occasionally, subsidy programs permit these applicants to qualify for starter new homes. There is usually less competition from conventional loan seekers in this market segment and less price sensitivity. There also tends to be much more customer (that is, real estate broker) loyalty to lenders and sales representatives who provide good, consistent service.

High Income Applicants. These loan applicants have high disposable income and assets. This usually permits flexible decision making regarding when to buy and how much to borrow. Since they usually live in high-cost housing areas, these applicants usually require loans in amounts above the FNMA, FHLMC, FHA, or GNMA ceilings. These applicants are typically professional, executive, or upper-income white-collar workers. In many cases, the household has two incomes. This market is least affected by recessions. Accordingly, the mortgages are normally less costly to service, because there are fewer delinquencies. The higher loan balances generate higher origination fees and more profitable servicing-fee income but less late-fee income. These applicants are also good prospects for second mortgages.

Virtually all mortgage bankers are forced to originate only *conforming loans* (loans eligible for sale to FNMA or FHLMC, or in a GNMA pool, if they are FHA or VA loans). However, an occasional institutional investor may be in the market to purchase *nonconforming loans* (high-balance loans). If the mortgage banker is able to originate and sell loan balances in excess of those acceptable to FNMA, FHLMC, or GNMA, there is a profitable opportunity. Having access to investors who purchase high-balance loans can be very profitable in luxury housing areas, because there is usually less competition. However, Realtors and builders who serve this market (and their customers) require greater and more sophisticated service, so that loan officers need to devote additional time to reaching these customers and consumers.

Types of Loans

The perception of a changing need or attitude among investors historically has led to new types of mortgages. Thus, the popularity of commercial mortgages with equity participations (kickers) as hedges against inflation led to the development of a shared-appreciation mortgage for residential loans. Similarly, the clear preference of investors for intermediate-term over long-term bonds led to the development of growth equity mortgages, paying off in 11 to 15 years. The introduction of special loan programs is a twofold test, first with investors, then with borrowers. Again, if the mortgage banker can sell it, he can usually originate it.

The adage "sell first, originate second" has long been the guiding principle of mortgage banking loan production. In recent years, the large choice of different loan types that are sold to FNMA and FHLMC, either as whole loans, as participations, or as collateral for the sale of FNMA and GNMA mortgage-backed securities, presents a new challenge. As the middleman between the homebuyer and the mortgage investor, the mortgage banker must maintain a balance between the two conflicting demands. Whatever compromise is effected, the test of market acceptance dictates what type of product can be originated in volume. Fixed, low-rate, assumable 30-year loans are the clear choice of most homebuyers. Variable, high-rate, non-assumable, short-term loans are the distinct preference of mortgage investors.

When interest rates are high relative to the recent past, homebuyers seem to be more willing to accept loans that are alternatives to fixed-rate, long-term mortgages, particularly if they may prepay without a penalty. However, when rates are low, homeowners overwhelmingly opt for fixed-rate loans. The major alternative mortgage products available in the marketplace and the respective investor and borrower considerations are set forth in Table 5.

In addition to the reactions of investors and consumers, pricing and marketing considerations are important in differentiating product lines. Mortgage originators should decide their pricing strategy in light of their own corporate objectives, resources, and calculated responses to market competition. Issues such as length of the commitment period, up-front commitment fees, whether to play the market, whether to buy coverage and whether to hedge mandatory deliveries with futures must be examined. Adequate reporting systems are, of course, mandatory.

In originating spot and builder loans, certain origination methods will complement the products being offered. The field sales force is a key element, particularly with many hard-to-understand mortgages. Loan officers should have a thorough knowledge of their products. Providing adequate services requires sufficient training. Training, therefore, is a key element in the unique product knowledge required for the successful loan officer.

In determining a product-mix strategy, managers should review frequently whether the specific product mix represents a good balance in terms of current volume, cost control, administrative feasibility, commitment fees required, sales stability, and profitability. Markets are continually changing in their needs and preferences, and the continuing proliferation of different loan types means that future change is assured.

The mortgage banker should be aware of new types of mortgages as they appear in the marketplace and educate personnel in the application and implications of new products. While the many and varied types of loans present a challenge to loan officers, they also present an opportunity, since the customer is even more dependent on loan officers to describe the choices and explain the variations.

The impact of a new product on all areas of the company should be thoroughly explored before the first loan is originated; problems should be anticipated and solutions thought through. Too often, several new mortgage products are originated, applications taken and closings effected, and then problems occur which could have been avoided had adequate research been undertaken first.

External and internal controls are necessary to control the quality and compliance aspects of various mortgages, particularly the more exotic mortgages. While HUD, GNMA, FHLMC, FNMA and state agencies may determine the lender's external controls, internal controls should be fitted to the needs of management. Additionally, financial controls should be carefully monitored for volume and profitability by type of mortgage, customer, and location.

Table 5 • Major Alternative Mortgage Products

Product	Investor Considerations	Borrower Considerations
Adjustable-rate mortgage (including ARMs and AMLs)	Product protects investor from long-term changes in the cost of money; however, if the index selected does not reflect changes in the lender's cost of funds (or if the lender does not build in an adequate profit margin), long-term profit may be less than with a standard fixed-rate mortgage.	Amount of future payments is unknown and risk is that increases will be beyond the borrower's ability to pay. In limited cases, the loan balance may be increased above the fair market value of the property.
Balloon mortgage	Due to a shorter term than most other mortgage types, these provide a good asset/liability match. Often, these mortgages are more risky than others as a result of the shorter and nonamortizing terms.	Balloons do not provide long-term security since they must be paid off in a short period of time. In periods of rising interest rates, borrower may have difficulty refinancing or selling the property.
Graduated-payment mortgage (including graduated-payment, adjustable-rate mortgage)	Yields in the first years are lower than on other mortgage products.	More borrowers can qualify due to the lower initial payments. Negative amortization payments may increase the loan balance above the fair market value of the property. In the GPARM, there is a possibility of a graduation of payments and an interest rate increase above the borrower's ability to pay.
Growing equity mortgage	Due to the shorter term of these mortgages, the lender has a better asset/liability match.	Although there is usually a cap on payment increases, the risk that the borrower will be unable to make the payment still exists. Borrowers can achieve the same goals of earlier payoff and decreased interest expenses without legally obligating themselves to increased payments by simply paying more money each month and by applying it to the principal balance.

Interest-rate buy-down	With permanent buy-downs, there is a risk that the loan will not be paid off within the assumed period (12 years), decreasing the return on the loan. When the seller provides buy-down funds, there is a risk that the actual value of the property is less than the loan amount.	With the lower initial monthly payments, more borrowers can qualify for mortgages; however, there is a risk that in the case of temporary buy-downs, the borrower may not be able to afford the increased payments.
Pledged account	When the seller provides funds for the pledged account, there is a risk that the actual value of the property is less than the loan amount.	(Same as Interest-rate buy-down)
Second mortgage	In the case of foreclosure on the first mortgage, the second lien would not be satisfied. In the case of balloon second mortgages, there is a risk that the borrower will not be able to pay the amount due at maturity.	This type of mortgage enables a homeowner to obtain some of the equity from the property without the need to refinance the first mortgage. For homebuyers, seconds facilitate assuming a low-interest first mortgage.
Wrap-around mortgage	Lenders may be able to obtain yields that are above current market rates.	Interest rates on the total outstanding debt is usually less than current market rates.
Reverse-annuity mortgage	If the payments are deferred until maturity, the borrower may be unable to afford them at that time.	Homeowners would be provided with a means of converting the equity in their homes into cash.
Shared-appreciation mortgage	There is no assurance that the property value will appreciate sufficiently to compensate for the below-market rate and the decreased cash flow.	The below-market rate of these mortgages makes them affordable for a larger number of borrowers.

Source: Federal National Mortgage Association, 1982.

Determining one's lending strategy, therefore, is a matter of choosing the type of customer one wishes to serve, organizing the appropriate method(s) to fill the customer's needs, and providing the particular competitive loans which match the current demand of consumers and investors, thereby enabling the mortgage banker's customer to be rewarded for a better job.

—— Chapter 12 ——————————————

The Value of Mortgage Banking

John W. Starke
Managing Director
Westchester Mortgage Company

Introduction

Mortgage bankers have dominated the secondary mortgage market for 30 years by using a combination of salesmanship, administrative efficiency, and considerable leverage. The increasing importance of the secondary mortgage market has stimulated interest in the value of mortgage-banking firms, as portfolio lenders have sought to acquire mortgage-banking methods. Also, large mortgage bankers have added to their servicing portfolios by purchasing other mortgage bankers and servicing portfolios. The question of the economic value of mortgage banking is important not only to buyers and sellers of firms, but also to a firm's management for corporate planning.

In general, mortgage bankers perform two functions: loan production and loan servicing. Loan production can be subdivided into origination, warehousing, and marketing. *Origination* is the process of soliciting business from the home builder or real estate broker, taking the loan application, processing the loan for underwriting, and closing the loan. *Warehousing* is the process of financing the closed loan until it is sold to the permanent investor. *Marketing* is the process of selling the loan to the permanent investor.

Mortgage-loan servicing is basically the process of collecting the monthly payment from the mortgagor, remitting the payment to the permanent investor, and handling other contacts with the borrower for the investor (delinquencies, assumptions, escrow accounts, and the payments of real estate tax and insurance premiums).

Approaches to Value

The historical market for mortgage bankers has exhibited a wide range of prices for both operating firms and for portfolio servicing. Economic uncertainty, the lack of good market information, changing participants, and speculation are the major contributors to the wide range of prices.

For these reasons, the market approach to valuation provides a range of potential values. It does not establish a point estimate. While any point estimate of value should be bounded by actual market experience, the other appraisal methods—income approach and cost approach—are more useful for valuing mortgage banking.

Income Approach

The traditional method employed to value a going business is the income approach: projecting future net income and discounting to present value. Often the sources of future-income projection are the firm's financial statements for several preceding years. In general, past performance (measured by accounting net income) is not indicative of a mortgage-banker's future performance. Accounting rules allow enough discretion in the treatment of certain expenses that firms can manage earnings. Further, mortgage bankers can operate in three basic, different modes to manage earnings: (1) originate loans and hold the servicing; (2) originate loans and sell the servicing; and (3) do not originate loans but buy servicing.

A firm may switch quickly from one mode to another, depending on its corporate goals. If a firm originates and holds servicing, it typically will have a low reported income (possibly a loss) in the early years of operation. However, the firm will build up a servicing portfolio that can provide stable future earnings, even if originations are depressed.

If a firm originates and sells the servicing, it should show high current income from the sale of the servicing. Since no servicing portfolio is created, which would otherwise be a future servicing cash flow, future income is dependent on the firm's ability to originate loans or buy servicing in future years.

If a firm purchases servicing, it buys a servicing annuity and creates an asset that must be amortized. To the extent that the annual amortization of the purchase price is less than the alternative actual cost of originating loans for the portfolio, a buyer of servicing can increase the rate of his net-worth formation.

Servicing can be bought in a variety of ways. The common method is a sale of a block of servicing in which the price is negotiated in private. Sometimes a block of servicing will be offered to a large number of bidders and sold to the highest bidder. Servicing may also be purchased on a loan-by-loan basis. In this case, the buyer may be purchasing a loan and selling the same loan while retaining the servicing. Finally, servicing can be obtained by purchasing an entire mortgage-banking company.

Business Plan

Because there are different methods of operation used by mortgage bankers, a potential purchaser should request management to prepare a business plan to forecast future income. The business-plan approach may be the best way to evaluate a firm that possesses a unique attribute (such as personal contacts in a local market or with investors). The drawback to forecasting future income is that single-forecast business plans tend to be optimistic. Hence, the value of the cash flow may be inflated. For this reason, alternative projections of business plans can provide a perspective on both risk and value.

Ultimately, the choice usually is not *whether* to buy a specific mortgage banker, but *how much* it will cost to enter the industry. Mortgage banking is a competitive industry with many participants. The alternative to buying a specific firm in order to acquire mortgage-banking technology would be purchasing the components separately.

Cost Approach

The cost approach is used often to value mortgage companies. The value of the firm is the cost of purchasing the components of the first: the market value of the net assets, the production and servicing organization, and the servicing portfolio.

The value of the servicing portfolio is often the largest asset; hence, it requires special attention. The income approach is the usual method of valuing a servicing portfolio.

Application of Methods

To illustrate the income and cost approaches, consider the case of Goode–Prospect Mortgage Company. The firm was started 10 years ago by 2 former loan originators; they remain the principal managers. Initially, the firm sold most of the servicing it originated; later it retained servicing. Now the servicing portfolio has grown to 5,000 loans with a remaining principal balance of $200 million.

Last year Goode–Prospect originated $40 million of new production, and production this year will be $60 million. The firm has two origination offices and six loan originators. The owners believe that the firm is poised for rapid growth; they plan to increase production by $40 million a year for the next 4 years. However, the firm would be more successful if it had a strong parent. Since the owners believe that a financial institution could use the escrow funds more effectively and provide the firm with more reliable inventory financing, they are offering the firm for sale at a price of $4 million.

The prospective purchaser is Regional Bank, a medium-sized bank not currently active in mortgage lending. How should Regional evaluate Goode–Prospect?

A projected balance sheet for the end of this fiscal year is shown in Table 1 and a projected income statement in Table 2. The following evaluation of Goode–Prospect uses the income and cost approaches.

Table 1 • Goode–Prospect Mortgage Company: Projected Balance Sheet

Assets	
Cash	$ 150,000
Loan Inventory	12,000,000
Fixed Assets (net)	50,000
Other Assets	30,000
Total Assets	$12,230,000
Liabilities	
Loan Inventory	$11,400,000
Other Bank Notes	400,000
Total Liabilities	$11,800,000
Owners' Equity	$ 430,000

Note: The firm also holds funds in escrow for borrowers totaling $3,000,000.

Table 2 • Goode–Prospect Mortgage Company: Projected Income Statement

Income	
Origination Fees	$ 600,000
Net Interest	10,000
Gain on Loans Sold	150,000
Servicing Fees	680,000
Other	60,000
Total Income	$1,500,000
Expense	
Personnel	$ 980,000
Occupancy	150,000
Utilities	110,000
Travel	18,000
Data Processing	20,000
Other	52,000
Total Expense	$1,330,000
Net Income	$ 170,000
Tax	78,200
After-tax Net Income	91,800

Income Approach

Analysis Method

The income approach forecasts the corporate cash flow, using a defined business plan, and then discounts the after-tax cash flow to present value. Recognizing that the probability of achieving one specific business plan is low, the evaluator should examine several business plans. There is always a trade-off between the level of effort to develop a forecasting model and the precision of the model. This evaluation uses simple forecasting rules, supplied by Goode–Prospect.

Assumptions

The following assumptions for the business plan are summarized in Table 3:

1. The management of Goode–Prospect Mortgage Company plans rapidly growing loan production for four years, and then anticipates a steady-state loan production for six years.

2. All servicing is retained. Management assumes that loans will run off at 8 percent a year.

3. The average loan balance remains constant at $50,000. This is a simplifying assumption for the purpose of illustration. This assumption neglects the impact of inflation on new-loan production. A more sophisticated model might assume that future average loan balances increase at some inflation rate. (Note: This is an example of the trade-off between the effort to develop the model and the precision of the model.)

4. To give value to the servicing portfolio, assume that it will be sold at the end of 10 years at a price of 1.2 percent.

5. The net cost of origination includes the net income (or loss) from all origination fees, and expenses warehouse interest-rate spread, gain or loss on the sale of loans, and all costs of production. The firm expects to produce loans at a 0.4 percent net loss.

6. Gross servicing income (including servicing fees and other income) is 42 basis points.

Table 3 • Business-Plan Assumptions

Beginning Portfolio	
Amount (millions)	$200
Number of loans	5,000
Production	
Volume for 10 years (millions)	$100, 140, 180, 220, 260, 260, 260, 260, 260, 260
Average new loan	$50,000
Servicing run-off	8% per year
Net cost of origination (percent of volume)	0.4% of loan production
Gross servicing income	0.42% of average servicing volume
Cost of servicing ($ per loan)	60, 55, 50, 45, 45, 45, 50, 50, 55, 55
Fixed expense	$150,000, increasing 10% a year
Net sale value of servicing	1.2% of ending servicing amount
Tax rate	46%
Escrow amount	1.5% of servicing amount
Escrow earnings rate	8%
Purchase price	$4 million
Tax amortization	$3 million, 10 years straight-line

7. The cost of servicing will decline for a time (because of improved efficiency), before increasing again because of inflation.

8. The bank will derive value from the escrow funds at the net rate of 8 percent. Escrow funds are 1.5 percent of the servicing amount.

Projected Cash Flow

The cash flow associated with this business plan is shown in Table 4. Each year net income increases as servicing volume grows. The plan assumes that at the end of 10 years, the servicing portfolio is sold at a price of 1.2 percent of remaining principal.

The value of the firm is the total expected net cash flow discounted to present value.[1]

In this case, the total cash flow is the current net worth, the annual after-tax cash flow, and the net proceeds from the theoretical sale of servicing in 10 years. Using a 15 percent discount rate, the present value is $4,564,000. Inasmuch as this calculation shows that the firm is worth more than the $4 million asking price, management is confident that the firm is reasonably priced.

The fundamental risk of this estimate is the probability of actually achieving the business plan. All sorts of calamities could depress earnings: low production, high costs, marketing losses, or a drop in the value of servicing (at the end of 10 years). Of course, management could argue that the business plan is conservative and that the firm will exceed this expectation.

To give some perspective to the value of the firm, assume that the growth of new loan production stops in the second year and stays constant for three years before growth resumes. This could happen because of a general slowdown in the housing market rather than because of a fault of management. Further, assume that the earnings rate on escrows falls to 5 percent, and the net cost of origination increases to 0.6 percent of the amount produced.

The cash flow for this assumption is shown in Table 5. Notice that the servicing portfolio and net income grow more slowly. The result is that the present value of the cash flow is reduced to $1,451,000 for the slower growth scenario.

The Value of Servicing

The value of a mortgage-servicing portfolio is the *expected net present value of the future after tax cash flow from all sources associated with the servicing portfolio.*

Expected value means that the evaluator must define a probability distribu-

---

[1] A good reference on the theory of present value is *Financial Theory and Corporate Policy* by T. E. Copeland and J. F. Weston, (Reading, Mass.: Addison-Wesley Publishing Company, 1979).

Table 4 • Goode–Prospect: Business Plan

Year	1	2	3	4	5	6	7	8	9	10
Loan Production										
$Millions	100	140	180	220	260	260	260	260	260	260
Average Servicing										
$Millions	234	335	468	631	821	1,015	1,194	1,358	1,510	1,649
#	5,600	7,552	10,148	13,336	17,069	20,904	24,431	27,677	30,663	33,410
Average Escrow										
$Millions	4	5	7	9	12	15	18	20	23	25
Income Statement—$000										
Net Origination	-400	-560	-720	-880	-1,040	-1,040	-1,040	-1,040	-1,040	-1,040
Servicing Income	936	1,341	1,874	2,524	3,282	4,059	4,775	5,433	6,038	6,595
Servicing Expense	-336	-415	-507	-600	-768	-941	-1,222	-1,384	-1,686	-1,838
Net Operating Income	200	366	646	1,044	1,474	2,079	2,513	3,009	3,312	3,718
Escrow Income	281	402	562	757	985	1,218	1,432	1,630	1,811	1,979
Sale of Servicing										19,785
Purchase Amortization	300	300	300	300	300	300	300	300	300	300
Tax	83	215	418	690	993	1,378	1,677	1,996	2,219	11,583
Net Income	398	553	791	1,111	1,466	1,918	2,269	2,643	2,904	-5,887
Present Value	4,564									

Table 5 • Goode—Prospect: Delayed Growth

Year	1	2	3	4	5	6	7	8	9	10
Loan Production $Millions	100	100	100	100	140	180	220	260	260	260
Average Servicing $Millions	234	315	390	459	542	659	806	982	1,163	1,330
#	5,600	7,152	8,580	9,893	11,502	13,782	16,679	20,145	23,733	27,035
Average Escrow $Millions	4	5	6	7	8	10	12	15	17	20
Income Statement—$000										
Net Origination	-600	-600	-600	-600	-840	-1,080	-1,320	-1,560	-1,560	-1,560
Servicing Income	936	1,261	1,560	1,835	2,169	2,635	3,224	3,926	4652	5,320
Servicing Expense	-336	-393	-429	-445	-518	-620	-834	-1,007	-1,305	-1,487
Net Operating Income	0	268	531	790	811	935	1,070	1,359	1,787	2,273
Escrow Income	176	236	293	344	407	494	605	736	872	998
Sale of Servicing										15,960
Purchase Amortization	300	300	300	300	300	300	300	300	300	300
Tax	-57	94	241	384	422	519	632	826	1,085	8708
Net Income	233	410	583	751	796	910	1,042	1,269	1,574	-5,438
Present Value	1,451									

tion for the future life of the loan portfolio. *Present value* means that future cash flows must be discounted to the present, using the firm's internal cost of capital. *After tax* means after corporate tax. And *all sources* means that cash flows associated with escrow funds and ancillary forms of income, such as late charges and insurance sales, should be included in the calculation.

For ease of understanding, most evaluators divide the sources of cash flow into net operating income and escrow income. The net operating income includes all of the income and expenses typically associated with the operation of a mortgage-servicing company except escrow income. Net operating income is also defined pretax.

Servicing Income

The principal source of income to a mortgage banker is the servicing fee. The servicing fees for single-family loans typically range from 25 basis points to 50 basis points. The servicing fee may be much lower for large income-property loans. Also, servicing fees may be defined in terms of a fixed dollar amount per loan for special servicing contracts. Over time the amount of the percentage servicing fee is reduced as the loan balance amortizes.

Other servicing income is earned primarily from late charges, miscellaneous fees, and insurance premiums. Late charges are earned on loans for which the monthly payment is received after the fifteenth of the month. The typical late charge on FHA/VA loans is 4 percent of the principal and interest not received by the fifteenth of the month each and every month.

Lenders may also collect a fee for handling assumptions on existing loans assumed by new buyers of the property mortgaged. This fee may be a fixed dollar amount, or it may be as much as 1 percent of the amount of the loan assumed. The amount of assumption fees depends on the status of the current real estate market and whether loans can be legally assumed in the state where the loans are located.

Another valuable source of income is the premium received for the sale of various types of insurance to mortgagors. The most common types of insurance sold are credit life and accident and health insurance. Some lenders have also been successful in selling hazard insurance.

A final category of income is the fee received for performing some special service for a party to the mortgage. An example of this kind of fee would be the 235-recertification fee currently paid by FHA for 235 loans.

Servicing Cost

The regular costs of servicing cover such tasks as collecting the monthly payment, remitting the payment to investors, preparing reports, collecting and maintaining escrow accounts, and paying real estate tax and insurance premiums. Another regular expense is the cost of managing delinquencies and foreclosures. These costs depend on the delinquency rate associated with the specific loan portfolio and the costs of foreclosure in the local region.

There is some evidence that the collection and foreclosure portion of servicing declines as loans mature because borrowers learn to pay on time to protect the growing equity in their homes. Since the average cost of collection and foreclosure is in the range of 30 to 50 percent of the total average servicing cost, the average cost of servicing may decline for older loans.

Other special costs can occur because of the type of loan or the requirements of the investor. FHA 235 loans require special annual contacts with the borrower to recertify the borrower for the government subsidy. Loans located in some jurisdictions may require more frequent or more complicated payments of real estate taxes. Some investors require periodic inspection of the property.

Loans sold to investors using GNMA securities incur special costs because of the requirement that the investor must receive timely payment of principal and interest, whether or not the funds are collected from the borrower. This means that the servicer/security issuer must advance funds not received by the fifteenth. Thus, there is an interest charge to finance the funds advanced until the monthly payments received from late-paying or delinquent borrowers make up the cash deficit.

In some cases, the servicer incurs other costs that are not recovered from the cash flow from the pool of mortgages. In the case of foreclosure on FHA loans, the servicer incurs a cost of one-third of the acquisition cost of the property, and may lose an interest cost, which is the difference between the rate on the mortgage-backed security and the debenture rate paid by FHA from the time of foreclosure until the acquisition of the property. In the case of prepayment of VA loans, the servicer may not collect part of a month's interest from the borrower, but the servicer must still pass the entire month's interest through to the certificate holder.

Surveys by the Mortgage Bankers Association indicate that the current average annual cost of servicing is in the range of $50 to $60 per loan. However, the cost falls slightly, then levels out as the number of loans serviced increases (see Figure 1). The average annual cost for most large servicers is in the range of $40 to $50 per loan. Since the industry's average-cost curve appears to be sloping downwards, the marginal cost must be below average cost over the range of activity for most firms.

The usual method of projecting servicing costs into the future is to multiply the annual servicing costs per loan by an inflation factor. In the past, the inflation factor for the cost of servicing has been less than the consumer price index because mortgage bankers have experienced economies of scale and increasing productivity in servicing from automation. Some costs, such as the interest costs associated with advancing funds to GNMA pools, or the costs of severely delinquent loans, are a function of other variables such as the interest rate or local economic conditions.

Figure 1 • Industry Cost of Servicing

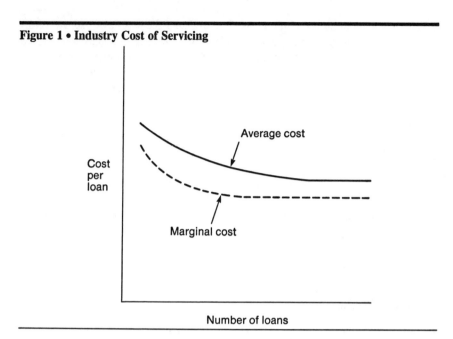

Escrow Income

Most lenders collect a portion of the annual real estate tax and insurance payments each month and hold these funds in escrow until the payment is due. The funds are held usually in interest-free accounts, thus giving the lender the use of the balances. A recent trend has been for some states to require that lenders pay the borrower interest on the average escrow balance. (The issue of interest on escrows may be a major consumer issue during the 1980s.)

Another source of escrow funds is the float on the monthly principal and interest that the mortgage banker collects and remits to the permanent investor. Borrowers typically pay between the first and fifteenth of the month, and the funds are due to the investor between the fifteenth and the twenty-fifth of the month. It is not unusual for the mortgage banker to hold these funds for an average of 10 days. This source of funds is commonly called the *P&I float*. In the case of mortgage-backed securities, the P&I float may still exist, but often it is overwhelmed by the cash advanced to certificate holders because of late payments.

Even though escrow funds may be held in accounts that do not bear interest, the lender may use the funds as compensating balances to support inventory warehousing, or as compensating balances for some other purpose. If the funds are held in a commercial bank, the value of the funds to the bank is the average amount of the escrow funds (net of the bank's reserve requirements) times the bank's marginal cost of funds; this is typically the Fed funds rate.

The usual modelling technique used to evaluate the worth of escrow funds to a mortgage banker is to simulate a cash flow by assuming a net earnings rate on the funds, and a growth (inflation) rate for taxes and insurance escrow accounts. The value of escrow funds is uncertain, despite the deceptive mathematical precision of multiplying an earnings rate by a growing average balance. Interest rates are unpredictable, and increasing consumer activism makes the payment of interest on escrows likely in the future. Even a change in the method of payment of real estate taxes to twice per year instead of once per year cuts the average balance in half.

After-Tax Value

Because the price of purchased servicing is capitalized for tax purposes and amortized over the expected remaining life of the loans, the tax paid is reduced during the amortization period. After-tax cash flow is the sum of after-tax accounting income and the purchase-price amortization.

Expected Value

Expected value is the product of the annual cash flow multiplied by the probability that the loan will exist in each future year. A loan may terminate prior to maturity because it is paid off early or because it is foreclosed. The industry standard for discussing loan-termination probability has been the FHA

Table 6 • FHA Survivor Table (survivorship and decrement table as of December 31, 1980)

Section 203 30 Year Term U.S. Totals

Policy Year	Survivors Beginning of Policy Year	Policy Year	Survivors Beginning of Policy Year
1	1000000	16	422262
2	988801	17	395391
3	951721	18	368412
4	900902	19	341548
5	849650	20	315028
6	798389	21	289085
7	746755	22	263923
8	697850	23	239719
9	651913	24	216619
10	610999	25	194742
11	574860	26	174176
12	539977	27	154982
13	507481	28	137195
14	477147	29	120825
15	448795	30	99898

Note: Based on aggregate insurance and termination experience for home mortgages insured since 1957.
Source: U.S. Department of Housing and Urban Development.

mortality schedule (see Table 6). This schedule shows the probability that a loan will stay on the books until a certain year. It is derived from an average of FHA termination statistics for approximately 20 years. HUD revises this schedule periodically.

While the FHA payoff schedule appears mathematically precise, real-life experience shows that the actual termination rate of a group of loans will vary widely from the FHA experience. Some parts of the country show high mobility, and loans prepay much more rapidly. In times of high interest rates, loans prepay more slowly because mortgagors wish to obtain the value of a low coupon rate mortgage. Also, conventional loans and VA loans show different prepayment patterns.

The seventies and the early 80s were characterized by a wide range in actual prepayments. At one point, loans were prepaying at the rate of 10 or 20 percent a year. Several years later, the rate of prepayment had dropped to 3 percent per year. Conventional wisdom explained the change by the dramatic increase in interest rates; the mortgagor thus had less ability to refinance or purchase another house.

To account for different expectations on loan mortality, the mortgage industry has adopted the convention of referring to prepayment expectations relative to the FHA schedule. A loan that is expected to prepay at the same rate as the FHA experience is said to follow a 100 percent FHA curve. A loan that is expected to prepay sooner might follow a 200 percent FHA curve. Conversely, a loan that is expected to prepay more slowly (have a longer average life) might follow a 50 percent FHA curve. These different curves are computed by multiplying the age-conditional probability of payoff by the percentage factor, then recalculating the cumulative payoff probability.

Cancellation Risk

Most servicing contracts contain provisions allowing the investor to cancel the contract for cause (not fulfilling other provisions of the contract). Cancellation by the investor without cause usually requires the investor to pay a cancellation fee. The typical cancellation fee is 1 percent of the remaining loan balance.

Servicing contracts for mortgage-backed securities usually may be cancelled only for cause. Thus, the servicing on loans sold as mortgage-backed securities is more secure than servicing that may be cancelled without cause. The risk of cancellation increases if the value of the servicing is higher than the cancellation fee, or if the investor is no longer interested in maintaining the correspondent relationship.

There are two ways to model the risk of cancellation. One method postulates a probability of cancellation that can be used to increase the payoff distribution. An extreme form of this approach would be to assume all income ends at some point; for example, in two years.

The other method is to increase the discount rate to reflect the risk of cancellation. While highly subjective, it may be the best way to handle an unspecified risk (such as the new FNMA servicing contract, wherein servicing may be cancelled if unforeseen events occur). While neither approach is entirely satisfactory, common sense dictates that servicing subject to cancellation is worth less than servicing that can be cancelled only for cause.

Present Value

The present value is the projected after-tax cash flow discounted at the marginal cost of capital. While present value is a fairly simple concept, it is often misapplied because of the way servicing portfolios are purchased. Escrow funds from the servicing portfolio are often used as compensating balances for the loan to purchase the servicing. Because the amount of the escrows usually equals or exceeds the purchase price, the buyer can offer 100 percent compensating balances. This reduces the nominal cost of borrowing. Some evaluators confuse the cost of capital with the cost of borrowing for a specific transaction and use the low nominal rate of cost of capital as the discount rate. The correct application of the present-value method uses an average of the after-tax cost of debt and the owner's return on equity, weighted by the market values of each. The present value is therefore the sum of the projected after-tax cash flows discounted by the marginal cost of capital.

Computing Present Value

The assumptions for Goode–Prospect's servicing portfolio are shown in Table 7. The forecast of cash flows and the present-value computation is shown in Table 8. In this example, the present-value calculations are based on the total remaining cash flows even though only 15 years are displayed.

The value of servicing is calculated to be $2,612,000 or 1.3 percent of the remaining principal balance. The components of this value include $2,102,000

Table 7 • Servicing-Portfolio Assumptions (standard case)

Loan balance	$200 million
Number of loans	5,000
Servicing fee	42 basis points
Other income	$10 per loan
Cost of servicing	$55
Escrow earning rate	8%
Escrow growth rate	5%
Escrow balance	$3 million
Cost inflation rate	5%
Payoff rate	100% of FHA experience
Tax rate	46%
Amortization method	10 years, sum-of-years-digits
Discount rate	15%

Table 8 • Goode–Prospect: Standard Case Economic Value of Servicing: Cash Flow Forecast—($000)

Year	1	2	3	4	5	6	7	8	9	10	11	12	13	14	15
Fee Income	775	726	676	627	579	534	492	454	419	385	354	324	296	269	243
+ Other Income	49	46	43	41	38	35	33	31	29	28	26	24	23	21	20
− Servicing Cost	274	272	269	265	260	255	250	247	244	240	237	234	231	228	224
= Net Operating Income	550	500	451	403	357	314	274	238	204	172	143	114	88	63	39
+ Escrow Balance	239	237	222	206	202	199	195	192	190	187	185	183	180	178	174
− Tax	144	142	135	127	126	127	129	132	138	144	151	137	123	111	98
= Cash Flow	645	595	538	482	433	386	341	298	257	216	177	160	145	130	115
Amortization	475	427	380	332	285	237	190	142	95	47	0	0	0	0	0
Average Number Loans	4,876	4,598	4,329	4,059	3,795	3,546	3,317	3,115	2,928	2,751	2,586	2,432	2,288	2,148	2,006
Average Balance ($MM)	194	181	169	157	145	133	123	113	105	96	88	81	74	67	61
Average Escrow ($MM)	3.0	3.0	2.8	2.6	2.5	2.5	2.4	2.4	2.4	2.3	2.3	2.3	2.3	2.2	2.2

Present Values ($000)

Net Operating Income	=	2,102
+ Escrow Income	=	1,338
− Set-up Cost	=	0
− Tax	=	828
= Servicing Value	=	2,612
Percent of Principal	=	1.31

net operating income, $1,338,000 escrow value, and $828,000 tax. The escrow value represents 39 percent of the pretax income.

To gain some perspective on the risk of accepting this calculation as the estimate of value, consider another scenario: lower inflation. Suppose that inflation drops so that costs rise more slowly, loans pay off faster, and the earning rate on escrows is less. For example:

Cost inflation rate	2%
Escrow growth rate	2%
Escrow earning rate	5%
Payoff rate	200% of FHA experience

The cash flow projection for the lower inflation case is shown in Table 9. In this case, the value of servicing is $1,816,000, or 0.9 percent of the remaining principal. Obviously, a dramatic reduction in value results from changing a few assumptions.

The Cost Approach

The value of the firm, using the cost approach, is the sum of the value of the servicing portfolio, the net market value of the assets, and the value of the organization. The value of the servicing portfolio was computed in the previous section. This section describes an approach to valuing the net assets and the organization.

Net-Asset Value

Analysis of a mortgage banker's balance sheet uses the standard principles of financial analysis: marking assets and liabilities to market, eliminating assets of doubtful value, and searching for hidden assets and liabilities. The value of furniture, fixtures, and leases may require a specific appraisal if these assets are significant.

The principal hidden asset is the servicing portfolio. Most mortgage bankers do not show any asset value for the servicing portfolio unless the servicing was purchased from someone else. Even then, the amount capitalized usually does not reflect the market value of the servicing. The best procedure is to subtract any servicing value from net assets and evaluate the portfolio separately.

The accounting convention has been to value loan inventory at the lower of cost or market. As a prospective purchaser, Regional Bank should decide whether pricing loans above par is acceptable. Occasionally, a mortgage banker may have mortgage loans or mortgage-backed securities classified as long-term investments. These items should be valued at market.

Not reported on the balance sheet is the fact that Goode–Prospect has com-

Table 9 • Goode—Prospect: Lower Inflation Economic Value of Servicing—Cash Flow Forecast—($000)

Year	1	2	3	4	5	6	7	8	9	10	11	12	13	14	15
Fee Income	754	665	581	503	432	370	318	274	237	204	175	151	129	110	92
+ Other Income	47	42	37	33	28	25	21	19	17	15	13	11	10	9	8
– Servicing Cost	263	239	215	192	170	151	134	120	108	97	87	78	70	63	56
= Net Operating Income	539	469	404	344	290	244	205	173	146	122	102	84	69	56	44
+ Escrow Balance	143	130	106	83	73	65	58	52	47	42	37	34	30	27	24
– Tax	162	139	113	90	76	66	60	58	58	60	64	54	46	38	31
= Cash Flow	520	460	396	337	288	243	203	167	134	104	75	63	53	45	37
Amortization	330	297	264	231	198	165	132	99	66	33	0	0	0	0	0
Average Number Loans	4,733	4,212	3,719	3,255	2,832	2,460	2,143	1,881	1,656	1,456	1,281	1,128	995	873	758
Average Balance ($MM)	189	166	145	126	108	93	79	69	59	51	44	38	32	27	23
Average Escrow ($MM)	2.9	2.6	2.1	1.7	1.5	1.3	1.2	1.0	0.9	0.8	0.7	0.7	0.6	0.5	0.5

Present Values ($000)

Net Operating Income =	1,875
+ Escrow Income =	517
– Set-Up Cost =	0
= Tax =	576
= Servicing Value =	1,816
Percent of Principal =	0.91

mitted to make loans to applicants at below-market rates and has not offset these commitments with forward-delivery commitment. That is, the firm is *net long* and would incur a loss if all of the loans close and prices stay the same. Goode–Prospect is speculating that rates will improve by the time the loans close.

If the loans ultimately close at a price that results in a loss after the firm has been sold, the new owner suffers an unanticipated loss. Regional Bank may elect to participate in the speculation or to place all of the potential loss on the current owners by escrowing part of the purchase price as a reserve against loss, or by reducing the value of the assets by the expected loss.

Mortgage bankers usually do not have gains or losses from liabilities, because the debt is usually short term. If there were long term debt, then Regional should consider recognizing any gains or losses in the value of the debt when computing net-asset value.

Some firms might have pension plans that could be overfunded or underfunded. Evaluation of a pension liability should be done by a professional actuary.

In the case of Goode–Prospect, the net-asset value can be taken as the amount of the equity—$430,000—assuming that the assets are fairly stated and that the purchaser approves of the risk of the commitment to loan applications.

Value of the Organization

One measure of the value of the organization is the cost to duplicate its parts: the management team, the origination and servicing capability, and the momentum that comes from being an existing operation.

The management of Goode–Prospect consists of the two original owners, who make all of the production, marketing, and financing decisions. To attract and support two comparable managers for a year while they assembled a similar team might cost $150,000 apiece, or $300,000. The origination capability consists of two branch offices. The price paid for branches varies widely. In this case, the evaluator knows that establishing similar branches has recently cost $100,000 apiece. Thus, the value of this capability is estimated to be $200,000. The cost of duplicating the servicing operation is estimated to be the cost of the personnel for one year. The firm's records show that the servicing-personnel cost for one year is $200,000.

This leaves the value of having an operating entity now instead of a year from now. One measure of this value is the value that will be added to the firm next year. If the firm originates $100 million in new servicing (worth 0.75 percent after tax if sold), and earns $100,000 in after-tax income, the value of the organization existing now instead of one year from now is $850,000.

Adding together all of these costs:

Management	$ 300,000
Origination	200,000
Servicing	200,000
Existing Now	850,000
Organization Value	$1,550,000

Value of the Firm

The value of the firm, using the cost of the parts method, is

Net Asset Value	$ 430,000
Organization Value	1,550,000
Servicing Value	2,612,000
	$4,592,000
Rounding	$4.6 million

This value is an estimate of the cost to duplicate the firm. The value of the firm to the purchaser may be higher or lower depending on the cost of servicing, the purchaser's tax rate, and the perceived advantages to the purchaser.

Comparison of Values

The value of any business may be different for different persons. One person may see stagnation where another sees opportunity. These different views can create different values.

The offering price of $4 million for Goode–Prospect may appear cheap to someone who believes that the business plan can be achieved or that the firm can be purchased for the cost of the parts. But the price is outrageous to someone who expects the delayed-production scenario.

If Regional Bank wants only to acquire mortgage-banking capability, it could hire the talent separately and not invest in the servicing portfolio. That is, Regional Bank might acquire the equivalent of Goode–Prospect's origination and servicing capability for $700,000, if the bank can wait a year for the purchased components to begin working together. On the other hand, a large mortgage banker, experiencing economies of scale in servicing, might view the servicing revenue as the only valuable asset. In such a case, the value of the origination capability would be marginal, and a large mortgage banker would find no value in the servicing personnel at all.

A potential buyer should define how the mortgage banker and the servicing portfolio will be used. This makes the concept of a business plan very important to an evaluation. Equally important is the need to evaluate alternative scenarios to gain perspective on the business risks.

The cost approach is useful for comparing the price of a mortgage banker with the cost of purchasing or assembling a similar firm. At times when there is a wide range of actual market prices because of economic uncertainty, poor market data, and speculation, a cost approach valuation using the same assumptions as informed buyers and sellers is a good proxy for fair market value. Of course, there will be times when the prerequisites for establishing a fair market value do exist, and the range of prices will narrow.

Both the income approach and the cost approach provide a methodology for valuing mortgage banking. Despite the appearance of computerized precision, both approaches depend on assumptions about unknown future events. Many different assumptions may be postulated. Some may be unreasonable in the view of most purchasers (a market set of assumptions), but value is necessarily in the eye of the beholder. Thus, each assumption should be examined carefully. Also, it is important to postulate alternate assumptions to gain perspective and to understand the range of business risks. The lesson is to understand the methods and to understand the assumptions.

—— Chapter 13 ——————————————————

Market Analysis

Richard L. Mower
President and Chief Executive Officer
Transamerica Mortgage Company

Dennis M. Wiggins
President
Sybran Corporation/Mortgage Data Service

The phrase most commonly used to describe the desirability of real estate is "location, location, location." For the mortgage banker, the location of originating (or purchasing) offices and the competition in those locations may determine whether volume and cost objectives are attained. Thus, the choice of a specific location can have a significant impact on a firm's long-run success. To effectively make that choice, a detailed market analysis is required.

The purpose of market analysis is to evaluate mortgage-origination activity and the behavior of competitors in a given market location, so that successful strategies for achieving company goals in these locations can subsequently be developed. This chapter is divided into two sections: (1) the demand characteristics of mortgage markets, and (2) the supply aspects of the companies that provide mortgage credit in those markets. Demand questions concentrate on the quantitative and economic aspects of a location: What is the loan volume? What are the types of loans originated? What is the average loan size? Who has what market share? What trends are discernible? What is the delinquency and foreclosure experience? What is the unemployment rate? What are the foreclosure and usury laws? Supply questions focus on the analysis of competitors and involve qualitative as well as quantitative judgments: What are the primary competitors trying to do? Why? How are they performing? What strategies are they pursuing? What can we learn to benefit our operation?

Market Demand: Analysis of a Location's Economy

A major ingredient in the success of an individual enterprise—from the neighborhood restaurant to IBM and Exxon—is an in-depth analysis of the potential markets for its product or service. For a mortgage banker, a realistic analysis leads to strategic considerations of the types of loans and services to offer, the territorial scope of activities, and the expected profit potential.

255

Just as proper market analysis contributes to a firm's long-term profitability, market information and data are the keys to undertaking a successful market analysis. Without access to reliable information and data, management must act, or react, blindly in a highly competitive business environment. Samuel Johnson said, "Knowledge is of two kinds: We know a subject ourselves, or we know where we can find information upon it." In a dynamic market situation with aggressive and competetent competitors, the thoughtfully managed enterprise must "find information upon it" by turning to professional sources of market data.

A firm in the mortgage banking business has the aim common to all businesses: to secure the highest financial return from the time and capital invested. Achievement of this aim in the mortgage business comes from maximizing the return on mortgage originations and servicing.

A decade ago, there was little study of quantitative mortgage market data as the basis for judgments about the efficiency of current performance or the attractiveness of future expansion. Few firms had the proper information and the techniques of analysis to decide if their existing operations were efficient, if they should expand into new markets, or if they should abandon some existing markets for greater concentration of effort in others. There are many good real estate and mortgage markets in the country. For an individual firm to take best advantage of them, it must:

Know whether it is doing an effective job in its existing markets.

Be able to select potential markets that satisfy corporate objectives.

Determine which markets should be abandoned.

Many mortgage firms use a three-tiered system of market analysis: economic factors, external factors, and demographics. A brief statement of the variables involved in each of these categories will suggest both their interrelationship and their importance in market analysis.

Economic Factors

There are numerous economic factors that mortgage-banking management should review when assessing its firm's performance in existing markets or studying new markets for expansion.

Market-Share Percentage.   One of the most important review factors is *market-share percentage*. Market-share percentage is vital because it measures the performance of the firm in closing mortgages relative to the potential the market offers. If a market expands by 15 percent in a given year, and the firm's share expands by only 8 percent, the firm is failing to maximize the profit opportunity of that market, even though it may have exceeded the previous year's activity and met corporate sales goals. Management should measure the performance of each office and the firm as a whole *only* in the context of their unique markets. Market-share data, which are widely used in virtually every other industry, are now increasingly used to measure a mortgagee's performance.

Mortgages Originated. A second important economic factor in the mortgage-origination business is the *total number and dollar volume of mortgages originated* in a market area. There are more than 300 major geographic mortgage markets in the country, each with a different level of mortgage activity. A time series analysis showing the growth of each local market of interest during the previous three to five years provides essential information on the current level of activity as well as the trends in that market, including the growth of spot and builder mortgage activity.

Average Mortgage Size. A third important economic factor is the *average mortgage size* of mortgages originated in a market. Commercial bankers often state that it costs as much to process a $20,000 automobile loan as it does a $2 million business loan. Similar economies of scale are found in mortgage banking. As the size of a mortgage loan increases, so does the expected present value of profit generated from originating and servicing the loan. Given the choice of several new markets for expansion, those with the highest average mortgage size should be more attractive because of their higher profit potential per loan.

Secondary-Market Activity. A fourth important economic factor is the *level of secondary-market activity* that occurs in a given market. A high level of secondary-market activity usually means that lenders in a given area are not dependent on local sources of money, that they price loan originations to the reality of prices available to every qualified mortgage seller in the secondary market, and that they are likely to maintain origination activities even during times of tight money.

Competitive Quotient. A fifth important economic factor is *the competitive quotient,* especially when one is studying markets for possible expansion. The competitive quotient reflects such factors as the number of firms operating in a market; the types of operations run by competing firms (service- or price-oriented operations); the existence of any special business relationships or linkages with other local enterprises (bank ownership of a particular firm, links among local realtors, preferred bank lending to some competitors); the market share of the competition; the nature of the individual competitors themselves; and whether a competitor's market share may be vulnerable to an aggressive new competitor. In theory, with perfect information, all markets reach the same level of competition. In reality, certain markets are more competitive than others. This reality underscores the need to have good market data to help pinpoint those markets which offer the greatest potential.

Spot and Builder Activity.   A sixth important factor is *the amount of spot and builder (tract) activity* in each market. Markets which at first appear to offer great potential for spot lending may not actually have such potential, because several of the leading lenders may be captives of construction companies or may have contractual obligations to handle such business. Market-share analysis should differentiate between spot and builder activity, because the total size of the spot market as distinct from new-mortgage origination should influence production strategy.

Types of Mortgages Originated.   A seventh important factor is *the type of mortgages being originated* in a market area. For example, if a firm wants to move into a market in which adjustable-rate mortgages (ARMs) represent a sizeable portion of overall activity, that firm must have the ability to originate and service such mortgages. When management reviews a given market, it should analyze the volume of business attributable to a given type of mortgage, the number and variety of different mortgages being originated, the key competitive factors for each type of mortgage (index and interest rate, for example) and market-share data.

Based on these economic factors, the following simplified approach to market analysis is used by some of the leading firms in the mortgage and real estate industry for branch location study. It can also be applied to a review of the performance of branch offices. The aim of the simplified approach is to establish a profit-potential ranking of markets for possible expansion. This is accomplished through the preparation of spreadsheets analyzing each of the individual areas, using the following method:

Step 1: Make an assumption as to the share of the prospective new market that you think you can obtain initially, 3.5 percent, say, with due regard for such factors as the size and growth rate of the market and the extent, caliber, and competitive quotient of those firms already in the market. (As an example, see Table 1, the Tucson SMSA report from one of the co-author's FHA/VA residential mortgage-origination reports.)

Step 2: Multiply the percentage of market share you assign to yourself by the overall size of the market, using the figures on number and dollar amount of mortgages originated, as shown in the sample report. The product of the multiplication provides the numbers of mortgages you originate and the gross dollar value of those originations.

Step 3: Take the average mortgage (loan) size for that market overall and determine what revenue you may expect to derive from one such mortgage, using standard company or industry averages. If you conclude that your company routinely originates larger or smaller mortgages than the competition does, factor that size into your calculations.

Step 4: Multiply the number of mortgages you expect to make, taken from Step 2 above, by the revenue per mortgage, taken from Step 3, to get the total gross revenue you would be receiving if you were in that market area.

Step 5: Estimate the costs of doing business in the market. Subtract these costs from the gross revenue figures derived in Step 4. The resulting figure is your estimate of potential profit for that market. Alternatively, each market over a three-year period can be analyzed, using an increasing market-share percentage based on the relative competitive factors of each market being examined.

Step 6: Rank the markets by the profit potential of each as reflected in Step 5.

Step 7: Study the historical analysis of each of these economic factors to determine which market areas currently offer the greatest potential.

External Factors

The second tier of market analysis requires that external factors be introduced, after economic factors have been reviewed and summarized. External factors are costs and benefits that do not directly affect the pure economics of financial transactions as goods trade in the market place. For example, the costs of pollution, or the benefits (or costs) of product-design safety are costs/benefits borne by all of society and not reflected in the price of the particular product as it trades in the marketplace. (This is true except when the consumer directly associates a cost or benefit with a given firm or product.)

Experienced Personnel. One such external consideration is the ability and availability of experienced personnel to achieve the potential of a market in which a firm is located. This includes their willingness to relocate to a new market, if required. In many instances, the availability of competent people may be the most important factor determining a firm's decision to open a new branch office.

Limitations and Requirements. A second external factor is unique limitations or requirements of a firm. These include such things as the amount of capital available and the method of a firm's operations: spot loans or builder loans, for example.

General Market Climate. A third external factor is the general business climate of various markets. For example, laws regarding foreclosure and delinquency and those restricting certain types of business activities or limiting access to geographic markets have an important, if indirect, effect upon the costs of doing business in a particular market. The level of personal and business taxes, and the time, difficulty, and cost of obtaining necessary operating permits also have an important influence.

Table 1 • Sample Report: Mortgage Data Service FHA/VA Residential-Mortgage Origination Reports

Market Rank	Lender Name	Number Loans	Total $ Amount	Market Share	Average Loan Size	GPM $ Amount	Tract $ Amount	% Share of Tract
					Year to Date			
1	Colwell Financial Corp.	586	35,268,722	10.71	60,185	2,535,650	27,623,110	19.60
2	Manufacturers Hanover Mortgage Corp.	594	35,175,202	10.68	59,217	1,499,350	7,293,810	5.17
3	Margaretten & Co.	586	33,419,392	10.15	57,029	2,675,600	7,734,342	5.48
4	Waterfield Mortgage Co., Inc.	531	29,686,499	9.01	55,906	2,896,275	11,134,928	7.90
5	Great American Mortgage Co.	407	25,556,400	7.76	62,792	4,308,230	23,979,800	17.01
6	Suburban Coastal Corp.	352	20,572,560	6.24	58,444	1,863,860	1,691,440	1.20
7	Colonial Mortgage Service Co.	298	16,093,350	4.88	54,004	839,580	1,976,690	1.40
8	Countrywide Funding Corp.	235	14,011,238	4.25	59,622	1,244,900	778,650	0.55
9	U.S. Homes Mortgage Corp.	202	13,545,555	4.11	67,057	0	13,052,580	9.26
10	H.S. Pickrell Co.	199	11,962,770	3.63	60,114	1,080,350	7,448,140	5.28
11	ICM Mortgage Corp.	180	10,695,300	3.24	59,418	1,549,100	8,657,900	6.14
12	Western American Financial Corp.	156	9,377,100	2.84	60,109	118,850	107,280	0.07
13	First Federal S & L	135	8,067,220	2.45	59,757	0	1,355,570	0.96
14	Criterion Financial Corp.	107	7,386,271	2.24	69,030	2,385,020	5,286,801	3.75
15	Centralfed Mortgage Co.	88	6,455,600	1.96	73,359	66,550	5,901,560	4.18
16	General Electric Mortgage Corp.	103	5,829,775	1.77	56,599	759,810	3,207,725	2.27
17	Bancwest Mortgage Corp.	101	5,366,913	1.63	53,137	0	1,719,783	1.22

#	Company						
18	Weyerhaeuser Mortgage Co.	79	4,795,173	1.45	60,698	136,860	458,080	0.32
19	Valley National Mortgage Corp.	78	4,321,759	1.31	55,407	51,900	637,650	0.45
20	Valentine Mortgage, Inc.	49	3,198,870	0.97	65,283	0	693,410	0.49
21	Rainier Mortgage Co.	55	2,797,270	0.84	50,859	190,200	466,320	0.33
22	First Gibraltar Mortgage Corp.	52	2,590,210	0.78	49,811	267,780	537,780	0.38
23	First California Mortgage	28	2,083,505	0.63	74,410	229,380	1,683,325	1.19
24	Territorial Bank	31	2,015,950	0.61	65,030	236,450	1,302,800	0.92
25	Lomas & Nettleton	39	1,931,550	0.58	49,526	0	80,000	0.05
26	Anchor Equities Ltd.	31	1,817,440	0.55	58,627	122,750	100,000	0.07
27	First Interstate Bank of Arizona	28	1,675,070	0.50	59,823	115,300	127,550	0.09
28	First Financial S & L	73	1,655,070	0.50	22,672	0	1,627,347	1.15
29	Arizona Trust Co.	28	1,429,850	0.43	51,066	0	1,429,850	1.01
30	Seafirst Mortgage Corp.	29	1,310,600	0.39	45,193	76,000	58,400	0.04
31	Home Federal S & L	21	1,246,150	0.37	59,340	0	0	0.00
32	Sutter Trust Co.	10	830,200	0.25	83,020	0	0	0.00
33	Greentree Acceptance Corp.	31	787,669	0.23	25,408	0	749,869	0.53
34	General Electric Credit Corp.	9	713,400	0.21	79,266	0	237,500	0.16
35	Lincoln Financial Corp.	10	574,570	0.17	57,457	0	0	0.00
36	Fleet Mortgage Corp.	9	510,710	0.15	56,745	0	0	0.00
	Other	73	4,480,054	1.36	61,370	370,300	1,763,736	0.00
	Total Market	5,623	329,234,937		58,551	25,620,045	140,903,726	1.25

Source: Copyright 1983 by Sybran Corporation, 1301 20th Street, NW, Washington, D.C. 20036.

Geographic Considerations. A fourth external factor includes the various geographic considerations. In addition to the direct costs of travel by management and staff to various markets, there are more indirect costs: the problems of managerial direction and oversight associated with operating at a distant location rather than in a nearby market area. Movement of personnel may also be difficult. Many firms feel there is a synergistic benefit to operating in a region where the firm's reputation is well established, even if that means ignoring attractive but more distant markets, at least over the short term.

Demographic Study

The third and final tier of market analysis is the demographic study. This is the least important of the three, because in a competitive market each of the demographic factors and trends is fully integrated in, and reflected by, the *efficient market,* as shown by the number of firms and the overall level of activity in the market. When some firms' analysts consider the number of households in an area, or its population trends, employment levels, etc., they are often ignoring the important fact that all of these elements are reflected in the efficient market and in the level of market activity.

Market demographics are therefore used to support economic and external factors in a market analysis. They should not be considered primary data. The critical issue is the size of the mortgage market in a given area. Two of the other important demographic elements in a given area are:

Business Diversity and Growth. A broad and expanding base of service and manufacturing firms is the ideal; least desirable is an industrial community dominated by one corporation or industry.

Population Profile. Demographic data on population growth, the size of various age groups, the growth of household formations, the growth of income, occupational diversity, and numbers and educational backgrounds provide insights into the habits and preferences in a market area and clues as to the market's growth potential. Information on the amount, condition and patterns of growth of the number of housing units in the market is usually also valuable.

Demographic data, available from numerous firms, should be used to confirm trends and to obtain further details about a market selected through economic analysis.

Summary of Market Demand

First, consider the economic factors of available markets; then rank each market against the criteria imposed by the economic factors. Demographic information may be added to deepen insights about those markets which appear to be the firm's best choices. The changing dynamics of mortgage markets require that mortgage originators use market analysis as a vital tool for achieving corporate objectives.

Market Supply: Analysis of Competitors

Like other businessmen, mortgage bankers gain a competitive advantage if they can anticipate how competitors are likely to behave in different situations. The preceding market-demand analysis should have identified the primary competitors in both existing and potential locations, as well as the economic potential of these locations. While a competitor may be recognized as a mortgage company, a savings and loan association, or a commercial bank, or may be in some other general category, each type of competitor should be analyzed in terms of its motivation and performance.

Motivation

Ownership structure, values, goals, and expectations are often the primary factors in understanding what a mortgage-banking entity is trying to do. Analysis of a competitor, therefore, begins with an appraisal of ownership and management.

Ownership. Entry into the mortgage-banking business involves a relatively small amount of capital. The number of competitors is large. The ownership structure is diverse. An understanding of the motivation of a specific competitor, therefore, requires comparisons of the advantages and disadvantages, as well as the implicit objectives, of the various combinations of ownership structure: public versus private, institutional versus corporate, stock versus mutual ownership, and independent versus captive companies (see Table 2).

Cutting across these ownership comparisons and evaluations of trade-offs is the need for further appraisals to determine whether there is a concentration of individual equity ownership. Is the competition widely or closely held? There is also the further question: is the competitor a financially large or a small entity? Obtaining information about, or actually knowing the individuals who own competing organizations also helps in determining whether competitors are trying to build up a servicing portfolio of the company for future sale, to enhance profitablity in certain market areas, to minimize tax liability, to achieve market expansion/or penetration, to complement other activities, or to achieve some goal that is identified with an individual owner or owners.

Management. Adequate competitor analysis should link ownership and management. While management ostensibly maximizes the criteria established

Table 2 • Public versus Private Ownership

Public	Private
Motivated to maximize stock price (earnings per share or dividends per share)	Motivated to minimize taxes, maximize cash flow per share or sales value of corporation or servicing portfolio
Subject to SEC regulations	Virtually unregulated
Concern with public image	Management compensation programs must be acceptable to private owners
Management compensation programs subject to stockholder review	Limited capital sources (depending on financial strength)
Access to many sources of capital	

Institutional versus Corporate Lender

Institutional	Corporate
Motivated to optimize regulatory performance indicators	Primary motivation is to maximize shareholders' wealth
Portfolio lender as well as secondary market lender	Typically mortgage banking only
Regulated	Virtually unregulated
Assured inexpensive cost of money	Cost of money depends on financial strength
Perk-oriented compensation structure	Incentive-oriented compensation structure
Advantageous tax treatment of earnings	Corporate tax rate applies
Concentrated regulated financial services	Diversified revenue base
Place high value on trust accounts	Relatively lower value based on trust accounts

Mutual versus Stock Organization

Mutual	Stock
Perk-oriented compensation structure	Incentive-oriented compensation structure
Earnings accountability of management not emphasized	Market value of stock and increase in earnings per share emphasized
Limited sources of capital growth	Varied sources of capital infusion

Captive Firm of Larger Company versus Independent Company

Captive	Independent
Complements other businesses	Focus on chosen businesses
Access to financial strength	Financial strength depends on capital base
Possible access to cheaper cost of money	
Restricted compensation programs	Cost of money depends on financial strength and reputation
	Unrestricted compensation programs

by ownership interests, in practice inconsistencies do sometimes develop. Frequently, there exists a degree of freedom to set or establish objectives designed to achieve overall ownership goals. The key here is the extent to which management is directly rewarded for achieving what ownership desires. Compensation programs that involve equity participation and/or large bonus plans are powerful incentives to management. Analysis of compensation programs can suggest whether management emphasizes loan volume, control of costs, or profitablity.

It is important to analyze management values in terms of the kind of company management is trying to become or to continue to represent. Oftentimes when annual reports are available, the president's letter or foreword explicitly states management's credo and objectives. Even without the aid of annual reports, a knowledge of the organizational structure and operations can reveal whether a competitor is national or regional in scope, aggressive or conservative, risk-adverse or speculative, or quality- versus quantity-oriented.

Performance

Volume. The first section of this chapter (market demand) identified competitors by market location, loan volume, market share of certain types of loans, and the degree to which these loans are sold to FNMA or FHLMC. The amount of current activity of GNMA mortgage-backed securities issued can also be gleaned from reports of various private companies and periodicals that publish MBS data for sale.

Financial. Analyzing a competitor's financial performance is more difficult than analyzing his volume performance because of the general unavailability of current financial statements. As noted, the ease of entry into the mortgage-banking industry had led to very fragmented competition, particularly on a national basis. Many lenders originate loans for their portfolio as well as for the secondary market, while others are subsidiaries of larger entities. Consequently, available financial data may not accommodate analysis of mortgage-banking operations. Further, many competitors are privately held, and no data are available.

However, publicly owned mortgage-banking companies do provide useful financial information, such as annual and interim reports. Thrift institutions involved in the secondary mortgage market are required by regulation to provide regular reports to various government agencies. These reports are available for analysis under the Freedom of Information Act, which applies to federal government-insured entities. Although annual reports of large holding companies, or parent corporations of firms operating in the mortgage market, may not divulge much about the financial status of a mortgage-lending competitor, the more detailed Form 10-K may have the necessary information. A prospectus for a potential public issue can also be an excellent source. Firms issuing commercial paper through an investment-banking firm provide considerable financial information that is sent out to potential buyers of the commercial paper.

Once data have been obtained, an in-depth analysis requires that footnotes to financial statements be read. Sometimes only a change in accounting treatment explains a reported "profit." Several key items that should be analyzed with footnotes in mind are the following:

Profitability.   What are the current profits relative to those of other firms of similar size? Is there a trend in profitability over the past years? Has the competition been profitable in tough years as well as good years? Has there been a change in accounting treatment that has created the "profit"?

Sources of Profit.   Where are the profits coming from? Loan-origination fees, servicing income, interest income, property-management fees, and appraisal fees are typical sources of income. By focusing on these, the analyst can determine what areas the competition stress. There may be nonrecurring revenue items (such as the sale of part of the loan-servicing portfolio or FNMA stock no longer required to be held).

Net Worth.   Has there been consistent growth of net worth over the past several years? If not, have dividends of a high percentage of earnings been paid out to either the parent company or to shareholders? Is there sufficient net worth to support the amount of originations the competitor is doing annually? Has there been a recent contribution of capital to the firm, either by a sale of stock or by the parent? Answers to these questions provide clues as to the underlying ability of the competitor to continue its strategy.

Debt-to-Equity Ratio.   These ratios can range from very high to very low, depending on the structure and size of an organization as well as on such underlying factors as ownership, source of debt, guarantees of debt, and source of capital. Generally, a secured debt-to-equity ratio is much higher than an unsecured debt-to-equity ratio. What is the relationship? What are the types and amounts of secured lending? The ability to incur a high debt-to-equity ratio is advantageous to the high-volume originator. Analysis of footnotes to financial statements provides insights as to the amount and cost of borrowings available to a competitor.

Inventory Held for Resale and Reserves.   The careful reviewer should compare loans held in inventory against the reserves carried for potential loss upon sale. If the secondary-market yields have increased since the report was issued, those reserves may not be sufficient to cover any loss incurred subsequent to the date of the report. Such analysis can be tricky, because it is usually not possible to know what investor commitments may be covering loans held in the inventory. Thus, an understanding of a competitor's marketing philosophy and pricing policy is important. If loan prices are guaranteed, a reserve for potential future losses should be established, based on the market or commitments on hand. If the amount of price-guaranteed loans in process exceeds the amount of investor commitment coverage, and potential future losses on loan sales are not reserved, future profits will be eroded.

Construction Loans Outstanding.   Knowing the amount of construction loans a firm has outstanding is useful in anticipating its future income or losses.

When real property is selling at a fast pace, construction loans can be an excellent source of income. Conversely, when real estate sales slow down, construction loans can be unprofitable and can even erode or extinguish a firm's capital. Relating the real estate economy to construction loans by location sometimes enables an analyst to detect a current or potential financial weakness.

Gain or Loss on Sale of Mortgage Loans. Consistent gains on the sale of loans typically indicate a sophisticated understanding of the hedging process. Marketing losses or smaller gains than those of other firms of similar size may indicate a lack of understanding of hedging or an overly aggressive pricing policy. Analysis of financial statements may reflect a major portion of marketing gains coming from sales that release the right to service loans. Servicing-released activity could reveal a potential customer or a financial problem.

Net Interest. Analysis of net interest income and expense should reveal a competitor's cost to finance inventory held for resale. The spread between the mortgage interest rate and the warehouse interest rate may explain the pricing of the product and the timing of the sale of mortgages. If a negative spread exists, turnover (how quickly loans are being sold) is a particularly important measurement. Historically, in mortgage-company financial statements, the largest source of income, other than loan-servicing income, has been the net interest income earned from financing the loan inventory. Understanding the sources and costs of borrowing is valuable in analyzing the originating strength of the competitor.

Summary of Market Supply

Unlike the analysis of market demand, an in-depth analysis of market supply—those companies that provide mortgage credit in a given mortgage market—requires access to financial data oftentimes not readily available, if available at all. Even without access to financial data, however, it is quite possible to know who the owners and managers of a specific competitor are, how a competitors management is structured and rewarded, and what the implied values and goals are. Where available, financial information should be analyzed to determine the competitor's profitability, sources of revenue, capital resources, borrowing capacity, and accounting practices.

Measuring effective performance in existing locales or evaluating the desirability of potential mortgage markets involves analysis of the absolute size of the market, the average loan size and type, the relative share of the market, the amount of nature of competition, the availability of competent personnel, and favorable demographics. While analyzing a given competitor's financial performance is usually very difficult, understanding his motivation is just as important as financial or operating considerations.

—— Chapter 14 ———————————————————

Purchase and Sale of Servicing Portfolios

Hunter W. Wolcott
President
Reserve Financial Management Corp.

One viable tool for achieving corporate objectives available to servicer/participants in the secondary mortgage market is the purchase or sale (or both) of mortgage servicing rights. The volume of servicing portfolios purchased and sold annually among servicers amounts to billions of dollars. This secondary market in servicing rights has existed for many years and is growing. The nearly complete adoption of conforming loan documentation and uniform servicing standards has added a measure of standardization and liquidity to servicing portfolios, which in turn has permitted the growth in volume.

Trading in mortgage portfolios challenges the traditional view of mortgage banking correspondent relationships, in which mortgage loan servicing forms an extension of highly personalized relationships. With the advent of FNMA, FHLMC, and GNMA, the secondary market has evolved from the personalized correspondent system to the impersonal, standardized world of loan sales and homogeneous mortgage-backed securities transactions in which the primary motivation is price. This chapter discusses this secondary servicing market, emphasizing the execution of actual transactions, their negotiation, and the details of closing portfolio purchase and sale transactions.

The Market

Although there are many ways to view the size of the servicing market, a conservative approach is to equate it with the volume of mortgage servicing done for others. Viewed in this way, the servicing market in December, 1983 was approximately $565 billion (measured by dollar balances serviced), or about 31 percent of the total amount of U.S. mortgage debt of $1,824 billion. (1) The market also appears to be growing rapidly. The top 100 savings and loan servicers experienced a growth of $52 billion, or a remarkable 128 percent in 24 months. (2)

Furthermore, there is evidence that sales of servicing portfolios (secondary transactions) are also increasing. In a recent survey of 2,600 servicers, respondents who serviced over $67 billion (about 12 percent of all loans serviced for others) reported that they had completed acquisitions of $9.9 billion of servicing in 1982. These same respondents budgeted over $15 billion for acquisitions during 1983, an increase in purchase appetite of over 55 percent. (3)

Another way to look at the secondary servicing market is to determine who are the buyers and who are the sellers. Analysis of a recent survey of the 100 largest mortgage servicers as compiled by *The American Banker* (for mid-year 1983) provides some insights (see Table 1).

This compilation illustrates a growing concentration of servicing in the hands of deposit-gathering institutions. The true concentration is undoubtedly even greater, because the *American Banker* compilation included only 2 of the top 25 S&L mortgage servicers as of June 30th, 1983. All 25 would easily have made the Top 100, if included. Notwithstanding this suggestive empirical evidence, there are also conceptual reasons to expect servicing to be most valuable to depository institutions because of their broader powers for investment. As pointed out in Chapter 12, The Value of Mortgage Banking, compensating balances and mortgagor relationships are two servicing attributes; both are likely to be more valuable to depository instititutions than to independent mortgage bankers.

Servicing as a Corporate Investment

Holding or purchasing mortgage loan servicing is a corporate investment, and as such should be analyzed with the same thoroughness as any other investment. In fact, servicing might require more attention. Whereas many investments can be adequately evaluated at discrete intervals, the reinvestment process caused by repayments, maturities, and foreclosures requires constant attention. Proper analysis, as with any investment, requires determining the rate of return on (or present value of) servicing, and comparing it to available alternatives, taking account of relative risks. This analytical approach is appropriate whether the decision to be made is to purchase servicing, sell servicing, or

Table 1 • Servicing Volume

Type of company servicing	No. of Companies		% of Dollars	
	12/82	6/81	% 82	% 81
Banks, S&Ls, affiliates	64	45	65.7	48.9
Other (including private)	22	45	19.2	38.5
Diversified financial companies	9	5	8.9	6.2
Real estate and related	5	5	6.2	6.4
	100	100	100.0	100.0
Total			$245.1B	$188.4B

maintain the existing size of the current portfolio. It is not a simple exercise; many variables must be taken into account. Of particular importance are: (1) the expected cost of servicing, (2) the tax implications, and (3) the expected delinquency and prepayment patterns. These considerations and others are discussed in Chapter 12.

Required Current Portfolio Information

The expected return or present value of a servicing portfolio depends on projections involving considerable uncertainty: the future course of prepayments, delinquencies, and servicing costs. When making such forecasts over extended time horizons, the best one can do is to use educated intuition. It is therefore extremely important that the factual information that does exist concerning a servicing portfolio be made available for study and use.

Although gathering factual information about a portfolio would appear to be an obvious first step before deciding to buy, it is improperly handled so often that it calls for some discussion. Few serious, qualified sellers of servicing will have any difficulty in providing the necessary information. Any reluctance or inability to provide data can be a sign of problems, lack of commitment by the seller, or other issues. The current portfolio information listed below is the *minimum* required to form the basis for portfolio valuation judgements.

1. Breakdown by *Investor:* GNMA MBS by pool; GNMA direct; FNMA/FHLMC by pool or plan and, if FNMA, by region; housing authorities; and private investors.
2. Breakdown by *Loan Type:*
   a. Type of Property: one-to-four-family multifamily, residential, commercial, etc.
   b. Type of Lien: first, second, wrap, etc.
   c. Type of Loan: FHA (by Section of the Act; 203, 221(d)(2), 245, 265, etc.), VA, Conventional with PMI, without, etc.
   d. Type of Payment Plan: Level payment fixed rate, adjustable rate (by interval and basis of adjustment, capped or uncapped, etc.), GEM, GPARM, etc.
3. Breakdown by *Location,* usually by state.
4. Breakdown by *Loan,* usually through a detailed trial balance report showing unpaid principal, interest rate, remaining loan term, service fee, monthly P and I and T and I payments, date-paid-to, escrow balance or overdraft, and non-service-fee revenues.

Historical Portfolio Information

Current portfolio information presents a ''snapshot'' of the portfolio at an instant in time. While this information is absolutely essential to valuation, it can be misleading if it is taken outside its historical context. Astute management usually gathers the following information:

1. Historical escrows: At least twelve months by type of loan. Escrows in many jurisdictions are highly seasonal, and reliance on any period shorter than a year can be misleading. In addition to examining the bank statements for segregated PITI funds and the effect of float upon actual escrows held, it is advisable to examine recent escrow analyses for all major tax jurisdictions. These analyses may highlight imperfect escrow practices that can be improved to minimize tax escrow erosion in vulnerable areas.

2. Historical delinquency and foreclosure data: Monthly delinquency, REO, and foreclosure activity should be analyzed. Delinquency and foreclosure costs are among the largest expenses of servicing. Examination of these costs can suggest changes in the manner in which loans are underwritten and provide insight as to the attitudes of courts, insurers, and investors.

3. The ownership history: If the portfolio was not originated by the seller, one should make sure it has not been subject to adverse selection on the basis of quality, expected longevity, or other factors.

Field Examination

Purchase agreements customarily contain warranties and remedies concerning certain material misstatement of facts. As a practical matter, however, few buyers and sellers would suggest that contract remedies should substitute for pre-closing diligence. The time allotted between final agreement and closing is often limited, so it is important to verify as much data as possible well in advance. Sophisticated buyers customarily use a streamlined field examination routine in which even the most complex portfolios can be evaluated for material errors, omissions, accuracy, and completeness.

After evaluating servicing as a long-term investment, management may discover advantages to becoming both a buyer and seller of servicing. If, for example, a company presently services 10,000 loans in Ohio and another 1,000 in 15 other states, those 1,000 loans may be worth more to some other company. Profitability might be improved by selling the servicing (at the right price) in the other states and reinvesting the proceeds to originate or buy more Ohio loans.

Executing the Purchase or Sale

The Buyer's Perspective

An aggressive, professional approach to buying servicing involves: (1) defining in advance the type and characteristics of the servicing desired; (2) researching and identifying prospective sellers who own or control such servicing; (3) approving at the appropriate policy level the procedures to be used for valuation, contracting, closing, and funding servicing purchases; and (4) soliciting offers to sell servicing that will be accepted for a specific, limited period of time. The offering package should also include guidelines for the size of offers to be considered and the types of loans desired.

1. Considerations in targeting sellers: There is presently an increase in both the number and type of companies involved in the mortgage-banking industry. Some grow and prosper, some fail and sell, and others become part of larger groups. Since there is little benefit in soliciting sellers who are not owners, good research is essential. Depending upon the type of servicing desired, efficiency may be gained from concentrating research and solicitation efforts on a particular type of holder, such as small independents or S&L service corporations.

2. Considerations in selecting the type of servicing are outlined in Table 2.

The Seller's Perspective

Sellers can also benefit from a formal plan to sell servicing. Such a plan should include selection of the proper servicing for sale; an appraisal of the full market value of the servicing targeted; a marketing strategy to maximize value for the type, the number, and the nature of desired bidders, and for limits on the price, the timing and terms, if any; research to identify the prospective bidders who have the willingness and ability to be competitive; preparation and distribution of marketing materials; and formalization of the procedures for the evaluating, contracting, and closing stages of the sale.

The solicitation from potential buyers should be uniform in content and timing. If the list of prospective bidders has been sufficiently well researched, one solicitation with an announced deadline should suffice. The bidders list should be kept small for two reasons. First, there is value in maintaining confidentiality during initial selling discussions, particularly in sales involving large amounts or in turbulent markets; and, second, some buyers will not commit themselves to the labors required for truly competitive bidding unless they are convinced that the bidding is a serious, well-considered, and well-targeted effort. The list of offerees should contain only those sellers with adequate qualifications. The transfer of a portfolio can be complex for professionals and even more difficult for the inexperienced. For example, if one's plans call for the sale of a large, multi-state portfolio of GNMA servicing, one would be ill-advised to consider a buyer who had never handled such a transfer before. The last thing a seller wants is a bungled closing, investor rejection, incomplete documentation handling, or some other last-minute issue to stand between him and his money.

A primary consideration, therefore, is whether the buyer can do what the seller wants. A secondary consideration is whether the buyer should do it.

Table 2 • Selecting Servicing

GNMA Pool

Pros	Cons
FHA insured/VA guaranteed with assumability, mandatory escrows, uniform terms.	Costs involved with pool advances.
Ability to select seasoned, assumable loans with probable lower pay-off rates than conventional loans.	Potential loss exposure on foreclosures from $500 to $5,000/case.
.44% net service fee.	Rigorous servicing, transfer and closing procedures.

FNMA Whole Loans (Conventional or FHA/VA)

Pros	Cons
Standardized mortgage instruments.	Risk of forced sale may cause exercise of termination of servicing without cause provision.
High degree of standardized underwriting requirements.	Conventional loans have an historically higher pay-off rate.
Amount of servicing available in the marketplace.	Limited transferability after purchase.
	FNMA's across-the-board enforcement of due-on-sale clause.
	Inability to hold all escrows.
	FNMA varying policy of fees on sale or transfer detracts from value.

FHLMC

Pros	Cons
Standardized mortgage instruments.	Conventional loans with historically higher pay-off rate.
Lower loan-to-value ratios and foreclosure expenses than FNMA.	FHLMC's across-the-board enforcement of due-on-sale clause.
No risk of arbitrary transfer of servicing without cause.	

Other Investors

Pros	Cons
Protection from loss exposure.	Non-standard mortgage instruments.
Flexibility in servicing methods.	Necessity of tailored reports.
Potential fees from renegotiated loans at time of assumption.	Risk of portfolio consolidation.
	Risk of consideration upon transfer.

Pipeline*/Over-the-Counter Whole Loans†

Pros	Cons
Availability of warehousing differential, when positive.	Very labor intensive in loan audit, shipping, credit review.
Possibility of marketing gains if purchase well managed.	Probability of some credit losses.
Purchase price of servicing may be includable in marketing gain or loss and therefore deductible.	Sellers may adverse select poorer quality loans.
	Difficult to buy in large size.
	Probability of unshippable loans being acquired is much higher than through originations.
	Price competitive.
	Purchase programs assist those who are competing with one's own originators, splitting volume, and keeping acquisition and field prices high.

Note: The geographic considerations for these acquisitions should reflect stated corporate strategy.
*Pipeline Loans: As defined in the chapter entitled, "Inventory Philosophy, Reporting and Control," pipeline inventory consists of all unclosed loans with outstanding price quotes to which the company is committed for some time period.
†Over-the-Counter Loans: Loans originated by others, which are offered to the company for purchase immediately following closing (time element significant).

Money is important, but it is not the only issue in a servicing sale. The price may be so closely bid that other considerations become more important.

It is usually sufficient for an offering to contain 20 to 50 prospective bidders. The Federal Home Loan Bank Board call-report tapes can be analyzed to identify S&Ls that have been aggressive in purchasing or selling servicing. Albeit less accessible, similar information may be gathered concerning commercial banks and mortgage bankers.

An extremely large portfolio offered for sale to a narrow offeree base may depress prices to the detriment of the seller. Offerings of $100 million to $500 million presently draw from the very largest base of possible buyers. Amounts over and under that size limit participation somewhat, and the very largest and smallest portfolios require unique sales strategies.

Timing will also have an impact on target size, as selling into a temporarily saturated market may produce unsatisfactory prices. Saturation can occur very quickly, because even one buyer, temporarily out of the market, can cause a significant change in prices. Therefore, the timing and size of the sale should be given deliberate attention.

With a few exceptions, investors do not philosophically approve of "trafficking" in servicing. If the sale has a valid business purpose and if it does not damage the investor's interests, many investors will permit it on a conditional basis. It is not in the investor's best interest to lock-in a servicer who cannot economically service his loans, or who experiences a change in ownership or strategy. Nevertheless, investor policies influence the economics of a sale. The policies of the major secondary market investors listed below are subject to frequent change and should be checked prior to any proposed sale.

Currently, GNMA has a flexible policy permitting transfer of MBS I servicing to qualified new issuer/servicers upon payment of a set pool fee and provision for appropriate documentation. GNMA requires that a sale have a valid business purpose. (There is very limited experience with MBS II pools at the time of this writing.)

FHLMC permits transfers on a wholesale basis. Unlike GNMA, which is typically just a guarantor, FHLMC is an active buyer and seller of loans and is often the owner of the serviced mortgages. The fee is currently minimal.

FNMA presently charges a transfer fee based upon circumstances. FNMA does not quote this fee in advance, but it can be substantial and can seriously affect the profitability of a sale. FNMA also has the right to terminate servicing at any time without cause for payment (currently equal to twice the servicer's annual servicing compensation). These two factors increase the risk of buying FNMA servicing considerably, and purchasers should consider the value of their FNMA servicing to be *net* of these items unless otherwise protected by written guarantees from sellers. In the opinion of many servicers, this policy, and the attendant uncertainty of future FNMA changes, reduce the attractiveness of FNMA loan sales relative to other options.

Insurance companies have traditionally adopted rather relaxed policies with respect to their servicers. Their servicing agreements typically give them an absolute right to cancel agreements at any time without penalty, whether or not a sale or transfer is taking place, but they do not often exercise that power. In many cases, the value of the originations (current and prospective) that the new servicer can provide has been the determining factor in negotiations. Industry practices are changing rapidly (particularly in the life companies), and it is likely that transfer policies will change.

Savings & Loans and savings banks have long had policies of requesting transfer fees on sales of servicing. Many are eager to take back outside loan servicing, particularly in light of recent increases in servicing values. A seller's best tactic with these investors is a frank confrontation of the potential issue.

Closing the Purchase or Sale

Crucial in the closing and transfer proceedings is the advice of experienced legal, tax, and accounting professionals, who should be included in the transaction planning as early as feasible. Failure to anticipate all possibilities can result in delays, extra costs, and, sometimes, unconsummated transactions.

A good purchase agreement is fundamental. Some of the items customarily included:

1. Recitals to explain the intent of the parties.

2. Description of what is being sold: servicing rights (in detailed exhibits), escrow accounts, the mortgages (GNMA), advances recoverable, accounts receivable.

3. Evidence of sale, assignments, certificates, etc.

4. Purchase price: computation and payment; payment for loans delinquent at closing; those brought current later; those which go into foreclosure later; pipeline loans defining a cutoff date; closing date.

5. Tasks to be performed by the buyer: to pay for the servicing, to perform under the agreements, to accept and administer escrows, and to accept and discharge other obligations, such as to investors and guarantors.

6. Tasks to be performed by the seller: to deliver the servicing loans, to deliver all escrows, to turn over fees and ancillary income received after cutoff date, to service properly through closing.

7. Consents: who will get them, when, who will pay the fees or cost of consent or termination penalties, consequences of failure to get consents required.

8. Warranties of the seller: that the information is complete and accurate with no misstatements or omissions; that the seller owns and has authority to sell and deliver free of lien or claim; that the sale does not violate any contracts or regulations; that the seller will file all notices and reports required; that there are no defaults or actions jeopardizing the servicing or the ability to sell it; that the escrows are maintained in accordance with law, regulations, mortgage

terms and servicing contracts and on deposit in the appropriate accounts; that no litigation or governmental action, pending or threatened, exists, nor any basis therefor; that the loans were made in conformity with state and federal law; that they are enforceable in accordance with their terms; that there are no accrued liabilities with respect to actions taken prior to closing date.

9. Conditions precedent to closing: verification of correctness of representations; compliance with conditions, such as consent; opinion of counsel for buyer and seller in satisfactory form.

10. Delivery of documents: trial balances; status of all defaulted loans; complete supporting files, origination papers, ledgers, tax records, flood and hazard policies, title policies, insurance endorsements, loss draft authorizations, FHA commitments, VA CRVs, and all reports made to GNMA, FNMA, FHA, and VA.

11. Indemnification: seller indemnifies for loss, cost and damage (including reasonable attorney's fees) resulting therefrom; misrepresentation; breach or nonfulfillment of any warranty or convenant; defects in mortgage documents (including those subsequently discovered); subsequent events such as investor termination; errors in servicing, such as misquoted payoffs, misapplied payments, failure to file timely notices; costs of completing foreclosures in process or for loans ninety days or more past due at closing; limitation on indemnification period; notifications, accounting and proof of losses; holdback or indemnity funds, who holds, who gets interest, how claims are handled and when they are returned.

12. Other: notifications regarding timing and responsibility, supplementary information as reasonably required, broker's fees, interim payments to investors during closing process, exhibits setting forth all relevant portfolio and supporting data.

Some postclosing liability is common between seller and buyer, and the negotiation of contingency items is an important part of contract talks. To avoid litigation, one key is to minimize the areas of uncertainty before funds pass. Field examination, discussed earlier, is a fundamental part of buyer due diligence in this stage.

Upon completion of a definitive purchase and sale agreement, investors, existing servicers in the case of a consolidation, or other primary parties at interest should be notified and consents solicited where applicable. The approach used to acquire consent can be as much an art form as a skill, and depends upon the specific investors involved. In general, however, knowledgeable investors look to present and future economics in determining whether or on what terms consent is given. Mortgagors, FHA, PMI companies, hazard-insurance companies, accident and health insurance companies and other insurance companies are not parties to the transaction, but sending proper notification to them is essential.

If some of the servicing is for loans still in the pipeline, other issues should be taken up. First, the handling of the original mortgage, and the interim warehousing lien, of the seller can be a serious concern. If these are improperly handled, the buyer could find himself becoming a creditor of the seller or incurring unnecessary costs. A good attorney is a must. The second issue is that of audit and control. Pipeline purchases, almost by definition, involve loans on which documentation is incomplete. Frequently, the seller is the more poorly capitalized company. Good control of the purchase package and postclosing documentation follow-up is mandatory.

The closing of GNMA I pool servicing transfers contains most of the above steps except the negotiation phase of dealing with investors. GNMA's policies are customarily uniform and published. The GNMA pool servicing transfer checklist is provided in the following appendix.

Summary

Increasingly, servicing is being viewed as just another investment. The increasing uniformity of servicing standards, loan documentation, and computer support has greatly reduced the cost of transfering servicing. In general, if management feel that servicing is more valuable than the "market," they should buy (or hold) servicing, whereas management who feel that market prices are higher should sell servicing. Nonetheless, servicing transactions are still relatively complex and require much careful planning.

APPENDIX: GNMA SERVICING TRANSFER CHECKLIST

A. *Pre-Closing Requirements*
1. Fully executed Purchase Agreement to include Seller's representations and warranties as prescribed
2. Review of Mortgage Portfolios for (also function of new custodian-recertification of pool):
    a) Note and proper endorsements
    b) Original mortgages
    c) Assignment to GNMA
    d) FHA or VA insurance or guaranty certificate
    e) Title insurance policy and proper endorsements
    f) Hazard insurance policy
    g) Flood insurance policy, if required
    h) Letter agreement guaranties and other documents relating to GNMA securities
    i) Other documents, as required (e.g., RESPA form, Truth-in-Lending Disclosures, etc.)

3. Written request for GNMA approval
4. Receipt of GNMA approval/payment of $250.00 per pool fee
5. Post-approval, pre-transfer submissions to GNMA:
   a) Corporate Resolution of Seller approving request for transfer
   b) New HUD 1715 (Custodial Agreement) executed by Buyer and Custodian for each pool
   c) New HUD 1707 (Servicing Agreement) executed by Buyer for each pool
   d) New HUD 1709 & 1720 (P&I)(T&I) executed by Buyer and new Custodian for each pool
   e) Executed Assignment Agreement in form prescribed by GNMA with GNMA approval of consolidated forms b–d
6. GNMA Execution of Assignment Agreement for transfer of servicing
7. Notice to borrowers of transfer
8. Requests for endorsement of hazard and casualty insurance
9. List of taxing authorities for new servicer
10. Endorsement of Mortgage Notes from seller to buyer
11. Following GNMA signing of Assignment Agreement, seller must submit to GNMA:
    a) Copy of release of documents from prior custodian
    b) Updated 1706 for each pool certified by new custodian
12. Endorsement of Mortgage Notes from buyer in blank
13. Preparation of individual mortgage assignments from seller to buyer
    a) Request for GNMA approval of blanket assignments
14. Preparation of individual mortgage assignments from buyer to GNMA

B. *On Or Before Closing Requirements*
   1. Certified trial balance of each mortgage identified by GNMA pool number and loan number
      a) Current balance
      b) Balance required for P&I custodial account (GNMA guide, Sec. 4.11)
      c) Current balance for T&I custodial account (GNMA guide, Sec. 4.13)
      d) Due date of next P&I payment
      e) Due date and amount of each delinquent payment
      f) Amount of sellers P&I and T&I advances
   2. Notification to FHA (Form #92080)
   3. Most recent tax receipts
   4. Copy (microfiche) of seller's most recent T&I custodial account analysis
   5. Individual YTD loan ledgers and definition of transaction codes
   6. Previous year's loan ledgers
   7. IRS forms 1041, K-1, 1099

C. *Documents To Be Delivered at Closing*
   1. Original notes properly endorsed
   2. Original recorded mortgages (Deeds of Trust, etc.)
   3. Original Title policy, together with endorsements, if applicable
   4. Delivery of mortgage insurance certificate (FHA), guaranty certificate (VA)
   5. All recorded assignments, as applicable
   6. Recordable replacement assignments from buyer to seller
   7. Seller's certified Corporate Resolution and Incumbency Certificate
   8. Buyer's certified Corporate Resolution and Incumbency Certificate
   9. Opinion of attorney for seller
   10. Opinion of attorney for buyer
       a) Check of states of qualification of buyer
   11. President's certificate as to representations and warranties
   12. Copy of 1710A for each pool
       a) Reconciliation of pool principal to security price
   13. Copy of 1710D
   14. Certification by mortgage pool as to warranty that 1710A's, 1710D and reconciliations are true and correct
   15. Updated certified 1706
   16. Certification and schedule of unreimbursed advances
   17. Schedule of documents which are not in custodial bank's possession
   18. Escrow Agreement with custodian bank
   19. Letter Agreement with custodian bank
   20. Buyer's receipt for documents
       a) Schedule A – excepted notes
       b) Schedule B – excepted assignments
   21. Delivery of:
       a) Balance required for P&I custodial accounts as of cut-off
       b) Actual balance of T&I accounts as of cut-off
   22. Evidence of GNMA approval of custodian bank HUD 1715
   23. The custodian bank release of documents
   24. Delivery of loan payments to buyer after transfer date
   25. Payment of purchase price to seller
D. *Post-Closing Requirements*
   1. Substitution of recordable assignments from seller to buyer; to GNMA for all pooled mortgages
   2. Acknowledgement by custodian of receipt of new assignment and release of old assignment
   3. Recording of assignment from seller to buyer
   4. Delivery of loan payments after transfer date received by seller after cut-off
   5. Notice to GNMA certificate holders of assignment
   6. Statement of interest paid (YTD) to borrowers

7. Buyer to reimburse seller for seller's P&I advances
8. Buyer to reimburse seller for T&I advances
9. Buyer to pay seller for delinquent mortgages (3 months or more) which are brought current, if applicable
10. Seller to pay buyer for costs of completed foreclosures, if applicable
11. Follow-up on hazard insurance endorsement
12. Seller, upon deposit of buyer, will make first payment to GNMA security holders following closing
13. Follow-up on recording and delivery of possession of assignments from seller to buyer
14. Follow up on documents defects:
    a) Missing 1708s (request for release of documents)
    b) Erroneous assignments
    c) Erroneous title insurance
15. Follow-up on notes and mortgage guaranties and insurance of loans in foreclosure
16. Completion of all final certifications

— PART TWO —— SECTION B —

Originating and Marketing Policies

—— Chapter 15 ——————————

Production-Department Management

Robert B. Ferguson, Jr.
President and Chairman of the Board
Security Pacific Mortgage Corporation

This chapter provides a detailed overview of managing a residential loan-production department that makes loans to individual buyers on new and previously owned houses. These loans, closed in the primary retail market, are meant to be eligible, through proper underwriting and documentation, for sale in the secondary mortgage market. Planning, directing, and controlling this effort is the main theme of this chapter, with emphasis on incentive systems, the production–marketing interface, organization, pricing, control, and coordination.

Determining Goals and Objectives

Traditional mortgage-banker operations produce loans for resale in the secondary mortgage market (with the retention of servicing rights) in order to produce long-term cash flow streams. From a production viewpoint, the most common success measurement of this effort has been the increase in the size of mortgage-servicing portfolios. However, an increase in servicing volume may not necessarily be the primary goal of modern-day mortgage-banking companies. Bottom-line profits are now frequently stressed over production volume and the servicing portfolio's size. Such trade-offs and their relative importance need to be established as corporate goals, so that the production department can establish its targets. Most production departments are not able to produce loans for servicing at a profit from the fee income generated. Management must therefore determine what cost it is willing to incur per increment of volume. This decision depends not only on what value the producer places on servicing, but also on what net interest the producer expects to earn (or lose) on loans while they are warehoused, and the gain (or loss) on the sale of a loan. A producer placing a value of two points on new servicing, while expecting to break even on both warehousing and marketing, would be willing to generate new loans only until the additional cost of doing so also equalled two points. As long as the sum of warehousing gains, marketing profits, and servicing value is greater than origination costs, the producer has an incentive to expand volume. If origination costs are greater, management has an incentive to cut back new-loan production.

Two other related decisions are: (1) whether to originate or buy loans, and (2) whether to retain servicing with respect to the first decision. The after-tax cost of originated servicing should be calculated and compared to the after-tax cost of purchased servicing to determine which production strategy, or combination of strategies, should be pursued. The fact that a producer can immediately write off origination cost for tax purposes, but must amortize the price of purchased servicing will have a significant effect on this decision. However, at times the cost of either method may be deemed too high, and the production effort will be changed accordingly. With respect to the second decision, it is top management's responsibility to establish a balance between the need for current profit and the need for future profit.

Acknowledging that it costs more to produce a loan than the origination fee will cover, many mortgage bankers sell their originated loans servicing-released in order to recoup or offset the net cost to originate. In fact, some companies have a well-defined strategy to sell two or three new loans servicing-released, in order to retain one new loan for servicing at some overall origination profit. Others may price their loans at less than market to attract volume, recouping part of their built-in pricing loss by selling off a portion of their volume servicing-released.

Production management must know the corporate goals for the volume desired, the type of volume desired (originated and/or purchased) and the cost constraints to be observed. Additionally, corporate management should make known its strategy for the production department: is it to be national, regional or local in scope? To ensure that the production department pursues objectives that satisfy corporate goals, the incentive systems of the department must be complementary.

Incentives

Management

The method in which the manager of the production department is compensated should reflect the desired corporate direction. Aside from salary, bonus, and profit-sharing considerations, the company may reward the production manager for gross volume, volume exceeding some standard, value of servicing added, costs within budget, or some combination or variation of these. Again, there is a trade-off between volume and cost, and both production objectives and production incentive systems should reflect the trade-off decided upon. Normally, an incentive plan for the production manager is tied to the profits of the department. Since the cost of origination normally exceeds the income, "phantom" calculations are sometimes made which give the production department credit for servicing as though it had been purchased from them by management or the servicing department.

Complementary accounting systems should be made for the revenues which should be credited to the production department. In addition to origination and miscellaneous loan fees, production may be credited with servicing value added, net warehouse interest, or the extent to which loans are originated at a price greater or less than that established by the marketing or the investor-sales department. Likewise, decisions must be made on what to charge production. In addition to direct expenses, charges may be made for home-office production overhead and/or overall corporate overhead, or for losses suffered on uninsured or nonguaranteed loans. These deliberate accounting decisions, as well as the tradeoff between volume and cost, should be reflected throughout the production department's incentive system.

Usually found only in large companies, the regional manager reports directly to the production manager and is responsible for the organization effort in his or her given territory, which normally consists of specific branches. The incentive compensation should be consistent with that of the manager's superior. Compensation may be given to reward him or her for administrative achievement, (control of expenses or attainment of certain productivity standards as well as for achieving production milestones).

Incentive programs for branch managers are quite varied. In the small office, the manager has the status of a senior solicitor, and the manager may share to a greater extent in profits he or she generates than in those generated by the loan officers working in the branch. Bonuses may be paid for expense control or for achieving production-volume milestones. In larger offices, the branch manager may have true manager status. A number of producers may report to this manager. In this environment the manager's major effort may be spent on training and scheduling rather than on calling on a group of clients. Accordingly, the branch manager of a large office may participate to a larger extent in profits or discount overages collected than does the small-office branch manager.

Loan Officers

Compensation programs for loan officers run the gamut from fixed salary plus a car allowance and expenses to commission only. The major advantage of straight salary is that it is easy to compute and understand. It is effective in holding good people during poor production periods and is very popular. The principal disadvantages to this method are: (1) that it is not acceptable to the high-volume producer, thus resulting in high turnover of good producers, and (2) that costs are incurred that are independent of the volume generated.

At the other end of the spectrum is the straight-commission solicitor. The principal advantages of straight commission are that it gives top pay for top production, provides an ongoing, built-in incentive, and keeps loan officer personnel costs at a minimum. This plan is prevalent in very high-volume markets. It also tends to hold down expenses in a market that is contracting. The principal disadvantages to straight commission are that it builds little employee loyalty and quickly discourages people if production efforts are not high.

A more common compensation program is a combination of straight salary and a commission arrangement. A program such as this may pay a fixed salary, but when a production level is reached that warrants an override, it may also provide for additional income based on volume. Such a commission plan may also provide incentive for the collection of excess discounts or fees. A combination program like this can instill employee loyalty and discourage high turnover. It provides a floor income and rewards top producers at the same time.

Solicitors may also be provided with company automobiles or car allowances or limited expense accounts. For those for whom it is considered important to maintain an image and style—builder-developer loan specialists—these compensation benefits may be provided. Fringe benefits, such as insurance, profit-sharing, etc., need to be evaluated on a competitive basis and are for all employees in the organization, not just those in the production department.

Organization

The production department's primary responsibility is to produce loans that can be sold in the secondary mortgage market at a desired volume and price. The marketing department's primary responsibility is to ensure that all loans produced are in fact sold and purchased by institutional investors in the secondary market at a desired price and in a timely manner. The organizational relationship between these two departments varies from company to company.

In some companies, the marketing department is independent of the production department and is on a co-equal status. In others, the marketing manager reports directly to the production-department manager. In the latter case, the production manager would also have responsibility for selling loans. In any event, communication between the needs of customers in the field and the needs of institutional investors in the secondary market is critical for a successful joint venture.

Because a cardinal principle of mortgage banking is to sell every loan that is originated, the investors' requirements determine what the production department is allowed to originate. The marketing department establishes the types of loans, interest rates, terms, and discount points that the company is seeking.

Obviously, the organization of a mortgage-banking company can and does vary from firm to firm. The most significant variation is in the organization of the marketing function. However, a typical production department—one without marketing responsibility, originating a high volume of residential loans through a branch system—usually resembles the organization shown in Figure 1.

The typical branch office is concerned only with originating loans, processing loans in a timely manner, and closing them in compliance with price, interest rate, and regulatory regulations/guidelines. Thus, a typical branch would consist of a branch manager, loan officers, loan processors, and loan closers. Essentially, the organization of the production department supplies the structure necessary to carry out the firm's production objectives and values. Whether the intent is to a national, regional, or local lender, the geographic coverage of a company's origination operation reflects the company's intent. If the strategy is to originate only high-balance loans, offices are located only in areas likely to generate such loans. If the strategy is to originate only relatively high-discount loans, offices are located in high government-loan-volume areas, typically blue-collar neighborhoods, where the prices of homes reflect lower loan balances and where discount overage is normally obtained.

Figure 1 • Production-Department Organization

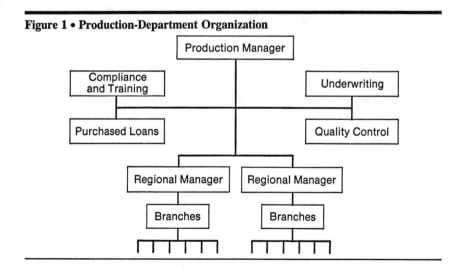

If the production department seeks builder business, there may be builder specialists on the staff, and geographic coverage may be concentrated in areas where new homes and subdivisions are being constructed. Indeed, if there is a construction-loan officer or manager, the builder-oriented part of the branch may not be in the same location as the residential-loan production branch.

Whatever the strategic considerations, a branch production system must fill the functions of the following line and staff positions, even though staff functions are commonly centralized in the home office:

Regional Manager

The regional manager reports directly to the production manager. Responsible for the origination effort in a given territory, the regional manager is also accountable for adequate loan documentation and compliance with corporate procedures for the territory. This manager is usually responsible for approving all office space and leases, hiring and firing branch managers, approving branch personnel compensation changes, planning territories and products, budgeting, informing branches of the latest prices, and generally overseeing the entire application, processing, closing, and documention effort for an entire region.

Branch Manager

In companies without a regional manager, the branch manager reports directly to the production manager. A branch can vary in size from two to twenty or more people. The branch manager is responsible for administrating the branch and for originating and/or purchasing loans in a specific geographic territory. The branch manager is normally charged with calling on realtors and builders in the territory to inform them of the company's products and to encourage them to use the company's services. The manager and/or the solicitors must be intimately familiar with the products, terms, and prices provided by the company in order to see that loan applications and the attendant processing towards closing are handled in a professional and timely fashion. The manager and/or his solicitors may also call on other mortgage-banking firms to purchase loans on a servicing-released basis.

Underwriting

The residential loan underwriting section should be autonomous. Its primary function is to objectively determine the overall qualification of both borrower and collateral for corporate and investor loan requirements. There should be no pressure by loan-origination personnel on the underwriter.

The organization of an underwriting section begins with the chief underwriter, under whom there are underwriters whose duties are specialized, usually by the type of loan: government, conventional, second mortgages, and assumptions. Underwriting personnel should have a full understanding of loan origination, current loan programs and processing. The chief underwriter usually reports to the production management, which is responsible for the quality of loans as well as for volume.

The underwriting section is responsible for the creation and management of a company underwriting manual (used by the underwriters and loan originators as a guide to quality control in production). The underwriting section is also responsible for the approval of appraisers and their appraisals. Each mortgage seller/servicer should have its own list of approved appraisers who meet stipulated criteria. Once an appraiser is approved, there should be a constant review of his or her work for quality control.

The underwriting procedure will vary by type of loan, owing to the absence of one or more of the procedure steps. The process as a whole consists of the following: the appraisal (company approval of the appraiser, completeness of the report, accuracy of the mathematics, and quality of the report); the loan program (program prerequisities, accuracy of mathematics, and special requirements); the collateral (quality of construction, size of requirements, aesthetics, and condition); and the borrower (stability of employment, stability of income, credit history, previous housing experience, down payment availability, and motivation for ownership).

After review, a decision is made to approve, approve with contingency, or disapprove the loan. Many mortgage lenders require that a disapproval be reviewed by the chief underwriter prior to final decision. Some government-insured or -guaranteed loans may eliminate some of the mortgage banker's responsibility for one or more of these steps. The trend, however, is toward more and more mortgage-banker responsibility for the entire underwriting process. The overriding theme of the underwriting procedure can be summed up in one word: stability. The collateral should have stability of value, and the borrower should have stability of employment, location, life-style, and income to qualify for the requested loan.

Quality Control

Quality control personnel usually report directly to the production manager and, like the underwriting section, should not be subject to pressure from origination personnel. Quality control audits a percentage of incoming loans for adequate documentation and reverifies information contained on various forms. It compares loan documents for consistency, accuracy, and completeness. It spot checks all offices for proper procedures and compliance with company and other required policies.

Compliance and Training

This group is responsible for compliance with the numerous local, state, and federal regulations. It ensures that procedures are written, promulgated, and updated and that training is given to all affected personnel. In addition to conducting training classes for loan officers and clerical personnel, this unit periodically visits branches and other originating mortgagees to review the procedures and forms being used.

Purchased Loans

The purchasing of loans originated by other mortgagees or loan brokers is typically centralized in the home office. This department ensures that loans purchased are eligible for sale according to the marketing department's specifications and that loans comply with applicable agency and insurance requirements. Personnel in this section should work closely with the quality control department to minimize the purchase of poorly documented or delinquent loans.

Atypically, branch loan-servicing and construction-loan functions may also be located in a branch, usually in a staff position reporting to the branch manager for administrative purposes but to the appropriate party within the home office for line instructions. In such cases, the branch organization chart may resemble the one shown in Figure 2.

The servicing duties assigned to branch-office personnel are those that normally cannot be done other than by someone in the immediate neighborhood of the borrower. Property inspections, insurance inspections, and loss-draft processing are more efficiently performed by local personnel than by someone in a remote home office. In many companies, a designated employee is responsible for servicing duties and acts as a liaison between the branch and the main servicing office.

Branch office production personnel should be knowledgeable about servicing needs for several reasons: an awareness of causes of delinquency will create a better understanding of underwriting; the branch office is ideally suited to handle the necessary credit documents for credit qualification of mortgage-loan assumptions; and pay-off requests can create very valuable new-loan leads.

Collection of delinquent accounts and foreclosure actions are functions which should be carried out only by loan administrators. Where it is not cost efficient to create branch or satellite servicing offices, a predetermined fair al-

Figure 2 • A Typical Branch-Office Servicing and Construction-Loan Functions

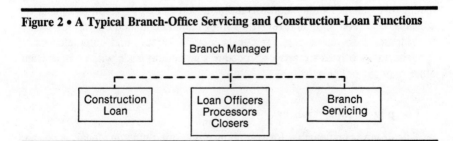

location of costs for the servicing functions performed can properly reward the branch for its efforts on behalf of the loan-administration department.

Some mortgage bankers provide builders with construction financing in order to capture the builder's end-loan business. Construction lending requires a specialist, strict policies and procedures, and underwriting guidelines.

Large mortgage-banking firms may have a regional office system for permanent and construction-loan underwriting, but most require home- or central-office approval. The construction-loan submission from the branch or satellite office, therefore, must be complete, timely, and accurate. Normally, a construction loan specialist in the branch is accountable to the home office for line purposes and to the branch manager for administrative purposes. The construction-loan package is more involved and demanding than is that for a residential loan, and therefore requires more expertise and tighter controls. The construction loan is subject to specified approval procedures, including home-office loan-committee approval.

Branch Administration

In addition to supervising the branch loan officers and clerical personnel, the branch manager must ensure that the office is organized in such a manner that a clerical staff of loan processors and loan closers can support and maintain the origination of loans efficiently.

Many mortgage companies and thrift institutions write personal and/or commercial lines of insurance on borrowers and others. This is in addition to the insurance products written on the portfolio loans, which are usually solicited by mail at the home office. Good coordination between the branch residential and insurance personnel can bring about good penetration of mortgagor accounts with homeowners' coverage.

Processing the Loan

The first step in the creation of a new mortgage is the application. Methods of obtaining the application information vary widely, from taking a loan application at the realtor's or builder's office, to taking the application at the prospective purchaser's residence. Whichever method is selected, there should be a face-to-face interview by the loan officer before any processing begins on the application.

During the interview, statements must be solicited in compliance with the Equal Credit Opportunity Act. Rights under financial privacy regulations should be explained, and, if possible, estimates of the cost of complying with the Real Estate Settlement Procedures Act should be delivered to the prospective borrower. Any required fees or deposits must be collected and properly receipted (credit report, appraisal, commitment fees, etc.).

After all required information is complete, the application should be analyzed to determine the probability of making the requested loan. If the analysis is negative, either further data must be obtained or the loan rejected. If positive, the application is processed to validate preliminary information. All necessary verifications or validations should be mailed to the proper addresses, not hand-carried. Incoming verifications must be compared to the data received from the applicant. When all documents are in the file, a review is made of the adequacy of the documentation and the file is submitted to the lender's underwriting staff or the appropriate government agency.

Closing the Loan

The closing process begins after the borrower's loan application has been completed and approved by the FHA, VA, or conventional underwriter. The actual closing will be conditioned on the receipt of the approval commitment and compliance with any conditions contained in that commitment. The closing agent must clear all contingencies prior to disbursing funds.

Closing agents are attorneys, title companies, or escrow agents. Their primary duties are to close the loan in accordance with the instructions issued by the mortgage lender and to insure title and lien position. Mortgage lenders must assure themselves that the closing agents who handle their closings do so with expertise and fidelity. The expertise is determined through experience and recommendation, and the fidelity is normally accomplished through an indemnity agreement given to the mortgage banker by the title company. The indemnity agreement insures the mortgage banker against loss from fraud or intentional mishandling of the loan proceeds by the closing agent.

Detailed closing instructions, along with the closing check or draft, are issued to the closing agent, together with any contingencies of closing. Once the closed loan documents are deemed accurate and complete, the closed loan package is sent on to shipping for investor purchase.

Customers

Just as the marketing department calls on institutional investors, the branch offices call on realtors and builders. Loans secured from a calling effort on realtors fall into three broad categories: government loans, conventional loans, and loan transactions involving assumptions.

What the realtor needs on behalf of his seller/client is the lowest discount points, convenient application processing, quick loan approval, and closing. Inasmuch as government loans are standardized, rates, underwriting, and closing documents will be the same from lender to lender for a particular type of loan. Occasionally friendship, past experience, or loyalty will have some influence on securing business; however, these hard-to-qualify characteristics simply serve as tie-breakers, for the best price usually prevails.

With conventional loans, the realtor would like to obtain: the lowest fixed rate and the longest term possible; the fewest loan and closing documents; quick appraisal, underwriting approval, and closing. With conventional loans, certain nonstandard characteristics become important, such as very high maximum-loan balances, assumability, lack of prepayment penalties, etc.

An additional loan is often needed with assumption transactions to complete the purchase, a second mortgage or a wrap-around loan, for example. Amortized second mortgages have been very popular among both realtors and sellers in the primary market and investors in the secondary market. The wrap-around loan is a second mortgage behind a low-interest-rate first mortgage, affording the buyer a blended rate on both the first and second mortgages. Finally, the realtor needs certain swing or bridge loans, generally very short term in nature, to facilitate the purchase of a home in one area while awaiting the sale and liquidation of equity on a home in another area. These accommodations are normally supplied by commercial banks and frequently are of too short a term to offer for secondary-market resale. The fees involved are normally high, and the mortgage banker may possibly acquire brokerage income by referring a customer to a financial institution interested in making these loans.

In dealing with the home builder, the mortgage banker has special risk considerations thrust upon him. Builders normally require that large dollar amounts be available to them over extended periods of time. Traditionally, builders do not view a commitment as mandatory delivery. They tend to view the commitment as a standby, meaning that if terms available in the current market are worse than those of the commitment, delivery is made. If terms available in the current market are more favorable than those of the commitment, delivery is made elsewhere. Where the exposure span on a single realtor loan is limited to about 60 days, builders frequently want commitments that cover 12, 15, or 18 months on very competitive terms and prices, with little cash paid in advance. If a builder is willing to take a commitment that contains some variable discount terms, he realizes that the VA rate will probably change several times over the course of the commitment. He therefore desires to have a discount established that would give him a floor, regardless of what the market does. Large-volume business from a builder is very desirable because it is easier to process and deal with one sponsor than to deal with numerous small realtors. The risks are, however, quite large, and the mortgage banker can frequently lose many times the value of any servicing that will be produced. When dealing with a volume builder, great care must be taken to assess the risks and rewards carefully.

Pricing

A previous chapter has discussed the primary risk in inventory management for the mortgage banker: exposure to interest-rate volatility of the loans in the pipeline. Generally, two broad categories of loans exist, which imply different pricing and control techniques for the production department: government loans and conventional loans.

Government loans include a variety of loan types: the FHA and VA fixed-payment loans, FHA graduated-payment loans, FHA adjustable rate loans, interest-rate buy-downs, 15-year and 30-year loans, builder operative loans, etc. The list continues to be augmented. However, the principal government loans have been the 30-year FHA 203(b) and VA loans. Because these loans have been sold via GNMA mortgage-backed pools for many years, and GNMA pools typically afford the mortgage originator of FHA and VA loans the best prices, the current GNMA pool price (which is widely publicized) usually determines the prevailing origination price in the field.

Conventional loans embrace an even larger variety of terms and features. While the 30-year fully amortized loan is considered the standard, even its due-on-sale and call provisions may vary. Other types of conventional loans offer a sometimes confusing variety of features or combination of features: 15-year term, graduated payment, full amortization, negative amortization, adjustable interest rate keyed to an index, shared equity, second mortgages, wrap-around or blended rates, interest-rate buy-downs, etc.

Conventional loans also have more variety than do government loans with respect to legal documents, usury-law restraints, loan-to-valve ratios, private mortgage-insurance requirements and maximum loan limits. Clearly, conventional originations should be matched closely to the marketing department's investor commitments. While origination fees and discounts tend to be the same among competitors, interest rates change frequently and usually reflect the current FNMA or FHLMC pricing.

While GNMA pool prices may determine field prices on standard government loans and FNMA and FHLMC may determine interest-rate quotes on conventional loans, the manner in which price is quoted, its duration and timing, delivery requirements, provisions for interest rate changes, special variations, and management considerations may vary widely among competitors.

Pricing Communication

Prices may be established in several different manners. They may be published in widely distributed circulars or limited, in-house memos. They may be obtained by telephoning for a quote from the marketing department. They may be derived or given by using some commonly known and accessible index, such as the FNMA mandatory price or the current coupon GNMA price for delivery in two months, etc. They may be allocated to a branch and therefore fixed as to price, number of loans, expiration date, etc. They may be quoted as market, with no firm price over time. Finally, they may be published via a network of computer terminals.

The more formal the procedure, the tighter the control. The major advantage to the production department in establishing firm prices is the certainty provided the loan officer; the disadvantage is the difficulty in changing the price quickly. The more the necessity for changing prices, the more paperwork the publication system mandates. Calling for quotes or using an index maximizes quick responses to price changes but puts a premium on control mechanisms. Allocation of an investor commitment to a branch or region establishes good control but may not be competitive with market changes. Finally, quoting at market minimizes liability but may not be competitive when others quote firm prices over a specified time period.

Duration

Whichever method is chosen, variations occur in the duration and timing of price quotes. Prices may be quoted for an absolute number of days irrespective of interest changes, or for x days at a specified interest rate, or for as long as the official FHA/VA rates stay the same, etc. These fixed-duration quotes are commonly referred to as *point guarantees*. The longer the time period covered by a point guarantee, the greater the risk. Point guarantees usually have the effect of originating many loans when market prices deteriorate beyond the guarantee price, and producing few loans when prices improve substantially. The mortgage banker's commitment is assumed to be ironclad, while the seller, realtor, or builder makes no commitment to assure closing whatsoever. This one-way street has traditionally existed and persists with builders, sellers, and realtors.

Timing

Whatever the manner of establishing the price and its duration, the actual implementation of the pricing system may vary widely on when a price is established. Prices may be established at the time of application for a loan by the prospective buyer, at the time the loan is submitted for approval for the FHA or VA or the underwriter, after approval, when closing documents are drawn, or at the actual closing. Sometimes point guarantees are given for a set period of time; 15, 30, and 60 days are the more popular time periods. Normally, the further down the list one goes before pricing a loan, the more certain one is that the loan will close. The realtor or seller of the property pressures for a price very early in the process, while the mortgage originator, if competition allows, resists quoting until the last possible moment.

Delivery

Prices established for branches and/or loan officers may apply to individual loans or to specified dollar bulk commitments. They may also allow optional, or best-efforts, delivery, or require mandatory delivery. The pricing mechanism must make mandatory- versus optional-delivery requirements abundantly clear.

While mandatory-delivery commitments reflect the willingness of investors to accept lower yields for certainty of delivery and offer better prices to originators than do optional deliveries, optional deliveries allow the originator to hedge his position better relative to the competitive marketplace. Obviously, marketing and production must work together closely to constantly monitor the pipeline to determine which loans will probably close and which will not.

Interest-Rate Changes

Price quotes for branches and/or loan officers may be independent of, or dependent on, subsequent interest-rate changes, particularly changes in the official VA rate. When rate changes occur, the former price may expire, may require renegotiation, or may be determined by a previously agreed-upon formula. Obviously, liability is minimized with the first two procedures, although the loan(s) may be lost. A formula may enable one to hold onto a loan, but it is necessary to know how the formula affects the marketing effort. One common formula is called a yield-equivalent formula, in which the price of the loan with the new interest rate is adjusted to obtain the same yield to the price quoter (originator) as existed at the old interest rate. Suppose an originator commits to buying a loan with a 13 ½ percent coupon at a price of 93. This loan yields the originator 14.77 percent (according to FNMA's "Mortgage Yield Conversion Tables and Supplemental Amortization Tables," 4th Edition). If coupon rates rise to 14 ½ percent, the originator might agree (or might be required) to buy this loan to generate the equivalent yield. This would require the originator to buy the loan for a price of 98.5. This process would probably become easier if the VA were to free the administered VA rate to move with the market. Other formulas are a variation on this theme, either providing more or less adjustment, *capping* and *flooring* any possible price changes. The important management point to remember is to match production liabilities with investor commitments containing similar provisions.

Variations

By design, some companies skew their pricing to reflect a high price for high-balance loans and a lower price for small-balance loans, reflecting the implied servicing value of the loans. Some companies will discourage a certain type of loan or loans with lower than acceptable minimum balances by pricing at less than market. Most companies will pay less for a nonowner loan than for a loan on an owner-occupied residence, while others will penalize condominiums but not single-family detached homes. Some companies will establish the same pricing for both originated and purchased loans to prevent internal morale problems, while others will pay a higher price for purchased loans because of their perception of less risk. Many companies will change pricing systems as the market changes, and, more importantly, as competition forces change.

Management Considerations

In comparing pricing alternatives with the corporation's strategy and the production-department's objectives, management should attempt to:

1. Minimize liability. The longer the duration of the price quotes, the greater the risk. The more the pipeline is not covered by matching investor commitments, the more exposure to interest-rate risk. The greater the use of mandatory-delivery commitments, the greater the risk posed by cancellation of loans in process. A good pipeline reporting system is a must.

2. Obtain recourse. While usually not obtainable from realtors on spot loans originated, recourse should be negotiated for all builder loans, and loans purchased which become unsaleable for reasons of documentation or delinquency, or which must be repurchased subsequent to a sale to an investor for fraud or other pertinent reasons.

3. Maximize administrative ease. Pipeline reporting procedures should be easily implemented, particularly the cancellation of loans in process. Bulk commitments are easier to track than are loan-by-loan quotes.

4. Integrate incentive systems. Sharing in the discount underage (loss) will tend to discourage loan officers' closing of loans at a price higher than approved or quoted. Sharing in overage will reward both the producer and the company.

5. Analyze the strategies used by the competition to determine if they pursue one or more of the following: penetrate the market, skim the cream, exclude the competition, meet the competition, anticipate interest rates, push unique product lines, bait and switch.

Who is the dominant lender and why? What modifications to the current pricing system are called for? Is the pricing strategy short- or long-term?

Limiting response to competition is always a difficult task and a major undertaking. Reaction should be tempered by the following lessons of experience:

1. Competition does not always guess the market correctly. His cheap money will not be driven out by meeting unrealistic prices.

2. The economics of mortgage originating and selling apply equally to all competitors. Eventually uneconomic pricing has to change, or there is one less competitor around.

3. The mortgage market is extremely large. It is not necessary to make every loan in an area in order to be successful. Every loan is not a good loan.

4. Customers (realtors and builders) often allege that the competitors' prices are better or that their processing is superior, etc. The important point to remember is that they are telling your competition the same thing about you.

5. The first loss is usually the smallest loss. People costs are the largest controllable cost for a mortgage banker. If uneconomic price competition persists, cutting back rapidly in a slow market or territory will enable terminated employees to find jobs with other companies more easily than if there is a delay while economics catch up with the rest of competition.

Layoff fast!

Reporting and Control

Production reports on applications taken, loans closed, and sources of business should be prepared as needed. Usually weekly, monthly, and annual figures are maintained. These reports show the quantity of business produced, not the quality. Productivity reports may indicate processing time and units produced per person or solicitor by office, region, and department, and typically show the cost of producing a unit. These reports frequently serve as a basis for the compensation programs discussed earlier and offer an efficiency comparison within the industry.

Financial reports continue to be the key element of any business enterprise. Production-department progress against the budget is essential. A breakdown of major items would include fee income collected, ancillary income, compensation expense, and detail on controllable expense items. Regional and branch managers should also be provided with these reports covering their respective units and be held accountable for their progress against the budget.

A control system for documents is necessary to see if the loans closed are receiving proper attention for timely verification, sale, and delivery to the institutional investor.

Productivity should be measured by quotas, standards, and budget targets. Such productivity measures are important methods of validating a given strategy. An analysis of market penetration can reveal how the competition is doing and whether production is at a satisfactory level.

Within the branch office, determination should be made of the number of loans produced per employee, the loans originated per producer, and other statistics, including average loan size, loans brokered, discount earned or lost, compensation expenses per loan, and the cost of servicing added to the portfolio. Further, the branch should have a profit or loss statement prepared and reviewed monthly.

To compare these standards to those within the industry, statistics are available from the Mortgage Bankers Association of America. Occasionally, direct comparisons from one company to another are available; however, care must be taken not to discuss prices or the fixing of prices in any way.

Coordination with Agencies

The production department must get along with numerous governmental agencies. Winners do not emerge from a battle with regulatory authorities. The production manager needs to know the heads of the various FHA and VA offices. Branch managers and processors need to know the underwriting and appraisal chiefs, and the clerks should get to know the clerks within the agencies.

The production manager must deal with FHA both on the local and the national level. Interfacing occurs in production and servicing. Locally, branch offices must secure timely and accurate appraisals, prompt underwriting and credit approvals, and take advantage of new programs as they are promulgated. With the advent of FHA's direct endorsement program, company underwriters must maintain a close liaison with each FHA office to keep themselves current on criteria that FHA considers acceptable to approve applications.

On the Washington level, nonsupervised lenders must obtain FHA's approval for opening new branches. FHA's mortgage review committee conducts periodic hearings to determine whether mortgage bankers brought before it will remain approved mortgagees. The Mortgage Bankers Association of America maintains a close liaison with FHA at the national level to inform the members of new programs and assist with special programs that need to be handled on a national level.

The Veterans Administration exists to help eligible persons who served in the armed forces of the United States. As with FHA, the production department must deal with VA on a local basis for certificates of reasonable value (appraisals), prompt underwriting and credit approval, and periodic review of the mortgage banker's participation in the automatic guaranty program.

Certain local housing authorities must be dealt with when they receive special bond money for targeted programs within the local community. The primary problem normally encountered is securing an adequate allocation.

Occasionally, it is necessary to deal with state and federal labor departments, equal employment opportunity commissions, the Office of Federal Contract Compliance, the Federal Trade Commission and others. The laws and regulations of these bureaus must be complied with. The larger the company, the higher the profile, and the more likely the company will be selected for a compliance review.

Conventional loans are subject to many more state and local laws than are FHA and VA loans, and new programs concerning adjustable-balance mortgages, shared equity, adjustable-rate mortgages, and others should be carefully covered by an attorney with the consumer-affairs department of the affected states.

Conclusion

Whether the production department is centralized or decentralized and whether it originates loans by branch operations or through the purchase of loans, successful production-department management is characterized by:

Knowledge of corporate/department objectives.

An understanding of the measurements of performance and how they affect management and departmental personnel compensation.

Good administration and control of the technical aspects of originating loans
   and attendant documentation requirements.

Good service to customers: accurate and "as advertised."

Tough-minded determination, communication, and monitoring of loan pric
   ing.

Good financial and operational reporting and control systems.

Satisfactory professional relationships with lending agencies.

Inventory Philosophy, Reporting, and Control

F. Allen Graham
Executive Vice President
Bloomfield Savings and Loan Association, F. A.

This chapter discusses the management of the *mortgage-loan inventory* (pipeline). The management technique endorsed is a hands-on, or constant-monitoring, type. This can be achieved in any number of ways, but the end result should be the development of a reporting and control system through which the mortgage banker can adequately project and secure an appropriate position in the secondary market to cover the mortgage inventory as loans are originated, priced, and closed.

Commitments in the secondary market are, to a large extent, predictable. That is, the dollar amount, the purchase or sale price, and expiration date are all known and agreed to in writing. Only when an investor becomes unable or unwilling to fulfill his contractual obligations is the commitment position of a mortgage banker not of a known, fixed quantity and value. The make-up of an inventory position, however, changes constantly because loans are applied for, approved or disapproved, and closed daily. The key to profitability is the successful balancing of a fixed short position (commitments) against an ever-changing long position (inventory).

Inventory Defined

The set of all loans for which an application has been taken make up the *pipeline*. There is some disagreement about what subset of the pipeline constitutes the inventory, but in this chapter, *inventory* is defined as all uncommitted closed loans plus all unclosed loans with outstanding price quotes. The inventory, then is a subset of all loans in the pipeline, as shown in Figure 1.

In Figure 1, the two areas in capital letters comprise the inventory. Inventory is that part of the pipeline that one either owns or is committed to own at a set price. It has not yet been allocated against a commitment to sell. It is against these loans that the commitment position is evaluated; the inventory and commitment positions together form a *net market position*. Other loans in the pipeline do not generate the same kind of market exposure as the inventory

Figure 1

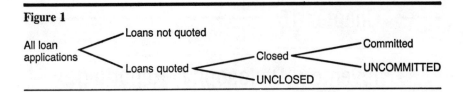

position. Loans in process that are *floating* (not quoted) are indicative of business yet to come, but until they are quoted there is no market exposure other than a possible obligation to close the loan at some price. Likewise, once closed loans are committed to a particular investor, the gain or loss on their sale is fixed and becomes an indicator of past performance.

Identifying Risks

Inherent in the pricing and managing of a mortgage inventory are two major, interrelated risks. One is the originator's risk of obtaining the loans on which he quotes a rate or discount. Current market practice does not obligate the mortgagor to actually close his loans with a mortgage banker, and as a result the mortgage banker cannot be assured that he will have a loan with a specific coupon rate and term that he can profitably deliver to an investor. The other risk involves committing to a mortgagor to close his loan at a fixed rate, discount, and term without an offsetting commitment to sell that loan at a similar fixed rate, discount, and term. Unlike the mortgagor, the mortgage banker is obligated to honor his commitment. Risk-taking involves the possibility of tremendous profits (or unmanageable losses). Top management must decide what level of risk they are comfortable with, and commit the company to this desired level of risk.

Origination Risks

To assess the risks of origination, a reasonable estimate must be developed of the percentage of quoted loans an originator will close according to the terms that he has originally committed (or quoted) to the potential borrower or seller. For example, assume an originator is currently quoting and committing to close FHA/VA loans at a specific rate and discount. The commitment is a firm quote for 60 days. What will the results be if economic forces cause the market discount to increase or decrease greatly if the pegged VA rate is changed during that 60-day commitment period?

Estimates of the *attrition* or *fallout rate* (applications which do not mature to closed loans) must be continually updated. An understanding based on historical data of the normal fallout rate of applications according to the type of loan, the geographic area, and the rate movements is helpful for understanding the attrition rate of existing applications. The effect that the source of the loans will have on the attrition rate must also be clearly understood. For example, a large commitment from a single builder creates a different risk than do individual commitments to many loan applicants on existing properties. These statistics and conclusions must be documented and analyzed on a daily basis to enable the originator to develop a projection of the volume of loans that he can reasonably expect to close.

Selling Risks

Once a formula is developed that will accurately predict the mortgage inventory which will close, the originator must consider the sale of that inventory. Here the originator considers the type of coverage desired (if available): mandatory-delivery commitments or standby or optional-delivery commitments. The advantage of mandatory-delivery commitments is that mortgages can usually be sold at better rates and discounts than with optional-delivery commitments. However, the originator must deliver to the mandatory commitment, in spite of the fact that he may not have the loans or may not be able to produce the loans at the commitment price.

The advantage of optional-delivery commitments is that the originator may choose whether or not to deliver the loans. In a period of falling interest rates, an originator could disregard an optional commitment and sell loans to other investors (or even the same investor) at higher prices. However, optional-delivery commitments, if available at all, generally require upfront fees substantially higher than do mandatory commitments. The mix of mandatory and standby commitments which a mortgage banker chooses is one tool by which management can alter risk exposure.

After the originator decides the type of coverage desired, it must go through a selection process as to where that coverage is to be obtained. A clear policy must be developed and adhered to as it relates to critiera used in obtaining commitments to sell mortgages. Criteria must be developed for the financial status and credit of dealers, institutions, brokers, and banks with whom the originator deals. Volume limitations and credit standards must be established. Diversification among the sources to which the originator sells is a means of risk management.

Inventory Exposure

A good loan control system monitors and records the whole pipeline, not just the inventory, even though the exposure on unquoted loans is much less than that on the inventory. The need for volume forecasts, document tracking, and document preparation makes such a system desirable.

The inventory is defined as closed, uncommited loans and nonclosed, quoted loans. Net exposure is measured by matching this inventory to the investor commitment position. Still, this topic would not merit a separate chapter were it not for the crucially important fact that the inventory is not a static position. Unlike the commitment position, the inventory is changing daily. Some changes are simple: quotes expire, new quotes at different prices or rates are issued, loans close, and applications are cancelled. Other, less frequent, changes may have far more impact: VA rate changes can increase or decrease the worth of a large percentage of the inventory, or a general awareness on the part of prospective buyers of declining (or rising) interest rates can change the cancellation rate. Such factors can radically alter the nature of an inventory position.

Inventory exposure can be broken down into four categories: mechanical, strategic, market, and administrative. *Mechanical exposure* refers to the reporting system itself, while *strategic exposure* refers to the risks inherent in a particular strategy of doing business. *Market exposure* covers the possible damage caused by an adverse economic or financial market. *Administrative exposure* encompasses management's "tinkering" with the system. Strategic and market exposure have a much greater consequence on overall performance than do the other two categories, although any one of the four types of exposure can result in devastating losses.

Mechanical

Whether a loan control system is manual or automated, it is important to understand the weakness involved in a reporting sequence. No matter how sophisticated a marketing system is, if the inventory data on which it is based are inaccurate, the system will be inefficient. Mechanical exposure is comprised of clerical error, system inefficiency, inadequate computer support, and procedural confusion.

Clerical error can be minimized but never eliminated. Inventory systems can range from totally manual to almost fully automated. Input and transcribing errors are most common in a manual system, but even the most advanced computer system requires that data be input initially, and continually updated by an operator, whether at the branch or home office. There are three ways to inhibit clerical error. First, all people involved should understand what the numbers mean, how their performance affects the company, and how to spot errors or inconsistencies. Second, procedures should be established for all situations, and the people concerned should be aware of such procedures. Third, the need for follow-up and crosschecking should be emphasized. Activity reports prepared at the home office should be forwarded to the branch office for verification, and vice versa. Error reports and inconsistencies should be reviewed by and with appropriate management personnel.

System inefficiency is the least visible aspect of mechanical exposure. Once a system has been established, the people using the system tend to learn to live with it, even when market changes dictate other measures. An inventory control system can be inefficient in a number of ways, the most apparent of which is the timeliness of the inventory information. When interest rates were relatively stable, it was not uncommon for a mortgage banker to update his inventory position less than once a week. Now, because of the extreme volatility in interest rates, it is a virtual necessity for management to obtain information on inventory changes on a much more frequent basis. Another possible inefficiency is the delay between the need to change origination prices and the actual implementation of the change.

Document control is another area where a poorly designed system can cost time and money. It is important that all loan documents be on hand, verified, and put in the required order so that loan packages are ready for delivery as soon as possible after closing. To take full advantage of market swings, immediate delivery of loans may be required. All loan-processing audit procedures and document follow-up should be directed towards this end.

While timeliness of information is of paramount importance, the amount of information available is also a concern. Some systems provide such data as the average cost of loans in the pipeline, the estimated closings over the upcoming 30-day period, the value of the inventory, and the cancellation rate. The importance of these reports depends upon the particular marketing strategy employed. Any overall marketing strategy must take into consideration the limitations of the inventory control system.

A corporate policy should cover every situation that comes up in processing and closing a loan, selling a loan, and shipping a loan. Confusion can result when personnel in the corporation do not understand the policy in the same way. For example, there may be conflicting ideas of what to do after such events as a rate change or the expiration of a quote, or when to report a new deal (or quote). This problem is especially prevalent with a large branch production system and a large middle-management group.

Strategic

In order to have a successful marketing effort, an overall strategy for obtaining and closing loans must be developed in light of corporate objectives and attitude toward risk. This strategy must also take into consideration the marketplace in which the company competes. Pricing and product selection are the prime concerns in this area of strategic exposure.

Pricing. Controlling the inventory includes controlling the price at which that inventory is obtained. Setting rates or prices too competitively may achieve substantial volume but also may adversely affect immediate corporate earnings. Rates or prices set too conservatively may adversely affect origination volume and the morale of the production personnel.

Pricing decisions can also affect the quality of the inventory by making it more (or less) responsive to changing market conditions. Both the length and the terms of the quoting procedures are important. The longer a quote is outstanding, the harder it is to determine what the end product will be. One of the biggest risks for a mortgage bank that does a majority of its business in FHA-insured or VA-guaranteed mortgages is that the prevailing VA rate will change downward, forcing it to close a large percentage of its loans at a lower rate than anticipated. It also becomes harder to anticipate a fallout rate as the length of the quote increases.

Sometimes, when interest rates rise, originators quote interest rates lower than the prevailing FHA/VA rate in effect at the time of the quote. This is usually done in one of two ways. In the first instance, a fixed discount on a rate lower than the prevailing FHA/VA rate is quoted. This type of quote locks one into the rate regardless of swings in prices during the period of the quote. A less risky strategy is to quote an interest-rate spread; for example, 12 points or 2 percent below the prevailing FHA/VA rate at time of closing.

The obvious answer to limiting the risk on all quotes is to shorten the length of the quote. However, at this time, 30- and 60-day quotes are common. Thus, a policy of shorter quotes generally creates a reduced volume of loan applications. A mortgage bank, therefore, must decide how much risk it is willing to assume, based on its ability (1) to successfully market the loans, and, (2) to absorb losses if it fails.

Product Selection.   Consumer acceptance of the product is also important. Start-up costs, including fees for legal opinions and document drafts, as well as training for the origination staff and possible computer system modifications, can be very expensive (especially if the subsequent product is unacceptable to consumers). Conversely, adequate investor interest must be verified, either through prior commitments or widespread acceptance, so that there is a place to sell the loans once they are accumulated in inventory.

Most importantly with new or unusual products, but equally applicable to all loans, is concern over investor viability. If an investor is unable to fulfill a commitment to purchase loans, not only is any commitment fee already paid usually lost, but another outlet for the loans must be found. If the loans were originally tailored to the investor's needs (e.g., a special index for an ARM), it is that much more difficult to resell them.

The liquidity in a market for a new product is also a concern. Where there is limited investor interest, the pricing relationships between similar products will not remain constant. The price spread between GPM GNMAs and regular GNMAs has historically fluctuated between one and four points. FHA buy-down pools experience the same sort of fluctuation. Extreme fluctuation makes it ever more difficult to adequately cross-hedge loan quotations during the formation of a GNMA pool.

Builder Loans. Some mortgage bankers have been able to develop ongoing, profitable relationships with residential home builders. These relationships, however, are not without their own special risks. Many builders require a mortgage banker to commit to close their loans at predetermined prices, or within specified ranges, over a long period of time. There is a double problem in hedging the cost of this type of inventory.

First of all, many builders require some sort of price guarantee, such as a fixed price or a price cap, that keeps the mortgage banker from quoting all loans at current prices. Secondly, many builders are looking for commitments to close loans at below-market rates in order to sell their products. When an outstanding commitment is in place with a builder, loans are much more certain to be delivered at prices better than the market than when commitment prices are worse than the market. For example, a mortgage banker commits to close 13 percent FHA loans at 12 points when the market is 12 points. If the market starts to deteriorate to 18 points, the builder will make every effort to close and deliver loans at the committed price of 12. However, if the market improves, some builders may deliver their loans elsewhere at a better price. In this no-win situation, a mortgage banker who had not covered the commitment would have lost 6 points in the first scenario. In the second scenario, a mortgage banker who had sold before the loans closed would not have the loans to fill the commitment. To try to force the builder to deliver creates an adversary position in which the mortgage banker may win the battle but lose the war if the builder is lost as a customer. No matter how they are structured, most builder commitments have some extra element of risk. Before entering into such a relationship, a mortgage banker must be sure that the added production is worth the added risk. Often it is helpful to hypothesize a worst-case scenario to put the possible risk into perspective.

Diversification. A serious oversight in many corporate strategies is a lack of diversification in both commitments to sell and sources of product originations. The pitfall of too few investors is made more obvious if one of them fails with a large percentage of the total commitments outstanding. The opposite can happen if most of the originations are concentrated in a few areas, loan-origination personnel or builder accounts. Economic hardship or changing loyalties could easily jeopardize a relatively large portion of the pipeline.

Analysis

If, as stated earlier, the primary theme in inventory control is constant monitoring, surely a secondary theme is constant analysis. This analysis should, at a minimum, include: (1) constantly reverifying the fallout rate; (2) monitoring the results of all builder commitments to see the net cost of loans closed relative to the market; (3) tracking the average time a loan is in the pipeline; (4)

verifying that loans are being quoted at marketable prices and rates and that changes in the authorized price are being reflected at once in new originations; and (5) ascertaining that a profitable trend in loan sales has been and is established by the marketing personnel.

Market Exposure

The first two types of exposure discussed above, mechanical and strategic exposure, are mostly under the control of the originator. The next area of exposure—market exposure—refers to those adverse conditions beyond the control of the originator that negatively affect even prudent operations. Note the use of the word *prudent*. It is easy to say that business is poor because of the market. However, prudent business operations require that allowance be made for an adverse turn in the market. Although such a turn may catch you unaware (if you had known it was coming, it could have been taken advantage of), it should not catch you unprepared. Proper planning for the following contingencies can make the difference between slow business and out of business.

Yield Curves.   A normal yield curve has a positive slope and, therefore, "normally" short-term rates are lower than long-term rates. Mortgage bankers have always taken advantage of this opportunity by borrowing short term to finance their mortgage fundings between settlement and sale to an investor. However, there have been several protracted periods of time in the last few years when the opposite was true: short-term rates were higher than long-term rates, and what had been a steady source of income to subsidize the cost of loan originations became another expense. One way to minimize the effects of a negative borrowing spread is to insist that all loans be ready for delivery as soon as possible after closing. It is very helpful for any mortgage banker using FNMA or FHLMC coverage to be approved for accelerated delivery. Using this procedure, both agencies will accept, and fund, a loan delivery with less than full documentation if certain procedures are followed.

FHA/VA Rate Changes.   As discussed earlier, an FHA/VA rate change can significantly alter the loan-sale gain or loss of a company by changing the future interest rates at which most loans in the pipeline will close. A rate change up enhances the value of the pipeline loans, while a rate change down has the opposite effect. Two or more rate changes in quick succession can leave the smaller originator with only a few loans at the short-lived rate, possibly less than the minimum number needed to form a GNMA pool.

Speculation on an impending rate change, especially downward, has a direct impact on home buyer psychology. In anticipation of an upward rate change, realtors and borrowers will demand extraordinary service to close loans prior to the change. An anticipated downward rate change evokes the opposite reaction. In some cities, interest-rate forecasting has become a media event, with newscasters going so far as to advise prospective buyers on the course of rates. The elimination of the administered FHA rate by HUD has softened the impact of a rate change. However, the same results usually occur when interest rates change, because of market forces or a change in the administered VA rate.

Periods of Interest-Rate Volatility. In times of drastic market swings, drastic actions are sometimes necessary. Changes in the fallout rate estimates should cause a corresponding adjustment to the commitment position. The related problem of not having enough loans of the same interest rate to make a normal GNMA pool must be managed. Other whole-loan investor opportunities, such as FNMA, may offer the same price with no minimum requirements. Lastly, there is always the possibility of selling the loans servicing-released, with a premium for the servicing or, conversely, buying some loans servicing-released to augment a pool. With the many below-market-rate loans being originated, the sale of loans servicing-released has become much more common.

A rapid increase in rates does not go unnoticed by investors. It is very important that loans closed against a special investor commitment conform exactly with the terms of the commitment. As rates rise, investors tend to be much more discriminating in the loans they will accept at rates now substantially below the market. The easiest way to avoid this pitfall is to have all terms and conditions agreed to in writing by both parties at the outset.

A related problem to consider in a widely fluctuating market is the financial strength of the institutional investors dealt with. Many thrifts, in particular, have experienced severe cash flow problems and may not have the money to fund commitments when due.

Administrative Exposure

The fourth category of inventory exposure is administrative. Although corporate policy is set by senior management, it must be carried out through subordinates. Particularly in the areas of loan originations and marketing, abuses of authority, intentional or otherwise, can blunt the total corporate effort. Certainly there cannot be a rule to cover every situation. Since it is impossible in a company of any size for senior management to make every decision, some discretion must be given to the people running daily operations. However, the limits of this discretionary authority must be understood by all. Excess policy deviations seem to occur most often in price concessions to loan originators, deviations from quoting policy, speculative positioning in the secondary market, and entering into large builder commitments at very unfavorable terms.

Administrative exposure is but one facet of the larger problem of orchestrating the whole origination and marketing effort. The decisions on what risks to take and how aggressively to go after originations must form a composite strategy that reduces overall risk to the corporation to whatever level management is comfortable with and the company can reasonably afford. The marketing and origination strategies must be consistent with, and complement each other. If long-term quotes are given, they must be at levels that can reasonably be covered by a combination of standby and forward coverage. New products can be offered only to the extent that investors can be found for them. Management must make a determination of the worth of servicing vis-á-vis loan-sale gains. All of these considerations and many more are the concern of senior management and should be clearly understood at that level.

Once a policy or strategy is set conceptually, it must be implemented at all levels of the origination process. At this level it is vital that procedures be in place to ensure that corporate policy is carried out as envisioned.

Written Procedures. The best way to avoid misinterpretation of company policy is to have clear, preestablished rules for as many contingencies as possible, in both loan origination and marketing. This ensures that the overall corporate goals of risk versus reward are being properly achieved.

Written procedures should largely reflect standard operating procedures in both origination and marketing. For example, after a VA rate change, either up or down, discount points must generally be redetermined with the seller. A company should have a policy of going to the new market price or staying with the old price or some combination. Many companies issue a *point letter,* when they first take an application, that spells out the company's obligation in the event of a VA rate change.

Pricing procedures vary greatly from one mortgage banker to the next. The main questions, however, concern the time a price can be locked in and for how long. Other questions are: How should a change, in mortgagor, mortgage amount, or loan type, for example, be treated? What constitutes a new deal, or are the old points still valid?

Rules should be established governing the source of the origination. As discussed before, it is not wise to concentrate on only a few large sources. At the same time it is hard to pass up business. If builder commitments are written on a local or regional level, there must be strict rules on terms and maximum amounts, including special rules for loans that are assigned in. Since in most cases assigned loans are ready to close, it is usually important to close at current market and not, for example, at an aggressive price that was established to lure new applications.

While all of these decisions seem to be origination decisions, it is important to realize that it is just such decisions that determine the quality and quantity of the inventory. Inventory and marketing risk cannot be separated, although they may at times seem to be. There must be firm procedures in the marketing area to complement the origination process, just as rules for loan production are set within the limitations of the marketing effort. A clear understanding of corporate policy regarding coverage of the pipeline is mandatory. Generally, companies have a policy about mandatory coverage versus closed loans, and total coverage versus total loans, with some leeway left to the discretion of marketing personnel. This discretion includes the use of the cash market, the futures market, puts, calls, and the mix between them.

The corporate policy about who is authorized to enter into contracts, and to what extent, should be in writing. Although many companies have a marketing committee, it is essential that an individual have the authority to make spot decisions as necessary. The marketing committee is usually more an oversight committee. It is usually at this level that investors are approved, as well. Investor approval should be clearly understood and maintained. The allocation of responsibility and authority to the appropriate individuals should be completely understood. It should be written down and communicated.

Implementation of these policies, controls, and practices requires certain internal reports and internal audit procedures that show management the application of the corporate policies.

Internal Reports.   Reports are generated in two general areas. The origination and marketing area generates its reports of closed loans, loans in process, and investor commitments, for decision and control purposes. The controller or accounting section of the corporation records closed loans, mortgage-sale transactions and the economic results after a delivery has been consummated under a commitment. Commitments can be satisfied by the delivery of loans, thus matching the origination price to the commitment price paid at funding. Or commitments may be paired off or allowed to expire, in the case of optional delivery commitments, without the delivery of loans. When a commitment is paired off, the originator simply buys loans or securities which can be delivered to the commitment, thereby cancelling the commitment and creating an income or loss between the two prices.

As previously discussed, internal production reports should be developed that show the total loans in process. Production reports that report price obligations to close loans, or loans which are closed at specific rates or discounts, should be updated frequently. Reports of originations by loan offices, branch, and region of the corporation should be generated at least monthly. Internal reports on the outstanding investor commitment position should be updated frequently by the marketing department, and reconciliations should be produced at least weekly by the controller's department. The profit or loss that results when loans are delivered against an outstanding commitment should be reported by the controller's department, and the allocation of that profit or loss should be allocated by loan office, branch, or region, to allow management to assess the results of its pricing policies.

Notwithstanding the development and implementation of the best pricing policies and controls to manage those policies, certain deviations of price will occur because of competition or prudent business practices in order to satisfy the demands of existing customers or new business relationships. Clearly, a price- or rate-concession report must be developed at least monthly to allow management to assess the magnitude and extent of price or rate concessions.

Steps may then be taken to eliminate or control excessive concessions. The authority to make price or rate concessions must be limited: a loan officer or solicitor having none, a branch manager very little, and the bulk of the authority left with senior management. Senior management has a better overview of corporate objectives and usually does not become as emotionally involved in obtaining the loan and satisfying the customer's demand.

Overall marketing performance reports should be developed by the controller's department, which reports monthly and year-to-date results of marketing gains or losses. Detail should be provided by commitment, loan-origination type, and location.

Internal Audit. All mortgage-banking companies or originating entities should have an internal audit effort. The separation from corporate or origination personnel, as well as the quality of this effort, will vary from company to company, depending on the size and scope of the operation. Corporate origination and marketing policies should be audited by the internal auditor or the person responsible for the internal audit. This audit should concern itself with the overall compliance with corporate controls as they relate to pricing, commitment coverage, and all aspects of marketing. This report, which reports deviations or noncompliance with corporate policies or controls, should be given directly to the chief operating officer (or an internal audit committee). The extent of compliance with all the regulatory requirements and corporate policies should be reported. Where possible, the internal audit must be conducted by one who is not involved in any other management function.

Problem Loans. In spite of the knowledgeable management of clear, concise policies and procedures, problem loans still develop. A problem loan can take many forms: technical or documentation deficiency, such as a flaw in title or uninsurability as it relates to FHA or MI insurance or a VA loan guarantee; nonconforming to a maximum allowable loan balance or underwriting requirement; delinquency; foreclosure; or real-estate-owned. When this problem loan emerges, responsibility to cure the defect in the loan should be placed in the hands of one who is charged with overall management and not one whose duties are limited to origination and production goals. If a loan-production officer or branch manager is left with the responsibility of curing a loan deficiency, the job usually takes a low priority. The production person does not usually realize the adverse consequences of failing to deal with a problem loan immediately. Thus, corporate controls should provide immediate knowledge of a problem loan.

If all efforts fail to cure a problem loan, making it unmarketable in the secondary market, the mortgage-bank originator must have a predeveloped strategy to dispose of, or deal with, this loan. Although some companies are large enough to hold some problem loans as long-term investments, management should have the ability to dispose of its problem loans, thus preventing a catastrophic result when an excess number of such loans appear.

Problem Investors.   Dealing with a problem commitment represents a much more challenging and potentially harmful situation for the mortgage banker or seller. Many times the cause of a problem commitment can be traced to telltale signs which existed and should have been discovered upon close examination at the time the commitment contract was entered into. The primary reason for default involves one of the parties dealing beyond its financial capability to deliver or accept delivery, usually in a worst-case scenario situation. Analyzing the credit position and the investment philosophy of the other party allows the originating and selling entity to eliminate most problem commitments.

The more troublesome issue is to understand how to deal with the problem commitment when it rears its ugly head. One must first determine whether or not the problem is bona fide or represents a devious maneuver (an attempt to avoid honoring a commitment that has had bad economic results, for example). Assuming the problem is bona fide, then every effort should be made to concentrate on an immediate work-out arrangement. Accepting an immediate settlement or opting to process a long-term claim depends on the nature of the problem (size, amount, etc.) on one side and the financial standing of the party (company, broker, institution) on the other side.

Thus, the disposition of problem loans or commitments is a reality that many originators and participants in the secondary mortgage market have faced from time to time. The cost or loss suffered from these loans or commitments must be anticipated to a point where, when they occur, a catastrophic result will not follow.

Summary

Thus, the basic inventory philosophy must be one which creates a successful control and disposition of the inventory in the secondary market with servicing retained by the seller. Inventory control and disposition match prices, rates, and terms of the mortgages originated, with similar prices, rates, and terms of investor commitments. Many mortgage originators, because of size or other factors, always attempt to match specific loans with specific investor commitments. Others seek to match the aggregate of loans or application in the pipeline to the overall aggregate commitment position of both mandatory and standby commitments.

A pricing policy which is consistent, communicated, and enforced with all origination personnel is an absolute necessity before an effective inventory control system can be utilized. The discipline of a consistent pricing policy creates predictable results, and the need for the ongoing administration of this discipline cannot be emphasized enough. Once the pricing mechanism is in place, it then becomes a simple matter of communication of volume on a daily basis to the marketing department, or other person in the mortgage-banking operation who is able to identify the pipeline in process and the obligation of the mortgage banker to close loans at specific prices, rates, and terms.

Because the mortgage bank enters into a unilateral agreement with the mortgage applicant (the applicant may not qualify or close the mortgage), it is its judgement of the attrition (fallout) of the pipeline which probably becomes the single most important decision made by the mortgage bank during the inventory control process. Here it is important that the mortgage bank avail itself of historical data, clearly understanding the customs of the origination area (they vary in different cities or regions of the country), follow the marketplace for the current movement of interest rates, and project on a daily basis the future movement of rates. As the attrition rates change (which they do, as interest rates rise or fall or the overall economic conditions change), the mortgage bank must react and fine tune the commitment position.

Thus, it is the exercise of discipline in following a conservative pricing policy, and a hands-on management of the mortgage inventory (through proper reporting and control techniques) that creates a predictable result which is acceptable and meets the preestablished corporate objective. Speculation or flexible applications of policies and controls create unpredictable results and possible financial losses to the mortgage banker. The mortgage bank must establish a philosophy of inventory control which it understands and is comfortable with, and which produces corporate profits.

Chapter 17

Hedging Alternatives

William E. Long
President
Talman Home Mortgage Corporation

Every business has some degree of risk that must be identified and managed. Operating in the secondary mortgage market is no exception. Besides the risks of other businesses, mortgage bankers must manage the interest-rate risk, involving both long-term and short-term interest rates. Because mortgages are typically packaged and sold in million dollar units, just a small change in interest rates and the concomitant change in the prices of the mortgages can mean the difference between profit and loss.

The secondary mortgage market participant has many means of reducing, or hedging, the risk of interest-rate changes. These hedging alternatives should be well understood by management. This chapter discusses the need for hedging long-term interest rates, various ways to hedge in general, and the specific alternatives available for various types of mortgage loans.

The Need to Hedge

Interest-rate risk to the mortgage banker is price risk. Price risk is the potential change in the value of the mortgage product because of future changes in its sale price. Changes in sales prices reflect the movement of long-term interest rates. The primary creators of price risk are interest-rate volatility and the uncertainty of the future direction, timing, and effect of interest rates.

Interest Rate Volatility

Figure 1 (the dotted line) graphically portrays the effect of the volatility of interest rates on the sales prices of 8 percent GNMA mortgage-backed securities (MBSs), a proxy for the sales prices of FHA/VA mortgages and a good indicator for the relative movement of price for conventional loans as well. The prices shown range from a low of 58 percent of par to a high of 91 percent of par, a range or absolute price amplitude of 33 percentage points. Significantly, during this same time frame, prices changed direction 29 times.

**Figure 1 • Closing Price Levels for GNMA 8's and Current Coupon GNMA's
(monthly closing levels from January 1979 to December 1983)**

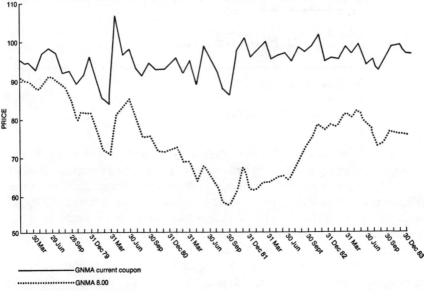

Source: Salomon Brothers Inc

Greater time exposure translates into greater volatility exposure. Because originating, processing, closing, and packaging a deliverable mortgage product usually consumes a two- to four-month period, price changes can be dramatic and can produce either ruinous losses or windfall profits to a nonhedger. For example, suppose a nonhedged mortgage banker agreed (committed) to fund $1 million of current coupon government mortgages within the next two months. If, say, the time period involved were from October 31 to December 31, 1979, and all the loans were actually funded, Figure 1 (the solid line) suggests that the mortgage banker could have "bought" his loans at about 90 percent of par and sold them at 95 percent of par, making a $50,000 profit directly attributable to the decline in interest rates (improvement in mortgage prices). If a longer time period were involved, say, October 31, 1979, to April 30, 1980, even more money could have been made, namely $170,000 (107 percent less 90 percent times $1 million).

However, if the two-month time period were from May 31 to July 31, 1981, a loss of $50,000 would have resulted. As above, if a longer time period were involved, say, from May 31 to September 30, 1981, a greater loss of $100,000 would have resulted.

Interest-Rate Uncertainty

The uncertainty of interest rates involves both economic and political guess-timates. The future direction of market-driven interest rates is clearly uncertain. Using Figure 1 again as a reference, when does a price movement become a trend? How much of a price movement? One half point? One point? When is a price movement merely an aberration? How does one "stop-loss" versus "wait for the windfall" versus "avoid whiplash," etc.? One prudent way to deal with an uncertain future is to "lock in" a future sales price, i.e., hedge immediately at some predetermined sales price.

However, as discussed in Chapter 16, Inventory Philosophy, Reporting, and Control, hedging an exact amount of expected loan production at current interest rates with an equivalent amount of current market investor commitments does not eliminate the uncertainty risk, because the effect of the future direction of interest rates on the loans in the pipeline (i.e., loans not yet closed that may become closed) is uncertain. Thus, it is necessary for the hedger to estimate uncertain future interest rates and their uncertain effect on the volume and pricing of loans to be hedged.

Coupled with these economic uncertainties is the political uncertainty of when official, federal-government-administered interest-rate changes will be made. With the deregulation of the FHA rate, the VA rate is currently the only government-administered mortgage rate. Politically inspired interest-rate actions tend to move quickly or lead when the direction of interest rates favors consumers/voters. With an increase in market interest rates, a politically managed rate lags the market, creating huge discounts (low prices) to equate mortgage yields with capital market yields.

The Ways to Hedge

All mortgage banking hedging alternatives have a common element: price protection. This protection can be afforded from investors' forward commitments for purchase of whole loans or participations, from Wall Street dealers for purchase of MBSs, from futures contracts and options, and from selling servicing released.

Forward-Delivery Commitments—Whole Loan

Institutional investor forward commitments for the purchase of residential mortgages have evolved from firm takeouts that require mandatory delivery over a lengthy period of time to forward optional-delivery or standby commitments to very short-term mandatory commitments. Currently, optional-delivery or standby commitments, if available at all, are significantly more costly than mandatory commitments.

A hybrid of the mandatory and standby commitment has evolved whereby delivery is required *if* loans are "purchased" and is described as "best efforts." With new products and the attendant uncertainty of origination volume, this arrangement provides the originator with a hedge that allows limited price protection, while it forfeits the windfall profits often available under a pure standby option.

The current high cost of optional-delivery commitments is significant for hedging purposes inasmuch as standby commitments close to market prices formerly represented the "ideal" marketing strategy: Originate loans to standby coverage. If the market improves, deliver loans to then obtainable mandatory commitments with better prices; if the market deteriorates, deliver to the standby. Today, mandatory-delivery commitments require a sure knowledge of deliverable loans and the ability to deliver loans in the required time frame. Forward-delivery commitments for whole loans are available from government agencies or private institutions. The primary government-related mortgage purchasers are FNMA and FHLMC.

Private investor forward commitments for fixed-rate 30-year loans are rare today. However, private buyers for 15-year fixed-rate government loans are not uncommon. Private investor standby commitments are generally not available.

Forward-Delivery Commitments—Participations

Forward commitments for delivery of participations in mortgage loans are usually transacted between thrift institutions, because the typical highly leveraged mortgage banker cannot afford to tie up capital in a participation interest. Traditionally, participations involve conventional, not government, loans and may be shown on the balance sheet as a contingent liability. They also often result from the restructuring or realignment of a thrift's existing portfolio.

For mortgage bankers, a tri-party participation is possible in which the minority participation is sold off to a third party, with the servicing retained by the originator. The assignment of interest to a third party does not release the originator from its obligations under the participation. Furthermore, the sale of both participation interests in a mortgage loan to other investors under a tri-party arrangement may subject the seller to securities regulations, requiring legal advice.

A participation interest is attractive to an investor because the seller-servicer is financially committed and "lives with" the loan over its servicing lifetime. Also, the requirement to maintain voluminous loan documents is eliminated. This latter feature has spurred the evolution of the 100 percent participation, because of specific document and accounting simplifications for both investor and servicer.

Forward-Delivery Commitments—MBSs

Forward-delivery commitments for the purchase of MBSs are issued by Wall Street dealers, government agencies, and private institutions. MBSs may be either GNMA guaranteed, FNMA/FHLMC guaranteed, or insured by a private mortgage insurance company.

GNMA

Basically, all government-insured (including Farmers Home Administration) or guaranteed mortgage loans are eligible to be put in GNMA MBS pools. Individual single-family pools may consist of the following types of mortgages:

- Level payment (FHA, FmHA or VA), either 15 or 30 years. All loans in a given MBS should have the same approximate maturity.
- Buydown mortgages (FHA or VA).
- Graduated-payment mortgages (FHA or VA).
- Growing-equity mortgages (FHA or VA).
- Mobile home loans (FHA or VA).

Any one pool must consist of mortgages within just one of these categories.

GNMA MBSs are typically sold to Wall Street dealers on a 30- to 90-day mandatory-delivery basis. Optional-delivery commitments are sometimes available, however, they are very costly and do not usually allow for much more than four- to six-month future delivery.

GNMA MBS prices generally are more competitive than FNMA or other whole-loan investor prices. Prices above par are obtainable for MBSs, not so for whole loans. Other advantages include: There is no fee required for mandatory GNMA MBS delivery, there is a high servicing fee, 30-day delinquent loans can be included in a GNMA MBS issue, and standbys are obtainable, albeit costly. The major disadvantage of GNMA securities is the requirement to make corporate advances to pass through uncollected principal and interest to the ultimate investors. Therefore, quality control and collection capabilities are important considerations.

In the GNMA MBS pooling process, the issuer must choose between the traditional GNMA I or the more recent GNMA II. The latter has some current advantages that should be considered from a marketing viewpoint: Loans with interest rates varying over a 1 percent range may be mixed within the same pool; multiple issuer pools are allowed, permitting participation by several originating firms unable to aggregate enough loans for a single custom pool; and the current minimum pool size is $250,000 versus $1 million for GNMA I pools. A change in payment date, however, alters the yield of the GNMA II slightly, and this may be reflected in a market price difference between GNMA I and GNMA II. Another major difference with GNMA II is the use of a central

Table 1

A comparison of GNMA I and GNMA II Mortgage-Backed Securities		
	GNMA I	**GNMA II**
Underlying mortgages	FHA, VA & FmHA loans	FHA, VA & FmHA loans
Pools	Single issuer	Custom (single issuer) and multiple issuer
Central paying agent	None—multiple monthly checks to investors	Chemical bank—single monthly check to investors
Transfer agent	Chemical bank	Chemical bank
Interest rate	All mortgages in a pool have the same interest rate (except mobile home pools)	Mortgages in a pool may have interest rates that vary within a 1 percent range
Guarantor	GNMA (full faith and credit of the U.S. government)	GNMA (full faith and credit of the U.S. government)
Guaranty	Full and timely payment of principal and interest plus prepayments	Full and timely payment of principal and interest, plus prepayments
Payment date	15th of the month	20th of the month

Source: GNMA Annual Report, 1983, p. 11.

paying agent, which may be advantageous to both issuer and investor. (For a summary review of GNMA I versus GNMA II, see Table 1.)

MBS pool advances for either GNMA I or GNMA II can require a significant capital commitment however and management should carefully review whether it has the resources and desire to make this commitment as well as the organization and procedures to minimize the amount of corporate advances.

FNMA

The FNMA MBS program builds upon the success of GNMA MBSs. In 1983, its second full year, FNMA issued more than $13 billion in commitments to guarantee its securities.

Unlike GNMA, FNMA guarantees MBSs backed by seasoned loans as well as by new production. Currently, the pools backing FNMA's securities can be composed of any of the following types of first mortgages:

• Conventional loans: 30-year, fixed-rate, fully amortizing; 15-year, fixed-rate, fully amortizing; Growing Equity Mortgages (GEMs) with 3, 4, or 5 percent payment increments; and "California" Variable Rate Mortgages (VRMs).

- FHA/VA loans: 30-year, fixed-rate, fully amortizing; and seasoned at least one year.

The minimum pool size is $1 million. Inasmuch as FNMA is continually refining its MBS program, it is necessary to check with the FNMA regional office for the most up-to-date information.

Conventional loans that exceed 80 percent loan-to-value ratios must be insured by a private mortgage insurance company.

Unlike GNMA MBSs, the issuer/servicer of a FNMA MBS can choose not to assume the risks of borrower default. If FNMA is not required to absorb these losses, its guaranty fee is 25 basis points. This choice is called the "regular servicing option." If FNMA assumes the total risk of loss from borrower default, the guaranty fee is 30 basis points. Under this "special servicing" option, the servicer must still make pool principal and interest advances, but the advances ultimately will be reimbursed by FNMA. These servicing options may influence the choice of loans placed in any one pool. Similar to GNMA II, interest rates varying over a 2 percent range may be included in FNMA MBSs.

FHLMC

The FHLMC MBS program is properly termed a "PC," or participation certificate. Originally designed to participate out pro rata interests in loans purchased by the agency, it evolved into a more traditional MBS through a pilot "SWAP" program, which in turn developed into a security outlet for new production as well.

In 1983, FHLMC issued approximately $19.7 billion in commitments to guarantee securities. Similar to FNMA, these MBSs may be backed by either seasoned or newly produced loans. Currently, these securities can be collateralized by the following types of residential first mortgages:

- Conventional loans: 30-year fixed-rate and 15-year fixed-rate, fully amortizing; private mortgage insurance is required on loans with greater than 80 percent loan-to-value ratios.
- FHA/VA loans: 30-year, fixed-rate, fully amortizing and seasoned at least one year.

Interest rates included in a pool may vary over a 2 percent range, allowing some flexibility in packaging. Minimum pool size is $1 million.

Currently, FHLMC also has two servicing options. If FHLMC does not assume the borrower default risk, the basic guarantee fee is 20 basis points; however, on large negotiated transactions, this fee can be significantly lower. If FHLMC assumes total risk of loss from borrower default, the guarantee fee is 25 basis points. Under this latter option, the servicer still makes interest advances, but the advances ultimately will be reimbursed.

FHLMC's MBS design requires the pass-through of interest only, rather than principal and interest, and security holders receive a single monthly check, regardless of the number of issuers or certificates.

Other Price Protection Alternatives

GNMA Futures

The GNMA futures market should not be confused with the traditional forward standby market in GNMA MBSs. A futures contract is not a standby. With a futures contract one *must* either deliver a security, buy another security to satisfy delivery, or offset one's sell position by buying back the futures contract sold earlier. One has an obligation to do something; a standby does not impose this obligation.

Another important consideration in the use of a mortgage futures contract is margin. There are separate requirements for both initial and maintenance margin. Initial margin is usually only 1 to 2 percent of the amount hedged, regardless of interest rate changes. Maintenance margin, however, is very significant when interest rates go in an unanticipated direction. This is because cash or its equivalent must be posted in an amount that represents the difference between the market price at the initiation of the contract and the current price of the contract. Maintenance margin calls require a continuing involvement by management and detailed record keeping by the marketing and accounting departments.

Among the advantages of a futures market are continuous trading on an exchange floor; firm prices displayed instantaneously; instantaneous offset at any time during the contract without any need to renegotiate terms of the commitment; the existence of a clearing house that prevents a "renege" by the other contract party, minimizing the credit risk; and a narrow price spread—typically $\frac{1}{32}$ of 1 percent—between the bid and ask prices.

The mortgage originator/seller generally uses the futures market in two situations: when the futures price is better than alternative prices and when it provides price protection for a portion of his pipeline. A futures position may be preferable to a standard mandatory forward commitment under several conditions: if there is a possibility that less than the required minimum amount will actually close (possibly prohibiting issuance of an MBS); if the futures price is better than the cash market price; if the "basis" improves while the hedge is on (for a discussion of "basis" see Chapter 7, Role of Interest Rate Futures); or if it is easier or more economical to offset the futures position.

Hedging conventional mortgages with futures is different from hedging government mortgages. Not only is the conventional secondary market less liquid, but conventional mortgages also exhibit different interest rate and price movements than do FHA/VA mortgages. Because government loans are the collateral for GNMA MBSs, the correlation of conventional loans with GNMA MBSs is not as similar and therefore presents additional basis risk. Attempting to hedge non-FHA/VA loan production with GNMA securities is a form of cross-hedge. Cross-hedging can be very inexact and costly and should be carefully evaluated to determine if it is an acceptable hedging alternative.

In addition to providing a hedging alternative, the mortgage futures market also offers trading opportunities. However, trading transactions require unusual expertise and do not truly represent nonspeculative hedging within a mortgage banking operation.

Hedging with futures is not riskless. While it eliminates the major risk of absolute price exposure, it substitutes the smaller, more measurable and manageable relative price risk. Finally, it can be very tempting to convert a true hedge position into a speculative position. It is crucial that a hedging strategy incorporate discipline.

Other Futures Contracts

The unique success of the GNMA futures contract has resulted in a proliferation of other interest rate hedging instruments, which cover the spectrum of interest rate maturities. Long-term U.S. Treasury bond futures contracts have been developed to provide a hedging instrument for corporate treasurers and other bond portfolio managers such as pension fund managers. Often, the T-Bond market proves to be a better hedging mechanism for the mortgage banker than is the traditional GNMA futures contract. Such cross-hedging, however, generally requires a very high degree of expertise and sophistication for the mortgage originator attempting to hedge his loan inventory.

Futures contracts in commercial paper and CDs also provide short-term interest-rate hedges. Since mortgage warehouse lines are often tied to commercial paper, commercial paper futures provide a potential hedging mechanism for short-term bank borrowings.

Options Market

An option to deliver in the mortgage market, e.g., a standby commitment, is an option to sell, i.e., a "put." An option to buy loans, or a "call," is the opposite. Exchange-traded put and call options, from the mortgage originator's viewpoint, offer limited risk with no margin or mark-to-market constraints. By paying a "premium," or set fee, the originator buys price protection. Unlike mortgage standby commitments, the put option has a residual value that can be sold at a price. Alternatively, writing a call on a GNMA MBS position can provide premium income to offset price declines in GNMA MBSs or other inventory. A strategy to buy put options does not surrender potential price appreciation; however, a strategy to sell call options does, because if interest rates fall, the security can be "called away" from the call's seller.

The added sophistication required to deal in options again calls for careful evaluation on the part of the user. Any serious futures market or options market user should study and understand rate movements in both the cash and futures market. Once a person has hedged, price correlation and basis movement are the key determinants for profitability. The user must determine the normal basis relationship between the two markets, the probable effect of interest-rate changes on the basis, the anticipated direction of these changes, and the anticipated effect on total net profit. At all times, the decision maker must be able to take a futures or options price and translate that into a cash price for mortgages. Differences in delivery time, delivery procedures, and coupon rates complicate the decision process.

Hedging with options is not costless. Unused options should be viewed as the cost of doing business or the cost of insurance protection that—as their name implies—preserves certain options.

Servicing-Released

Traditionally, selling loans servicing-released has been confined to the marginal or start-up mortgage banker or mortgage broker. Today, it is not uncommon for established mortgage originators to sell all or part of their servicing rights on an ongoing basis. Philosophies vary, but the most common reasons for servicing-released sales seem to be a disinterest in servicing certain categories of loans (or loans in general) or a means to provide capital.

Specific Hedging Alternatives

FNMA

FNMA purchases a sometimes bewildering array of mortgage loan types. To sell to FNMA, the originator must obtain a commitment. The types of commitments and the various mortgage types currently eligible for delivery thereto follow:

- *Mandatory delivery.*
    1. FHA-insured or VA-guaranteed (FHA/VA) first mortgages.
        a. FHA/VA growing-equity mortgages (GEMs) may be delivered under any FHA/VA commitment.
        b. FHA/VA graduated-payment mortgages (GPMs) may be delivered under GPM commitments only.
    2. Conventional fixed-rate first mortgages, including participations.
    3. Conventional adjustable-rate first mortgages (ARMs) and graduated-payment adjustable rate mortgages (GPARMs), including participations. GPARMs can be delivered to certain preapproved ARM commitments.
    4. Conventional fixed-rate second mortgages, including participations.

The allowable period for each type of loan can vary. (FNMA sellers should consult the most recent FNMA requirements for each type of loan and commitment, as they may change at any time.)

- *Optional delivery.* Optional-delivery commitments are issued for ARMs and GPARMs that conform to stipulated standard plans (subject to change at any time).
- *Standby commitments.* Standby commitments may be requested for either a 9- or 12-month term. The commitment will be issued without a yield and must be converted to a mandatory-delivery commitment as specified before the lender can deliver under it. A fixed-rate standby commitment may be used for FHA/VA, FHA/VA GPM, conventional first mortgages and participations in conventional first mortgages. An ARM standby commitment may be used for adjustable-rate mortgages or graduated-payment, adjustable-rate mortgages under any of FNMA's standard plans.

  The standby commitment is converted at the yield required for that type of mandatory-delivery commitment on the day the lender requests the conversion. For ARM commitments, the margin in effect on the day the commitment is converted applies to the mandatory-delivery commitment.

- *Resale and refinance commitments.* Individual commitments may be requested for a new conventional mortgage on property financed by an existing FHA, VA or conventional fixed-rate mortgage that FNMA owns, or in which FNMA owns a participation interest. The commitment yield is based on the remaining balance and note rate of the old mortgage and the addional amount requested for the new mortgage and the type of new loan—an ARM, GPARM or a conventional fixed-rate mortgage. Since this yield reflects a blend of the old and new terms, it usually specifies a yield that is below current market rates. Delivery is at the lender's option within a specified time period from the date of the commitment.
- *Negotiated commitments.* Conventional GEMs are negotiated on a commitment-by-commitment basis, as are all acceptable variations to FNMA's numerous standard plans.

FHLMC

FHLMC also purchases may different mortgage loan types pursuant to various commitments. Currently, the types of commitments and the loans eligible for purchase thereunder are as follows:

- *Mandatory delivery.*
  1. Conventional fixed-rate first mortgages, including whole loans and participations.
  2. Conventional adjustable-rate first mortgages (ARMs).
  3. Conventional fixed-rate home improvement second mortgage participations.

4.   Conventional fixed-rate 15-year loans, including participations.

As with FNMA, the allowable delivery period may vary (FHLMC sellers should verify the most recent requirements with the appropriate FHLMC office).

*   *Optional delivery.*

FHLMC issues optional-delivery commitments for:

1.   Conventional first fixed-rate mortgages.
2.   ARMs.

Optional-delivery commitments also vary as to allowable delivery periods.

GNMA MBSs

GNMA MBSs represent the dominant secondary market outlet for FHA/VA production for most originators. Since the deregulation of the FHA rate, GNMA MBSs are generally sold based on a guaranteed coupon rate for each issue, i.e., the issuer guarantees to deliver a specific interest rate, irrespective of future interest rate movements.

Delivery to GNMA MBS commitments may be satisfied by any of these alternative methods:

1.   The MBS issuer actually delivers the MBS to the dealer.
2.   If permitted by the terms of the MBS commitment, the issuer buys another MBS issued by some other company for delivery to the dealer.
3.   The issuer "buys back" his position from the same dealer he sold to at a market price, thus offsetting his delivery obligation.

Alternatives 2 and 3 are useful when forward commitments are in excess of delivery capabilities, when loans will be delivered late, or when a better commitment can be obtained elsewhere.

FNMA/FHLMC MBSs

Virtually all 30-year fixed-rate conventional loan production today is marketed through issuance of MBS securities. Because the payment delay period for a FNMA MBS is 55 days as compared to 75 days for a FHLMC MBS, the capital markets currently pay a slight premium for a comparable new issue FNMA MBS.

Unlike GNMA MBSs, foreclosure risk can be avoided with FNMA/FHLMC securities, for which FNMA and FHLMC require a higher guarantee fee. This translates into a lower servicing fee for the issuer/servicer. However, no delinquent loans can be placed in a FNMA/FHLMC conventional security pool, unlike GNMA MBSs, thereby creating an occasional shipping problem for conventional loans that become delinquent in warehouse.

FNMA/FHLMC MBSs are sold on a guaranteed coupon basis and on an immediate forward or optional delivery basis. Inasmuch as the issuer guarantees delivery of a specific interest rate, he must deliver under three basis strategies:

1. The MBS issuer purchases mandatory delivery commitments over the 30 to 90-day period during which he can best project production and satisfy delivery requirements.
2. If there is an insufficient volume of originated loans to fill mandatory commitments, an issuer can buy back his commitments to deliver and take his loss or windfall profits.
3. Anticipating rising interest rates, he agrees to deliver MBSs on a mandatory or optional basis over the next four to six months with the intention of buying back one coupon if necessary and reselling his higher rate production against a new coupon.

FNMA/FHLMC MBSs allow the mixing of interest rates over a given interest rate, generally ¼ to ½ percent. Rapid interest rate movement sometimes results in greater interest rate differentials, however, triggering one of three other hedging alternatives:

1. The MBS issuer includes higher coupons than necessary in one pool.
2. The MBS issuer sells loans servicing released.
3. The MBS issuer buys loans in the wholesale market, if available, to complete his pool.

Conduit Companies

Major individual companies have established mortgage conduit entities, which purchase whole loans from various originators, pool them and then issue conventional MBSs with the pool as collateral—hence the term *conduit*. Usually, the individual collateral mortgage loans are insured by a private mortgage insurance (MI) company. An MI also usually insures a portion of the pool and sometimes acts as trustee and/or administrator as well.

Conduit companies usually permit only a short time for delivery of the individual mortgages. Most issues are pooled within a short time period, and delivery is virtually always on a mandatory basis.

Conduit companies typically purchase nonconforming loans, i.e., loans that exceed the FNMA/FHLMC maximum loan amounts for individual loans. Accordingly, they offer the most readily available alternative for hedging high loan balance conventional protection.

Typically, conduit companies purchase the following types of mortgages (always check the most recent directives):

- One family detached.
- Two- to four-unit dwellings.
- Low-rise condominiums.

- Townhouses.
- *De minimus* PUDs and PUDs.

Notably, they usually do not purchase high-rise condo properties, leasehold properties, or manufactured housing.

Private Investors

Traditional or private investors (thrift institutions) have generally issued whole-loan and participation commitments. Today, investors tend to prefer mortgage loans that afford a short-term and/or variable-rate advantage, such as the following:

- ARMs.
- Five-to seven-year balloons.
- Fifteen-year fixed rate, level payment, fully amortizing.

Occasionally, a nonthrift private investor—for example, a pension fund or life insurance company, seeks the same investment. While pension funds do not normally seek 30-year products, occasionally an originator may be successful in negotiating a mandatory or best efforts commitment. In these rare situations, very competitive 30-year commitments may be obtained.

Second Mortgages

Whole loan sales are the most common way to sell second mortgages in the private sector. While FHLMC does not make a market for second mortgages at this writing, FNMA does invest in both whole loans and participations of second mortgages. FNMA mandatory commitments are available on a posted, daily basis. Although there is no standard second mortgage standby program, the FNMA negotiation department does custom tailor the specific types of second mortgages originated.

Traditionally, second mortgages have been purchased by either portfolio lenders, small mortgage brokers, or finance companies. Today, due mostly to improved underwriting and mortgage insurance coverage, second mortgages can be sold as either whole loans, participations or securities.

Recently, some high-volume originators have issued second mortgage private placement pass-through securities in which they have mixed loans with varying interest rates at a net rate that allows for a servicing fee. However, as with other private placements, there are additional costs in the form of trustee fees, pool insurance, legal fees, and underwriting costs that must be evaluated.

Summary

Every mortgage banking entity is in a unique situation because of its marketplace and its product mix. Marketing philosophy, however, determines the acceptable interest-rate exposure. The cost and availability of mandatory and standby commitments usually determine the hedging strategy that can best be implemented. A detailed understanding of available alternatives and disciplined implementation of a plan will ensure the most effective use of hedging alternatives. To be successful, management must be familiar with and accept the advantages and disadvantages of each alternative.

Chapter 18

Collateral Management

Joycelyn Harris
President
Builders Mortgage Company

The primary function of collateral management—commonly called *shipping*—is to deliver *(ship)* warehoused loans to investors in accordance with the terms of individual investor commitments. The succesful collateral manager must know not only the investor commitment requirements, but also the technical detail required for adequate loan documentation and compliance with the warehousing bank's requirements. This chapter discusses the loan delivery aspects of investor commitments, the types of loan delivery, the necessary documentation and commitment procedures, and quality controls.

Investor Commitments

The most significant requirement of an investor commitment is whether it requires mandatory delivery or whether delivery is optional (on a standby basis). Mandatory-delivery commitments *must* be filled within the specified time period for designated loan types at set prices, yields, and dollar amounts. Partial delivery or nondelivery to a mandatory commitment may result in the company losing approval to do business with an investor, such as FNMA or FHLMC, or with a major Wall Street dealer selling GNMA securities. In contrast, optional-delivery commitments allow for delivery or nondelivery of loans with forfeiture of any commitment fee paid being the only cost of nondelivery.

Mandatory-delivery commitments always have a better price than do optional-delivery commitments at a given point in time. Furthermore, because there is usually a smaller commitment fee for short-delivery mandatory commitments (30 rather than 60 days) and/or a better price for the loans, the marketing or production departments of a mortgage bank will usually attempt to take advantage of these better prices by using as many short-term mandatory-delivery commitments as possible. This may pose a problem to the collateral department if loans are slow in coming in or poorly documented. Given expiring mandatory-delivery commitments in any volume at all, the primary problem of collateral management can become the management of shipping deadlines.

Preferably, a realistic time frame to develop shippable loans is taken into account when the mandatory commitment is entered into.

A mandatory-delivery requirement is a standard feature of commitments for GNMA and FNMA mortgage-backed securities (MBS). When a commitment to sell a GNMA or FNMA MBS to a Wall Street dealer is negotiated, it is assumed to be a mandatory delivery, unless explicitly noted as an optional-delivery commitment, in which case the price and fees will not be as attractive. Whereas one can buy back one's commitment to sell a GNMA MBS, or buy another GNMA MBS to fulfill the mandatory-delivery requirement, there are currently no such alternatives for FNMA MBS, or other FNMA mandatory-delivery commitments.

Every investor commitment has specific loan delivery requirements or shipping specifications. Whenever FNMA, FHLMC, or GNMA is involved—either as an investor or as a guarantor—the requirements are specified in the guidebooks. Other investor commitments may include delivery requirements in the purchase contract or in a commitment letter, or may refer to accepted FNMA/FHLMC guidelines. These guidelines have come to be the accepted industry standards. Anyone responsible for loan delivery must have direct access to the most recently published FNMA and FHLMC lending and selling guides.

FNMA and FHLMC

Both FNMA and FHLMC issue mandatory- and optional-delivery commitments for recently closed loans. The terms of each mandatory commitment vary according to the agency involved. FNMA and FHLMC currently issue *mandatory-delivery commitments* for:

Conventional fixed-rate first mortgages, including whole loans and participations.

Conventional adjustable-rate first mortgages (ARMs).

In addition, FNMA purchases on a mandatory basis:

FHA-insured or VA-guaranteed (FHA/VA) first mortgages, including growing equity mortgages (GEMs).

FHA/VA graduated-payment mortgages and conventional graduated-payment mortgages (GPARMS).

Participations in ARM first mortgages.

FHLMC purchases on a mandatory basis:

Conventional fixed-rate second mortgages, including participations.

Conventional fixed-rate home-improvement second-mortgage participations.

FHLMC issues *optional-delivery commitments* for:

Conventional first fixed-rate mortgages.
ARMs.

FNMA issues optional-delivery commitments for:

ARMs.
GPARMs.

FNMA also issues resale and refinance commitments for both fixed- and adjustable-rate conventional first mortgages to replace mortgages owned either in whole or in part by FNMA.

FNMA issues standby commitments for:

FHA/VA GPM and conventional fixed-rate first mortgages
Conventional adjustable-rate first mortgages

FNMA and FHLMC have minimum commitment amounts, which change from time to time. In FNMA's programs, the lender must deliver eligible whole loans or participation interests in an amount equal to at least 90 percent of the commitment amount. In FHLMC's programs, the lender must deliver eligible mortgages in an amount equal to the commitment amount, plus or minus $10,000. Failure to deliver a mandatory commitment is considered a breach that may result in the suspension or termination of FNMA's or FHLMC's contract with the offending party.

FNMA's three-month resale and refinance commitments currently provide for delivery at the seller's option. These commitments must be for a specified loan in the seller's servicing portfolio or in some other FNMA servicer's portfolio.

FNMA standby commitments, usually for 9- or 12-month terms, provide no yield or price protection, and each must be converted to a mandatory-delivery commitment at the then-existing market rate and fee in order to be able to deliver to it. Either all or part of the commitment may be converted.

Each commitment contains certain specific information that must be noted, and the person with direct responsibility for fulfillment of commitments must have a method of keeping track of the commitments to be filled. That specific information is:

Name of purchaser.
Name and number of lender.
Identifying number of contract or commitment number.
Type of eligible loans.
Delivery: optional or mandatory.

Commitment period.

Commitment date.

Expiration date.

Yield required, price or interest rate.

Amount of commitment.

Commitment fee.

Signature of authorized officer(s).

FNMA's accelerated-delivery plan and FHLMC's preferred-seller program allow sellers to deliver whole mortgages with incomplete documentation. The plans are especially useful when a mandatory-commitment expiration date is imminent, when there is a negative interest spread in the warehouse (warehouse interest is greater than interest received on loans), or when the amount of loans in the warehouse line becomes excessive. With use of accelerated delivery, the seller must deliver any remaining documentation to FNMA within 90 days. If outstanding documentation is not delivered in a timely manner, FNMA may require the seller to repurchase the loan.

The preferred-seller program is currently applicable only to conventional fixed-rate home-mortgage purchase programs. It is designed to reduce documentation submission requirements and to shorten the period of time between the delivery date and the funding date for sellers that have demonstrated, and continue to demonstrate, satisfactory performance and adherence to the delivery, purchase, servicing and accounting requirements of FHLMC.

The current trend at FNMA and FHLMC is to minimize documents required for purchase, thus decreasing somewhat the urgency of follow-up. Indeed, inasmuch as FHLMC requires only the note and purchase schedules, there is little follow-up required. (Complete underwriting and closing documents must be available for shipment upon request.) For GNMA MBSs, GNMA allows extensions to its 90-day requirement to forward documents to the custodian. This trend towards minimizing documents required for purchase is consistent with the move towards shorter mandatory commitments. Nonetheless, the collateral department must ensure that documentation is fully complete on each loan.

Secondary market investors other than FNMA and FHLMC (thrift institutions, insurance companies, retirement or pension trusts, and public revenue-bond funds), have specific guidelines for their delivery requirements; however, most of these requirements are usually very similar to one of the types of delivery outlined by FNMA or FHLMC.

Constant review of a commitment control log or report is necessary to keep track of delivery schedules and missing documents and to monitor the timely purchase and documentation of loans delivered. Extra man-hours required for documentation follow-up may interfere with timely delivery of new loans. When monitoring purchases, the funds received, with proper adjustment for interest and servicing fees, should be compared to the price and terms specified in the commitment to verify accuracy.

Types of Loan Sales

Whole Loan and Participation Sales

The sale of a whole loan assigns the entire beneficial interest or ownership of an individual mortgage loan to an investor. The loan documentation required is usually extensive. The seller of a whole loan, as servicer, may act as custodian of the loan documents not delivered.

The sale of a participation is the sale of a pro-rata interest in a whole loan. Generally, the sale is from 50 to 95 percent of the ownership in the loan. The loan documentation required for the sale of a participation is minimal, as can be seen from the Table 1. The seller retains an interest in each loan, generally 5 to 50 percent, and remains responsible for the file containing all documents and exhibits.

Obviously, delivering a participation is much less involved than is delivering a whole loan. Therefore the time required to ship participations is less; additionally, there is no follow-up required for missing documents.

Mortgage-Backed Securities (MBSs)

MBSs may be guaranteed by GNMA, FNMA, FHLMC, or by private institutions. The pool of mortgages underlying GNMA MBSs consists of FHA-

Table 1 • Required Documentation for Sale of a Whole Loan or a Participation

Whole Loan	Participation
Submission vouchers	Copy of note
Note	Schedule of loans
Recorded mortgage or deed of trust	Participation certificate
Guaranty or insurance certificate	
Assignment	
Title policy/evidence	
Leasehold information	
Evidence of hazard insurance	
Plat of survey	
Flood insurance, if applicable	
Loan application, if applicable*	
Truth-in-lending form, if applicable*	
Appraisal, if applicable*	

*Not FNMA or FHLMC.

insured and/or VA-guaranteed loans in an aggregate minimum amount of $1 million; for FNMA and private issues, the pool consists of either first or second fixed-rate conventional loans of varying maturities and interest rates; and for FHLMC, the pool consists of first-lien fixed-rate conventional home loans. FNMA also offers MBSs collateralized by seasoned FHA/VA loans.

The documentation required to issue GNMA MBSs is much less than that required for delivering whole loans, although more than that required for participations. A well-organized collateral department can issue GNMA certificates totalling millions of dollars in the same amount of time it takes to deliver several hundred thousand dollars of whole loans.

This increase in shipping efficiency is directly attributable to the limited initial documentation required to ship GNMA pools. The *initial* documentation required by a pool custodian (usually a commercial bank) consists of mortgage notes, unrecorded assignment to GNMA, and any intervening assignments. While such partial documentation makes it easier to ship GNMA pools quickly, it also necessitates follow-up on missing documents. To obtain the final pool certification from the custodian—which must be forwarded to GNMA within 90 days—the GNMA issuer must forward the balance of the documents to the custodian within this time frame. The additional documents consist of the recorded mortgage or deed of trust, title policy, and insurance or guaranty certificate for each loan.

While GNMA pools exclusively feature government loans, FNMA and FHLMC act as guarantors/issuers of mortgage securities backed by conventional loans. These conventional mortgage-backed security programs are very similar to GNMA pools, after which they are modeled. Both GNMA I and GNMA II have minimum pool and certificate sizes comparable to FNMA/FHLMC conventional programs. However, only GNMA II has a central paying agent like its conventional counterparts (a central paying agent acts as a central collection point for monies from servicers, and remits monthly payments to pool certificateholders), and allows a range of interest rates in the pool. An advantage over GNMA programs that currently exist for the seller of conventional pools is even less required documentation: Note, private mortgage insurance certificate, and unrecorded assignment.

Documentation

After satisfying investor delivery requirements on a timely basis, the second most important shipping requirement is control of documentation. Recognition by management of the importance of this documentation is essential for an efficient ongoing operation, one in which loans are delivered promptly and warehouse lines maintained with a constantly rotating flow of loans, thus avoiding overage loans in the warehouse line. (Warehouse agreements typically allow no more than six months for any one loan to stay in the line.) Documentation includes the setup of the new loan file, control of the warehouse funding package, and follow-up to complete the delivered loan file.

New Loan Files

In order to establish uniformity and efficiency in packaging loans for shipment, incoming new-loan files should be received in a specified order, with a properly marked checklist indicating documents and exhibits. Loan documents (consisting of mortgage insurance, note, assignment, deed of trust, title policy, and the truth-in-lending disclosure) should be on one side of the folder with any required closing exhibits placed immediately under these documents. Beneath these should be the credit package (consisting of the loan application, credit report, and all required verifications and exhibits supporting the application, including the good-faith estimate, the fair-lending notice and the property appraisal). A checklist located on the other side of the folder allows for easy review and checking of the loan documents and credit package. Loan analysis forms, transmittal letters, worksheets, and other loan-related papers not actually a part of the loan, are usually under the checklist. The checklist is also used to indicate which documents and exhibits are missing.

As each incoming new loan is logged, and missing documents and exhibits indicated, the loan goes through a quality review. Questionable loans may be flagged for internal audit. A record of each loan selected for internal audit should be maintained. As loans are shipped to investors or placed in mortgage-backed securities pools, or in participation pools, the date shipped and type of commitment is indicated on the loan log so that follow-up mail can be easily sorted and forwarded.

Thoroughness in noting missing exhibits and documents at the time new loans are received, and accuracy in logging loose daily follow-up mail makes the ongoing task of maintaining lists of outstanding exhibits and documents due from branches an efficient function. The cooperation and assistance of title companies and escrow agents in promptly providing documents for closed loans enable branch offices to forward items to the collateral department in a timely manner. Good communication and cooperation between branch offices and the collateral department in these matters is a necessity.

Warehousing-Funding Package

In addition to the new-loan file used for shipping purposes, a warehouse-funding package is required by the warehousing bank to support any funding draft or check which has been issued. The documents and exhibits required in the warehouse-funding package are specified in the warehousing agreement (usually the note, truth-in-lending disclosure, evidence of guarantee or insurance, assignment and evidence of hazard and flood insurance). The warehouse package may be forwarded to the bank by branch origination offices as documents are drawn, or by a central document production area. A period of 30 to 60 days is usually allowed by the warehousing agreement to obtain and forward the recorded deed of trust or mortgage and title policy, to the warehouse bank.

Warehousing agreement provisions for delivery of the notes and other documents that are collateral for bank loans vary. Many agreements will allow delivery only by specific methods, and only directly to another commercial bank or to FNMA, FHLMC, or a previously approved Wall Street firm (for mortgage securities). Many banks do not allow delivery directly to a mortgage-banking company.

Equally as important as the working knowledge of individuals is an up-to-date library of manuals and guidebooks. Since the instructions and requirements for loan delivery change frequently, it is important to correctly update the guidebooks and any internal procedures that contain reference to the guidebooks immediately upon receipt of a change.

Quality Control

In addition to the internal audit function (discussed in the chapters entitled "Production Department Management" and "Inventory Philosophy, Reporting and Control"), quality control is an essential function of every firm which operates in the secondary mortgage market. The purpose of quality control is to assure management, and the investors who purchase loans and mortgage-backed securities issued by the company, that the company's personnel comply with accepted standards, procedures, guidelines and regulations, and originate quality loans.

In quality control, incoming new loans are reviewed as they are received for accuracy, correctness and consistency of names, addresses and legal descriptions on the various exhibits and documents in the file. The type and amount of mortgage insurance, if required, is verified. The note and deed of trust or mortgage are reviewed, and signatures and notary acknowledgement are checked. The title policy form, exceptions, and endorsements are reviewed. If applicable, the HUD 1 settlement statement is compared to the lender's closing instructions, and the amount of fees and charges reviewed. The presence of exhibits and other evidence required as a condition of closing is verified. If the loan has been previously approved by a company underwriter, it may not be necessary to review the credit package during the quality review. However, a closed loan not previously reviewed by the company (a loan being purchased) should include a quality review of the credit package and appraisal.

The loan application is reviewed for completeness. The information provided by the credit report, verifications, and other exhibits supporting the application is compared to the applicable sections of the application. Required evidence of income for self-employed borrowers is verified, and analysis of allowed income amount checked.

Conventional appraisals are reviewed according to company instructions, if not previously reviewed by underwriters. If there is a list of approved appraisers, the name of the appraiser is noted. Accuracy of census tract numbers and flood-insurance compliance may be checked for each loan, or a percentage of loans may be spot-checked. Additionally, third-party reports of sales in a given market area are reviewed to verify the accuracy of comparables shown on the appraisal.

Any loan about which there are questions, or which appears not to conform to any company procedures, is flagged for internal audit. This may be part of a specified percentage of loans audited or an addition to that percentage.

Indemnification letters from title insurance companies that underwrite policies for agency title companies or closing agents, from which a mortgage company accepts policies, should be periodically reviewed. Loan-origination branch offices should be provided with a list of title companies or closing agents whose policies are acceptable to the company.

Follow-Up

The importance of follow-up on outstanding documentation involving closed loans, whether in inventory or delivered for purchase, cannot be emphasized too strongly. Accurate identification and filing of documents improve the efficiency of the collateral department, assist in timely delivery of loans to meet commitments, and enhance the company's reputation for satisfactorily meeting committed obligations.

The manager of the collateral department should schedule regular periodic review of the new-loan log, the list of outstanding documents and exhibits due from originators, and documentation due investors and pool custodians. Origination branch managers should be advised on a regular basis of the outstanding documents due from the branch.

Reports

The collateral department is usually operated as a budgeted cost center. Operating figures should be reviewed monthly, and an extensive quarterly review should be made of budget variances, cost-per-loan-shipped, inventory turnover, and commitment fees for mandatory or optional delivery of loans.

Inventory reports prepared, or contributed to, by the collateral department are a daily report of new commitments, a daily report of new loans in warehouse, a daily report of loans allocated, a daily report of unallocated loans in inventory, a weekly commitment position report, a weekly or monthly report of loans delivered, and a monthly report of loans sold.

A collateral department report that should be prepared for the production department is the weekly list of missing loan documents and exhibits. A response should be expected from each branch office each week. Review of the outstanding items should be coordinated with the production department at least once a month.

Summary

Collateral management involves responsibility for mortgage loans from the time the loans are funded until they are purchased by the investor and all required follow-up documentation is completed. A well-managed department ensures that each investor commitment is filled on time, particularly mandatory-delivery commitments. It minimizes loan delivery expense by maximizing the number of loans shipped out of warehouse per department employee. Delivering more MBSs and participations than whole loans enhances this efficiency ratio. Assuming loans are not purposely held in warehouse, a good measure of the collateral department's efficiency is warehouse turnover or the dollar amount of loans shipped per year, divided by the average warehouse amount. The higher this number, the less the inventory interest expense and the greater the department's efficiency.

—— PART THREE ——

Administration of the Servicing Portfolio

Loan Administration

George I. Wilson
Executive Vice President
The Lomas & Nettleton Company

After a loan is originated by the production department and sold to an investor by the marketing department, the loan-administration department (also known as the loan-servicing department) must service that loan for up to 30 years. The primary responsibility of the manager of the loan-administration department is to service the loans in the servicing portfolio in full compliance with the various investors' requirements. The objectives are to service all loans in a timely manner and at a profit.

This chapter focuses on the traditional responsibilities involved in servicing whole-mortgage loans. It does not address the unique requirements posed by mortgage-backed securities (MBSs). It discusses the importance of the servicing agreement between the servicer and the investor, analyzes the organizational choices and primary responsibilities of a servicer, notes the various constituencies the servicer must relate to, and, finally, reviews desirable servicing reports, standards, and data-processing applications.

The Servicing Agreement

The *servicing agreement* is the basic contract between the investor as principal and the servicer as agent. It sets forth the minimum requirements for a mortgage servicer, including duties, fees, and audit requirements. Beyond these minimum requirements, however, there is an unwritten investor requirement applicable to all good mortgage servicers that says, "We want you to service this loan just as if it were your own."

In addition to being a servicing agent, a mortgage servicer acts in a fiduciary role as a trustee. Except for servicing fees and late charges, the funds received by the servicer from the homeowner either belong to the investor or are escrow funds (sometimes called *impounds*) to be set aside for payment of insurance and taxes. Controls are needed so that trust funds are used only for payment of tax bills and insurance premiums, and so that principal and interest collected are remitted to investors on a timely basis.

In developing these controls, the loan administrator should standardize the requirements of the servicing agreement and incorporate as many as possible into systems and procedures, relying on an exception sheet or log to monitor daily transactions.

In every servicing agreement there are both standard provisions and others that are subject to negotiation between investor and servicer.

Standard Provisions

Legal Requirements

1. Warranties of Servicers. When the servicer sells loans to an investor, certain warranties are made: that full and complete title is insured; that the full amount of principal has been advanced; that all insurance premiums are paid; that there is a valid title policy; that the loan is not in default; that the instrument has been duly recorded; that the mortgage and loan secured thereby comply with the usury laws. There may also be other specific warrants required by the investor. If any of the loans fail to comply with the warranties, the investor can exercise his option under a repurchase clause in either the loan commitment or servicing agreement to have the servicer buy back the loan, or, in some instances, to cancel the servicing agreement.

2. Cancellation Provisions. There are two basic cancellation provisions: for cause and without cause. Investors may cancel for cause if the ownership of the servicing company is materially changed, the servicing company declares bankruptcy, or the servicing company cannot perform under the contract. Cancellation without cause usually results in the payment of a previously negotiated penalty fee to the servicer, based on a percentage of the unpaid balance at the time of transfer, or related to the earnings of the servicer over a period of time. The loan administrator should negotiate this cancellation fee for as large an amount as possible when the original contract is consummated.

3. Interest on Escrows. Several states require that an investor pay interest on escrows. While the amount of interest is governed by state law, the servicing agreement should designate whether interest on escrows is to be paid by the servicer or by the investor.

Servicer Security

1. Approval by Federal Agencies. Investors usually require that servicers be approved by FHA and VA. Loss of FHA/VA approval may result in cancellation for cause by an investor.

2. Fidelity Bond. The servicer is usually required to have fidelity coverage to protect against theft, embezzlement, forgery, and mysterious disappearances. Any claims filed must be reported to all investors, thereby allowing each investor to determine if the servicing agreement should be cancelled.

3. Errors and Omissions Charge. To protect against failure to provide prop-

erty insurance, investors insist that the servicer obtain errors-and-omissions coverage. The prime purpose of errors-and-omissions coverage is to protect the servicer from loss by fire, windstorm, or failure to obtain flood insurance (where required); or to pay property taxes, special assessments, ground rent, or other disbursements from the escrow accounts required by the servicing agreement.

4. Audit of Performance. The servicing agreement usually permits the investor to audit the servicer's records during regular working hours and requires the servicer to furnish annual reports, certifications as provided for in the standard Single Audit Program for Mortgage Bankers, and other special audits.

Security of Investment. The investor is concerned that the property securing the mortgage remain in satisfactory condition; accordingly, he is concerned about the following:

1. Insurance. On standard residential loans the investor requires in-force fire, and extended or homeowner's coverage. The servicing agreement should spell out the minimum Best's Guide rating acceptable to the investor.

Any property located in a flood plain should carry flood insurance. In certain locations, earthquake insurance may be required. Regardless of the insurance required, the servicer should see that any property damage incurred is repaired and that the loss draft is released to the homeowner when the property is again acceptable.

2. Property Taxes. Unpaid property taxes take legal precedent over the mortgage lien. The servicer is required to see that all taxes on mortgaged properties are paid in a timely manner.

3. Inspection Requirements. The investor may require a servicer to see that properties are properly maintained and may also require inspections under the following circumstances: a fire or flood loss; an act of God, such as a hurricane or tornado; a delinquency for 60 days or more; or a special request made by the investor.

Accounting for the Funds. The servicer has the responsibility to maintain and protect the integrity of the homeowner's mortgage payments. Those funds must be deposited promptly in Federal Deposit Insurance Corporation- or Federal Savings and Loan Insurance Corporation-insured accounts. The technical description of the custodial account must be written in such a way that it protects the investor and the mortgagor up to the maximum amount of FDIC or FSLIC insurance per mortgagor. The funds are held in trust for the investor (interest and principal) and the homeowner (escrow or impounds). Unless otherwise required by state law or investor requirements, the principal and interest and escrow funds are held in the same custodial account.

In addition, the servicing agreement specifies which party is entitled to the following fees and in what amounts:

1. Service Fees. These are sometimes also spelled out in a loan commitment.

2. Late Charges. The amount of late charges on any loan is governed by both the amount shown in the security instrument and by state laws. The security instrument also sets forth the time at which a late charge can be assessed. Both FHA and VA mortgages currently provide for a 4 percent late charge calculated on the total monthly payment due, including the escrow portion. FNMA permits the servicer to charge late charges on conventional loans on the monthly interest and principal portion only.

Property-management fee. As a result of foreclosure action, the servicer of the original mortgage may be responsible for assisting the investor in the disposition of the property. If the property is rented, the servicer may be entitled to a fee for handling the collection of rents.

4. Miscellaneous Fees. A servicer is usually entitled to collect from the mortgagor certain fees resulting from changes, such as assumption fees, insurance substitution fees, and returned check fees. The servicing agreement usually spells out whether these fees remain with the servicer or are shared with the investor.

Rather than forward copies of tax receipts, insurance policies, inspection reports, etc., to the investor, the servicer should certify periodically that taxes and insurance premiums have been paid and inspections have been completed.

Desirable Provisions

Processing Loss Drafts. The servicer is responsible for the rehabilitation of the property to maintain the collateral value of the investor's investment. Inasmuch as the investor is named in the mortgage clause of the insurance policy, the investor's name also appears on the insurance-loss draft. The servicing agreement should grant the Power of Attorney to the servicer to endorse loss drafts on behalf of the investor. In the absence of a power of attorney, a mortgage servicer must forward each insurance-loss draft to the investor for endorsement.

Escrow Overdrafts. The servicer's responsibility to advance corporate money to the escrow account when it is overdrawn should be spelled out in the contract. Without this agreement, the investor advances the necessary funds to pay taxes and insurance on delinquent accounts. FNMA advances funds, as do some other investors, after it has been determined that the servicer cannot obtain the funds from the mortgagor.

Foreclosure Costs. Investors can expect some loss as the result of foreclosures. If it is intended that the servicer bear any portion of this cost, this provision should appear in the servicing agreement. Without such specification, the total net cost of foreclosure must be borne by the investor. GNMA, FNMA, and FHLMC, as investors, currently have no provision in their servicing agreements requiring a portion of the foreclosure cost to be borne by the mortgage servicer.

Control of Escrow Funds. The control of escrow deposits allows a servicer to generate a warehousing credit line. Unless the servicing agreement specifies that the investor controls escrow funds, escrow funds are controlled by the servicer.

Some FNMA and GNMA contracts provide for escrow funds to be held by the investor, with only a portion thereof under the control of the mortgage servicer. Usually, however, FNMA, FHLMC, and most private investors allow the servicer to control the escrow funds, so long as the funds are deposited in a bank satisfactory to them.

Organization and Primary Responsibility

Even with well-designed systems that incorporate key provisions of the servicing agreement, a manager is only as efficient as are the supervisors under his or her control. Proper results stem from a combination of systems and people. Until recent years, the requirements of the mortgage servicer remained pretty much unchanged. Recently, however, the changes are not only rapid and more far-reaching, but continuous. Organizing for change, therefore, is a prelude to organizing for efficiency.

Most mortgage servicers organize around the following functions or combinations thereof: loan accounting and cashiering (many servicers also have a mortgage-backed security department): collections and foreclosure; and escrow administration and customer services. There are many variations. Some companies combine the accounting function with corporate accounting; others combine the insurance department with the insurance agency; and customer services may consist of a person in each department. Larger mortgage servicers may have additional special departments: personnel, data processing, printing, mail and machine, word processing, file room, etc.

Is it better to centralize functions as much as possible in one location? Not always. Centralized collections, for example, may increase telephone long-distance costs compared to more decentralized operations. Combining all cashiering in one location may delay mortgage payments, thus increasing delinquencies. Centralizing all functions also requires personnel to have a wider knowledge of state laws and customs. On the other hand, the centralization of functions usually costs less, and, depending on the strength of management personnel, furnishes better control. The consolidated operation also normally requires a smaller management team.

Whatever the organization, the primary responsibilities within each functional entity must be carried out. The following overview takes up the most significant considerations relating to each.

Loan Accounting and Cashiering

Control of Cash Received

One of the most important responsibilities of the mortgage servicer is to control the flow of cash from the homeowner to the custodial account to the investor. All checks should be deposited daily in a clearing account, and subsequently transferred to the appropriate custodial accounts.

Some mortgage servicers use a lockbox bank to pick up payments, compare the payments to the payment media, deposit the funds into the clearing account, and furnish the details of the payments received for posting. The bank's fee for this service is either billed to the mortgage servicer or charged against compensating balances. The mortgage servicer must work closely with the bank to clear exceptions and assure that payments are processed promptly.

Some companies do not use a lockbox bank because they do not want to release the security of handling mortgage payments to an outside company or because they feel they can process payments more efficiently themselves. They want to be sure that the payments are processed as received. As all exceptions must be processed by them anyway, they find the additional cost of opening mail and processing payments acceptable.

Types of Remittances

Years ago, the remittance report was a list of receipts containing loan numbers and amounts. The total amount minus the service fee was remitted monthly. Subsequently, investors requested from the mortgage servicer an account of only the exceptions. Using a forecast of what was expected, the totals of delinquent payments and prepaid installments were reconciled in order to arrive at the funds remitted. This method is called *single debit*. Currently, the aggregate exception system (AES) is popular among some investors. With the AES, the mortgage servicer is expected to reconcile in the aggregate, as opposed to an individual single debit for each interest rate, state, service fee, or type of loan. Many investors require that funds be remitted more than once a month.

Disbursements for Taxes and Insurance

As homeowners make a mortgage payments, a portion is held in escrow for taxes and insurance. As taxes or insurance premiums become due, funds may come from several escrow custodial accounts. Rather than disburse a check for each tax or insurance payment, most mortgage servicers use a *disbursement clearing account*. One check from each custodial account is deposited in a disbursement clearing account, and a single check is sent to the tax collector or insurance company. Once funds are disbursed, the system should prevent the disbursement from being made again. Obtaining refunds from insurance companies or tax collectors for double payments is time-consuming, and the escrow account remains incorrect until the adjustment is made.

Disbursements may sometimes overdraw the escrow funds held on behalf of the homeowner, usually as a result of delinquent mortgage payments. Some mortgage servicers advance their own funds and make the disbursements; others holdup the disbursement until either the investor or the homeowner advances the funds.

Billing the Subsidy

Certain loans are subsidized by the federal government; others are subsidized by the homeseller or builder (buy-down loans). The agreement to pay the government subsidy is a contract between the federal government and the investor. The servicer, on behalf of the investor, agrees to collect and combine the mortgagor's portion of the total payment with the subsidy payment from the federal government and apply these funds as a full mortgage payment. In order to obtain the subsidy funds, the servicer requests from the government the total funds due each month. The servicer is responsible to the government for keeping adequate backup to support the request. All overbillings must be refunded to the government, even if the overpayments have not been collected from the mortgagor.

Subsidy payments are based on the ability of the mortgagor to pay. As the income of the mortgagor changes, the subsidy also changes. Each year a recertification of income is furnished by the mortgagor and confirmed by his or her employer. A fee added to the monthly billing forwarded to the Federal Housing Administration repays the servicer for the cost of obtaining the recertification, confirming its accuracy, and recalculating the subsidy payment amount. The servicer is also required to keep records of the total subsidy funds paid each calendar year, as well as the total amount paid for the life of the subsidized loan.

Collection and Foreclosure

Investors view delinquent ratios as a measure of a servicer's efficiency, and with good reason. Delinquencies lower the yield on their investment.

Collection Procedures

The best method of collecting unpaid accounts is face-to-face contact, at the mortgagor's home or in the servicer's office. But visiting the homes of all delinquent accounts can be very costly, and servicers use this method only for serious cases. Mailing notices to mortgagors is usually ineffective. The notice is easily ignored, with the result that the servicer does not obtain the reason for delinquency from the mortgagor. Notices normally serve to collect only from those who would pay anyway but forgot to make the payment on time.

After face-to-face contact, telephoning is usually the next best collection method. Telephone calls made during the early evening hours usually find mortgagors at home and produce the best results. Collection personnel should be informed each day of all payments processed, in order not to waste their efforts on paid accounts.

Mortgage servicers are often faced with the question of whether to use branch offices for collection efforts or to consolidate the collection personnel in one location. Several factors should be considered. A central location can usually be managed with fewer personnel. However, if the mortgagors are outside the local telephone area, long-distance costs must be considered. Contacts with the delinquent mortgagors can also be made by contracting with outside companies.

Some mortgage servicers prefer to have a servicing office in a local area, as long as the number of loans serviced in the area warrants it. Branch offices allow servicers' employees to make face-to-face contacts and property inspections, take advantage of local telephone rates, and counsel mortgagors in a local office. Many servicers feel that a more complete and reliable report is obtained by their own people; others prefer to use outside companies.

FHA and VA regulations, as well as many investor servicing agreements, require a servicer to determine the reason for delinquency and the ability of the mortgagor to reinstate the mortgage and, if at all possible, to have a face-to-face contact before considering foreclosure. In many cases a workable repayment plan can be agreed upon by mortgagor and servicer. Documentation of all transactions or agreements between the mortgagor and the servicer is required to allow a foreclosure review committee to approve or disapprove the beginning of foreclosure action, should the delinquency continue.

Forebearance agreements can be formal or informal. Formal forebearance is outlined in writing and signed by both mortgagor and servicer. Informal forebearance agreements are usually made by telephone when a homeowner promises to repay the delinquent payments or portions thereof on specific dates. Once a forebearance agreement is made, the mortgage should not be considered as past due if the payments agreed upon are current.

Property Inspections

Properties should usually be inspected under the following circumstances: notification of damage caused by fire, wind, or flood; an act of God in the area, such as hurricane, tornado, or flood; a special request by the investor; or an account delinquent for two payments.

Inspection of a property for which payment is two months or more delinquent can serve two purposes: A personal contact can be made with the homeowner; and the servicer can, at the same time, determine if the property is occupied and in acceptable condition. FHA regulations require the servicer to visit the property if no contact is made within 45 days after the payment is delinquent. This procedure determines at an early date if the property has been abandoned, in which case a great deal of damage can occur, especially in freezing weather. The property should be inspected monthly for as long as the account remains delinquent.

The property-inspection report should be made a part of the servicer's records. If maintenance is required because of vacancy, most servicers also file photographs taken before and after board-ups.

Foreclosure

Many servicers have a foreclosure review committee to review each case before foreclosure action is begun. The committee usually consists of employees who are not responsible for the day-by-day collection activities. They review all information obtained and determine that all available steps have been taken to prevent foreclosure. The committee determines if the mortgagor considered selling the property, recasting the loan, releasing the property by signing a deed in lieu of foreclosure, or exercising other available options. If the servicer has done everything possible to prevent foreclosure, without results, the committee releases the case to the foreclosure department to begin action. Once the determination is made to foreclose, foreclosure should be instituted as quickly as possible and be carefully controlled.

Foreclosures should be conducted by qualified attorneys, preferably those specializing in foreclosure. Mortgage servicers should expect a monthly report on the status of each loan being foreclosed for them. This report should be used to update the information on the mortgage servicer's record and bring attention to any delays.

The method used to obtain title to the property varies with state requirements and the types of documents used when a loan is originated. Most investors prefer to obtain title by having the mortgagor deed the property to them. Obtaining the title through a deed in lieu of foreclosure is more economical, inasmuch as attorney's fees, and advertising and court costs can be saved. Most investors, as well as the FHA, require the servicer to discuss the possibility of signing a deed in lieu with the delinquent mortgagor before considering fore-closure.

If the mortgagor does not sign a deed or the investor cannot get clear title, foreclosure is necessary. In some states the foreclosure is judicial, requiring action by the courts. The foreclosure attorney files a petition with the court, lists in a local publication, sues to obtain judgment, and obtains a court order to sell the property in order to satisfy the judgment.

In some states a deed of trust is used, which names a trustee who has title to the property until the debt is satisfied. When the mortgagor fails to fulfill his obligation, the investor notifies the trustee to sell the property in order to satisfy the debt. Notices are posted in designated areas prior to the public sale of the real estate. If the foreclosure sale is held for the amount of the delinquent payments only, the purchaser may assume the existing mortgage. In most cases, the foreclosure is held to eliminate the total debt, including the unpaid principal balance and accrued interest.

Redemption periods, designed to allow the mortgagor to pay off the debt and maintain possession of the property, are required in some states. After the foreclosure sale is held, the title is not vested in the purchaser until the re-demption period has lapsed. Redemption periods may be three months, six months or one year, depending on the requirements of the state and the legal documents signed by the mortgagor and investor at closing.

The selection of a knowledgeable attorney is the key to proper and timely foreclosures. Investors rely on the mortgage servicer to know the foreclosure requirements and to select an attorney who can protect their interests through-out the foreclosure action.

Any unusual delays in the foreclosure processing may require a notification to the investor. Once the property is foreclosed and conveyed to the investor, government agency, or private mortgage insurance agency, the filing of the appropriate claim should be expedited. Particular care should be taken to see that the mortgage servicer is reimbursed for all funds to which he is entitled.

Escrow Administration

Investors usually require the servicer to have a system that assures them that no properties serviced for them become uninsured. Failure to have property insurance could cause the investor to lose the security if the house is destroyed by fire.

Payment of property taxes when due is also required, because a tax lien takes precedence over the mortgage. FHA, VA, and some conventional mort-gages stipulate that funds must be collected, as part of the mortgage payment, and held in escrow for the payment of taxes and insurance. The escrow account may also contain funds for FHA or private mortgage insurance premiums, flood insurance premiums, or ground rent. The servicer should see that every lienable item can be paid from the escrow portion of the mortgagor's monthly payments.

The cost of maintaining the escrow-administration department requires management attention. In recent years, the escrow department has become more costly because: (1) taxing authorities are collecting taxes more frequently; (2) more insurance policies are now written on a one-year basis; and (3) homeowners are substituting policies more often. To reduce the expense of the disbursement processing, many servicers provide tax collectors with computer tapes identified with the servicer's loan number. Some insurance companies are also able to use such tapes for insurance premium requests.

The escrow-administration department for a large mortgage servicer typically consists of a tax department, an insurance department, and an escrow payment analysis department. A higher quality of work can be accomplished when responsibilities are grouped to produce specialists. This division of labor allows for promotion possibilities and cross-training. Cross-training, or learning more than one specialty, effectively counters the primary disadvantage to specialization, namely, reliance on key individuals who may become sick, take vacations, or resign.

Tax Disbursements

To avoid penalties, property taxes must be paid when due. The escrow-administration manager should make certain that the facts are accurate when a new loan is set up on the system (legal description, tax due date, tax penalty date, etc.); have a procedure for requesting tax bills when the tax collector indicates that a request is desired; pay bills promptly when received; have a procedure for requesting bills not included in the original disbursement; and follow up promptly on any outstanding checks.

Tax collectors may not always cooperate as the mortgage servicer feels they should. If the tax bills are difficult to obtain, many servicers place the burden on the homeowner. Notification to the homeowner should produce the tax bill. If the tax bill is received too late to pay without penalty, the penalty should be charged to the homeowner.

Tax service companies can be employed to obtain tax bills, code them with the servicer's number, and deliver them to the servicer for payment. Such companies reimburse the servicer for tax penalties incurred because of the company's error in requesting bills from the tax collector, or failure to obtain tax bills.

Insurance Coverage

Most servicing agreements require fire and extended-coverage insurance; some require flood, earthquake, or other hazard insurance. Once coverage is obtained, the mortgage servicer must be certain it continues. Most investors require that the servicer hold the original policy to prevent cancellation. Upon notice of cancellation, the mortgage servicer should immediately seek other coverage. Generally, investors will require: (1) enough insurance to cover the mortgage balance, and (2) a mortgage clause naming either them as mortgagee or the servicer.

Any delays in paying insurance premiums increase the workload of the insurance department. Soon after the due date on the policy, the mortgage servicer receives a late notice, then a cancellation notice, then a call from the agency, then a contact from the insurance underwriter, etc. It is essential, therefore, that the insurance department have sufficient employees and adequate procedures to process premium notices promptly for payment.

The responsibility of the mortgage servicer is not complete when the premium is paid on an acceptable policy. All claims must be controlled as well. The investor or servicer is named on the loss draft. Therefore, the mortgage servicer must be sure repairs are complete before funds are released to the homeowner.

Some mortgage servicers have adopted the *single-interest insurance* plan, which protects them if a homeowner fails to insure mortgaged property. If such a plan is adopted, most investors require the mortgage servicer to: (1) notify the homeowner each year on the anniversary date of the policy, (2) collect and hold escrow funds to pay the insurance premiums, and (3) disburse escrow funds as the approved invoices are received. The cost of complying with these requirements, plus the premium required for the single-interest policy, usually does not provide a sufficient saving to warrant the adoption of this procedure.

Lienable Items

The recorded first mortgage usually provides protection for the mortgagee's investment. However, there are some items that can take precedence over the first mortgage: tax liens, special assessments, and mechanics liens.

Tax liens and special assessments are usually sent to the mortgagor. Most mortgagors notify the servicer controlling the escrow account, who then increases the mortgage payments to cover escrow requirements. If the servicer is not notified, the taxing authority notifies the mortgagee when the lien is placed on the property. The mortgagee then notifies its servicer, who is responsible for payment of the lien or assessment and is reimbursed by the mortgagor.

When notified that a tax sale is to take place, the mortgage servicer should make prompt contact with the taxing authority to redeem the tax bill. If the property has already been sold for taxes, the servicer must make contact with the purchaser to redeem the property so that the investor has his security restored.

Analysis of Escrow Accounts

FHA and VA regulations and many servicing agreements require an annual escrow analysis as well as a report to the mortgagor of transactions affecting the escrow account. The best time to analyze the account is as soon as possible after payment of the largest disbursement (taxes). Any delay in preparing the analysis usually produces a larger adjustment to the monthly payment.

The escrow account should be analyzed whenever the tax or insurance disbursement results in an overdrawn account. The servicer must advance funds to cover overdrawn accounts in order to continue FDIC or FSLIC protection. Prompt analysis usually results in the receipt of funds from the homeowner and a refund to the servicer of funds advanced.

When the escrow analysis reveals a shortage of funds in the account, some servicers request prompt payment of the funds from the mortgagor. Others increase the monthly payments to bring the account into balance by the due date of the next tax bill. The analysis statement sent to the mortgagor should clearly show how the shortage occurred.

When there is an overage in the escrow account, the servicer may credit funds to the mortgagor in one of three ways: by mailing a check to the mortgagor; by decreasing the monthly payments so that the overage is disbursed before the next analysis date; or by notifying the mortgagor so that he can choose whether or not to leave the funds in the escrow account. Servicers are permitted to hold two monthly payments in excess of the requirements before considering the escrow account as having an overage. FHA regulations require the servicer to notify any mortgagor with an overage and to request a reply about how he wishes to use the funds. Certain state laws require the servicer to refund overages within thirty days after the account is analyzed.

The escrow analysis should be used to audit the efficiency of the servicing departments. Large overages or shortages may mean delays in processing, incorrect monthly payments used, insufficient funds collected at closing, improper collection of shortages, improper control of tax bills on unimproved properties, or delays in applying insurance refunds.

Relating to Those Outside the Company

The Investor

A servicer is under contract to an investor. Servicers are hired as experts to make decisions and keep investors informed of any substantial problems in connection with their mortgage loans. Many mortgage-servicing companies fail to inform the investor early enough when a problem occurs.

Because the income of the mortgage servicer is dependent upon service fees paid by the investor, the investor is the servicer's number one customer. Failure to comply with investor requirements usually results in cancellation of servicing for cause, and a loss of income.

The Mortgagor

The mortgagor is a customer also. The mortgage servicer has a responsibility to the mortgagor for the mortgagor's funds placed in escrow and for an annual accounting, including the amount of taxes and interest paid for income tax purposes.

Errors made by a mortgage servicer, an insurance agent or taxing authority increase costs when the escrow analysis or the accounting of the trust funds is sent to the homeowner, because time must be spent to respond adequately to the mortgagor's inquiry or complaint. The mortgage servicer should be equipped to supply accurate complete information in a reasonable time in order to minimize the costs caused by these errors.

Even when the mortgage servicer performs in an exemplary fashion, homeowners ask for explanations. A servicer should carefully review the questions asked, whether in response to an auditor's confirmation, the annual reconciliation of the escrow account, or a payment change as a result of an escrow analysis. The nature of the replies required should tell the servicer if employees are performing as they should, or if, in fact, an internal problem exists. Through this resource, management can learn much about both employee performance and the effectiveness of procedures.

Government Agencies

Most servicing agreements require a servicer to be approved by the FHA and the VA. In order to be approved, a servicer must comply with FHA and VA regulations. Although they may not always be consistent with investor requirements, the servicer must always comply with these regulations and legal requirements. Servicers should continually review every change in regulations, and in the requirements of government agencies in order to ensure prompt updating of systems and procedures.

State Laws and Regulations

In recent years, states have enacted many laws that affect mortgages, and, of course, mortgage servicers. These laws concern such things as usury, maximum late charges, and payment of interest on escrows. Some states have spelled out in detail the notifications that must go to homeowners before foreclosure, the notices that must appear on annual statements, etc. Although these laws and requirements are too numerous to delineate here, servicers must always be alert to changes in state laws and must comply with them, unless the state laws allow more leniency than do federal regulations or investor requirements.

Insurance Agents and Tax Collectors

When it is the responsibility of the mortgage servicer to obtain bills for taxes and insurance, and to pay them in a timely manner, it is necessary to deal with tax collectors and insurance agents. The insurance agent is really an agent of the homeowner and acts on the homeowner's behalf. The mortgagor should select the insurance agent of his choice and understand the requirements imposed by the servicer for the insurance policy. Mortgage servicers should organize their remittance procedure so that the insurance company or agent is able to identify remittances without returning a copy of each insurance bill with the check. Each mortgage servicing company should prepare a list of insurance requirements to be furnished to insurance agents so that they will be aware of the disbursing procedures.

Tax collectors are primarily interested in following the regulations laid down by their municipality or county. Mortgage servicers should know the date for requesting bills, the order in which the bills should be requested, the tax due date, and the penalty date, in order to minimize difficulties with the tax collector. It is usually advantageous to have employees in the local area available to obtain miscellaneous tax bills in order to avoid penalties. If this is not possible, arrangements can usually be made with someone in the local tax department to research and obtain such bills.

Most tax collectors are anxious to cooperate with mortgage servicers. Good cooperation between the tax collector and the mortgage servicer is essential. Tax collectors and insurance companies are turning more and more to automated processing of payments, in which computer tapes containing the servicer's records are sent to the taxing authority. In some states, mortgage servicers may purchase tax-service contracts from a tax-service company, as discussed earlier.

The servicer is not always required to pay taxes or insurance premiums. When the mortgage requires no funds to be placed in escrow for such payments, the mortgagor is responsible for these disbursements. The servicing agreement usually requires the servicer, however, to verify annually that the property taxes have been paid and that there is a valid insurance policy containing a mortgagee clause.

Reports, Standards, and Data Processing

Management should concentrate on exceptions to determine which loans require attention. Carefully planned reports are therefore a must. These reports are of two general types:

Reports Showing the Total Work Flow of Activity

1. Number of loans paid off this month and year-to-date, in comparison to prior year.
2. Number of assumptions this month and year-to-date, in comparison to prior year.
3. Number of delinquencies and foreclosures this month and year-to-date, in comparison to prior year.
4. Number of uncleared loss drafts by age.
5. Late charges billed, collected, and waived.
6. Head count by department.
7. Activity report by department, showing beginning balance, receipts, ending balance, and items completed during the period.

Reports Showing the Exception Cases

1. List of loans three full payments delinquent that are not in foreclosure
2. Open items of tax and insurance
3. List of accounts not analyzed for 13 months
4. Status of loans in foreclosure where action is delayed
5. Any exception that can be programmed against standards

Comparison of reports between periods reveals trends. Investors watch the delinquency ratios to evaluate mortgage servicers, although the delinquency ratio is only one gauge of the efficiency of a mortgage servicer.

Standards

No one can outline the exact requirements for a normal operation in all mortgage-servicing companies. Only comparison of one period to another in the same company brings satisfactory answers. For example, mortgage servicers usually know the cost of servicing in their shops. Comparison with another company only brings questions: Is data processing cost included? Does the insurance agency do any function of servicing? Is corporate accounting included? Does the cost include amortization of acquisition costs? When comparing delinquent ratios, do they use the same delinquency cutoff date?

There are a few rules of thumb that are commonly used to evaluate the efficiency of a mortgage servicer:

1. How many loans serviced per person can be called standard?

   If all employees are counted, including operating personnel of data processing, accounting, and insurance, each employee should handle from 600 to 650 loans.

2. How many mortgages can be handled by each collection person?

   There is virtually no way of associating the number of loans in a geographic area with the collection requirements. The measurement should be made using the number of delinquent contacts required by the collection personnel. Counting all employees involved, the work load should be 700 to 750 per person.

3. Looking at the insurance department as a separate entity, how many loans can be handled by each clerk?

   If all persons are counted, including management, file control, and customer-related problem solving, each person should handle 3,700 to 3,900 loans.

4. If a lockbox bank deposits all items that match and sends all others to the cashier to make a determination, what percentage can a mortgage servicer expect as exceptions?

   If the company is on a monthly billing, 9 to 10 percent is average. On the other hand, if a mortgage servicing company uses a deck of cards or coupon book, the exceptions will be 14 to 15 percent.

5. How can a company tell if the late charges collected are in line with those of other companies?

   This figure varies because of the types of loans, balances, and efforts placed on collection. A good rule of thumb is 15 percent of the service-fee income should be late charges. This figure is increasing slowly as mortgage payments increase.

The Role of Data Processing

The computer is a tool that can increase productivity. Most mortgage servicing companies use a computer for payment processing, disbursing escrow funds, and preparing analyses. The computer, however, can do much, much more. Full automation should reduce personnel costs. The fewer the employees required to perform detailed tasks, the better the use performance. Since investors, tax collectors, and insurance companies increasingly use computer reporting, it is now possible for one computer to talk to another one to transfer funds automatically. The computer can also report to management exactly where the problems are in an organization.

The value of loan administration increases as does the need for flexibility in servicing new mortgage programs. A firm's ability to service loans properly is an asset to the production personnel responsible for originating new mortgage loans in today's marketplace.

Proper loan administration satisfies the requirements of the investor, furnishes accurate accounting information to the mortgagor, and complies with the requirements of the FHA, VA, private mortgage insurer, state statutes, and applicable federal laws. The mortgage servicer who pays close attention to investor and agency requirements, uses the management tools available, and remains flexible to change, finds mortgage servicing both a challenge and a very rewarding profession.

PART FOUR

Financial Management

Chapter 20

Financial Planning

Delbert R. Ellis
Senior Vice President
First Federal Savings and Loan of Arizona

As in other businesses, the functions of management in mortgage banking are to plan, organize, execute, and report. Long-range plans and budgets are the mechanisms employed to carry out these functions. By measuring results against plans and budget assumptions, management is able to assess progress (or the lack of it) in meeting objectives, and to direct attention to problems or opportunities. Thus, long-range plans and budgets are major tools of financial planning for mortgage bankers.

Financial planning involves projecting both long- and short-term profitability. Budgets plan and control profits on a short-term basis, while strategic plans pursue profits on a long-range basis. Budgets reflect what should be attained under estimated current prevailing circumstances, while strategic plans go farther ahead and therefore need to be more flexible than budgets in measuring performance under varying conditions of operations.

This chapter addresses the need of the well-managed mortgage banking firm to formulate a strategic plan, to determine the capital requirements for the plan, to relate long-term strategic objectives to short-term budgets, and to install appropriate controls and reports to monitor performance.

Strategic Planning

Planning Process

Effective financial planning begins with the formulation of a strategic plan. This plan, or planning process, seeks to answer the following questions:

1. Where are we today?
2. What are our resources?
3. Where would we like to be?
4. At what point do we want to reach this future performance level?
5. What are our alternatives?
6. How are we going to get to our desired results (the specific plans or strategies)?

Question one involves an analysis of organizational strengths and weaknesses, current market and share position, analysis of the competition, current trends within the industry, and possible opportunities and obstacles.

Question two involves an assessment of present resources, both financial and human, that are in place or are obtainable by the organization.

Question three requires the development of long-range goals and objectives that are believed to be both feasible and desirable. These objectives and goals are usually expressed in terms of commonly used measures of performance: net income, increase in the net present value of the servicing portfolio, desired return on investment, employee productivity per loan, etc. This objective–goal formulation phase of planning should specify corporate objectives and provide a schedule for their attainment; establish an operational definition of each objective; specify measures to be used in evaluating progress; and eliminate (or provide the means for solving) conflicts between goals—that is, decide what to do when progress towards one goal requires sacrificing progress towards another.

Question four constitutes the formulation of a desired schedule for achievement of these goals. It also involves communication to all within the organization of the desired schedule. It means assigning to a specific individual or group the responsibility for progress toward and eventual attainment of the goal. Expected measures of performance should be established and used to monitor the progress and take corrective action when necessary.

Question five assesses available alternatives to reach desired corporate objectives. These alternatives should be put in order of desirability, after accounting for return versus risk, and minimum adverse consequences.

Question six is perhaps the most difficult and requires a higher degree of creative thinking. It involves designing the specific methods, procedures and strategies to attain objectives. Required tasks are identified and assigned to designated individuals or groups. Managers are then provided with relevant tasks and objectives and informed as to the criteria which will be used to evaluate performance.

Key Assumptions

Implicit in the planning process is the consideration of both the external and the internal factors that will influence the corporation's ability to reach its desired objectives. Some key assumptions that must be made include the following:

1. A general economic and industry forecast, including: the general rate of inflation, household formations, housing starts, demographic growth areas, and short- and long-term interest rates. The assumed relationship of interest rates will dictate a positive or negative warehouse interest spread.

2. Total loan-origination volume anticipated during the period in the geographic areas of operation, and the anticipated market share. This assumption

should specify the total number of loans produced as well as the dollar amount so that the average loan size originated may be derived. The average cost to originate or to purchase new loans should be projected.

3. Servicing-portfolio runoff will be affected by future interest rates. Therefore, a forecast of probable portfolio runoff under several interest-rate scenarios should be made and then compared with expectations regarding future loan-production ability to replace and increase servicing-fee income in the same interest-rate environment.

4. New loan production less portfolio runoff should be added annually to the beginning service portfolio. An assumed average cost to service, average service fee, other portfolio income, average interest rate, and average loan size serviced, will yield estimates of future portfolio profitability and growth in the net present value of the servicing portfolio.

5. An assessment of human resources available to obtain the desired corporate objectives. If insufficient, the commitment required to assure the availability of the qualified people is required.

Contingency Plans

If the external environment changes unpredictably, and the necessary ability to adapt does not occur, the organization cannot reach its objectives. Contingency planning is necessary to allow an organization to change assumptions and alter strategy or modify objectives when changes occur. Contingency plans should provide an analytical basis to measure the effect of changing conditions on the original objectives and suggest alternative strategies to achieve the desired objectives. Such plans are useful in pointing out gaps that may or will exist between desired objectives and realistically achievable objectives.

In contingency planning, management must ask What if questions. For example, What if loan production is only 75 percent of plan? What is the effect on loan-production income and expenses, warehouse spreads, servicing portfolio, and the like?

Steps involved in developing contingency plans are as follows:

Refining What if events (not part of the plan but could occur).

Estimating probability of events.

Assessing adverse consequences.

Devising alternative plans to protect against adverse events or to take advantage of them.

Determining Capital Requirements

Ownership and Size

Effective financial planning and implementation require an analysis of existing and potential sources of capital. Capital availability may, in many cases, be a function of ownership structure and size. If a company is publicly owned, it has the choice of a public stock issue. A privately owned company does not have this option, without a conscious decision to go public. However, either may opt for a private placement. Also, it may be easier for a public company to issue long-term debt, particularly if the company is large and profitable when compared to a private company. More sophisticated methods of raising capital (convertible debt, preferred stock, long-term debentures or bonds, for example) are also more feasible for larger, well-capitalized firms.

Institutional owners of mortgage banking firms have access to nonequity public funds which they may use to invest in, or to lend to, a subsidiary. Mutually owned institutions (such as mutual savings and loan associations and savings banks) are more circumscribed in raising additional capital than are stock institutions (commercial banks and stock S&Ls). Stock institutions have the option of selling shares of stock to the public; mutuals do not. However, being regulated, institutional owners are subject to compliance with regulations, laws, and audits to which nonregulated owners are not subject. Regulations may prevent an institutional mortgage banker from incurring additional debt, or lending on certain collateral or to certain individuals.

Obviously, the larger and more profitable one is, irrespective of ownership, the easier it is to arrange short-term borrowings or private placement of long-term debt. Only public companies, however, have the full range of debt and equity options (assuming they are profitable) to raise capital.

Cash Flow Projections

Cash flow projections by the mortgage banker will determine the capital generated or consumed by a given level of loan production and assumed interest-rate scenario. The capital generated or consumed is then compared to desired objectives and available resources to suggest either revisions in the objectives or strategy, or the need for additional capital.

For assumed economic conditions, the loan-origination department should project anticipated volume and the number of branches required. New branches usually require additional capital. Pricing subsidies, if applicable, should be established, and the choice made of retaining all loan production for servicing, or selling portions of it in order to provide a more favorable cash flow and income level. Virtually all production considerations affect the required capital of the company, reflecting the regulatory net-worth requirements of doing business with FNMA, GNMA, and FHLMC, as well as the cash requirements dictated by operating factors, particularly if new branches are planned.

The warehousing of loans awaiting delivery to permanent investors imposes capital requirements. The amount of capital necessary is influenced by (1) the ability to turn the inventory, (2) changing investor purchasing patterns, (3) management decisions to build inventory, and (4) the relative interest spread on warehoused loans. Loans held in the inventory may have a further impact on capital requirements if risk-avoidance techniques, such as hedging, are being used, and margin requirements are imposed. In addition, problem loans which develop because of delinquency may have to be margined down while in the inventory. Management policies regarding forward-commitment coverage, and the building of inventory to fill forward commitments, will also affect the warehousing requirements.

Marketing strategies which require fees for forward commitments in hedging activities require capital for fees and margin calls. The sale of participations requires additional capital. The cost of risk-avoidance must be considered in estimating the required capital associated with a marketing plan.

Servicing activities of the organization impose yet more capital requirements; in particular, for advances on GNMA or other pass-through securities. In addition, the foreclosure of problem loans requires corporate capital until settlement of the foreclosed loans is reached. The potential to purchase blocks of loans for servicing is another area that must be considered in capital planning.

Taxes must always be considered. Both state and federal income taxes, as well as real estate tax payments due on delinquent loans (which require cash advances), should be carefully projected.

Budgeting

Relation to Strategic Plan

The budget is the tactical implementation of the strategic plan for a given time, such as a year. The budget must, therefore, be consistent with the goals and objectives set forth in the strategic plan and be compatible with available capital resources.

Goals and Objectives

The principal aim of budgeting is increased profits. This goal must be communicated to every individual who participates in budgeting. In order to obtain maximum cooperation, this philosophy must be communicated to all employees. In addition to establishing profit objectives, the budget provides an overall plan of coordinated action and a basis for comparing actual performance with anticipated results. It measures adherence to a previously charted course and highlights departures from the original plan.

The budget fixes the responsibility for achieving each estimated result on a particular individual or department. Employees should be encouraged to attain objectives set by the budget. There is no better method of coordinating financial production and operating results than through budgetary control.

Effective budgetary control strengthens the systems of internal control. Frequent comparisons of projected and actual figures serve to check the correct recording of transactions and events in the accounts. Errors are often disclosed as the result of a department head questioning charges made to his operation.

A well-defined, flexible budget cushions the effects of adverse developments. If unexpected events cause decreased production, expenses can be reduced promptly when operating results are evaluated and compared with preplanned results. Ideally, a budget provides for coordinated efforts by all sections of a business. It serves as a communication tool that enables each section to know its role in achieving overall objectives.

One of the most important advantages of budgeting is the aid it affords in planning working capital needs and cash availability. Financial planning, whether on a long- or short-term basis, is largely founded on anticipated operating results.

Forecasting Loan Volume

For a mortgage banker, the key factor in projecting anticipated operating results is the forecast of loan-production volume, involving as it does assessing the economy as a whole, analyzing trends in the mortgage industry, and weighing the outlook for a particular company in particular markets with finite resources.

Information regarding general economic factors may be obtained from the local and national press, from various indicators published by the U.S. Government Printing Office, from economic articles, or from consultants. Mortgage trends may be assessed through articles in magazines of the mortgage banking, commercial banking, savings and loan, and savings banking industries and special studies conducted by these industries, as well as the surveys and publications of FNMA, FHLMC, the Federal Reserve Board, and the Federal Home Loan Bank Board.

The outlook for a particular company and its expected future production volume requires a detailed analysis of each market area it serves. Before looking to the future, however, it is necessary to assess the past.

1. Start with an analysis of past production activity in each market area, by month if possible. What were dollar volume, number of loans, type of loans, average-size loan originated, number of loan officers, number of loans closed per originator, total direct-labor cost per loan and the annual trend in these averages?

2. Review these data with each branch manager and regional manager, as applicable. If purchasing loans, review past history with the responsible manager. Negotiate anticipated volume for the branch for the coming year. (Recognize that branch managers have an optimistic bias.) Project fixed and variable expenses.

3. Aggregate the volume for each market area the company is in and the resultant total revenues and expenses.

4. Project centralized production-department expenses (production manager, underwriting, etc.). Determine projected net contribution of production to overhead and profit.

5. Using the expected number of loans originated, the assumed average size per loan and inventory turnover, determine the addition to the loan portfolio.

6. Estimate servicing-portfolio runoff, average loan size serviced, average servicing fee and cost-per-loan to arrive at resultant servicing contribution.

7. Estimate net warehouse interest spread, average size of the warehouse, and expected gain or loss on loans sold. Project collateral-department, marketing, and general and administrative expenses to determine net contribution of these functional areas.

8. Add the net contribution from ancillary activities, such as insurance brokerage, data-processing fees, etc.

9. The aggregation of all net contributions by function by month should constitute the preliminary budget for the coming year.

Throughout the budget process of review and projection, due consideration should be given to just how essential each line item in the budget actually is.

The primary variable expenses in mortgage banking consist of interest and personnel costs. These costs are by far the most significant expenses in a mortgage banker's profit and loss statement. This fact underscores the importance of the loan volume forecast, since variable costs by definition reflect the expense impact of loan volume.

Implementation and Monitoring

The actual installation of the budget system is usually preceded by a planning period given to matters which often do not seem to be involved. The following checklist includes most items that should be considered during the planning period.

1. Prepare an organizational chart.
2. Assign responsibility for preparation of the preliminary budget.
3. Determine management reports to be prepared.
4. Decide what production estimates are to be made, by whom, and when. Additional estimates will be required in areas that are directly related to production when the volume forecast is adopted, such as the warehousing, shipping, marketing, servicing, administraion, etc.
5. Analyze the types of loans and other services to be produced.
6. Substantiate production estimates by relating them to past experience or to changed current conditions.
7. Review adequacy of resources to produce estimated production.
8. Estimate expected profits in relation to production and determine return on invested capital.
9. Revise the preliminary budget by refining estimates of production and expenses, utilizing one or more of the following techniques:

     a.   Increase income by increasing fees, adding or changing services, expanding markets, or increasing volume by lowering prices.

     b.   Develop standard costs for all products.

     c.   Determine minimum fixed overhead.

     d.   Determine variable costs in relation to production increases or decreases.

     e.   Determine break-even points.

     f.   Analyze desired asset-turnover ratios and equity requirements.

10.   Prepare final individual budgets for each phase of operations.

11.   Once the budget is installed, prepare summary reports comparing the budget with actual operating results.

12.   Analyze reasons for variances.

13.   Take corrective action, if needed, to ensure that budget objectives are attained. If assumed budget conditions, and therefore objectives, have changed drastically, consider changing the budget; not, however, more often than every six months.

Analysis of the monthly variance from the budget and prior years' performance is an ongoing management responsibility. Complementary management reports should be clear and concise and focus on important ratios, such as loans produced or serviced per employee, warehouse turnover, etc.

Controls

Cost Accounting

Cost accounting has attained its greatest application in manufacturing. However, as an orderly process of compiling detailed cost information about business operations, it is as essential to the mortgage-banking and service industries as it is to manufacturing enterprises. Thus, the cost systems needed in mortgage banking are not fundamentally different from those required in manufacturing organizations.

The cost system should be custom designed to meet specific organizational requirements. The two basic cost accounting systems used in product-producing industries are specific order costs and continuous process costs. The first is generally best suited to the commercial-lending or income-property part of the mortgage-banking industry. In income-property lending, each project is different in its requirement and specifications from every other project. Because of this, there is need for a system of compiling cost data that identifies and segregates each element of cost applicable to each project. Some of the advantages project costs offer to the mortgage banker are: (1) the ability to determine proper gain or loss for each project; (2) the ability to improve techniques in estimating future profits; and (3) the ability to evaluate the cost control performance of the manager responsible for the project.

Continuous-process cost procedures are more appropriate for the residential lending business, which is engaged in continuous production. The accumulation of various costs by identified continuous-process centers enables measurements of revenues and cost-per-loan-processed, etc.

Responsibility Centers

As previously stated, the principal aim of budgeting is to increase profits through control of operating costs and expenses. This control may be achieved by incorporating responsibility centers into the internal accounting and reporting systems. Responsibility centers are usually broken down into profit centers and cost centers. With a profit center, say a production branch office, the manager is primarily accountable for profits. With a cost center, say a loan-servicing department, a manager is primarily accountable for controlling costs. Generally, profit centers differ from cost centers in that the manager is held accountable for generating revenues as well as controlling costs.

Responsibility centers should include four main elements:

1. Revenues, costs, and expenses should be classified into clearly defined functional groupings, such as origination fees, salaries, benefits, rent, etc.

2. Departments and operating centers should be identified in terms of the managers responsible for the respective operations; branch managers, data processing, etc.

3. Quantitative goals or objectives should be established for each specific departmental responsibility; revenues-per-loan-closed in a branch, cost-per-loan-serviced in a servicing department, etc.

4. There should be timely compilation and reporting of actual versus budgeted revenues; costs and expenses; and profits, as applicable.

Since responsibility centers separate cost and expenses according to the scope of responsibility of individual managers, effective control dictates that each manager be keenly aware of exactly what costs are charged to him in operations under his jurisdiction. Accounting arrangements should conform to the organizational chain of command of the company. The budgets for a group of subordinate supervisors can be combined into a total for all units under the direction of a senior executive.

Profit or cost centers utilized for accumulations may not always conform to these managerial authorities and responsibility by divisions. In such instances, it is important that the chart of accounts be revised to provide information that clearly reflects the span of control for each level of management.

Controllable Items

Generally, fewer responsibility centers and classifications are needed in service businesses than are ordinarily required in a manufacturing business. Employee costs are often the largest single element to be controlled. To illustrate, consider some of the prime factors for a service organization that influence the operating cost of doing business. In a typical mortgage-banking operation, one-third of the operating costs are employee costs. Therefore, controlling employee costs requires that management select personnel with the skills necessary to provide the desired quality and quantity of service while controlling utilization and productivity of the personnel selected.

Another significant cost factor is interest expense, which for the average mortgage banker usually accounts for 40 percent of operating costs. Utilizing trust and escrow accounts to price an effective warehouse bank line should be common practice wherever feasible. The utilization of an unsecured note program can, at times, be more economical than bank line arrangements. Also, with proper cash management techiques (lockboxes, etc.), compensating balances will be enhanced.

The system of classifying revenues, costs, and expenses for budgetary control purposes should indicate the specific sources of the principal components of these items. Expenses, such as travel and promotion, which combine charges for payroll, vouchers, etc., are not adequate for control. Thus, the account classification should be developed in a manner that will clearly show management those separate costs that stem from labor, supplies consumed, journal entries, etc. Likewise, revenue sources should be clearly specified.

Reports

The development of a reporting system that generates a mass of financial data serves no useful purpose until the data are transformed into effective management reports. Reports should enhance the ability of managers to make good decisions. Financial staff and operating management must constantly strive to understand which factors are important and require attention. It is up to management to determine what reports they need. Management reports should monitor the following:

1. Performance versus objectives.
2. Compliance with policies and regulations.
3. Organizational responsibilities.
4. Areas of risk exposure and liabilities.
5. Financial returns on selected indices (equity, assets, etc.).
6. Unit performance (per loan, per employee, per loan officer, etc.).
7. Performance timetables for specific items.

Reports of this type will provide management with additional information beyond measuring the actual financial results of operations against budgets.

Management is often directly involved in the activities of business promotion and is usually in direct contact with production, marketing, etc. Consequently, little time may be available for the study of reports and evaluation of operating conditions. Reports should therefore tell management just what they want and need to know in a form that is readily comprehensible. The analysis of data in reports should highlight exceptions and motivate the manager to take suitable control action. These performance reports, prepared and issued at monthly intervals, are essential to effective cost control. Often it is important to report certain key data on a more current basis. For example, when there is a major and rapid change in interest rates, a current analysis of loan inventory versus investor purchase commitments can focus the need for management action.

A list of key reports that a mortgage banker might consider follows:

1. For the production department and each branch office:
   a. Narrative of significant items
   b. Comparison of actual performance versus budgeted performance
   c. Loan volume and interest rates by type of loan closed
   d. Fees and gains or losses on loans closed
   e. Loans to servicing, brokered and servicing-released
   f. Unit performance and averages
   g. Personnel costs and productivity
2. For the marketing department (loans closed for sale in the secondary market):
   a. Volume of production at various stages in the pipeline compared to investor commitments, reflecting the price of the loan versus the price of available commitments
   b. Delinquent and foreclosure loans in warehouse
   c. Price and volume by types of loans closed and those nonclosed loans on which prices have been committed.
   d. Loan closing and investor purchase activity.
3. For servicing:
   a. Type of loan in the servicing portfolio with average servicing fee, ancillary income and insurance; average cost per unit; average loan size serviced.
   b. Unit costs reflecting productivity, such as loans serviced per employee, etc.
   c. The amount, loan type, and geographical breakdown of delinquencies and foreclosures.
   d. The loans delivered to the portfolio for servicing; runoff information for amortization; payoffs; and foreclosures.
4. For banking:
   a. The daily cash position and borrowing position, secured and unsecured.
   b. Profitability.
   c. Credit-lines usage, turnover and compensating balances.

5. For construction lending, builder activity and lines:
   a. Builder activity and line usage.
   b. Project's profitability.
   c. Delinquent interest, aging.
   d. Builder cash flow analysis, credit forecast and equity adequacies.

Communications

While the budgeting of business operations involves a knowledge and application of special techniques, its most important feature is communication. In establishing a budget program, the budget technician is only the catalyst; the line executives and managers have a key role in successful budgeting. All members of the management team should understand the budget's principal features and support its use and application. Loan volume forecasts should be developed, based on discussions with branch managers and regional production managers. As mentioned, any tendency by branch managers to either underestimate, or, at the other extreme, overestimate levels of future production must be tempered into most-probable numbers as budget estimates are assembled.

The final authority to approve the budget rests with the chief executive officer. Similarly, all department and divisional budgets must have the approval of the respective managers of those units. Most of the detail, rationale, and computations of budgets can be developed by a budget coordinator, but the program is not likely to achieve good results unless the department managers are involved and accept the budget as an equitable performance evaluator.

Internal Controls

While internal controls are particularly important for transactions involving cash receipts and cash payments, the concept of internal controls is so important that it affects all aspects of the business. It includes all measures taken by an organization for the purpose of: (1) protecting its resources against waste, fraud, and inefficiencies; (2) ensuring the accuracy and reliability in accounting and operating data; (3) securing compliance with company policies; and (4) evaluating the level of performance in all divisions of the company.

Since most business decisions are based on accounting data, a system of internal control provides assurance of the dependability of the accounting data used to make those decisions.

Internal auditing should be routinely performed to ensure that company policies and procedures are being followed. The internal audit staff serves a useful purpose in auditing various branch-office locations or departments to ensure that quality control procedures of the various departments are being followed. Internal audit staffs can also ensure compliance with risk-avoidance procedures such as hedging, construction lending controls, etc.

Analysis

Origination

Information on unit costs should be produced monthly, providing data for the current month and year-to-date, reflecting such items as numbers of loans closed per-loan-origination employee, loan-origination cost per loan, etc., to provide meaningful information as to productivity and to suggest trends.

There should be a procedure for valuing the total production effort. Production that is brokered is immediately valued by its sales value, but production delivered to servicing should be valued by using present-value techniques. Present-value information should determine whether to originate loans for servicing, or to buy loans for servicing. Additional information developed should include branch-office break-even, insurance sales penetration at the branch level, fee income and discount overage or underage, construction-loan activity at branch levels, additional revenues generated, department underwriting expenses, and loan cancellations and pricing activity.

Marketing

Analysis of discount gains and losses should be identified by functional activity (produced by the branch in the origination process or produced by the marketing department in its committing and selling activity). This analysis can guide the company regarding the setting of prices for branches or for purchased loans.

The marketing department should also be measured for effectiveness by the fees written off as a percentage of loans sold and total marketing costs of the department. This should be expressed in basis points (1 basis point equals 1/100th of 1 percent) for production volume handled.

Servicing

Analysis of unit costs in the servicing department is essential to assess productivity. These measurements can be based upon the number of loans serviced per employee and/or the dollar amount of loans serviced per employee and/or the costs-per-loan-serviced. The costs per loan can be broken down further: salary costs, data processing costs, foreclosure costs, etc. Likewise, measurement of income can be expressed in basis points or revenues per loan for service fees as well as other income.

Additional items which can be useful in analysis include compensating balances per loan, penetration of insurance as a percentage of both loans originated and loans serviced by type of insurance, advances for pools serviced, etc.

Warehousing

Measuring the effectiveness of the warehousing department should focus on turnover of the inventory, such as average number of days in the warehouse, and warehouse turnover per year. Warehouse usage, interest spread, aging of loans and compensating balances also should be monitored.

Overhead

The allocation of indirect expenses, such as general and administrative (G&A) overhead, represents a problem for virtually every company, not just mortgage bankers or companies and institutions involved in mortgage banking. The choice is between direct allocation, indirect allocation, or period cost. Normally, direct costing is followed wherever identifiable. Otherwise, nondirect-allocable G&A expenses may be allocated on an indirect basis, such as number of employees in a department, as a percentage of the total square-foot usage of department, as a percentage of total square footage, etc. The trick is to relate indirect expenses to the appropriate department.

Whatever expenses are not allocated on a direct or indirect basis must be accounted for on a period-cost basis: these expenses may be charged to the company as a whole or to a department for the period involved (normally a month). Whether charged to a specific profit or cost center, all G&A expenses should be subject to the same scrutiny that managers on an incentive program give to costs affecting their compensation.

Thus, effective financial planning for a mortgage banker focuses on the primary objectives of the enterprise, whether they be earnings-per-share, or growth in the net present value of the servicing portfolio, or other objectives. Cash flow projections determine capital requirements, while budgets provide short-term guidance for management, augmented by a total system of controls, reports, and ongoing analysis.

—— Chapter 21 ————————————————

———————

Short-Term Financing Requirements and Capabilities

Roswald K. McMullen
Senior Vice President
Mortgage and Trust, Inc.

The need for financing is a fact of life for the mortgage-banking company which typically maintains a mortgage-loan inventory which is large relative to its owners' equity. In order to generate a growing portfolio of serviced mortgage loans, the mortgage banker must take a short-term ownership position in "permanent" mortgages. This inventory must be financed with capital from some source, and it is vital that the mortgage banker be able to increase or decrease his inventory position on short notice, as market conditions dictate. Thus a short-term borrowing arrangement with full prepayment privileges is desirable, at least for a significant portion of debt.

Some mortgage bankers are very active in short-term lending for construction and development. This activity may be financed with borrowed capital, and whether matching assets and liabilities or taking a risk position, such borrowing should be on a short-term basis. In addition, some large mortgage bankers provide warehousing for small mortgage bankers, with the objective of acquiring the servicing. This activity should also be financed with short-term borrowed capital.

In the ordinary conduct of business, the mortgage banker may also have a temporary need for operating funds not related to inventory position in order to finance such transactions as advances to escrow accounts or mortgage-backed securities pools. In such instances, the availability and wise use of short-term financing can help the mortgage banker make the most of opportunities for profit or growth.

The purpose of this chapter is to review the various short-term financing alternatives, including goals and management considerations in the use of such facilities, features to look for and those to avoid, and the management of such financing opportunities for maximum profitability.

Management Considerations

In considering the use of various short-term financing alternatives, the mortgage banker should seek to minimize cost, administrative burden, and risk of

377

corporate assets, while maximizing flexibility in the use of the facility. It is important to recognize the value, as compensating balances, of the many demand-deposit accounts he or she controls and make optimum use of them in arranging for credit. It is also important to consider the balance-sheet impact of the various financing alternatives. Specific factors contributing to these considerations are discussed in the following paragraphs.

Interest Rate

Since mortgage-banking companies are typically very highly leveraged, interest expense tends to be among the highest, perhaps the highest expense item on the statement of earnings. Thus the potential exists for very significant savings with proper management of borrowings to minimize interest expense. To illustrate, a hypothetical mortgage-banking company, with a net worth of $4,000,000 and a debt-to-equity ratio of eight to one, can increase return on equity by 4 percent per year by saving an average of 1/2 of 1 percent interest on each dollar borrowed. Similarly, if the same mortgage-banking company originates $100 million in mortgage loans during a year and has experienced a 1 percent per annum positive interest spread, he can add 1 percent to his annual return on equity by keeping each loan in inventory for an extra two weeks before delivery to a permanent investor (assuming the 1 percent positive spread continues).

The stated interest rate for the short-term financing facility is of paramount importance; but in order to minimize the amount of interest expense, the mortgage banker must recognize that, in addition to the stated interest rate, many factors contribute to the effective interest rate.

The *stated interest rate* is that rate agreed upon between the mortgage banker and the lender. The best tool available to the mortgage banker to minimize this rate, in addition to good credit and collateral, is compensating balances. There are many different arrangements whereby the mortgage banker receives a reduced rate in exchange for bank balances on deposit. The mortgage banker should do some comparison shopping among the various approaches available to determine which stated rate will be the lowest, on a January-to-December average, net of credit for compensating balances, under whatever formula the commercial bank employs.

The agreed-upon interest rate, and the formula for giving credit for balances, are very important elements in the negotiation of any credit-line pricing; however, other vital elements should also be clearly understood by both parties from the outset. The bank's method of calculation and frequency of billing for interest are examples of this. Is a 360- or 365-day basis used? How often are principal reductions credited? If the stated rate bears a fixed relationship to the bank's prime rate or some other index (floats), how often are changes in the index reflected?

The desirable response will depend on the mortgage bank's intended use of the facility, its perception of future interest-rate movements, and its basic business philosophy. If the rate on underlying collateral floats relative to an index, the mortgage banker will probably prefer a credit line that does the same, assuring a positive spread. However, if the mortgage bank's collateral is fixed (as to rate) for a specified term, it may prefer to arrange credit with a rate similarly fixed for a like term.

Is interest paid in advance or in arrears? How often is interest paid? In addition to interest, does the bank charge any fee for administering the credit arrangement? If compensating balances are an element in pricing, how are available balances calculated? Would such balances be better applied to the purchase of bank services (such as lockbox or computer services)? The answer to each of these questions will have an important effect on the mortgage banker's choice of credit facility.

A very important element of effective interest is the accuracy of the lender's calculation. Like any bill to be paid by the mortgage banker, the correctness of mathematical calculations should be verified, as well as the stated rate employed in calculating interest charged by the bank or other lender.

The rate of interest paid is by far the most important single element in the choice of a short-term credit facility, but it must be considered in light of other terms, conditions, and effects of the arrangement.

Flexibility and Administrative Ease

The extent to which use of the facility is placed in the control of the mortgage banker is very important. For example, the flexibility to increase or decrease the amount borrowed on a daily basis as the mortgage banker's business dictates is a great advantage.

By contrast, the necessity to plan for, and manage, maturity dates adds an administrative burden that the mortgage banker may prefer to avoid. Similarly, the ability to withdraw or substitute collateral makes it easier for the mortgage banker to use the facility in the ordinary operation of business. The mortgage banker may be willing to make some concessions in interest rate in exchange for such administrative convenience.

Other questions the mortgage banker should address in evaluating a credit facility are as follows:

> What assurance is given of the continued availability of the facility, and to what extent is it under the mortgage banker's control? The mortgage banker needs assurance that the credit will be available for the duration of its need, as long as it continues to meet certain guidelines under its control. Probably more than any other characteristic of a credit line, this one tends to be implicit rather than firmly documented. If the mortgage banker has a good relationship with the lender and a high degree of confidence regarding its business and its value to the lender, it

may be comfortable with such a tacit agreement. Otherwise, continued availability should be covered in the documentation.

What items of collateral documentation must be furnished? The lender will require sufficient documentation to perfect the security interest in the collateral in the event of the mortgage banker's default, but anything beyond that should be critically evaluated. Undue administrative burdens must be avoided. The lender should remember that it is primarily making a loan to the mortgage banker, not to the underlying builder, developer, or homeowner, and should put at least as much emphasis on the first two *Cs* of credit (character and capacity) as on the third (collateral).

Can the collateral be freely accessed or moved to facilitate formation of a mortgage-backed securities pool or the shipment of a loan to a permanent investor? If the mortgage banker employs the credit facilities of many commercial banks, it may desire to move large blocks of mortgage loans from various banks into a single bank which is to be the custodian on a mortgage-backed securities pool. The arrangement must permit re-banking in this manner, paying off the first bank(s) and borrowing from the second, to facilitate the orderly formation of the pool, establishment of the custodial arrangement, protection of the guarantor's interests and delivery of the mortgage-backed securities to the purchaser.

Standard practice in the sale of whole loans to permanent investors permits the forwarding of collateral under control of the commercial bank lender to the investor versus payment directly to the bank. This should be agreed on from the outset.

Will the administrative capability of the lender enhance or detract from the value of the facility? The lender will be an administrative extension of the mortgage banker's office, and the efficient execution of these duties is vital.

Is marking-to-the-market required? When a credit facility is collateralized by permanent mortgage loans, the lender may require adjustments in the amount borrowed to: (1) maintain a relationship to market value when such value declines, or (2) keep the amount of security constant when principal payments are received. Conversely, if market values are moving up, the mortgage banker may desire the capability of increasing the borrowing on the same collateral. On the other hand, the mortgage banker may prefer to avoid the necessity of any such adjustments.

Risk of Corporate Assets

The mortgage banker should seek to risk as few corporate assets as possible in exchange for a credit facility. Although the lender will usually require the general credit of the corporation, it may in some instances be possible for the mortgage bank to limit its liability to those specific mortgage loans or other assets which are directly pledged as collateral for the borrowing. Even when the mortgage-banking company is generally liable on the credit, the mortgage banker's best interests will be served by minimizing those assets which are directly pledged as security for the line.

Even though a line of credit may be secured by specific assets, there are other common techniques frequently used by commercial banks to broaden the base of assets that can be used to satisfy the line of credit. Two of these are cross-collateralization and the right of set-off. *Cross-collateralization* enables the lender to claim the security pledged for one loan in satisfaction of another. The *right of set-off* gives him the privilege of claiming any cash in the bank's custody (other than that of a fiduciary nature, such as escrow accounts) in satisfaction of the line of credit. The mortgage banker should be aware of these concepts, and he or she should know whether protection in this form is afforded the lender under the particular credit arrangements.

The loan-to-value ratio is another point to be considered in evaluating the risk to corporate assets in a credit arrangement. The lender will want to be assured that the borrower's equity in a particular asset is commensurate with the risk inherent in the asset. For example, there is more perceived risk in owning a land development project (or a loan on such a project) than in owning a single-family residence (or a loan on such a property). Therefore, the warehouse lender may require the mortgage banker to have a larger equity interest in the former than in the latter. Conversely, the mortgage bank that is employing leverage by pledging such assets to secure bank credit should be aware of prudent lending limits so that it can make maximum use of such leverage if it so chooses.

The stability of the lending institution should also be considered in evaluating risk to the mortgage bank's assets. The mortgage banker is well advised to keep in mind that the secured lender is responsible for safeguarding the collateral as well as lending on it. If the lender is not financially sound or is only marginally so, the lender may be tempted to use the mortgage banker's mortgage loans or mortgage-backed securities in other transactions in its business. For example, a mortgage banker who has surrendered GNMA mortgage-backed securities to a GNMA dealer in a repurchase arrangement, needs assurance that the dealer will not "borrow" the securities to satisfy delivery requirements on another transaction. Careful underwriting of the financial condition of all lenders will enable the mortgage banker to deal with chosen lenders with confidence that such situations will not occur.

Even though the financial stability of the lending institution may give the mortgage banker no cause for concern, the safekeeping and collateral-handling duties of the lender require certain administrative capabilities. The mortgage bank must satisfy itself that the lender possesses these capabilities. Otherwise it may find that its collateral is at greater risk than necessary simply because of the lender's administrative inefficiencies.

The risk of loss of corporate assets cannot be avoided in a borrowing arrangement, but the mortgage banker must be certain that the risk is no greater than necessary and certainly no greater than contemplated in the initial transaction.

Short-Term Financing Alternatives

There are many possible approaches to meeting the mortgage banker's short-term financing needs. Each offers its own advantages, while at the same time possessing certain disadvantages. At this juncture, it is advisable to review the goals of the mortgage banker in seeking short-term financing:

Minimum cost.

Maximum flexibility.

Minimum risk of corporate assets.

Maximum administrative ease.

Continued availability.

These goals are met to differing degrees in the various financing alternatives described in the following discussion.

Bank Lines of Credit

By far the most universally used short-term financing method is the line of credit with a commercial bank. In a prearranged agreement, the bank agrees to make a certain amount of credit available to the mortgage banker under certain prescribed conditions. The agreement may be very formal, with every condition carefully documented, but it can also be extremely informal, based entirely on a verbal conversation and understanding. The degree of formality depends on the relationship between the bank and the mortgage banker, the size and financial characteristics of the mortgage banker, and the established policies of both firms. Regardless of the degree of formality, there should be an understanding regarding term of the agreement, interest-rate structure, collateral and its documentation, loan-to-value ratios, compensating balances, and resources for ultimate payoff of each amount borrowed.

Since the typical mortgage bank is extremely dependent on credit facilities, it should have bank lines available that are renewed well in advance of expiration. A typical arrangement is a one-year agreement with renewal for another year, arranged three months before expiration. As discussed earlier, the level of assurance and degree of documentation of such continued availability that the mortgage bank requires, will depend on its relationship with the bank and the level of its confidence regarding its business and its value to the bank, as well as availability of credit from other sources.

There are a multitude of pricing mechanisms that have been used in establishing the interest rate on bank lines of credit for mortgage bankers. Most of them involve a base price, such as the bank's prime rate, the bank's cost of funds, its quoted adjusted-TCD rate, or some well-publicized and readily determinable rate (such as the federal funds rate, LIBOR, or the quoted rate on some money market instrument). From this base price, a reduction is then made to give credit for compensating balances that the mortgage banker has on deposit with the bank. The formula for giving such credit may take any one of several forms. The bank may simply require that the average level of balances be maintained at a certain percentage of the line amount, and/or a certain percent of *usage* (the outstanding balance at any time), in order to maintain a certain rate; or the formula may be a straightforward one, giving the mortgage banker credit at an agreed-upon rate for the actual balances in the bank during the period. The latter arrangement leaves the mortgage bank more in control of its price, since it knows exactly what the effect will be of each movement of funds into or out of the bank. On the other hand, if the mortgage banker's compensating balances are small relative to the total banking needs, fluctuations in the amount of balances may tend to be material, creating an undesirable volatility in balances available to support the line. In such an instance, the mortgage banker may prefer an arrangement wherein credit is based on average balances, thereby leveling the rate.

Credit given for compensating balances will be based on *available balances*: the net amount of money on deposit after subtracting required reserves, funds in process of collection, and balances required to support checking account services (such as processing checks and deposits, and maintaining the account). Most commercial banks will agree to furnish a copy of this calculation to the depositor. The mortgage banker should obtain a copy of the calculation on each such account maintained, for the purpose of making comparisons between banks and verifying accuracy.

Unless a mortgage banker is in control of large amounts of compensating balances, the interest rate on bank lines will probably be higher than that on other forms of short-term borrowing discussed below. However, the advantages of bank line borrowing are numerous and include the following:

1. Dealing with a professional lender. Inasmuch as the lending of money is a primary line of business with commercial banks, the mortgage banker will have the opportunity to establish a business relationship that will be continuing in nature. The continued availability of such a credit facility is more likely to exist than with other arrangements.

2. Greater flexibility. Being a professional lender and cash manager, the commercial bank is better equipped than is the mortgage banker to absorb the day-to-day fluctuations in cash flow that are inherent in the business, thereby providing the mortgage banker with the privilege of varying borrowing up or down at will and on a daily basis.

3. Custodial efficiency. The commercial banker will usually be well-staffed and equipped to efficiently handle the movement of collateral so necessary in the marketing and delivery of mortgage loans and the formation of pools of mortgage-backed securities.

4. Related services. The mortgage banker is a frequent user of other bank services, such as lockbox processing and custodial services. A significant de-

posit and debt position with the bank tends to solidify the relationship and the efficient accomplishment of these services.

5. Convenient location. Since there are banks in virtually every city, the bank tends to be physically convenient as compared with other lenders, facilitating the movement of collateral, deposit of funds, formation of mortgage-backed securities pools, prompt credit for principal reductions, and general administrative ease.

For these reasons, the mortgage banker may find it advantageous to deal with a lead bank which is physically located in his home office city.

The mortgage banker should consider the relative merits of a centralized relationship with one bank as compared with a decentralized approach, in which independent arrangements are made for credit lines with various banks. There is an obvious advantage to the mortgage banker in the competitive environment created by dealing independently with more than one commercial bank. Terms arranged with each bank can be used to evaluate those offered by the others, and the knowledge that this concept is employed will cause the banks to be more aggressive in pricing the line of credit. Additionally, the mortgage banker may receive comfort from the knowledge that there is no one lender that can unilaterally terminate the entire credit arrangement.

On the other hand, the mortgage banker may find that the terms of the credit line are more favorable if the banker is assured of being the exclusive lender. Basically, however, the major advantages to a single-bank arrangement are administrative. All of the bank accounts are in the same institution, facilitating the movement of funds among accounts, and messenger service must only be provided to one banking location. Uniform requirements contribute to easier monitoring, and simplified training of personnel is made possible.

The size of the mortgage banker and the size of the commercial bank may be controlling factors in this decision. Because of the bank's lending limit, a large mortgage bank may find that its needs cannot be served by one bank alone. It must, therefore, make use of multiple banks to guarantee the availability of adequate warehousing at all times. A compromise arrangement is for one bank to be the lead bank and to participate in credit arrangements with several other banks for the benefit of the same borrower. All of the collateral is deposited with the lead bank under a custodial arrangement, and each bank is given an interest in the collateral pool through a pooling agreement. This greatly simplifies the formation of a mortgage-backed securities pool, inasmuch as all documents are already in the lead bank, which is assumed to be the pool custodian. All necessary demand-deposit accounts are placed in the lead bank, and any balances needed in the other banks to support borrowings are furnished by the lead bank, at the instructions of the mortgage banker, under a *due-to/due-from account*. This arrangement achieves the goal of administrative simplification while retaining the competitive advantages of multiple-bank credit arrangements. One caution: it should be agreed at the outset that the free movement of funds among the banks will be under the control of the mortgage banker.

One variation of the bank line of credit is the purchase line. This arrangement is technically a purchase by the bank of the mortgages or securities, with a written or implied agreement from the mortgage banker to repurchase the collateral at a later date. All documentation is the same as that in the regular bank line, except that there is no promissory note executed by the mortgage banker, further simplifying the administrative work attendant to the arrangement. Although the bank is technically looking to the underlying mortgagor for payment, the transaction is essentially a financing arrangement (as opposed to a sale of mortgages) and is accounted for as such by the mortgage banker.

A bank credit line agreement will usually specify that a certain type of collateral (permanent single-family mortgages, short-term construction loans or land development loans) is to be financed with the line. The mortgage banker will probably find that a credit line designated for construction and land development loans commands a higher rate of interest than one designated for permanent mortgages. The basic reason for this is that the banks tend to evaluate and underwrite the credit risk based on the underlying property and mortgagor rather than on the credit of the mortgage banker. The mortgage banker needs to be aware of this tendency and discourage it where his credit warrants such consideration.

The commercial bank normally requires that the amount borrowed under the line of credit be limited to a conservative proportion of the market value of the underlying collateral. In the case of credit lines secured by permanent mortgages or mortgage-backed securities, in which there is an established, liquid secondary market, with readily available quotations of market value, the bank's maximum loan is normally limited to that market value or slightly less. If such loans or securities are covered by an investor commitment, the bank's maximum loan is likely to be the net proceeds to be realized by the mortgage banker upon delivery. The bank may require that a certain percentage of loans or securities banked under the line be covered by such commitments. For loans or securities not covered by investor commitments, the bank may desire that any decreases in the market value of the loans or securities be matched by decreases in the amount borrowed. This marking-to-the-market is designed to maintain assurance that resources are available for the ultimate liquidation of the loan, but the requirement increases the administrative burden to the mortgage banker. A reasonable solution is to build in tolerance by borrowing less than full market value initially (the difference is sometimes referred to as a *haircut*), then making no adjustments until the market has declined by twice the amount of the haircut. For example, say the current market price for the product is 98 percent of par. The mortgage banker borrows, say, 96 ½, allowing a 150-basis-point haircut, representing the mortgage banker's equity in the loans. No reduction in his bank loan would then be made until the market value had declined by 3 percent. This arrangement provides continuous protection for the bank, because all new banking carries the 1½ percent cushion to help offset any declines in the market value of loans banked earlier. At the same time, the mortgage banker's administrative burden is lessened because required adjustments are minimized.

The degree of marking-to-the-market required depends greatly on the total financial condition of the mortgage bank, the net market position of its entire portfolio (which the commercial banker may want to monitor) and its relationship with the bank. Consistency in marking-to-the-market arrangements permits increases in the amount borrowed in the event of upward movements in market value.

Credit lines secured by construction or development loans, in which there is no orderly secondary market, may lead the bank to insist on a *take-out*, which is a commitment from a recognized lender for permanent financing on the property. If no such protection is present, the ultimate liquidation of the bank's loan will probably come from the mortgage banker's funding of a permanent loan on the property. In such cases, the bank will be entitled to assurance that:(1) the property will qualify for such a loan; (2) the mortgage banker's construction or development loan bears a reasonable proportion (not more than 70 to 75 percent of the value of the property); and (3) the construction or development work is proceeding at a pace consistent with the advances being made on the loan. Given such assurances, the bank should be willing to fund the entire amount of the mortgage banker's investment in such loans. In the event repayment of the construction or development loan becomes doubtful because of problems befalling the underlying builder or developer, a cooperative understanding is necessary between the commercial bank and the mortgage banker. If the amount borrowed continues to bear a reasonable ratio to the net realizable value of the property, the commercial banker should be willing to continue the loan and neither require repayment nor put its lien of record. During the workout period, the bank must be kept advised of progress and, in the event of foreclosure, should be willing to directly finance the mortgage banker's ownership and completion and/or sale of the property.

Problem loans in the mortgage banker's inventory of permanent loans give rise to different considerations. These loans, which are held primarily for sale, become unsaleable when collectibility problems arise. Such loans may become involved in foreclosure, or even bankruptcy, proceedings. They may also become unsaleable because of nonconformity with the requirements of the investor for which they were intended. Because of the long-term nature of such loans, a commercial bank cannot be expected to finance a mortgage banker's ownership of such assets under a short-term line of credit. Other arrangements can, however, be made to the mutual satisfaction of both mortgage banker and commercial banker in the comparatively rare case in which this occurs. The mortgage banker should take the initiative to advise the bank of this situation and ask for arrangements to finance ownership of the loan outside the regular line. Such arrangements will probably include scheduled principal reductions, protection for the bank in the event of loss of value for any reason, and some agreement as to the expected term of the bank's involvement.

The mortgage banker should be prepared to finance the ownership of unsaleable permanent loans through long-term sources of financing (long-term debt or permanent capital). When bank debt is used, the bank may prefer to finance problem loan activity, as well as certain other activities of the mortgage banker, through the use of an unsecured line.

The *unsecured* (working capital) *line of credit* is very useful, particularly for the small mortgage-banking concern, in filling short-term working capital needs, such as advances to GNMA pools, escrow advances, and even the purchase of supplies and equipment. On an unsecured line, the bank is looking to all of the assets of the corporation, and sometimes to those of its owners, for repayment, and will employ various techniques to assure, or at least encourage, repayment:

1. Claims on future servicing income. (Because servicing rights are generally not assignable, it is impossible to perfect a security interest in them. The banker can, however, take an assignment of the proceeds on any future sale of such rights.)

2. Pledge of corporate stock by major shareholder or parent company.

3. Guaranty by parent company of net-worth level of mortgage-banking company.

4. Subordination by parent company of its loans to those of the bank.

The unsecured line, while very useful in certain situations, may be expected to bear a higher interest rate to compensate the bank for its perceived higher risk.

It is also important to the mortgage banker's cash-management program that day-to-day reductions in debt be permitted as cash flow permits. The commercial bank line of credit is the best tool to provide this capability. The commercial bank can also provide a vital service in minimizing borrowing by permitting the mortgage banker to borrow only the funds needed to bring the balance in the operating bank account to zero. There are several techniques for doing this, including the following:

1. Disbursement of loans and advances with drafts rather than checks. The draft is technically a collection item and not an unconditional promise to pay. Therefore it does not overdraw the account when it arrives at the bank. The maker of the draft is contacted for approval of the draft, giving the opportunity to borrow funds to cover the draft.

2. The zero-balance account. The mortgage banker's operating bank account is adjusted up or down to zero each day by an offsetting adjustment in the amount borrowed from the bank against collateral on deposit.

3. The controlled disbursement account. Combining features of drafts and the zero-balance account, the controlled disbursement account features *check presentment advisory service*, whereby the bank agrees to process against the customer's account on a given day only those items which are presented for payment before a designated time, say, 6:00A.M. on that day. This permits the

mortgage banker to determine by mid-morning the amount of such items that must be considered in banking for each day.

The use of these and similar techniques for minimizing borrowings will help to solidify the mortgage bank–commercial bank relationship and to establish the commercial bank as the central source of short-term borrowings. Commercial bank lines of credit should be considered the foundation, not simply one alternative source, of the mortgage banker's short-term financing arrangements. The other sources of short-term financing to be discussed should be viewed as supplementary to the basic relationship with the commercial bank, with consideration given to their potential effects on bank borrowing capacity and available compensating balances.

Documented Discount Notes

The technique of borrowing short-term funds with the documented discount note (DDN) involves a three-way arrangement among the mortgage banker, the commercial bank and the purchaser of commercial paper. The commercial banker serves as the pivot point in this arrangement.

The mortgage banker keeps collateral in the form of mortgage loans on deposit with the commercial bank, under a normal warehousing arrangement. From time to time, the mortgage banker may issue DDNs for sale in the commercial paper market, in amounts up to the total value of such collateral. While the DDNs are actually issued by the mortgage banker, they are backed by a letter of credit issued by the commercial bank. The DDNs are sold in the marketplace, either by the bank or an independent commercial broker, and proceeds of the sale are used to pay down the warehouse line, making a portion of the mortgages available to collateralize the letter of credit. Upon maturity of the DDN, the bank makes an advance under the warehouse line of credit sufficient to repay the purchaser of the DDN, the letter of credit expires, and the mortgages again collateralize the credit line.

Although the DDN is technically issued by the mortgage banker, the purchaser of such paper is actually looking to the commercial bank, through its letter of credit, for repayment. As the name implies, DDNs are issued on a discounted basis; maturities are for a fixed term from 1 to 45 days, and rates tend to be considerably better than those available on normal bank lines of credit. The primary advantages of DDNs over the normal warehouse line of credit are the following:

1. Rates. Even after compensating the bank for the letter of credit, administrative services, and marketing, the rate should be considerably less than the bank prime rate.

2. Compensating balances freed.

3. Fixed rate for term. Since DDNs are issued at a discount for a definite term, the rate is effectively fixed, rather than floating, for that term. If the

mortgage bank feels that rates are moving upwards, it will issue notes with longer terms. During a period of declining rates, shorter terms will be employed.

Disadvantages are as follows:

1. Maturity date management. Since DDNs are issued for fixed terms, the mortgage banker must plan such maturities so that mortgages are available for sale in the secondary market when business conditions dictate, while at the same time issuing DDNs for the optimum term to minimize the rate and lessen the administrative burden.

2. Prepayment of interest. DDNs are issued on a discounted basis, and the impact on the effective interest rate will vary with the term of the issue. The mortgage bank will want to assure itself that, even after adjustment for this factor, the effective rate is preferable to that available on straight debt.

Since the purchaser of the DDN is looking to the bank for repayment, it is not necessary that the DDN carry a favorable rating from one of the rating agencies, although such a rating does enhance the marketability of the paper. While the DDN represents an attractive compromise between the bank line of credit and an outright issue of commercial paper, the bank's letter of credit is subject to the same lending limits as is a direct loan. Therefore no additional borrowing capacity is created with the arrangement. The choice of the bank is very important. The larger and more creditworthy the bank, the lower the interest rate should be.

The documented discount note is an excellent tool to supplement the mortgage banker's bank line borrowing arrangement, affording the opportunity to reduce interest rates and free balances, while preserving the relationship with the commercial bank.

Commercial Paper

Mortgage-banking companies with a high volume of permanent-loan originations and a large and secure capital base have found it attractive to issue their own commercial paper in the form either of a collateral trust note (CTN) or a mortgage-backed note. These instruments are distinguished from DDNs in that they are issued directly by the mortgage banker without a commercial bank letter of credit. Like DDNs (and unlike normal corporate commercial paper), they are collateralized by a pool of long-term mortgages, mortgage-backed securities, or similar instruments, which are placed in the custody of a trustee bank and are further secured by back-up lines of credit from one or more banks. A successfully marketed issue of CTNs must have a favorable rating from a recognized rating agency and requires extensive technical documentation. These requirements necessitate the outlay of very large initial costs (in the form of legal and accounting fees, printing and administrative expenses), as well as an enormous investment of time and effort on the part of management and staff. The involvement of several outside entities is required, including the rating agency, the investment bank, the commercial bank, and the trustee bank, in addition to attorneys and independent certified public accountants. Because of the tremendous initial outlay, the mortgage banker must carefully study the feasibility of the effort to ascertain that the continuing volume of inventory to be financed in this manner will be large enough that the interest savings will justify and recover the initial cost over a reasonable period of time, preferably in the first year.

The large mortgage banker who successfully creates an issue of CTNs can expect to realize substantial interest savings during normal economic times when commercial-paper rates are favorable to short-term bank rates.

There are four advantages of this method of short-term borrowing, relative to other methods:

1. Rate. The interest rate is lower than that of commercial bank lines of credit.

2. Expanded lines of credit. The amount of credit available in the commercial-paper market is not subject to a lending limit. However, since CTNs are further secured by back-up lines of credit from one or more banks, they are to some extent subject to the lending limits of the back-up banks.

3. Reduced compensating balance requirements. The balances required to support the back-up lines of credit are considerably less than those needed for direct borrowings.

4. Fixed rate for term. As in the case of DDNs, because commercial paper is to be issued at a discount for a definite term, the rate is fixed for that term. Depending on the mortgage bank's perception of interest-rate movements, it may issue paper for a longer or shorter term to take advantage of this feature.

The disadvantages are as follows:

1. Initial cost. The entry cost may make the entire issue unfeasible. The mortgage bank needs to assure itself that volume will be great enough so that the high entry cost will be more than offset by interest savings over time.

2. Maturity date management. As in the case of DDNs, commercial paper is issued for a fixed term; therefore, maturity dates must be carefully planned to permit the orderly delivery of mortgages or securities to secondary-market purchasers.

3. Tendency to abandon bank lines. The low interest rate available to CTNs creates the temptation to make it the exclusive warehousing tool, effectively severing bank relationships. This could prove disastrous when commercial-paper rates are higher than bank rates. A mortgage banker should generally never abandon bank lines. The mortgage banker may have to revert to bank borrowings in the future if interest lines cross, and the bank line should be retained as a back-up to the commercial paper.

4. Prepayment of interest. As in the case of DDNs, commercial paper is issued at a discount, causing interest on the issue to be paid in advance. Depending on the terms of the issue, this has a varying impact on the effective interest rate.

Repurchase Arrangements

Most commonly used with GNMA mortgage-backed securities, the repurchase arrangement, or *repo*, as it is commonly called, is a very attractive financing technique. The mortgage banker sells the mortgage-backed security to a securities dealer or commercial bank (through the securities trading department), and simultaneously agrees to repurchase the same securities at a definite future date at a fixed price. The transaction has all the characteristics of a financing transaction, and is accounted for and reported as such, rather than as a sale. The two transfers of ownership are not made of record, but the security dealer does take physical possession of the certificates, which are usually issued in the name of the mortgage banker, along with the necessary assignment form, executed in blank, to make a complete transfer of ownership should repurchase not be made as agreed. The arrangement may be for any term, but is most commonly utilized for a term of 30–180 days. Wherever possible, maturity should coincide with the date of delivery of a mortgage-backed security to the purchaser. The rate charged by the securities dealer will approximate commercial banks' cost of funds for money borrowed for a similar term, plus a small add-on.

Advantages to the mortgage banker of the use of repurchase agreements are as follows:

1. Favorable rate, with no compensating balance requirements.
2. Credit lines are expanded, since lending limits are not a factor.
3. Inexpensive documentation. Since there is no note or security instrument between the mortgage banker and the purchaser, no documentation is required other than the security itself and the assignment form.

Disadvantages are as follows:

1. Inventory inaccessible. When used for unsold inventory, the securities are not available for delivery into the secondary market should conditions so dictate. For this reason, the repurchase agreement is more commonly used to finance sold inventory awaiting deferred delivery.
2. Loan-to-value ratios. To further secure his position and eliminate the need for detailed underwriting on the mortgage banker's credit, the purchaser of the securities will pay less than their current market value in a repurchase arrangement. Of course, if the securities being conveyed are sold, with eventual delivery to be made to the same securities dealer, the purchase/repurchase price will logically be set to match the net proceeds due upon the eventual sale.

Variations

Innovative and imaginative mortgage bankers, as well as commercial bankers and investment bankers, continue to create variations on the basic methods of providing short-term financing alternatives. Each variation is designed to better fill a particular need, eliminate a shortcoming, or capitalize on a certain feature of an existing method. A few of the more popular variations:

1. The *gestation-period repo*. Not actually a repurchase agreement at all, this arrangement recognizes that once a GNMA mortgage-backed securities pool is complete, issuance of the securities approved, and the issue date passed, it is only a matter of time before the actual certificates will be issued and available for a true repurchase agreement. At this stage, the underlying mortgage loans are considered more desirable security than otherwise. Therefore some commercial banks are willing to reduce the interest rate during this time, usually not more than a two-week period.

2. *Conduit* or *syndicate for issuance of commercial paper*. Through the formation of a single-purpose corporation for the issuance of commercial paper, several medium-sized mortgage bankers can realize some of the advantages of a direct issue of commercial paper, although actually issuing DDNs. The formation of such as issuer is usually coordinated by a commercial bank, in cooperation with an investment banker. This arrangement typically involves purchase of DDNs by the issuer from several different mortgage bankers, and issuance of rated commercial paper by the issuer, backed by letters of credit from the commercial bank, which are in turn secured by the pledge of mortgage loans or mortgage-backed securities. The issuer can be made bankruptcy-proof, thereby permitting a longer term (up to 270 days). An additional advantage of such a pooled effort is a continued presence in the marketplace, making possible a lower rate.

3. *Prewarehousing line of credit*. Used when mortgage loans are closed in locations distant from the commercial bank, this arrangement permits borrowing temporarily without complete documentation, until all loan papers arrive. It would typically be available for no more than five days, would require evidence of funding of the loan, and would carry a slightly higher interest rate than the fully secured line of credit.

4. *Delayed interest payment*. Normally, banks will require payment of interest on a monthly basis, in arrears. Negotiated deviations from this schedule will have a varied effect on the interest rate, depending on time and rate levels. For example, payment quarterly in arrears will save approximately 15 basis points when the monthly payment base rate is 12 percent. At lower rates, the savings is less; at higher rates, more.

Alternatives

Mortgage bankers have been innovative not only in creating variations in borrowing methods, but also in devising alternatives to borrowing that eliminate certain of the disadvantages while retaining at least a majority of the advantages:

1. *Participations.*   For the mortgage banker engaged in construction and development lending, an alternative to bank borrowing or other short-term debt is to participate out to a bank or other investor some portion of the construction or development loan. As the name implies, this arrangement allows another lender to participate in the ownership of the loan, permitting the mortgage banker to continue in control of the builder's business, while minimizing risk. The mortgage banker will do all the required administrative work, with the participant merely advancing funds as required. The mortgage banker will make certain that all necessary permits are obtained and fees paid, will do the site approvals and job inspections, disburse funds, and see that the job is completed free of liens. The mortgage banker will retain a portion of the points or loan fees charged, and possibly some override on the interest rate. The participation can be for any percentage of the total construction loan and, as such, replaces the need for the mortgage banker to borrow money in order to fund the loan. In the event the loan becomes a problem loan, it will be the job of the mortgage banker to work out of the problem, and the participating investor can be expected to cooperate to the fullest during this workout period.

2. *Callable Preferred Stock.*   Although technically a form of equity, callable preferred stock has been used by some mortgage bankers as a suitable alternative to intermediate-term debt. The usual issuer of such stock is relatively large, with a good credit rating, and is a subsidiary of a larger, publicly held company. By issuing preferred stock, the mortgage bank has improved its balance sheet, reduced its risk and assured itself of financing for an intermediate term, usually three to five years. The price paid for the privilege is a commitment to the longer term, nondeductibility of interest for federal income-tax purposes, and a more firmly set interest rate (not necessarily a disadvantage). Preferred stock bears a fixed dividend rate, with the issuer retaining the right to redeem the stock after a certain number of years upon payment of a premium. Generally, such an issue would call for a reduced premium each year thereafter.

Preferred stock can be an effective tool for the mortgage bank, depending on its perception of interest rates and money needs over an intermediate period of time.

In selecting the most appropriate alternatives for short-term financing needs, the mortgage banker must explore all available avenues and consider each one not only in light of its effect on profitability, but also in terms of flexibility of use, risk of corporate assets, impact on administrative responsibilities, and continued availability of the facility. The mortgage bank must seek to make optimum use of the demand deposits under its control, while honoring the fiduciary nature of the funds. Above all, it must honor the terms of the credit arrangement so that its entire business, the liability side as well as the asset side, remains under its control and not that of its creditors. As Benjamin Franklin once put it, "Remember this saying, *'The good payer is lord of another man's purse.'* He that is known to pay punctually and exactly to the time he promises, may at any time, and on any occasion, raise all the money his friends can spare."

Chapter 22

Accounting Policies

James H. Hammond, Jr.
Partner
Peat, Marwick, Mitchell & Co.

This chapter discusses the significant accounting policies applicable to mortgage originators/sellers in the secondary mortgage market. Generally accepted accounting principles are applicable to all transactions entered into by these enterprises. This chapter focuses on those major transaction cycles unique to a secondary mortgage market operation and does not include all transactions that may be entered into by an enterprise. The discussion includes descriptions of the transactions, applicable generally accepted accounting principles, and suggested financial statement presentations and disclosures. At the end of the chapter there is a sample set of financial statements and related notes.

Mortgage Loans Held

Loans Held for Sale or Market Recovery

All, or almost all, of the loans owned by a secondary mortgage market seller (seller) are held for sale during the normal business cycle, either as individual loans, as collateral for mortgage-backed securities, or as mortgage-backed securities. Occasionally, some owned loans may be held for longer periods. Generally accepted accounting principles (GAAP) provide for the use of the lower of cost or market valuation method for loans held for sale. Such a valuation method most clearly represents the economic realities of the seller's operations. Mortgage loans held for sale have characteristics similar to both accounts receivable and merchandise inventory. Consequently, mortgage accounting principles are drawn from the principles for valuation adjustment for receivables, and also those for reduction of carrying values to the lower of cost or market for inventories. The cost method for valuing loans held for sale is not acceptable, because it does not reflect subsequent reductions in market values. It fails to meet the *conservatism, accrual,* or *measuring-of-unfavorable-event* principles of accounting.

Sellers may hold mortgage loans or GNMA securities for extended periods of time if they expect a favorable long-term interest trend. Although these loans may technically not be held for sale during the seller's normal operating cycles,

395

such loans should also be valued in accordance with the lower of cost or market method prescribed for loans held for sale.

Loans Held for Long-Term Investment

Accounting practices followed by commercial banks, savings and loan associations, insurance companies, and others support the use of the cost method of valuing mortgage loans held as long-term investments, since these institutions contemplate holding the loans to maturity. Occasionally, originator/sellers may choose to make such investments.

Mortgages transferred into a long-term investment category by sellers must be transferred at the lower of cost or market at the date of transfer. Because the transfer to long-term investment terminates any necessity to further write down such loans in the event of subsequent market declines, it is inappropriate to adjust such loans for any subsequent market recovery. If some event occurs to permanently impair value, a further reduction in carrying value may be necessary. Any difference between par value of the loans transferred to long-term investment and carrying value, as determined above, should be accreted and recorded in income, using a method of amortization that provides for a level yield over the terms of the investments. Inasmuch as mortgage loans are rarely outstanding for their full terms, due to normal amortization, payments-in-full, foreclosures, etc., accretion may be based on the estimated life of the loan instead of its stated term.

Loans Sold under Repurchase Agreements

As a means of financing a portion of their inventory, some sellers temporarily transfer such loans to banks or other financial institutions under repurchase agreements. When the loans are marketed to permanent investors, they are reacquired from the banks and sold to the investors. The loans may also be temporarily transferred without a formal repurchase agreement, but the circumstances indicate that an informal agreement exists (that is, all marketing efforts are made by the seller, not the bank; the positive or negative interest spread is the property of the seller; fluctuations in loan market values are the risk of the seller; uncollectible loans are reacquired by the seller; and the seller routinely reacquires all or almost all of the loans from the bank and resells them to permanent investors). While loans transferred to banks under such *sold loan lines* may technically be sales, the existence of a formal repurchase agreement, or the existence of evidence of an informal repurchase practice, indicates that the risk of market loss is retained by the seller and that such transactions are essentially financing in nature and should be accounted for as such. Therefore, the seller should value all such loans at the lower of cost or market. GNMA certificates sold under repurchase agreements should also be valued at the lower of cost or market, unless they are investment and not inventory.

Definition of Lower of Cost or Market

Current Industry Practice

Sellers generally have two types of loans held for sale: those loans that have been originated specifically to fill existing investor commitments, and those loans originated on a speculative or uncommitted basis to fill future investor needs.

Mortgages, like other assets, are initially recorded at cost. *Cost* is generally considered to be the cash or fair value of other assets given in exchange for the asset acquired. While outlays incident to the acquisition, as well as the outlay for the asset itself, are generally considered to comprise the cost of an asset, secondary mortgage market participants generally have not attempted to capitalize the administrative costs involved in the origination of a mortgage. Prevailing industry practice is to recognize only the charging of an origination fee, usually 1 percent of the mortgage amount, to cover some, or all, of these origination costs.

Most sellers reduce the carrying value of their loans-for-sale to market when market value is less than cost. Generally, such valuation computations are made in the aggregate, either in total or by type of loan, so that any potential losses are reduced by potential gains before a write-down is recorded. However, some companies do calculate the write-down on an individual-loan basis without offsetting gains against losses.

Computation of Market

Market value of mortgage loans and mortgage-backed securities should be computed by type of loan, with separate computations made for residential and commercial loans. When calculating the lower of cost or market, either the aggregate or individual-loan basis may be used. (The method used should be disclosed in the financial statements.) The computation of market is a two-tiered calculation: first, those loans held subject to existing commitments (committed loans); and second, those loans held on a speculative basis (uncommitted loans).

Committed Loans and GNMA Securities

Market value for loans and mortgage securities covered by investor commitments should be computed based upon commitment prices. These loans must meet the specific terms of the commitments. Loans that do not meet the requirements of the commitments, or for which there exists a reasonable doubt as to acceptance, should be considered uncommitted loans for the calculation of market value.

Uncommitted Loans

Computations of market value for uncommitted loans should be based on the market within which the seller operates and should reflect the following considerations:

1. To the extent that commitments obtained after, or shortly before, balance-sheet date represent market conditions existing at year-end, market-value computations should be based on these commitment prices
2. General market prices and yields sought by the seller's normal market outlets for particular types of loans
3. Quoted GNMA security prices, or other public market quotations for long-term FHA/VA loan rates
4. FNMA currect market prices for eligible government and conventional loans.

Uncommitted Mortgage-Backed Securities

The seller may hold mortgage securities for trading purposes. If the trust holding the seller's loans collateralizing the securities may be readily terminated and the loans sold directly, the securities may be valued at either the current mortgage-security price or the current whole-loan price, depending upon the seller's sales intent. Other securities should be valued at the lower of cost or market.

Costs Associated with Bulk Purchases

Sellers sometimes acquire large blocks of existing mortgage loans. Some capitalize certain costs associated with these purchases as costs of future servicing income and amortize them over the estimated life of the loans. The costs to be capitalized should be excluded from the cost of the mortgages for the purpose of computing the lower of cost or market.

Valuation Dates and Subsequent Changes in Market Conditions

Valuation Dates

Valuations are made at the close of all stockholder reporting periods, including those for interim financial statements. Temporary market declines may not be provided for in interim financial statements if market conditions have actually improved subsequent to the interim reporting period. Otherwise, material market changes subsequent to the valuation date should be considered subsequent-period events and included in the notes to financial statements.

Subsequent Recoveries of Previous Write-Downs

As previously noted, the lower of cost or market valuation procedure for sellers combines elements of receivable and inventory valuation. Traditionally, inventory-valuation concepts require that items which have been written down below cost be considered cost for subsequent accounting purposes. Conversely, receivable valuation reserves are determined for each reporting period independently, so that receivables are carried at current realizable value. It is acceptable for a seller to calculate the lower of cost or market value at each valuation date independent of any previous calculation. Thus, mortgage loans written down in one accounting period (other than those held for long-term investment) need not be carried at such reduced value in a later period, if their market value has partly or completely recovered. However, the carrying value of the portfolio, once written down, should not be written up to a value in excess of its original cost.

Bulk Purchases and Sales of Loans and Servicing Rights

Some sellers make bulk purchases of mortgages. The purpose of these bulk purchases is generally to put together a pool of mortgages for the issuance of a GNMA mortgage-backed security servicing-retained. Purchasers often enter into this type of transaction with full knowledge and expectation that the cost of the mortgages will exceed the selling price. However, they are willing to complete the transaction in order to obtain the future servicing income. These transactions have many attributes of the direct purchase of mortgage-servicing contracts.

It is common practice to capitalize the direct costs associated with the purchase of mortgage-servicing contracts and to capitalize the amount of the purchase price allocated to the serviced mortgage portfolio. These costs are amortized over the average life of the loans included in the pool of loans.

Because of the similarities to an outright purchase of servicing contracts, GAAP provides for the capitalization of the excess of cost over selling price in connection with the bulk purchase and sale of mortgages servicing-retained by the seller, subject to the following conditions and limitations:

At the time the transaction is initiated, a definitive plan should exist. This plan should include the estimated excess of cost over selling price with reasonable support for such estimate.

The commitment from the investor or underwriter should be received in close proximity (generally 30 days before or after) to the date the mortgages are purchased.

The amounts deferred should not exceed the present value of the net amounts of future servicing revenue, after deducting expected servicing costs.

Obviously, the types of bulk purchase and sale transactions described above must be *at arm's length* to warrant deferral of the excess of cost over sales price. For example, if two parties both buy and sell mortgages to each other, the transactions may be deemed to be related and, therefore, not at arm's length.

Determination of the amounts which can be deferred is difficult and subject to judgement. The estimates of future revenue should include probable ancillary income such as late charges, insurance commissions, and related fees. The cost to service should also reflect estimates of increases in future costs resulting from inflation, etc. The cost to service should be established on a full-absorption basis (direct costs plus indirect costs and allocations of overhead) for each seller before arriving at any conclusions as to the amount of costs that may be deferred and amortized. Since each seller has a separate and distinct cost structure, no specific rules can be set.

GAAP provides that, inasmuch as servicing revenue is earned and reflected in income on an accelerated basis (based on unpaid principal of the mortgages), amortization of the deferred costs should be made at a rate directly related to net servicing income. The deferred costs should be amortized over the remaining period of net servicing income.

GNMA Mortgage-Backed Securities (MBSs)

Operating Procedures

An issuer assembles a group of mortgages sufficient to collateralize the amount of the mortgage-backed securities (MBSs) to be issued and places the mortgage documents in trust with a custodian, usually a commercial bank. Thereafter, all collections, including prepayments, of principal and interest relating to these mortgages are deposited in a custodial account. Disbursements are made from this account to security holders for principal and interest; GNMA for a guarantee fee (currently 0.06 percent of principal balance); and the issuer for the servicing fee (currently 0.44 percent of the principal balance).

Issuers of GNMA MBSs currently have two options for payment to investors of collections for principal and interest:

	Example
Description	*Dates*
OPTION I—45 Day Procedure (Internal Reserve Method):	
Date of issue of GNMA MBS	February 1
Date of first payment to security holder	March 15
Date of mortage balances on which amount of first payment to security holder is calculated	January 1

Issuer starts collecting payments from mortgagors on February 1 for pass-through to security holder on March 15, or 45 days later.

	Example
Description	*Dates*

OPTION II—15 Day Procedure (Concurrent Date Method):

Date of issue of GNMA MBS	February 1
Date of first payment to security holder	March 15
Date of mortgage balances on which amount of first payment to security holder is calculated	February 1

Issuer starts collecting payments from mortgagors on March 1 for passthrough to security holder on March 15, or 15 days later.

Under Option I, the issuer is required to deposit in the custodial account an amount equal to the interest collected on all mortgages in the pool for the month prior to pooling. Under Option II, the issuer is not required to deposit in the custodial account the one month's interest. Under either option, issuers must pass through to security holders a stated amount each month. If this amount is not collected, the issuer must advance corporate funds to make up the difference.

Under the 45-day procedure, the issuer has from February 1 to March 15 to collect payments from mortgagors. During this time, the issuer collects a full month's principal and interest from mortgagors, plus a part of another month's principal and interest. The total can be used to pay the specified amount due security holders on March 15. This usually eliminates the issuer's need for advancing corporate funds.

Under the 15-day procedure, payment to the security holder must be made by March 15. Consequently, the issuer has only 15 days to collect the funds due security holders. This may not be enough time to collect all payments, and, therefore, advances from corporate funds are usually necessary. Any advances are repaid daily with collections received from mortgagors after the 15th of the month.

Initial Deposit of Interest in Custodial Account

The nature and treatment of the amount initially deposited in the custodial account under Option I have been the subject of considerable discussion. One proposal is that the full amount of this interest be included in the cost of the mortgages pooled for purposes of computation of the gain or loss on the sale to the security holders. This approach seems inappropriate because of the following:

The primary reason an issuer is dealing in GNMA MBSs is to expand his servicing portfolio.

The GNMA MBS servicing fee is in excess of the typical fee received from other investors.

The normal costs of acquiring these mortgages are expensed; therefore, this additional element of cost to obtain servicing should more properly be matched against the higher future income.

GAAP provides that the initial lost interest should be treated as cost incurred to secure mortgage servicing revenue, and that such a cost should be deferred and amortized over the average life of the related mortgages. This one month's interest deposit under the internal reserve method is an out-of-pocket disbursement, and the full amount will not be recovered.

Because of the special requirements and risks imposed upon the issuer by the program, specific factors must be considered in determining the appropriateness of the amount deferred in each situation. These factors are: normal servicing rate currently in effect, expected servicing costs, expected foreclosure costs and losses, and expected need to advance funds to the pool in excess of the required one month's interest referred to above.

The issuer of GNMA MBSs must bear the costs and losses of foreclosure. Because of government insurance and guarantees, such losses should be limited. In addition, the issuer must bear the interest cost of funds advanced to the custodian to meet payments due holders of the securities on which scheduled installment collections have not been received. Excess collections of principal received from the mortgagors are distributed to the security holders. In order to defer any portion of the initial deposit required in connection with Internal Reserve GNMA MBS pools, it must be clearly demonstrated that there is a reasonable basis for an assumption that the premium-servicing income will provide sufficient revenue to cover the cost of foreclosures, foreclosure losses, any interest on additional funds that may have to be advanced to the pool, and the absorption of the amortization of the amount deferred. Recent experience indicates that industry-wide normal servicing income amounts to 37½ basis points, with the result that GNMA MBS premium-servicing income of 6½ basis points is calculated as follows:

Mortgages yield ½ of 1% in excess of yield on securities issued		50	basis points
Less: GNMA insurance	6		
Normal servicing fee	37½	43½	basis points
Premium-servicing income		6½	basis points

If premium-servicing income does not cover interest on additional funds expected to be advanced to the pool and expected costs of foreclosures and foreclosure losses, that portion of the deferred amount which is not recoverable from the premium-servicing income should be charged to operations by including the unrecoverable amount in the computation of gain or loss on the sale of the GNMA MBS.

If the servicing of the mortgages subsequent to pooling is performed by someone other than the issuer of the security, in order to determine the appropriateness of an amount to be deferred by the issuer, the costs of foreclosure, foreclosure losses, and interest on additional funds expected to be advanced must be estimated in order to demonstrate that the differential between the fee paid to the servicer and the fee received by the issuer of the GNMA MBS is sufficient to cover the amortization of the deferred amount. Obviously, if no portion of the servicing fee is to be received by the issuer, no amount can be deferred.

Accounting for Futures Contracts

Initial cash margin payments required by commodity brokers and/or the futures exchange should be recognized as assets at the inception of futures contracts. Changes in the market value of outstanding futures contracts should be recognized as gain or loss in the period of the change, unless the contracts qualify as a hedge for a present exposure or the contracts relate to a qualifying anticipated transaction. To qualify in either case, futures contracts should be matched with identifiable assets, liabilities, firm commitments, or anticipated transactions.

To the extent futures contracts are a hedge, changes in market value are reported as adjustments of the carrying amount of the hedged item. The cumulative change in the market value of a contract that relates to a qualifying anticipated transaction generally is included in the measurement of that transaction when it occurs.

Allowances for Loan Losses

Individual Evaluation Method

The allowance for loan losses should be based on an individual evaluation of the recoverability of individual loans and properties. Allowance determination should take into consideration the facts and circumstances in existence at the time of the evaluation and reasonable estimates of future economic conditions. The allowance should not be determined on the basis of percentages of loan balances, income, or other similar general bases.

Because of the many factors which can effect recoverability, the estimated loss on an individual loan or property may not be the same as the ultimate loss actually sustained. While the individual evaluation method, like all estimation methods, inherently lacks precision, it best achieves the ultimate objective of determining an allowance for losses, which is, in the aggregate, reasonable in the context of the financial statements taken as a whole.

Timing of Evaluations

Management should reevaluate the allowance for loan losses on a continuing basis. Adjustments should be made on the basis of a reevaluation of the loans for all reporting periods, including those for interim financial statements.

Mortgage Origination Costs

The typical seller originates first-mortgage loans on new and used homes through real estate brokers, agents, builders, and developers, and by direct contact with home buyers. Currently 1 percent of the principal amount of the loan is charged as an origination fee for loans guaranteed or insured by agencies of the U.S. government. Origination fees for conventional residential loans vary from 1 percent upward.

GAAP provides that the deferral of origination costs is clearly not preferable to the flow-through of such costs to current operations. Accordingly, sellers should not change to the deferral method of accounting for the types of costs described below, except in the very narrow circumstances involving bulk purchases and sales of mortgage loans. Similarly, sellers incurring the following costs for the first time should not adopt the deferral method of accounting for these costs:

Excess of in-house mortgage-loan origination costs over loan origination fee income.

Excess of interest paid over interest received during the period mortgages are held, pending sale to investors.

Excess of purchase price over sales price of mortgages purchased and subsequently sold

Under present accounting and tax practices, all income and costs in connection with origination of new mortgages are reflected in current operations, including interest income and interest expense during the warehousing period and gains and losses from sales of mortgages.

A change to the deferral method for origination costs is deemed a change in accounting method under APB Opinion No. 20, which requires that the new method be preferable to the old method. However, the flow-through method is usually preferable, for the following reasons:

The prevailing negative opinion of the profession towards deferral of these types of costs.

The long-standing industry practice followed by sellers of expensing origination costs as incurred.

The practice followed by other industries with similar activities.

Excess of Purchase Price over Sales Price of Mortgages Purchased and Sold

Many sellers typically obtain, by payment of a fee, investors' commitments to purchase mortgages, and then originate sufficient mortgages to fill the commitments. Other sellers originate mortgages without a commitment and hold them until an investor can be located. In both circumstances, any spread between purchase and sales price of the mortgage loans is traditionally reflected in current operations. GAAP provides that the present accounting practice for these transactions is appropriate and should not be changed, even though economic conditions may cause losses on sales during certain periods. These losses cannot be deferred.

Revenues

The primary sources of income for traditional mortgage bankers are loan-administration fees, origination fees, and interest income. Additionally, income is received from commitment fee, gains from the sales of loans, real estate commissions, insurance commissions and advisory fees.

Loan-Administration Fees

Loan-servicing fees come from the interest portion of the monthly payment collected from mortgagors. Each investor has a specific fee for servicing a particular loan. This fee is deducted from interest collected to determine the net remittance of interest to the investor. Additional servicing income is also obtained from borrowers in the form of late-charge penalties and fees for special services rendered.

Occasionally, a mortgage banker sells, or commits to sell, loans at a servicing fee that is significantly different from rates currently prevalent in the industry. Assuming the fee is lower, the loans are generally sold at prices higher than otherwise available. The result is the recognition of increased income at the time of sale, offset by reduced servicing income to be recognized in future periods. In other cases, a seller may act as a broker and sell loans servicing-released (no servicing income to be collected, nor is the seller to perform any servicing functions) at prices higher than otherwise available. This results in the recognition of increased income (or reduced loss) at the time of sale.

When loans are sold servicing-released, no adjustment of the sales price should be made. However, if loans are sold at a servicing-fee rate that is significantly different (higher or lower) from rates currently prevalent in the industry, an adjustment to the sales price is required whenever the impact on operating results is significant. Such adjustments result in deferred credits or debits against servicing-fee income over future years. Any such adjustment should be made as of the date the sale of the loans is recorded and any resulting gain or loss is recognized. In addition, if normal servicing fees are expected to be less than estimated servicing costs over the estimated life of the mortgage loans, the expected loss on servicing the loans should be accrued at the sale date.

Loan-Origination Fees

Fees representing reimbursement of the seller's costs of processing mortgage-loan applications, reviewing legal title, and performing other loan-origination procedures, should be recognized as revenue when the loan is made. Any fees in excess of the amount considered to be a reimbursement of loan-origination costs shall be recognized as deferred income. Fees representing reimbursement for the costs of specific services performed by third parties with respect to originating a loan (such as appraisal fees, credit reports, etc.), should be recognized as revenue when the services have been performed.

Interest Income

Fees Relating to Loans Held for Sale

Commitment fees received for guaranteeing the funding of mortgage loans to borrowers, builders, or developers, and commitment fees paid to permanent investors to ensure the ultimate sale of the loans, should be recognized as revenue or expense when the loans are sold to permanent investors (or when it becomes evident that the commitment will not be used). Because residential-loan commitment fees ordinarily relate to blocks of loans, fees recognized as revenue or expense as the result of individual-loan transactions should be based on the ratio of the individual-loan amount to the total commitment amount.

Fees for arranging a commitment directly between a permanent investor and a borrower (loan-placement fees) should be recognized as revenue when all significant services have been performed. In addition, if a commitment is obtained from a permanent investor before or at the time a related commitment is made to a borrower, and if the commitment to the borrower requires a simultaneous assignment of the commitment to the investor, and a simultaneous transfer to the borrower of the amount received from the investor, the related fees also should be accounted for as loan-placement fees.

Fees Relating to Loans not Held for Sale

Fees for guaranteeing the funding of a mortgage loan to acquire or develop land or to construct residential or income-producing properties should be recognized as revenue over the combined commitment and loan periods, using the best estimate of these periods. The straight-line method should be used during the commitment period to recognize the fee revenue, and the interest method should be used during the loan period to recognize the remaining fee revenue. If the original estimate of the combined commitment and loan periods is revised significantly, the remaining commitment fee should be recognized as revenue over the revised period. Additional fees received as a result of changes in the period should be recognized as revenue over the revised period.

Standby-commitment and gap-commitment fees for issuing a commitment to fund a standby or gap loan should be recognized as revenue over the combined commitment and loan periods. The straight-line method should be used during the commitment period to recognize the fee revenue, and the interest method should be used during the loan period to recognize the remaining fee revenue. Any additional fees received when the loan is made shall be recognized as revenue over the loan period.

If a loan commitment expires without the loan having been made, or if a loan is repaid before the estimated repayment date, any related unrecognized fees should be recognized as revenue or expense at that time. The Financial Accounting Standards Board is currently studying the diversity of fee recognition as provided for under GAAP for mortgage bankers and other types of lenders. This study may result in some changes under GAAP for all lenders.

Recognition of Interest Income

Interest income should be recorded monthly. For mortgage loans held in warehouse, interest income is usually accrued as earned, based on the contract rates of the mortgages (as opposed to interest recovered in cash).

For interim loans, interest income should also be accrued monthly. Many construction-loan commitments include a provision for capitalization of monthly interest into the principal balance of the loan (an *interest reserve*). Interest reserves are sometimes exhausted before maturity because of unexpected rises in interest rates. When this occurs, the seller must either increase his commitment to provide for further capitalization of interest, or prevail upon the borrower to pay the monthly interest out-of-pocket.

Discontinuance of Recognition of Interest Income

Interest revenue is not recognized:

When the amount of any final loss can be determined with a high degree of precision (as upon final settlement).

When certain specified events occur (such as interest or principal is a certain number of days past due, cost overruns are at a certain percentage, foreclosure proceedings are being initiated, etc.).

When judgment—often involving an evaluation of total loan recoverability—indicates that any additional interest would not be realized.

Postponing the discontinuance of interest recognition until a loss can be determined with precision conflicts with both general practice and theory.

Table 1 • Sample Secondary-Market Seller and Subsidiaries
(consolidated balance sheets, December 31, 19XX and 19XX)

Assets	19XX	19XX
Cash	$ 412,918	$ 563,235
Marketable securities, at cost (market value $206,000 in 19XX and $410,000 in 19XX)	200,000	400,000
Receivables:		
Due from financial institutions— pledged	2,511,526	1,517,912
Notes and accounts	700,786	389,945
Interest	366,042	242,099
	$ 3,578,354	$ 2,149,956
Less allowance for doubtful receivables	100,000	70,000
Net receivables	$ 3,478,354	$ 2,079,956
Mortgage loans held for sale, at cost, less allowance for market losses of $350,000 in 19XX and $150,000 in 19XX— pledged	$13,102,472	$ 7,685,562
Construction and development loans, at cost, less allowances for losses of $250,000 at 19XX and $150,000 in 19XX— pledged	11,219,635	5,452,575
Real estate and property acquired by foreclosure, at cost, less allowance for losses of $550,000 in 19XX and $300,000 in 19XX and accumulated depreciation of $110,000 in 19XX and $108,000 in 19XX—pledged	2,924,336	1,678,176
Federal National Mortgage Association stock, at cost (market value $400,000 in 19XX and $425,000 in 19XX)	202,245	206,905
Furniture, equipment and leasehold improvements, at cost, less accumulated depreciation and amortization	185,264	104,627
Other assets:		
Purchase servicing, at cost, less accumulated amortization	103,605	208,376
Interest on Government National Mortgage Association mortgage-backed security pools, at cost, less accumulated amortization	121,750	92,250
Other	14,175	12,082
	$ 239,530	$ 312,708
	$31,964,754	$18,483,744

Liabilities and Stockholders' Equity	19XX	19XX
Liabilities:		
Notes payable:		
Banks—secured	$28,025,152	$16,040,696
Other—unsecured	500,000	100,000
	$28,525,152	$16,140,696
Accounts payable and accrued expenses	1,224,480	696,080
Unearned loan origination and commitment fees	668,923	465,541
Income taxes	193,455	99,231
	$30,612,010	$17,401,548
Stockholders' equity:		
Common stock of $1 par value. Authorized 1,000 shares; issued 800 shares	$ 800	$ 800
Additional paid-in capital	288,370	288,370
Retained earnings	1,063,574	793,026
Total stockholders' equity	$ 1,352,744	$ 1,082,196
Commitments		
	$31,964,754	$18,483,744

Table 2 • Sample Secondary-Market Seller and Subsidiaries (consolidated statements of earnings and retained earnings, years ended December 31, 19XX and 19XX)

	19XX	19XX
Revenues:		
Loan administration	$ 695,093	$ 664,564
Loan origination and brokerage:		
Gain on sale of mortgage loans, net*	582,342	431,030
Loan origination fees	730,490	689,420
	$1,312,832	$1,120,450
Interest, net of interest expense of $1,426,832 in 19XX and $948,250 in 19XX	$ 523,139	$ 251,961
Insurance commissions	174,405	177,640
Other	96,313	98,842
	$2,801,782	$2,313,457
Expenses:		
Personnel	$1,260,810	$1,064,210
Occupancy	126,000	105,400
Equipment rental and expense	98,063	83,286
Office supplies and expense	140,090	97,167
Travel and business promotion	117,675	85,600
Provision for losses on:		
Construction and development loans	100,000	75,000
Real estate and property acquired by foreclosure	250,000	100,000
Other	219,156	75,745
Total expenses	$2,311,794	$1,686,408
Earnings before income taxes	$ 489,988	$ 627,049
Income taxes	219,440	304,830
Net earnings	$ 270,548	$ 322,219
Retained earnings at beginning of year	793,026	470,807
Retained earnings at end of year	$1,063,574	$ 793,026
Earnings per common share†	$338.19	$402.77

*Provisions for market losses on mortgage loans held for sale should be included in this account for financial statement purposes.
†Not required for private company.

Not recognizing interest revenue is related to the question of whether principal and interest will be collected. As stated in FASB Statement No. 5, "Contingencies that might result in gains usually are not reflected in the accounts since to do so might be to recognize revenue prior to its realization," and ARB No. 43, "Profit is deemed to be realized ... unless the circumstances are such that collection of the sales price is not reasonably assured."

Some accountants believe that, even though the recognition of interest is discontinued, interest revenue should be "grossed up" with an offsetting charge to an expense account. They believe that this presentation will more clearly reflect the planned income from the portfolio, as well as provisions for possible losses from that plan. GAAP supports the view that it would not be appropriate to include such amounts in interest revenue in the financial statements, because such a presentation would contradict economic reality.

Table 3 • Sample Secondary-Market Seller and Subsidiaries (consolidated statements of changes in financial position, years ended December 31, 19XX and 19XX)

	19XX	19XX
Funds provided:		
Net earnings	$ 270,548	$ 322,219
Add items not requiring funds:		
Provision for losses on:		
Receivables	30,000	10,000
Mortgage loans held for sale	200,000	100,000
Construction and development loans	100,000	75,000
Real estate and property acquired by foreclosure	150,000	—
Depreciation and amortization of furniture, equipment		
and leasehold improvements	10,500	9,000
Other depreciation and amortization	132,000	135,000
Funds provided from operations	$ 893,048	$ 651,219
Increases in:		
Notes payable	$12,384,456	$4,771,168
Accounts payable and accrued expenses	528,400	63,028
Unearned loan origination and commitment fees	203,382	—
Income taxes	94,224	30,500
Decreases in:		
Cash	150,317	—
Marketable securities	200,000	—
Real estate and property acquired by foreclosure	—	628,316
Other, net	47,838	—
Total funds provided	$14,501,665	$6,144,231
Funds used:		
Increases in:		
Cash	$ —	$ 100,000
Receivables	1,428,398	1,000,615
Mortgage loans held for sale	5,616,910	2,917,005
Construction and development loans	5,867,060	1,999,985
Real estate and property acquired by foreclosure	1,498,160	—
Furniture, equipment and leasehold improvements	91,137	65,190
Other assets, net	—	35,009
Decrease in unearned loan origination and commitment		
fees	—	26,427
Total funds used	$14,501,665	$6,144,231

Financial Statement Presentation and Disclosure

The following presentation and disclosures are currently required by GAAP in the financial statements of sellers:

Disclosures

Sellers using either a classified or unclassified balance sheet should distinguish between mortgage loans and mortgage-backed securities held for sale, and mortgage loans and mortgage-backed securities held for long-term investment.

Table 4 • Sample Secondary-Market Seller and Subsidiaries (notes to consolidated financial statements, December 31, 19XX and 19XX)

(1) *Summary of Significant Accounting Policies*
   (a) *Principles of Consolidation*
        Note: (See Note B)
   (b) *Marketable Securities and Federal National Mortgage Association Stock*
        Note: (See Note B)
   (c) *Mortgage Loans Held for Sale*
        Mortgage loans held for sale are valued at the lower of cost or market as determined by outstanding commitments from investors or current investor yield requirements calculated on the aggregate loan basis.
   (d) *Construction and Development Loans*
        Construction and development loans are carried at disbursed amounts less an allowance for estimated losses. The Company originates and services these loans for its own investment or for sale to institutional investors. The Company was servicing approximately $22,600,000 in 19XX and $11,100,000 in 19XX, in construction and development loans in which institutional investors had purchased 50% participation. Only the Company's participations in these loans are carried in the accompanying consolidated financial statements.

        The accrual of interest income on construction and development loans is discontinued when, in management's opinion, it is not reasonable to expect the income to be realized.
   (e) *Real Estate and Property Acquired by Foreclosure*
        Real estate and property acquired by foreclosure is valued at the lower of cost or market.
   (f) *Federal National Mortgage Association (FNMA) Stock*
        Note: (See Note B)
   (g) *Revenue From Sale of Mortgage Loans*
        Gains or losses resulting from sales of mortgage loans are recognized at the date the loans are shipped to investors.
   (h) *Loan Administration Income*
        Loan administration income represents fees earned for servicing real estate mortgage loans owned by institutional investors, net of the amortization of interest advances on Government National Mortgage Association (GNMA) mortgage-backed security pools and the cost of purchased servicing. The fees are generally calculated on the outstanding principal balances of the loans serviced and are recorded as income when earned.
   (i) *Loan Fees*
        Loan fees are recognized as income as follows:

Type of Fee	Method
Land acquisition, construction, development, standby and gap-loan fees	Deferred and amortized to income over the combined commitment and loan period
Residential and commercial loan commitment fees	Upon completion of sale of loans to investors
Residential loan origination fees	When collected
Commercial loan placement fees	When the Company has no remaining significant obligation for performance
Other fees	When the services have been performed

Table 4 *(continued)*

(j) *Other Assets*

The cost of purchased servicing is amortized in proportion to the related estimated net servicing income over the estimated life of the mortgages.

In accordance with the regulations governing the administration of GNMA mortgage-backed security pools, the Company had made nonrefundable deposits in custodian accounts for certain pools in amounts equal to the first month's interest collected. Such deposits are amortized in proportion to the related estimated net servicing income over the estimated life of the mortgages.

(k) *Furniture, Equipment and Leasehold Improvements*
Note: (See Note B)

(l) *Income Taxes*
Note: (See Note B)

(2) *Marketable Securities*
Note: (See Note B)

(3) *Construction and Development Loans*
The principal amounts of construction and development loans on which the accrual of interest had been discontinued at December 31, 19XX and 19XX was $1,727,849 and $561,855, respectively.

(4) *Federal National Mortgage Association Stock*
As of December 31, 19XX and 19XX, the Company was required to be owner of record of 10,000 and 9,000 shares with aggregate costs of $190,000 and $180,000, respectively, of the common stock of FNMA in order to comply with the FNMA servicing agreement. As of these dates, the Company met the stock-holding requirements.

(5) *Purchased Servicing*
The following summarized the changes in this asset for the year 19XX and 19XX:

	19XX	**19XX**
Balance at beginning of year	$208,376	313,747
Amount capitalized during the year	—	—
Amount of amortization during the year	105,371	105,371
Balance at end of year	$103,605	$208,376

(6) *Notes Payable to Banks*
Amounts due from financial institutions, mortgage loans held for sale, construction and development loans and real estate and property acquired by foreclosure are pledged to secure notes payable to banks.

The Company maintains compensating balances for its bank lines. The compensating balance requirements, which at December 31, 19XX and 19XX approximated 20% of the lines in use, have been met as is customary in the mortgage banking industry, primarily by trust funds on deposit in special bank accounts for mortgage loans serviced for institutional investors. The terms of the bank lines call for interest rates (10% to 10 ½% at December 31, 19XX and 19XX) between ½% and 1% above the banks' prime rates.

(7) *Income Taxes*
Note: (See Note B)

(8) *Loan Administration*
The Company was servicing approximately 11,000 and 10,000 loans owned by institutional investors aggregating $165,000,000 and $140,000,000 at December 31, 19XX and 19XX, respectively. Related trust funds of approximately $2,400,000 and $2,000,000 at December 31, 19XX and 19XX, respectively, on deposit in

Table 4 (concluded)

special bank accounts are not included in the accompanying consolidated financial statements. The company carries blanket bond coverage of $750,000 and errors and omissions coverage in the amount of $2,500,000.

The Company has issued mortgage-backed securities guaranteed by GNMA under the provisions of the National Housing Act. At December 31, 19XX and 19XX, the principal amount of these securities outstanding was approximately $20,000,000 and $15,000,000, respectively, which also represents the approximate principal amount of the related mortgages that serve as collateral for the security and are being serviced under this program. In keeping with the economic substance of these transactions, the issuance of the mortgage-backed securities and simultaneous placement of the related mortgages in trust have been accounted for as a sale of the mortgages; accordingly, neither the mortgages receivable nor the securities payable appear on the consolidated balance sheets.

(9) *Commitments*

In the ordinary course of business, the Company had issued commitments to builders to purchase approximately $2,000,000 and $1,500,000 of mortgage loans at December 31, 19XX and 19XX, respectively, at amounts which approximate market prices at the time of closing. In addition, the Company had issued standby commitments for $350,000 and $275,000 and gap commitments for $800,000 and $500,000 as of December 31, 19XX and 19XX, respectively.

In addition the Company has purchased commitments from permanent investors to take future delivery of approximately $2,500,000 and $2,000,000 of the above mortgage loans at December 31, 19XX and 19XX, respectively, at amounts which approximate market prices at the time of closing.

Note: (See Note B)

Note B: These notes to consolidated financial statements include only those disclosures unique to secondary mortgage market sellers and do not include all disclosures necessary for a fair presentation in accordance with generally accepted accounting principles.

The method used in determining the lower of cost or market value of mortgage loans and mortgage-backed securities (i.e., aggregate or individual-loan basis) should be disclosed. The amount capitalized during the period in connection with acquiring the right to service mortgage loans, the method of amortizing the capitalized amount, and the amount of amortization for the period should also be disclosed.

Sample Financial Statements

The following material (see Tables 1–4) illustrates the format of financial statements of sellers. It is recognized that alternative formats exist for presentation in accordance with generally accepted accounting principles, and no attempt has been made to illustrate format or language for all situations.

— PART FIVE —

Investor
Considerations

— Chapter 23 ——————————————

Analyzing Warehousing Credits

Kurt Kettenmann
Vice President
Bankers Trust Company

Warehousing, asset-based lending, inventory financing, revolving credit—all are terms describing the subject matter of this chapter: extending short-term secured lines of credit to enable mortgage bankers to fund mortgage loans, and inventory them, until the loans are purchased by institutional investors. The commercial banks that extend this type of credit are known as *warehouse lenders*. Warehouse lenders are primarily concerned with the lending risks, the character and creditworthiness of the borrower, and the quality of the collateral.

This chapter views these concerns from the perspective of the warehouse lender. It covers choosing the customer, understanding the risks of warehouse lending, and monitoring those risks. It looks at the borrower and raises general credit questions about the lender-borrower relationship: track record, management, resources, financial performance, and compliance with loan agreements. It also analyzes the mortgage-banking customer as an operating entity, and suggests specific functional inquiries concerning loan origination, warehousing, inventory management, marketing loan administration, personnel development and training, and other business activities. It reviews necessary documentation and the types of secured lending available to mortgage bankers, and, finally, discusses the reports and audits required to manage the warehouse-lending relationship.

Choosing the Customer

Each warehouse lender should have a strategy for soliciting customers according to preestablished criteria. Normally, these criteria are those of geography, the size of the servicing portfolio, and compensating balances, management experience, and net worth.

Warehouse lenders may choose to stay in their own local area—maintaining close proximity to the customer, to lend only in certain states, or to lend on a national basis.

Lenders may have minimum loan and compensating-balance requirements, which determine the acceptable size for a warehousing relationship.

Given the thin capitalization of many mortgage bankers, many lenders do business with only those companies that have demonstrated performance over several years of interest-rate changes. They typically require a minimum number of years together for the management team.

Finally, many warehousers seek comfort in a minimum net-worth requirement, reasoning that when a mortgage banker obtains a warehouse loan, the warehouser has assumed the same interest-rate risk as has the mortgage banker. The only differential in risk for the warehouse lender is the tangible net worth, plus the present value of the servicing portfolio of the mortgage banker, which becomes the warehouse lender's margin before it, too, suffers a loss. As noted, capital is typically small in relation to debt for a mortgage banker. Therefore, total adjusted net worth as a percentage of debt becomes an important variable.

Warehouse Lending Risks

The primary risk to a warehouse lender is the same as that confronted by the mortgage banker: the interest-rate risk. (The interest-rate risk is discussed in Chapter 16, Inventory Philosophy, Reporting, and Control, and Chapter 17, Hedging Alternatives.) It is the risk that the sale of mortgage inventory will result in a loss. Inventory losses may be caused by failing to hedge, hedging with too many mandatory-delivery investor commitments, or hedging with nonviable commitments. Secondary areas of risk include: inadequate loan documentation, problem loans, and mortgage-bank cash flow problems.

Price Risk: Nonhedged Inventory

During 1980, market yields rose in a period of six weeks by 2¼ percent. Since each percent change in interest rates equals from 5 to 7 discount points, the loss incurred by unhedged mortgage inventory during this time period could have been almost 16 points. With a debt-to-equity ratio of 10:1 or more, the typical mortgage banker may not have been able to survive such an unhedged loss.

Price Risk: Overhedged Inventory

During 1981, mortgage yields declined more than 3½ percent in a period of six weeks, normally a profitable occurrence for mortgage bankers. An ostensibly conservative mortgage banker, who covered 100 percent of his pipeline (loans not yet closed) with mandatory-delivery commitments during this period, would have found himself obligated to deliver loans he did not have. Pipeline loans would have cancelled, because prospective borrowers could obtain cheaper mortgages elsewhere. Either buying loans for delivery, or offsetting his position with mortgage-backed security (MBS) dealers, could have resulted in a loss of over 20 points. Few businesses can withstand such losses in any volume.

Price Risk: Nonviable Investor Commitments

An investor commitment to purchase mortgages is only as good as the intent and financial ability to honor it. Drastic changes in interest rates call both attributes into question. The reputation and fiscal soundness of the investor issuing the commitment are therefore prime concerns to the warehouse lender. If the commitment amount is large relative to the investor's net worth or investable funds, or the investor is losing money, or interest rates have risen dramatically since the commitment was issued, the possibility of a renege exists. A *renege* occurs when the investor either refuses or cannot purchase loans delivered pursuant to a commitment. Obviously, a renege that occurs during increasing market yields can result in substantial inventory losses and is therefore a legitimate concern for the warehouse lender.

Secondary Risks

Inadequate loan documentation is probably the other risk most frequently confronted by warehouse lenders. While still a price risk, it is less, inasmuch as documentation problems usually occur on an exception, loan-by-loan basis and not on the wholesale basis experienced by investor commitments. Documentation problems can result in loans not being eligible for current commitments, being repurchased from filled commitments, becoming nonsaleable, requiring new documents, or requiring updated old documents. In virtually every case, additional time and cash, as well as marketing losses, result.

Problem loans occur because of inadequate documentation, delinquency or foreclosure, legal actions, and fraud. All of these occurrences involve workout situations and substantial periods of time.

Corporate cash flow problems can result from inventory price losses, losses from inadequate documentation, problem loans, or other operating demands or losses. Other operating demands or losses intrude on the warehouse lender when there is a sudden lack of working capital to continue the business, as in margin calls on futures contracts or advances on GNMA pools.

Monitoring Inventory Risks

The best way to identify mortgage inventory risks is to monitor net exposure, as defined in Chapter 16, Inventory Philosophy, Reporting, and Control. The net exposure measurement alerts warehouse lenders to problems caused by failure to hedge (a net exposure less than zero implies that more investor commitments are needed, for example).

The anatomy of the net exposure criterion, as well as the nature of the net exposure itself, is important insofar as mandatory delivery and optional delivery commitments are segregated. The amount of mandatory delivery commitments should generally not exceed the amount of closed warehouse loans, plus the amount of pipeline loans one can confidently expect to close within the 30 days immediately following. The warehouse lender should track the mortgage banker's estimates of loans closing in the next 30 days on a continuing basis, so that it has some feel for the amount of mandatory commitments the mortgage banker purchases. If the net exposure measurement indicates more commitments than loans, and those commitments are mandatory, the warehouse lender may safely assume that potential problems exist.

Documentation, problem loan, and cash flow problems are best highlighted by adequate reporting, good communications, and analysis of the general characteristics and specific performance of the borrower.

Analyzing the Risks

There is no standard format with which to analyze the risks posed for the warehouse lender. There are, however, certain general questions that should be asked about the borrower and certain specific inquiries that should be directed to the functional areas of a mortgage banker.

Character, Credit, and Capacity

The most important dictum in warehouse lending is Know Your Customer. To develop this knowledge, the warehouse lender needs to know the company's history, management, available resources, and compliance with loan agreements. Answers to the following questions enable the warehouse lender to appraise the borrowing relationship:
1. History of the company:
   Number of years in business.
   Type of ownership: corporate, partnership, etc.
   Product lines.
   Management philosophy.
   Recent business activities and acquisitions.
   Credit rating of agencies, if applicable.
2. Management:
   Key individuals known to bank.
   Age, tenure and compensation.
   Depth and competence of middle management.
   Industry reputation.
   Competent marketing personnel.
   Years together as a management team.
3. Available resources:
   Net worth and working capital.
   Lines of credit and borrowing capacity.
   Cash flow from servicing portfolio.

Compensating balances.
Equity or private-placement debt potential.
4. Compliance with loan agreements:
Warehousing and security agreements.
Servicing agreements.
Covenants and restrictions.

Financial Analysis

Adequate financial analysis requires three years of audited financial statements from an acceptable accounting firm plus subsequent interim reports. These data should reveal any capital deficiencies, questions to be answered about specific assets and liabilities, trends in income and expenses, and improvements needed in financial reporting procedures and practices.

Capital

The capital for a mortgage banker consists of both its book net worth and the off-balance-sheet value of its mortgage servicing portfolio. Book net worth minus unacceptable assets, such as prepaid commitment fees, loans due from officers, mortgage inventory valued over market, etc., determines tangible net worth.

Tangible net worth is the factor used by most banks to determine *leverage ratios* (the total dollar amount of credit lines to be extended to the mortgage banker as a multiple of adjusted or tangible net worth). The primary leverage factors analyzed are the following:

1. Total available lines, plus other liabilities:tangible net worth
2. Total available lines, plus other liabilities:tangible net worth plus net present value of servicing portfolio

Acceptable ratios range from 10:1 to 25:1 for the former, and from 10:1 to 15:1 for the latter, depending on the standards of the warehouse lender and the mortgage-banker's product line and approach to secondary-market risk. A 25:1 ratio (number 1), for a customer engaged exclusively in the production of FHA/VA loans, may be justified, whereas a ratio of 2:1 or 3:1, for a customer engaged in land development, may be warranted. A nonspeculative approach to marketing also favors a higher ratio than that obtainable for more speculative approaches.

In Chapter 14, Purchase and Sale of Servicing Portfolios, real value is represented by the servicing portfolios of the mortgage banker. Typically, prices paid for servicing portfolios range from 1 to 2 percent of the outstanding principal balance. Thus, a $100 million servicing portfolio represents from $1 to $2 million (before tax). Because the servicing portfolio is an important factor in appraising the capital base of a mortgage banker, the warehouse lender should insert a no-sale covenant into the warehousing agreement.

Financial Statements

Adequate analysis of a mortgage banker's financial statements requires the following:

Assets

Evaluate receivables and investments.
  Age receivables.
  Are loans valued at cost or market or other?
  Warehouse loans covered by commitments?
  Strategy for pipeline coverage? marketing philosophy?
Determine asset turnover.
Analyze repurchase agreements.
Analyze investor commitments.
  Relative size of investors?
  Relative size of MBS dealers?

Liabilities

Analyze all credit lines and debt obligations.
  Commitment terms?
  Usage and payback.
Analyze bank services: lockbox, custodian, etc.

Income and Expenses

Overhead: stable, growing, or declining?
Income: stable, growing or declining?
Warehousing spread: gain or loss?
Marketing: gain or loss? why?
Cash flow analysis.
  Debt coverage?
  GNMA MBS advances?
  Commitment fees?
  Purchase of servicing?
  Margin?

Net cost of production? trend?
Servicing cost per loan? trend?

Reporting Procedures and Practices

Identify key management information reports.
Review accounting and financial reporting system.
Review CPA's management letter.
Determine compliance with agency requirements.
Review adequacy of internal audit procedures.

Operational Analysis

If the first dictum of warehouse lending is Know Your Customer, the second is Be Sure You Know. A personal acquaintance with management and a detailed knowledge of the customer's operations are necessary to monitor operating performance and to permit recognition of early warning signals. The following functional areas should be investigated by the warehouse lender:

Loan Origination. Determine nature of policies, practices, and procedures relating to the loan origination, documentation, and the pricing operation.

1. Review any existing procedural manuals or key policy correspondence or memoranda
2. Determine by whom and how loan prices are established for origination purposes: are they controlled centrally, regionally, or locally, through head office, regions, or local branches?
3. Identify and review the primary sources of loans: spot-market brokers, commission sales representatives, builder programs, and others.
4. Review the procedure for monitoring and controlling loans in pipeline, from application through closing.
5. Determine principal type of loans originated and closed.
6. Review loan-closing practices to determine if loans are: (1) closed through title company, attorneys, or other closing agents; (2) funded through drafts, or other payment methods.
7. Determine how, when, and for what period prices are quoted.
8. Review method for compensating loan-production staff: are commissions, salaries, or other compensation methods used.
9. Review composition of loan production expenses to determine if corporate overhead is included or excluded, highlight any unusual items.
10. Review composition of loan-production income.
11. Review loan-underwriting practices to determine the existence and the

source of credit criteria: is it established by investor commitment, government agencies, branch management, or by another method.

12. Review pipeline volume, cancellation rate, and anticipated funding practices.
13. Determine loan-origination market area: regional, local, or national.

Warehousing and Inventory Control. Review and evaluate warehousing and inventory control procedures and practices for loans held for sale.

1. Determine if investor commitments are obtained in advance of loan closings and if loans in inventory are matched to specific commitments prior to shipment to investors.
2. Assess nature and extent of information maintained on closed loans.
3. Determine if loans are controlled manually or through computer tracking systems.
4. Determine and review method of warehousing loans with funding institutions.
5. Review inventory mix, yield, and age.
6. Assess marketability of loan inventory.
7. Determine policies and procedures for handling under-market loans.
8. Review delinquency position and delinquency-management practices.
9. Review and evaluate loan-shipping practices and determine how investors make payment for acquired loans.

Marketing and Inventory Management. Determine procedures and practices for marketing loan inventory and managing inventory exposure.

1. Determine method used to obtain investor purchase commitments.
2. Review nature and extent of investor commitments.
3. Review practices for determining, monitoring, and managing inventory exposure.
4. Identify the primary manager involved in marketing the company's position.
5. Determine the extent of senior management's review of marketing activities, strategy, and commitment position.
6. Review investor and dealer profiles.
7. Review the experience, training, and development of key marketing personnel.
8. Determine the level of authority of key marketing personnel.
9. Review the company's trading position to determine if trading is done to protect its commitment position or to build profits.

Loan Administration Review and evaluate the company's loan-administration operation and servicing portfolio.

1. Determine the magnitude of the servicing portfolio and assess its growth over the past three years by volume and number of loans.
2. Reconcile the change in portfolio: additions versus deletions and repayments.
3. Determine the portfolio mix by loan type, servicing-fee rate, and geography.
4. Evaluate the composition of servicing revenues and expenses.
5. Determine the average cost of servicing per loan, and assess the profitability of the portfolio.
6. Review the investor servicing profile.
7. Identify the servicing processing method: equipment used internally or through outside agency or institution.
8. Review the loan payment practices to determine if payments are made through the use of coupon cards and lockboxes.
9. Review the number and location of servicing offices and determine the number of employees involved.
10. Determine the nature, scope, and quality of delinquency control and management.
11. Review the foreclosure policies and practices.
12. Assess the quality of the servicing portfolio.

Personnel Development and Training. Conduct a review of personnel development and training practices:

1. Identify and interview key operating managers and determine the nature and extent of their prior business experience and special qualifications for current responsibilities.
2. Evaluate the extent of staff development, training and rotation, mobility and turnover.

Other Business Activities. Determine nature and extent of other business activities and assess their impact on traditional mortgage-banking operations:

1. Identify and interview the key managers responsible for other business activities.
2. Assess the extent of senior management's involvement in other business activities.
3. Review and comment on the operating procedures and controls of other significant business entities.

Compliance. Determine the extent of company's compliance with the terms, conditions, and spirit of relevant loan agreements.

Documentation

The lender's attorney usually confirms that the clearances necessary to do business in various states have been obtained. A uniform commercial code (UCC) search should be made to ascertain if there are any encumbrances of the borrower's assets. A bank may file a U.C.C.–1 financial statement, covering all of the borrower's right, title, and interest in and to all collateral documents to be pledged pursuant to the terms of the warehousing agreement, and all of the borrower's books and records relating thereto.

Warehousing Agreement

The warehousing agreement sets forth the terms and conditions of the borrowings, in addition to the basic procedures for advances and repayments. The security agreement establishes the bank's position as a secured lender, as well as its secured interest in the collateral, and defines the lender's rights and remedies in the event of default.

While these agreements vary in size from institution to institution, a clear understanding of the terms contained in the warehousing agreement facilitates the relationship between the bank and the mortgage banker. The agreement should cover in detail:

Parties to the transaction.

Definition of terms.

Interest rate.

Maximum line of credit.

States in which properties may be located.

Collateral acceptable for pledge.

Basis for interest on advances.

Procedure for advances.

Commitment coverage requirements.

Opinions required from borrower's counsel, acceptable to the bank, that the borrower is a valid entity in its present form (corporation, partnership, etc.), and that no actions exist against borrower before any court or administrative agency which might result in any material, adverse change in the borrower's condition.

Certified resolutions of the board of directors authorizing delivery and execution of the warehousing agreement and note.

Collections on pledged mortgages.

Status reports.

Incidents requiring redemption from pledge.

Events of default.

Covenants, representations, and warranties covering: standing within states and with agencies, and quality of collateral to be pledged. Compliance with the Real Estate Settlement Procedures Act and Equal Credit Opportunity Act, Federal Truth-in-Lending Act, Regulation Z, etc.

Termination date.

Termination by either party (with or without cause).

Renewal or extension.

In addition, the warehousing agreement usually incorporates in it, or has as part of the agreement, a separate schedule which spells out the collateral documents required for an advance to be made. Prior to the initial advance, the administration officer of the bank should contact or visit the appropriate personnel of the borrower to review the entire operational procedure from the submission of a document package to the final repayment.

Collateral

Although the warehousing agreement spells out a complete package acceptable to the permanent investor, a bank usually advances based upon a minimum collateral package:

1. Original mortgage note (or bond).
2. Certified copy of mortgage (or deed of trust).
3. Assignment in blank (in recordable form).
4. Settlement statement as required under RESPA.

The settlement statement provides the information on the price (or cost) at which the loan was closed. This is necessary if the cost is one of the factors in determining the amount to be advanced.

The remaining pertinent documents may accompany this package, or they may be sent along with the transmittal letter and shipping instructions at a later date to be incorporated with the initial documents and shipped to the investor.

The necessary signature cards and corporate resolutions must be obtained to open the bank accounts necessary to manage the relationship in an efficient manner. Detailed instructions are outlined giving time limits for the receipt of document packages for funds to be advanced or for repayments for funds to be credited or transferred on the same day.

The high velocity of collateral turnover in today's marketplace puts a premium on a cooperative working relationship between the borrower and the bank.

Types of Secured Lending

The primary types of secured short-term lending to mortgage bankers are: (1) direct warehousing, (2) warehouse participations, and (3) warehouse pooling. Secondary types of secured lending, usually involving back-up or standby lines or credit, are documented discount notes (DDNs), repurchase agreements (repos), and commercial paper. Finally, in any warehousing relationship, there are special customer needs that may be handled under a warehousing agreement or a separate loan agreement. These special needs are for uncommitted loans, loans in foreclosure, and real estate-owned (REO), special loan types, and specific working capital needs.

Direct Warehousing

As its name implies, *direct warehousing* is the extension of secured credit by a specific warehouse lender to a specific mortgage banker. Credit is extended on a loan-by-loan basis as each loan is funded, either by a check from the warehouse lender, or by a draft drawn on the warehouse lender and charged to the preapproved mortgage banker's warehouse line or credit. In each case, predetermined mortgage-loan documentation becomes the collateral for the credit extension.

When a package of mortgage loans is accumulated in warehouse for delivery to an investor commitment, the mortgage banker furnishes delivery instructions to the warehouse lender, together with any additional documentation required by the investor. The warehouse lender then assembles the complete package and ships it to the investor under a trust receipt. The investor normally makes payment directly to the warehouse bank. The bank in turn reduces the outstanding loan balance and credits any excess funds to the account of the borrower. The warehouse line is then available to repeat the process.

Participations

When the mortgage banker has reached the legal or policy lending limit of the warehouse lender, the direct warehousing bank (the lead bank) usually seeks other lenders to participate in the warehouse credit.

The participating banks perform their normal credit check of the mortgage banker before entering into a participation agreement with the lead bank. Participants also satisfy themselves that the lead bank is handling the collateral properly and monitoring the customer satisfactorily. Participants deal directly with the lead bank and not with the mortgage banker. Normally, the lead bank handles all collateral and disburses the mortgage banker's escrow funds among participants or substitutes its own balances for distribution to participants. The lead bank makes the necessary monthly interest payments to the participating lenders. Usually, the lead bank retains an override to compensate for the additional paperwork it performs for the participants.

Participants are attractive to many lenders (as high-quality credits available for investment without the need for the large staff normally required for direct warehousing).

Pooling

Pooling is a variation of the participation concept in that the mortgage banker negotiates individually with each lending bank on pricing. However, it deals with only a single bank (agent bank) for the collateral. The agent bank is agreed upon among all lenders in the pool. Each lending bank has a pro rata interest in the entire collateral pool. Mutual agreement is required among the warehousing banks on the method used for advances and any mark-to-the-market requirements.

Pooling avoids the danger (present in a participation arrangement) of having all one's eggs in one basket. If a single bank were to change its policy or decide it no longer wished to lend to the mortgage banker, the mortgage banker's direct relationship with several banks would permit filling the void directly or obtaining assistance to bring in a substitute bank.

The advantages to the warehouse lenders are significant. All of the borrower's collateral is housed in one place for simplicity of control and audit. All of the borrower's commitments can be related to this single pool of collateral for pricing purposes. This minimizes the historical control problems caused by double warehousing and the use of favorable commitments with more than one bank.

Standby Letters of Credit and Backup Commitments

Occasionally, when the mortgage banker desires either to obtain cheaper financing or to relieve the amount of his warehouse line, the mortgage banker issues documented discount notes or repurchase agreements. In the past, if it were large enough, the mortgage banker issued commercial paper. In each instance, a warehouse lender has to provide either overall lines or standby letters of credit (at least equal to the securities issued) to assure full protection to investors who purchase repos or commercial paper.

Documented Discount Notes

Documented-discount-note (DDN) financing consists of the promissory notes of the mortgage banker, which are accompanied by an irrevocable letter of credit from a commercial bank. The notes are sold in the commercial-paper market by either the commercial bank or a broker. The purpose of DDNs is to permit the mortgage banker to use the underlying credit of the bank that issues the letter of credit in order to obtain cheaper financing.

With DDN financing, the mortgage banker enters into an agreement with a commercial bank, under which the bank permits optional direct borrowings similar to a conventional warehousing line, or agrees to issue letters of credit to accompany the DDNs. DDNs are backed by the pledge of a pool of mortgages, and the total amount of credit is determined by a formula applied to the collateral. The collateral generally consists of VA and FHA mortgages for which there are purchase commitments, either in the form of whole mortgages or GNMA securities. The collateral may be held by either the bank or a custodian. Ordinarily, borrowings are not anticipated, but the option is with the mortgage banker. If it is cheaper to use the warehouse line at a given time, the mortgage banker will probably exercise this option.

The advantages of DDNs to the mortgage banker are lower costs, fixed terms for fixed periods of time, and the freeing of a portion of the compensating balances to support other activities. From the bank's point of view, DDNs can fund the mortgage banker's warehousing needs during tight periods, and there is fee income for issuing the letter of credit (or for the marketing of the notes if the bank handles this aspect), in addition to the normal balance arrangements for the back-up lines.

Repurchase Agreements (Repos)

When a mortgage banker owns a GNMA MBS, he can enter into a repo agreement with a securities dealer. A *repo* is an agreement in which the dealer agrees to purchase the MBS for a specific time period and price, and the repo issuer agrees to repurchase the MBS at the end of the agreed-upon period. Repos can be arranged for time periods ranging from days to months. To the mortgage banker, repos usually represent lower financing costs, ready availability, and either no or little required compensating balances.

To the warehouse lender, this financing alternative presents only two problem areas: (1) if the market deteriorates, the repo dealer may make margin calls on the repo issues, and the mortgage banker may have difficulty in obtaining enough cash; and (2) if repos are used by mortgage bankers to finance uncommitted inventory when market prices are falling, the resultant losses could be disastrous.

Commercial Paper

Commercial paper is an unsecured promissory note issued at a discount from face value with a stated short-term maturity. Technically, mortgage bankers do not issue unsecured commercial paper. They issue collateral trust notes (CTNs). In CTN programs, an indenture is established, whereby the trust department of an independent bank acts as trustee and holds the mortgage loans that serve as collateral. The total amount of CTNs to be issued is backed by lines of credit from commercial banks.

Although popular in the 1970s, today there is only one known CTN program in place, and the CTN concept has been effectively replaced by DDN programs.

Other Customer Needs

The short-term financing needs of most mortgage bankers encompass more than the bread-and-butter warehouse lending secured by FHA/VA mortgages and covered by commitments from FNMA or major GNMA MBS dealers. These other, nonstandard needs, include the following:

Uncommitted lines. This credit facility is designed for warehouse loans that are not covered by investor commitments. Because such an inventory position is speculative, the amount of credit should be limited to the borrower's net worth and creditworthiness. Normally, the warehouse lender charges a premium of from 1/4 of 1 percent to 1 percent more than committed warehousing for this type of credit, as well as advancing less than would be obtainable for committed loans.

Foreclosure and real estate-owned (REO) lines. Sometimes, loans in warehouse become delinquent. They are therefore not eligible for purchase by some investors and enter the foreclosure process. Whether loans are in the process of foreclosure or have completed foreclosure to become REOs, lines of credit usually need to be designated for this purpose to relieve the pressure on working capital. Pricing of this line of credit reflects the practice followed for uncommitted loans.

Special loans. Oftentimes, mortgage bankers originate nonconforming loans (loans not eligible for purchase by FNMA or FHLMC or guarantee by GNMA). Inasmuch as the investors who purchase these loans are of a lesser financial stature, the warehouse lender must be cognizant of the investor's financial capacity behind the commitment to purchase these loans. Pricing of this line usually parallels that used for uncommitted and foreclosure and REO lines.

Working capital. While this chapter focuses on secured lending, it would be myopic not to recognize that the mortgage banker usually ties-in his unsecured needs with his secured lending requirements.

Typical working capital needs include the following:

1. Funds for loan closings, particularly when a draft system is used in which the draft hits the warehouse bank before the loan collateral arrives.

2. Monthly advances to GNMA MBS pools, when mortgagor payments are insufficient at the remittance date to completely pay MBS investors.
3. Escrow and foreclosure advances, when taxes and insurance premiums must be paid.
4. Commitment fees, required to provide protection for warehouse and pipeline loans.

Most unsecured lenders relate maximum credit extension to the type of exposure and to the borrower's unencumbered net worth. It is not uncommon to seek to minimize exposure by obtaining a pledge of corporate stock or personal guarantees of the principals. This type of credit extension is usually the most expensive borrowing for normal operating needs.

Required Reports

The minimum reports that the warehouse lender should review systematically:

Weekly. A commitment report should cover all commitments in detail, MBS pair-offs, reverse repos and unsold inventory. Figure 1 is a sample form used for this purpose. If a mortgage banker automates this information, the need for a special form would be eliminated.

Monthly. Three reports are required: (1) loan production and commitment analysis report, with a breakdown of closed loans and pipeline loans indicating commitment coverage, profit or loss, and exposure; (2) mortgage-loan inventory warehoused and loans in process (Figure 2 details various warehouse lines, their use and production volume); and (3) monthly profit and loss statement.

Quarterly. Delinquency reports should be reviewed; these show portfolio breakdown of loans, corresponding with MBA of America's *National Delinquency Survey,* which is published quarterly. There should also be a review of unaudited interim financial statements.

Annually. Financial statements, prepared by an accounting firm satisfactory to the lender, should be analyzed.

Audits

Some warehouse lenders have a separate auditing department to make periodic visits to the borrower for audit purposes, while others use the same group that handles the lending function. In either case, the audit function is an on-

Figure 1 • Commitment Report

Name ———————————————————   Week of ————————

Type	Investor or broker	Commitment no.	Expiration date	Amount ($000)	Coupon rate	Price or yield

MBS PAIR-OFFS

Investor or broker	Commitment no.	Expiration date	Rate	Amount ($000)	Bought or sold	Net position

Reverse REPOS/unsold GNMA securities

Investor	Type	No. days	Repo. period	Amount

NAME: CBT position

(————————— contracts)

going one. In both cases, frequent personal contact is desirable. A constant monitoring of the borrower's daily activity should be maintained to alert the warehouse lender to any adverse changes:

Changes in the servicing portfolio from investor cancellations, sale of servicing, purchase of servicing, and excessive runoff (foreclosure, amortization, etc.).

Excessive delinquencies and foreclosures.

Involvement in unrelated accounts.

Speculated marketing positions.

Figure 2 • Mortgage Loan Inventory

NAME

WAREHOUSED AND LOANS IN PROCESS
WEEK OF:

(000s OMITTED)

WAREHOUSE LINES

LINE AMT. & (OUTSTANDINGS)

Line Amt.	Bankers ($ MM)	OUTSTANDINGS			
TOTAL FHA/VA WAREHOUSED					
TOTAL CONVENTIONAL LOANS WAREH.					
TOTAL FHA-GPMs WAREHOUSED					
OTHER					
TOTAL					

A. TOTAL WAREHOUSED ALL BANKS: _____

B. WAREHOUSE INVENTORY

PIPELINE

	CONV.	FHA/VA	GPM	TOTAL
C. APPLICATIONS IN PROCESS				
D. READY TO CLOSE (60 days)				
E. COMMITMENTS TO PURCHASE				
TOTAL A + C				

Operating losses over several quarters.

Growth in excess of management's capacity.

Changes in senior management.

Substantial increases in marketable loans.

Noncompliance with the warehousing agreement.

An on-site audit of a mortgage-banking customer provides a general overview of the customer's internal operating policies, procedures, and practices. It also serves the following purposes:

1. Periodic review and updating of internal reports and controls.
2. Identification of changes in policies, practices, and procedures.
3. Highlighting of operating problems not reflected in internally generated reports.
4. Evaluation of funding and collateral management procedures and practices.
5. Determination of compliance with bank agreements and collateral-control requirements.

Summary

This chapter has reviewed the risks in warehouse lending from the viewpoint of the commercial banker. It sets forth a risk-management stragety of knowledge of one's customer; knowledge of its operations in detail, as well as its needs and problems, by personal knowledge of management; thorough analysis of the lending risks and the customer's operating procedures and performance; use of adequate documentation; systematic review of required reports; and use of on-site audits.

—— Chapter 24 ————————————————————

Analyzing and Monitoring Originators and Servicers

Allen P. Miller
Regional Vice President
Federal National Mortgage Association

Norman H. Peterson
Manager, Loan Acquisition
Federal National Mortgage Association

This chapter reviews the analyses that take place before and after a relationship between a lender and an investor is established. It is written from the perspective of a prudent investor and is intended only to present a framework within which to operate. The discussion applies equally to mortgage bankers, savings and loan associations, and commercial banks. Little distinction is made among them in the analysis of lender capabilities, although relevant differences are pointed out in applicable sections.

Production Capability and Portfolio Needs

One of the fundamental criteria used to determine if there is a basis for a business relationship is whether the lender can supply the type of loan that the investor is interested in buying. Another criterion is whether the lender can supply a sufficient loan volume to maintain a mutually beneficial relationship.

Many originators have expertise or other attributes that cause them to specialize in certain types of loan originations. A lender may produce mostly commercial loans, while the investor is interested primarily in residential. An investor may want FHA/VA loans, but the lender may have no experience with government loan programs or may not want to get involved in the rules and regulations associated with those programs. The investor may be interested only in purchasing participations, but the originator may not be in a position to retain a participation share, and can sell only on a whole-loan basis. An investor may be attracted to the higher yields and shorter maturities of second mortgages, but the lender's servicing department may not be prepared for the more intensive servicing efforts associated with seconds. Adjustable loans may furnish an investor with the chance to match maturities of assets and liabilities, but the servicer's automated systems may not be ready to accommodate them.

Consideration should also be given to potential loan volume. Should a minimum volume be based on unwritten but reasonable expectations, or should it be a contractual obligation?

Past Record

Basing a decision on past performance is certainly no guarantee of future satisfaction. However, an investor considering a long-term relationship with a lender should look at a company's record and the quality of its personnel. The investor should evaluate the method of production, control of that production, and the experiences of others who have dealt with that lender.

Management Strength. The desirable characteristics of management include experience, depth, and integrity. Unfortunately, these qualities are difficult to measure. There are, however, some reasonably reliable indications. There should be a review of the institutions with which the lender does business, along with the nature and tenure of that relationship. As there are numerous trade associations in the secondary mortgage industry, the lending company's reputation and participation in the industry can be an indicator of management's commitment to the industry. The company should also have been able to adapt to new products and operational techniques as conditions have changed. One can probably best assess management by how the company has performed, and the performance and potential of management is the central theme of the discussions that follow.

Method of Production. There is no right or wrong way to obtain production. Companies have successfully originated loans through branch offices, agents, or brokers. Some buy closed loans. Others pursue a combination of these alternatives.

Branch Offices. Whether owned by the lender or of the franchise variety, branch offices are usually the easiest to control. The quality and type of production are more dependable, and there is usually more stability in branch personnel. Lenders can structure compensation packages that will help balance the quantity and quality of production. In addition, home office personnel can perform on-site audits of all phases of a branch's operation.

Agents. Agents who are contractually bound to the lender offer some of the benefits of branches. There can be a sense of long-term relationship, and, it is hoped, a greater dedication to quality than might be inherent in a mortgage-broker relationship. However, since agents are usually not paid exclusively by a single lender, and are usually not subject to an intensity of audit of owned branches, there is less control.

Wholesale Purchasers.   Such purchasers of loans may have ongoing contracts with lending firms or may purchase on a spot basis. These companies may be portfolio lenders that buy loans to hold permanently or temporarily, as market conditions dictate. Even if the wholesale purchaser is buying strictly for resale, the fact that it owns the loan for some period of time (and will probably service the loan after resale) gives a degree of comfort to investors dealing with this type of lender.

Production Control.   Whatever the method of production, a critical item to consider is the lender's quality control commitment and procedures. Lenders with branches can perform unscheduled on-site branch audits for closed loans, as well as for loans in process. Unless otherwise expressly authorized, this is more difficult if agents are being used. Thus the production sources, and the steps the lender takes to ensure that it is getting what it paid for, should be examined by the investor.

The lender's methods for controlling loan quality should be examined. How loans are processed, underwritten, funded, warehoused, and shipped should be periodically reviewed by an internal audit department and the results reported to management. A quality control system that monitors the accuracy of the documents relied upon to make loans should also be in place. Among other items, this system should provide for spot reviews of appraisals, credit reports, and verifications of deposit and employment.

Appraisal reports can be checked by ordering a new appraisal or by having another appraiser do a field review and comment on the original appraisal and valuation conclusion. Ordering another appraisal is expensive and not necessarily the best approach. Field reviews can often supply good information. Having a staff appraiser do the review is acceptable. However, competency of the review appraiser is more important than whether a staff or a fee appraiser is used. Some metropolitan areas have a cooperative automated data base from which recent sales can be obtained to determine the accuracy of market valuations.

Quality control spot-check credit reports should be ordered from a different agency than the one which issued the initial report, preferably one that uses different repositories. Verifications of deposit and employment should be audited by sending a copy of the original verification to the employer or depository institution with an attachment that requests a confirmation of the information on the form.

Internal Audit

The internal audit system should include an audit of a random selection of loans (both originated and purchased). The procedures should be in writing, and logs of the status of data for each loan selected should be maintained. This function should be performed by personnel outside the production department.

Also, the analysis should be completed by those experienced enough to recognize discrepancies and their implications. The system should provide for reporting significant discrepancies to the appropriate executive officer, taking appropriate action where necessary, and notifying the investor, if applicable. The establishment (and maintenance) of such a system requires an allocation of resources and a dedication to the production of quality loans. The use of discretionary spot checks can be a good indicator that the lender recognizes the risks associated with differing conditions and sources of loans. As in the origination process, the lender should be concerned with the experience and reputation of the appraiser and the credit bureau in the review process.

Some regulatory agencies of supervised lenders perform stringent audits. If the investor has knowledge of the types of tests performed by these agencies, some reliance can be placed on those systems. However, the quality of the tests varies widely (agencies primarily involved in secondary mortgage market operations typically conduct the most thorough, comprehensive, and knowledgeable audits). Thus, the fact that a supervising agency audits a supervised lender is not a substitute for an ongoing, verifiable quality control system.

Performance Verification.   Other investors with which the originator is doing business can often provide useful information. This is especially true if another investor has been purchasing similar types of loans. Even though it is rare to receive detailed information on operating performance, such as repurchases or delinquency and foreclosure percentages, sufficient information sometimes can be obtained to get a feel for the investor's view of the lender.

An investor endeavoring to do business with a lender can usually obtain permission from the lender to contact other institutions for information regarding its performance. While information received in this manner can prove very beneficial, the wise investor will not place total reliance on these reports.

If a mortgage banker uses a warehouse line, that source may know more about the lender than any other outsider. The warehouser knows the financial condition, current production levels by type, unrecognized marketing losses or gains, general marketing philosophy, and the extent of problem loans or backup lines. Such inside information can provide insight to the warehouser's opinion of the mortgage banker.

Financial Condition

Whatever the relationship, there is a general need for the lender to maintain a degree of financial stability. If transactions between investors and the lender rely on warranties and certifications for performance and standards, the investor must be even more careful regarding financial condition. Audited financial statements for nonsupervised lenders should be required, as they are the best source of accurate, comprehensive data.

Some mortgage bankers are subsidiaries of large companies or financial institutions, and often do not have individual financial statements separate from those of the parent. A decision must be made on whether to require separate statements. Counter statements of financial institutions provide bare information, but the detailed reports they submit to regulatory agencies give a much better indication of financial condition. The reports required by regulators are available from the lenders, the regulators themselves, or from various independent, private reporting entities. Once the way to obtain acceptable financial information is determined, that data must be analyzed and deficiencies or strong points noted.

Net worth should be adjusted, where applicable, by reducing it by those assets whose book values are greater than their market values. Net worth, represented by specified and acceptable-quality assets, helps give the investor comfort that the lender has the staying power to honor the contractual warranties the lender has made. The minimum net worth desired may change, depending on the type of product the lender will supply, and the nature of other contractual provisions.

As with the financial statements, some mortgage bankers want investors to rely on the net worth of the parent or that of a related company. Such arrangements may prove satisfactory, but the investor should consider the possibility that one of the reasons for the establishment of the subsidiary lender is avoidance of liability by the parent.

Another financial item of importance is the adequacy of working capital. In the normal course of business, servicers are required to make substantial advances on behalf of the investor, for obligations under mortgage-backed securities pools and participation pools, delinquent tax payments, or the necessity of bringing a first-mortgage holder current when the investor holds the second mortgage. The servicer must have sufficient liquid capital so that it can be relied upon to make the necessary advances in a timely manner.

Quality of Servicing

It is relatively easy for an investor to determine which lenders have a long-term view of the company's prospects and which do not. Unlike originations, the servicing portfolio reflects more than a snapshot in time. It represents the culmination of what could be years of operation. The size, mix, and delinquency and foreclosure statistics of the portfolio reveal the profile of the lender. An investor's yield may depend on the quality of servicing.

Servicers are expected to provide investors with sufficient portfolio information so that investors can make comparative analyses of other lenders with similar portfolios. Verification of this information with other investors is also possible.

The quality of the servicing effort is usually as good as the people managing and performing the tasks. Companies that have expended the resources to attract and retain qualified personnel, and to acquire up-to-date systems and automated equipment, are likely to have superior servicing capabilities.

Those servicers concerned about the maintenence of high-level servicing performance are likely to have established well-written internal procedures. Investors are moving toward publishing *what* is supposed to be done, but leaving *how* to do it to the servicer. If servicing expertise is likely to drop with the departure of a few key people, it is imperative that the benefit of their experience be available to those who must still get the job done. Written procedures will survive the departure.

The same principles regarding quality control that apply to production also are pertinent to servicing: there must be an internal system so that the servicer's management can monitor the level of performance. In addition, management should recognize that a lesser degree of direct investor control of some servicing functions calls for increased servicer monitoring of those functions. An example of this is the practice of servicers in using service bureaus for mortgagor contact or property inspections. Unless the servicer spot checks the results it receives by having another service bureau or its own staff check the original reports, the servicer may be too late in discovering serious deficiencies for which it is responsible.

Other areas that should be covered in a servicing quality control system are timely payment of taxes and insurance premiums, response to routine mortgagor inquiries, contact with delinquent accounts, decisions on commencement of foreclosure action or forebearance plans, timeliness of the foreclosure process, claim filing, disposition of acquired property, cash handling, and investor accounting and remitting.

Monitoring Servicing Performance

Once the decision is made to start purchasing loans from a particular lender, the investor must have systems for checking performance. The investor should verify that it is receiving the anticipated return on investment (timely remittances and acceptable rates of delinquency and foreclosure), and that other servicing aspects are being handled as expected.

Cash Flow Analysis

This section presumes that the investor will share in delays of payments caused by delinquency, and losses caused by foreclosure and real estate-owned (REO) disposition. By reviewing routine servicing reports, the investor should be able to judge the number of total delinquents in the portfolio and the seriousness of each delinquency. Reports to the investor should also include the degree to which formal forebearance plans have been implemented. To get meaningful data, the investor should be careful to compare the raw numbers of a particular servicer's portfolio with those of other servicers of similar portfolio mix. For example, one servicer's portfolio might consist primarily of conventional loans, while the majority of another's might be government-backed loans. Any comparison between the two should take the differences into account. Other variables might be portfolio age or differing geographic locations.

If mortgagors' payments are remitted to the investor as they are received rather than their all being due on a particular date, the investor should know how the servicer's remittance schedule during the month compares with others. The investor should take care not to establish a system by which the servicer is rewarded for late remittances. This can happen when there is no incentive for collecting and remitting as soon as possible. Some servicers wait until the late charges are payable before serious servicing efforts begin. In addition, servicing fees should be paid by the investor for current loans only. There should be no remittance delays resulting from ancillary insurance disputes or other servicer sideline activities with mortgagors.

On loans which have completed foreclosure, and for which the servicer is responsible for REO dispositions, the investor should get regular status reports. These reports should include the marketing efforts to sell the property and the extent of losses or gains expected. Servicers in many geographic areas have not, until recently, had any experience in this function. The investor should satisfy itself that all prudent steps are being taken.

Routine Servicing

The servicer has the responsibility for handling mortgagor needs and accounts occurring in the normal course of business. Disgruntled mortgagors seem to have a way of finding out the investor's name, especially if the assignment of the loan is a matter of public record. The investor should make sure that the servicer is made aware of, and responds to, borrower complaints.

The investor may want to contribute to the decision-making process for some servicing functions. This might occur in large hazard-insurance loss cases, in which investors may want to approve servicer recommendations for the restoration of the property. The investor may also want to be the decision point on partial releases of security or disposition of real estate-owned. In addition, for properties located in states imposing substantial penalties for delays in processing payoffs, investors want assurance that reconveyances and satisfactions are being handled in an expeditious manner.

Custodial or impound accounts for payment of taxes or insurance premiums can be monitored by receiving account detail from the bank and comparing it with mortgagor records. This item is very difficult to control if the funds are not kept in a separate custodial account for the particular investor.

The investor can perform periodic on-site audits of the servicer's activities and sample a representative number of cases for each function the servicer performs on behalf of the investor. The results of the audit can be used to make improvements in deficient areas.

Whatever monitoring methods are chosen, the investor's reaction to material deficiencies discovered as a result of monitoring should be consistent with the nature of the relationship, that is, the lender should understand that a relationship that gives great latitude and flexibility can increase the adverse consequences resulting from poor performance. The investor also has the responsibility not to overreact to a relatively minor occurrence.

Types of Reports

The reliance and responsibility placed on the lender is usually so great that it is incumbent upon the investor to stay abreast of the servicer's internal organization and changes in activities. The following lists some of the reports a lender might be required to submit:

1. Change of corporate status. This could include a change in ownership or in the relation to affiliated companies.
2. Change of officers and key personnel. In large or small companies, a few people may be the driving force for past successes.
3. Changes in financial conditions. In addition to the annual financial statements, material changes that could affect the mortgage banker's ability to carry out responsibilities should be reported.
4. Auditor's internal control report to management. This can give additional insight to the lender's operations, insight that is not generally available elsewhere.
5. Quality control system findings and the lender's corrective actions. An investor should expect that spot checks would result in an occasional problem.
6. Remittance reconciliations. It should be verified that the amount due was the amount sent.
7. Custodial-account reconciliations. The funds in the accounts should balance with what borrowers have paid.
8. Loan-service reports. These could include delinquency and foreclosure data, as well as paid-in-full loans.

The nature of these reports can vary widely and be overviews or detail accounts, but they should be required on a regular basis.

Primary Problem Areas

Some problems seem to be chronic. The investor should nonetheless be aware of them and must attempt to keep them to a minimum, with a view to eventual solutions.

Lack of Knowledge about Investor Requirements. Lender personnel, whether in production or loan administration, are usually working with different investors at the same time. Originating and servicing loans can be difficult enough, even if only one loan type and investor is involved. With the complexity of product and the numerous investors currently in the market, overlooking some requirements may be difficult to avoid.

Relationship of Underwriters to Production Department. There can be a conflict between producers of loans and the department whose job it is to underwrite credit and property risk. If either of these departments becomes the dominant force, risky loans may be made or profitable loans that should be made may be declined.

Quality Control System is Considered a Necessary Evil. Those lenders who establish and maintain a good system on their own volition deserve commensurate recognition.

Degree of Home-Office Involvement with Branches. There is a fine balance in home office involvement between ensuring good product and service from a branch, and discouraging a spirit that will enhance production in the branches. A lending firm that takes an even-handed approach will probably do the best job for investors.

Communications with Mortgagors and Other Departments. Good lines of open communications must be established between the servicer and the mortgagors and within the servicer's organization itself. Dissatisfied mortgagors are avoided when timely and accurate responses are given and when one department does not contradict another. Ultimately, dissatisfied mortgagors may contact the investor, causing it to spend time on problems which should have been resolved by the servicer.

Future Considerations

As the nature and operations of investors change, so do those of lenders. As important as the relationships between lenders and investors have been, they will become more important as the trend to larger and fewer financial service centers continues. Investors look for stronger fiduciary relationships with proven and financially sound lenders. As investors require more specialized products and services, successful lenders are able to deliver. For example, adjustable-rate mortgages (ARMs) were among the many new financing techniques that became more important to investors and portfolio lenders. Lenders successful in marketing and administering ARMs demonstrated the ability to adapt to a changing environment and investor needs. Modifications to procedures cut across lenders' entire operations. Training of origination personnel, as well as real estate brokers, had to be accomplished. Mathematical skills and systems were refined. There were changes in title insurance, mortgage insurance, and hazard insurance that had to be learned. Loans were set up differently on the books and were serviced with new considerations. Servicing personnel had to be educated to the new array of terminology and procedures and be able to explain them to mortgagors.

Investors that chose their sources of production carefully will have the highest probablity of meeting their portfolio objectives. As other new loan types are developed in the future, those lenders who demonstrate the ability to excel during times of change will become more necessary to investors. Hence, the ability to evaluate loan-origination relationships and to monitor loan-servicing relationships will become increasingly important.

Conclusion

Certain information should be obtained, questions asked, and responses evaluated before entering a business relationship with a lender, so that there will be beneficial results for both. The lender and the investor should have loan portfolio needs and loan-production capabilities that complement each other. The past record and the management of the lender are probably the most critical items to evaluate before (and during) a business relationship. The financial condition of the lender should be examined to ensure that it can fulfill contractual obligations.

Various monitoring techniques and reports should be used to make sure that the investor is receiving the quality of product and the servicing performance expected. Areas of typical, ongoing problems should be constantly reviewed to minimize disruption and ineffectiveness. A view to the future reinforces the need for care in establishing associations that will endure through the challenges to come.

Chapter 25

Liquifying Portfolio Loans

Richard A. Dorfman
Managing Director
Lehman Commercial Paper, Inc.
Shearson Lehman/American Express, Inc.

Existing portfolio loans are a large and growing segment of mortgage and mortgage-backed security offerings in the secondary mortgage market. Spurred by encouraging accounting changes and government mortgage agencies, many depository institutions are converting their portfolio loans into cash or liquid securities via these offerings and then reinvesting the cash or borrowing against the liquid securities to obtain cash for reinvestment. This process of conversion to cash is called *liquifying* in this chapter, whether by the sale of loans or by hypothecation. The primary technique of liquification recommended is the exchange of rate-insensitive assets, i.e., fixed-rate mortgages, for cash that is subsequently redeployed into carefully chosen investment alternatives, some of which are rate sensitive.

This chapter notes the important effect of alternative accounting treatments on liquification techniques, describes the several phases necessary to plan and execute a liquification, discusses the benefits of portfolio segmentation to a loan seller, and compares the advantages of hypothecation versus loan sales.

The Importance of Accounting Policies

Selling a mortgage loan portfolio is technically a severence of risk of the seller from the mortgages sold. Under Generally Accepted Accounting Principles (GAAP), a true portfolio sales triggers the immediate recognition of the profit or loss of that sale. Below-market yields of mortgage portfolios require large sales discounts to achieve a market yield for prospective portfolio loan investors. Deep-discount loan sales can bring recognition under GAAP of discount losses so large as to preempt any consideration of a portfolio sale. GAAP presents many portfolio lenders with a dilemma: Sell at a loss that would recognize instant insolvency, or do nothing and experience almost certain gradual insolvency. Resolution of the dilemma comes from two strategies: adoption of Regulatory Accounting Principle (RAP) accounting and pursuit of long-term portfolio hypothecation.

The sale of a portfolio usually generates the greatest amount of immediate

447

cash for reinvestment, and financing for the same portfolio is inherently more expensive. This basic recognition is the rationale behind RAP that a federally chartered savings and loan association or savings bank can elect annually to defer gains or losses on the sales of assets and amortize such deferrals over the average life of each loan group or the stated life of each security sold. This regulation enables effective restructuring by avoiding complete recognition of sales discounts upon sale and amortizes recognition of sales discounts over extended periods. Deferred discount expenses can thereby be offset by enhanced earnings on the assets acquired through reinvestment or from other earning assets. RAP sales probably have accounted for a major number of portfolio loan offerings.

Unfortunately, RAP benefits conflict with GAAP, and any savings institution that uses RAP to defer sales discounts cannot receive an unqualified auditor's report, because RAP accounting does not fairly represent the balance sheet as defined by GAAP. Furthermore, neither the Controller of the Currency nor the Federal Deposit Insurance Corporation (FDIC) has authorized RAP sales, while many states have been slow to adopt RAP deferral for state-chartered institutions. Stock-form associations also cannot use RAP because of their need for a "clean" auditor's letter. Therefore, for the banks and associations that cannot, or will not, elect RAP-deferred selling, the liquification alternative is to finance portions of the mortgage loan portfolio. Financings, when skillfully structured, can be nearly as efficient as sales in terms of net cash received. As will be discussed later in this chapter, financings in the form of "paythrough" bonds, are an alternative to portfolio sales.

Another significant source of loan portfolio offerings has been sales of merged portfolios. When such mergers are accounted for under the purchase accounting method, the assets and liabilities of the merged institution are valued at market as of the merger date, with the result being the elimination of the net worth of the merged institution. The market discount of the merged assets, as measured by the difference between book value and market value, is shifted to a goodwill asset and amortized. Traditionally, goodwill has been amortized over forty years, but accounting abuses involving the creation of noneconomic earnings forced the amortization period to the weighted average life of the merged assets. (In certain instances involving public offerings of stock, the goodwill amortization period has been even shorter.)

Valuation of a portfolio at market enables a sale of the portfolio at a later time at a higher value than the purchase book value, markets permitting. Any gain on sale of the portfolio is recognized under GAAP.

Planning a Liquification

Liquifying a mortgage portfolio requires numerous decisions in the evaluation process that can result in either success or failure. The decisions required during sequential phases include the following:

Analytical Phase

1. What is the purpose of the liquification? Profit, gap closure, liquidity?
2. What accounting technique will be used? GAAP (realize discount loss), RAP (amortize loss), purchase accounting (mergers), sale, or financing?
3. Which loans are available for liquification? How many and what types that are not encumbered have good documents, timely payments, and scheduled amortizations?
4. Are complete and accurate loan data available? This is often a problem with merged or purchased loans.
5. Can adequate data processing tapes be generated? This is essential for segmentation strategy.
6. What are the primary characteristics of the portfolio? What are the weighted average term and maturity, types, and location? Are they conforming or not, owner occupancy or not, due-on-sale or not?
7. How many homogeneous subgroups can be identified?

Strategic Phase

1. What is the minimum remaining life for loans in the portfolios? Typically, loans with fewer than five years' remaining life should be held in portfolio because of heavy amortization.
2. Which investors are buyers in the current market? From time to time, whole-loan investors provide favorable pricing above the securities markets for conforming loans. Nonconforming loans must be directed to appropriate investors as whole loans or participations or through conduits.
3. As to conforming loans, what security should be chosen for conventional loans best sold as securities? FNMA or FHLMC? What are the financial, market, and servicing characteristics of each?
4. As to loans chosen for securitization, what pooling strategies are best? This is often the most critical consideration. Segmentation analysis is required, according to market activity for *(a)* coupon range, *(b)* relationship of loan coupons to security coupons (servicing spread), *(c)* comparison of highest cash value (minimum servicing spread) to lowest cash value plus present value of future servicing income (maximum servicing spread) in a RAP sale or bond, *(d)* highest cash value for a merger sale, and *(e)* multiple issues per coupon advisable to segment maturities.
5. In a GAAP accounting context, can the portfolio provide for the sale of matching profits and losses, with the residue eligible for financing?
6. In a financing context, has the impact of long-term debt on the balance sheet been evaluated?

Reinvestment Phase

1. Will the reinvestment assets funded by the proceeds of liquification be immediately available? A liquification and reinvestment analysis is re-

quired to evaluate meaningful economic results (gap closure, real economic income increase, etc.), to reject unrealistic amortization and reinvestable cash flow assumptions (ultra fast or slow), to weigh the effect of the reinvestment rate on amortization and interest; and to establish objectives for minimum rate of return.
2. If reinvestment is to be delayed, is a sound hedge program in place to protect the value of the interim position?

Execution Phase: Sale of Loans, MBSs, or Bonds

1. Is there a group of investors responsive to the segmentation strategy? Is there excessive reliance on too few bidders? Are the bidders reliable and creditworthy? Are there any undisclosed buyer or seller conditions?
2. Has the market been systematically cultivated to prepare for one's offerings and to maximize competitive forces among a sufficient number of bidders? Are funding procedures and dates clear? Has provision been made for pool "fallout"?

The above questions are preliminary to an overview of the extremely detailed considerations encountered in a portfolio liquification program. Weakness at any point of planning or execution can negate the entire program. Portfolio lenders should stress these phases to determine if the full range of activities can be managed internally or if an outside expert adviser is appropriate.

Portfolio Segmentation

Of the financial and operational issues mentioned above, none is more essential to obtaining the maximum price of a portfolio than segmentation. Segmentation of a mortgage loan portfolio is defined as the disaggregation of a portfolio and its reaggregation into the optimal number and type of subgroups to maximize the aggregate value of the entire offered portfolio. In the majority of portfolio sales, the sum of the market value of a carefully segmented portfolio is significantly greater than the value of the same portfolio taken as a whole.

The reason for the enhanced value through segmentation is that most portfolios are heterogeneous, consisting of many loan types, coupon ranges, maturity ranges, due-on-sale clauses, loan-size ranges, property locations, and owner-occupancy variations. When a diverse portfolio is offered to a single investor, the investor prefers some portions of the portfolio to others. He, therefore, is willing to pay a higher price for some portions and a lower price for others. To the extent that portfolio sellers accept bids based on gross-aggregate-weighted average characteristics, the likelihood of lower portfolio prices is enhanced. Someone who acquires a portfolio based on gross aggregates across an entire portfolio is subsequently able to segment the portfolio and resell the segments, often at considerably higher prices.

The segmentation process involves the statistical breakdown of a given portfolio into very small, relatively homogeneous minipools. (Sophisticated analysts often discern 100 or more minipools in portfolios of $50 million or more.) The minipools are then reassembled into larger subgroups for sale of blocks of whole loans to certain investors, who may be in the market intermittently, at prices better than those the loans could command as securities. Whole-loan transactions typically consist of the portions of a portfolio ranging from 5 to 15 years' remaining contract maturity.

The market basis for the occasional ability to sell whole loans at a net price above securities is, in part, the prepayment assumption used as a pricing factor. The securities markets typically and historically have used the 12-year prepaid life convention. However, with the advent of the ability to convert older portfolio loans to FHLMC PCs and FNMA MBSs, security pools of far shorter contract maturity can be offered. The early attempts of securities dealers to require the 12-year convention in bid pricing was inconsistent with the reality of certain short-life pools. Currently, whole loans having a 12-year weighted average life and a 15-year maximum contract term typically sell at a 7-year prepayment assumption. The lessened prepayment assumption from 12 to 7 years dramatically increases the price at which loans are sold. Market knowledge still permits intermittent whole-loan opportunities that compete successfully with the corresponding securities pricing for a given loan coupon and maturity combination.

Securities remain and will likely grow as the primary vehicle for portfolio loan sales. Currently, the primary vehicles for such securitization are the FNMA MBS and the FHLMC PC. Each of these agency programs carries the ability to sell the securities based on portfolio loans to a vast public market. Neither the FNMA nor the FHLMC program is U.S. government full-faith-and-credit paper. However, they both are widely traded as agency issues, and they currently enjoy approximate equality of pricing in the open market, with some preference to FNMA coupon for coupon.

Securitization transforms illiquid portfolio loans into liquid securities. In the case of the FHLMC PC and the FNMA MBS, "swaps" that generate no gain or loss are involved. The securities received by a portfolio holder as a consequence of a PC or MBS swap are based on exactly the same loans held prior to the swap. The swap triggers no accounting recognition of gain or loss, because the underlying loans have not been sold.

Sample Segmentation

Let us assume the following portfolio data:

Date	November 22, 1982
Portfolio aggregate balances	$154,378,000.00
Weighted average coupon	9.205 percent

Weighted average term to maturity	252.7 months
Servicing retained	0.25 percent p.a.

This portfolio can be priced on its described average aggregates. Let us assume that the agreed price-to-yield index would be the FNMA posted net yield of 12.875 percent, plus a 1.0 percent fee. The gross portfolio value would be 77.51 percent of par, assuming the specified index and a prepayment assumption of 144 months.

Segregating the loans, the same portfolio could be sold as follows:

Whole loans (at FNMA index)	$80,917,000	79.607 percent of par
CMBS	73,461,000	80.420 percent of par
Total	$154,378,000	79.994 percent of par
Difference (percent)		2.484% of par
Difference (dollars)		$3,834,000

The elementary segmentation shown above enhanced the net proceeds sale of this portfolio by an impressive 2.484 percent.

Segmentation segments the portfolio into rate and contract maturity groups. For the sake of this example, acceptable FNMA investment parameters are assumed and consistently applied.

Balances ($000)

	Months Remaining		
Loan Coupon (percent)	Less Than 180	Less Than 240	More Than 240
11.000	—	2,526	4,500
10.500	—	3,176	3,950
10.250	1,082	1,941	3,450
9.875	453	962	1,021
9.500	9,438	12,834	23,969
9.000	10,144	9,616	31,435
8.500	2,163	4,722	5,136
8.250	1,444	7,651	—
8.000	3,146	3,934	—
7.878	4,122	1,563	—
Total	31,992	48,925	73,461
Weighted average coupon	8.891	9.114	9.402

The matrix above provides the statistical basis for addressing the known portfolio characteristics as of November 22, 1982, with the following segmentation of whole loans and FNMA MBS offerings:

I Whole Loans

Pool No.	Balances ($1000)	Weighted Average Coupon	Weighted Average Term (months)	Price (FNMA)
1	$ 5,973	9.664	179	83.98
2	5,000	9.500	179	83.30
3	10,144	9.000	179	81.22
4	5,753	8.251	179	78.14
5	5,122	7.899	179	76.72
6	5,702	10.722	239	86.63
7	5,000	9.863	239	82.33
8	10,737	9.500	239	80.54
9	9,616	9.000	239	78.09
10	12,373	8.345	232	75.10
11	5,497	7.964	210	73.96
Total	$80,917	9.027	212	79.607

II FNMA MBS

Pool No.	Balances ($1000)	CMBS Coupon (percent)	Excess Servicing	Price (percent par)
1	$ 4,500	10.50	0	88.00
2	3,950	10.00	0	85.50
3	3,450	9.50	0.250	83.00
4	24,990	9.00	0.015	80.75
5	31,435	8.50	0	78.75
6	5,136	8.00	0	76.75
Total	$73,461	8.850	0.017	80.42

Note: Excess servicing income has been minimized to produce the highest cash value on sale.

III Summary

Total Pools	Balances ($1000)	Price (percent par)
17	$154,378	79.99

The above simplified segmentation strategy produces a price enhancement of 2.48 percent or par, or $3,834,000. A more refined treatment could produce superior results, especially with a break-out of FNMA MBS pools 4 and 5 further segmented by maturity ranges.

Portfolio Financings (Hypothecations)

An alternative to portfolio loan sales under any accounting method is the related technique of long-term financings and hypothecations. The benefit of hypothecation/financing is that GAAP permits market discounts to be deferred during the life of the financing. This is because GAAP treats sales discount expense as additional interest expense as long as the transaction generates cash on the financing of a collateralized debt instrument, not on the sale of the collateral portfolio.

The broad subject of mortgage-backed pools is treated elsewhere in this book. This chapter confines itself to the place of such bonded debt in the liquification of an existing portfolio, specifically the "paythrough" techniques. Paythroughs are deemed to be the preferable long-term financing technique, because the expert compilation of a paythrough bond usually approximates the financial efficiency of a RAP sale for a GAAP seller. This efficiency is best created in a collateralized mortgage obligation (CMO) which applies the benefits of segmentation analysis to a series of paythrough bonds with the cash flow from the underlying mortgages directed to pay off the bonds in a sequential order.

CMO bonds have become increasingly important as liquification vehicles because of investor appeal. Many investors interested in purchasing whole loans of intermediate term find the CMO attractive, because it is essentially like a discounted loan purchase, with the added benefit of enhanced creditworthiness. This added benefit occurs because the scheduled and unscheduled amortization of the loan collateral is paid through to the bondholder, just as if the investor owned the loans. The paythrough of amortization reduces the need for higher overcollateralization and collateral value maintenance that characterizes traditional mortgage-backed bonds. Nonetheless, the total CMO issue should represent a satisfactory credit risk to the bond investor. For a CMO issue, the loan collateral is shown as a segregated (in trust) asset—there is no sale triggering recognition of loss—and as a liability on the other side of the balance sheet.

Putting together a CMO bond involves the same segmentation techniques illustrated above in the sale context. Just as loan sale pools should be targeted to a known market, bond pools should be configured from a disaggregation/reaggregation exercise directed to known investors. The statistical procedures used to assemble a CMO bond allow also for sophisticated bond structures of the multitranche type. For the purpose of this chapter, an elementary paythrough is examined (single tranche).

The following example illustrates the financing of a larger heterogeneous loan portfolio as of April 15, 1983.

ABC Bank Portfolio Bonds

Issue	$1000	Percent	Term	Price*	Servicing
1	18,061	9.305	283	87.75	.250
2	28,996	7.827	178	75.95	.250
3	30,280	9.536	301	77.19	.250
4	14,040	9.664	274	87.17	.250
Total	91,377	8.968	254	80.42	.250

Estimated Fee Summary*

Legal fees	$ 60
Rating fee	20 (pool 3)
Additional expenses	20
Total	$100

*All prices contain a 15 basis point (BP) reduction of coupon for 10 percent stop-loss insurance. Note: Underwriting and placement fees have been omitted. These could range from one point to far more, depending on the public or private nature of the placement and the inherent risk involved for the investment banker.

The bond pools presented above have been configured to obtain favorable prices based on differing pool mortality assumptions. While all bond pricing is illustrated from a single issue date of April 15, 1983, consideration was given by the actual issuer to issuing the bonds in series to accommodate his desire to reinvest the bond proceeds in commercial mortgage loans over time.

Interest Expense Projections for Paythrough Bonds: Bond Pool 1 ($000)

Face amount $18.061 million
Bond coupon 8.905%
Price 87.75

Year	Coupon Interest	"Discount" Recognition	Total
1	$1,480.97	$ 350.41	$1,831.38
2	1,232.40	333.46	1,565.86
3	992.56	326.50	1,319.06
4	758.05	318.50	1,076.55
5	529.89	309.25	839.14
6	309.32	297.59	606.91
7	100.58	276.71	377.29
Total		$2,212.42	

Note: It is assumed that ¹⁄₇ of loans are called annually and are purchased at par from the collateral pool by ABC Bank. Price represents a yield of 12.17 percent based on a remaining term of 283 months and a 60-month prepayment assumption.

Interest Expense Projections for Paythrough Bonds: Bond Pool 2 ($000)

Face amount $28.996 million
Bond coupon 7.427 percent
Price 75.95

Year	Coupon Interest	"Discount" Recognition	Total
1	$2,062.66	$ 588.55	$2,652.21
2	1,884.27	566.76	2,451.03
3	1,712.41	546.23	2,258.64

Year	Coupon Interest	"Discount" Recognition	Total
4	1,546.72	526.89	2,073.61
5	1,386.82	508.69	1,895.51
6	1,232.37	491.58	1,723.95
7	1,083.04	475.51	1,558.55
8	938.52	460.44	1,398.96
9	798.51	446.31	1,244.82
10	662.73	433.06	1,095.79
11	530.91	420.65	951.56
12	402.80	409.02	811.82
13	278.18	398.05	676.23
14	156.88	387.55	544.43
15 (10 months)	40.43	314.24	354.67
Total		$6,973.53	

Note: A 5 percent prepayment constant is assumed. Price represents a 13.0 percent yield based on a remaining term of 178 months and a 96-month prepayment assumption.

Interest Expense Projections for Paythrough Bonds: Bond Pool 3 ($000)

Face amount $30.28 million
Bond coupon 9.136 percent
Price 77.19

Year	Coupon Interest	"Discount" Recognition	Total
1	$2,685.40	$ 404.39	$3,089.79
2	2,526.77	387.69	2,194.46
3	2,374.64	371.95	2,746.59
4	2,228.63	357.13	2,585.76
5	2,088.39	343.18	2,431.57
6	1,953.56	330.07	2,283.63
7	1,823.82	317.78	2,141.60
8	1,698.85	306.26	2,005.11
9	1,578.34	295.48	1,873.82
10	1,462.01	285.42	1,747.43
11	1,349.57	276.05	1,625.62
12	1,240.74	267.35	1,508.09
13	1,135.28	259.28	1,394.56
14	1,032.92	251.85	1,284.77
15	933.42	245.00	1,178.42
16	836.54	238.74	1,075.28
17	742.06	233.04	975.10
18	649.76	227.88	877.64
19	559.41	223.25	782.66
20	470.82	219.12	689.94
21	383.78	215.48	599.26
22	298.11	212.31	510.42
23	213.63	209.56	423.19
24	130.18	207.15	337.33
25	47.71	204.68	252.39
26 (8 months)	2.24	16.77	19.01
Total		$6,906.86	

Note: A 5 percent prepayment constant is assumed. Price represents a yield of 13.10 percent based on a remaining term of 301 months and a 144-month prepayment assumption.

Interest Expense Projections for Paythrough Bonds: Bond Pool 4 ($000)

Face amount $14.04 million
Bond coupon 9.264 percent
Price 87.15

Year	Coupon Interest	"Discount" Principal Repayments	Total
1	$1,201.02	$ 276.02	$1,477.04
2	1,003.17	271.99	1,275.16
3	808.43	266.27	1,074.70
4	618.97	259.64	878.61
5	434.34	251.76	686.10
6	255.82	242.73	498.55
7	84.09	232.92	317.01
Total		$1,801.33	

Note: It is assumed that ½ of the loans are called annually and are purchased at par from the collateral pool by ABC Bank. Price represents a yield of 12.74 percent based on a remaining term of 274 months and a 60-month prepayment assumption.

While the cost of financing the portfolio for its expected life should be compared to alternative borrowing costs, the determination to finance a portfolio is not principally directed at generating long-term borrowed funds. Borrowing funds may be less expensive through alternative sources, such as FHLB borrowings. The point here is that the holder of a portfolio such as the one depicted pays a price to shift interest-rate risk to the bond investor. In this case, the holder used the proceeds to acquire interest-sensitive commercial loan assets to effect gap closure. Therefore, the price of such a financing includes the implicit cost of locking in asset and liability matches to stabilize earnings in the future.

Segmentation, Schematics, and Summary

Segmentation in the portfolio liquification process is the foundation of value enhancement. The following schematics summarize the issues involved in segmentation. Figure 1 illustrates a typical diverse portfolio. Figure 2 illustrates the disaggregation and reaggregation of the most important portion of a mortgage loan portfolio, one-to-four-unit conventional home loans, that represent the largest portion of a typical savings institution's portfolio.

This chapter has outlined only the essentials of portfolio loan liquification. Taken as a whole, the process is in fact a long and complex chain of events commencing with data analysis and running through final reinvestment of the proceeds. In a sense, the process is never really ended, as savings institutions and other portfolio holders increasingly recognize the financial management potential of the existing portfolio. The techniques are now available to continually monitor and manage portfolio mortgage loans for optimum impact on the balance sheet and earnings statement.

Figure 1

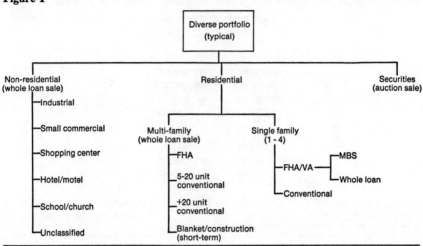

Figure 2

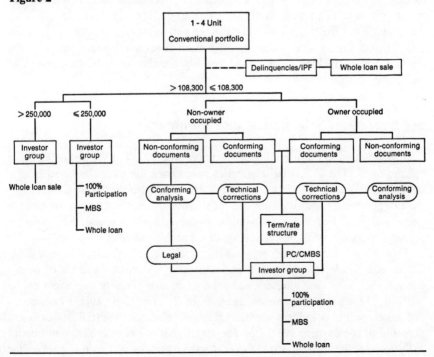

Chapter 26

Mortgage Investment Determinants

William W. Bartlett
Vice President
Shearson Lehman Mortgage Securities
Shearson Lehman/American Express, Inc.

Foreword

As with other fixed-income investments, the primary reasons for investing in mortgages or mortgage-backed securities (MBSs) are yield, liquidity, and preservation of capital. Because of the unique characteristics of mortgages, however, the factors bearing on the interaction of these investment determinants are often less predictable than are those affecting other fixed-income investments. This chapter explores key mortgage-related investment determinants, such as product diversity, liquidity, and risk—both market and credit risks—as they relate uniquely to alternative investments in whole-loan mortgages versus investment in MBSs versus investment in bonds. Along with relevant accounting and tax considerations, other topics discussed are forecasting the availability of funds and funding forward commitments. The chapter is written from the perspective of the institutional mortgage investor.

Product Diversity

The secondary mortgage market taken as a whole—mortgages offered in the secondary market both as whole loans and in securitized form—offers a wide variety of maturities, a diversity of yield and risk tradeoffs, and even choices of fixed and variable rates.

Maturities: Long- and Short-Term. The shortest maturities (usually twelve to eighteen months) are typically offered with construction loans, although residential mortgages may be packaged as MBSs, which are available in short-term certificates (5-year maturity with an expected 3.5-year average live); intermediate certificates (12-year maturity with an expected 8-year average life); and long-term certificates (30-year maturity with an assumed 12-year average life). An increasingly popular type of MBS that offers a series of sequential pay-through certificates is the collateralized mortgage obligation (CMO). To date, however, the preponderance of securitized mortgage issues

459

have been based on 30–year stated maturity mortgages with an assumed 12-year average life.

Yield and Risk Diversity.   Construction loans carry a high level of perceived risk, and are preferred by some sophisticated mortgage lenders, because they offer a relatively high rate of return. Less sophisticated investors may prefer long-term GNMA MBSs, which are perceived as virtually riskless because of the full-faith-and-credit guarantee of the federal government. Also, the existence of an actively traded dealer market assures liquidity for GNMA MBSs, in contrast to the extreme illiquidity in a construction- or commercial-loan investment.

Fixed versus Variable Rate.   Diversity may be offered through a choice of a fixed-rate or variable-rate investment in mortgages. While the securitized forms of mortgage investment are predominantly fixed rate, there is a wide range of adjustable-rate mortgage types offered within the whole-loan market. Increasingly, the majority of construction and commercial permanent loans float according to an index: the bank prime rate, or to the yields on Treasury bills.

Mortgages versus Mortgage-Backed Securities

In deciding whether to buy mortgages as whole-loan packages or to buy them in securitized form the investor should balance the higher yield of the whole-loan investment against the greater liquidity and reduced risk associated with securitized mortgage offerings. The lower yield associated with securitized mortgages reflects the benefit derived from the agency guarantee (on securities issued by GNMA, FNMA, FHLMC) or the private mortgage or pool insurance on other types of MBSs. The yield offered on an MBS should be carefully evaluated to determine if it represents fair yield value compared with other MBSs of like or even better quality. For example, some builder bond offerings have been sold at yields lower than GNMA MBSs in spite of their lesser liquidity and the lack of the federal government full-faith-and-credit guarantee.

MBSs versus Bonds

MBSs have historically sold at higher yields than have corporate or government bonds of like maturity. MBSs as a generic group represent a two-tiered market, and federally guaranteed (GNMA) and federally sponsored (FNMA, FHLMC) MBSs generally trade at lower relative yields than the privately issued mortgage-backed bonds and pass-through certificates. (While some privately issued MBS securities that are GNMA-collateralized have been exceptions to this rule, they have been sold primarily to noninstitutional investors at yields below the GNMA yield. These private issues build in a substantial front-end marketing expense to pay commissions to Wall Street brokers who sell MBSs to the general public rather than the institutional market.)

Recently, the introduction of CMOs with a multiclass-maturity structure has enabled CMOs to be sold at yields below that of MBSs with the traditional 30-year stated maturity. Typically, the lower aggregate average yields of CMOs reflect the favorable yield on shorter maturities, particularly those with a steep positive yield curve, and some degree of call protection on the longer maturities.

Liquidity Lends Intrinsic Value

The liquidity associated with MBSs, compared to whole-loan investments, reduces market risk to the extent that the investor correctly perceives the right time to buy or sell and does so quickly. Execution time varies considerably with different types of mortgage investments and is a function of the breadth of the secondary market available for a given type of mortgage investment. In 1983, some $85 billion of federal-agency-sponsored, original securities were issued, while the total number of additional secondary trades was several times that of the original issues, amounting to hundreds of billions of dollars annually.

GNMA, FHLMC, and FNMA securities are all traded in a primary dealer market, where blocks of several million dollars may be bought and sold in minutes. Such liquidity is possible because the primary dealers buy and sell as principals (not as agents or on a best-efforts basis). Of equal importance, the bids and offers are made on relatively narrow spreads, where the difference between the bid and offer prices is usually less than one quarter of a point.

Standardization Is Key.   The reason the GNMA, FNMA, and FHLMC securities trade so quickly in the dealer-sponsored secondary market is the fungibility resulting from standardization. These securities all bear uniform terms (with respect to maturity and structural characteristics), conditions, and guarantee features, which enables them to be traded with a minimum of information. The high liquidity and fungibility of the GNMA, FHLMC, and FNMA securities enable MBSs to be bought and sold quickly at minimal liquidation expense (at a relatively low dealer spread).

Privately issued MBSs have less liquidity than do federally sponsored agency securities because the dealer market often performs on a best-efforts basis and at a wide dealer spread (up to one point). If a seller insists on quick execution, or if the market is sluggish, the dealer spread may even widen. Private MBSs are often originally sold at yields only slightly above those of the agency-sponsored MBSs, but on resale they are often traded at substantially higher yields. Thus, the investor should consider carefully the need for liquidity when purchasing the less frequently traded MBS issucs.

Whole-loan mortgage offerings have much less liquidity than MBSs and are frequently disposed of through a broker (rather than a dealer) market on a best-efforts basis. Liquidation of a whole-loan position can take up to several days to achieve and requires substantially more information about the characteristics of the loans being offered. Some forms of whole-loan offerings that have a high degree of standardization (seasoned conventionals on standard FHLMC documents) may be purchased by a dealer for his position as principal. But if there is no standard documentation, the dealer would require at least a spot check of the documentation and a listing of the characteristics of the loans before making a *for position bid*.

Loan Participations

Loan participations also typically offer a higher yield than do MBSs. The seller retains an ownership position in the loan package, generally 10 percent, and sells the balance on a standard document referred to as a *participation agreement*. The participation purchase has certain advantages: the seller retains an investment position in the package, thus assuring his interest in maintaining a good payment record; and the documentation for delivery and settlement is simplified, because the buyer need not take delivery of the loan files, just the participation agreement. The participation agreement is really a form of trust agreement, whereby the seller retains the loan files as custodian for the buyer, or the seller may deliver the loans to an acceptable third party for custody.

A disadvantage of purchasing loans under a participation agreement is that it may not be possible later to securitize the portfolio if it is part of a participation.

Risk Considerations—Market versus Credit

Liquidity is but one factor in the greater intrinsic value of the securitized form of mortgage investing; the other is the presumption of reduced risk. Risk, however, has two components: credit risk (which may be virtually eliminated in the securitized form) and market risk (which also may be lower for the securitized form because of the reduced liquidation time required). Historically, more money has been lost in market risk than in credit risk, whether or not the mortgage investment was securitized. Therefore, it is relatively more important to be able to sell out of a position quickly if prices decline.

Among mortgage investors there tends to be a much greater preoccupation with the credit risk of the individual mortgage collateral, in spite of the fact that loss due to market or interest rate risk has far outweighed credit-related loss due to delinquency (slow and delayed payments) or foreclosure (loss of principal).

Market Risk

The longer the term to maturity of the investment, the greater is the holding risk and the less the liquidity in a rising interest-rate environment. The holding risk is greater with long-term securities for two reasons: the greater price volatility of the longer maturing security, and the loss of a positive spread between the fixed return on the asset versus the probable rising cost of variable-rate liabilities. Because a long-term security must change price by a greater amount than must a short-term security to maintain yield parity, increased maturity represents increased risk. To illustrate, assume a market in which short-term yields are at 10 percent and long-term yields are at 13 percent. Further assume the yield level of the whole fixed-income market increases by 200 basis points (or 2 percent) so that a 5-year maturity investment trades at 12 percent and a 20-year maturity investment at 15 percent. The 5-year maturity would be discounted by 7½ points in dollar price, while the 20-year maturity would be discounted 12 points to achieve the same 2 percent yield adjustment.

The risk of the loss of a positive spread on holding a long-term investment is simply an opportunity loss if the investment is held against matching funds. However, if the fixed-return investment is carried against short-term funds with a rising replacement cost, disaster may result. Proper asset-to-liability matching therefore becomes a critical ingredient in reducing market risk. It is the principal investment determinant for banking and thrift institutions, but it is less so for insurance companies and pension funds (who have a less volatile liability base).

Market timing is also an important consideration in making mortgage investments. Typically, long-term investments of any kind are best bought when rates are at a secular high; short-term investments are the better bet when rates are low. However, when market conditions are stable, the most common strategy is to extend to the longest maturity in an effort to obtain the best yields available at the time.

Call Protection

Call protection may be built into a corporate bond by imposing a contractual obligation on the issuer so that the bonds may not be prepaid for some specified period of time, usually 5 to 10 years. By contrast, a mortgage can be paid off without a prepayment penalty at any time the house is sold, or, in many instances, refinanced. Therefore, it is difficult to estimate the true average life of a mortgage investment.

The lack of call protection in mortgage-related investments is of particular concern because prepayments on mortgages with high coupons (and the highest book yields) prepay principal fastest in declining interest-rate cycles. Mortgages with low coupons (and the lowest book yield) pay off the slowest when rates are rising. One solution is to invest in seasoned, low-coupon, deep-discount portfolios at current market-rate yields. If the portfolio amortizes at a slow prepayment rate, there is de facto call protection, and the original market-rate yield is preserved. If the pool should prepay at a relatively faster rate, the realization of accelerated discount improves the yield.

CMO Protection

The CMO is structured with multiclass maturities. To understand how a CMO differs from traditional MBSs, picture a $10 million pool of mortgages backing the various types of mortgage securities. With the pass-through structure, the principal and interest payments made monthly on each of the mortgages are paid through monthly to the certificateholders just as they are received—thus the term *pass through*. In the case of the CMO, the principal and interest payments are not passed through monthly but are typically paid every six months (or semi-annually).

Several CMO certificates with sequential maturities may be issued. For example, a $10 million CMO is issued with three maturity classes, C–1, C–2 and C–3. All of the principal payments from the $10 million pool are directed entirely to the C–1 certificate until it is paid off in full. C–2 and C–3 receive *no* principal payments until C–1 is entirely paid off. When C–1 is paid in full, all the principal payments from the mortgage pool are applied to C–2 until it is paid off, and so on. The result is a multiclass-maturity MBS which may look as follows:

Certificate	Amount	Stated Maturity	Average Life
C–1	$2.15 million	5.0 years	3.2 years
C–2	$3.50 million	12.5 years	8.6 years
C–3	$4.35 million	30.0 years	20.4 years

The CMO structure is popular because the overall yield on all maturities of the CMO is less than that of the standard 30-year maturity, 12-year average life MBS.

Credit Risk

The best substitute for personal, knowledgeable, and direct loan underwriting is a guarantee or insurance. The introduction of FHA insurance in the 1930's first opened the possibilities for a secondary market. With the introduction of GNMA MBSs, reliance on the federal government's full-faith-and-credit guarantee eliminated fear of the loss of principal. Further, these pass-through certificates oblige the issuer to advance delinquent mortgage payments. Thus, any erosion of investment yield through delay in receipt of funds is eliminated. This required-payment feature means that an MBS has a more assured yield than does the underlying mortgage.

Private mortgage insurance placed on whole-loan offerings also eliminates a major portion of the credit risk associated with secondary-mortgage purchases. Perhaps as important as the risk benefit provided by the insurance itself is the knowledge that the mortgage insurer has done a thorough underwriting job on the loan before it was insured. The lower the percentage of insurance for a given loan-to-value ratio or on a specific pool, the more important become the mortgage characteristics, the real estate market in which the properties are located, and the reputation of the seller/servicer. Key questions: What are the underwriting practices of the originator? What is the delinquency experience of this originator with whole loans or pools previously placed in the secondary market?

Another approach to reducing credit and underwriting risk with bulk sales of mortgages is overcollateralization. For example, a $100 million mortgage bond offering may be collateralized by a pool consisting of $110 million of mortgages, an overcollateralization of $10 million. The benefit of such over-collateralization is that the principal payments made on the extra $10 million of mortgages are available to cover any shortfall resulting from delinquencies within the underlying pool. In effect, the extra collateral represents a reserve for the bond issue.

Privately underwritten offerings of mortgage-backed bonds use a combination of private mortgage insurance on each loan (generally insuring them to a 75 percent loan-to-value equivalent), pool insurance (generally 5 percent of the face amount of the pool), and special-hazard insurance to protect the investor from risk of principal loss, in addition to overcollateralization.

Other Yield Considerations

Fee income, which is normally associated with whole-loan purchase commitments, can be an important addition to the yield considerations. Industry convention is that each one point of fee income adds about ¼ percent to the effective yield of the investment. Fees may, for certain institutions, be taken directly into earnings in the fiscal year in which they are received. Other investors may elect to (or be required to) treat the fee as original-issue discount and amortize it over the estimated average life of the mortgages provided. Except for optional-delivery contracts on GNMAs, or certain specialized MBS offerings, fees are generally not available with purchases of securities.

Interest-rate-sensitive mortgages (where the rate on the mortgage changes periodically in accordance with a predetermined index) have become increasingly available. These adjustable-rate mortgages, or ARMs, lessen market risk by adjusting yield return as market conditions change. There is a vast array of different types of ARMs, and it is beyond the scope of this chapter to review them in detail. The predominant forms adjust to an index related to the yield on 1-, 3-, or 5-year government securities. Some have caps on the maximum amount the rate can adjust at one time (or over the life of the loan), although such interest-rate-capped ARMs offer less market-risk protection than do un-capped ARMs.

Mortgages with maturities shorter than the predominant 25 or 30 years are gaining acceptance. With shorter maturities, mortgages offer better market risk protection. Some 15-year, fully amortized mortgages and the early ownership mortgage (EOM) are being securitized.

The EOM is a mortgage which is typically set up as a 30-year amortizing loan with an annual payment escalator of from 3 to 7½ percent. The payment escalator results in an automatic acceleration in the reduction of principal. The actual maturity of the mortgage is usually reduced to 13 or 16 years, depending on the percent at which annual principal payments are increased. These features provide greater value stability, because the same level of market interest rates can be offset by a smaller price change than would be necessary for a longer maturity.

Forecasting Funds Available for Investment

Developing a forecast of future investable cash flow is an essential part of any secondary-market investment program. There are four sources of funds that may be available:

1. Return of principal and interest from existing investment.
2. A contractual source of funds (such as life insurance premiums or contributions to a pension plan).
3. Demand or savings deposits held by a depository institution.
4. Purchased funds such as the issuance of CDs or the sale of other money market instruments such as commercial paper, or, in the case of some financial institutions, money market deposit accounts.

Except for mortgage-related holdings, return of principal and interest (P & I) on existing investments is usually the most predictable source of cash flow. Other sources of funds that are relatively stable are: (1) savings deposits or (2) the contractual sources of funds (such as insurance premiums and pension contributions).

Although month-to-month variations in the aggregate base of such funds may be small, trends over long periods of time can cause cyclical changes in the aggregate base. In recent years, people have dramatically changed their patterns in buying life insurance, for example, which has caused a secular change in the availability of whole-life premiums available to insurance companies for investment. This kind of pattern takes place over years, however, and does not affect month-to-month forecasting. Such changes in long-term trends must be identified as they occur, because they obviously affect the viability of long-term investment commitments.

Forecasting becomes a highly sophisticated art when short-term, purchased funds are involved. Factors such as savings patterns and the willingness (and ability) of competitive institutions to pay a higher rate to attract funds can cause major, short-term swings in the availability of purchased funds. Even such factors as a superior (or inferior) advertising campaign to attract consumer savings dollars can be as important as is the willingness to pay a competitive rate for the funds.

The volatility of the types of funds to be used for investing is also a critical consideration. Highly volatile funds must, of necessity, be supported with a substantial liquidity reserve to offset a temporary reduction in short-term, purchased funds. The liquidity reserve can be liquidated with minimal market risk if the investments held are short-term, liquid assets. Long-term assets may also be a source of liquidity if they are eligible to be sold to a primary dealer under a sale and repurchase agreement (a *repo, agreement*), such as U.S. government securities, obligations of agencies guaranteed by the U.S. government, GNMA, FHLMC PCs, and FNMA pass-throughs. Corporate and municipal securities typically are not good sources of repos because of their lesser liquidity in the secondary market.

Forward-Delivery Transactions

Most secondary-market investments may be bought (or sold) for forward delivery. GNMA, FHLMC, and FNMA mortgage-backed securities are regularly traded on a 60- to 120-day forward-delivery basis. Straight mortgage investments may be committed six months or even more into the future.

The advantages of committing forward for delivery of securities are increased flexibility in planning future investments; the ability to sell the commitment prior to funding; and the ability to hedge changes in interest rates.

The ability to commit funds for forward commitment enables the portfolio manager to lock-in a desired investment rate before the investment is actually available for funding. In periods of declining interest rates, this improves portfolio performance and permits the orderly disposition of a future stream of cash flow with adequate decision time to select preferred investments.

If the market outlook changes prior to the funding date for the investment, the forward commitment (for purchase of securities) may be sold without an actual funding ever taking place. Of course, any profit or loss is realized on the originally scheduled funding date. The advantage of the forward-delivery market is that a profit can be preserved if prices start to decline prior to the original settlement date. Conversely, losses may be reduced by selling the commitment as soon as possible rather than being forced to wait for settlement.

Another advantage of forward commitments is that they may be suitable for hedging transactions in the financial futures market, a subject taken up at length elsewhere in this *Handbook*.

Disadvantages

Disadvantages of forward-delivery transactions include the risk of nondelivery of the contracted investment at the scheduled settlement. The risk of nondelivery is minimized when dealing with major securities dealers in GNMA, FHLMC, or FNMA securities. If the originator of the security fails to deliver to the dealer, the dealer remains obligated to make good on the trade at settlement. Forward transactions committed directly with the primary originator or with a financially weak intermediary can be risky if the market improves and the seller can sell elsewhere for a better profit. This contingency suggests restricting forward-delivery transactions to well-capitalized, reputable dealers and originators.

With whole-loan transactions, nondelivery of a forward commitment can become a very real consideration. The economic incentive to not deliver is almost irresistible to a nonregulated entity such as a developer or real estate syndicator. Fortunately, because of the discipline imposed on mortgage originators participating in the dealer-sponsored, forward-delivery markets for GNMA, FNMA, and FHLMC securities, nondelivery is now a minimal problem with reputable mortgage bankers and savings and loans who participate in these markets.

Credit risk is also increased with a forward-delivery transaction involving nonsecuritized mortgage-investment projects or income-property loans. The investor cannot exercise much control over a mortgage or real estate investment until his funds are actually invested in the transaction. Therefore, if property-management competency, occupancy, or other economic factors bearing on the viability of a real estate investment deteriorate between the commitment date and the funding date, it may be difficult to back away from the investment without incurring a lawsuit. In the meantime, the investor is generally unable to exercise control to alter the factors contributing to a deteriorating situation.

Accounting Considerations

Accounting procedures for most institutions are dictated by regulation and/or by generally accepted procedures adopted by accountants. Accounting for mortgage-related securities is unique in the treatment of discount or premium in relation to actual or expected-life assumptions. With newly issued mortgage-backed securities, discount is amortized and premium is accreted to the accepted average life expectancy of the security, with any adjustments based on actual prepayment experience made annually as an addition to or subtraction from income. Mortgage investments with a stated maturity of 30 years are typically treated for accounting purposes as though they have a 12-year assumed average life; mortgages with 15-year maturities as though they have a 7-year average life; and 40-year terms carry an 18-year average life. Investments with other maturities use an average life established by generally accepted industry practice and regulatory considerations.

Because the actual average-life experience of a given mortgage-related investment cannot be determined (except with the passage of time), actual prepayment experience that is slower or faster than that assumed for accounting purposes has an impact on income. This phenomenon is referred to as *speed*.

Discount with High Speed

For example, assume $1 million GNMA MBSs purchased at a price of 94 prepay faster than the 12-year average-life assumption. Accepted accounting procedure is to set up the 6 points discount ($6,000) to be straight-line amortized, or taken into income, at the rate of $500 a year ($6,000 ÷ 12 = $500). If the mortgage prepays more than 1/12th in the first year, there is more than $500 of discount realized, or earned, in the first year. An adjustment may be made at the end of the accounting period, which results in an increase in income and an increase in yield over book.

Discount with Slow Speed

A discount with slow speed, conversely, results in an actual prepayment experience slower than anticipated, resulting in realization of less than a $500 discount in the first full year. The adjustment is then a deduction from income and a reduction in book yield.

The accounting treatment for premiums is the reverse of that for discounts. If the MBS were purchased at a price of 106, each year $500 of premium is expensed. If the mortgage prepays faster than expected, more than $500 in premium expense must be realized, resulting in a reduction in income and yield.

The rule of thumb, then, is: Discount + High Speed = Higher Yield; Premium + High Speed = Lower Yield.

Seasoned loan portfolios are often priced at a yield to maturity or to an average weighted term to maturity. In this case, the discount is amortized to the weighted maturity, and any prepayment is an addition to income.

In the examples above, for simplicity, straight-line amortization was used. Other methods of accounting may be used (subject to regulatory constraint), such as the level-yield sum of the digits.

Tax Questions

Accrued Interest

Whether or not interest accrued and added to principal should be recognized as income for tax purposes requires the review of two IRS rulings. Revenue

Ruling 77–135 deals with interest added to principal in the context of a graduated-payment mortgage, and Revenue Ruling 80–248 deals with interest added to principal in the context of a reverse-amortization mortgage. Both rulings stress that the accounting method selected (cash versus accrual) determines whether interest is taxed in the year incurred or in the year it is actually paid.

Accrual-Basis Taxpayer

For an accrual-basis taxpayer, all events that fix the right to receive income occur when the required performance occurs; payment is due; or payment is made, whichever happens earlier. Performance therefore occurs when the lender allows the borrower to use the lender's money. Hence, if interest is added to principal (compound interest) in an ARM, and the lender is on the accrual basis, the lender has to report as income all interest on that loan, including the interest that was added (accrued) to the principal.

Cash-Basis Taxpayer

Under the cash method, partial payments for the discharge of indebtedness are, in the absence of an agreement to the contrary, applied first towards the reduction of interest due and then toward principal. Thus, if the cash method of accounting is used, GPM interest may be included in the income of the mortgagee for the taxable year in which it is actually or constructively received, and it is deductible by the mortgagor in the year paid. The addition of the unpaid interest to the note does not constitute a payment or receipt of interest. For the early years of the mortgage term, when the monthly payment does not fully cover the interest owed, the entire amount represents interest and may be included in the income of the mortgagee when received, and deducted by the mortgagor when paid. That part of the interest owed but not paid is not included in income by the mortgagee until received, and it is not allowed the mortgagor as a deduction until paid.

In subsequent years, following recasting of the loan, to amortize accumulated negative amortization added to the loan principal and to increase the payments so that they then exceed the current interest charge owed, the excess is to be applied to reduce the current balance of the loan. This excess is applied first to discharging the unpaid balance of the loan that represents accumulated interest carried over from prior years. At that time, it is included in income by the mortgagee and deducted by the mortgagor as interest.

Summary

The mortgage market offers a wide diversity of products. Mortgages packaged in securitized form by the federally sponsored agencies (GNMA, FNMA, and FHLMC) represent about half of all mortgages sold in the secondary market and are the most actively traded by the Wall Street dealer community. With the introduction of the CMO, investors have a diversity of maturities to choose from with a fair degree of call protection in the long-maturing certificates. The CMO has also led to a surge in privately issued (nonfederal-agency-sponsored) mortgage-backed securities.

The investor seeking maximum yield and maturity diversity should also consider the whole-loan (nonsecuritized) segment of the market. Most current whole-loan offerings are adjustable-rate mortgages indexed to the commercial bank prime rate or to Treasury bond yields. Institutional investors not having in-house mortgage underwriting capability may buy participations in whole loans that are packaged and serviced by institutions intimately familiar with mortgage underwriting procedures.

Market and credit-risk considerations are important for the institutional mortgage investor to analyze. Market risk has been the cause of far greater loss to mortgage investors than credit risk. Liquidity is a key factor in reducing market risk. With increasing standardization of the mortgage instrument and a secondary market larger than the corporate or municipal bond market, liquidity is excellent for mortgage-backed securities, particularly those issued by the federally sponsored agencies. The breadth of the secondary mortgage market has grown to the point where there is considerable liquidity in whole-loan offerings as well.

Market risk can also be substantially reduced with proper matching of assets to liabilities (by investing in maturities that correspond as closely as possible to the average maturity of the liabilities used to carry the investment). Investing in interest-rate-sensitive, or adjustable-rate, instruments is also an excellent way to mitigate market risk.

Credit risk may be lessened with mortgage insurance. With the case of federal-agency-guaranteed MBSs, it may be virtually eliminated. Good loan-by-loan underwriting is the cornerstone to reducing credit risk with mortgage instruments. If one is not buying agency-backed paper, one should carefully check out the delinquency experience of the servicing portfolio of the seller.

The secondary market has come of age. The determinants of the secondary mortgage market are essentially the same as those of any other: yield, liquidity, and the preservation of capital. Because of its size and diversity, the mortgage market offers perhaps more variables to these basic determinants than does any other fixed-income market available today.

Chapter 27

Determining the Yield

Dexter E. Senft
Vice President, Fixed Income Research
The First Boston Corporation

In order to understand and analyze mortgage-related securities, it is necessary to understand how mortgages operate. Therefore we shall briefly examine the types of mortgage loans in existence today, their cash flows, and certain other aspects relevant to the analysis of pass-through securities.

What Is a Mortgage?

By definition, a *mortgage* is a pledge of property to secure payment of a debt. Typically, property refers to real estate, which is often in the form of a house; the debt is the loan given to the buyer of the house by a bank or other lender. Thus a mortgage might be a pledge of a house to secure payment of a bank loan. If a homeowner (the *mortgagor*) fails to pay the lender (the *mortgagee*), the lender has the right to foreclose the loan and seize the property in order to ensure that it is repaid.

The form that a mortgage loan takes could technically be anything the borrower and lender agree upon. Traditionally, however, most mortgage loans were structured similarly. There was a fixed rate of interest on the loan for its entire term, and the loan was repaid in monthly installments of principal and interest. Each loan was structured in such a way that the total payment each month (the sum of the principal and interest) was equal, or *level*. We shall refer to this type of loan arrangement as a *traditional mortgage loan*. In a traditional mortgage loan, the terms to be negotiated are the interest rate and the period to maturity. Interest rates vary with the general economic climate, and maturities range from 12 to 40 years, depending on the type of property involved. Most mortgages on single-family homes carry 30-year maturities.

Figure 1 illustrates the breakdown of monthly payments between principal and interest on a 30-year, 10 percent traditional mortgage. At first, the mortgage payment is mostly interest. The principal portion increases over time until, at maturity, the payment is almost entirely principal. At all times, however, the sum of the principal and interest payments is the same. Notice that over the course of the loan the borrower pays more dollars as interest than as princi-

Figure 1 • Monthly Mortgage Payments: Interest/ Principal (30-year 10 percent conventional loan)

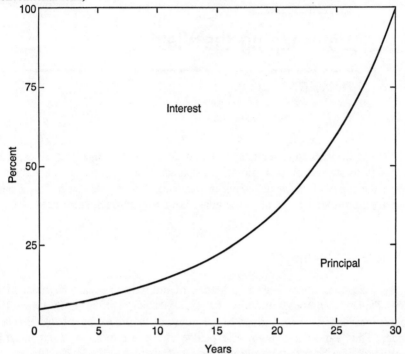

pal—in fact, total interest is more than twice total principal in this example.

The principal portion of each monthly payment is used to reduce the amount of the loan outstanding. In mortgage terms, the loan is *amortized* over 30 years, and the principal payments each month are known as *amortization payments*. The amount of the loan that is outstanding at any time is known as the *mortgage balance*. In any month, the interest payment equals the interest rate (expressed monthly) times the mortgage balance at the beginning of the month (see Table 1). Often the mortgage balance is expressed as a ratio or percentage of the original loan amount, in which case the mortgage balance runs from 1 (or 100 percent) initially, to 0 at maturity. Figure 2 shows how the mortgage balance for several possible loans would decline over time. Another way to view the mortgage balance is as the amount of the house value the home buyer does not yet own. The amount of a home's value that is owned is referred to as the *homeowner's equity*. *Equity* can be defined as the difference between the current value of the home and the mortgage balance; as the mortgage balance declines, the equity rises. Equity also increases if the current value of the home increases, due to home improvements, inflation, etc.

Sometimes a mortgagor may want to make a monthly payment that is greater

Table 1 • Sample Payment Schedule: Traditional Mortgage (10 percent interest rate, 30-year [360-month] term)

| Month | Mortgage Balance | | Monthly Payment | Interest | Principal |
	Dollars	Decimal			
0	50000.00	1.00000			
1	49977.88	.99956	438.79	416.67	22.12
2	49955.58	.99911	438.79	416.48	22.30
3	49933.09	.99866	438.79	416.30	22.49
4	49910.41	.99821	438.79	416.11	22.68
5	49887.55	.99775	438.79	415.92	22.87
6	49864.49	.99729	438.79	415.73	23.06
7	49841.24	.99682	438.79	415.54	23.25
8	49817.80	.99636	438.79	415.34	23.44
9	49794.16	.99588	438.79	415.15	23.64
10	49770.33	.99541	438.79	414.95	23.83
100	46567.88	.93136	438.79	388.48	50.30
101	46517.16	.93034	438.79	388.07	50.72
102	46466.02	.92932	438.79	387.64	51.14
103	46414.45	.92829	438.79	387.22	51.57
200	38697.88	.77396	438.79	323.44	115.34
201	38581.57	.77163	438.79	322.48	116.30
202	38464.30	.76929	438.79	321.51	117.27
203	38346.05	.76692	438.79	320.54	118.25
300	20651.61	.41303	438.79	174.30	264.48
301	20384.93	.40770	438.79	172.10	266.69
302	20116.01	.40232	438.79	169.87	268.91
303	19844.86	.39690	438.79	167.63	271.15
355	2140.13	.04280	438.79	21.31	417.47
356	1719.18	.03438	438.79	17.83	420.95
357	1294.72	.02589	438.79	14.33	424.46
358	866.72	.01733	438.79	10.79	428.00
359	435.16	.00870	438.79	7.22	431.56
360	0.00	.00000	438.79	3.63	435.16

Note: Each month, the interest payment is $\frac{1}{12}$ of 10 percent of the mortgage balance. The principal payment is the total payment less the interest due. The principal balance is reduced by the amount of the principal payment.

than the amount actually due, with the idea of applying the excess payment to further reducing the loan. Such excess principal payments are called *prepayments* and may be made for several reasons (these reasons will be discussed in detail later). Prepayments result in a direct reduction of the mortgage balance and a direct increase in the amount of equity. Another way to define mortgage balance is to say that it equals the original loan amount less the total amount of amortization and prepayments to date.

A mortgagor who fails to make a mortgage payment is said to be *delinquent*. Delinquencies can have a variety of causes—the homeowner may have died, become unemployed, bounced a check, or simply forgotten to make the pay-

Figure 2 • Examples of Mortgage Balances for Various Loans

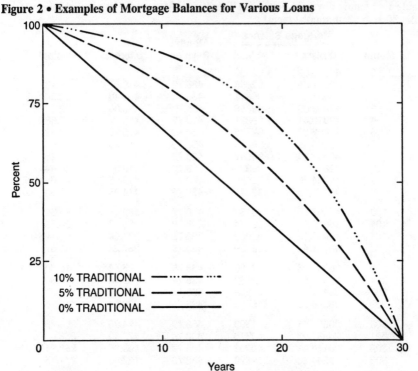

ment. The mortgagee then reminds the homeowner that the payment is overdue and attempts to collect the money. If the matter is not resolved quickly, the mortgagee may assess the mortgagor with a late payment charge. Sometimes there is no quick solution, and the mortgagor may become more than one month in arrears. Although most lenders are willing to allow a borrower a few months leeway, in extreme cases it may be necessary for the bank to foreclose the loan, in which case the property is taken from the mortgagor and sold in order to pay off the loan.

Qualifying for a Mortgage

Borrowers who are interested in obtaining mortgage loans must meet certain standards set by the lender in order to be considered creditworthy. The first thing a lender checks is whether the borrower has any other loans or obligations outstanding; if so, these will diminish the borrower's ability to make mortgage payments. Next, the lender determines the income and net worth of the borrower. Many mortgage lenders use these classical rules of thumb to determine whether or not a borrower's income is adequate for the mortgage:

1. The total mortgage payment (principal and interest) should not exceed 25 percent of the borrower's total income less any payments owed for other obligations.
2. Total mortgage payments plus other housing expenses should not exceed 33 percent of the borrower's income less payments for other obligations. Other housing expenses include such items as taxes, insurance, utilities, and normal maintenance costs.

Of course, these percentages may vary depending on the lender and the circumstances. In particular, borrowers with relatively high net worth and/or liquid assets will find lenders to be more flexible. Also, in times of high interest rates and tight money, lenders have been known to bend these rules somewhat in order to maintain a certain level of business.

The buyer is usually required to make a down payment on the property in order to qualify for the mortgage. The down payment might range anywhere from 5 to 25 percent of the purchase price. The reason for requiring a down payment is that, in the event the lender is forced to foreclose the loan and sell the property, the mortgage balance will be more easily recovered. In other words, there is room for error if the property is sold—even if it cannot bring the original purchase price on the market, there can still be enough to cover the debt. Lenders use the term *loan-to-value ratio,* or LTV, to express the amount of protection on the mortgage. LTV is calculated as the ratio of the mortgage balance to the market value of the property and is expressed as a percentage. The lower the LTV, the less the loan amount relative to the property value, and the greater the safety.

The LTV ratio tends to decrease over time. For example, if a buyer makes a 10 percent down payment on a property and mortgages the rest, the LTV is initially 90 percent. Over time, the mortgage balance declines (from amortization and prepayments), while the property value tends to increase due to inflation. Both of these changes serve to lower the LTV.

As with income requirements, down payment and LTV requirements depend on certain circumstances. These include not only the net worth of the borrower but the condition and marketability of the property and the availability of credit. Higher LTV ratios are associated with newer, more marketable properties, and with easier credit and lower interest rates.

An important (if not obvious) conclusion about qualifying for a mortgage is that it becomes harder when interest rates rise. Because of the income and LTV requirements, smaller mortgage balances are affordable when rates rise, and yet this is also the time when inflation, and therefore home purchase prices, is rising. As a consequence, all but those buyers with large amounts of cash or equity are squeezed from the market.

Servicing

Among the jobs that mortgage lenders must perform in order to ensure that borrowers make timely and accurate payments are: sending payment notices, reminding borrowers when payments are overdue, recording prepayments, keeping records of mortgage balances, administering escrow accounts for payment of property taxes or insurance, sending out tax information at year-end, and initiating foreclosure proceedings. These functions are collectively known as *servicing the loans.* Many times the original lender, known as the *mortgage originator,* is the one who services the loan, but this is not always the case. Sometimes the mortgage is sold to someone else, and the servicing of the loan may or may not go along with the mortgage.

In the event that one party owns a mortgage and another services it, the servicer receives a fee (the *servicing fee*) for the trouble. Servicing fees usually take the form of a fixed percentage of the mortgage balance outstanding. Although the percentage may vary from one servicer to the next, it is usually in the area of .25 percent to .50 percent. Small servicing-fee percentages are usually associated with larger commercial property loans, and larger percentages with smaller residential loans. From the point of view of the owner of the mortgage, the servicing fee comes out of the interest portion of the mortgage payment. For example, if party A owns a 10 percent mortgage being serviced by party B for a three eighths of 1 percent fee, then A is really earning 9⅝ percent (10 percent minus three eighths of 1 percent) on the loan.

In addition to servicing fees, there are occasionally other fees that the servicer may keep. For example, some servicers are entitled to keep late-payment penalties paid by the borrower, foreclosure penalties, and certain other penalty fees. The specific types and amounts of fees that servicers are entitled to receive are set forth in a servicing agreement between the mortgage owner and the servicer.

Where Does Mortgage Money Come From?

Figure 3 shows the originators of mortgage loans in the United States over the last decade. The largest single originating group has been the savings and loan industry. Savings and loans, together with savings banks and credit unions, constitute the *thrift industry*—so-called because its funds come from the savings accumulated by thrifty depositors. Commercial banks make up the second largest group of originators, and, as in thrift institutions, the money they put into mortgages comes primarily from deposits. The third major source of mortgage loans is the mortgage-company sector, or mortgage banks. Unlike savings banks or commercial banks, mortgage banks do not have depositors. They are in the business of finding other sources of mortgage money, such as thrifts or insurance companies, and making it available for housing construction

Figure 3 • Originators of U.S. Mortgage Loans: 1972-1982

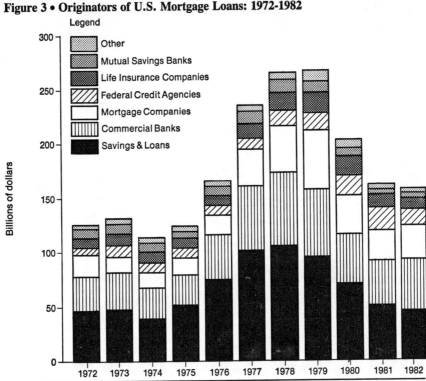

and ownership; mortgage bankers' profits come from servicing the loans they originate, plus any profit that can be made from buying and selling the mortgages. The lesser originators of mortgages are the insurance companies, pension funds, and various federal, state, and local entities empowered to make mortgage loans.

Knowing who originates mortgages, however, does not really answer the question of where mortgage money comes from. The real lenders of mortgage money are those who *own* mortgages, who are somewhat different from those who create them. Mortgage bankers, for example, generally do not want to own mortgages at all—once they create them, they sell the mortgages to someone else. Figure 4 breaks down the ownership of mortgages in the United States by type of holder over the past 13 years. The thrifts and commercial banks prove to be the major holders of mortgages, but there are several other notable ones. Life insurance companies, for example, have owned between 9 percent and 16 percent of all mortgages over the past decade, with a trend toward holding less. Individuals and others have owned 13–16 percent fairly consistently. The owner category with by far the largest growth is mortgage pools, which went from almost zero in 1970 to over 10 percent by 1982.

Figure 4 • Mortgages by Type of Holder: 1970-1982

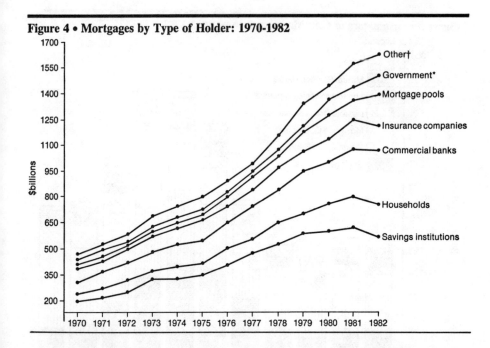

What are these pools? Essentially, they are collections of mortgages of which shares, or participations, are resold to someone else. (In this sense, mortgage pools as an ownership category is not very informative.) Mortgage pools will be examined later in greater detail.

What Types of Properties Are Mortgaged?

Virtually all forms of real estate have been mortgaged. These properties fall into several categories. First, property (and the mortgage on it) can be classified as either residential or nonresidential, depending on whether or not people use the property primarily for living. Residential properties include houses, apartments, condominiums, cooperatives, and mobile homes. These do not necessarily have to be someone's primary residence—for example, summer homes and skiing condominiums are classified as residential properties. Residential properties are subdivided into one-to-four family dwellings and multifamily dwellings for the purposes of Federal Reserve statistics.

Nonresidential properties are subdivided into commercial properties and farm properties. The commercial category encompasses a wide variety of properties, such as office buildings, shopping centers, hospitals, and industrial plants.

Figure 5 shows the outstanding amounts of mortgage debt in various years

Figure 5 • Mortgages by Type of Property: 1970–1982

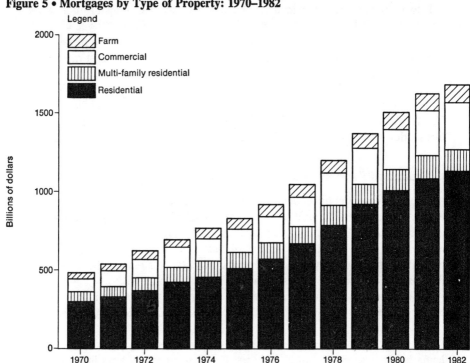

broken out by type of property. For the past 30 years, roughly three of every four mortgage dollars went to finance residential property, and of that amount, more than 80 percent went to one-to-four-family dwellings.

Nontraditional Mortgages

The decade of the 1970s saw the advent of many new and different varieties of mortgages. Unlike traditional mortgages, most of these *alternative mortgage instruments* (AMIs) do not have level monthly payments, but employ some other (often complicated) scheme.

What was the impetus for the creation of AMIs, and in what ways are they superior to traditional mortgages? The answers to these questions are related to the level and behavior of mortgage interest rates. In the 15 years ending in 1979, mortgage rates doubled, from roughly 6-percent levels to 12-percent levels, and by 1981 they had almost tripled, to 17 percent. More importantly, the volatility of these rates increased tremendously. Moves of 1 percentage point between the time a loan application was made and the time the loan was closed were not unheard of in 1979. The interest climate resulted in a great deal of risk to both borrower and lender. The rate that seemed plausible one week might be out of line the next week. (Not to mention the next 30 years.) High interest rates combined with the rapid inflation in housing prices to make home financing difficult in general, and all but impossible for the first-time buyer. AMIs were created as a way of coping with these problems.

There are literally dozens of different types of AMIs, each with its own peculiar twist. Their names, which are often abbreviated, include GPMs, VRMs, ARMs, PAMs, PLAMs, GEMs, FLIPs, and SAMs. The remainder of this section will discuss some of the salient features of the more popular AMIs.

Graduated Payment Mortgages (GPMs)

The only essential difference between the GPM and the traditional mortgage is that the payments on a GPM are not all equal. *Graduated payment* refers to the fact that GPM payments start at a relatively low level and rise for some number of years. The actual number of years that the payments rise and the percentage increase per year depend on the exact type or plan of the GPM. The five major GPM plans work as shown in Table 2 below.

At the end of the graduation period, the monthly payment is held at its existing level for the remainder of the mortgage term. Table 3 shows the payment schedule on a $50,000, 10 percent, Plan III GPM.

The attraction of a GPM is the small payment in its early years. A first-time home buyer who might not be able to afford payments on a traditional mortgage might be able to afford the smaller payments of the GPM, even if both loans were for the same principal amount. Eventually, when the graduation period has ended, homeowners with GPMs make up the difference by paying larger monthly amounts than the traditional mortgages require. The originators of GPMs reason that most home buyers, particularly young, first-time home buyers, have incomes that will increase at least as rapidly as the mortgage payments increase. Thus they should always be able to afford their monthly payments. Table 4 compares the initial and final payments of a traditional mortgage with the five GPM plans, assuming all mortgages have a $50,000 balance and a 10 percent interest rate. Notice that the lowest initial payment is on the

Table 2 • Major GPM Plans

Plan	Term to Maturity (years)	Years That Payments Rise	Percentage Increase per Year
I	30	5	2.5%
II	30	5	5.0
III	30	5	7.5
IV	30	10	2.0
V	30	10	3.0

Table 3 • Mortgage Payment Schedule for a $50,000 Plan III GPM (30-year term, 10 percent mortgage rate)

Year(s)	Monthly Payment
1	$333.52
2	358.53
3	385.42
4	414.33
5	445.40
6–30	478.81

Note: Plan III GPMs call for monthly payments that increase by 7.5 percent at the end of each of the first five years of the mortgage.

Plan III GPM, and in this example it is about $100 less per month than the traditional mortgage in the first year. It is perhaps not surprising that Plan III GPMs are the most popular and have accounted for more than 80 percent of all GPMs originated in late 1978 and early 1979. The Plan III GPM is the only plan to offer a 7.5 percent graduation rate; this is the maximum graduation rate that federally chartered banks can currently offer.

Because GPMs have smaller initial payments than do traditional mortgages, they do not pay down their mortgage balances as quickly. The interesting feature of GPMs is that in their early years they do not pay down any principal at all—in fact their mortgage balances actually *increase* for a short period of time. Technically, we would say that they experience *negative amortization* at the outset. To see how this works, consider the first monthly payment on the GPM in Table 3.

Interest due for month one is 10 percent per year for one-twelfth year on $50,000 balance.

$= \$50,000 \times \frac{1}{12} \times \frac{10}{100} = \$416.67$

Payment on GPM $= \$333.52$

Principal paid $= \$333.52 - \$416.67 = -\$83.15$

New mortgage balance $= \$50,000 - (-\$83.15) = \$50,083.15$

Table 4 • Comparison of Initial and Final Payments: Traditional Mortgage versus GPMs ($50,000, 10 percent, 30-year mortgages)

Loan Type	Initial Payment	Final Payment
Traditional	$438.79	$438.79
GPM Plan I	400.29	452.89
GPM Plan II	365.29	466.22
GPM Plan III	333.52	478.81
GPM Plan IV	390.02	475.43
GPM Plan V	367.29	493.60

Another way of viewing this situation is as follows: The amount paid on the mortgage ($333.52) was insufficient to cover even the interest due on the loan ($416.67), so the shortfall ($83.15) is lent to the mortgagor. Thus the new mortgage balance is the sum of the original balance plus the new loan:

$$\$50,000 + \$83.15 = \$50,083.15$$

Of course, the mortgage balance must eventually be reduced to zero. The annual increases in the mortgage payment eventually catch up to and overtake the amount of interest due, and at that time the mortgage balance begins to decrease. In Table 5, the mortgage balances (expressed as ratios to the original loan amount) are shown at the end of each year, for all five GPM plans, as well as for a traditional mortgage. Notice that a 10 percent Plan III GPM has

Table 5 • Graduated Payment Mortgage (GPM) Factor Comparison for 10 Percent, 30-Year Loans

Year-End Factors	Traditional Mortgage	Plan I 5-Year 2.5 Percent	Plan II 5-Year 5.0 Percent	Plan III 5-Year 7.5 Percent	Plan IV 10-Year 2.0 Percent	Plan V 10-Year 3.0 Percent
0	1.00000	1.00000	1.00000	1.00000	1.00000	1.00000
1	.99444	1.00412	1.01291	1.02090	1.00670	1.01241
2	.98830	1.00615	1.02258	1.03769	1.01214	1.02335
3	.98152	1.00582	1.02845	1.04949	1.01615	1.03258
4	.97402	1.00281	1.02987	1.05526	1.01853	1.03985
5	.96574	.99678	1.02612	1.05383	1.01909	1.04484
6	.95660	.98734	1.01640	1.04385	1.01759	1.04725
7	.94649	.97691	1.00567	1.03282	1.01376	1.04669
8	.93533	.96539	.99381	1.02064	1.00732	1.04277
9	.92300	.95266	.98071	1.00719	.99796	1.03504
10	.90938	.93860	.96623	.99233	.98532	1.02299
11	.89433	.92307	.95025	.97591	.96902	1.00606
12	.97771	.90591	.93258	.95777	.95101	.98736
13	.85934	.88696	.91307	.93773	.93111	.96670
14	.83906	.86602	.89151	.91559	.90913	.94388
15	.81665	.84289	.86770	.89113	.88484	.91867
16	.79189	.81733	.84140	.86412	.85802	.89082
17	.76454	.78910	.81233	.83427	.82838	.86005
18	.73432	.75792	.78023	.80130	.79564	.82606
19	.70094	.72347	.74477	.76488	.75948	.78851
20	.66407	.68541	.70559	.72464	.71953	.74703
21	.62333	.64336	.66230	.68019	.67539	.70120
22	.57833	.59692	.61449	.63108	.62663	.65058
23	.52862	.54561	.56167	.57684	.57277	.59466
24	.47370	.48892	.50332	.51691	.51326	.53288
25	.41303	.42631	.43885	.45071	.44752	.46468
26	.34601	.35713	.36764	.37757	.37491	.38924
27	.27197	.28071	.28897	.29678	.29468	.30595
28	.19018	.19629	.20207	.20752	.20606	.21394
29	.09982	.10303	.10606	.10892	.10816	.11229
30	.00000	.00000	00000	.00000	.00000	.00000

a balance that rises through the end of the fourth year, at which point it declines to zero over the next 26 years. It is interesting to note that the mortgage balance does not go below 1.0 until some time in the 10th year. Figure 6 is a graph of the mortgage balances for a traditional mortgage and a Plan III GPM.

GPMs were first introduced by the Federal Housing Administration (FHA) in November 1976, although various legal and technical matters prevented any large-scale issuance until late 1978. In April 1979, GPMs became eligible for pooling into GNMA pass-through securities, and since that time GPMs have accounted for roughly 25–30 percent of all FHA-insured mortgages.

Pledged-Account Mortgages (PAMs)

Pledged-account mortgages are structured so as to resemble GPMs from the borrower's point of view, and traditional mortgages from the lender's point of view. This is engineered by using some or all of the down payment on the property to create a pledged savings account that not only becomes collateral on the loan, but also is used to pay off the mortgage. The borrower makes mortgage payments that are initially small; withdrawals from the savings ac-

Figure 6 • Comparison between a Plan III GPM and a Traditional Mortgage

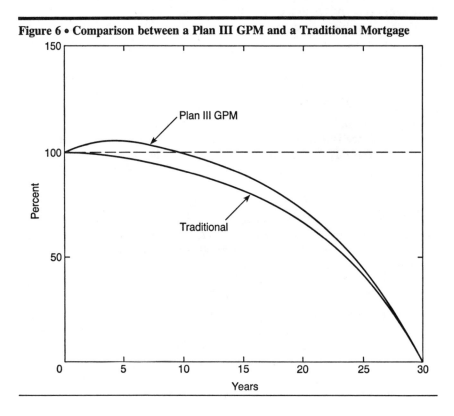

count are made to supplement the payments. The bank, which receives the sum of the two amounts, gets a level stream of payments, just as it would with a traditional mortgage.

Figure 7 shows a sample PAM mortgage scheme for a buyer who is interested in a $55,000 house and who has down-payment money of $8,767.50. With a traditional mortgage, the buyer would get a mortgage for $46,232.50 (the house price less the down payment). Assuming a 10 percent interest rate, this would require a monthly payment of $405.73. In the PAM example, $5,000 of the down-payment money is applied to the house directly (leaving $50,000 to be mortgaged), and the remaining $3,767.50 is used to create the pledged savings account, which returns the passbook savings rate (assumed to be 5¼ percent in this example). In the first year of the PAM mortgage, the homeowner pays only $327.89 per month, and an additional $110.90 is taken from the savings account each month. The out-of-pocket monthly expense during the first year is $77.84 less than the traditional mortgage, a saving of 19.2 percent. After each of the first five years of this PAM mortgage, the payment from the borrower rises (6 percent in this case), and the saving relative to the traditional mortgage decreases. As with a GPM, when the graduation period is over, the monthly PAM payment is greater than the payment on the traditional mortgage. (The savings in the early years are paid for in the later years.)

While all of this goes on at the borrower's level, the bank receives a constant monthly sum of $438.79—precisely the amount that the monthly payments on a traditional mortgage of $50,000 would be and the amount the homeowner pays out-of-pocket in years 6 through 30, after the savings account is exhausted. From the bank's point of view, the total indebtedness of the borrower equals the mortgage balance less whatever money is in the savings account. Because money is withdrawn from the savings account faster than the mortgage balance is paid down, the total indebtedness of the borrower rises for the first 5 years. This is analogous to the rise in the mortgage balance of a GPM during the period of negative amortization. If, in this example, we assume that the property value remains at $55,000 (no inflation or improvement), the LTV ratio of the mortgage will rise for five years. If the bank had a maximum LTV ratio of 85 percent, then this PAM would not be feasible because even though it is low enough in the first year, the LTV rises above .85 in years two through nine. An LTV maximum of 90 percent would be met, however. In making PAM loans, therefore (and GPMs as well), the lender must examine the maximum possible LTV that the loan can reach in order to determine whether the loan meets the lender's standards or whether additional cash for a down payment or mortgage insurance is called for.

The PAM loan is really an ingenious way of trading net worth (or assets) against income. The borrower who has sufficient cash on hand, but faces an income or cash flow shortage for the first few years, uses the cash to create the savings account, which subsequently subsidizes the monthly payments and lowers the out-of-pocket cost. The price the borrower pays for this privilege is that

Figure 7 • Traditional and PAM Mortgages
Traditional Mortgage

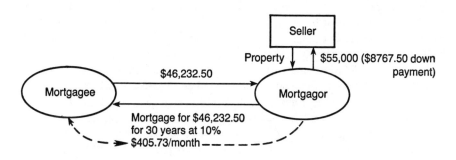

PAM Mortgage

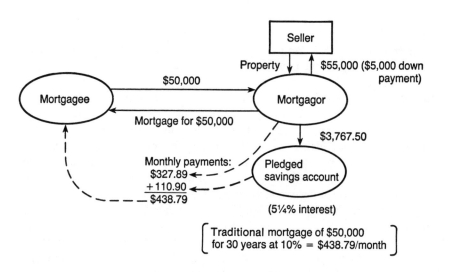

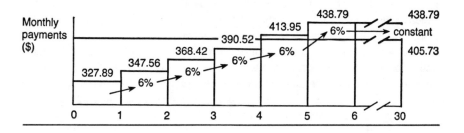

the interest rate on the savings account generally does not yield as much as the mortgage rate costs. The additional cost of a PAM loan over 30 years equals the difference between the mortgage rate and the savings passbook rate on the savings balances for the period of graduation. As with GPMs, however, the PAM could be the best buy in the long run, despite these added costs, because the costs are repaid in the later years of the mortgage. If inflation is sufficiently high, the homeowner repays current benefits with inflated future dollars.

Like GPMs, PAMs come in a variety of packages with different terms to maturity, graduation periods, and graduation rates. Because PAMs are designed to meet constraints on income-to-expense ratios and LTV ratios and take into account such factors as mortgage insurance, property insurance, and taxes, the actual payment schedules vary somewhat from the simple pattern shown in Figure 7. Although PAMs do not have the same popularity as GPMs right now (primarily because they have not been eligible for FHA insurance), the PAM is an interesting form of AMI that deserves closer attention in the future.

Buy-Down Loans

The buy-down loan is very similar to the PAM loan just described, except that it is the seller, not the buyer, who places cash in a segregated account that is subsequently used to augment the buyer's mortgage payments. When newly constructed property is financed in this fashion, the loans may be referred to as *builder buy-downs*, since the seller is the home builder. In general, these loans derive their name from the fact that the seller is using cash to buy down the mortgage rate from a high level to a lower level for some period of time.

The buy-down loan is very attractive from the buyer's point of view because it provides the benefit of a PAM loan or a GPM at someone else's expense. It might seem that the seller could pass along the cost of the buy-down to the buyer by increasing the price of the house; although this may occur to some small extent, it is not true in general because the mortgage lender places constraints on the maximum LTV ratio. The seller of the home cannot arbitrarily hike the price of the property, lest there be a difference of opinion with the lender, who bases the LTV ratio on the appraised value of the property.

What motivation does the seller have, then, to give up part of the profit on the sale in order to create a buy-down loan? And would it not be simpler just to reduce the price of the property? The answer to both these questions is that the buy-down loan is very often the only financing vehicle that can get the property sold, because it is the only type of loan that potential buyers may qualify for. Consider a comparison of two possible ways of financing a $60,000 house (see Figure 8), using as alternatives a 30-year traditional loan and a buy-down loan. In both cases, it is assumed that the prevailing mortgage interest rate is 16 percent, that the home buyer has $10,000 down-payment money, and that the home builder is willing to give up $3,000 of its profit. The buy-down loan shown in the exhibit is of the *3–2–1 variety,* meaning that the buyer pays

Figure 8 • Traditional and Buy-Down Loans
Traditional LTV = 83.3%

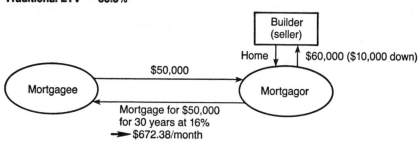

Builder lowers sale price by $3,000: LTV = 78.3%

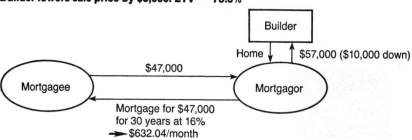

Builder buys down interest rate:

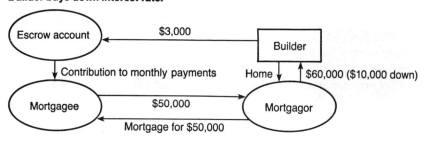

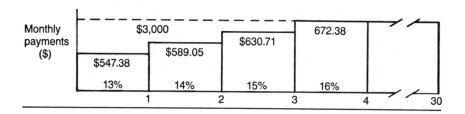

3 percent less interest the first year (13 percent in this case), 2 percent less the second year, 1 percent less the third year, and all of the mortgage payment thereafter.

If the builder contributes no money to the sale, the monthly payment (on a $50,000 traditional loan) is $672.38. If the builder simply contributes $3,000 to the purchase (by selling the house for $57,000) the monthly payment on the $47,000 loan is reduced to $632.04. If the $3,000 is used to buy down the interest rate from 16 percent according to the 3–2–1 plan, however, the initial monthly payment is only $547.37 and graduates to $672.38 after three years. The buyer of the house can now apply for a loan based on a monthly payment that is roughly 14 percent less than the payment would have been if the price of the property had simply been lowered. Since the seller is the one who is buying down the rate, no increase in down payment is required. Furthermore, if the escrow account in which the seller's funds are placed pays some rate of interest, then not all of the $3,000 will be necessary to buy down the rate (for example, if the account pays 8 percent, then only about $2,700 would be needed). Thus the buy-down loan can be a cheaper alternative for the seller as well.

Growing Equity Mortgages (GEMs)

The GEM loan surfaced in the early 1980s, largely in response to investor demand for a mortgage instrument with less market risk. Specifically, it was designed to have a shorter life than the usual 30 years, accomplished by a graduating series of mortgage payments over time. As the homeowner's payments graduate, his mortgage balance is reduced more quickly than usual, which leads to the *growing equity pattern* implied in the name of the loan.

GEMs are mathematically similar to GPMs, but have a few important differences at the practical level:

1. A GEM loan has payments that graduate for its entire life, unlike the GPM, whose payments rise for only the first 5 or 10 years.
2. The first year's payment on a GEM is the same as that on a traditional 30-year loan, whereas the GPM starts with a much smaller payment. The GEM, therefore, has no negative amortization.
3. Since the GEM starts with 30-year amortization, but also has graduating payments, its balance is extinguished very quickly. The GPM, with its initial negative amortization, is designed to amortize over exactly 30 years.

Table 6 compares the payments and mortgage balances of a traditional loan, a GPM, and a 3 percent GEM (that is, a GEM whose payments rise 3 percent each year). In each case, the loan is for $50,000 at 10 percent. Note that the GEM's payments graduate like the GPM's, except that they start from a higher level (the level of the traditional loan). The GEM's mortgage balance initially

Table 6 • Mortgage Balances and Total Annual Payments for Various Mortgages
10 percent loans, $50,000 initial balances

	Traditional Mortgage		PLAN III GPM		3.0% GEM	
Year-end	Mortgage Balance	Total Payment	Mortgage Balance	Total Payment	Mortgage Balance	Total Payment
1	49,722	5,265	51,045	4,002	49,722	5,265
2	49,415	5,265	51,885	4,302	49,250	5,423
3	49,076	5,265	52,475	4,625	48,557	5,586
4	48,701	5,265	52,763	4,972	47,617	5,754
5	48,287	5,265	52,691	5,345	46,398	5,926
6	47,830	5,265	52,192	5,746	44,864	6,104
7	47,325	5,265	51,641	5,746	42,979	6,287
8	46,767	5,265	51,032	5,746	40,698	6,476
9	46,150	5,265	50,359	5,746	37,975	6,670
10	45,469	5,265	49,616	5,746	34,758	6,870
11	44,717	5,265	48,795	5,746	30,987	7,076
12	43,885	5,265	47,888	5,746	26,600	7,289
13	42,967	5,265	46,886	5,746	21,524	7,507
14	41,953	5,265	45,779	5,746	15,681	7,732
15	40,832	5,265	44,557	5,746	8,984	7,964
16	39,594	5,265	43,206	5,746	1,334	8,203
17	38,227	5,265	41,714	5,746	0	1,351
18	36,716	5,265	40,065	5,746		
19	35,047	5,265	38,244	5,746		
20	33,203	5,265	36,232	5,746		
21	31,167	5,265	34,009	5,746		
22	28,917	5,265	31,554	5,746		
23	26,431	5,265	28,842	5,746		
24	23,685	5,265	25,845	5,746		
25	20,652	5,265	22,535	5,746		
26	17,301	5,265	18,879	5,746		
27	13,599	5,265	14,839	5,746		
28	9,509	5,265	10,376	5,746		
29	4,991	5,265	5,446	5,746		
30	0	5,265	0	5,746		

declines like the traditional loan's, but decreases more rapidly in its later years, becoming extinguished by the end of year 15.

The GEM does not directly attempt to make qualification for a mortgage any easier on prospective borrowers. On the contrary, it demands the same ability to afford traditional loan payments, plus the graduations in the later years. This may have served to discourage potential borrowers from GEM loans, despite the fact that the payment graduation rate is usually small. On the other hand, GEM borrowers could take comfort in the knowledge that they would own the property free and clear in much less time than with a traditional loan. GEMs do address the qualification issue indirectly, however, through their shorter lives. Mortgage lenders are often willing to reduce their interest rate in return for the GEM's shorter payback period. This would serve to make the initial GEM payments lower than those on traditional 30-year loans, and could win over some borrowers.

Midgets

The *midget* is the term of endearment used by Wall Street to refer to a level-payment, fixed-rate loan originated with fewer than 30 years to maturity. In some sense, therefore, midgets do not really belong in a discussion of AMIs. They are included here, though, because of their successful introduction to the securities market around 1982 and the reasons behind it.

By the time midgets were introduced, the GEM loan had already proven that there was an appetite for mortgages with shorter maturities. The GEM accomplished the shorter life with graduating payments, whereas the midget took the more direct approach of using a traditional structure to amortize fully in only 15 years. What really made midgets appealing, however, was a quirk in mortgage mathematics that surfaces with high interest rates: going from a 30-year amortization schedule to 15 years produces a smaller increase in monthly payment at higher interest rates than at lower rates.

To illustrate, suppose we are comparing midgets to traditional 30-year loans when rates are at 10 percent, and again when rates are at 18 percent. At 10 percent, the traditional loan payment on a $50,000 mortgage is $438.79, versus $537.30 for a comparable midget. The midget requires almost $100 more per month, or an increase of 22.5 percent. However, at 18 percent, the 30-year loan payment is $753.54, whereas the midget payment is $805.21, an increase of less than $52 per month or 6.9 percent. Thus, at high interest rates, the midget has tremendous psychological appeal; when a borrower is about to commit to payments that seem high in an absolute sense, a small increase becomes easy to rationalize when it means cutting the life of the loan in half. By the same token, one might also expect that the popularity of midgets should wane in an environment of falling interest rates.

Variable-Rate Mortgages (VRMs)

The VRM was one of the first AMIs to emerge and remains popular today because of the advantages it affords to both borrowers and lenders. The chief difference between a VRM and a traditional mortgage is that the VRM has no fixed interest rate. Instead, the rate is variable, and depends on the level of interest rates in general. This type of mortgage is created by tying the mortgage rate to some index related to government borrowing, cost of funds, inflation, and so on. Sometimes one will see the term *ARM* (adjustable-rate mortgage) used to describe a loan with similar features.

There are various rules governing how often and by how much the mortgage rate on a VRM may change. These rules may vary slightly from one lender to the next, although they are basically similar in design. As an example of a typical VRM, let us consider the provisions of those initially issued by Home Savings and Loan Association in California, the first lender to issue a pass-through security backed by VRMs:

1. The mortgage rate is based on the weighted average cost of savings index published by the Federal Home Loan Bank of San Francisco. In general, the spread between the mortgage rate and the index rate is held constant (when the index changes, the VRM changes equally). However, the provisions that follow may prevent this from happening all the time.

2. The mortgage rate may change (up or down) only once in any six-month period and may not be changed at all during the first six months.

3. The mortgage rate may not change (up or down) by more than 0.25 percent (25 basis points) at a time, no matter how much the index changes. Combined with provision number 2 above, this means that the VRM rate may not change more than 0.5 percent per year.

4. The rate must change at least 0.1 percent (10 basis points) at a time, except to bring the rate to a level previously impossible because of the 25-basis-point limitation. For example, suppose the index rises five basis points from its initial level. The VRM rate does not rise because it cannot rise by 10 basis points. However, suppose the index rises 30 basis points from its initial level. The VRM will rise 25 basis points (the maximum rise) after six months, and may then rise another 5 basis points in another six months.

5. The VRM rate may not rise by more than 2.5 percent above its initial level, no matter how much the index rises. In addition, state usury laws may prevent the VRM rate from exceeding a certain rate.

6. Increases in the VRM rate are optional on the part of the lender. Decreases, however, are mandatory.

7. Within 90 days of any time the VRM rate is increased, or at any time the VRM rate exceeds its initial level, the borrower may prepay the loan in whole or in part with no prepayment penalty.

8. Whenever the VRM rate is increased to a rate higher than its initial level, the borrower may elect to keep his monthly payment constant by extending the maturity of the mortgage. However, the new maturity may not be more than 40 years from the origination date (if the original VRM had a term of 30 years, it cannot be extended by more than another 10 years). If a borrower extends the maturity of his loan and if the VRM rate is subsequently decreased, the lender may decrease the maturity by a comparable amount.

As the last provision indicates, VRMs may have varying maturities as well as varying rates. For example, suppose a borrower obtains a $50,000 VRM for 30 years with an initial rate of 10 percent. This requires monthly payments of $438.79. Suppose the rate rises after six months to 10¼ percent. By doing nothing, the borrower will have a new monthly payment of $447.99. On the other hand, electing to keep paying $438.79 (which is the buyer's option), extends the mortgage maturity an additional 5 years and 1 month to assure repayment of the debt. Should the VRM rate rise to 10½ percent in another 6 months, the borrower could no longer keep paying the same monthly amount because that change would add another 11 years and 9 months to the maturity, making a total of 46 years, 10 months from origination, which is too long. The borrower could extend the mortgage to a total of 40 years from origination, but no further.

It is impossible to calculate the exact amortization schedule for a VRM because it depends on the patterns that the interest rate and maturity follow. Figure 9 shows one possible course that a VRM might take and footnotes the various decisions made by the lender and the borrower along the way. Even with the same origination date, initial rate, and index, two VRMs may follow different courses if either the lender *or* the borrower makes different decisions because each affects the payment pattern. In deciding whether or not a borrower meets the qualifications of creditworthiness on a VRM, lenders usually examine the worst-case scenario—that is, the case in which the VRM rate rises as much as possible as soon as possible.

With all of these complexities, it may not be immediately obvious why the VRM is so popular. The reason lies in the fact that it reduces risk for the lender, who passes on some of the benefit in a lower initial mortgage rate. In making mortgage loans, lenders face the risk that interest rates will rise. Since mortgage lenders usually have short-term liabilities (deposits) matched against their long-term assets (mortgages), rising interest rates mean greater costs and no offsetting increase in revenues. The VRM serves as a hedge against rising rates by permitting revenues (mortgage payments) to fluctuate with the lender's costs. Without the VRM hedge, lenders tack on a premium to the mortgage rate to compensate for the greater risk they face. Thus the VRM reduces the lender's risk, and the borrower can get a preferential rate, often as much as one fourth to three fourths of 1 percent less than a traditional mortgage.

VRMs are especially attractive to lenders in periods of rising interest rates because they are able to raise the mortgage rate. Because high interest rates go hand-in-hand with tight money, borrowers often take loans in the form in which they are most readily available. Therefore, we would expect VRMs to increase in popularity in a year in which interest rates are high and rising for the entire year. This is exactly what happened in 1979. In California, where VRMs first gained widespread acceptance, VRMs grew from roughly 20 percent of originations, in early 1978, to more than 40 percent in 1979, based on surveys by the Federal Home Loan Bank of San Francisco. Nationwide acceptance of the VRM continued to grow in the years that followed as interest rates moved to record highs and their wild fluctuations encouraged both lenders and borrowers to minimize risk.

Price-Level-Adjusted Mortgages (PLAMs)

The PLAM loan is a new breed of mortgage that surfaced in 1982. It resembles a cross between a GEM and a VRM, and is the first AMI to address the concept of real rate of return. Most securities and loans are negotiated in terms of nominal returns, from which inflation must be subtracted. For example, if a security returns 10 percent, but inflation is 8 percent, the real return is only 2

Figure 9 • VRM: An Example

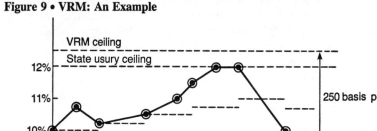
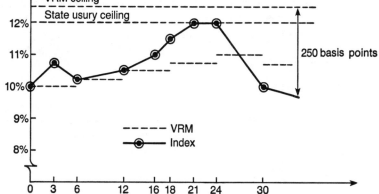

Month

0	Index = 10 percent VRM of $50,000 for 30 years at 10 percent = $438.79/month
3	Index = 10¾ percent VRM rate does not change (since less than six months since settlement).
6	Index = 10¼ percent Borrower may elect to *(a)* pay $447.99/month (rate increases to 10¼ percent—maximum allowed) or *(b)* pay $438.79/month *and* extend maturity by five years, one month (i.e., term increases from 354 to 415 months). [Assume *(a)* is chosen.]
12	Index = 10½ percent Borrower may elect to *(a)* pay $443.14 *and* extend mortgage by only 4 years, 11 months (to bring mortgage to 40 years past settlement) or *(b)* pay $448.33/month. [Assume *(a)* is chosen.]
16	Index = 11 percent VRM rate cannot increase (since it increased less than six months previously)
18	Index = 11½ percent Borrower has no option (since maturity is at 40 years). Lender elects to increase VRM rate by the 25 b.p. maximum to 10¾ percent. Monthly payment is $452.94.
21	Index = 12 percent VRM/usury ceilings apply to VRM rate only.
24	Index = 12 percent Notice that VRM rate increased to 11 percent, even though the index decreased in the ensuing time period. Monthly payment is $462.75.
30	Index = 10 percent VRM rate decreases to 10¾ percent. Borrower decides to prepay $5,000. However, lender decides to reduce maturity to 30 years (past settlement). Hence, payments are now $419.87/month (instead of $406.96 with a 40-year maturity).

. . . and so on.

percent. The PLAM loan is based around an inflation index, such as the consumer price index, which is used to increase both the homeowner's monthly payments and the outstanding mortgage balance. In this way, payments are kept equal in terms of purchasing power and the PLAM lender is assured of realizing a real rate of return at some fixed spread over the inflation rate.

Actually, there are several forms of PLAMs which have been proposed under various names, and no particular form has yet emerged as the dominant structure. Table 7 illustrates one of the simplest PLAMs and points out the principles involved. The table assumes that the lender has determined that a

Table 7 • Example of Price-Level-Adjusted Mortgage (PLAM)

Real interest rate	4.50%
Inflation rate	8.00%
Maturity (months)	360
Initial loan amount	$50,000

Month	Total Payment	Payment Breakdown Interest	Payment Breakdown Principal	Inflation of Balance	New Balance
1	254.97	188.71	66.27	321.70	50,255.43
12	273.61	199.51	74.10	340.12	53,128.86
24	295.50	211.80	83.70	361.06	56,395.11
36	319.14	224.59	94.55	382.87	59,795.11
48	344.67	237.86	106.81	405.50	63,323.04
60	372.24	251.59	120.65	428.91	66,970.44
72	402.02	265.73	136.29	453.01	70,725.78
84	434.18	280.23	153.96	477.73	74,573.87
96	468.92	295.01	173.91	502.92	78,495.21
108	506.43	309.98	196.45	528.45	82,465.24
120	546.95	325.03	221.91	554.11	86,453.53
132	590.70	340.03	250.68	579.67	90,422.71
144	637.96	354.79	283.17	604.84	94,327.45
156	689.00	369.12	319.87	629.27	98,113.07
168	744.12	382.78	361.33	652.56	101,714.11
180	803.65	395.48	408.17	674.20	105,052.62
192	867.94	406.86	461.07	693.61	108,036.25
204	937.37	416.54	520.83	710.10	110,555.98
216	1,012.36	424.02	588.34	722.86	112,483.63
228	1,093.35	428.75	664.60	730.92	113,668.97
240	1,180.82	430.08	750.74	733.18	113,936.41
252	1,275.28	427.23	848.05	728.34	113,081.25
264	1,377.31	419.34	957.97	714.88	110,865.41
276	1,487.49	405.36	1,082.14	691.04	107,012.54
288	1,606.49	384.09	1,222.40	654.79	101,202.46
300	1,735.01	354.17	1,380.84	603.78	93,064.87
312	1,873.81	313.99	1,559.82	535.29	82,172.12
324	2,023.72	261.72	1,761.99	446.18	68,031.09
336	2,185.61	195.24	1,990.37	332.84	50,073.83
348	2,360.46	112.11	2,248.35	191.12	27,647.02
360	2,549.30	9.52	2,539.77	16.24	0.00

real rate of return of 4.5 percent is to be achieved, and that inflation (as measured by the index) is running at 8 percent per year over the 30-year life of the loan. The mortgage balance is initially $50,000.

The initial monthly payment is based on a 4.5 percent interest rate, and works out to only $254.97, which is far below the required payment on a traditional loan. If there were no inflation, the principal balance would be reduced by the same amount as on a traditional 4.5 percent loan. However, inflation does exist, and at a rate of 8 percent per year, the initial $50,000 goes up by $321.70 in the first month. This amount is added to the old balance less the principal paid in to give the new balance. Finally, the payment for the next month is increased at the same inflation rate.

The results of all of these machinations are evident. The monthly payment grows to over $2,500 by the end of the loan, and the mortgage balance negatively amortizes to as much as $113,000 after 20 years. While these figures are startling in absolute magnitude, two things should be kept in mind:

1. The total monthly payment *in constant dollars* is always the same. The final payment looks large, but in terms of purchasing power it is equivalent to the initial payment.
2. The mortgage balance, when expressed *in constant dollars,* is the same as a traditional 4.5 percent mortgage would have been at all times.

Note that the PLAM in the example is purely hypothetical because in reality the 8 percent inflation rate would not remain constant. In periods of low inflation, the monthly payments would remain more or less constant, whereas with high inflation the payments could easily mushroom.

The PLAM loan represents a novel approach to mortgage finance inasmuch as it attempts to place a constant burden on the homeowner (in terms of purchasing power) while providing the lender with a fixed return over inflation. However, it is easy to see why borrowers and lenders might shy away from the PLAM. Two problems can arise if the index used for determining the payment schedule rises faster than either housing prices or personal income:

1. If the homeowner's income does not keep pace with the index, he will have trouble meeting the rising monthly payments and could default on the loan.
2. If the property value does not keep pace with the index, the LTV ratio could increase, potentially above 100 percent. This would mean that if the property were sold, there might not be sufficient money to pay off the mortgage.

While it is too soon to tell for certain, it appears unlikely that the PLAM can proliferate beyond the more aggressive borrowers and lenders until inflation is brought under stricter control or an index well-suited to both home prices and personal income is developed.

Shared-Appreciation Mortgages (SAMs)

The SAM loan is another innovation of the early 1980s brought about by high interest rates, and it uses inflation as a way of paying for part of the property. The basic terms are fairly simple. The mortgage lender agrees to provide funds at a greatly reduced rate of interest. In return, the borrower agrees to share part of the increase in the property value with the lender when the loan matures, when the property is sold, or at some other specified time.

At the inception of the SAM program, a one-third participation was popular—the lender would reduce the interest rate by a third (in a period of 15 percent interest rates, for example, the home buyer would obtain a loan at 10 percent) in return for one third of the appreciation in the property value. Over time, the formulas behind SAMs have varied somewhat from the one-third mix. In periods such as 1981, when interest rates were rising in concert with inflation falling, SAM lenders needed to compensate for the imbalance by lowering the percentage reduction in the interest rate, raising the percentage of property appreciation to be shared, or some combination of both.

Table 8 shows the consequences of a SAM loan, assuming the home buyer remains in the home for five years. If the actual percentage increase in the property value (the inflation rate) is close to the prevailing level of interest rates, the cumulative savings over the first five years for the home buyer are roughly the same as the value surrendered at the end of the period. (This example assumes the one-third-type SAM and expresses all costs and benefits in comparable terms.) If inflation turns out to be lower, the homeowner wins in the long run because there is less appreciation in value to surrender; if actual inflation is greater, the homeowner loses. Of course, the homeowner will never

---

Table 8 • Traditional Loan versus Shared-Appreciation Mortgage (SAM)

Traditional loan: $50,000 for 30 years @ 15 percent.
One-third SAM: $50,000 for 30 years @ 10 percent, one third of appreciation due on sale.

Assume: Inflation rate = 12 percent (1 percent per month).
Homeowner sells after five years.
Original down payment = $10,000.

	Traditional Loan	SAM	SAM Benefit
Monthly payment	($ 632.22)	($ 438.79)	$ 193.43
Total value of payments for five years (assuming 15 percent time value)	(55,998.58)	(38,865.61)	17,132.97
Value of house today	60,000.00	60,000.00	—
Value of house in five years	109,001.80	109,001.80	—
Mortgage balance in five years	(49,360.31)	(48,287.16)	1,073.15
One third of appreciation due to bank on SAM		(16,333.93)	(16,333.93)
Net benefit of SAM in five years (B + E − F)			1,872.19

have a problem coming up with the funds to pay the lender if the property is sold because they can be taken from the proceeds of the sale. In the event that the SAM matures, or whenever the lender must be repaid without the property being sold, it may be necessary for the homeowner to obtain new financing on the property in order to obtain the required funds.

The attractions of the SAM loan are great to both borrower and lender; the borrower is able to purchase the otherwise unaffordable home, and the lender has a potentially lucrative equity kicker, depending on the rate of inflation. Two factors, though, have prevented SAMs from becoming more popular than they already are. First, although the SAM is simple in concept, the fine print can be onerous. The complications created by property additions or home improvements, for example, can cloud the issue of which portion of the overall increase in property value is really due to inflation and shareable with the lender. Second, SAMs are difficult to package into units and sell as securities because there is such a broad range of formulas and other parameters being used to create them. It is difficult to have mass production of an item for which there is no standardization of parts. Access to the securities markets, which is vital as a liquidity source for mortgage originators, is effectively denied without a fungible product.

Pass-Through Securities

As we saw previously, the holders of mortgages and the originators of mortgages are not always the same groups. For different reasons, a holder of a mortgage may want to sell all or part of his or her interest to someone else. In the past, the only way to do this was to sell whole loans, which meant transferring the title and various other legal documents to the buyer. Even though the servicing may have remained with the originator of the mortgage, buyers of whole loans faced many of the legal complications and paperwork of mortgage ownership. Perhaps more importantly, there was not a great deal of liquidity in the whole loan market, and buyers ran the risk of potential losses if they were ever forced to sell their mortgages quickly. Finally, there were very few small buyers of whole loans, because the details and paperwork involved made larger holdings more economical. The introduction of the pass-through security brought about a means of buying and selling mortgages that was cleaner and, in many respects, superior to the whole loan market.

A *pass-through security* is created when one or more mortgage holders form a collection, or *pool* of mortgages and sell shares or participations in the pool. The pool may consist of as few as one to as many as several thousand mortgages. Each mortgage continues to be serviced by its originator or other servicer, not by the security holders. A trustee is assigned to hold the titles of all mortgages in the pool and to ensure that all mortgages and properties are in acceptable form and that payments are properly made. Essentially, the cash flow from the pool of mortgages, which consists of principal and interest less servicing and other fees, is distributed to the security holders in a pro rata fashion. These securities get their name from the fact that the cash flow from the pool is "passed through" to the security holders by the mortgage servicers.

Although all pass-through securities have the same basic structure described above, there is a wide variety of pass-throughs available that differ substantially in their fine print. Aside from the fact that there are different issuers of pass-throughs, the securities may vary in one or more of the following ways:

1. The nature of the component mortgages.
2. The method for determining and distributing payments to security holders.
3. The guarantees on the security and the mortgages.

We will discuss each of these in general, occasionally using an actual security as an example.

The Underlying Mortgages

Because a purchaser of a pass-through owns a share of the cash flow from the mortgages in the pass-through pool, the nature of those mortgages is of paramount importance in determining the value of the security. In particular, the following factors should be examined when analyzing the components of a pool:

1. Types of mortgages or AMIs.
2. Distribution of mortgage rates versus pass-through coupon.
3. Distribution of mortgage maturities.
4. Number and size of mortgages.
5. Geographic distribution of mortgages.
6. Creditworthiness of mortgages.

The first three factors directly affect the amount of monthly cash flow from a pool and the breakdown between principal and interest. The last three factors contribute to the regularity, predictability, and risk of that cash flow. A key word in the above factors is *distribution*. It is not enough to know only the level (or average level) of the mortgage rates, maturities, etc.; one must also know the range and diversity of levels on the individual mortgages. For example, there may be two pools with average mortgage rates of 11 percent. In one pool, this could mean that all mortgages have 11 percent rates, while in the other, there could be a range of rates from 10 percent to 14 percent. The actual pattern affects the amount of cash flow as well as its predictability.

Type of mortgage is an important determinant of cash flow because different types of mortgages have different amortization patterns. A pass-through pool consisting of GPMs, for example, would have negative principal amortization in its early years. In general, the more progressive the AMIs in a pool (meaning the more they lower the initial payments from that on a traditional mortgage), the less principal gets passed through in the early years of the security (with more principal in the later years).

The mortgage interest rates, curiously, do not affect the amount of interest passed through to the security holders because the holders earn the coupon rate on the security at all times. The mortgage rates usually vary from the coupon rate, with any excess of mortgage rate above coupon rate being kept by the mortgage servicer and/or the security issuer. Mortgage interest rates are important to the investor because they affect the principal amortization schedule. Higher mortgage rates mean slower amortization of the loan (less principal in the early years, more in the later years). This is true regardless of the mortgage type or maturity. Servicers generally like high mortgage rates and/or low coupon rates so as to maximize the difference, which is their servicing fee. Investors, on the other hand, tend to want higher coupon rates (more interest paid to them) and lower mortgage rates (faster amortization).

The distribution of mortgage maturities is important in the same regard as the mortgage types and interest rates. The longer the maturity, the more time over which the principal is amortized and therefore the less amortization is passed through in the early years of the security. The maturity date of a pass-through is generally stated to be the date on which the last component mortgage is fully repaid. The investor must not assume that all of the mortgages in the pool mature on the same date. Each issuer has its own limitations as to the allowable distribution of mortgage maturities in a pool—typically the maturities must all lie in a one-year time span. Nonetheless, the average maturity of the component mortgages, and therefore the average maturity of the pool, is almost always shorter than the stated maturity of the pool. Any difference that does exist becomes increasingly important over time.

The greater the number of mortgages in a pool, the more regular and predictable its cash flow. If it were not for prepayments, predicting pass-through payments would be easy as long as one knew the components of the pool. Prepayments are often voluntary (and occasionally unanticipated) payments of principal that vary with each individual mortgage. The greater the population of mortgages, the more the law of averages applies and historical behavior can be used as a standard to estimate future experience. Although issuers rarely disclose the exact number of mortgages in a pool, it can be estimated by dividing the size of the pool by the average size of the mortgages. The size of the mortgages is often indicated by issuers, and in many cases there is a maximum size that allows one to establish a minimum number of mortgages for the pool.

Geographic distribution is important because it affects the likelihood and predictability of prepayments. Certain areas of the country are popular (and others unpopular) among pass-through investors, so pools that are highly concentrated in a particular region will be evaluated accordingly. From the standpoint of predictability, however, the more geographical diversification the better. This is because certain events that precipitate prepayments and defaults, such as natural disasters or factory closings, are local in nature and would have a greater impact on regionalized pools than on diversified pools.

Finally, there is the matter of creditworthiness. The creditworthiness of a pool can be greater than that of the mortgages because of pool insurance and payment guarantees that go beyond mortgage insurance alone. (These will be explained more fully later.) Still, the strength of the mortgages determines in large part the strength of the pool. In the absence of payment guarantees, the stronger the credit of the individual mortgages, the more valuable the security. However, payment guarantees can alter this perspective. For example, if an issuer agrees to pay off in full any loan that defaults, the investor may begin to hope for defaults and prize pools consisting of low-quality mortgages.

By far the biggest problem in evaluating the underlying mortgages of a pass-through pool is obtaining information on them. The information available and the ease with which it can be obtained varies from issuer to issuer. Suffice it to say that in general there is never enough information available to the investor. In time, securities investors and dealers may persuade issuers to make more detailed data available.

Payments to Investors

The methods by which pass-through issuers collect, determine, and distribute payments to security holders is a somewhat complicated topic. It involves examining closely who pays what to whom and when, as well as who is entitled to which part of the payments. Rather than discuss this subject in general, we shall choose an actual type of pass-through as a model. The most obvious choice for the model is the GNMA (Government National Mortgage Association) arrangement because GNMAs have consistently constituted more than 75 percent of all outstanding pass-throughs.

The flow of money in a GNMA pass-through security is fairly simple and is illustrated in Figure 10. Each pool has one originator and servicer, who each month collects principal and interest payments from the mortgagors. The originator/servicer sends checks to investors and reports payments and principal balances to GNMA. The servicer keeps .5 percent (50 basis points) of the outstanding principal balance each month as a gross servicing fee (this comes out of the interst passed through to the investors). From the .5 percent fee, the servicer remits .06 percent (6 basis points) to GNMA as a guarantee fee, thereby leaving .44 percent (44 basis points) as the net servicing fee.

The timing of payments is shown in Figure 11. Mortgage payments are due from the homeowners on the 1st of each month and are sent to the investors on the 15th of the month. Prepayments might be made by homeowners at any time during the month, so a cutoff date must be established. For GNMAs, any prepayments received by the servicer up to the 25th day of a month will be passed through on the 15th of the following month. Because GNMAs are securities that are routinely bought and sold in the secondary market, the servicer

Figure 10 • The Pass-Through Process for GNMA Securities

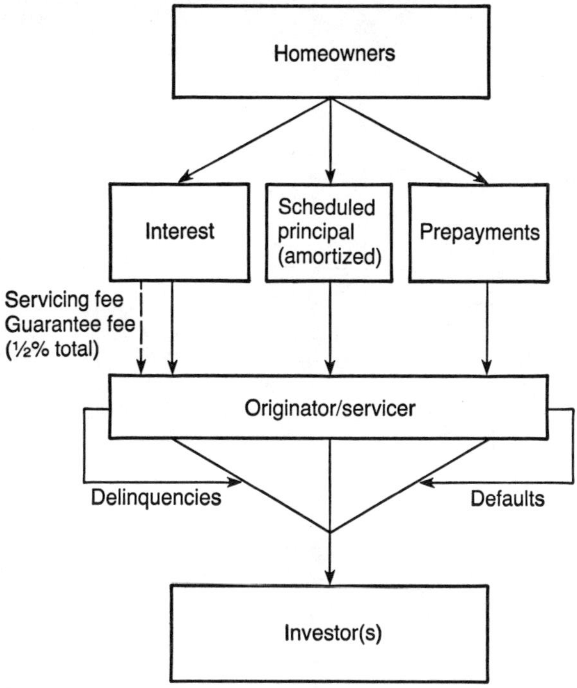

must have some way of determining whom to pay. The method used is to remit a check each month to the owner of the securities registered as of the 30th day of the prior month. This date is known as the record date because payments are received by holders of record on that date.

Notice that an investor who buys a GNMA on the first of a month (or who buys a new GNMA) does not receive the first payment until the 15th day of the following month. How many days does such an investor have to wait before receiving the payment? Let us assume that the month is 30 days long; this is the standard assumption made by Wall Street dealers with regard to all corporate, agency, and municipal securities, no matter how many days are really in the month. The number of days that elapse from the 1st of one month to the 15th of the next month is therefore 44. Because pass-throughs are a monthly payment security, the investor would expect to receive a payment after 30 days, and every 30 days thereafter. Clearly, then, the first payment on a GNMA is delayed by 14 additional days. The only problem is that many a GNMA trader, salesperson, or investor will tell you that GNMAs have a 45-day payment delay. It is difficult to imagine how this phrase was started—even if you count the first 30 days, the total wait is only 44 days. The real shame is that this misconception was subsequently inherited by all other types of pass-throughs.

Figure 11 • Timing of Payments for GNMA Securities

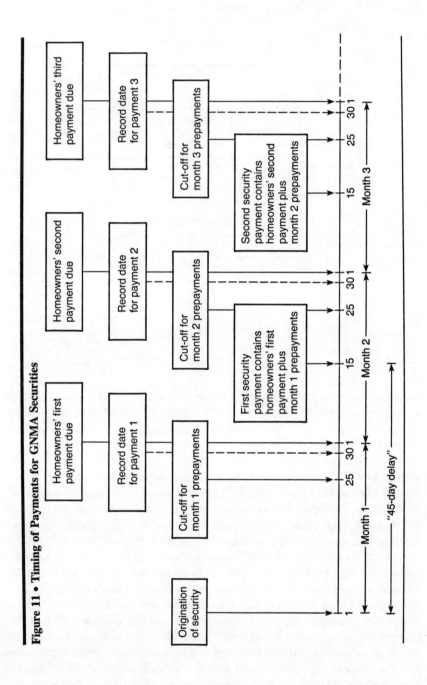

As a result, the analyst must always subtract 31 from the stated payment delay in order to obtain the real delay or penalty. For example, the pass-throughs issued by the Federal Home Loan Mortgage Corporation (FHLMC, or Freddie Mac) are said to have a 75-day delay in receipt of the initial payment. For analytical purposes (computing yields, etc.) this equates to a penalty of $75 - 31 = 44$ days.

Guarantees

To date there are four types of guarantees that have been placed on pass-through securities in order to elevate their creditworthiness above that of whole loans. These are:

1. Guarantees on interest payments.
2. Guarantees on principal payments.
3. Mortgage-guarantee insurance.
4. Hazard insurance.

Not all types of guarantees apply to each type of pass-through, and investors should determine the exact nature of any guarantees before purchasing these securities.

A *guarantee on interest payments* is a promise that investors will receive interest earned on the outstanding principal balance of the security on a timely basis. This means that investors are assured of collecting interest due whether or not is was actually collected by the servicer (whether or not the homeowner actually paid it). It also means that if principal payments fall in arrears, the investor is guaranteed to receive interest due on the entire unpaid principal balance, despite the fact that the mortgage balance would have been less if the principal payments were up to date. Pass-throughs that have guarantees of timely interest payments are said to be *modified pass-throughs*.

Some pass-throughs guarantee the timely payment of principal as well as interest. Such securities are said to be *fully modified*. A fully modified pass-through therefore assures investors that they will always receive payments as if there were no delinquencies.

Certain private issuers of pass-throughs are effectively prevented from offering modified or fully modified securities because of a legal technicality: although the issuance of a pass-through normally constitutes a sale of assets (which is what is desired), the existence of any guarantees as to principal or interest keeps the mortgages on the issuer's balance sheet as a contingent liability. In order to avoid this problem, private pass-through issuers have purchased one or more types of insurance to compensate the investor for the absence of direct guarantees.

Mortgage-guarantee insurance, or pool insurance, is a policy that insures against defaults on the part of the homeowners. It is limited in scope, typically to 5 percent of the initial principal amount of the mortgage pool. *Hazard in-*

surance, on the other hand, covers certain physical risks, such as earthquakes and floods, which may not be covered by the insurance policies of the property owners. Hazard insurance is also limited in scope, often to 1 percent of the initial pool size.

Guarantees, either outright or in the form of insurance, can only benefit a security's creditworthiness, although it should be remembered that a guarantee is only as strong as the guarantor. GNMA securities have by far the strongest guarantee, since they are fully modified and guaranteed by the U.S. government.

Prepayments

The analysis of pass-through securities would be fairly straightforward if it were not for the existence of prepayments. If no prepayments took place, the cash flow generated by a pass-through security would be the aggregate cash flow from all of the underlying mortgages less the servicing and guarantee fees kept by the originator and/or issuer. Although there might be some degree of uncertainty as to the exact composition of a pool in terms of mortgage interest rate and maturity mix, these would usually be known accurately enough to forecast pass-through payments with a high degree of precision. With cash flow out of the way, the analyst's sole concern would be the creditworthiness of the security.

A prepayment occurs whenever a monthly mortgage payment is made in excess of the amount actually due. The amount of the excess payment is applied directly to the outstanding principal balance, and therefore serves to extinguish the loan earlier than its original maturity date. Usually a prepayment means that an entire mortgage loan was repaid. It is rare that a property owner decides to prepay only a portion of an outstanding loan, especially in a climate of rising interest rates and/or tight money. There are several possible causes for prepayments, among which are the following:

1. *Sale of the property*—the original property owner uses part of the proceeds from the sale to repay the mortgage loan.
2. *Refinancing*—if interest rates fall, the property owner may obtain a new mortgage loan at a more favorable rate and use the proceeds to retire the original mortgage.
3. *Disaster*—in the event the property is destroyed by fire, flood, or other disaster, insurance proceeds may be used to repay the mortgage. A homeowner may die, and the survivors may repay the mortgage from life insurance proceeds.

In addition to these causes, investors of fully modified or insured pass-throughs will receive prepayments in the event of a default on one or more of the underlying mortgages. In general, an investor is unaware of whether any principal prepayments were caused by mortgage retirements or defaults. On average, though, defaults have accounted for a relatively small percentage of total pass-through prepayments.

Some mortgage lenders discourage property owners from prepaying their loans by imposing a prepayment penalty. This often takes the form of an additional six months of interest charges and may decline to zero over some period of time. Depending on the exact structure of a pass-through security, prepayment penalties may be distributed to the security holders or kept by the mortgage servicer or issuer. This question does not arise with GNMA securities, however, since neither the FHA-insured nor the VA-guaranteed mortgages comprising GNMAs permit prepayment penalties to be charged.

It is tempting to assume that a prepayment would always be desirable from the point of view of the security holder. However, this is not the case. The security holder should compare the investment opportunities available with any prepaid dollars to the coupon rate being earned by the dollars that are not prepaid. When the coupon is higher, prepayments are undesirable. An equivalent analysis is the comparison of the market value of the security to par. If the security is valued at a premium, then each dollar of principal value is worth more in security form than as cash (when it is prepaid). One form of prepayment that is almost always detrimental to the investor is refinancing. The property owner will generally not refinance unless interest rates are low enough to make it worthwhile. However, this is precisely the case in which the prevailing interest rate is lower than the coupon rate (the security is selling at a premium), and therefore the prepayment is undesirable to the investor.

One final point concerning the fine print on pass-through prepayments is the interest on prepaid principal. Suppose a homeowner prepays the mortgage on the second day of the month. The mortgage lender ceases to earn interest on the prepaid amount but does not pass through this payment until the end of the month. Depending on the particular security, the investor may or may not earn a full month's interest on the prepaid amount. This problem is less significant for larger pools and/or pools with fewer prepayments, since the percentage of mortgages experiencing this problem will tend to be lower.

Measuring Prepayments

The cash flow to an investor from a pass-through security consists of three parts: coupon income, principal amortization, and prepayments. The first two of these are predictable quantities, since they are determined by the characteristics of the mortgages making up the pool. Prepayments, however, are inherently unpredictable, since they depend on the actions of individual property owners. Nonetheless, if large numbers of mortgages are aggregated, the prepayments that do occur tend to become spread out over time. Although a prepayment tends to be an all-or-none event at the individual mortgage level, it may represent the return of only a small percentage of total principal at the pool level. Thus a mortgage pool may have prepayment activity ongoing over its entire period to maturity. The level of this prepayment activity is referred to as the *prepayment experience rate* of the pool, and it may be measured in several different ways. In any event, the prepayment experience rate as measured by any standard need not be constant over time. In fact, prepayment experience tends to fluctuate in conjunction with various economic indicators.

Before explaining how prepayments are measured, some terminology is required. We already know that *mortgage balance* is the ratio of the remaining principal amount on an individual mortgage loan to the original loan amount. This ratio generally runs from 0 to 1, although certain AMIs (GPMs) may permit it to exceed 1. In an analogous fashion, we define the *pool factor* of a pass-through security to be the ratio of the outstanding principal balance of a pool to its original principal amount.

If a mortgage pool had no prepayments, then at any point in time its pool factor would be the same as the mortgage balance on the underlying mortgages. (If the component mortgages were of different types, interest rates, or origination dates, then the pool factor would represent a weighted average of the individual mortgage balances.) On the other hand, if prepayments did occur, the pool factor would be less than the mortgage balance. In effect, the mortgage balance measures the remaining principal on loans that have not prepaid, whereas the pool factor accounts for prepaid loans as well.

Figure 12 illustrates this distinction between mortgage balance and pool factor. It assumes a pool is originally constructed of 20 identical mortgages for $50,000 each, giving a pool size of $1 million. At the end of 10 years, half of the loans are assumed to have prepaid, and the balance on each remaining loan is $40,000. Thus the pool contains $.4 million principal at that time. The mortgage balance is 0.4 million/0.5 million, or 0.8, whereas the pool factor is 0.4 million/1 million, or 0.4. A measurement for prepayments now suggests itself; prepayment experience may be expressed as the amount by which the pool factor has declined relative to the mortgage balance. In other words, it is the amount by which the pool factor is different from what its value would have been if no prepayments had occurred. We define the overall prepayment rate for the 10-year period as the ratio of the pool factor to the mortgage balance: 0.4/0.8 = 0.5, or 50 percent. This of course merely reiterates what we already knew—that half of the loans had prepaid. In practice, however, we are neither given the number of loans composing a pool nor the sizes of the individual loans, so that the prepayment rate must be imputed by dividing the pool factor (which is always known) by the mortgage balance (which can be computed based on the known or assumed characteristics of the underlying mortgages).

A subtle problem arises with mortgage pools containing a mixture of mortgage types, interest rates, and/or maturity dates. In order to perform the cal-

Figure 12 • Sample Pool Factor Computation

Original mortgage pool

20 mortgages at $50,000 = $1,000,000

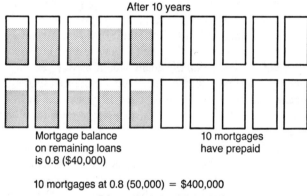
After 10 years

Mortgage balance
on remaining loans
is 0.8 ($40,000)

10 mortgages
have prepaid

10 mortgages at 0.8 (50,000) = $400,000

$$\text{Pool factor} = \frac{\text{Remaining balance}}{\text{Original balance}} = \frac{400,000}{1,000,000} = 0.4$$

culation described above, it is necessary to know the average mortgage balance on the loans in the pool. If the pool originally contained a mixed bag of loans, this average mortgage balance would vary depending on exactly which loans survived (did not prepay). For example, if a pool originally contained half 8 percent loans and half 10 percent loans, the average mortgage balance would depend on how much of each type prepaid. Unfortunately, this information may not be available. For better or worse, it is commonplace to assume that all of the loans in a pool have common characteristics (the above pool could be viewed as if it were entirely composed of 9 percent loans). These characteristics would be viewed as immutable until such time as information to the contrary becomes available. This assumption causes the calculation of prepayment rates to be somewhat imprecise, although with long periods to maturity it is rarely a problem.

SMM Experience

In examining the prepayment rate of a pool, it is not enough to know simply the number of mortgages that have prepaid. One must also consider the amount of time involved. In the previous example, we could say that since 50 percent of the mortgages terminated over a 10-year period, the average prepayment rate was 5 percent per year. A similar prepayment measurement is the single monthly mortality, or SMM, prepayment rate of the pool. SMM differs from the calculation above in two respects:

1. The SMM rate reflects average prepayments per month rather than per year.
2. SMM expresses the amount of mortgages that prepay relative to the amount of mortgages outstanding, not the original amount.

The second point is worth elaborating. If a mortgage pool had 75 percent of its mortgages prepay after only two months, it would be tempting to compute the SMM rate as 37.5 percent. In fact though, the SMM rate would be 50 percent. After one month at 50 percent SMM, half of the loans would prepay. In the second month, half of the *remaining* loans would prepay, leaving 25 percent of the original pool, which is the desired result. In the first example, in which half of the loans in a pool prepay in the first 10 years, the SMM rate works out to roughly 0.58 percent. Typical SMM-experience rates for mortgage pools are 1 percent or less.

Notice that the SMM experience for a pool is an average prepayment rate and does not imply that prepayments take place every month. In fact, pools containing relatively few mortgages will rarely have prepayments, and when prepayments do occur, they will tend to be for a relatively large percentage of the pool. Investors should be careful to notice any difference between the *cumulative prepayment rate* (the average rate of prepayment since the pool's inception) and the *interim experience rates* (the prepayments during the past six months, prepayments for each calendar quarter, etc.).

Figure 13 graphs the pool factor for a pass-through security containing 30-year, 10 percent mortgages at various SMM prepayment rates. The higher the prepayment rate, the more quickly the pool factor declines. Notice that the line labeled 0 percent SMM represents no prepayments (it is the schedule for the mortgage balance).

SMM is an appealing way to measure prepayments because of its simplicity, but it is not in any way a predictive model. In other words, there is no basis (yet) for supposing that the historical prepayment rate should be continued into the future. Certain studies of mortgage termination behavior have resulted in the discovery of prepayment patterns. These patterns can be built into a prepayment model, and individual pools can be evaluated *relative* to this norm. The best known prepayment model and the measurement employed by most institutional investors is known as *FHA-experience*.

Figure 13 • Mortgage Balances at Various SMM-Experience Rates (10 percent mortgage, 30-year maturity)

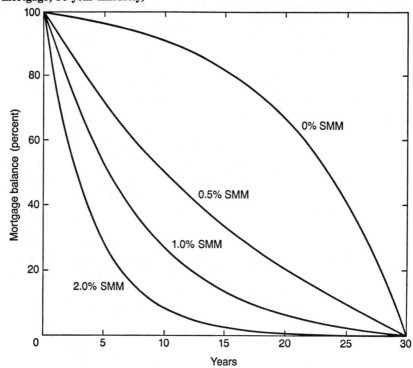

FHA-Experience

The Federal Housing Administration (FHA) was established in 1934 to encourage the improvement of housing standards and to provide a system at the national level for mortgage insurance as an aid to home builders, buyers, and mortgage lenders. In the process of performing these tasks, FHA has accumulated a wealth of historical information on the mortgages it insures, including data on mortgage terminations. Each year the actuarial division of the Department of Housing and Urban Development (HUD) performs a statistical analysis of the FHA data going back to 1957. The results of this analysis have become the basis for the FHA-experience model.

Technically, there are several varieties of FHA-experience corresponding to mortgages insured under different sections of the National Housing Act. Each section applies to loans for different property types and for various terms to maturity, and so on. In fact the full HUD analysis breaks down prepayments by mortgage type and by state. The most commonly insured FHA loan, though, is the Section 203 single-family loan, and when the term *FHA-experience* is used without further qualification, it generally means the most recent HUD study on Section 203 loans for the United States as a whole.

FHA-experience takes the form of a decimal-balance table, which indicates for each year in the life of a mortgage the probability that it will survive (not prepay or default) to that point. For example, consider the figures from Table 9, which shows the standard FHA-experience balances used during each of the years 1974 through 1982. According to the 1982 data, a Section 203 mortgage had a 98.87 percent chance of surviving until the end of 1 year, a 55.59 percent chance of lasting 10 years, and so on. Notice that only 12.7 percent of all such mortgages are expected to reach their 30-year maturity. From the decimal-balance table, one can compute the percentage of mortgages expected to terminate in any given year. By spreading these terminations out over the entire year, one can then compute expected terminations per month. (In fact the HUD study allows one to differentiate between terminations due to prepayments and terminations due to defaults. For the purposes of pass-through analysis, though, these can be lumped together and are usually referred to simply as prepayments.)

It should be mentioned that not all of the decimal balances are based on actual mortgage prepayment data. Table 9 shows the year through which the mortgage data were taken. For instance, the 1982 study used data through the end of 1981. Since the data started in 1957, the latest study had only 25 years of information on which to base 30 years of prepayment estimates. Therefore, the last five years of data in the 1982 study are extrapolations of the earlier data.

Mortgage market participants measure the prepayment rates of pass-through pools in terms of percentages or multiples of FHA experience. A pool conforming to the FHA prediction is said to prepay at 100 percent FHA experience. Pools prepaying at twice the normal rate are said to be 200 percent FHA pools, and so on. A pool experiencing no prepayments at all is said to be a 0 percent FHA pool. Figure 14 graphs the pool factor of a new 10 percent pool as a function of time for various FHA-experience rates. Notice that the 0 percent FHA line is identical to the 0 percent SMM line in Figure 13.

Historically, there has been some controversy as to the exact interpretation of FHA-experience multiples. In fact, the investment community reversed itself in 1979 and changed the standard computation. To illustrate with an example, suppose we are given a four-year-old mortgage pool and are asked to determine the proportion of mortgages that would prepay during the next year at a 200 percent FHA-experience rate. We know that at 100 percent FHA experience, the decimal balance table goes from .85050 after four years to .79771 after five years—a decrease of .05279. According to the old (and currently obsolete) computation, at 200 percent FHA, we would have expected to see a decline of 2(0.05279), or .10558, in the mortgage population. The accepted procedure currently is somewhat more sophisticated. To begin with, we look at the proportion of mortgages normally expected to survive between years 4 and 5. This

Table 9 • Historical FHA-Experience Decimal Balances (U.S. total, Section 203, 30-year original term)

FHA Experience as of year	1974	1975	1977	1978	1979	1980	1981	1982
0	1.00000	1.00000	1.00000	1.00000	1.00000	1.00000	1.00000	1.00000
1	.99191	.99161	.99187	.99186	.99163	.98993	.98880	.98874
2	.96707	.96360	.96246	.96246	.96063	.95036	.95172	.95146
3	.93425	.92884	.92207	.92253	.91892	.89668	.90090	.90224
4	.89564	.88920	.87666	.87740	.87289	.84139	.84965	.85050
5	.85425	.84692	.82972	.82978	.82380	.78728	.79839	.79771
6	.81060	.80291	.78252	.78267	.77424	.73430	.74676	.74343
7	.76702	.75907	.73765	.73746	.72756	.68304	.69785	.69050
8	.72598	.71727	.69570	.69490	.68357	.63459	.65191	.64055
9	.68712	.67760	.65710	.65566	.64264	.58952	.61100	.59573
10	.65033	.63991	.62084	.61921	.60480	.54752	.57486	.55590
11	.61292	.60122	.58638	.58432	.56885	.50836	.53998	.51924
12	.57933	.56710	.55449	.55128	.53486	.47196	.50748	.48586
13	.54425	.53168	.52325	.51945	.50245	.43794	.47715	.45613
14	.51381	.50038	.49416	.48841	.47118	.40612	.44880	.42939
15	.48959	.47585	.46766	.45781	.44062	.37635	.42227	.40537
16	.46484	.45116	.44448	.42724	.41034	.34810	.39540	.38373
17	.44151	.42569	.42482	.39639	.37997	.32085	.36842	.36415
18	.41619	.40123	.40754	.36496	.34940	.29436	.34156	.34635
19	.39159	.37756	.38276	.33247	.31866	.26865	.31504	.33018
20	.36869	.35508	.35881	.30121	.28761	.24400	.28910	.31564
21	.34821	.33585	.33574	.27130	.25808	.22061	.26394	.30267
22	.32618	.31176	.31357	.24286	.23015	.19842	.23973	.28773
23	.30415	.29154	.29230	.21598	.20390	.17776	.21663	.27110
24	.28212	.21732	.27197	.19075	.17940	.15861	.19745	.25299
25	.26010	.25110	.25256	.16724	.15669	.14092	.17418	.23370
26	.23808	.23088	.23410	.14548	.13580	.12465	.15499	.21370
27	.21606	.21066	.21657	.12551	.11673	.10975	.13720	.19344
28	.19404	.19044	.19997	.10734	.09948	.09618	.12083	.17331
29	.17202	.17022	.18429	.08464	.07767	.07880	.09990	.14821
30	.15000	.15000	.17000	.06200	.05590	.06140	.07900	.12674
Data through	1971	1972	1975	1976	1977	1979	1980	1981

Figure 14 • Mortgage Balances at Various FHA-Experience Rates (10 percent mortgage, 30-year maturity)

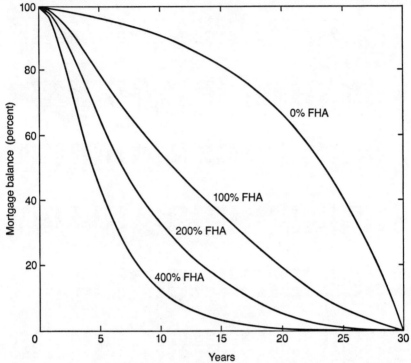

is given by the ratio of the decimal balances: 0.79771/0.85050 = .9379 (or 93.79 percent). Now at an arbitrary prepayment rate we compute the ratio of survivors by raising this number to the power of the FHA multiple—in this case, we square it. Thus we have $(.9379)^2$, which is roughly 88 percent of the mortgages expected to survive. Therefore, 12 percent of the outstanding mortgages would be expected to prepay in year 5. Note that these two procedures will give equivalent results at 0 percent FHA and at 100 percent FHA, but different results for everything else.

Unlike SMM experience, which merely quantifies prepayments, FHA experience represents a normal rate of prepayments as measured on actual mortgages. It allows for different paydown rates depending on how old the mortgage is. For example, the number of terminations in the second year can be seen to be roughly three times the rate in the first year. This is an appealing notion, since the circumstances leading to a default, refinancing, or other reason for termination would seem rather unlikely to crop up in the first 12 months of a mortgage. It turns out that the FHA-experience data imply a generally increasing conditional probability of termination with time. More simply stated, the older the mortgage, the more likely it is to terminate.

As with SMM experience, FHA experience can be measured either cumulatively or as an interim prepayment rate for some specific time period. Pools
with cumulative prepayment rates that are above average are often referred to
as *fast-pay securities,* and slower than average cumulative prepayments indicate
a *slow-pay pool.* Surprisingly, the average prepayment rate for most pass-
through securities does not turn out to be 100 percent FHA. Figure 15 is a
graph of the monthly average (interim) prepayment rates, expressed as multiples of FHA experience for three large sectors of the pass-through market:
GNMA single-family securities (Section 203), GNMA graduated-payment securities (Section 245), and FHLMC participation certificates (conventional
mortgages). The graph shows that the prepayment rate for the market as a
whole can vary substantially with time. Except for GPMs, the securities in the
exhibit have prepaid faster than 100 percent FHA in some periods and slower
than 100 percent FHA in others. This is why the concepts of fast pay and slow
pay are (or should be) relative to the universe of securities outstanding and not
the 100 percent FHA standard.

Figure 16 is a graph similar to Figure 15 but expressed in SMM terms. The
GNMA mobile-home sector is also shown on this chart. Again, there is considerable fluctuation in historical rates of prepayment, and no one number suggests
itself as "the" appropriate prepayment rate.

Pros and Cons of FHA Experience

Perhaps the greatest asset of FHA experience is the fact that it is widely
accepted and utilized among pass-through dealers and institutional investors.
The introduction of any alternative model for prepayments must first combat

Figure 15 • Monthly Interim FHA-Experience Rates

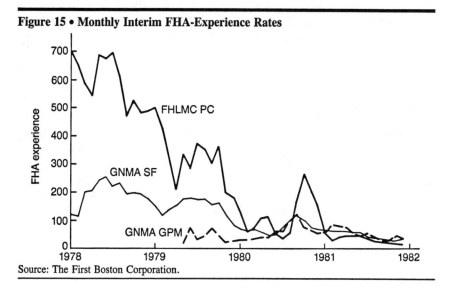

Source: The First Boston Corporation.

Figure 16 • Monthly Interim SMM-Experience Rates

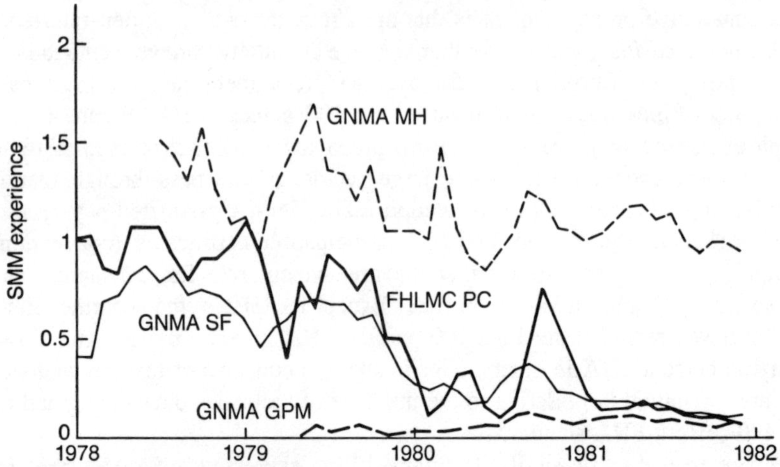

Source: The First Boston Corporation.

the traditional usage of FHA experience, and if the pass-through market is anything, it is a market of tradition.

The best mathematical selling point for FHA experience is the fact that it is founded on the basis of the actual historical behavior of mortgage prepayments and therefore embodies a pattern of increasing termination probabilities known to be representative. This underlying pattern is preserved even if multiples of FHA experience are being used to quantify or predict a pool's behavior.

This is not to say that FHA experience is without its drawbacks, however. One disadvantage, which is probably better described as an abuse, is that the original HUD study quantified prepayments on Section 203 loans, but FHA experience is being applied as a predictor for prepayments on virtually all types of 30-year loans. The applicability of termination data computed for level-payment mortgages to graduated-payment mortgages (to choose one example) is at best questionable and at worst seriously misleading when employed in a predictive capacity.

A second disadvantage to FHA experience is the fact that the data upon which it is based are old. Since the HUD study utilizes information beginning in 1957, most of the mortgages in the study carried relatively low interest rates in comparison with today's levels. Furthermore, the prepayment trends that are built into the decimal-balance table are largely a reflection of mortgage behavior in the 1950s and 1960s, when the economic and social climate were vastly different from that of the 1980s. One outcropping of this age problem can be seen in the HUD analyses of terminations by state. In the late 1970s, it became evident to most mortgage analysts that certain regions of the country—most notably the Southwest, California, and Florida—were experiencing faster mortgage prepayments than the rest of the country by virtue of their strong economic growth and population influx. The FHA-experience data, however, would have indicated just the reverse. In fact, recent HUD figures showed the fastest prepaying states to be Maine, Vermont, and New Hampshire.

A third problem often cited with regard to FHA experience is its ignorance of variables that are known to have significant influences on prepayments. The only parameter considered by the FHA-experience model is the age of the mortgages. The most notable parameter *not* in the HUD study is the mortgage interest rate. As one might expect, mortgages carrying higher interest rates tend to be more likely candidates for prepayments, especially during periods of declining interest rates, when refinancing becomes attractive. Several other variables, including the level of interest rates (yields) in general, the level of housing activity (housing starts), and seasonal factors are known to play an important part in determining prepayment activity. These too are absent from the FHA-experience model, although for predictive purposes that may actually be considered an advantage. If one's goal is to calculate a yield based on assumed prepayments, it is less than appealing to have to forecast interest rates and/or housing starts in order to obtain an answer.

One final complaint about FHA experience is that it gets revised every year. This requires that new yield tables be printed and distributed each time the updated decimal balances become available, resulting in a short period of confusion as to which numbers are correct. Since the alternative (of having no future updates) is even less palatable than the problem itself, this is a problem more investors are willing to live with.

The ultimate test of any prepayment model is its ability to successfully describe the historical prepayment behavior known to have taken place and the ease with which it can be used to predict future prepayments. On these grounds, FHA experience is about as good as most alternative models. It is interesting, though, that the SMM model, which is obviously simpler than FHA experience (no parameters versus one), is actually more effective in describing the behavior of certain mortgage pools. In fact, SMM was conceived in 1978 by The First Boston Corporation as an attempt to more accurately quantify yields on FHLMC PCs.

Figure 17 is a scatter diagram of age versus FHA-experience rate for all of the FHLMC PCs that had been outstanding for at least six months in mid-1978. There was a rather strong indication from the data that FHA experience (measured cumulatively) tended to decline on PCs over time. Because the FHA-experience data have a built-in acceleration of expected prepayments, the idea that PCs might simply have constant paydown rates in absolute percentage terms suggested itself. The dotted line on the exhibit is where pools would lie if they were to prepay at a constant 1 percent SMM rate; the correlation was obvious and tantalizing. The final test of SMM came when First Boston measured its standard error in describing the pattern of FHLMC PC factors versus the error from FHA experience. SMM was found to reduce total squared error

Figure 17 •

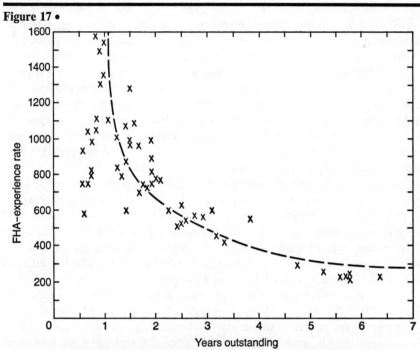

Note: This chart, originally prepared in 1978, shows how the idea for the SMM prepayment model was conceived. Each *x* represents a FHLMC PC; the FHA-experience rate of the PC is plotted versus its age. The older pools were the slower prepaying pools. The dotted line shows where the *x*s would be if all pools prepaid at a rate of 1 percent SMM. The fit to the actual data was tantalizingly close.

by anywhere from 50 percent to 75 percent for various PC pools. As a consequence, SMM gained popularity as a prepayment measurement, especially for conventional and high-coupon mortgage issues, and is used today as an alternative approach to FHA experience for production of yield tables.

Factors Affecting Prepayments

Figures 15 and 16 showed that prepayment rates can vary considerably over time. Much effort has been spent by both the financial and academic communities to discover the causes of this variation, in an effort to understand which direction prepayments might go in the future. Although an in-depth analysis is beyond the scope of this report, the fundamental factors affecting prepayments will be described.

The first step is to recognize that there are two distinctly different kinds of prepayments: those resulting from refinancing, and all others. Figures 15 and

16 are misleading because in showing average prepayment rates for entire market sectors, these figures lumped refinancings together with other prepayments whose behavior is inherently quite different.

Prepayments due to refinancing are confined to those mortgages with higher interest rates, and therefore to pass-throughs with higher coupons. Specifically, refinancing only occurs when the mortgage interest rate is higher than prevailing rates, making it economical for the borrower to take out a new loan and pay off the outstanding one. The greater the savings available from refinancing—that is, the greater the spread between the existing mortgage rate and the refinancing rate—the greater the enticement to prepay the loan.

Figure 18 bears this out by charting prepayments (in SMM terms) on a spectrum of GNMA coupons over a 15-month period beginning in July, 1982. In the bottom part of the chart is a graph of prevailing GNMA yields over the same period. What we see is that when interest rates are high, there is no incentive to refinance and prepayments are quite similar in magnitude for all coupon levels. As interest rates fell in the second half of 1982, however, prepayments rose dramatically, but rose most sharply for the highest coupons. This is in keeping with the fact that the highest coupons represented the greatest profit potential for refinancing. Note also that for coupons at or below the low point in interest rates, relatively little increase in prepayments took place, and what increase did occur is explainable from other factors.

It is interesting to ask why high-interest mortgage prepayments have not increased even more after a drop in interest rates. After all, what reason do borrowers have for *not* refinancing when the opportunity presents itself? There are several reasons, not the least of which is that people are greedy, and when a homeowner sees rates falling, he is often tempted to wait in the hope that rates will fall even further before making his move. In fact, it is typical for refinancing prepayments to reach a peak not when interest rates bottom out, but some months afterward when it becomes apparent to these homeowners that it is now or never. Another factor that limits refinancing activity is the upfront cost. A borrower cannot simply walk into the bank and renegotiate the mortgage loan at a lower rate. Usually a new loan application is required, involving certain fees and points which must be paid in advance. Even if these fees could be recovered in a short time, in the form of lower monthly mortgage payments, borrowers who do not have the upfront money are effectively denied access to refinancing. Also, the existence of any prepayment penalties could be an effective deterrent to refinancing until rates fall far below the old mortgage rate.

Let us now turn to the *all other* category of prepayments. After taking account of refinancing activity and subtracting the resulting prepayments from the total amount, what remains are those prepayments resulting from housing turnover, natural disaster, default, etc. The variation in these prepayments is caused by three types of factors: seasonal, cyclical, and regional.

Seasonal factors exist because people tend to shop for houses when the

Figure 18

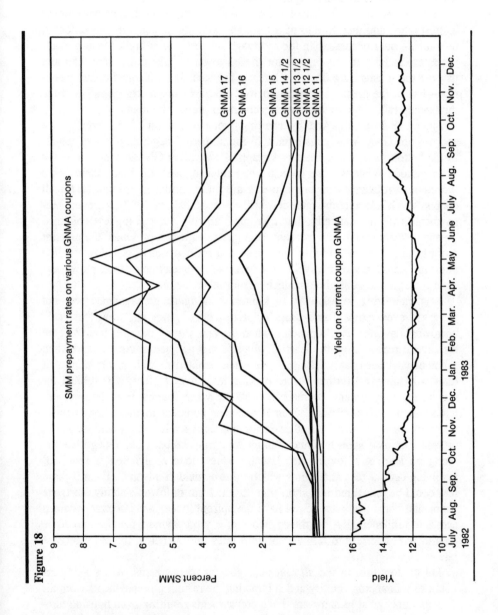

weather is nice and to stay at home when it is not. This results in a tendency for prepayments to be greatest in late spring and early summer and lowest during winter. The seasonal effect can be quite strong—on some conventional mortgages, prepayments have been twice as high in summer as in winter.

Cyclical factors include all of the variables related to the strength of the economy. When the economy is strong, prepayments increase because new homes are being built, unemployment is low, and people can afford to shop for houses. Conversely, in a weak economy, many families have higher priorities than shopping for a new house, and prepayments tend to fall. If the economy were to get too weak, however, many people would not be able to afford their mortgage payments, defaults would rise, and prepayments would increase on pass-throughs where the issuer guarantees timely payment of principal.

Regional factors also play an important role. Certain areas of the country tend to be more prosperous than others. For example, the Sun Belt region of the South and Southwest is relatively immune from any economic plight of the rest of the country because of large population growth and robust local economies. Prepayments therefore tend to be higher and less variable in this region.

Another regional factor influencing prepayments is the applicability of due-on-sale regulations. Due-on-sale (DOS) refers to the ability of a mortgage lender to require repayment of a loan upon sale or transfer of the property. Most conventional loans originated in the last 10 years have such clauses (FHA-insured and VA-guaranteed loans do not), but in several states the courts have ruled them unenforceable. When DOS either does not exist or is unenforceable, the mortgage does not have to be repaid when the property is sold or transferred; instead, it can be "assumed" by its new owner, meaning that the new owner simply continues making payments on the loan. Thus, prepayments are avoided. Buyers of mortgages and mortgage securities naturally prefer loans that are *good due-on-sale,* meaning loans originated with DOS clauses in states where DOS is enforceable.

Unfortunately, there is no short explanation of which states and loans are good DOS. Determining whether or not a mortgage is assumable involves looking at the type of loan, the state where it was originated, the origination date, the property sale date and the type of lending institution (federal- versus state-chartered S&L, commercial bank, etc.). Furthermore, controversy can exist even with these data, and the applicable laws are changing. Potential mortgage investors should therefore consult with their investment advisors on the applicability of DOS before commiting any funds.

When all of the explanatory variables are taken into account, one finds that there are some prepayments that never vary. They constitute a sort of "background noise" level below which prepayments cannot go. Such appeared to be the case in late 1981 and early 1982, when all explanatory variables were adverse: interest rates were high, the economy was weak, and the weather was cold. Figure 18 shows that, as of mid-1982, prepayments in different GNMA coupons were all crunched to around this base level, which was slightly higher than zero. What accounts for this behavior? There are some prepayments that result from natural disaster and death of the homeowner, and these are both small in quantity and random in occurence. It is this base level which we are probably seeing at the low point on the prepayment charts. This is important to remember when forecasting prepayments. It means that even the most pessimistic outlook must allow for some small prepayment rate.

Average Life, Half-Life, and Duration

Buyers of mortgages and pass-through securities are generally interested in two statistics that summarize the nature of their investments. The first of these is the yield, or rate of return, of the investment, which is a subject we shall discuss shortly. The other is the life of the investment, or the span of time over which the rate of return is realized.

One could argue (correctly) that since the cash flow of a 30-year pass-through security extends all the way to 30 years (barring complete extinction of the pool beforehand), the life of the security is 30 years. However, as Figures 13 and 14 showed, most of the principal amount in a mortgage pool is retired, due to amortization and prepayments, well before that time. Investors found it desirable to quantify the effective lifetime of a pool in a way that accounted for its principal paydowns. There are three traditional approaches to this problem: *average life, half-life,* and *duration.*

Half-life is probably the easiest of the three measurements to explain. The half-life of a security is the number of years that must elapse before half of the principal is repaid. Figure 19 illustrates the half-life concept by graphing the total principal payments (amortization plus prepayments) that would be received from a 30-year, 9½ percent GNMA security at 200 percent FHA-experience. The half-life of the security is 6.5 years and is indicated by a vertical line. When depicted in this fashion, half-life has a simple, geometric interpretation: It is the vertical line that divides the graph into equal portions. In other words, the two shaded regions on the exhibit have areas that are equal.

One of the drawbacks of half-life is that it fails to consider the actual timing of principal payments. Suppose, for example, that in the previous exhibit all of the principal outstanding in year 7 was prepaid at that time. This would have the effect of squeezing the portion of the graph lying to the right of the half-life line into a tall, narrow band. Most investors would agree that such a cash flow has a shorter life than it did before. However, the half-life statistic would not change. Because all of the squeezing occurs after the halfway point, nothing happened to affect the half-life measurement. Half of the issue is still retired by the end of 6.5 years. Although this example is somewhat perverse, it does indicate the need for a more sensitive measurement of the effective term, and average life provides such a measurement.

The *average life* of a security is the average number of years that each

Figure 19 • Half-Life of a $1 Million GNMA 9½ Percent Security (200 percent FHA-experience assumed)

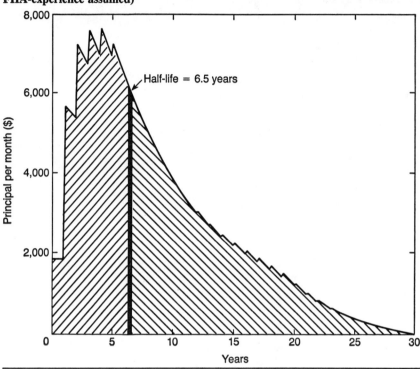

principal dollar will be outstanding. Stated differently, it is the number of years that each dollar in a pass-through pool can be expected to survive. Mathematically, the computation of average life is somewhat more difficult than of half-life. Average life is computed as the weighted average time to repayment of all of the principal paydowns, using as weights the dollar amounts of the pay-downs. Like half-life, average life has a geometric interpretation, which is shown in Figure 20. The graph shows the same cash flow as does Figure 19, but this time we consider the horizontal axis to be a seesaw. Each payment is a weight on the seesaw. The greater the payment, the heavier the weight. Average life turns out to be that location on the axis where the fulcrum of the seesaw must be placed in order to make it balance. In this example, average life works out to about 8.2 years.

Unlike half-life, average life is sensitive to any shifts in the timing of principal repayments. For example, if the security were to prepay in year 7 as previously supposed, the seesaw would become imbalanced to the left. In order to restore balance, the fulcrum would have to be shifted left to compensate. This is equivalent to saying that average life decreased, as expected.

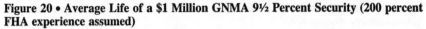

Figure 20 • Average Life of a $1 Million GNMA 9½ Percent Security (200 percent FHA experience assumed)

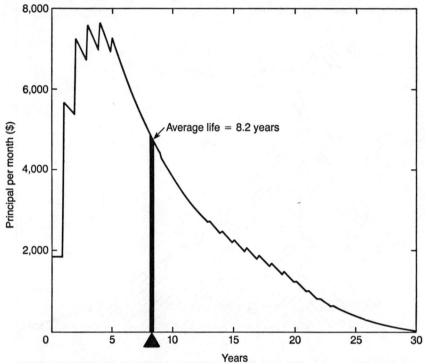

It should be noted that both average life and half-life tend to decrease as the mortgage pool ages. At each point in time, average life and half-life measure the term of the *remaining* dollars in the pool. Obviously, each measurement must go to zero by the time the pass-through matures. Figure 21 graphs the average lives of a GNMA 9½ percent pass-through over time at various assumed rates of experience. The higher the prepayment rate, the shorter the average life becomes, although as time elapses, the differences in average life (for different prepayment rates) become smaller.

Average life is typically longer than half-life for pass-through securities because of the nature of the cash flow. Pass-throughs generally return more dollars in their early years than in their later years. This keeps the half-life short, but the leverage on the seesaw provided by the few dollars going out to the later years keeps the average life from getting as small.

Despite its greater difficulty in computation, average life is generally regarded to be superior to half-life as an estimate of the effective period over which returns are generated. Average life is quite sensitive to changes in a pass-through's prepayment assumption and/or its age. Although average life is

Figure 21 • Average Life of a GNMA 9½ Percent Security (assuming various prepayment rates over first 15 years)

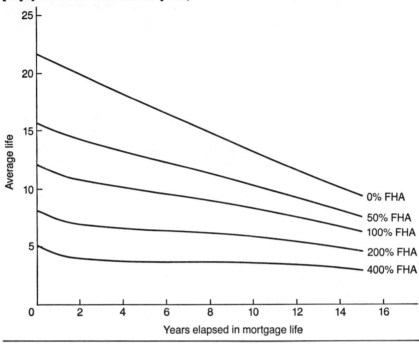

not as accurate a measure of volatility as it is purported to be, it should continue to be used (in conjunction with yield) to arrive at an overall evaluation of an investment.

Probably the best measure of a security's life, however, is a number known as *duration*. While it is a calculation that was first employed in 1938, it lay largely unutilized until the mid-70s, when it became the focus of the immunization and dedicated bond portfolio studies going on at that time. Many institutional investors are familiar with duration and often prefer it to average life.

The calculation of duration is analogous to that of average life, with two important differences:

1. Where average life looks at repayments of principal only, duration looks at all payments, whether principal or interest.
2. Where average life uses the nominal payment amounts, duration looks at all payments in present value amounts.

These distinctions between average life and duration might best be summarized as follows: average life is the average amount of time it takes to recover a dollar of principal amount; duration is the average amount of time it takes to recover a dollar of price.

Figure 22 illustrates duration in a manner analogous to the way Figure 19 illustrated average life. Notice that both principal and interest components appear on the graph. And because all future payments appear as present values, the graph trails off very rapidly after the early years. As before, the duration can be found as the point where the graph would balance if the horizontal axis were a seesaw.

Unlike average life and half-life, duration depends not only on the cash flow of a security but on its price as well. Actually, the security's yield is used as the discount rate in calculating present values of future cash flows, but the price determines this yield. Well, almost. We shall see in the following sections that a pass-through can have several yields even at one price, and it therefore can have several durations. Suffice it to say for now, though, that once a cash flow is determined or assumed for a security and a price set, only one yield and one duration exist.

It turns out that with a slight modification, duration can be used as an exact volatility measure for pass-throughs (or other securities). When duration is divided by a simple factor involving the security's yield per payment period, we get a number known as *modified duration*. Like duration, modified duration is measured in years. What we mean by a *volatility measure* is a number that quantifies the relative change in price of a security for a given small change in yield. The larger the price change, the greater the volatility. Modified duration is just such a number. If one pass-through has a modified duration which is twice that of another, then for an equal change in yield it will have twice the change in price.

Figure 22 • Duration of $1 Million GNMA 9½ Percent Security (200 percent FHA experience assumed)

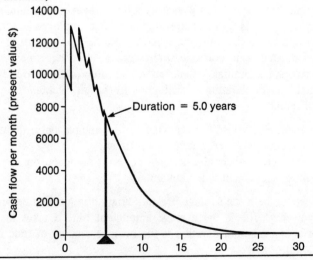

Investors are often uncomfortable with volatility measures denominated in years; they prefer more familiar numbers such as: yield value per $\frac{1}{32}$, or price change per 10 basis points, etc. Measuring volatility in years is like measuring gasoline in pounds. It is a precise specification, but in units which are unfamiliar. As investors acquire experience with duration (and modified duration), however, the awkwardness will fade and the use of these units will become second nature.

Yield Measurement

There is very likely no market as rich in controversy as the pass-through securities market when it comes to the subject of yield. The selection of the correct yield for a given pass-through at a given price is virtually the name of the game. Yet for all of the possible yields a security might have, there is really only one way to mathematically arrive at that yield. The various models, prepayment rates, and other assumptions determine the amount and timing of the cash flow received by the investor. Given the cash flow, however, there is very little freedom in determining the corresponding yield.

The yield of any investment is a measurement of its equivalent rate of return. Mathematically, yield should be viewed as a discounting rate used to compute present value. An investor who buys a security spends some amount of money in order to receive a series of future payments. In the case of pass-throughs, these future payments may not be known with certainty. In any event, when these future payments are converted to present-value equivalents and summed, the result should be the known market price. Yield (or, more properly, yield to maturity) is the discount rate that makes this relationship true.

The yields that are quoted for pass-through securities fall into two general categories: mortgage yield and cash flow yield. Mortgage yield is based on certain simplifying assumptions that force a definite cash flow into the yield calculation. As such it is useful only for very rough comparison purposes and should not be viewed as a true rate of return. Conversely, cash flow yield, which is often referred to as HTG yield, is based on cash flow assumptions chosen by the investor as being appropriate for the particular security and is generally more difficult to compute.

Mortgage Yield

Mortgages were bought and sold as whole loans by mortgage bankers and thrift institutions long before high-speed computers made the computation of yields easy. Fifty years ago, one did not have the luxury of being able to speculate as to the yield impact of the future prepayment rate of a mortgage or a mortgage pool. In fact, such prepayment models as FHA experience and

Table 10 • Pass-Through Yields and Corporate Bond Equivalents

GNMA 15

Prepaid In	8 Years		10 Years		12 Years		15 Years		18 Years		20 Years		25 Years	
Price	GNMA Yield	For CBE	GNMA Yield	For CBE	GNMA Yield	For CBE	GNMA Yield	For CBE	GNMA Yield	For CBE	GNMA Yield	For CBE	GNMA Yield	For CBE
75	21.44	+98	20.88	+93	20.55	+90	20.27	+88	20.13	+86	20.08	+86	20.02	+86
76	21.11	+95	20.58	+90	20.26	+87	20.00	+85	19.86	+84	19.81	+84	19.76	+84
77	20.80	+92	20.29	+88	19.99	+85	19.73	+83	19.60	+82	19.55	+81	19.50	+81
78	20.49	+89	20.00	+85	19.71	+83	19.47	+81	19.35	+80	19.30	+79	19.25	+79
79	20.19	+87	19.73	+83	19.45	+81	19.22	+79	19.10	+78	19.05	+77	19.00	+77
80	19.80	+84	19.45	+81	19.19	+78	18.97	+77	18.85	+76	18.81	+75	18.76	+75
81	19.60	+82	19.18	+78	18.94	+76	18.72	+75	18.61	+74	18.57	+73	18.53	+73
82	19.31	+79	18.92	+76	18.69	+74	18.49	+73	18.38	+72	18.34	+72	18.30	+71
83	19.03	+77	18.66	+74	18.44	+72	18.25	+71	18.15	+70	18.13	+70	18.03	+70
84	18.75	+75	18.41	+72	18.20	+70	18.02	+69	17.93	+68	17.80	+68	17.85	+69
85	18.48	+73	16.16	+70	17.97	+69	17.80	+67	17.71	+67	17.68	+66	17.64	+66
86	18.21	+71	17.92	+68	17.74	+67	17.58	+66	17.50	+65	17.47	+65	17.46	+65
87	17.95	+68	17.67	+66	17.51	+65	17.37	+64	17.29	+63	17.26	+63	17.22	
88	17.69	+66	17.44	+65	17.29	+63	17.15	+62	17.06	+62	17.04	+62	17.02	+62
89	17.44	+65	17.21	+63	17.07	+62	16.95	+61	16.88	+61	16.86	+60	16.81	+60
90	17.18	+63	16.98	+61	16.85	+60	16.74	+60	16.69	+59	16.66	+59	16.64	+58
91	16.94	+61	16.75	+60	16.64	+59	16.54	+58	16.49	+58	16.47	+58	16.45	+57
92	16.69	+59	16.52	+58	16.43	+57	16.35	+57	16.30	+56	16.28	+56	16.26	+55

93	16.46	+57	16.32	+56	16.23	+56	16.16	+55	16.12	+55	16.10	+55	16.08 +54
94	16.22	+56	16.10	+55	16.03	+55	15.97	+54	15.93	+54	15.92	+54	15.90 +53
95	15.99	+54	15.89	+54	15.83	+53	15.78	+53	15.75	+53	15.74	+53	15.72 +52
96	15.76	+53	15.69	+52	15.64	+52	15.60	+52	15.58	+51	15.67	+51	15.56
97	15.53	+51	15.48	+51	15.45	+51	15.42	+50	15.41	+50	15.40	+50	15.39 +49
98	15.31	+50	15.28	+49	15.26	+49	15.25	+49	15.24	+49	15.23	+48	15.23 +48
99	15.09	+48	15.08	+48	15.08	+48	15.07	+48	15.07	+48	15.07	+48	15.07 +48
100	14.88	+47	14.89	+47	14.90	+47	14.90	+47	14.91	+47	14.91	+47	14.91 +47
101	14.66	+46	14.70	+46	14.72	+46	14.73	+46	14.74	+46	14.75	+46	14.75
102	14.45	+44	14.51	+45	14.54	+45	14.57	+45	14.59	+45	14.59	+45	14.60 +45
103	14.24	+43	14.32	+43	14.37	+44	14.41	+44	14.43	+44	14.44	+44	14.45 +45
104	14.04	+42	14.14	+42	14.19	+43	14.25	+43	14.28	+43	14.29	+43	14.30 +43
105	13.84	+41	13.95	+41	14.03	+42	14.09	+42	14.13	+42	14.14	+42	14.16 +42
106	13.64	+39	13.78	+40	13.86	+41	13.94	+41	13.98	+41	13.99	+41	14.07 +40
107	13.44	+38	13.60	+39	13.70	+40	13.78	+40	13.83	+40	13.85	+41	13.88 +41
108	13.25	+37	13.42	+38	13.52	+39	13.63	+39	13.69	+39	13.71	+40	13.74 +40
109	13.06	+36	13.25	+37	13.38	+38	13.48	+38	13.55	+39	13.57	+39	13.60 +39
110	12.87	+35	13.08	+36	13.22	+37	13.34	+38	13.41	+38	13.43	+38	13.47 +39
111	12.68	+34	12.92	+35	13.06	+36	13.20	+37	13.27	+37	13.30	+37	13.34 +27
112	12.49	+33	12.75	+34	12.91	+35	13.05	+36	13.13	+36	13.17	+37	13.21 +37
113	12.31	+32	12.59	+33	12.76	+34	12.91	+35	13.00	+36	13.04	+36	13.08 +36
114	12.13	+31	12.43	+33	12.61	+34	12.78	+34	12.87	+35	12.91	+35	12.96 +35

Source: The First Boston Corporation.

SMM did not even exist. As a result, yields on mortgages were obtained by looking up the instrument in a yield book—often having to interpolate between available results to compensate for fractional coupon rates or prices.

Most yield books for mortgages contained columns of numbers corresponding to various years to prepayment. (See Table 10.) It was assumed that a mortgage or mortgage pool would experience no prepayments at all for the indicated number of years, at which time it would prepay in full. The yield obtained would depend on how much time elapsed before the pool terminated. Figure 23 depicts this situation for a 30-year mortgage assumed to prepay in 12 years. Two things should be noticed in this illustration. First, we are no longer dealing with a 30-year investment; the cash flow shown goes out no farther than 12 years. Second, this pattern is similar to that of an ordinary 12-year bond, which suggests that mortgage yields might be approximated using existing yield computations for corporate or government bond issues. Unfortunately, the cash flow in Figure 23 is different from that on straight debt in three respects, which are strong enough in combination to render the traditional bond yield books unusable:

1. The cash flow for the mortgage yield is monthly as opposed to the semiannual cash flow on ordinary bonds.
2. The mortgage cash flow returns some principal (in the form of amortiza-

Figure 23 • Cash Flow from $1 Million GNMA 9½ Percent Security (under 12-year prepayment assumption)

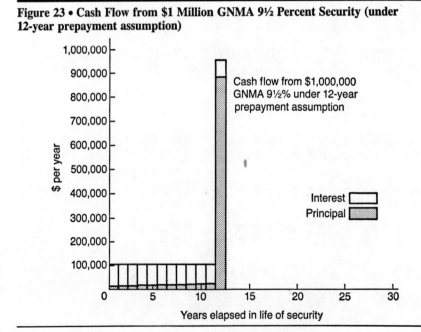

tion) over the entire period, whereas for straight debt all principal is repaid at maturity.
3. The existence of a servicing fee prevents the mortgage cash flow from being level up to its termination date, where straight debt pays level coupons.

In the event that the mortgage yield is being computed for a pass-through security, a fourth difference exists—payment delay. The longer the investor must wait to begin receiving payments, the lower the investor's net yield will be, other things being equal. This effect is not quantified in traditional bond yield tables, since bonds ordinarily have no payment delays.

Table 10 makes it clear that the choice of the number of years to prepayment is critical in determining the mortgage yield when the price is significantly different from par. Unfortunately, there was no way to know a priori when a mortgage investment was going to terminate, so some type of assumption had to be made. Over time, the mortgage industry evolved certain standard assumptions, which would be used in deciding the years to prepayment when there was no compelling reason to choose another number. These standards, still in use today, are displayed in Table 11. The table shows that for 30-year mortgages, 12 years was the accepted standard prepayment assumption. Generally, mortgages with shorter original terms had shorter prepayment assumptions.

The pass-through securities market adopted mortgage yield as its standard from its inception in the early 1970s. The standard assumptions regarding the term to prepayment have been left intact. Of course, pass-throughs require additional assumptions regarding servicing fee and payment delay in order to

Table 11 • Standard Assumptions behind Mortgage Yield

Security type	Years to Maturity	Years to Prepayment	Servicing Fee	Payment Delay (days)*
GNMA†				
Single-family	30	12	½%	45
Graduated payment	30	12	½	45
Buydown	30	12	½	45
Mobile home A	12	5	2½	45
Mobile home B	15	7	2½	45
Mobile home C	18	9	2½	45
Mobile home D	20	10	2½	45
Project Loan	40	18	¼	45
FHLMC PC	30	12	0	75
FNMA	30	12	0	55
Private Issuers	30	12	⅜	55

*Notice that the actual time penalty for each security is 31 days less than the stated payment delay.
†Assumptions for GNMA-2 securities are the same as shown except that the payment delay is 50 days.

determine yield. Each type of security has its own particular parameters for the yield formula, and these parameters are detailed in the Appendix.

What does it mean when we say that the mortgage yield is the pass-through market standard? Essentially there are three ways that mortgage yield is used as a standard. First, because mortgage yield is the accepted norm, it is often referred to using the security name itself. For example, *GNMA yield* means mortgage yield on GNMA securities (using the parameters appropriate for GNMAs), and *FHLMC yield* means mortgage yield for FHLMC PCs. Second, mortgage yield is the standard for quotations among security dealers. This means that trades done on a yield basis will be billed by computing a price using mortgage yield formulas. It also means that yields appearing in newspaper quotations or other market literature are mortgage yields. The third way in which mortgage yield is used as a standard is in yield maintenance trades. In the pass-through securities market, buyers often purchase securities for forward delivery, meaning that the trades will settle at some future date, usually from one to four months later. In some cases, it is not possible to guarantee to the buyer receipt of the exact coupon requested; this is because the securities the buyer receives may not have been created yet. In these situations, the buyer and seller agree that if another coupon is substituted, the price of the trade will be adjusted to maintain the original yield to the buyer, using the mortgage yield as the standard. In other words, the actual delivered coupon at the adjusted price has the same mortgage yield as the original coupon at the original price.

Drawbacks of Mortgage Yield

Before discussing cash flow yield, or HTG yield, it is appropriate to point out two problems with mortgage yield. It was these problems that led to the need for an alternative yield mechanism.

First, the cash flow assumptions underlying mortgage yield are viewed as unrealistic. The possibility of all the remaining principal balance prepaying on just one date may be reasonable for individual mortgage loans, but it is not reasonable for a mortgage pool. Because the pool has large numbers of mortgages contributing to the cash flow, its prepayments will tend to be spread out over time.

The second problem is more serious and yet is not realized by many market participants. Mortgage yield for a given type of security is always based on the same assumptions of years to prepayment and years to maturity, regardless of the actual age of the underlying mortgages. For example, GNMA 8 percent single-family securities, which were issued primarily in the mid-1970s, have mortgage yields based on 30 years to maturity and 12 years to prepayment, regardless of the fact that many of these issues have 25 years or less of remaining term. In fact, according to the rules, the yields of these issues would still be quoted based on this 30/12 system, even when they are 20 years old and only have a 10-year remaining term. This ignorance of mortgage age has the effect of seriously understating the true yield of older, deep-discount securities. In fact, if left unchecked, this problem will be magnified every year as the existing population of pass-throughs continues to age. The market will undoubtedly be forced at some point to reevaluate its standards, but for those who prefer not to wait there is another solution.

HTG Yield

Cash flow yield, or HTG yield, differs from mortgage yield in that the underlying cash flow is made to be as realistic as possible. This means accounting for all known factors, such as the age of the underlying mortgages, as well as projecting reasonable estimates for future prepayments. Prepayments are usually specified in the form of a percentage FHA- or SMM-experience rate. The name *HTG* is short for Honest-to-God and was coined in 1977 by The First Boston Corporation. It was intended to suggest, if somewhat unsubtly, a superior estimate of the true yield of a pass-through. Unlike mortgage yield, there is more than one HTG yield for a given pass-through at a given price. In fact, there are infinitely many HTG yields depending on the prepayment assumption used; no one prepayment model or experience multiple is cast as the standard, although market conditions inevitably make some assumptions appear to be more reasonable than others. Perhaps the greatest asset of HTG yield is its ability to evolve with a changing market environment

Table 12 is an example of an HTG yield table for a GNMA security. Separate sections are produced for each age assumption on the underlying mortgages. In this particular format, yields at various FHA-experience rates are calculated in addition to the GNMA yield (mortgage yield). Also, each column of yields is followed by the average life of the security under the given assumptions.

Several points can be made using this one table. First, notice that as FHA-experience increases, average life decreases. This serves to raise the HTG yield at discount prices and to lower it for premium prices. Second, notice that increasing the mortgage age (thereby decreasing remaining term) has the same effect because this too decreases remaining average life. Finally, notice that GNMA yield is insensitive to either of these effects. There is only one GNMA yield at a given price because neither age nor assumed prepayment rate enter into the mortgage yield computation.

The investor or analyst who has been accustomed to mortgage yield might find a quite different world in terms of HTG yield. The values of pass-throughs, both relatively and absolutely, are subject to change in the HTG analysis, particularly for older securities, higher assumed prepayment rates, and/or deeper discount prices. As an example, Table 13 shows how the GNMA market looked in both GNMA yield and HTG yield perspectives at the end of

Table 12 • Example of an HTG Yield Table

GNMA 9½ Servicing Fee ½ percent Mortgage Rate 10 percent Payment Delay 45 days Mortgage Age (yrs) 4 Years to Maturity 26

HTG Yields for Various FHA-Experience Rates

Price	GNMA Yield	0	50	100	150	200	250	300	400	500	600	800	1000
70.000	15.01	14.36	15.57	16.82	18.09	19.37	20.66	21.94	24.50	27.02	29.51	34.36	39.07
75.000	13.86	13.31	14.24	15.20	16.19	17.18	18.18	19.18	21.16	23.13	25.07	28.85	32.53
80.000	12.82	12.38	13.07	13.78	14.51	15.25	16.00	16.74	18.23	19.70	21.16	24.00	26.77
85.000	11.87	11.54	12.02	12.52	13.03	13.55	14.07	14.59	15.64	16.67	17.70	19.70	21.65
90.000	11.00	10.78	11.08	11.39	11.70	12.02	12.35	12.67	13.32	13.97	14.60	15.86	17.07
95.000	10.20	10.09	10.22	10.36	10.51	10.65	10.80	10.95	11.24	11.54	11.83	12.40	12.96
100.000	9.45	9.46	9.45	9.44	9.42	9.41	9.40	9.39	9.37	9.35	9.32	9.28	9.24
105.000	8.75	8.87	8.73	8.58	8.44	8.28	8.13	7.97	7.66	7.35	7.05	6.44	5.85
110.000	8.09	8.33	8.07	7.80	7.53	7.25	6.97	6.68	6.11	5.54	4.97	3.86	2.77
115.000	7.48	7.83	7.46	7.08	6.70	6.30	5.90	5.50	4.69	3.88	3.08	1.49	-.06
Average life (years)		18.15	13.19	10.08	8.02	6.59	5.56	4.79	3.73	3.05	2.58	1.97	1.61

GNMA 9½

Servicing Fee ½ percent
Mortgage Rate 10 percent
Payment Delay 45 days

Mortgage Age (yrs) 6
Years to Maturity 24

HTG Yields for Various FHA-Experience Rates

Price	GNMA Yield	0	50	100	150	200	250	300	400	500	600	800	1000
70.000	15.01	14.55	15.74	16.99	18.26	19.55	20.86	22.13	24.83	27.48	30.12	35.33	40.42
75.000	13.36	13.46	14.38	15.34	16.32	17.32	18.33	19.35	21.41	23.46	25.51	29.56	33.53
80.000	12.32	12.49	13.18	13.89	14.62	15.36	16.11	16.87	18.40	19.94	21.47	24.50	27.48
85.000	11.37	11.62	12.10	12.60	13.11	13.63	14.15	14.68	15.75	16.83	17.90	20.03	22.13
90.000	11.00	10.83	11.13	11.44	11.75	12.07	12.40	12.73	13.39	14.06	14.72	16.05	17.36
95.000	10.20	10.11	10.25	10.39	10.53	10.68	10.82	10.97	11.27	11.58	11.88	12.49	13.08
100.000	9.45	9.45	9.44	9.43	9.42	9.41	9.40	9.39	9.37	9.34	9.32	9.27	9.23
105.000	8.75	8.84	8.70	8.56	8.41	8.26	8.10	7.95	7.63	7.32	7.00	6.36	5.74
110.000	8.09	8.28	8.02	7.76	7.48	7.20	6.92	6.64	6.06	5.47	4.89	3.72	2.56
115.000	7.48	7.76	7.39	7.01	6.63	6.23	5.84	5.43	4.61	3.79	2.96	1.30	-.34
Average life (years)		16.46	12.23	9.51	7.66	6.36	5.40	4.67	3.66	2.99	2.53	1.92	1.55

1981. The prices used are actual bid side quotations, ages are approximate average values for each coupon, and the prepayment assumption of 75 percent FHA-experience was moderately bullish in posture at that time.

The investor or analyst who looked only at GNMA yields would see a pattern of generally increasing yields as coupon rates rise. This might seem appropriate, since it is typical in the fixed income markets for higher coupon issues to yield more, due primarily to tax considerations, reinvestment potential for incoming cash flow, and/or call protection. In the pass-through market, however, one would not always expect these traditional relationships to hold. It is true that GNMAs (or other pass-throughs) priced over par should carry a substantial yield premium as compensation for the risk that the issue could be prepaid with the investor suffering a loss in market value. However, it is also reasonable to expect very low coupon pass-throughs to carry high yields to compensate for a risk specific to such securities, known as prepayment risk. As Table 12 demonstrates, the HTG yield of a deep-discount pass-through is highly sensitive to the precise prepayment assumption used. For example, a 4-year-old GNMA 9½ at par has a difference in yield of only one basis point between the assumptions of 50 percent FHA-experience and 100 percent FHA. However, if the security were priced at 70, the difference in yield between the two assumptions is 125 basis points. The penalty for guessing wrong on the future prepayment rate is therefore far greater for low-coupon pass-throughs that carry deep-discount prices.

Returning to Table 13, notice that the pattern of HTG yields (using 75 percent FHA and ages appropriate for each coupon level) is closer to the way one might expect to see it. It is the intermediate coupons that yield the least. High coupons yield more because of the risk of prepayments speeding up when their prices go above par. Lower coupons yield more to compensate for the risk that prepayments may be less than predicted.

Obviously the GNMA yield and the HTG yield columns paint very different

Table 13 • GNMA Market Analysis as of December 31, 1981

Coupon	Price 12/31/81	GNMA Yield	Assumed Age (years)	HTG Yield
6½	55¾	14.79	9	18.57
7¼	57¾	15.26	6	18.12
8	60⅞	15.41	5	17.74
9	65¼	15.57	3	17.19
10	70⅜	15.55	2	16.68
11	75⅜	15.57	1	16.28
12½	83¼	15.55	1	15.98
13½	88⅜	15.58	1	15.85
15	94¾	15.88	0	15.95
16	98⅜	16.19	0	16.21
17	102⅞	16.32	0	16.28

Note: GNMA yield and HTG yield are calculated based on monthly compounding. HTG yield assumes mortgages have ages as shown and that prepayments are at 75 percent FHA.

pictures of the world, in both absolute level of returns and relationships between coupon sectors. One always prefers to go with the picture that makes the most sense to the observer, and for this reason, HTG yield analysis has become very popular.

Corporate Bond Equivalent Yield

Pass-through securities have a built-in advantage over traditional corporate or government debt in that they make monthly payments of principal and interest as opposed to semiannual payments. Investors always prefer payments to be more frequent and/or begin sooner, since this gives them more time to reinvest the payments to earn additional income.

Both pass-through yield and HTG yield are computed on the basis of monthly compounding, and as such they do not reflect this advantage over other securities. If one wishes to compare pass-throughs with corporate or government bonds, it is necessary to put all yields on an equal footing with respect to compounding. This is usually accomplished by adjusting the pass-through's yield upward to compute its corporate bond equivalent yield, or CBE.

Table 14 contains CBE adjustments for monthly-pay securities. The entries in the table are in the form of basis point add-ons. As an example, let us consider GNMA 17s at a price of 102⅞, which is where they were at year-end 1981. (See Table 13.) Table 14 indicates that for the GNMA yield of 16.32 percent, the adjustment is 57 basis points, giving the GNMA CBE yield of 16.89 percent. Similarly, the HTG yield of 16.28 percent (based on 30-year term, 75 percent FHA) has a CBE adjustment of 56 basis points, giving an HTG CBE yield of 16.84 percent.

Notice that the adjustment does not depend on whether the starting yield is a mortgage yield or an HTG yield. All that matters is the absolute level of the initial yield. The mathematics are such that any monthly-pay security will use the same table of adjustments for comparison to any semiannual-pay security. The exact formula for computing CBE values can be found in the Appendix.

The amount of the CBE adjustment rises very quickly as yield levels increase. The additional yield value in pass-through securities versus corporate bonds is therefore substantially more than it first appears during periods of high interest rates. Investors must remember to make this adjustment (or to use yield tables with the adjustment already built in) when operating in more than one market.

Parity Price

Bond investors are accustomed to the fact that at a price of par, the yield to maturity of a bond is equal to its coupon rate. They are probably also aware

---

Table 14 • Yield Adjustments for Corporate Bond Equivalents

Yield Range	BP	Yield Range	BP
8.02– 8.30	+14	13.84–14.00	+41
8.31– 8.58	+15	14.01–14.17	+42
8.59– 8.85	+16	14.18–14.33	+43
8.86– 9.11	+17	14.34–14.49	+44
9.12– 9.37	+18	14.50–14.65	+45
9.38– 9.62	+19	14.66–14.81	+46
9.63– 9.86	+20	14.82–14.97	+47
9.87–10.10	+21	14.98–15.12	+48
10.11–10.33	+22	15.13–15.28	+49
10.34–10.55	+23	15.29–15.43	+50
10.56–10.77	+24	15.44–15.58	+51
10.78–10.99	+25	15.59–15.73	+52
11.00–11.20	+26	15.74–15.88	+53
11.21–11.41	+27	15.89–16.03	+54
11.42–11.62	+28	16.04–16.17	+55
11.63–11.82	+29	16.18–16.31	+56
11.83–12.01	+30	16.32–16.46	+57
12.02–12.21	+31	16.47–16.60	+58
12.22–12.40	+32	16.61–16.74	+59
12.41–12.59	+33	16.75–16.88	+60
12.60–12.77	+34	16.89–17.01	+61
12.78–12.96	+35	17.02–17.15	+62
12.97–13.13	+36	17.16–17.29	+63
13.14–13.31	+37	17.30–17.42	+64
13.32–13.49	+38	17.43–17.55	+65
13.50–13.66	+39	17.56–17.69	+66
13.67–13.83	+40	17.70–17.82	+67

Example: If GNMA yield is 16.32 percent, adjustment is 57 basis points. Therefore the corporate bond equivalent is

$$16.32 + .57 = 16.89 \text{ percent}$$

---

that for pass-through securities, this relationship does not hold true. As Table 12 shows, at a price of par, both mortgage yield and HTG yield are less than the coupon rate, and in fact HTG yield decreases for higher prepayment rates. The cause of this phenomenon is the payment delay. It can be shown mathematically that at a price of par, yield equals coupon only if there is no payment delay. (This is why the relationship is true for ordinary bonds.)

As it turns out, there is a unique price for which yield (both mortgage and HTG) equals coupon regardless of prepayment rate. This price, known as the *parity price* of the security, is always less than par and is typically in the range from about 98½ to 99½. The parity price will be lower for higher coupon rates and/or greater payment delays.

Parity price is the analog to par in the pass-through market. Since a price of par is greater than the parity price, yields are less than the coupon rate and will decline as average life decreases, which accounts for the pattern in Table 12. An exact formula for parity price can be found in the Appendix.

Taxation

Like corporate and government bonds, pass-through securities are generally taxable. (The small quantity of pass-throughs issued in the municipal sector should be disregarded for the purposes of this section.) One does not often find a discussion of the tax aspects of pass-throughs, though, for two reasons. First, most pass-through buyers are tax-exempt institutions, such as pension funds, for whom the topic is not relevant. Second, there is some ambiguity as to exactly how pass-throughs should be taxed, which sections of the tax code apply, and so on. What follows here, therefore, is First Boston's present understanding of the tax aspects of pass-throughs, which at the very least should be checked with the reader's tax counsel.

There is no question that the coupon income from a pass-through represents ordinary income and is taxed as such. The controversy arises in the treatment of gains or losses on the return of principal due to amortization or prepayments. With ordinary bonds, such gain or loss would represent capital gain or loss, and would be long term if the holding period (the time from purchase to the date of the principal payment) was more than six months. This capital gains treatment is not afforded to pass-throughs on the grounds that to qualify for such treatment, the obligor of the security (the party responsible for making the payment) cannot be a natural person. The thinking is that the obligor of a pass-through is the collection of property owners whose mortgages compose the pool, and since property owners are usually individuals, the capital gains treatment does not apply. Therefore, any gains on amortized or prepaid principal are ordinary income, regardless of holding period. This is definitely a tax disadvantage for pass-throughs and perhaps explains why so few taxable investors own them. It may be some consolation that this adverse treatment applies only while the security is being held. If the security is sold, any gain or loss on the remaining principal balance once again becomes capital gain or loss, and is long term for holding periods of more than six months.

As if the tax treatment of pass-throughs were not complicated enough, it gets worse for GPM pass-throughs. As we have seen, GPMs experience negative amortization over their first few years, so their monthly payments are substantially smaller than for traditional mortgages. Taxable buyers of GPMs who are on an accrual basis must pay income taxes on the entire amount of interest that would have been paid on a traditional loan, even though only part of that interest was actually received. In other words, taxes are due on monies not received. The interest shortfall is treated as a deferred interest item by the tax payer. Since taxes have already been paid on it, it is not taxed when actually paid. Should a GPM pool exhibit prepayments, the first dollars of prepayments are used to reduce any deferred interest outstanding. It should come as no surprise that GPMs are even less attractive than ordinary pass-throughs to taxable buyers.

Prepayment Consistency

Imagine that you are an investor trying to choose between two GNMA pools
for purchase into your portfolio. Both are GNMA 8s, both are about 3½ years
old, both were issued by Philadelphia mortgage bankers, and both are offered
at a price of 65 (14.33 percent GNMA yield) in May 1981. An investigation
of the historical prepayment rates reveals that although both pools are above
average in speed, one pool has prepaid at an average of about 200 percent of
FHA experience and the other at a truly fast-pay pace of more than 600 percent
FHA. Which pool would you choose?

Because the pools appear identical in most other respects, many investors
would automatically choose the fast-pay pool. Some investors, noting that at
600 percent FHA the HTG yield of such a security is more than 33 percent,
would pay a substantial premium for the fast-pay pool. Other investors would
take the position that future prepayments might not be as good as 600 percent
FHA, but they would still favor the fast-pay pool because of its established
trend of high prepayments. However, a recent study by The First Boston Corporation has revealed that the historical performance of a GNMA pool is in
general a poor indication of its future performance, and it is entirely possible
that the 200 percent FHA pool described above would be the superior investment.

Table 15 details the payment history as of May 1981 of two actual GNMA
pools that have the characteristics just described. The total payment each month
consists of three components: coupon (mortgage interest less servicing and
guarantee fees), amortization, and prepayments (including defaults). Coupon
payments and amortization for a month are predictable from the pool factor at
the beginning of the month. Prepayments are the only unknown component,
and it is the prepayments that ultimately make pass-through investments attractive or unattractive. (Usually, buyers of discount pass-throughs want prepayments, and buyers of premium securities do not.) Notice that the prepayments
of the 200 percent FHA pool are strikingly regular through May 1981. The
numbers from month to month are still unpredictable, but in 41 of the 43 periods, the dollar amount of prepayments was at least $1000 (per million dollars
original principal amount). The fast-pay pool, on the other hand, had more
than 99.9 percent of its prepayments occur in the first three months following
its issuance; an investor who purchased the pool after April 1978 in expectation
of fast prepayments would have been very unpleasantly surprised. Most people
who could see the actual prepayment records would conclude that, if anything,
the 200 percent FHA pool has the better chance for future prepayments. Both
pools in this example are extreme cases, and by no means do all comparisons
work out this way. Nevertheless, examples like this are not so rare either, and
the possibility of this phenomenon should be cause for concern among investors.

Because it would be extremely cumbersome for an investor to examine the detailed prepayment history of every pass-through pool before buying or selling it, it would be nice if there were some way of summarizing the *consistency* of historical prepayments in a single index. First Boston devised just such an index, which is referred to simply as *C*. This is not a perfect substitute for the detailed history, but it is a step in that direction. The possible values of C range from 0 to 100, where low numbers mean inconsistent prepayments, and high numbers mean consistent ones. In Table 15, the first pool has a C-value of 84, and the second pool (the fast-paying pool) has a value of only 15. Our experience with C indicates that values of 80 or more should be considered very consistent, and pools with C-values under 20 should have their prepayment rates viewed skeptically. C is based on a computation that considers the standard deviation of a pool's monthly prepayment record in relation to the maximum possible deviation the pool could have had. Also, C is adjusted for the effect of time. Pools that have not been outstanding very long can hardly be viewed as having established much of a trend, and their C-values will be mathematically constrained to being close to 50. Conversely, a pool with a very high or a very low consistency must by definition be a pool that has been outstanding for a reasonably long time. The precise definition of C appears in the Appendix.

Figure 24 displays the pattern of consistency as of May 1981 for the three largest sectors of the pass-through market: GNMA single-family (fixed payment), GNMA graduated payment, and FHLMC PC pools. In each case, the bracket with the single largest amount of pools has a C of about 85—apparently an optimistic note. Notice, however, that each of the GNMA securities has a significant amount of pools with lower consistencies, whereas the FHLMCs are all clustered at the high end of the scale. What is the reason for this?

The Law of Averages

There are two major differences in the composition of GNMA and FHLMC pools. First, FHLMCs are composed of conventional loans instead of the FHA/VA loans in GNMAs. It is not clear why this would make any difference as far as consistency is concerned. The other difference is pool size, and this can indeed make a difference. The average GNMA single-family or GPM pool is issued with an original balance of about $2 million, which means the pool contains about 50 loans (assuming an average loan size of around $40,000). Freddie Mac pools, though, contain several thousand mortgages, generally totaling more than $100 million, which gives PCs an advantage as far as consistency is concerned—the law of averages.

Mortgage prepayments and defaults, although influenced by seasonal and cyclical factors, are essentially random events. If a single homeowner whose mortgage is in a GNMA pool of 50 loans should move and prepay the loan, say after living in the home for about three years, the GNMA will show a prepayment rate of about 550 percent FHA for that month. (If the prepayment

Table 15 • Prepayment Histories of Two Actual GNMAs

		Cash flow from $1 mil GNMA 8 (No. 19886)					Cash flow from $1 mil GNMA 8 (No. 17730)				
		Pool Factor	Amort	Prepay	Coupon	Total Payment	Pool Factor	Amort	Prepay	Coupon	Total Payment
1977	Oct	1.00000	$644	$ 1,078	$6,667	$ 8,389	1.00000	$634	$ 60	$6,667	$ 7,361
	Nov	.99828	648	4,540	6,655	11,843	.99931	639	84,661	6,662	91,962
	Dec	.99309	650	6,147	6,621	$13,417	.91401	589	489,030	6,093	495,712
1978	Jan	.98629	650	8,593	6,575	15,819	.42439	284		2,829	3,113
	Feb	.97705	649	6,823	6,514	13,986	.42410	286		2,827	3,114
	Mar	.96958	649	2,298	6,464	9,411	.42382	288		2,825	3,114
	Apr	.96663	652	9,215	6,444	16,312	.42353	290		2,824	3,114
	May	.95676	651	3,024	6,378	10,053	.42324	292		2,822	3,114
	Jun	.95309	653	7,070	6,354	14,077	.42295	294	22	2,820	3,136
	Jul	.94537	653	3,697	6,302	10,652	.42263	296		2,818	3,114
	Aug	.94102	655	10,398	6,273	17,326	.42233	298	22	2,816	3,136
	Sep	.92996	652	12,679	6,200	19,531	.42201	300	24	2,813	3,137
	Oct	.91663	648	10,648	6,111	17,407	.42169	302	24	2,811	3,137
	Nov	.90534	645	7,850	6,036	14,530	.42136	305	24	2,809	3,138
	Dec	.89684	644	20,228	5,979	26,851	.42103	308		2,807	3,115
1979	Jan	.87597	634	11,079	5,840	17,553	.42073	310		2,805	3,115
	Feb	.86426	630	3,291	5,762	9,683	.42042	312		2,803	3,115
	Mar	.86034	632	5,506	5,736	11,874	.42010	315		2,800	3,115
	Apr	.85420	633	5,466	5,695	11,794	.41979	315	26	2,799	3,140
	May	.84810	633	11,483	5,654	17,770					
	Jun	.83598	629	6,822	5,573	13,024					
	Jul	.82853	628	9,417	5,524	15,569					

Year	Month										
	Aug	.81849	625	8,302	5,457	14,384	.41945	318	25	2,796	3,140
	Sep	.80956	623	8,212	5,397	14,232	.41910	321		2,794	3,116
	Oct	.80072	621	9,604	5,338	15,563	.41878	324	25	2,792	3,141
	Nov	.79050	618	7,238	5,270	13,126	.41843	327		2,790	3,116
	Dec	.78264	617	12,506	5,218	18,340	.41811	329		2,787	3,116
1980	Jan	.76952	611	11,339	5,130	17,081	.41778	331		2,785	3,116
	Feb	.75757	607	5,659	5,050	11,316	.41745	334		2,783	3,116
	Mar	.75130	606	21	5,009	5,636	.41711	336		2,781	3,116
	Apr	.75068	611	1,553	5,005	7,168	.41678	338		2,779	3,117
	May	.74851	614	3,047	4,990	8,651	.41644	340		2,776	3,117
	Jun	.74485	616	1,219	4,966	6,801	.41610	343		2,774	3,117
	Jul	.74302	619	3,728	4,953	9,300	.41576	345		2,772	3,117
	Aug	.73867	620	4,637	4,924	10,182	.41541	347		2,769	3,117
	Sep	.73341	621	1,917	4,889	7,427	.41506	351		2,767	3,117
	Oct	.73088	623	6,655	4,873	12,151	.41471	353		2,765	3,118
	Nov	.72360	622	2,231	4,824	7,677	.41436	355		2,762	3,118
	Dec	.72074	625	3,377	4,805	8,807	.41401	358		2,760	3,118
1981	Jan	.71674	626	29	4,778	5,433	.41365	360		2,758	3,118
	Feb	.71609	630	8,030	4,774	13,434	.41329	363		2,755	3,118
	Mar	.70743	628	5,054	4,716	10,398	.41293	365		2,753	3,118
	Apr	.70175	628	5,752	4,678	11,058	.41256	368		2,750	3,118
	May	.69537					.41219				

FHA-experience rate 208%
Prepay. consistency 84
Original pool size $14.8 mil
Mortgage banker in Philadelphia

FHA-experience rate 637%
Prepay. consistency 15
Original pool size $1.0 mil
Mortgage banker in Philadelphia

Figure 24 • Consistency Patterns

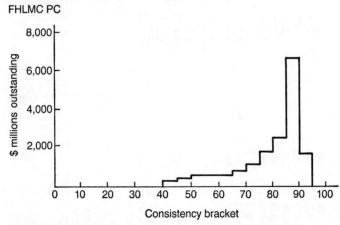

FHLMC PC

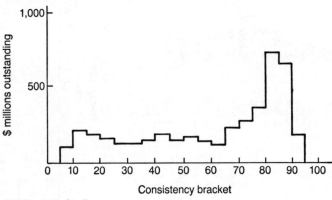

GNMA graduated payment

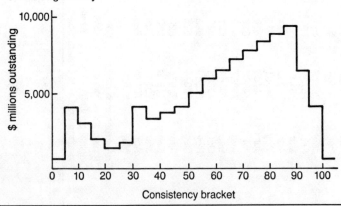

GNMA single family

occurs before three years, the FHA multiple is even higher.) The statistical value of a forecast for the other 49 loans based on this one event is dubious. In a FHLMC pool, however, single events are not statistically significant; in order to establish a prepayment trend, large numbers of mortgages must be involved. The law of averages makes a forecast based on this trend more reliable, and as a consequence, the consistency of month-to-month prepayments should be higher.

Referring to Table 15 again, it should come as no surprise that the first (consistent) pool had an original principal amount of $14.8 million, large by GNMA standards, and the second pool had an original size of only $1.0 million. There is another cause for high consistency in mortgage prepayments, and that is the lack of prepayments altogether. Obviously, if a pool never has any prepayments, it is behaving as consistently as possible. A statistical analysis of the pass-through universe reveals a negative correlation between consistency and average prepayment rate for all sectors of the market. In other words, the more consistent pools tend to be the slower paying ones. This does not mean that every fast-pay pool is going to be inconsistent, but it does mean that a fast-pay consistent pool is relatively hard to find.

Arguments against Consistency

Though there are several possible flaws in the consistency concept, consistency has withstood these challenges in most cases. First, it can be argued that inconsistency results from having a poor prepayment model—in this case, FHA experience. Obviously, if a prepayment model could perfectly predict future prepayments, all pools would behave consistently, and if a model were terrible, pools would tend to prepay randomly. The reason consistency is meaningful under FHA experience is not because FHA experience is a great model (it is not), but because it is the premier model being used by investors and dealers. It is FHA experience that makes pools fast-pay in people's minds, so it is the FHA consistency that counts.

Another argument is that one-month periods are too short for pools to behave consistently and that more consistent patterns would emerge if longer periods were examined. This is reasonable, but untrue. We repeated the consistency measurement on all pass-throughs using three-month, six-month, and one year periods, and in most cases consistency actually was worse. Part of the reason for this is that high consistency mathematically requires many time periods—a pool's prepayment history has only one-twelfth the number of annual periods as monthly periods. But the fact that most six-year and older pools have lower quarterly consistency than monthly consistency shoots down this argument quite clearly.

A third argument is that interest rates and seasonal factors have caused prepayments to fluctuate to a degree that destroys consistency. Again, this is a good possibility, but there is evidence against it. We took several thousand pools at random and ranked their prepayments relative to one another for each period. In other words, the prepayment rates were expressed as percentiles instead of absolute paydown rates. (The pools, in effect, were graded on a curve.) It turned out that the average change in the pool's percentile from one period to the next and the standard deviation of such changes were close to the values one would have obtained with a series of random numbers. This implies that no information is added (indeed, little even seems to be present) by accounting for overall market behavior.

One good argument against consistency is its failure to discriminate among pools based on the times at which prepayments occurred. In other words, two pools with all features alike, except that one had gradually increasing prepayments and the other gradually decreasing prepayments, would show the same value for C. By the same token, the fast-pay pool in Table 15 would be equally inconsistent (but no doubt more attractive to investors) if its large prepayments had occurred in the most recent three months instead of the first three months. All that can be said is that no one index can fully describe a series of numbers. We do not believe that this type of behavior is common or that it poses a serious problem, but of course some sort of prepayment acceleration index could be invented. A more attractive alternative is to examine recent prepayment experience in addition to overall consistency.

An Alternative

If consistency proves that historically fast-paying pools should not be relied upon to provide high future prepayments (in the absence of other information), how should they be viewed? Based on a statistical theorem proved by Charles Stein in the early 1960s, it can be shown that for most GNMA pools, a better guess for future prepayments is the average prepayment rate for the market, or even better, the average rate for similar pools of the same coupon. In other words, historical prepayment rates of individual pools are of little or no value in detecting the fast-pay GNMA pools of the future. First Boston advocates that investors obtain more information about specific pools before considering any trade at a price other than the going price for ordinary pools of the same type and coupon. Table 16 shows the sort of information First Boston generates on every GNMA and FHLMC pool. In addition to the pool's overall prepayment rate and consistency, prepayment rates for the past three months, six months, and one year are shown (other periods could also be chosen) to provide a feel for whether the prepayments have been coming or going. In conjunction with consistency, these prepayments give a good picture of the pool's behavior and get around the last problem cited earlier. The pools circled on the exhibit are the ones appearing in Table 15.

As long as there are pass-throughs, there will be pools that prepay faster or slower than average. However, a pool's historical prepayment rate alone is not a good indicator of which pools will be the fast-pay pools of the future. The

Table 16 • Prepayment Consistency Report for Pass-Through Securities; Data as of May 1981

Pool Number	Coupon	Type	Dated	$MM Outstanding	FHA EXP for Past			FHA to Date	C
					3 Months	6 Months	1 Year		
7071	8½	SF	9/75	.82	2	2	2	57	45
8655	8½	SF	4/76	.82	0	113	58	93	65
12337	8	SF	10/76	.88	2	2	2	45	45
15569	7½	SF	2/77	.72	2	1	158	155	68
17730	8	SF	1/78	.41	0	0	0	637	15
17993	7½	SF	12/77	2.40	0	15	49	146	65
19662	8	SF	9/77	3.26	77	121	109	115	69
19886	8	SF	10/77	10.29	168	109	102	208	84
20013	8	SF	1/78	1.73	2	2	45	92	64
20995	8	SF	11/77	1.72	0	71	109	85	54
27754	9	SF	2/79	3.74	1	116	64	81	53
28005	8½	SF	12/78	.86	24	427	308	197	46
29336	9	SF	6/79	.96	283	142	76	61	6
38892	11	SF	1/80	.98	3	3	157	137	20
39112	11	SF	2/80	.97	0	266	200	178	7

Source: The First Boston Corporation.

consistency index is a useful tool in making more reliable forecasts for individuals pools. In the absence of a consistency index, investors are advised to concentrate primarily on pool size because there tends to be safety in large numbers. In any event, the concept of the fast-paying GNMA should be taken with several grains of salt.

Risk versus Reward

We have shown that pass-through securities are more complex in nature than the typical corporate or government bond and are capable of posing formidable problems to the back office of an institutional investor. Not only are payments routinely composed of odd amounts of principal and interest, making it difficult to simply round off to the nearest million, but payments are received monthly. Furthermore, the prospect of calling individual mortgage bankers to track down errant checks for those issuers that have no central payment mechanism is less than appealing. Finally, the challenge of negative amortization on GPMs or of taxation is sufficient to scare off many a would-be buyer.

The pass-through market compensates investors for their trouble by offering relatively high yields in comparison to comparable-quality corporate or government issues. Figure 25 is a graph of the yield of U.S. Treasury 8¼ percent due 1990 versus the yield of GNMA 8s, using both GNMA yield and HTG yield (100 percent FHA assumed) since 1975. Both issues are virtually risk-free from a credit point of view, since the GNMAs are government guaranteed. Both have similar coupons and reasonably similar average lives. Yet the difference in yield (using the HTG figures) has averaged 130 basis points and has been as wide as 550 basis points.

There is more to the high yield of GNMAs than mere compensation for difficulties in bookkeeping. High reward in the securities markets almost always spells high risk. All pass-throughs embody five different forms of risk, which are as follows:

1. Market risk.
2. Credit risk.
3. Liquidity risk.
4. Reinvestment risk.
5. Prepayment risk.

Market risk is the risk that the market price of a security may change adversely in the future on either an absolute or a relative basis. As such, market risk embodies the volatility of the security's price as well as the yield relationship, or spread, to other issues. Pass-throughs historically have nearly as much volatility as long-term Treasury bonds, and the spreads in the pass-through market are influenced by traditional factors in the fixed-income market as well as external factors, such as housing turnover and mortgage issuance. Thus,

Figure 25 • Historical Relationship of GNMAs versus Treasuries

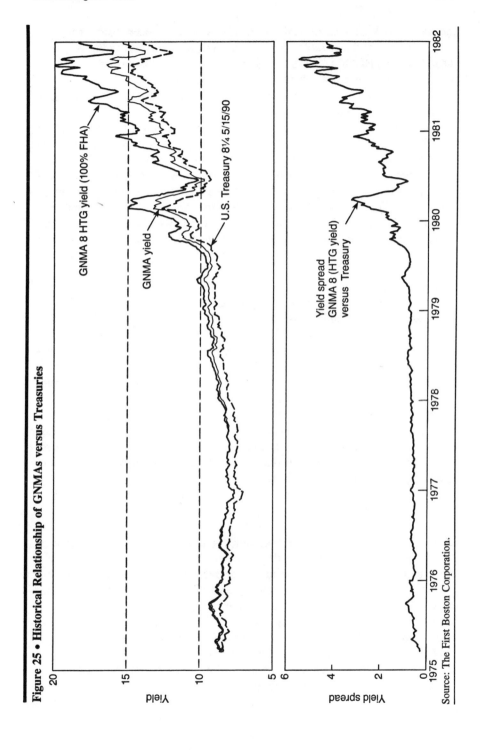

Source: The First Boston Corporation.

the market risk of pass-throughs is relatively high as debt instruments go.

Credit risk, or the risk of default, is not a factor for GNMAs but is a consideration for FHLMCs, FNMAs, and privately issued pass-throughs. Each issuer must be evaluated much like any other corporate issuer, but for FHLMC and FNMA there are certain indirect government ties that make these analyses somewhat more uncertain. Uncertainty is risk.

Liquidity risk is the risk that an investor may sustain a loss if forced to quickly sell an asset. In the fixed-income market, liquidity risk is often quantified in terms of the spread between the bid and offered sides of the market (the difference between the prices at which dealers will buy and sell the security). Treasury issues are generally the most liquid, with bid-offer spreads ranging from as little as $\frac{1}{16}$ of 1 percent or less for short maturities to about one-fourth point on long bonds. GNMAs typically fall in the one-fourth to one-half point range depending on the particular coupon, and other pass-throughs are in the one-half point plus range depending on the issuer. On average, then, liquidity is not as good as for Treasury issues and is sometimes comparable to corporate issues.

Reinvestment risk describes the uncertainty pass-through investors face in being able to put incoming cash flow to work at a favorable rate. Mathematically, one cannot realize a rate of return equal to the yield unless the cash flow can be reinvested at that rate on average. Pass-throughs are not the only securities with reinvestment risk—indeed, most securities have some degree of reinvestment risk. However, pass-throughs do tend to have high degrees of reinvestment risk for two reasons. First, pass-throughs tend to provide much of their return in the early part of their life. More cash flow up front is desirable only when it can be put to work favorably. Thus the realized returns of pass-throughs have a greater dependence on reinvestment potential than do the returns for many other issues. Second, and perhaps more important, is the double-whammy effect in pass-throughs—the fact that prepayments tend to be negatively correlated to interest rates. This means that the investor is most likely to receive the greatest cash flow from a pass-through at precisely the time when reinvestment opportunities are the worst.

Finally, there is prepayment risk, which is unique to the pass-through market. The previous exhibits have demonstrated that yields on pass-throughs can be extremely sensitive to the actual prepayment rate. At the same time, our consistency studies show that historical prepayment rates often do not count for much. Investors demand extra return from pass-throughs, especially those at deep discounts or high premiums, largely to compensate for the uncertainty in yield created by the need to forecast future prepayments.

Prepayment risk can be analyzed graphically using a technique developed by First Boston to compare pass-throughs with other types of securities. Figure 26 displays such an analysis, known as a *yield-duration plot,* as of mid-October, 1983. The graph plots yield on the vertical axis against duration on

Figure 26 • Yield-Duration Plot for Various GNMAs

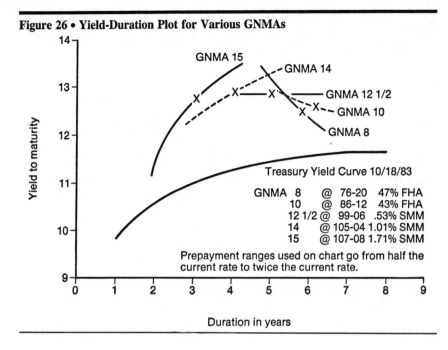

GNMA 8   @   76-20   47% FHA
      10   @   86-12   43% FHA
      12 1/2 @   99-06   .53% SMM
      14   @ 105-04 1.01% SMM
      15   @ 107-08 1.71% SMM

Prepayment ranges used on chart go from half the current rate to twice the current rate.

the horizontal axis. Any given security or cash flow at a specific price has only one yield and duration, and therefore can be represcnted by a point on the graph. When all of the actively traded Treasury bonds are plotted and a curve drawn through them (or nearly through them), the line labeled *Treasury Yield Curve* is obtained.

On top of this curve are added line segments representing various pass-throughs. Unlike Treasury bonds, pass-throughs cannot be shown as a single point on the graph because both yield and duration vary with prepayment rate. For this reason, yield-duration combinations are calculated for a variety of pre-payment rates, shown on the exhibit. This produces a segment of possible com-binations just for the one security. In addition, we place an *X* at the point representing each pass-through's yield-duration combination at its current pre-payment rate (also detailed in the exhibit).

Note that segments for discount pass-throughs, such as GNMA 8s, are sloped upward to the left. This is because higher prepayments produce shorter duration and higher yield. On the other hand, GNMA 15s, which traded at a premium on the analysis date, have a segment sloping upward to the right. This is because higher prepayments will shorten duration but lower yield. The exhibit gives a bird's-eye view of prepayment risk. The length of the line seg-ment for a pass-through is a measure of the uncertainty in yield and/or duration over the specified prepayment range. The slope of the line segment indicates the impact on yield for a given change in prepayment. Finally, the locations of the Xs on the segments show whether prepayments need to speed up or slow down for the various issues to have similar yields.

The Future: New Security Structures

The pass-through has been the dominant form of mortgage security since its inception by GNMA in 1970. However, by 1983 it had become apparent that there were alternative security structures which would be more appealing to certain types of investors, as well as potentially more profitable for mortgage-security issuers. At the heart of these new structures was the question of call protection.

Institutional investors are accustomed to securities that afford some degree of *call protection,* meaning that for some period of time the issuer cannot retire the debt. (Securities that can be retired but not with borrowed money are said to be *callable but not refundable.*) Many corporate bonds are issued with 5 to 10 years of refunding protection for the investor, and even then any debt that is retired may have to be repurchased at a premium to par. Pass-through securities, however, afford no call protection at all. Once a homeowner decides to prepay a mortgage, all security holders of an associated mortgage pool receive pro rata principal retirements at par.

It would seem that unless the rules of the game are changed at the home-owner level, it would be impossible to provide any call protection at the security level. Of course, a security could be designed with guarantees on the part of the issuer to reinvest or to continue making payments on prepaid principal, but this would violate the pass-through nature of such a security. Surprisingly, though, it is possible at the practical level to create security structures with *probable* call protection, even if not *guaranteed* call protection. The best example of such a structure is the collateralized mortgage obligation (or CMO) first issued in June 1983 by the Federal Home Loan Mortgage Corporation (FHLMC).

This CMO called for the creation of one mortgage pool and three different classes of securities, referred to as classes A-1, A-2, and A-3. Each class pays interest on its outstanding principal balance. However, the rules called for all collections of principal from the mortgage pool to be applied first to retiring the A-1 bonds, then the A-2s and finally the A-3s. In other words, the classes are to be retired in series; A-2 bonds will not be retired until all A-1 bonds are gone, and A-3 bonds go untouched until both A-1s and A-2s are extinguished.

This structure has several effects. First, it makes the A-1 securities extremely fast-pay and consistent in nature. Because only 21.5 percent of the securities sold are A-1 bonds, but prepayments on 100 percent of the mortgages are funneled through them, A-1s appear to have prepayments at a rate magnified to almost 5 times the normal rate. Second, the A-3 security appears to be

Figure 27 • FHLMC CMO Principal Retirements (dollars received semi-annually per $100 principal amount)

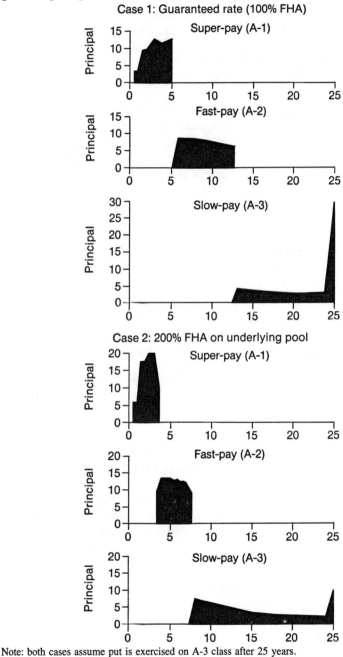

Case 1: Guaranteed rate (100% FHA)

Super-pay (A-1)

Fast-pay (A-2)

Slow-pay (A-3)

Case 2: 200% FHA on underlying pool

Super-pay (A-1)

Fast-pay (A-2)

Slow-pay (A-3)

Note: both cases assume put is exercised on A-3 class after 25 years.

very slow-pay. The A-3 bonds are in effect call-protected, not because they cannot be retired, but because the A-1 and A-2 bonds have to be retired first. Thanks to the studies of prepayments, their causes and variability, it is possible for investors to measure how long this pseudo call protection will last under various assumptions. Note that the A-2 bonds are a hybrid, with both a degree of call protection and a fast-pay nature once the call-protection period ends (once the A-1 bonds are gone). Figure 27 shows the principal retirement patterns of each CMO class at different assumed prepayment rates on the underlying collateral.

On top of this structure, FHLMC added two more features to its CMO. First, FHLMC guaranteed prepayments on the pool to run at least at a cumulative 100 percent FHA-experience on the mortgage pool. This creates a minimum paydown rate, and therefore a maximum maturity and average life for each class. (This is why Figure 27 does not have a cash flow under 100 percent FHA.) Second, FHLMC makes payments of principal and interest to security holders semi-annually rather than monthly, as with pass-throughs. This makes CMOs look more like traditional corporate bonds, and easier to account for on many investors' books.

Thus, while the CMO retains the pass-through philosophy at the pool level (all principal and interest less servicing spread are passed on to the various classes), it allows the issuer to discriminate at the security level as to who gets principal retirements and when. Since its issuance, the CMO structure has been copied and enhanced by other issuers, but the overall philosophy has remained the same. By adding a form of call protection and changing payment frequency, new investors, particularly pension funds, are attracted to the mortgage market. Through this increased demand, higher prices and better liquidity are obtained for mortgage securities, which ultimately permits lower interest costs to homeowners.

APPENDIX: FORMULAS RELATING TO MORTGAGES AND PASS-THROUGHS

The following formulas are provided for those who wish to calculate cash flows, average life, or yield for mortgages and pass-throughs. The following symbols are used (variables preceded by an asterisk [*] apply only to GPMs):

C = Coupon rate on security, as a percentage e.g.,   9.5
S = Servicing fee (total), as a percentage   0.5
D = Stated payment delay, in days   45
P = Security price, as a percentage   80.484
Y = Pass-through yield, as a percentage   12.5
N = Term to maturity, in years   30
M = Term to prepayment, in years   12

$*R$ = Percentage rate of payment graduation   7.5
$*A$ = Number of times payment graduates   5
$*B$ = Number of years between graduations   1

Definitions

Certain variables are now defined in terms of the inputs and/or other variables. We use lowercase letters to denote basic quantities (such as conversions of annual percentages to monthly decimals) and uppercase letters for more abstract quantities. (Again, asterisks denote variables necessary only for GPMs.)

$$i = \frac{C + S}{1200} \qquad n = 12N \qquad *r = \frac{R}{100}$$

$$s = \frac{S}{1200} \qquad m = 12M \qquad *a = A$$

$$y = \frac{Y}{1200} \qquad d = (1 + y)^{\frac{D-31}{30}} \qquad *b = 12B$$

$$F = \frac{1 + i}{1 + y} \qquad *K = \frac{(1 + y)^b - 1}{y} \qquad *U = (1 + i)^m$$

$$*G = \frac{1 + r}{(1 + y)^b} \qquad *L = (1 + r)^a \qquad *V = (1 + i)^{ab}$$

$$*H = \frac{G^a - 1}{G - 1} \qquad *Q = \frac{1 + r}{(1 + i)^b} \qquad W = (1 + y)^m$$

$$*J = \frac{(1 + i)^b - 1}{i} \qquad T = (1 + i)^n \qquad *Z = (1 + y)^{ab}$$

Formulas

1. Monthly mortgage payment.
   Let X = monthly payment per \$1 original mortgage amount. This formula applies only to traditional (level-payment) mortgages. For the formula on GPMs (initial payment only) see formula 5.

$$X = \frac{iT}{T - 1}$$

2. Mortgage balance.
   Let X = amount of mortgage remaining after k months per \$1 original mortgage amount (traditional mortgage only).

$$X = \frac{T - (1 + i)^k}{T - 1}$$

3. Principal payment.
   Let X = amount of principal paid in month k per $1 original mortgage
   amount (traditional mortgage only).

$$X = \frac{i(1 + i)^{k-1}}{T - 1}$$

4. Interest payment.
   Let X = amount of interest paid in month k per $1 original mortgage
   amount (traditional mortgage only).

$$X = \frac{i[T - (1 + i)^{k-1}]}{T - 1}$$

5. Mortgage yield.
   a. Yield to price for non-GPMs.

$$P = \frac{100}{d(T - 1)}\left[\frac{T(i - s)(W - 1)}{yW} + \frac{s}{1 + y}\left(\frac{F^m - 1}{F - 1}\right) + \frac{T}{W} - F^m\right]$$

   Special cases:

   (1) If $y = i - s$, then $P = \frac{100}{d}$.

   (2) If $y = i$, then $F = 1$. Substitute the value m in place of $(F^m - 1)/(F - 1)$ in the formula to avoid division by zero.

   (3) If $y = 0$, then substitute m for $(W - 1)/y$ in the formula to avoid division by zero.

   (4) If $i = 0$, then $P = \frac{100}{dn}\left[\frac{W - 1 + y(n - m)}{yW}\right]$.

   b. Yield to price for GPMs.
       For the sake of simplicity, we define four more quantities X, E_1, E_2, and E_3. The price is then computed in terms of these. For those who might be interested, X is the initial GPM monthly payment (per $1 principal), E_1 is the portion of the price attributable to gross principal and interest, E_2 is the value of servicing (to be subtracted out), and E_3 is the value of the residual security after m months. Note: This formula is valid only for the case in which the security is prepaid after all graduations have taken place ($m \geq ab$).

$$X = \frac{iV}{V + L + \dfrac{iLJ - rV}{1 + r - (1 + i)^b} - \dfrac{LV}{T}}$$

$$E_1 = \frac{XKH}{(1 + y)^b}$$

$$E_2 = \frac{sE_1}{i} + \left[\frac{s(F^b - 1)}{(1 + y)(F - 1)}\right] \times$$

$$\left[\frac{F^{ab} - 1}{F^b - 1} + \frac{XQJ}{(1 + r)(Q - 1)}\left(\frac{F^{ab} - 1}{F^b - 1} - H\right) - \frac{XH}{i}\right]$$

$$E_3 = \left[\frac{V}{T - V}\right] \times \left[1 - \frac{XJ(Q^a - 1)}{(Q - 1)(1 + i)^b}\right] \times$$

$$\left[\frac{(i - s)T(W - Z)}{yWZ} + \frac{s(F^m - F^{ab})}{(1 + y)(F - 1)} + \frac{T - U}{W}\right]$$

Now $P = \dfrac{100}{d}(E_1 - E_2 + E_3)$

Special cases:

(1) If $y = i - s$, then $P = \dfrac{100}{d}$.

(2) If $y = i$, three substitutions are necessary to avoid division by zero, as follows:

Replace	With	In Definition of
$\dfrac{F^b - 1}{F - 1}$	b	E_2
$\dfrac{F^{ab} - 1}{F^b - 1}$	a	E_2
$\dfrac{F^m - F^{ab}}{F - 1}$	$m - ab$	E_3

(3) If r and i have values such that $1 + r = (1 + i)^b$, then $Q = 1$ and two substitutions are necessary to avoid division by zero, as follows:

Replace	With	In Definition of
$\dfrac{iLJ - rV}{1 + r - (1 + i)^b}$	$L\left(\dfrac{ar}{1 + r} - 1\right)$	X
$\dfrac{XQJ}{(1 + r)(Q - 1)}\left(\dfrac{F^{ab} - 1}{F^b - 1} - H\right)$	$\dfrac{XJ}{(1 + y)^b}\left(\dfrac{G^a - 1 - aG^{a-1}(G - 1)}{(G - 1)^2}\right)$	E_2
$\dfrac{XJ(Q^a - 1)}{(Q - 1)(1 + i)^b}$	$\dfrac{aXJ}{(1 + i)^b}$	E_3

(4) If *both* $y = i$ and $1 + r = (1 + i)^b$, then in place of

$$\frac{XQJ}{(1 + r)(Q - 1)}\left(\frac{F^{ab} - 1}{F^b - 1} - H\right)$$

in the expression for E_2 substitute

$$\frac{XJa(1 - a)}{2(1 + r)}$$

(5) If $y = 0$, two substitutions are necessary to avoid division by zero.

Replace	With	In Definition of
K	b	E_1
$\dfrac{(i - s)T(W - Z)}{yWZ}$	$(i - s)T(m - ab)$	E_3

(6) If $i = 0$, then use the formula

$$P = \frac{100}{d}\left[\frac{rKH}{(1 + y)^b[bL - b + rL(n - ab)]} + \frac{W - Z + yZ(n - m - ab)}{yW(n - ab)}\right]$$

c. Price to yield computations.

There is no way to compute a pass-through yield directly from a price, so a technique known as *iteration* must be used to estimate the yield via successive approximation. Each yield estimate is converted to a price (based on the foregoing), which is compared to the known price. As an initial (but very crude) approximation with which to begin the process one can use

$$Y = \frac{2C + \dfrac{12(100 - Pd)}{5M}}{1 + \dfrac{Pd}{100}}$$

The second approximation can be taken as some small difference from the first one. Now suppose we have two yield approximations, Y_1 and Y_2, and prices for each of these, P_1 and P_2, respectively. Then

$$Y = Y_2 + \frac{(Y_1 - Y_2)(P_2 - P)}{P_2 - P_1}$$

This approximation is tested, and if it is not sufficiently close to the known price, the process is repeated until the yield has been determined to the desired degree of accuracy.

d. Standard assumptions.
Several of the input parameters take on standard values for the purposes of computing street-practice pass-through yields. For non-GPMs, these parameters are servicing fee, payment delay, term to maturity, and term to prepayment. At the present time, the values assumed for various non-GPMs are as follows:

Type of Security	Value to Assume for			
	S	D	N	M
GNMA				
Single-family	.50	45	30	12
Mobile home, type A	2.50	45	12	5
Mobile home, type B	2.50	45	15	7
Mobile home, type C	2.50	45	18	9
Mobile home, type D	2.50	45	20	10
Project loan	.25	45	40	18
FHLMC–PC	0	75	30	12
FNMA	0	55	30	12
Privately issued (Connie Macs)	.375	55	30	12

At present, the only GPM security is issued by GNMA. The assumptions for GPMs are the same as for GNMA single-family securities plus values of 7.5 for R, 5 for A and 1 for B.

6. Corporate bond equivalent yield.
Let Y be any yield (in percentage terms) computed on the basis of monthly compounding. Then the corporate bond equivalent (CBE) yield for Y is

$$CBE = \left[\left(1 + \frac{Y}{1200}\right)^6 - 1\right] \times 200$$

7. Parity price.
The Parity Price (PP) for a pass-through security is the price at which the yield (mortgage yield or HTG yield) equals the coupon rate.

$$PP = \left(1 + \frac{C}{1200}\right)^{\frac{31-D}{30}} \times 100$$

8. Calculation of prepayment rate.
Suppose we want to calculate the prepayment on a pass-through between months m and n (0 ≤ m < n). Let

F_m = pool factor in month m
F_n = pool factor in month n
B_m = mortgage balance (per $1) in month m
B_n = mortgage balance (per $1) in month n

(See Formula 2 for a calculation of mortgage balance.)

$$\text{Define } R_m = \frac{F_m}{B_m} \text{ and } R_n = \frac{F_n}{B_n}$$

The decimals R_m and R_n represent the number of mortgages in the pool that have not yet terminated (been prepaid).

a. FHA experience.

Let $\{G_i\}$ represent the fraction of mortgages in a pool expected to survive (not be prepaid) at the beginning of year i. These values are given by the FHA-experience decimal balance table. Now we define for $K = 0, 1, \ldots, 360$.

$$i = \frac{K}{12} \text{ truncated to an integer (i is a year number)}$$

$$j = K - 12i \text{ (j is the month number within the year)}$$

$$g_K = G_i\left(\frac{G_i+1}{G_i}\right)^{j/12}$$

The values $\{g_K\}$ are the values $\{G_i\}$ "filled in" by month; g_K is the predicted amount of mortgages expected to survive K months. Now, the FHA-experience percentage is given by

$$\text{FHA} = \frac{100(\log R_n - \log R_m)}{\log g_n - \log g_m}$$

b. SMM model.

The percentage SMM paydown is given by

$$\text{SMM} = 1 - \left(\frac{R_n}{R_m}\right)^{\frac{1}{n-m}}$$

Among the advantages of the SMM model are its simplicity and the fact that it can be computed for mortgages of any original term to maturity.

9. Prepayment consistency.

Suppose P is a pass-through pool that has been outstanding for K periods ($K \geq 2$). Let Y_i denote the interim prepayment rate in the ith period, $i = 1$ to K. Mean interim prepayment for pool P is

$$M_p = \frac{1}{K}\sum_{i=1}^{K} Y_i$$

Standard deviation of prepayments for pool P is

$$\sigma_p = \left[\frac{1}{K}\sum_{i=1}^{K}(Y_i - M_p)^2\right]^{1/2}$$

Note that prepayment rate (by any model) is never negative in a period. Therefore, the series $\{Y_i | i = 1, K\}$ is a series of K nonnegative numbers with mean M_p. In general, the maximum standard deviation for a series of K nonnegative numbers with mean M_p is the series $\{KM_p, 0, 0, \ldots, 0\}$, where there are $K - 1$ zeros. Define the standard deviation of this series as σ_{max}. Then

$$\sigma_{max} = M_p\sqrt{K - 1}$$

The *lumpiness*, L, of a series is its standard deviation divided by the maximum possible standard deviation for a nonnegative series with the same number of elements and the same mean. Thus

$$L_p = \frac{\sigma_p}{\sigma_{max}} = \frac{\sigma_p}{M_p\sqrt{K - 1}}$$

Consistency, or C, is given by the formula

$$C_p = \frac{(K - 1) - L_p(K - 2)}{K} \cdot 100$$

What this means is although L_p ranges from 0 to 1, C_p runs from 100 to 0 (respectively), but C_p is bounded by $100/K$ below and $100(K - 1)/K$ above. Thus, C_p can only approach 0 or 100 as K becomes infinite.

PART SIX

Specialty Lending

The Future for Alternative Mortgage Instruments

Richard G. Marcis
Senior Vice President
Trident Financial Corporation

Introduction

It was not that long ago that any borrower seeking funds to finance purchase of a home had to obtain a long-term, fixed-payment mortgage. At that time, that was virtually the only mortgage instrument generally available to the public.

The situation today is dramatically different. Borrowers now have the flexibility to choose among mortgages with changing interest rates, changing payments or changing principal. Moreover, since many of the new mortgage types can have a number of associated options, the number of specific mortgage forms has become quite extensive.

The development of new mortgage forms which serve as alternatives to the traditional long-term, fixed-payment mortgage is attributable to high and variable rates of inflation and interest rates that have created problems for both borrowers and lenders.

Prospective mortgage borrowers are confronted with the problem that in a period of high interest rates, their monthly payment obligations with the traditional long-term, fixed-rate mortgage may be too high relative to their incomes, thereby precluding them from purchasing a home. While the relative payments burden may decline through time as borrowers' incomes increase and monthly payments remain constant, the payment tilt of the burden in the early years of the mortgage may force some potential homebuyers to defer or downgrade their housing purchases while forcing others out of the housing market entirely.

Lenders, on the other hand, are confronted with interest-rate risks associated with unanticipated inflation. Rates of inflation in excess of anticipated rates results in higher short- and long-term interest rates. This increases the cost of funds to mortgage lenders. Since returns on long-term, fixed-rate loan portfolios cannot keep pace with rapid increases in costs of funds, mortgage-lending thrift institutions in recent years have experienced large reductions in net worth.

This has been caused by the losses incurred from costs of funds exceeding returns on mortgage portfolios.

For both lenders and borrowers, the long-term, fixed-rate mortgage has been largely incapable of coping with interest-rate risks attributable to unanticipated inflation. In response to the needs of borrowers and lenders, a number of alternative mortgage instruments (AMIs) have evolved in the marketplace in recent years. A relaxation of legislative and regulatory restrictions on mortgages and the depressed state of the housing market in 1979–1982 has given fillip to introduction of alternative mortgage forms. In response to the depressed state of the housing market and earnings problems experienced by savings and loan associations, the Federal Home Loan Bank Board passed regulations enabling FSLIC-insured associations to originate and invest in a number of different types of AMIs. Lenders, unsure of what mortgage form would find acceptance in the marketplace, responded to deregulation by experimenting with different mortgage forms. The depressed housing market over the 1979–1982 period also promoted lender inventiveness in structuring mortgages designed to increase the number of borrowers who could qualify for mortgage credit at high levels of interest rates.

After a brief review of the major categories of mortgage loans available today, this chapter will assess the mortgage instruments that are likely to evolve as standard mortgage instruments. The critical factors shaping the mortgage selection process will also be examined. The role that the traditional, long-term, fixed-rate mortgage may be expected to play in the future is also examined. Finally, since the changes discussed have the potential for substantially altering the nature of and the motives for homeownership, this article will review and evaluate these considerations.

Current AMI Activity

For purposes of discussion, AMIs can be classified in several basic categories:

Adjustable-rate mortgage (ARM). The common feature of an ARM is a variable interest rate that varies according to some preselected index or reference rate. The adjustments are made at the end of a predetermined period which may be as short as three months or as long as five years.[1]

Graduated-payment mortgage (GPM). This mortgage has scheduled monthly payments that start out at a low level relative to a level-payment, fixed-rate mortgage, but rise later. The graduation rate, the term of graduation, and the interest rate are fixed throughout the life of the loan.[2]

---

[1]This category includes all loans with flexible-rate features such as adjustable mortgage loans, variable-rate mortgages, and renegotiable-rate mortgages

[2]Although most GPM plans have negative amortization features, this is not always the case. For example, some GPMs have a pledged-account feature (a designated savings account is utilized to pay that portion of the interest payments that is not covered by the monthly payment.

Price-level-adjusted mortgage (PLAM). The interest rate is fixed, but the outstanding balance and monthly payments vary according to changes in some price index.

Reverse-annuity mortgage (RAM). A stream of monthly payments is provided to homeowners through an annuity purchased by a loan against the owner's accumulated equity in the home.

Shared-appreciation mortgage (SAM). Under this mortgage plan, the borrower agrees to share the appreciation in the value of the property financed by the loan with the lender, in return for a below-market interest rate.

Growing equity mortgage (GEM). This loan carries a fixed interest rate and a scheduled annual increase in monthly payments. Since the increase in monthly payments is applied to retirement of the principal, the final maturity is shortened considerably.

Within each of these loan categories there exists a variety of special features tailored to the specific needs of individual borrowers or lenders. For example, with respect to ARMs, there are numerous variations associated with different indices, different rate-adjustment periods, and, in some cases, limitations on the amount of periodic or cumulative interest-rate changes that are permitted. Some plans permit changes in interest rates to be reflected in changes in monthly payments, the terms of the loan, the outstanding balance of the loan, or some combination of these. Still other plans may hold payments constant for a set period of time even if interest rates increase. In this case, negative amortization occurs as unpaid interest is added to the loan balance.

Hybrid AMIs incorporating features from two or more general loan types have also evolved. One such mortgage plan integrates the adjustable-rate feature of the ARM and the low initial- and graduated-payment features of the GPM. These GPM-ARM hybrids also have a number of options. Some have payments rising by a set amount each year in the early years, others hold the low payments constant for a 3-, 4- or 5-year period. However, all variants of this plan involve some amount of negative amortization since there is a deferral of some part of the interest owed during the early years of the loan.

Thus, there is a great diversity in mortgage alternatives currently available. This system stands in sharp contrast to the previously prevailing mortgage finance system, which was dominated by a single, uniform mortgage instrument—the long-term, fixed-rate mortgage.

AMIs and the Selection Process

The proliferation of mortgage instruments has benefitted consumers to the extent that borrowers are able to find mortgages tailored to their individual needs and requirements. The proliferation of mortgage alternatives has, on the other hand, caused a degree of confusion for borrowers and portfolio investors as well as for lenders, with some reduction in the efficiency of the mortgage acquisition process. Borrowers, for example, find it harder to compare mortgages because of the differences in terms and conditions. Undoubtedly, some of the mortgage features have been difficult for the typical consumer to understand. Portfolio investors, especially those who are not traditional mortgage investors, have also experienced some confusion because of the diversity of current mortgage alternatives.

A winnowing process can be expected to follow the current proliferation of mortgage products, where some of the currently available mortgage products will fall out of use as they find little consumer or investor acceptance. This self-selection process should reduce mortgage alternatives to a more limited number of options.

There are several factors that will be instrumental in determining what mortgage alternatives will survive. These include: the degree of protection provided lenders from interest-rate risk, the degree of payment stability provided borrowers, and saleability in the secondary market. For any given mortgage form to gain widespread acceptance, it will have to reconcile these oftentimes conflicting needs of lenders, borrowers and investors.

The needs and requirements of lenders are by now only too well known. Inflation of the magnitude experienced over the past several years has resulted in unexpectedly high interest rates and unexpected increases in costs of funds to lenders. Since yields on their portfolios of existing mortgage assets have been below current market rates and portfolio yields are not responsive to changing market rates of interest, many lenders have been in a position of having to pay more for funds than the interest income from the mortgages the funds support. Thus, lenders value mortgages with adjustable-rate features that will protect them against unexpected increases in market rates of interest.

Lenders also desire servicing simplicity. While many AMIs are no more difficult to service than the traditional fixed-rate, level-payment mortgage, some mortgage instruments do impose additional servicing burdens. Care should be taken in structuring the AMI so that the mix and frequency of changing rates, payments, loan balances, and other loan terms are not so cumbersome and complicated as to impose costly servicing burdens on lenders' back offices.

The needs and requirements of borrowers are also important variables in determining what mortgage instruments will survive. While borrowers may be expected to have a variety of specialized financial needs and requirements based on their individual circumstances, a general requirement for most borrowers is for some degree of stability and predictability in mortgage payments. Stability and predictability of payments aid family financial planning. They also minimize the possibility of increased delinquencies and defaults in the event families are confronted with unexpectedly large increases in monthly payment requirements which exceed their ability to pay. Because of the potential for increased delinquency and default, lenders would find it to their advantage to protect borrowers from sharp increases in mortgage-payment requirements.

Depending on their individual circumstances, consumers may also place a high value on other mortgage features. For example, some borrowers emphasize low initial payments as an important feature, while others place a high value on assumability. However, consumer-survey data and casual observation suggest that most consumers place primary emphasis on stability and predictability of monthly payment.

Finally, the realtive marketability of AMIs in the secondary market is also important in determining what mortgage instruments will survive. Because secondary-market investors have provided an increasing share of mortgage credit in recent years, it is important that the mortgage instrument be marketable. If the mortgage market is to continue to grow, the mortgage instrument should be saleable not only to traditional mortgage investors (such as the federally assisted housing-finance agencies, savings and loan associations, mutual savings banks, and commercial banks), but to nontraditional mortgage investors (such as pension funds and life insurance companies) as well.

Because of their different investment needs and requirements, no one mortgage instrument or set of mortgage features is likely to appeal to all portfolio investors. Some investors emphasize investments with variable yields which are responsive to changes in inflation. Other investors place emphasis on certainty of rates of return. Thus, the former group would prefer mortgages with rate-adjustable features while the latter would emphasize investments with fixed terms and rates.

It is generally acknowledged that standardization of mortgage terms and conditions would facilitate marketability. Portfolio investors, especially those who have not traditionally invested in mortgages, undoubtedly have found the variety of mortgage products currently available confusing. Lack of familiarity with the mortgage instruments has probably hampered their willingness to purchase AMIs.

Some degree of uniformity and standardization of mortgage instruments is also desirable so as to enable AMIs to be pooled as collateral for mortgage-backed, pass-through securities which can then be sold in the secondary market. Mortgages with generally similar terms and features can be more readily pooled as collateral for pass-through securities than can AMIs with differing terms and conditions. Pass-through securities promote the efficiency of the secondary market by enabling investors to buy large blocks of mortgages without having to be bothered with the loan-origination and administration problems that are involved in handling individual mortgages.

The federally sponsored housing finance agencies—the Federal National Mortgage Association (FNMA) and the Federal Home Loan Mortgage Corporation (FHLMC)—will continue to play an important role in determining the relative marketability of alternative mortgage instruments. Through their mortgage purchase requirements, FNMA and FHLMC define standards of marketability for AMIs. Some of the recent initiatives of both FNMA and FHLMC in establishing ARM purchase requirements have been important in shaping the form of lending programs offered by lenders. Even if lenders to not plan on selling AMIs to these institutions, loans originated to their purchase requirements will usually be more marketable than nonconforming loans because their purchase requirements may be adopted by other investors. While FNMA and other investors will purchase nonconforming AMIs on a negotiated, case-by-case basis, such procedures do not facilitate an efficiently functioning secondary market. Uniformity and standardization of mortgage instruments will enhance marketability by reducing investor confusion and by facilitating large dollar-volume mortgage transactions.

Evolving Mortgage Forms

For these reasons the number and variety of alternative mortgage forms currently available is diminishing as the oftentimes competing requirements of lenders, borrowers, and investors are resolved in a competitive market environment. The net result should be a limited set of mortgage designs, or dominant mortgage forms—in contrast with the proliferation of mortgage forms currently available. Given the specific needs and requirements of market participants, one can make some tentative projections about the likely form of the mortgage instrument that will come to serve as a standard.

This instrument in all likelihood will be the adjustable-rate mortgage. The need for lenders to be protected against interest-rate risk is critical. Without this, lenders would probably substantially reduce their support of the mortgage market. However, the adjustable-rate mortgage will also have to provide some protection for borrowers against rapid fluctuations in monthly payments. Consequently, ARMs with annual limitations in the amount of rate and/or payment changes permitted will become a common feature of ARMs. For example, a one-year adjustable-rate mortgage may have a 2 percent limit on annual-rate movements with, say, a 6 percent limit on total rate changes over the life of the instrument. With these types of rate-change limitations, borrowers are at least protected against sharp upward movements in payments over short periods of time (as well as over the life of the mortgage).

It appears that lenders have also become more adept at competitively pricing ARMs. Initially, ARMs were priced at initial-rate levels that were not much different than rates on long-term, fixed-rate mortgages. Without the incentive of initially lower mortgage rates to compensate them for the payment-variability risks associated with ARMs, borrowers have typically opted for the long-term, fixed-rate mortgage product.

Gradually, lenders have learned how to overcome consumer resistance. They accomplish this by pricing ARMs competitively relative to fixed-rate mortgages so as to encourage consumers to choose ARMs. Lenders are now viewing ARMs as short-term instead of long-term assets and have begun to price them on that basis. Thus, many of the ARMs offered by lenders today offer initial rates several percentage points below rates on otherwise equivalent long-term, fixed-rate mortgages. While the yield differential will result in lower immediate earnings relative to long-term, fixed-rate mortgages, the greater yield variability over time should protect future earnings of lenders and thereby compensate them for the immediate yield differential. Consequently, today approximately half of all new loans are adjustable-rate mortgages, whereas two years ago, almost all new loans were fixed-rate mortgages.[3]

Conventional GPMs, on the other hand, have had only limited market acceptance to date and are likely to serve at best a minor role in the mortgage market. The fixed-rate feature of the GPMs make them relatively unattractive to lenders. Moreover, because of the negative amortization feature usually associated with GPMs, GPMs normally carry rates in excess of those offered on otherwise equivalent long-term, fixed-payment mortgages. This relatively higher rate makes them less attractive to many borrowers. However, since ARMs do not alleviate the inflation-induced distortions of borrowers' payments burdens, the low initial-payment and graduation features of the GPM may become a standard option available with ARMs in high interest rate periods.

Growing equity loans will also survive the shakeout of mortgage products but, like GPMs, will serve a minor role in the mortgage market at best. They will not play a major role in the mortgage market because the benefits accrue primarily to borrowers, with few benefits for lenders. They, like GPMs, may be thought of as "boutique mortgages" with specialized features that appeal to a limited number of borrowers with special financing requirements. Thus, they will find a niche in the mortgage-finance system as a specialized mortgage instrument, but will not achieve widespread popularity.

Reverse-annuity mortgages, price-level-adjusted mortgages, and shared-appreciation mortgages are not likely to achieve any level of significance in the marketplace. These mortgage forms are handicapped by their complexity as well as their novelty, which will hamper their acceptance not only by borrowers but also by lenders and investors. They are also subject to some potentially unusual tax or accounting considerations which may severely circumscribe their use. Finally, there are some unknowns associated with each of the instruments which will also serve to limit their adoption in the marketplace. What happens, for example, if borrowers with shared-appreciation mortgages have not moved or sold their houses and the loans are approaching maturity? Will they be forced to sell their houses in order to provide lenders with their share of the appreciation on the properties? What happens with a price-level-adjusted mortgage if the borrower's income does not keep pace with inflation? The real payment burden may become excessive, leading to increased delinquencies and defaults. Thus, despite the attention these AMIs have received in the popular

---

[3]*Federal Home Loan Bank Board News* (December, 1983).

press in recent years, because of their complexity, novelty, and the accounting, tax, and legal questions that are raised, it is unlikely that they will be widely adopted in the marketplace.

Is There a Future for the Fixed-Rate Mortgage?

What role, if any, will the fixed-rate, long-term mortgage play in the mortgage markets of the future? Will it be obsolete? In contrast to those who maintain that the current volatile financial environment has made the fixed-rate, level-payment mortgage obsolete, a strong case can be made that the fixed-rate, level-payment mortgage is likely to coexist with adjustable-rate mortgages and other AMIs in the evolving mortgage-finance system.

The fixed-rate, level-payment mortgage has one crucial feature, which is that borrowers know with certainty what their future mortgage payments will be regardless of current interest rates. This feature will ensure its survival in the evolving mortgage market. Since most borrowers are risk-averse, they will, other things being equal, generally prefer fixed-rate loans to variable-rate loans.

However, this does not imply that fixed-rate loans will be available on the same basis as in the past. They will, for example, be priced differently than in the past. Lenders who originate and hold fixed-rate loans assume all the interest-rate risk, and from now on they will require compensation for assuming such risk. This compensation will be in the form of an interest rate sufficiently high to cover the interest-rate risk assumed in making such loans. Consequently, rates on long-term, fixed-rate mortgages will be at a premium relative to otherwise-equivalent variable-rate mortgages by an amount sufficient to cover the interest-rate risk inherent in making such a loan.

Thus, risk-averse borrowers who desire predictability and stability in mortgage payments (and are willing to pay a risk-adjusted rate) will find some lenders willing to offer fixed-rate mortgage loans. The demand for and supply of fixed-rate loans will obviously depend upon the relative attitudes of borrowers and lenders toward risk and their expectations of future levels of interest rates. Also, investor preferences for fixed-rate investments will be important in determining the availability of fixed-rate loans, since lenders will be less averse to originating fixed-rate loans if they know they can be sold to third-party investors.

In summary, adjustable-rate mortgages with provisions designed to protect borrowers against abrupt changes in payments will, in all likelihood, become the dominant mortgage form in the future. However, there will also be some volume of activity in fixed-rate instruments such as the traditional fixed-rate mortgage instrument, as well as the graduated-payment mortgage and the growing equity mortgage. However, the key to the availability of fixed-rate instruments in the future is their pricing. If lenders are free to offer a risk-adjusted rate, these loans will be available in the marketplace, but at a premium relative to adjustable-rate mortgages.

Impact of AMIs on the Housing Market

To the extent that adjustable-rate mortgages have enabled lenders to remain in the mortgage-lending market, the home-buying public and the housing market has benefited from the introduction of alternative mortgage instruments. Given the sharp increases in their costs of funds and the reduced market values of their long-term, fixed-rate mortgage portfolios, lenders would have effectively abandoned the residential mortgage market had they not been granted the authority to originate and buy adjustable-rate mortgages. While high interest rates have encumbered the mortgage market in recent years, the level of housing activity would have been even lower had new mortgage forms not been permitted.

However, widespread adoption of ARM instruments will impact consumers in other ways that they may find not to their liking. It will, for example, affect the costs and investment returns from homeownership.

For most of the 1970s, inflation worked to the benefit of borrowers. With fixed mortgage-payment schedules, borrowers' carrying costs remained fixed as their incomes and house values increased over time. As a result, many borrowers experienced high real investment returns from housing. Inflation reduced the real costs of their mortgage payments while it increased the value of their home in both nominal and real terms. Lenders, on the other hand, were left with the problem of rolling over short-term funds at higher rates.

However, with ARMs, the effects of inflation are redistributed. Borrowers bear the costs of inflation that are reflected in higher interest rates. The more frequent and greater the rate adjustments permitted, the greater the degree of interest-rate risk shifted forward to borrowers. Homeownership becomes riskier because all borrowers, not just new borrowers, are affected by changes in market rates of inflation reflected in higher interest rates. Since loan payments can rise, borrowers will need to budget for possible increases in monthly payments. This could be especially burdensome for highly leveraged borrowers.

ARMs will also negatively affect investment returns from housing. With ARMs, inflation will not only be reflected in increases in housing prices, but also in higher mortgage rates. The appreciation in housing should be offset by increased loan-payment requirements. Thus, ARMs hold the potential for increasing the costs of housing credit and thereby reducing the potential investment returns from housing.

These changes will require some tough adjustments on the part of consumers. Some consumers may find that because of the increased cost of housing credit, they can't afford to own a house. They will either postpone their housing purchase or decide not to purchase at all. Other borrowers will have to allocate a higher percentage of their incomes to housing costs than what has been the case in the past. Others will attempt to reduce their housing outlays by purchasing smaller housing units. The increased cost of housing will also encourage greater utilization of the existing housing stock through sharing arrangements within families or between families.

While consumers will adjust, the adjustments may not be easy. Consumers who have been accustomed to low real housing costs and a wide variety of housing options may find these adjustments difficult.

Summary and Concluding Observations

The mortgage-finance system is in a period of transition. The standard fixed-rate, long-term mortgage instrument has been upstaged by the introduction of a seemingly limitless number of alternative mortgage instruments. However, a shake-out of mortgage instruments should occur as the market strives for a more limited number of mortgages with standardized features or options. The needs and requirements of borrowers, lenders, and portfolio investors will be critical variables in the winnowing process.

It would appear that the adjustable-rate mortgage instrument will probably emerge as the dominant mortgage instrument. It will be likely to contain some provisions for protecting borrowers against rapid and sharp changes in payments (such as limitations on the size or frequency of rate changes). GPMs and GEMs will be available as specialized mortgage instruments which will appeal to a limited number of borrowers with specialized financing needs and requirements. RAMs, SEMs, and PLAMs suffer from a number of problems and are unlikely to achieve any significant share of mortgage market activity.

Fixed-rate mortgages will be available in the marketplace, but will be priced at a premium to compensate lenders for their inherent interest-rate risk. Since there are risk-averse borrowers who are willing to pay a premium rate in exchange for stability of monthly payments, fixed-rate mortgages will play some role in the mortgage market of the 1980s.

The mortgage-finance system may be significantly altered with widespread use of ARMs. By shifting interest-rate risk forward to homeowners, ARMs hold the potential for making homeownership riskier than it has been in the past. Homeownership will become riskier to the extent that mortgage holders, as well as new borrowers, will bear the cost of unanticipated inflation that is reflected in higher interest rates. Since monthly mortgage payments can increase, homeowners will need to budget for this possibility.

In addition to increasing real housing-consumption costs, mortgage payments that vary with inflation will also adversely affect investment returns from housing. Homeowners will no longer be able to rely on fixed monthly payments as they experience increases in wealth caused by appreciation in property values. The net investment returns from housing should be lower in the 1980s than in the 1970s.

Thus, housing expectations for the 1980s that are based on experiences of the 1970s may have to be scaled back to more modest dimensions. Housing-consumption costs will be higher, with lower real investment returns from housing. While consumers will adjust, the adjustments may be difficult for those who are accustomed to thinking in terms of earlier housing choices.

— Chapter 29 ————————————————————

Resort Timeshare Financing*

Robert E. Adams
Vice President, Investment Banking
World Wide Group, Inc.

Christopher W. Hart
Professor of Economics, Marketing and Tourism
School of Hotel Administration
Cornell University, New York

Resort timesharing is a relatively new concept and product. Since its introduction in the United States in the late 1960s, timesharing has experienced exceptional growth and increased consumer acceptance. While the industry often receives negative media coverage because of its unfamiliarity and the widely publicized high-pressure sales practices used at some resort sites, quality timeshare projects and experienced developers have emerged. Many lending institutions are interested in resort timeshare loans because of the high yields and short terms of secured timeshare loans and the impressive payment performance of the consumers who finance their purchase of timeshare weeks at quality resorts. Timeshare financing combines the various elements of construction, sale, and management risks involved in real property lending, consumer lending, and the management of hotel operations. Analyzing these risks in such a hybrid business requires sophisticated and experienced lenders.

This chapter presents a brief overview of the resort timeshare industry: its growth, consumer satisfaction, the various forms of ownership, the importance of exchange, and a current consumer profile. It discusses the development of investor interest in timeshare lending, the various types of lending, and the primary reasons for investor interest in timeshare loans. Finally, it focuses on the primary risks to lenders: the developer; the project; marketing; sales management; maintenance; and legal, regulatory, and administrative concerns.

---

*Written with the assistance of Stuart Marshall Bloch, Esq., an Editor-in-Chief of *Timesharing I* and *Timesharing II*, published by the Urban Land Institute.

Growth

Resort timesharing sales have grown dramatically, from about $100 million in 1973 to over $1.3 billion in 1983. There are currently about 800 timeshare resorts in the United States and 500 in foreign countries. In the United States, the majority of timeshare resorts are located in Hawaii, Florida, California, Colorado, South Carolina, and Texas. Timeshare projects are usually located in resort destinations; however, urban areas, such as San Francisco and New Orleans, are also successful sites.

About two thirds of the timeshare projects in the United States involve condominium apartments, townhouses, and villa-type buildings. Hotel and motel structures—normally conversions—represent about 30 percent of the industry. There are also timeshared recreational vehicle parks and campgrounds, as well as timeshared yachts and houseboats.

Consumer Satisfaction

There has been considerable negative publicity of the high-pressure sales and marketing methods utilized by some timeshare developers, which have had a definite negative impact on consumer attitudes. Abusive sales tactics have led to restrictive regulation.

Nonetheless, the timesharing *concept* itself has enjoyed generally favorable publicity and high customer satisfaction to date. Consumer satisfaction among purchasers of timeshare weeks has been very high. Only 4–5 percent of the respondents in a major timeshare consumer study said they were dissatisfied with their timeshare purchase; roughly 10 percent were ambivalent. (See Tables 1 and 2.) Purchasers' dissatisfaction can be grouped into the following categories: poor property management, inadequate unit design and facilities, poor amenities in the geographical area, misrepresentation of exchange and investment potential and lack of an adequate resale market.

Forms of Ownership

There are two basic legal types of timesharing programs: fee ownership and right-to-use. Each type provides the consumer with occupancy rights of one week or more, usually in a specific unit. Fee ownership conveys fee-simple interest in real property to the consumer, wherein an owner can sell, lease, or will his timeshare week. There are two types of fee ownership: tenancy-in-common and interval ownership.

Tenancy-in-common is a form of joint ownership of real property wherein all individual buyers of weeks in a particular unit are deeded an individual beneficial interest in the unit in perpetuity. Under common law in some states,

Table 1 • Consumers' Satisfaction with Timesharing Purchase: 1978, 1980, and 1982

General Satisfaction with Purchase	Percent of Respondents		
	1978	1980	1982
Very satisfied	40.1%	44.6%	32.7%
Satisfied	44.1	41.7	45.8
50–50	10.8	9.2	15.9
Dissatisfied	2.4	2.6	3.4
Very dissatisfied	2.0	1.9	2.2
Total	99.4%	99.9%	100.0%

Dissatisfaction with Timeshare Purchase	Percent of Respondents		
	1978	1980	1982
Size of unit	1.1%	1.2%	1.7%
Kitchen facilities	2.0	1.3	2.2
Bathrooms	0.0	0.8	1.2
Storage space	2.0	2.2	3.3
Furnishings	1.1	1.1	1.6
Quality of construction	2.0	1.2	1.7
Cleanliness of unit	4.1	2.9	2.3
On-site recreation	0.0	3.0	6.1
Nearby recreation	1.3	1.9	3.5
Recreation for children	4.1	4.6	6.6
Restaurants	4.9	5.6	8.1
Shopping	7.2	6.4	8.2
Responsiveness of management	4.1	4.3	5.5

Source: Richard L. Ragatz Associates, Inc.

a tenant-in-common may sue for partition of his individual interest from those of others. A suit for partition could result in the sale of a timeshared building and the sales proceeds divided among all the buyers of timeshare weeks. To prevent this, the mortgage or warranty deed should contain a covenant which prevents partition, if such a covenant is not contrary to state law. An interval ownership deed conveys a fee estate for a specified number of years, usually approximating the estimated economic life of the unit, after which all interval owners become tenants-in-common. The creation of this remainder interest ef-

Table 2 • Percentage of Purchasers Who Would Buy Again, Knowing What They Now Know: 1978, 1980, and 1982

Would Purchase Again	Percent of Respondents		
	1978	1980	1982
Yes	78.1%	72.5%	62.5%
No	14.0	12.4	19.0
Don't know	7.9	15.0	18.5
	100.0%	100.0%	100.0%

Source: Richard L. Ragatz Associates, Inc.

fectively thwarts the application of the legal rule against perpetuities that exists in some states.

The lender involved in a fee-simple project, should ask the following legal questions:[1]

1. Is foreclosure necessary to perfect a claim upon default? How much does it cost to effect a foreclosure? Do the sales documents allow the lender to obtain title if the customer defaults?
2. Do usury laws apply?
3. Do sales and mortgage documents comply with all applicable laws and regulations?
4. What is the property owner association's relationship to the lender in the event of customer default?

Right-to-use timesharing is essentially a prepaid occupancy program. Right-to-use can be a vacation lease, license, or club membership. The purchaser of a right-to-use week(s) does not receive title to the property but has the right to occupy or use his timeshare living unit for a specified term, usually ranging up to 40 years. After this period elapses, full ownership and rights to the building revert to the developer or seller. The right-to-use method is attractive because it is flexible and simple to document. It is most prevalent in conversion projects involving hotels and motels. However, right-to-use timesharing is usually more regulated than are ownership forms. Because right-to-use projects force the consumer to rely on the developer for adequate future service, many states require right-to-use developers to provide more consumer safeguards for potential bankruptcy or insolvency.

Lenders should be particularly careful when lending to right-to-use timeshare projects. A recent court decision in Florida involving a bankrupt right-to-use timeshare project asserted the supremacy of federal bankruptcy laws over state consumer-protection provisions. In this instance, buyers (and lenders who financed their purchases of right-to-use weeks) found their purchase contracts voided on the basis that such contracts were executory (i.e., they depended on the developer's considerable obligation to perform in the future). Therefore, the right-to-use contract was not an interest in real estate nor did it convey an ownership interest. In spite of nondisturbance clauses recognizing the interests of buyers of the right-to-use weeks that the state of Florida required the developer to have inserted in all applicable mortgages, the court deemed that these clauses did not create a protectible interest. Federal bankruptcy invalidated executory contracts.

In addition to the different types of ownership, the usage time period itself can be either fixed or floating. Floating periods can be used throughout the year or within a particular season, while fixed periods require the owner to return to

---

[1]Dennis G. Dunn, *Commercial Bank Lending to the Resort Timesharing Industry,* a thesis submitted in partial fulfillment of the requirements for graduation from the Stonier Graduate School of Banking conducted by the American Bankers Association at Rutgers University, New Brunswick, N.J., June 1982, pp 35–36.

Table 3 • Consumers' Reasons for Buying Timeshares: 1978, 1980 and 1982*

	1978	1980	1982
Exchange opportunity†	75.3%	71.4%	79.1%
Save money on future vacation costs	63.0	59.4	65.4
Investment or resale potential	38.0	38.8	38.0
Liked timeshare unit	30.0	30.4	27.7
Liked recreational facilities	38.6	28.6	24.7
Certainty of having accommodations	31.0	24.1	23.1
Opportunity to own resort property	27.1	23.1	18.8

*The questions used to gather this data limited respondent's choices to the categories shown—by no means a collectively exhaustive set of possible reasons for purchasing timeshare intervals.
†Responses were biased toward exchange opportunity because the samples were drawn primarily from lists of exchange organization members.
Source: Richard L. Ragatz Associates, Inc.

a given resort at the same time each year. Both floating and fixed weeks can be used for periods of less than one week, as well as in a combined fashion.

Timesharing Exchange

For most timeshare purchasers, the opportunity to exchange one's time period in the accommodations purchased for a period in a unit at another timeshare project enhances the flexibility and hence the attractiveness of timeshare ownership (see Table 3). Purchasers who join such organizations as Interval International (II) and Resorts Condominiums International (RCI), the two original exchange companies that continue to dominate the industry, and two newer firms, Vacations Horizons International (VHI) and Network One, are able to trade their time periods for the weeks of other exchange-organization members. As shown in Table 4, purchasers have been generally satisfied with the exchange organizations so far.

Consumer Profile

The number of timeshare owners has risen dramatically over the last five years (see Table 5). A poll conducted by the Gallup Organization, Inc., in April 1983, for the National Timesharing Council, indicates a growing con-

Table 4 • Consumers' Satisfaction With Exchange: 1978, 1980 and 1982

	1978	1980	1982
Very satisfied	60.0%	51.9%	54.1%
Satisfied	30.7	37.7	33.5
Dissatisfied	9.3	10.4	12.4
Total	100.0%	100.0%	100.0%

Table 5 • Number of People Who Own a Timeshare

1977	56,000
1978	120,000
1979	200,000
1980	270,000
1981	350,000
1982	425,000

Source: The Resort Timesharing Industry: A Socio-Economic Impact Analysis of Resort Timesharing.

sumer awareness and satisfaction with the timesharing concept. Also, 54 percent were familiar with the concept.

The 1983 Gallup Survey also found that the market for timesharing is upscale: college graduates, households headed by professionals and persons from upper-income families. The average income of purchasers is about $33,500 per year.

In spite of high interest rates (usually 14–19 percent), the vast majority of timeshare buyers finance their purchases rather than pay cash (see Table 6).

Financing

Initially, financing for timeshare projects came from private sources or from the developer's own personal resources. Financing was generally available only to developers with proven records. In the mid-1970s, consumer-finance companies willing to take a risk on the new concept began to finance timeshare receivables. However, the cost of these funds to developers and consumers was very expensive.

In 1980, the Federal Home Loan Bank Board issued regulations authorizing federal chartered savings and loan associations (S&Ls) to make unsecured consumer loans for both ownership and right-to-use timesharing forms. Both S&Ls and commercial banks are now very active in timesharing, particularly in the states with the highest timeshare activity: Florida, Texas, Hawaii, and Colo-

Table 6 • Source of Financing

Company from which timeshare bought	48%
Lending institution in home community	7
Lending institution in timesharing field	29
Other lending institution	12
Private source	2
Other	2

Source: Volume 1, Ragatz study (1980).

rado. Their financing roles range from purchasers of consumer end loans to acquisition and construction financing to participation as developers of timeshare projects.

Type of Financing

Consumer End-Loan Financing

Most timeshare consumer loans sold to institutional investors are either direct purchases or hypothecations. In a direct-sale situation, the consumer paper is typically sold at a discount to produce a required yield.

With hypothecation, the developer pledges the consumer paper in return for a line of credit. The individual consumer's monthly payments are applied directly to retirement of the developer's line of credit. Hypothecation offers favorable tax benefits for the developer, because borrowing, rather than selling, postpones or spreads out the tax consequences, justifying the installment method for reporting sales income. The interest paid on the hypothecation line, which is usually variable with some index, is also tax deductible. Because the developer borrows a percentage of the principal balance of the consumer receivables from the lender, he must wait until the consumer paper pays off to obtain his full profit. Typically, hypothecation results in less upfront cash than an alternative sale and keeps the developer on personal recourse for the life of the loan.

In contrast, if a developer sells his paper outright, the proceeds are taxable income. Outright sale, however, has a number of benefits: a developer can eliminate the risk of fluctuating interest rates; he can receive larger upfront financing proceeds; and personal recourse is frequently limited to a 10 percent reserve.

Lenders generally have restricted loans on timeshare consumer paper to a maximum of 10 years. Many lenders prefer timeshare paper on which the consumer has made one or more monthly payments.

Holdback reserves are also a standard part of end-loan financing. The holdback reserve can range from 3 to 10 percent or more of the financed amount. However, as the paper becomes seasoned, the amount of the holdback reserve is usually reduced, and a greater percentage of the consumers' loan payments go to the developer. In many instances, the lender may also require recourse against the developer, a security interest in the underlying real estate, and a personal guarantee from the developer or the corporate entity.

Acquisition and Construction Financing

Acquisition and construction financing is more difficult to obtain for timeshare developers than is consumer end-loan financing. The availability of acquisition loans is usually a function of the strength of the developer and his past record.

Construction loans are generally based upon some percentage of the anticipated sell-out of the project. Payback of the construction loan is based on either a certain release amount per completed unit or a lesser amount per week sold in each unit. From the developer's cash flow perspective, it is desirable for the lender to release each weekly interval as it is sold. However, because of the risk of ending up with multiple unsold intervals if the project does not succeed, most construction lenders release encumbrances on whole units (that is, 52 weeks in a given unit) only when a sufficient number of time periods have been sold to pay off the debt on the unit.

Joint Venture Financing

Some lenders also joint venture in timeshare projects, which enables them to obtain more control over the management and operation of the timeshare program. Joint-venture partners are willing to accept more of the financial risk for an attractive return on investment. In the typical arrangement, the investor provides acquisition and development funds, and assists in obtaining construction and permanent financing. The developer partner is relied upon to provide expertise in the areas of development, management, sales, and marketing.

Limited partnerships and public offerings of equity are also funding sources. Properly structured, the limited partnership can minimize exposure for participants and provide tax benefits as well.

Why Lend On Timeshares?

Timesharing's growth has whetted the interest of mortgage investors in lending to the industry, particularly to individual timeshare owners on a secured basis. The primary investment attractions include:

1. *High Yields*. Yields typically reflect those associated with the high-yielding consumer loan market rather than the long-term mortgage market.

2. *Short Terms*. Maturities range from 30 months to 10 years, most commonly from 5 to 7 years, fully amortized by monthly payments. Prepayments have been frequent.

3. *Matching of Assets and Liabilities*. Yields can be fixed or variable. The purchase price of loans can change over time with some index (say, prime +) or be fixed over time. Loans can be hypothecated (borrowed against by the developer) at a variable or fixed rate of interest with the underlying receivables fully amortizing the loan.

4. *Recourse to the Developer*. The developer personally/corporately guarantees the performance of the timeshare paper.

5. *Cash Reserves.* Typically, 10 percent or more of the developer's loan proceeds is set aside as a holdback to offset the developer's potential failure to replace/repurchase the loans in default.

6. *First-Lien Position.* The mortgage note is secured by a first-mortgage deed (for a fee-simple transaction).

7. *Usage Product.* The timeshare owner receives immediate value from the purchase but loses usage if in default on the mortgage.

8. *Affordable Product.* The original loan amount is small, as are the monthly payments, thus reducing the chance of default.

9. *Loan Payment History.* The industry has experienced very low default ratios.

10. *Diversification of Risk.* Many more buyers over a broad geographic area exist for a given amount of money invested.

11. *Extension of Present Business.* Timeshare receivables are secured by real estate.

Risk Analysis

Timesharing is an intensive cash flow business and is heavily negative during the early years of development. Because sales and marketing costs are high in timesharing, usually more than 35 percent, even a well-conceived project invariably requires substantial cash resources, and profits are not achieved until many years have passed. Inexperienced developers sometimes think they are going to make a fast return, and, operating under this misconception, eventually find themselves out of business. The critical risk area for a lender to evaluate first is the developer. The next most important areas are the project, management, and legal and regulatory concerns.

The Developer(s)

Adequate capital is necessary to fund development costs as well as to finance marketing costs, which can exceed 50 percent of a project's gross sales in its early stages. Further, if a construction mortgage exists, additional cash from each sale of a week must be applied as paydown on the loan or set aside to release an entire unit when sufficient sales have been made, depending on the construction-loan agreement. It is not unusual for weekly loan releases to run 25 to 40 percent of gross sales, or for entire units to be released only when sufficient monies have been escrowed to match the unit's construction cost.

A detailed, time-phased cash flow is an absolute requirement in assessing whether the developer has adequate capital. Outgo in the form of marketing, loan, and administrative costs is returned slowly and with a delay of cash from the receivables, which must be processed, approved, and funded after a particular sale has cleared the state's recision period.

Where does the capital come from? Financial strength must be supported by financial statements, tax returns, and verifications of assets and liabilities. Liquid net worth must jibe with required capital plus a contingency to allow for what may be overly optimistic sales projections.

What is the character of the developer? Is the developer really committed to a long-range timeshare proposition? What is the developer's staying power? Is there any litigation pending? Investigative reports should be conducted to support character and manner of prior business dealings. References and banking connections should be interviewed. The developer should also be experienced in timeshare marketing, sales, administration, finance, and management, or have acceptable professionals under contract in areas where firsthand experience is lacking.

What is the credit of the developer? What banking lines are in place? What is the available credit, secured and unsecured? Does capital plus unused lines of credit provide sufficient cash to carry the project to sellout?

The Project

Analysis of a given timeshare project should rigorously examine the market, project design, pricing, area competition, and sales and marketing methods. The market should be well defined in terms of the needs and growth potential of the area and analyzed as to seasonality, price sensitivity, and market segmentation.

Location

There are essentially two categories of resorts: destination and regional. Destination resorts usually have unique natural attractions, such as a famous beach or ski slope, and usually draw users by air transportation from a wide geographical area. A regional resort is generally more accessible by automobile. Regional resorts have at least two advantages over destination resorts: they are less vulnerable to increased transportation costs; and they have lower acquisition costs for choice sites. However, destination resorts do not usually need to create tourist demand or an identity.

According to the 1980 Ragatz study, 28 percent of timeshare purchasers own intervals that are within 150–249 miles of their home. The norm appears to be around 150 miles. Desirable factors for a successful timeshare project's location are the following:

Proximity to main highways and airports.

Accessibility to restaurants and convenience shopping.

Diversity of family-oriented activities.

Short distance from the area's major attraction.

Site within a few hours' driving time of a large urban concentration.

A community or club-like atmosphere.

Project Design

Project design should justify the proposed architectural style, the unit mix and configuration, the number of units, and the furnishings and amenities. The ideal timeshare project offers units of sufficient size to ensure the purchaser's comfort over a one- or two-week stay. It is designed, furnished, and constructed (or renovated) to very high standards. A level of quality acceptable to the typical hotel guest is in all likelihood not acceptable to a timeshare owner. Completed, well-maintained amenities are a definite attraction for a timeshare project.

The average price per week, gross sales per unit, and pricing discounts, as well as unit costs should be reviewed. The effect on sales or other competitive resort accommodations in the market area, including hotels and rental condominiums, should be evaluated. Because of high sales and marketing costs, prospect-generation techniques and costs, sales commissions, closing rates, recession or cancellation rates, and post sales monitoring programs should be carefully evaluated. Additionally, the timeshare project should be marketed and sold by an organization with a record of success in selling projects *ethically*.

Feasibility Studies

Feasibility studies should be evaluated for their objectivity and relevance. Sometimes, the feasibility study may be conducted by a consultant who is trying to justify a marketing, sales, or management contract with the developer.

An investor should be cautious in interpreting a study's findings for the following reasons:

1. Lack of timeshare expertise, reflecting the newness of the industry.
2. Lack of methodological expertise. The analytical skills to conduct rigorous studies are not always combined with experience in timesharing. A good sales and marketing plan is not always tantamount to an adequate assessment of overall viability of the project.
3. Bias. Consulting fees frequently include a percentage of sales, thereby motivating a consultant to render a favorable report. With such tie-in arrangements, a feasibility study merely echoes the developer's personal attitudes and beliefs.[2]

---

[2]"Financing the Time Share Project," Christopher W. Hart and Sara Pfrommer, *Real Estate Review*.

In general, a lender should never accept a feasibility study from any entity, however qualified, who is not otherwise independent of the project or developer.

Appraisals

Appraisals should also be performed by independent outside appraisers. An outside appraisal should determine the value of the collateral used to secure a timeshare loan. The appraisal of a timeshare project, however, is quite different from valuating other types of commercial and residential real estate. Appraisal experts disagree about the most appropriate method to valuate timeshare developments: Should value be based on the multiple of the sales price per interval or should unusually high sales and marketing costs be deducted? Additionally, should many non-real estate and intangible items, such as unit furnishings, housekeeping services, and exchange membership, be deducted from the sales price? This controversy becomes very significant when local jurisdictions assess the property-tax value of timeshare properties.

Marketing and Sales

A developer's marketing and sales programs[3] directly affect the quality of the consumer paper that a lender may finance. If a timeshare project is marketed and sold with well-founded and properly executed programs in a truthful and ethical manner, the consumer knows what he is buying and is content with his purchase. A contented buyer who finances his purchase is motivated to make his payments in a timely manner. Because marketing and sales practices affect the quality of a given project's consumer loans, a thorough and detailed analysis of marketing and sales techniques should be performed by prospective lenders to that project.

In addition, an on-site personal inspection should be conducted to evaluate marketing and sales practices. The sales line should be shopped by a lender's representative to determine if high-pressure tactics or misrepresentation exist. Salespeople should not tout investment return or equity buildup unless they and managers are registered with the SEC. Salespeople also should not promise nonexistent amenities, future buy-backs of the weeks sold or other items without prior approval by the state attorney general's office.

Management and Maintenance

Maintenance of a timeshare project often spells the difference between a marginal and a successful property. Timeshare owners usually have a greater interest in property management than do rental users. Postpurchase satisfaction

---

[3]In the parlance of the timeshare industry, marketing is the function which generates prospective customers (commonly called "ups") to the resort site, while sales is the actual selling function usually performed at the site by sales personnel.

of timeshare owners is important to both the lender and the developer. A purchaser paying on a multi-year contract may default if he perceives that the project is poorly managed, as evidenced by inept maid service and shoddy repairs, or by substantial increases in maintenance fees.

Key questions that need to be answered for a potential lender of a timeshare property:

Is the original design and construction adequate? In conversion projects, developers sometimes try to get by with cosmetic changes when structural defects are evident.

Are the unit furnishings being replaced on a specified timetable? The furnishing should be durable, and major furnishings should be replaced on a justifiable cycle.

Are the maintenance fees and replacement reserves sufficient? Many developers "lowball" maintenance fees to impress investors or boost sales. Underestimated maintenance budgets lead to long-run maintenance problems and hostility from timeshare owners.

Are the daily property-management functions handled by skilled professionals? While management companies with timeshare experience are desirable, competent hospitality managers can also assume these responsibilities.

Have the legal documents been drafted to avoid timeshare management problems for the developer and the association?

Legal and Regulatory Requirements

Federal, state, and local regulatory controls over timesharing are extensive. Federal requirements mainly involve disclosures, such as the Truth-in-Lending Act. State and local controls are usually more substantive. More than 20 states now have specific timeshare laws, which vary from basic consumer disclosure statutes to comprehensive and stringent laws requiring, among other things, bonding, escrow constraints, marketing and sales restrictions, and specific management requirements. Other states have adapted their subdivision or securities' statutes to include timesharing.[4] Additionally, some local communities place restrictive zoning or land-use controls on timeshare developments to ban timesharing outright or severely restrict sales and marketing techniques employed within that jurisdiction.

Lenders must be assured that the timeshare developer has fully complied with all legal and regulatory requirements. Existing and potential legislation should be carefully scrutinized for its effect on the viability of the project. Violations of statutes, or administrative rules and regulations, can affect the viability of a venture, while some illegal acts of the developer may expose the

---

[4]"Regulation of Timesharing," Stuart Marshall Block, *University of Detroit Journal of Urban Law*, Vol. 60, Issue 1, Fall 1982.

lender to liability. In reviewing a developer's compliance with applicable laws, a lender should require copies of state registration documents and opinions of counsel regarding state and federal limitations. The lender should also check with the state attorney general's office for consumer complaints or official dissatisfaction.

Administrative Processing

Lenders should monitor the developer's/project's operating and financial reports, including delinquency reports, new sales and cancellations, and cash reconciliations. The handling of escrow funds is particularly important. Lenders (and some state laws) require prompt deposit of escrow funds and tight control over escrow disbursements. The credit procedures a developer uses to determine credit worthiness of potential purchasers should also be closely reviewed by the lender.

Summary

The institutional lending community has recognized the investment opportunities in resort timesharing. Timeshare loans, if properly structured, are a short-term investment with a high return. However, the uninitiated lender must understand the hybrid nature of resort timesharing. Timeshare loans require the lender to step beyond traditional real estate underwriting procedures and incorporate other elements, such as consumer lending, marketing, and hospitality management.

APPENDIX: WHAT LENDERS LOOK AT IN EVALUATING A TIMESHARE PROJECT

1. *Developer*
    a) Corporate and individual financial statements and tax returns
    b) Credit and business references
    c) Company history (articles of incorporation, partnership agreements)
    d) Résumés of principals
2. *Location*
    a) Major nonproject amenities and attractions
    b) Tourism statistics
    c) Accessibility
3. *Project design*
    a) On-site amenities
    b) Feasibility study
    c) Appraisal

    d) Site plan

    e) Competition analysis

    f) Zoning compliance

4. *Financial information on project*

    a) Cash flow assumptions

    b) Actual operating history and projected monthly cash flow charts

    c) Existing debt schedules

5. *Marketing and sales*

    a) Résumés of principals showing timesharing experience

    b) Business references

    c) Marketing plan, including copies of mailers and sales brochures; pricing sheet; target market; sales methods

    d) Marketing agreements and exchange affiliation agreements

    e) Description of credit approval process and financing to be offered to purchaser.

6. *Management company*

    a) Résumés of principals showing timeshare/hospitality experience

    b) Management contract

    c) Detailed maintenance budget

    d) Replacement schedule

7. *Legal*

    a) All legal documentations, registrations and filings

    b) List of pending legal action with counsel's opinion

    c) By-laws of property association

    d) Title policy

    e) Consumer documentation: purchase agreement; note; deed of trust; credit application; good-faith representation; truth-in-lending form

8. *Contract servicing*

    a) Name of servicing agent, address, telephone number

    b) Description of collection procedures

    c) Copy of servicing agreement

    d) Aging schedule of accounts

    e) Repossession history

Index

A

Accounting principles,
  bulk purchase of loans, 399-400
  conservatism, accrual, or measuring-of-
    unfavorable-event principles, 395
  discount with high speed, 469
  discount with slow speed, 469
  excess of purchase price over sales price,
    404-5
  financial statement presentation and
    disclosure, 411-14
  futures contracts, 403
  GNMA mortgage-backed securities,
    400-403
  interest income, 406-10
  loan loses, 403
  loan-organization fees, 406
  loan servicing fees, 405
  loans held for long-term investment, 396
  loans held for sale or market recovery,
    395-96
  loans sold under repurchase agreements
    396
  loan value computation, 397
  long-term portfolio hypothecation,
    447-48
  mortgage origination costs, 404
  Regulatory Accounting Principle, 447-48
  secondary market, 395-414
Accounting Principles Board,
  Opinion No. 20, 404
  Opinion No. 43, 410
Accrual-basis taxpayer, 470
Accrual principle of accounting, 395
Accrued interest, 469-70
Acquisition and construction financing,
  583-84
Acquisition rate mortgages (ARMs), 61-62,
    66, 84, 153, 78-79, 258, 566, 570-71
  characteristics, 492-94
  Federal Home Loan Mortgage Corporation,
    202-203

Adjustable rate mortgages—*cont.*
  Federal National Mortgage Association,
    324
  future dominance of, 572-73
  impact on housing market, 573
  rating, 109-10
Administrative exposure,
  characteristics, 309-10
  definition, 304
  internal audit, 312
  internal reports, 311-12
  problem investors, 313-14
  problem loans, 312-13
  written procedures, 310-11
Advance-claims payment provision, 1-6
AES; *see* Aggregate exception system
After-tax,
  definition, 243
  value, 246
Aggregate exception system (AES),
    348
Agreed-upon interest rate, 378
Alger, George W., 138
All sources, 243
Allstate Insurance, 92
Alternative mortgage instruments (AMI),
    481-99
  adjustable rate mortgages, 566, 570-71,
    572-73
  buy-down loans, 488-90
  evolving forms, 570-72
  and fixed-rate mortgages, 572-73
  future of, 565-75
  growing equity mortgages, 490-91, 567
  graduated payment mortgages, 482-85,
    566, 571
  hybrid types, 567
  impact on housing market, 573-74
  midgets, 492
  origin, 481-82
  pledged-account mortgages, 485-88
  price-level-adjusted mortgages, 494-97,
    567

593

Alternative mortgage instruments,—*cont.*
reverse-annuity mortgages, 567
selection process, 567-70
shared-appreciation mortgages, 498-99,
567
types, 482
variable rate mortgages, 492-94
American Banker, 270
American Commodity Exchange, 76
AMI: *see* Alternative mortgage instruments
Amortize, 23
Amortization
negative, 483-85
payments, 474
APB; *see* Accounting Principles Board
Appraisals, timesharing, 588
ARM; *see* Adjustable rate mortgages
Arthur D. Little, Inc., 143
Assets, 380-81
Audit,
internal, 312
warehouse lenders, 432-35
Audit Guides for Audits of HUD-Approved
Nonsupervised Mortgages for Use by
Independent Public Accountants, 193
Average life measurement of investments,
522-27

B

Baby boom, 4-5
Banco Mortgage Company, 92
Bank of America, 59, 84, 85, 91, 151, 152
Bank holding company subsidiaries, 191
Bank lines of credit, 382-88
advantages, 383-84
agreement specifications, 385
check presentment advisory service,
387-88
due-to/due-from account, 384
haircut borrowing, 385
pricing mechanisms, 382-83
problem loans, 386
purchase line, 385
security for, 386
take-outs, 386
unsecured line of credit, 387
Bank-owned mortgage companies, 189
Bankers; *see also* Mortgage banking
call reports, 188
real estate authority, 188-89
regulation of, 187-88
sources of mortgage funds, 15, 478
state chartering laws, 179
Basis relationship in hedging, 132
Basket of mortgages, 111
Blind pool securities offerings, 51
Blue sky laws, 52, 55, 176-77, 208

Bonds, mortgage-backed, 152; *see also*
Mortgage-backed bonds
Bond markets, 151
Bond rating agencies; *see* Rating agencies
Borrower qualifications, 477
Branch managers, 288
Branch office administration, 291
Branch office administration,—*cont.*
closing a loan, 292
customers, 292-93
dealing with home builders, 293
dealing with realtors, 292-93
loan purchasing, 291-92
management considerations, 297
Budgeting,
forecasting loan volume, 368-69
goals and objectives, 367-68
implementation and monitoring, 369-70
strategic plan and, 367
Builder buy-downs, 488
Builder loans,
characteristics, 220-22
construction loans, 221-22
definition, 220
market demand, 258
risks, 307
secondary market qualifications, 221
versus spot loans, 224-25
Business plan approach to value, 236-37
Business relationship criteria, 437-40
Buy-down mortgages, 488-90
rating, 108

C

Cabinet Council on Economic Affairs, 54
California Variable Rate Mortgages, 320;
see also Adjustable rate
mortgages
Callable but not refundable securities, 552
Callable preferred stock, 393
Call protection, 463-64, 552
definition, 41
Call reports, 188
Cancellation risk, 247-48
CAP: *see* Certified Agency Program
Capital, 421-22
Capital markets, competition in, 22
Capital requirements,
cash flow projections, 366-67
ownership and size of company, 365-66
Capping price changes, 296
Cash advance capability, 105-6
Cash-basis taxpayer, 470
Cash flow,
after-tax, 346
analysis, 442-43
bonds, 85-86

Cash flow—*cont.*
  coverage, 119-20
  expected value computation, 246-47
  servicing loans, 240-50
  pass-through securities, 507-8
  present value, 248
  present value computation, 248-50
  projections, 366-67
Cash flow yield; *see* HTG yield
Cash forward market (TBA market), 76-77
Cash immediate market, 75-76
Certificate account, 106
Certified Agency Program, 194
CFTC; *see* Commodity Futures Trading
      Commission
Chartering of banks and savings and loans, 179
Cheapness, in hedging, 133
Check presentment advisory services, 387-88
Chicago Board of Trade, 76, 126
  regulation of securities market, 207-8
Chicago Mercantile Exchange, 126
Chicago Produce Exchange, 126
Civil Rights Act of 1968, Title VIII (Fair
      Housing Act), 163
Claims, private mortgage insurance industry,
      143
Clearing organization, 128-29
Clerical error, 304
Closed end credit transactions, 161
  rules for advertising, 162
Closing agents, 292
CMBS; *see* Conventional mortgage-backed
      securities
CMO; *see* Collateralized mortgage obligation
      bonds
Coinsurance program, 194-95
Coldwell Banker Real Estate Group, 92
Collaterial,
  department reports, 339-40
  mortgage-backed bonds, 111-13
Collateralized mortgage obligation (CMO)
      bonds, 65, 85-86, 91, 454
  definition, 115
  flexibility, 94
  origin, 552-54
  protection, 464
  versus mortgage-backed securities, 460-61
Collateral management,
  documentation, 336-38
  follow-up documentation, 339
  investor commitments, 331-35
  new loan files, 337
  quality control, 338-39
  types of loan sales, 335-36
  types of reports, 339-40
  warehousing-funding package
      requirement, 337-38
Collaterial trust notes (CTNs), 389-90, 403-31

Collection procedures, 350
Commercial paper,
  conduit for, 392
  financing by, 430-21
  types, 389-90
Commissions, 223
Commitment fees, 406
Commodities exchanges, 125-26
  role of clearing organization, 128-29
Commodities Exchange, Inc., 126
Commodities Futures Trading Commission
      (CFTC), 128
  regulation of securities dealers, 207-8,
      209
Community Reinvestment Act of 1977,
      164-65
Compensation,
  loan debt managers, 285
  loan officers, 286
Competitive quotient of market, 257
Competitor analysis, 263-67
  construction loans outstanding, 266-67
  debt-to-equity ratio, 266
  financial performance, 265
  gains or losses, 267
  inventory held, 266
  management qualities, 262-65
  motivation, 263-65
  net interest income, 267
  net worth growth, 266
  ownership structure, 262
  performance, 265-67
  profitability, 266
  sources of profit, 266
  volume of transactions, 265
Controller of Currency, 170, 448
Computers, 305, 359
Condominums; *see also* Resort timesharing
  definition, 181
  multifamily, 7
  percent of total housing, 19
  projects, 62-63
  state laws, 181-82
Conduits, 150-53
  commercial paper, 392
  companies, 152-53, 327-28
  conventional pass-throughs, 85
  definition, 152
  function, 26
  purpose, 151
Conservatism principle of accounting, 395
Contingency plans, 365
Contingency reserves, 144
Continuous-process cost procedures, 371
Construction loans, 583-84
  outstanding, 266-67
Consumer Credit Protection Act, 158
Consumer end-loan financing, 583

Consumer lending, compared to mortgage lending, 14
Consumers,
high income applicants, 229-30
low to moderate income applicants, 229
middle income applicants, 228-29
types of loans, 230-34
wholesale loan distribution to, 228
Contract months, 133
Conventional loans, 294
Conventional mortgage-backed securities, 211; *see also* Mortgage-backed securities
active management of pools, 94
evolution of concept, 89-91
private programs, 91-93
quality of guarantee, 94-95
reason for, 88-89
recent entrants, 92
role and market potential, 93
standardization, 93-94
Corporate bond equivalent yield, 537
Correspondent system of income-property lending, 218
Cost,
accounting, 370-71
of servicing loans, 243-44
Cost approach to value,
definition, 237
net-asset value, 250-52
Credit; *see also* Loans; Mortgage financing
alternatives to borrowing, 392-94
bank lines, 382-88
commercial paper, 389-91
conduit for issuance of commercial paper, 392
delayed interest payment, 392
gestation-period repo, 392
prewarehousing line, 392
qualifying for, 476-77
real estate-owned lines, 431
repurchase agreements, 391
special loans, 431
total demand for, 86
uncommitted lines, 431
unsecured line, 387
warehouse lending, 417-35
Credit crunch of 1960s, 10
Credit ratings for bond issuers, 97-124
Credit risk, 462, 464-65, 550
mortgage collateral, 115-18
qualifications, 101-2
Creditor, 158
Credit transactions, closed-end, 161
Crocker National Bank, 49
Cross-collateralization, 381
CTN; *see* Collateral trust note
Cumulative prepayment rate, 510; *see also* Prepayment

Current coupon, 76

D

Data processing, 359
DDN; *see* Documented discount notes
Dealer markets, 127-29
Dean Witter Reynolds, 92
Debt rating definitions, 122-24
Deeply discounted mortgage assets, 41
Delayed interest payment, 392
Delinquent, 475-76
Delinquent mortgage, 105-6
Demographics of housing, demand, 4-9, 262
Demonstration Program of Outreach and Delegated Processing, 194-95
Demonstration intermediation, 21
DEP; *see* Direct Endorsement Processing
Department of Housing and Urban Development, 46, 60-61, 63, 69, 71, 74, 156-57, 231, 247, 511, 516-17
approval of mortgages, 191-92, 193-96, 198-99
Certified Agency Program, 194-95
Coinsurance Program, 194-95
Demonstration Program of Outreach and Delegated Processing, 194-95
Direct Endorsement Processing, 195
loan processing programs, 194-95
operational requirements, 194
single family application process, 194
supervision of bank-owned mortgage companies, 189
Department of Labor, 50, 165-67, 211
Deposit accounts, 13
Deposit facility, 164
Depository institutions, regulation of 184-89; *see also* Thrift institutions
Depository Institutions Act of 1982, 169-72
Depository Institutions Deregulation and Monetary Control Act of 1980 (DIDA), 13, 171-72
Depository Institutions Deregulation Committee, (DIDC), 13-14
Deregulation of thrift institutions, 13-14
Destination resorts, 586-87
DIDA; *see* Depository Institutions Deregulation and Monetary Control Act of 1980
DIDC: *see* Depository Institutions Deregulation Committee
Direct Endorsement Processing (DEP), 195
Direct warehousing, 428
Disbursement clearing account, 349
Disclosure requirements, 411-14
Discounting, 469
Disintermediation,
cycle, 59

Disintermediation—*cont.*
thrift industry, 12-13
Diversification, 307
Documentation, 336-38
Document control, 305
Documented discount notes, 388-89,
429-30
Doing business statues, 175-76
Down payment, 477
Drucker, Peter, 217
Due-on-sale clauses, 170
regulation, 421
Due-to/due-from account, 384
Duff and Phelps, 98
Duration of investment, 525-27

E

Early ownership mortgage, 466
ECOA; *see* Equal Credit Opportunity Act
Economic factors in real estate market
demand, 256-59
Efficient market, 262
Employee Retirement Income Security Act
(ERISA), 50, 91, 165-67
regulation of pension funds, 210-12
Equal Credit Opportunity Act (ECOA),
157-59, 291, 427
Equity; *see also* Homeowner's equity
definition, 474
growing pattern, 490
ERISA; *see* Employee Retirement Income
Security Act
Escrow accounts,
administration, 352-55
analysis, 355
control, 347
costs, 353
insurance payments, 353-54
interest on, 344
lienable items, 354
overdrafts, 346
tax disbursements, 353
taxes and insurance payments,
348-49
Escrow income, 345-46
P and I float, 244
Exempted security, 169
Expected value, 240-43

F

Fair Housing Act, 163
Fannie Mae; *see* Federal National
Mortgage Association
Fallout rate of loan applications, 302-3
Farmers Home Administration (FmHA),
35, 46-47
nature of securities, 27

Farmers Home Administration—*cont.*
origin, 72
FASB; *see* Financial Accounting
Standards Board
Fast pay/slow pay classes, 49
Federal Deposit Insurance Corporation
(FDIC), 121, 164, 187-88, 345, 448
Federal Financing Bank, 27
Federal government,
aid to thrift industry, 12
deregulation of thrift institutions, 13-14
mortgage agencies, 16
mortgage innovations, 10
mortgage purchasers, 57-72
third-party mortgage loan guarantees,
23-24
Federal Home Loan Bank of San Francisco,
493, 494
Federal Home Loan Bank Board (FHLBB),
13, 64, 148, 155, 164, 169, 170, 172.
178, 198, 202, 207-8
funds redeployment strategies, 41
regulation of savings institutions,
184-86
timesharing rules, 582-83
Federal Home Loan Bank System (FHLBS),
64, 66, 184
Federal Home Loan Mortgage Corporation
(FHLMC), 85, 99, 41-42, 143, 148,
151, 152, 155, 156, 163, 167, 168, 230,
231, 318, 335-36, 347, 460, 461, 467,
569
adjustable rate mortgages, 202-3
alternative mortgage instruments, 566
charter act, 168-69
collateralized mortgage obligation
bonds, 91, 552-54
delivery commitments, 326-28
guaranteed mortgage certificate, 90
Guarantor program, 90-91
issuance of participation certificates,
89
loan types, 325-26
mandatory delivery commitments, 332
mortgage-backed securities, 321-22
mortgage loan approval, 198-99
mortgage/securities swaps, 44-46
nature of commitments, 333-35
operational requirements, 200
operation of, 64-69
optional delivery commitments, 333
origins, 58
origins of Mortgage Participation
Certificate, 58
participation certificates, 10, 12, 15, 16,
28, 31, 41, 42, 46-47, 54, 55
pools, 541, 545
product eligibility, 202-3
servicing portfolios, 275

Federal Home Loan Mortgage Corporation—
    cont.
  types of securities, 27
  yield, 532
Federal Housing Administration (FHA)
  approval of servicing agreements, 356
  endorsement program, 299
  establishment, 73, 139, 511
  graduated payment mortgages, 485
  issuance of principal, 145
  liquidity of mortgage, 26
  loans, 28, 35-39, 42, 57-58, 61, 62, 63, 69-70,
    226, 230, 247, 306, 315, 321, 323, 324-25,
    335-36, 430, 437
  loans for income property, 218
  loans to middle income applicants, 229
  loans to secondary markets, 26
  mortgage approval, 191-92
  mortgage pools, 201
  mortgages, 16, 75, 77, 83-84, 89, 92, 183
  operational requirements, 193-96
  operation of, 71-72
  property inspection rules, 351
  rate changes, 308-9
  rules on escrow accounts, 355
  third party guarantor, 23-24
  235 loans, 244
  types of loans, 294
Federal Housing Administration-experience,
    510, 511-18
  pros and cons, 515-18
  single monthly mortality, 514-15, 517-18
Federal housing finance laws, 150-71
Federally related mortgage loan, 163
Federal National Mortgage Association
    (FNMA), 99, 141-42, 143, 148, 151, 155,
    156, 163, 167, 230, 231, 247, 308, 318,
    335-36, 347, 460, 461, 467, 569-70
  charter act, 168
  commitment auction, 10, 12, 15, 16, 28, 31,
    35-39, 41, 42, 46-47, 54, 55
  conventional mortgage-backed securities, 91
  establishment, 58, 73-74
  interest rate policy, 296
  introduction of adjustable rate mortgages,
    61-62
  mandatory delivery commitments,
    324-25, 332
  mortgage-backed securities, 326-28
  mortgage-backed securities pools, 320-21
  mortgage loan approval, 197-98
  mortgage/securities swaps, 44-46
  nature of commitments, 333-35
  negotiated commitments, 325
  operational requirements, 200
  operation of, 60-64
  optional delivery commitments, 325, 333
  product eligibility, 201-2

Federal National Mortgage Association—*cont.*
  resale and refinance commitments, 325
  second mortgages, 328
  servicing contract, 248
  servicing portfolios, 275
  success, 59
  types of securities, 27
Federal policy,
  pass-through securities, 46-54
  recent developments, 54-56
Federal Register, 211
Federal regulation,
  bank-owned mortgage companies, 189
  banks, 187-89
  depository institutions, 184-89
  mortgage bankers, 190-91
  mortgage insurance companies, 203-4
Federal Reserve Act, 188
Federal Reserve Board, 53, 207
  Regulation B, 158-59
  Regulation C, 163
  Regulation T, 52, 208
  Regulation Y, 191
  Regulation Z, 160-62
  supervision of bank holding companies,
    191
  supervision of banks, 187
Federal Reserve System, 164
Federal savings and loan associations, 187
Federal Savings and Loan Insurance
    Corporation (FSLIC), 121, 164, 184, 345
Fee ownership, 578-81
FHA; *see* Federal Housing Administration
FHLBB; *see* Federal Home Loan Bank Board
FHLBS; *see* Federal Home Loan Bank System
Fiduciary, 167
Financial Accounting Standards Board
    (FASB), 45, 407
  Statement No. 5, 410
Financial analysis, 375-76
  borrowers, 421-23
  breakdown, 422-23
  capital net worth, 421-22
Financial planning,
  analysis, 375-76
  budgeting, 367-70
  capital requirements, 365-67
  classification of revenues and expenses, 372
  communications, 374
  contingency plans, 365
  continuous-process cost procedures, 371
  controllable items, 371-72
  controls, 370-74
  cost accounting, 370-71
  employee costs, 371-72
  interest expense, 372
  internal controls, 374
  marketing costs, 375

Financial planning—*cont.*
  origination, 374
  overhead costs, 376
  responsibility centers, 371
  reports, 372-74
  servicing costs, 375
  strategic plan, 363-65
  warehousing costs, 376
Financial statements,
  accounting requirements, 411-14
  disclosure requirements, 411-14
First Boston Corporation, 533, 546, 550
First Federal Savings and Loan of Chicago, 91
Fixed-duration quotes, 295
Fixed low rate assumable mortgages, 230-31
Fixed-rate mortgage,
  future of, 572-73
  rating, 102
Fitch Investor Service, 98
Floating loans, 302
Flooring price changes, 296
FmHA; *see* Farmers Home Administration
FNMA; *see* Federal National Mortgage
  Association
Forebearance agreements, 350
Forecasting funds, 466-67
Foreclosure,
  costs, 346-47
  frequency, 101
  procedures, 351-52
  state laws, 172-75
Forward delivery commitments, 467-68
  disadvantages, 468
  FHLMC mortgage-backed securities,
    321-22
  FNMA pools, 320-21
  GNMA mortgage-backed securities, 319-20
  participations, 318
  whole loan, 317-18
Freddie Mac; *see* Federal Home Loan
  Mortgage Corporation
Fully modified pass-throughs, 505
Funds redeployment strategies, 41
Futures contracts,
  accounting policies, 403
  certificates of deposit, 323
  commercial paper, 323
  GNMA, 322-23
  Treasury bonds, 323
Futures market,
  advantages, 322
  contract months, 133
  fixed income securities, 126
  GNMA securities, 71, 209
  hedge planning, 132-33
  history, 125-26
  initial margin, 134
  maintenance margin, 134

Futures market—*cont.*
  margin, 133-34
  market participants, 129
  open interest, 129
  operation of, 127-29
  purposes, 128
  regulation of, 128
  risk capital, 130
  role of clearing organization, 128-29
  speculation and hedging, 129-32
  volume, 129

G

GAAP; *see* Accounting policies; Generally
  accepted accounting principles
Gallup Organization survey, 581-82
Garn-St. Germain Depository Institutions Act
  of 1982, 13-14, 22, 169-71, 178-79, 185
  188
GEM; *see* Graduated equity mortgage
General and administrative overhead costs, 376
General Electric Credit Corporation, 92
Generally accepted accounting principles
  (GAAP)
  portfolio financing, 453-57, 447-48
  secondary markets, 395-414
Geographic considerations in real estate, 262
Gestation-period repo, 392; *see also*
  Repurchase agreements
Ginnie Mae; *see* Government National
  Mortgage Association
GMC; *see* Guaranteed mortgage certificate
GNMA; *see* Government National Mortgage
  Association
Good due-on-sale, 521
Government mortgage agencies, 16
  secondary markets, 26
  share of mortgage loans, 31
  relation to servicers, 356
Government loans, 294
Government mortgage insurance, 139
Government policy,
  pass-through securities, 46-54
  recent developments, 54-56
Government National Mortgage Association,
  89, 99, 100, 152, 155, 156, 163, 167, 168,
  218, 230, 231, 244, 273, 277, 306, 308,
  320-21, 323, 335-36, 347, 381, 460, 461,
  467
  adjustable rate mortgages, 84
  average life, 524
  bulk purchase in pools, 399
  cash forward market, 76-77
  cash immediate market, 75-76
  current coupon, 76
  delivery commitments, 326
  15-year security, 83

Government National Mortgage Association *cont.*
  futures trading, 126, 209, 322-23
  graduated-payment mortgage pass-through, 83
  guaranteed securities program start, 74
  interest rate volatility, 315-16
  mobile home program, 83-84
  mortgage loan approval, 197
  mortgage-backed pools, 294, 319-20
  mortgage-backed securities, 10, 12, 15, 16, 28, 35-39, 42, 46-47, 400-403
  nature of securities, 26-27
  newer programs, 78-84
  I and II securities, 70-71, 319-20
  operational requirements, 199
  operation of, 69-71
  origins, 58, 60
  pass-through program, 151, 502-5
  Phase II program, 84
  prepayments, 507, 540-48
  problems of pass-throughs, 77-78
  product eligibility, 200-201
  securities, 75-77, 397
  servicing portfolios, 275
  servicing transfer checklist, 278-81
  size of market, 93
  start of pass-through program, 74-75
  success, 59
  types of securities, 74-75
  vehicle for VA/FHA loans, 35-39
  Wall Street involvement, 78
  yield, 532, 533-36, 537
  yields on securities, 519
GPARM; *see* Graduated-payment adjustable rate mortgages
GPM; *see* Graduated-payment mortgages
Graduated equity mortgages, 108-9
Graduated-payment mortgages (GPMs), 72, 482-85, 566, 571
  negative amortization, 482-85
  pass-throughs, 83
  rating, 109
  tax treatment, 539
Grantor trust, 48-49, 84
Growing-equity mortgages, (GEMs), 320, 490-91, 567
Growing equity pattern, 490
GSI; *see* Nonmember subsidiaries
Guaranteed governmental mortgage pool certificate, 167
Guaranteed mortgage certificate (GMC), 90
  origin, 64
Guarantee on interest payments, 505
Guarantee on principal payments, 505
Guarantor program, 90-91

H

Haircut, 385
Half-size measurement of investments, 522-27
Hazard insurance, 505-6
Hedge planning, 132-33
Hedge ratio, 132
Hedging,
  basis relationship, 132
  cheapness, 133
  contract months, 133
  controls, 135
  FHLMC loans, 325-26
  FNMA/FHLMC delivery commitments, 326-28
  FNMA loans, 324-25
  foward-delivery commitments, 317-22
  futures trading, 129-32
  GNMA futures, 322-23
  GNMA mortgage-backed securities, 326
  in the secondary market, 315-29
  long-term Treasury bond futures, 323
  margin cost, 134
  means of, 317-29
  need for, 315
  options market, 323-24
  ratio, 132
  richness, 133
  servicing-released loans, 324
  time adjustment, 132-33
  timing, 133
High income applicants for loans, 229-30
High rate nonassumable short-term mortgages, 230-31
Holdback reserves, 583
Holding company subsidiaries, 187
Home builders,
  loan customers, 293
  risks of dealing with, 307
Home Federal Savings and Loan, 49
Home improvement loans, 65
Home loans; *see also* Loans; Mortgage financing
  definition, 185
  loan-to-value ratio limits, 186
  types, 186
Home Mortgage Disclosure Act of 1975, 162-63
Homeowner's equity, 474
Home Owners' Loan Act of 1933, 169, 185
Home Savings and Loan Association, Los Angeles, 85, 592
Housing,
  demographic demand, 4
  percentages of types, 19
  projected price increases, 17-18
  rehabilitation and upgrading, 7-9
  single-family detached, 19
Household formation,
  age distribution, 6-7
  new residential construction for, 5-6

Household formation—*cont.*
  single-person units, 6
Housing Act of 1983, 72
Housing and Community Development Act of
  1980, 172n
Housing and Home Finance Agency, 60
Housing and Urban Development Act of
  1968, 60, 69
Housing and Urban-Rural Recovery Act of
  1983, 156n
Housing demand,
  condominiums, 7
  demographics of, 4-9
  effect of migration, 6
  financial need of 1980s, 16-20
  five-year cycle, 9-10
  single-person households, 6
  types, 5
  use of existing stock, 7
Housing finance; *see also* Loans; Mortgage
    finance
  demographic demand, 4
  mortgage lending/investment process,
    23-31
  non-thrift industry sources, 15
  origins of demand, 4
  problems, 9-11
  thrift industry services, 12-14
Housing law,
  federal, 155-71
  state, 171-82
Housing market,
  forecasting trends, 368-69
  impact of alternative mortgage instruments,
    573-74
  size, 14
HTG (cash flow) yield, 533-37, 538
HUD; *see* Department of Housing and Urban
    Development

I-K

Income approach to value,
  analysis method, 238-40
  definition, 236
  projected cash flow, 240
  servicing methods, 236
Income-property lending,
  correspondent system, 218
  field, 218-19
  management characteristics, 219
  secondary market access, 218
Individual evaluation method of accounting,
  403
Inflation, 10
Initial margin, 134
Insurance,
  agents, 357

Insurance—*cont.*
  in escrow accounts, 348-49
  payments, 353-54
Interest income,
  commitment fees, 406
  discontinuation of recognition, 407-10
  loans held for sale, 406
  loans not held for sale, 406-7
  recognition of, 407
Interest payments guarantee, 505
Interest rate,
  agreed upon, 378
  changes, 308-9
  charges, 296
  expenses, 378-79
  futures contracts, 127
  periods of volatility, 309
  risk avoidance by hedging, 315-29
  stated, 378
  uncertainty, 317
  volatility, 114, 315-16
Interest-rate futures markets, 125-35
  advantages of contracts, 127
  dealer/futures markets, 127-29
  volume and open interest, 129
Interest reserve, 407
Internal audit, 312
  system, 439-40
Internal reports, 311-12
Internal Revenue Code, 49, 204
  section 4975
Internal Revenue Service, 165, 211
  regulation of mortgage securities, 204-5
  Revenue Ruling 77-135, 469-70
  Revenue Ruling 80-248, 470
International Monetary Market, 126
Interval International, 581
Inventory,
  monitoring risks, 419-20
  nonhedged, 418
  overhedged, 418
  price risk of nonviable investor commit-
    ments, 419
  reports, 339
  valuation, 398-99
Investment,
  definition of liquidity, 26
  security of, 345
  servicing portfolios, 269-81
Investment determinants, 459-69
Investment grade ratings,
  mortgage-backed bonds, 85
  mortgage pass-throughs, 84
Investors,
  payments from pass-throughs, 502-5
  problem, 313
  relation to servicing, 355-56
Issuer considerations, 120-21

Joint ownership of resort timesharing, 578-81
Joint venture financing, 584
Kansas City Board of Trade, 126
Karl, Max H., 139
Kickback penalties, 157n
Kidd, Phillip E., 3

L

Legal-investment statutes, 52, 55
Lenders Handbook, 196
Lending; *see also* Loans; Mortgage financing
   builder loans, 220-22
   construction, 221-22
   income-property, 218-19
   residential, 219-28
   spot loans, 222-24
   strategy, 214-34
   two primary types, 218-19
   types, 218-28, 230-34
   types of consumers, 228-30
   wholesale distribution, 226-28
Letter of credit, 105
Leverage ratio, 421
Lienable items, 354
Life Insurance companies
   ownership of mortgages, 479
   regulation of, 210
   sources of mortgage funds, 15
Liquifying, 447
Liquidity,
   definition, 26
   risk, 550
Loans; *see also* Alternative mortgage
     instruments;
   Mortgage financing
   accounting for losses, 403
   borrower qualifications, 476-77
   closing, 292
   collection procedures, 350
   committed, 397
   cost, 397
   cost of bulk purchases, 398
   delivery, 295-96
   due-on-sale regulations, 521
   duration of price quotes, 295
   fallout rate, 302-3
   fixed low rate assumable 30 year, 230-31
   floating, 302
   forebearance agreements, 350
   forecasting volume, 368-69
   gains or losses by competitors, 267
   good due-on-sale, 521
   held for long-term investment, 396
   held for sale or market recovery, 395-96
   hedging in secondary market, 513-29
   high rate nonassumable short-term 230-31
   interest income, 406-10

Loans—*cont.*
   investor commitments, 331-35
   mandatory/optional delivery commitments, 303
   market value, 397
   mortality, 247
   nonconforming, 431
   monitoring originators and servicers, 437-46
   prepayment, 247
   pricing, 293-96
   pricing communication, 294-95
   problem, 312-13
   purchasing, 290-91, 291-92
   recoveries of previous write-downs, 399
   resort timesharing, 583-85
   servicing factors, 240-50
   servicing-released, 324
   sold under repurchase agreements, 396
   source of mortgage money, 478-80
   types, 230-34
   types of sales, 335-36
   uncommitted, 398
   window period, 170
Loan administration, 343-59
   analysis, 424-25
   servicing agreements, 343-47
Loan inventory,
   administrative exposure problems, 309-13
   analysis, 307-8
   definition, 301-2
   exposure categories, 304
   fallout rate of applications, 302-3
   floating loans, 302
   mandatory-delivery commitments, 303
   market exposure problems, 308-9
   mechanical exposure problems, 304-5
   net market position, 301
   origination risks, 302-3
   optional-delivery commitments, 303
   pipeline, 301
   point letter, 310
   risks, 302-3
   selling risks, 303
   strategic exposure problems, 305-7
Loan officers, 286
Loan organization analysis, 423-24
   fees, 406
Loan-placement fees, 406
Loan pools, 102
Loan portfolios
   accounting policies, 447-48
   collateralized mortgage obligation bonds, 454
   conversion to liquid assets, 447-57
   hypothecations, 453-57
   paythrough techniques, 454
   planning a liquification, 448-50

Loan portfolios—*cont.*
  reinvestment phase, 449-50
  segmentation, 450-53
Loan production,
  definition, 235
  origination/warehousing/marketing,
    235
  portfolio needs, 437-40
Loan production departments,
  branch managers, 288
  branch office administration, 291-97
  branch office responsibilities, 287
  closing agents, 292
  compliance and training, 289-90
  coordination with government agencies,
    298-99
  goals and objectives, 283-84
  incentives of management, 285-86
  loan officers' incentives, 286
  loan procedures, 291-97
  management, 283-300
  management compensation, 285
  organization, 286-91
  purchasing of loans, 290-91
  quality control, 289
  regional managers, 288
  reporting and control, 298
  straight commission solicitors, 286
  underwriting section, 288-89
Loan servicing; *see also* Servicing
  definition, 235
  department, 343
  fees, 405-6
  methods, 236
Loan-to-value (LTV) ratio, 65, 145-46, 381
  buy-down loans, 488
  definition, 477
  limits, 186
London International Financial Futures
    Exchange, 126
Long-term financing, 453-57
Long-term investment, 396
Long-term maturities, 459-60
Long-term portfolio hypothecation, 447-48
Loss reserves, 144
Loss severity, 101
Low-coupon mortgage assets, 41
Low to moderate income applicants, 229
LTV; *see* Loan-to-value ratio

M

Management of loan production depart-
    ments, 283-300
Mandatory-delivery commitments, 65, 303,
    317-18
  FHLMC, 325-26
  FNMA and FHLMC, 332

Mandatory-delivery commitments—*cont.*
  FNMA loans, 324-25
  nature of, 331-32
Margin,
  in futures trading, 133-34
  initial and maintenance, 134
Marginability of pass-throughs, 52
Maintenance margin, 134
Market analysis,
  demand characteristics, 255-63
  purpose, 255
  supply characteristics, 263-67
Market demand
  average mortgage size, 257
  business diversity and growth, 262
  competitive quotient, 257
  demographic study, 262
  economic factors in analysis, 256-59
  efficient market, 262
  experienced personnel, 259
  external factors, 259-62
  general market climate, 259
  geographic considerations, 262
  firm limitations or requirements, 259
  market-share percentage, 256-57
  mortgages originated, 257-59
  need for analysis, 255-56
  number of mortgage markets, 257
  population profile, 262
  secondary market activity, 257
  simplified approach to analysis, 258-59
  spot and builder loan activity, 258
Market exposure,
  definition, 304
  FHA or VA rate charges, 308-9
  interest rate volatility, 309
  yield curves, 308
Marketing,
  capital requirements, 367
  costs, 375
  of loans, 235
Market risk, 462-63, 548-50
Market-share percentage, 256-57
Market supply, 263-67
Maturity intermediation, 21
MBB; *see* Mortgage-backed bonds
MBS; *see* Mortgage-backed securities
McCarthey, Crisenti, and Maffei, 98
Measuring-of-unfavorable-event principle of
    accounting, 395
Mechanical exposure,
  definition, 304
  types of problems, 304-5
Mechanics liens, 354
MGIC; *see* Mortgage Guaranty Insurance
    Company
MIC; *see* Mortgage insurance companies
Mid-America Commodities Exchange, 126

Middle income applicants for loans, 228-29
Midgets, 492
Migration of population, 6
MMIF; *see* Mutual Mortgage Insurance Fund
Mobile homes,
    GNMA program, 83-84
    percent of total housing, 19
Model Savings Association Act, 177
Modified duration, 526
Modified pass-throughs, 505
Modified weak-link theory of rating, 205-6
MMDA; *see* Money market deposit accounts
Money market certificates, 13
Money market deposit accounts (MMDA), 14
Money market funds, 14
Moody's Investors Services, 97-98
Mortgages; *see also* Adjustable rate mortgages;
    Alternative mortgage instruments; Early
    ownership mortgages; Mortgage
    financing; Participation certificates;
    Pass-through securities; Servicing
    average size, 257
    basket of, 111
    characteristics, 473
    delinquent, 105-6
    down payment, 477
    excess of purchase price over sales price,
        404-5
    FHA approval, 191-92
    FHA-experience, 511-18
    FHA requirements, 193-96
    fixed rate, 572-73
    fixed rate versus variable rate, 460
    formulas, 554-61
    graduated equity, 108-9
    graduated payment, 109
    history of secondary market, 73-84
    innovations by federal government, 10
    interest rate futures market, 122-35
    life of investment, 522-27
    loan-to-value ratio, 145-46, 477
    long and short term maturities, 459-60
    measuring prepayments, 507-9
    new instruments, 106-10
    originator, 478
    over-collateralization, 115-18
    ownership, 479
    participation certificates, 89-90
    pledged account/buy-down, 108
    pooling concept, 74
    qualifying for, 476-77
    recorded at cost, 397
    seasoned, 24
    second, 107-8, 328
    shared appreciation, 108, 498-99, 567
    spot or builder loan demand, 258
    term loans, 108
    thrift industry role, 12-14

Mortgages—*cont.*
    total demand for credit, 86
    total dollar volume, 257
    traditional loan, 473
    types of loans, 230-34
    types originated, 258-59
    versus mortgage-backed securities, 460
    Veterans Administration approval, 192-93
    VA operational requirements, 196
    yield and risk diversity, 460
Mortgage agencies, government; *see* Govern-
    ment mortgage agencies
Mortgage assets,
    deeply discounted (low coupon), 41
    liquidity, 26
Mortgage-backed bonds (MBBs), 85, 151-52
    creditworthiness, 113-14
    definition, 100
    quality of collateral, 111-13
    rating process, 110-14
    review process, 114
Mortgage-backed note, 389-90
Mortgage-backed securities (MBS), 12, 15, 16,
        63
    conduit companies, 327-28
    conventional, 87-95
    FNMA/FHLMC commitments, 326-28
    FNMA pools, 320-21
    FHLMC program, 321-22
    forward-delivery commitments, 319-22
    GNMA commitments, 326
    GNMA pools, 319-20
    issurance, 151
    liquidity, 461-62
    loan participation, 462
    private investor commitments, 328
    regulation of market, 204-12
    standardization, 461-62
    types of guarantees, 335-36
    uncommitted, 398
    versus bonds, 460-61
    versus mortgages, 460
Mortgage balance,
    definition, 474
    prepayments, 508
Mortgage Bankers Association, 244, 299
Mortgage banking,
    accounting policies, 395-414
    agents, 438
    application of valuation methods, 237
    approaches to valuation, 235-37
    branch offices, 438
    business plan, 236-37
    cash flow, 240-50
    competitor analysis, 263-67
    consumers, 228-30
    cost approach, 237, 250-53
    credit by warehouse lending, 417-35

Mortgage banking—*cont.*
  dealing with home builders, 293, 307
  dealing with realtors, 292-93
  dominance of market, 235
  economic value, 235-54
  escrow income, 245-46
  financial planning, 363-76
  financial stability, 440-41
  financial statement analysis, 422-23
  financial statement requirements, 411-14
  functions, 217-18
  income approach to value, 236, 238-40
  interest income, 406-10
  internal audit system, 439-40
  loan inventory management, 301-14
  loan mortality, 247
  loan production department, 283-300
  management strength, 438
  market analysis procedures, 255-67
  method of production, 438
  monitoring servicing and performance,
    442-44
  net-asset value, 250-52
  net long value, 252
  past record, 438-39
  performance verification, 440
  prepayment of loans, 247
  primary functions, 235
  problem areas, 444-45
  production control, 439
  quality of servicing, 441-42
  regulation of, 190-91
  rise in importance, 39
  servicing fees, 243
  short-term financing requirements, 377-94
  sources of loan money, 478-80
  sources of revenues, 405-6
  types of lending, 218-28
  types of reports, 444
  types of short-term lending, 428-29
  value comparisons, 253-54
  value of organization, 252-53
  value of servicing, 240-50
  wholesale, 226-28
  wholesale purchasers, 439
Mortgage bonding/investment process, 24-30
Mortgage companies,
  bank-owned, 189
  state regulation, 190-91
Mortgage credit; *see also* Credit
  adjustable rate plans, 61-62
  capital market competition, 22
  channels, 21
  conduit function, 26
  funds redeployment strategies, 41
  government secondary market purchases,
    57-72
  grantor trust, 48-49

Mortgage credit—*cont.*
  mandatory-delivery contracts, 65-66
  need for secondary markets, 22-56
  primary market instruments and
    participants, 23-24
  third-party guarantees, 23-24
  thrift institutions, 21-22
Mortgage-default insurance, 73
Mortgagee, 473
Mortgagee Approval Handbook, 193
Mortgage financing; *see also* Pass-through
    securities; Secondary Market; Servicing
  acquisition and construction, 583-84
  alternative mortgage instruments, 565-75
  bank authority, 188-89
  banks, 15
  buyer's right of revocation, 174
  closed-end credit transsactions, 161
  collateral management, 331-40
  consumer end-loan, 583
  due-on-sale regulations, 521
  federal laws, 155-71
  nature of transaction, 473-76
  holdback reserves, 583
  joint venture, 584
  legal issues, 155-82
  lending strategy, 217-34
  life insurance companies, 15
  loan production, 235
  overcollateralization, 152
  pension funds, 15
  prepayments, 506-7
  private industry, 137-53
  projected need, 16-20
  regulation of securities markets,
    204-13
  resort timesharing, 577-91
  state laws, 171-82
  terminology, 473-76
  transition period, 574-75
  types of property, 480-81
  window period loans, 170
  yield measurement, 527-39
Mortgage futures contracts; *see* Futures
    contracts
Mortgage-guarantee insurance, 505-6
  private, 137-53
Mortgage Guarantee Insurance Company,
    Milwaukee, 139
  secondary market program, 147, 149
  sponsorship of Residential Funding, 151
Mortgage insurance, 23-24
Mortgage insurance companies,
  rating, 105
  regulation of, 203-4
  required reserves, 204
Mortgage Insurance Companies of America,
    141, 149-50

Mortgage investment,
   credit risk and market risk, 462
   determinants, 463-64
Mortgage investors, 31
Mortgage lending/investment process,
   mortgage investors, 31
   primary markets, 23-24
Mortgage loans; *see also* Loans
   federally related, 163
   nonconforming, 28
   pass-through market, 26-28
   sales, 24-26
Mortgage loan approval,
   FHLMC approval, 198-99
   FHLMC operational requirements, 200
   FHLMC product eligibility, 202-3
   FNMA approval, 197-98
   FNMA operational requirements, 200
   FNMA product eligibility, 201-2
   GNMA approval, 197
   GNMA operational requirements, 199
   GNMA product eligibility, 200-201
Mortgage loan guaranty by FHA/VA, 191-96
Mortgage loan inventory; *see* Loan inventory
Mortgage loan pools, 102
Mortgage loan sales alternatives, 26
Mortgage market,
   effect of inflation, 10
   number in the United States, 257
Mortgage money availability cycles, 10
Mortgage pass-through certificates, 84
   definition, 99
   rating process, 100-110
Mortgage pay-through bonds, 100, 115-22
   advantages, 121-22
   cash flow coverage, 119-20
   collateralized mortgage obligations, 115
   credit risk, 115-18
   issuer consideration, 120-21
   key factors in evaluating, 115
   reinvestment, 118-19
Mortgage pools,
   average life, 522-27
   cash flow, 501
   components, 500
   creditworthiness, 502
   definition, 479-80, 499-500
   duration measure, 525-27
   FHA-experience, 512-18
   geographic distribution, 501-2
   growth, 31
   half-life, 522-27
   interim experience rates, 510
   lifetime, 522
   management of assets, 49
   modified duration, 526
   new security structures, 552-54
   prepayments, 508-9

Mortgage pools—*cont.*
   prepayment consistency, 540-48
   pool factor, 508
   single monthly mortality, 510
   volatility measure, 526-27
Mortgage origination costs, 404
Mortgage originators, 87
Mortgage securities, 150-53; *see also*
   Secondary market
   market, 99
   outlook, 54
   overview, 99-100
   rating, 98-99
   recent policy changes, 54-56
Mortgage/securities swaps, 44-46
Mortgage servicing portfolio, 240-43
Mortgage servicing rights, 269
Mortgage yield, 527-32
   drawbacks, 532-33
Mortgagor,
   definition, 473
   delinquent, 475-76
Mutual Mortgage Insurance Fund, 139
Mutual savings banks, 12-14

N

NASD; *see* National Association of
   Securities Dealers
National Association of Securities
   Dealers, 207-9
National Conference of Commissioners on
   Uniform State Laws, 52, 176, 179-80,
   181
National Credit Union Administration
   Board, 170
National Delinquency Survey, 432
National Futures Association, 209
National Housing Act of 1934, 60, 69, 139, 172
National Mortgage Association, 60
National Timesharing Council, 581
Negative amortization, 483-85
Negotiated commitments, 325
Net-asset value, 250-52
   servicing portfolio hidden asset, 250
Net interest income, 267
Net long, 252
Net market position, 301
Net worth, 421-22
Network One, 581
Net loan files, 337
New loan log, 339
New York, first mortgage law, 137-38
New York Futures Exchange, 126
New York Stock Exchange, 61
   regulation of securities dealers, 207-8
Nonconforming loans, 28, 431
Nonmember subsidiaries, 207

Nonresidential real estate, 480
  definition, 185
Nonsupervised mortgagee, 191-92
Non-swap securities; *see* Pass-through
  securities
Nontraditional mortgages; *see* Alternative
  mortgage instruments
Norwest Mortgage, Inc., 92
Notice of commencement, 180-81

O

Office of Controller of Currency, 170, 448
  bank supervision, 187-89
Open interest, 129
Open-market rates, 13
Optional delivery commitments, 65-66, 303,
  317-18
  FHLMC loans, 326, 333
  FNMA loans, 325, 333
Options market, 67, 68, 74
  hedging, 323-24
  regulation of, 209
  standby commitment, 323
Origination,
  costs, 404
  definition, 325
  financial planning, 375
  risks, 302-3
Over-collateralization, 115-18, 152
Overhead costs, 376
  Over-the-counter margin bonds, 52

P

PAM; *see* Pledged account mortgages
P and I float, 245
Parity price, 537-38
Participation agreement, 462
Participation certificates (PCs), 64-65,
  67-68, 393, 428-29
  definition, 26
  forward-delivery commitments, 318
  origins, 58, 89
  sales, 335
  versus mortgage-backed securities, 462
Pass-through securities, 499-506; *see also*
  Secondary market
  amount issued 1983, 31-35
  average life, 522-27
  blind pool loans, 51
  cash flow, 152, 507-8
  cash flow bonds, 85-86
  cash forward market, 76-77
  conduit function, 26
  conventional mortgage-backed securities,
    89-95
  corporate bond equivalent yield, 537

Pass-through securities—*cont.*
  credit quality and loss protection, 101-4
  credit risk, 550
  definition, 58, 99, 499-500
  deposit liabilities, 53-54
  development of market, 31-46
  duration measure, 525-27
  FmHA, 27
  Fast pay/slow pay classes, 49
  FHLMC, 27
  federal policy, 46-54
  federal quality standards, 49-50
  forms of risk involved, 548
  formulas, 554-61
  fully modified, 505
  funds redeployment strategies, 41
  geographic distribution, 501-2
  government agencies, 35-39
  government encouragement, 46-48
  GNMA, 26-27, 502-5
  graduated-payment mortgages, 83
  grantor trust, 48-49
  guarantees, 505-6
  half-life measurement, 522-27
  high ratings, 53
  HTG yield, 533-37
  implications for investor base, 41-43
  issuers/sponsors, 51
  life of investment, 522-27
  liquidity risk, 550
  marginability, 52
  market, 26-28
  market risk, 548-50
  measuring prepayments, 507-9
  modified, 505
  modified duration, 526
  mortgage-backed, 152
  mortgage pools, 31, 500-502
  mortgage/securities swaps, 44-46
  mortgage yield, 527-33
  new programs, 78-84
  new structures, 552-54
  parity price, 537-38
  participation certificates, 89-90
  payment to investors, 502-5
  pension fund law, 50
  pool factor, 508
  and prepayments, 506-7
  prepayment consistency, 540-48
  prepayment risks, 550-52
  private institutions, 27-28, 84-86, 91-93
  private volume, 59
  problems, 77-78
  rating financial strength, 104-5
  rating criteria, 152
  rating process, 100-110
  Reagan administration policy, 46-48
  recent policy changes, 54-56

Pass-through securities—*cont.*
  recourse arrangement, 53-54
  reinvestment risk, 550
  reverse purchase agreements, 44-45
  risk versus reward, 548-52
  sales of loans into secondary markets, 39-41
  SEC regulation, 51-52
  senior/subordinated classes, 49
  servicer's cash advance capability, 105-6
  single monthly mortality, 510
  start of program, 74-75
  state laws, 52, 55
  swap-adjusted, 39
  swap transactions, 59
  tax policies, 539
  tax treatment of recovered discount, 49
  Treasury-Yield Curve, 551
  Trust for Investment Mortgages, 48-49
  types, 74-75
  underlying mortgages, 500-502
  Wall Street involvement, 78
  yield-duration plot, 550-51
  yield measurement, 527-39
  varieties, 500
  volatility measure, 526-27
Pay-through bonds,
  advantages, 121-22
  rating, 115-22
PC; *see* Participation certificate
Pension funds,
  discretionary investment powers, 15
  ERISA regulation of, 210-12
  public employees, 212
  sources of mortgage financing, 15
Phase II program, 84
Pipeline; *see* Loan investory
PLAMs; *see* Price-level adjusted mortgages
Planned unit development projects, 62-63
Pledged-account mortgages (PAMs), 485-88
  rating, 108
Point guarantees, 295
Point letters, 310
Pool factor, 508
Pooling; *see also* Mortgage pools
  concept, 74
  definition, 429
  management, 94
Population,
  growth, 4-5
  migration, 6
Portfolio needs, 437-40
Postclosing liability, 277
Postwar baby boom, 4-5
Prepayment, 247, 506-7
  arguments against consistency, 545-46
  causes, 506
  consistency, 540-48
  cumulative rate, 510

Prepayment—*cont.*
  cyclical factors, 521
  definition, 475
  due-on-sale regulations, 521
  due to refinancing, 518-19
  experience rate, 508
  factors affecting, 518-22
  FHA-experience, 510-18
  HTG yield, 533-37
  interim experience rates, 510
  measuring, 507-9
  mortgage yield, 527-32
  penalty, 507
  regional factors, 521
  risk, 112, 550-52
  seasonal factors, 519-21
  single monthly mortality, 510
Present value,
  after tax, 248
  computation, 248-50
  definition, 243
President's Commission on Housing, 22
  recommendation on pass-through securities 46-54
Prewarehousing line of credit, 392
Price-level adjusted mortgages, 494-97, 567
Price protection, 315-29
Pricing,
  capping and flooring changes, 296
  control, 305-6
  fixed duration quotes, 295
  interest rate charges, 296
  point guarantees, 295
  timing, 295
  variations, 296
Primary markets,
  definition, 23
  mortgage insurance, 23-24
  private mortgage insurance industry, 144-47
  third-party loan guarantees, 23-24
Primary mortgage market instruments, 23-24
Prior approval commitment loans, 65-66
Private mortgage insurance industry,
  adjustable rate mortgages, 153
  claims function, 143
  Depression collapse, 138
  financial strength, 143-44
  growth since 1957, 139
  history, 137-39
  monitoring lenders, 142
  mortgage securities and conduits, 150-53
  operation of, 141-44
  primary market involvement, 144-47
  secondary market, 147-50
  shared risk concept, 146
  standardization of practices, 141-42
  types of reserves, 144
  underwriting function, 142-43

Private-sector mortgage securities, 84-86
Problem investors, 313
Procedural confusion, 305
Product selection, 306
Prohibited Transactions Exemption, 166n
Property,
  inspections, 351
  sale or transfer, 170-71
  taxes, 353
  types mortgaged, 480-81
PSA; *see* Public Securities Association
Public bond issues, 98
Public employees, 212
Public Employee Retirement Investment
  Security, proposed, 212
Public Securities Association, 208, 209
Purchase accounting, 44-45
Purchase line arrangement, 385
Put-and-call options, 323

R

RAM; *see* Reverse-annuity mortgage
Rating,
  adjustable rate mortgages, 109-10
  credibility, 97
  credit quality and loss protection, 101-10
  credit risk qualification, 101-2
  definition, 122-24
  financial strength of mortgage insurance
    companies, 104-5
  graduated equity mortgages, 108-9
  graduated-payment mortgages, 109
  information required, 206
  instruments assigned, 98
  leading agencies, 97-98
  modified weak-link theory, 205-6
  mortgage-backed bonds, 110-14
  mortgage pass-through certificates, 100-110
  mortgage pay-through bonds, 115-22
  mortgage securities, 98-99
  pass-through certificates, 152
  pledged account/buy-down mortgages, 108
  review process, 114
  savings and loan associations, 113-14
  second mortgages, 107-8
  securities, 205-6
  servicer's cash advance capability, 105-6
  shared appreciation mortgages, 108
  special-hazard insurance requirement, 206
  term loans, 108
Rating agencies,
  leading, 97-98
  rating definitions, 122-24
Reagan administration, 46-48
Real estate; *see also* Market demand;
  Market supply
  brokerage firms, 223-24

Real estate—*cont.*
  efficient market, 262
  market analysis, 255-67
  market demand analysis, 255-63
  market supply analysis, 263-67
  1920s boom, 138
  number of mortgage markets, 257
  residential/nonresidential, 185
  types, 480-81
Real estate investment trust, 48
Real estate-owned dispositions, 442-43
Real estate-owned lines, 198, 431
Real Estate Settlement Procedures Act, 156-57,
  161, 291, 427
  Amendments of 1975, 156-57
Real income, fluctuation in, 4
Real property, security interest, 174
Realtors, 292-93
Reconstruction Finance Corporation, 60
Redemption periods, 352
Refinance commitments, 325
Refinancing, prepayments due to, 518-19
Regional managers, 288
Regional resorts, 586-87
Regulation
  banks, 187-89
  bank-owned mortgage companies, 189
  depository institutions, 184-89
  housing finance, 155-82
  life insurance companies, 210
Regulation,
  mortgage bankers, 190-91
  mortgage insurance companies, 203-4
  pension funds, 21-12
  secondary market, 183-210
  securities dealers, 207-8
Regulation B of the Federal Reserve, 159
Regulation C of the Federal Reserve, 163
Regulation D of the Federal Reserve, 53
Regulation T of the Federal Reserve, 52,
  208
Regulation X of the Department of Housing
  and Urban Development, 156
Regulation Y of the Federal Reserve, 191
Regulation Z of the Federal Reserve, 160-62
Regulatory Accounting Principle, 447-48
Rehabilitation, 7-9
Reinvestment risk, 118-19, 550
Remittance reports, 348
Repo; *see* Repurchase agreements
Repurchase agreements, 391
  financing by, 430
  loans sold under, 396
Resale commitments, 325
Reserve requirements, 53
Residential construction and household
  formation, 5-6
Residential Funding Corporation, 92, 151

Residential lending; *see also* Loan production
        department
    builder loans and spot loans, 220, 224-25
    field of, 218-19
    management characteristics, 219-20
    spot loans, 222-24
    wholesale distribution, 226-28
Residential property, 185, 480
Resorts Condominiums International, 581
Revenue Ruling, 77-135, 469-70
Revenue Ruling, 80-248, 470
Resort timesharing,
    acquisition and construction financing,
        583-84
    administration processing, 590
    appraisals, 588
    companies, 581
    consumer-end-loan financing, 583
    customer profile, 581-82
    customer satisfaction, 578
    destination and regional types, 586-87
    development risks, 585-86
    exchange, 581
    feasibility studies, 587-88
    financing, 577-91
    growth, 578
    joint venture financing, 584
    location, 586-87
    legal and regulatory requirements
        589-90
    lender's evaluation, 590-91
    management and maintenance, 588-89
    market, 586
    marketing and sale, 588
    ownership and right to use, 578-81
    ownership forms, 578-81
    project design, 587
    reasons for loans, 584-85
    risk analysis, 585-90
Responsibility centers, 371
Revenues, interest-income accounting,
        406-10
Reverse-annuity mortgages (RAMs), 567
Reverse purchase agreements, 44-45
Revocation, buyer's right of, 174
Richness in hedging, 133
Right-to-use, resort timesharing, 578-80
Right of set-off, 381
Risk,
    avoidance by heding, 315-29
    investment types, 548-52
    in mortgage inventory management, 302-3
    resort timesharing loans, 585-90
Risk capital, 130
Risk management, 417-35
Rollinger v. *J. C. Penney Company* 171n
Rule 415 of the Securities and Exchange
        Commission

S

Salomon Brothers, 86
Sale or transfer, 170-71
SAM; *see* Shared appreciation mortgages
Savings and loan associations, 12-14
    chartering, 169
    federal, 187
    issuers of mortgage-backed bonds, 113-14
    lending powers, 177-79
    regulation, 184-86
    sources of loan money, 478
    state chartering laws, 179
Sears real estate subsidiaries, 92
Seasoned mortgages,
    definition, 24
    liquidity, 26
    sales of assets, 41
Secondary market; *see also* Pass-through
        securities
    accounting policies, 468-69
    adjustable rate mortgages, 61-62
    alternative mortgage instruments, 565-75
    amount of activity, 257
    bulk purchases, 399-400
    call protection, 552
    collateral management, 331-40
    collateral mortgage obligation bonds,
        552-54
    collateral mortgage obligation protection, 464
    commitment loans, 397, 398
    conduit function, 26
    costs of bulk purchases, 398
    credit risk, 464-65
    definition of lower cost market, 397
    development, 57-60
    documentation requirements, 336-38
    early ownership mortgages, 466
    FHA, 72, 71-72
    follow-up documentation, 339
    forecasting funds available for investment,
        466-67
    forward delivery transactions, 467-68
    goverment agencies, 26-28
    GNMA securities, 397
    goverment-related, 57-72
    hedging alternatives, 315-29
    institutions and instruments, 24-30
    investment determinants, 459-72
    lack of call protection, 463-64
    liquidity of mortgage assets, 26
    history, 73-84
    major functions, 59
    mandatory delivery contracts, 65-66
    market risk, 462-63
    mortgage-backed securities, 335-36
    mortgage loans held, 395-96
    need for, 22-56

Secondary market—*cont.*
new securities structures, 552-54
operation by FHLMC, 64-69
operation by FNMA, 60-64
operation by GNMA, 69-71
optional delivery programs, 65-66
origins, 147
participation sales, 335
private investors, 26
private mortgage insurance industry in,
147-50
private sector mortgage securities, 84-86
quality control, 338-39
risks, 548-52
sales of loans into, 39-41, 399-400
servicing portfolios, 269-81
start of GNMA, 74-75
tax policies, 469-70
thrift portfolio reconstruction, 59
types of reports, 339-40
valuation data, 398
Veterans Administration, 72
whole loan sales, 335
yield consideration, 465-66
yield measurement, 527-39
Second mortgages, 328
poor risk, 107-8
regulation of market, 183-213
Secondary Mortgage Market Enhancement
Act, 52, 55, 92, 169n
Securities,
callable but not refundable, 552
conventional mortgage, 87-95
exempted, 169
IRS requirements, 204-5
rating, 205-6
SEC requirements, 204-5
state laws, 176-77
Securities Act of 1933, 167-69
Securities Exchange Commission, 168
exemptions from regulation, 59
regulation of mortgage securities, 204-5
regulation of pass-through securities, 51-52
regulation of securities dealers, 207-8
Rule 415, 51
Securities Exchange Act of 1934, 168-69
Securities laws, 167-69
Securities market,
blue sky laws, 208
dealer regulation, 207-8
good delivery requirements, 208
nonmember subsidiaries, 207
regulation, 204-13
Regulation T, 208
Segmentation of loan portfolios, 450-53
Seiders, David F., 21, 47n
Selling risks, 303
Senior/subordinated classes, 49

Seraco, 92
Servicer performance bond, 106
Servicing,
after-tax value, 246
aggregate exemption system, 348
cancellation risk, 247-48
capital requirements, 367
cash flow analysis, 442-43
collection procedures, 350
control of cash received, 348
cost, 243-44, 375
data processing role, 359
disbursement clearing account, 349
duties of branch personnel, 290
escrow accounts, 352-55
escrow income, 245-46
expected value, 246-47
fee, 243, 478
forebearance agreements, 350
foreclosure procedures, 351-52
goal of management, 283-84
and government agencies, 356
hidden asset value, 250
income, 243
insurance agents and, 357
lienable items, 354
loan administration, 343-59
methods, 236
monitoring performance, 442-44
by mortgage originator, 478
nature of, 478
organization and responsibility, 347-48
present value, 248
present value computation, 248-50
property inspections, 351
quality, 441-42
relation to investor, 355-56
relation to mortgagor, 356
remittance report, 348
reports, 358
routine, 443-44
single-interest insurance, 354
standards, 358-59
state regulations, 356-57
subsidy payments, 249
tax and insurance disbursements, 348-49
tax collectors and, 357
value, 240-50
wholesale mortgage loans, 343-59
Servicing agreements,
accounting for funds, 345-46
cancellation provisions, 344
characteristics, 343-47
control of escrow funds, 347
definition, 343-44
desirable provisions, 344-47
escrow overdraft provision, 346
foreclosure costs provision, 346-47

Servicing agreements—*cont.*
 interest on escrow accounts, 344
 legal requirements, 344
 processing lost drafts, 346
 security of investment, 345
 servicer security, 344-45
 specification of fees, 345-46
 warranties of servicers, 344
Servicing portfolios,
 closing a sale or purchase, 276-78
 as corporate investment, 270-72
 field examination, 272
 GNMA checklist, 278-81
 historical information, 271-72
 market size, 260-70
 perspective of buyer, 272-73
 post-closing liability, 277
 purchase or sale of, 272-78
 required current information, 271
 secondary market in, 269-81
 seller's perspective, 273-76
Servicing-released loans, 324
Servicing rights, 269
Shared appreciation mortgages (SAMs), 108,
 498-99, 567
Shared risk concept, 146
Shelf registration procedures, 51
Shelter production mix, 7
Shipping; *see* Collateral management
Short-term financing,
 alternatives, 382-94
 alternatives to borrowing, 392-94
 bank lines of credit, 382-88
 callable preferred stock, 393
 collateral trust notes, 389-90
 commercial paper, 389-91
 conduit for issuance of commercial paper,
  392
 cross collateralization, 381
 delayed interest payment, 392
 documented discount notes, 388-89
 flexibility and administrative ease, 379-80
 gestation-period repo, 392
 interest rate expenses, 378-79
 loan-to-value ratio, 381
 management considerations, 377-81
 mortgage-backed notes, 389-90
 participations, 393
 prewarehousing line of credit, 392
 repurchase agreements, 391
 right of set-off, 381
 risk of corporate assets, 380-81
 variations on customary credit, 392
 warehouse lending, 417-35
 zero-balance account techniques, 387-88
Short-term lending, 377
 secured types, 428-29
Short-term maturities, 459-60
Single debit method, 348

Single-family detached housing, 19
Single-family nondetached housing, 19
Single-family insurance, 194
Single-interest insurance, 354
Single-person households, 6
Single-monthly mortality, 510
 and FHA-experience, 514-15, 517-18
Sold loan lines, 396
Special hazard insurance, 206
Speculation, 129-32
Spot loans,
 characteristics, 222-24
 commissions, 223
 definition, 220
 market demand, 258
 origination, 222-23
 size of market, 224
 versus builder loans, 224-25
 wholesale distribution, 226-28
Standard and Poor, 152
 rating agencies, 97-124
 securities rating, 205-6
Standardization of private mortgage industry,
 141-42
Standby commitment, 323; *see also* Optional-
 delivery commitment
Standby letters of credit, 429-31
Stated interest rate, 378
States,
 blue sky laws, 52, 176-77, 208
 doing business statutes, 175-76
 due-on-sale regulations, 521
 foreclosure laws, 172-75
 legal investment statutes, 52, 55
 mortgage company regulation, 190-91
 regulation of housing finance, 171-72
 regulation of life insurance companies, 210
 servicing laws, 356-57
 timeshare laws, 589-90
State savings and loan associations, 1-7, 79
Stein, Charles, 546
Straight commission solicitors, 286
Strategic exposure,
 builder loan risks, 307
 definition, 304
 lack of diversification, 307
 pricing control, 305-6
 product selection, 306
Strategic planning, 363-65
Subsidy payments, 349
Swap-adjusted sales, 39
Swap transactions, 44-46
 definition, 59
Syndicate for issuance of commercial paper,
 392
System inefficiency, 304-5

T

Take-out costs, 386

Tax collectors, 357
Tax disbursements, 353
Taxes in escrow, 348-49
Tax liens, 354
Tax policies,
 accrual-basis taxpayer, 470
 accrued interet, 469-70
 cash-basis taxpayer, 470
 graduated-payment mortgage, 539
 pass-through securities, 539
 recovered discounts, 49
TBA market; *see* Cash forward market
Tenancy-in-common timesharing,
 578-81
Term loans, 108
Third-party loan guarantees, 23-24
Thrift industry, 12-14
 definition, 478-79
 deregulation, 13-14
 drop in share of market, 42
 federal mortgage aid, 12
 money market deposit accounts, 14
 money market certificates, 13
 percentage of mortgage loans, 31
 sources of mortgage credit, 21-22
 types of intermediation, 21
 use of swap transactions, 45
Thrift portfolio, 59
TIM; *see* Trust for Investment in Mortgages
Timeshare law, 589-90
Timesharing; *see* Resort timesharing
Timing in hedging, 133
Title VIII of the Civil Rights Act of 1968,
 163
Trading volume, 129
Traditional mortgage loan, 473-74
Treasury bills, 126
Treasury bonds, 323
Treasury Department, 49, 60, 61, 63
Treasury Yield Curve, 551
Trust for Investment Mortgages (TIM), 48-49,
 94
 federal quality proposals, 49-50
 federal Reserve Board Regulation T, 52
 pension fund law, 50
 recent policy changes, 55
 SEC regulation, 51-52
 state laws, 52
Trust for Investment in Mortgages Act
 proposal, 50
Truth in Lending Act, 159-62, 427, 589
Truth in Lending Simplification and Reform
 Act, 159-60

U

UCA; *see* Uniform Condominium Act
Uncommitted loans, 398
Uncommitted mortgage-backed securities, 398

Underwriting,
 basic elements, 142
 private mortgage industry, 142-43
 residential loans, 288-89
Unearned premium reserves, 144
Uniform Condominium Act, 181-82
Uniform Land Transactions Act,
 172-75
Uniform Securities Act, 176-77, 208
Uniform Simplification of Land Transfers
 Act (USOLTA), 179-81
United States, population growth, 4-5
United States League of Savings Associations,
 175-76
Unsecured line of credit, 387
USOLTA; *see* Uniform Simplification of Land
 Transfers Act
Usury laws, 171-72
*Usury Laws and Modern Business
 Transactions,* 171n

V

VA; *see* Veterans Administration
Vacations Horizons International, 581
Valuation dates, 398
Variable rate mortgages, 320, 492-94; *see also*
 Adjustable rate mortgages
Veterans Administration,
 approval of servicing agreements, 356
 guaranteed loan program, 73
 interest rate charges, 296
 Lender's Handbook, 196
 liquidity of mortgages, 26
 loans, 28, 35-39, 42, 57-58, 61, 62, 63, 69-70,
  226, 230, 247, 306, 315, 321, 323, 324-25,
  335-36, 430, 437
 loans to middle income applicants, 229
 mortgage approval, 192-93
 mortgages, 16, 75, 77, 83, 89, 92, 183
 mortgage pools, 201
 operational requirements, 196
 origin, 72
 Prior Approval Loan Guaranty Program,
  192-93
 production department coordination,
  299
 rate changes, 308-9
 rules on escrow accounts, 355
 in secondary markets, 26
 third-party guarantor, 23-24
 types of loans, 294
Volatility measure of investment, 526-27

W

Wall Street,
 involvement in pass-through market, 78
 mortgage market, 86

Warehouse lenders,
  audits, 432-35
  choosing customers, 417-19
  definition, 417
  required reports, 432
Warehouse lending,
  agreements, 337-38, 426-27
  analysis and inventory control, 424
  analyzing the risks, 420-25
  backup commitments, 429-32
  capital requirements, 366-67
  collateral, 427
  collateral trust note programs, 430-31
  commercial paper, 430-31
  compliance record, 425
  costs, 376
  definition, 235
  direct, 328
  documentation, 426-27
  documented discount notes, 429-30
  financial analysis, 421-23
  foreclosure, 431
  funding package, 337-38
  knowledge of customers, 420-21
  loan administration analysis, 424-25
  loan organization analysis, 423-24
  marketing and inventory management
    analysis, 424
  monitoring inventory risks, 419-20
  nonconforming loans, 431
  nonstandard need of bankers, 431-32
  operational analysis, 423-25
  participations, 428-29
Warehouse lending—*cont.*
  pooling, 429
  price risk of nonhedged inventory, 418
  price risk of nonviable investor
    commitments, 419
  price risk of overhedged inventory, 418
  real estate-owned lines, 431
  repurchase agreements, 430
  review of personnel and training, 425
  risk management, 417
  risks, 418
  secondary risks, 419
  secured types, 428-29
  special loans, 431
  standby letters of credit, 429-31
  uncommitted lines of credit, 431
  working capital needs, 431-32
Warranties of servicers, 344
Whole loan sales, 335
Whole-mortgage loans, 343-59
Wholesale distribution,
  direct to consumer, 228
  of loans, 226-28
Wholesale mortgage bankers, 226-28
Window period loans, 170
Working capital, 387
  need, 431-32
Write-downs, 399

Y-Z

Yield duration plot, 550-51
Zero-balance account techniques, 387-88

NOTES

1986